UNDERSTANDING POVERTY

Understanding Poverty

Sheldon H. Danziger
Robert H. Haveman
Editors

RUSSELL SAGE FOUNDATION
New York, New York

HARVARD UNIVERSITY PRESS
Cambridge, Massachusetts, and London, England

To Eugene Smolensky,

Colleague, mentor, friend, former director of the Institute for Research on Poverty, and a major contributor to poverty research

Library of Congress Cataloging-in-Publication Data

Understanding poverty / Sheldon H. Danziger and Robert H. Haveman, editors.
   p. cm.
  Includes bibliographical references and index.
  ISBN 0-674-00767-0 (cloth)   ISBN 0-674-00876-6 (paper)
    1. Poverty. I. Danziger, Sheldon. II. Haveman, Robert H.

HC79.p6+
362.—dc21   2001040818

The paper used in this publication meets the minimum requirements of American National Standard for Information Sciences—Permanence of Paper for Printed Library materials. ANZI Z39.48-1992.

Contents

Contributors

Sheldon H. Danziger is Henry J. Meyer Collegiate Professor of Social Work and Public Policy and director of the Center on Poverty Risk and Mental Health at the University of Michigan.

Robert H. Haveman is John Bascom Professor of Economics and Public Affairs and research affiliate of the Institute for Research on Poverty at the University of Wisconsin–Madison.

Gary Burtless is John C. and Nancy D. Whitehead Chair in Economic Studies at the Brookings Institution in Washington, D.C.

Maria Cancian is associate professor of public affairs and social work and research affiliate of the Institute for Research on Poverty at the University of Wisconsin–Madison.

Mary Corcoran is professor of political science, public policy, social work, and women's studies at the University of Michigan.

Steven N. Durlauf is professor and chair of the Economics Department and research affiliate of the Institute for Research on Poverty at the University of Wisconsin–Madison.

Ronald F. Ferguson is lecturer in public policy at the John F. Kennedy School of Government and senior research associate at the Malcolm Wiener Center for Social Policy Research, Harvard University.

Richard B. Freeman is Herbert Ascherman Chair in Economics at Harvard University and faculty co-chair of the Harvard University Trade Union Program. He is also director of the Labor Studies program at the National Bureau of Economic Research, co-director of the Centre for Economic Performance at the London School of Economics, and visiting professor at the London School of Economics.

David R. Harris is assistant professor of sociology at the University of Michigan and assistant research scientist at the Institute for Social Research.

Lynn A. Karoly is senior economist and director of the Labor and Population program at RAND and research associate at the Institute for Research on Poverty at the University of Wisconsin–Madison.

Kara Levine is a graduate student in economics at the University of Wisconsin–Madison.

Glenn C. Loury is University Professor, professor of economics, and director of the Institute on Race and Social Division at Boston University.

John Mullahy is professor of population health sciences and economics at the University of Wisconsin–Madison.

LaDonna A. Pavetti is senior fellow at Mathematica Policy Research, Inc. in Washington, D.C.

Lee Rainwater is professor emeritus of sociology at Harvard University and research director of the Luxembourg Income Study.

Deborah Reed is research fellow and population program director at the Public Policy Institute of California in San Francisco.

John Karl Scholz is professor of economics and director of the Institute for Research on Poverty at the University of Wisconsin–Madison

Timothy M. Smeeding is Maxwell Professor of Public Policy and director of the Center for Policy Research at the Maxwell School, Syracuse University. He is also director of the Luxembourg Income Study.

Jane Waldfogel is associate professor of social work and public affairs at the Columbia University School of Social Work and research associate at the Centre for Analysis of Social Exclusion at the London School of Economics.

Barbara L. Wolfe is professor of economics and population health sciences and research affiliate of the Institute for Research on Poverty at the University of Wisconsin–Madison.

John Yinger is Trustee Professor of Public Administration and Economics at the Maxwell School, Syracuse University.

Preface

The chapters in this volume were initially presented at a conference held in May 2000 in Madison, Wisconsin. The Institute for Research on Poverty at the University of Wisconsin-Madison and the Office of the Assistant Secretary for Planning and Evaluation in the U.S. Department of Health and Human Services jointly sponsored the conference. The Russell Sage Foundation, the Charles Stewart Mott Foundation, the Annie E. Casey Foundation, and the Ford Foundation provided additional funding.

We gratefully acknowledge the encouragement of Eric Wanner, president of the Russell Sage Foundation. Barbara Wolfe, director of the Institute at the time of the conference, provided valuable advice regarding the content and scope of the conference and of the volume. Betty Evanson of the Institute was involved in all stages of the development of this volume, from conference planning and organization to the final editing of the chapters. Suzanne Nichols, director of publications at the Russell Sage Foundation, provided valuable assistance at all stages of the production process. Dawn Duren provided outstanding typing and formatting skills with her usual proficiency and smile.

Any views expressed in this book are those of the chapter authors and should not be construed as representing the official position or policy of any sponsoring institution, agency, or foundation.

S.H.D.

R.H.H.

Introduction: The Evolution of Poverty and Antipoverty Policy

SHELDON H. DANZIGER AND ROBERT H. HAVEMAN

In the 1960s, the United States experienced a long period of sustained economic growth, rising real wages, and low unemployment. Although the fruits of this prosperity were widely visible in the period between the Korean and Vietnam Wars, a combination of academic writings and magazine articles focused attention on those who were not benefiting from economic growth. President Kennedy, concerned with the extent of the poverty he had seen during the 1960 campaign, asked his economic advisers to prepare proposals to address the problem. President Johnson would later endorse these proposals and declare the War on Poverty in his 1964 State of the Union address. Within a few years, numerous pieces of legislation were drafted and enacted into law. They dramatically transformed the federal budget and the scope of the nation's social welfare policies. Many new programs were introduced (for example, Medicare, Medicaid, Head Start), and benefit levels were increased in many others (Social Security, Aid to Families with Dependent Children).

Now, as the new millennium begins, the nation has again experienced a period of sustained prosperity. However, unlike the mid-1960s, the topics now occupying center stage include reducing taxes on large estates, granting income tax relief, especially to high-income taxpayers, enforcing work requirements for welfare recipients, and ensuring that retirement and medical benefits for the older population are maintained. Public and presidential concern for the nation's poverty problem has been minimal for years, despite the long-standing labor market problems of less-skilled workers and the dramatic increase in income and wealth inequalities of the last quarter-century.

This volume focuses on the extent of poverty in the United States at the

1

end of the twentieth century. The authors look backward over the past four decades and tell us how the poor have fared in the market economy and what government programs and policies have and have not accomplished. They help us understand how a variety of economic, demographic, and public policy changes have affected the trend in poverty for all persons and selected demographic groups. Most important, they offer suggestions for changes in programs and policies that would reduce poverty and income inequality if the nation were willing to spend the resources to undertake them.

The Evolution of Social Science Thinking About Poverty

Since the mid-1960s, our understanding of the complex problems of poverty and inequality in the United States has changed substantially. This evolution reflects the research on the causes and consequences of poverty and the changes in the level and composition of poverty in response to economic changes, demographic changes, and public policy changes.

The 1960s

During this decade, Americans seemed convinced that government could combine scientific thinking and additional public resources to solve pressing national problems. The announcement of the War on Poverty made income poverty one of those problems. Income poverty was officially defined and measured, the best minds were gathered to develop proposals to address it, and a legislative agenda was prepared. Many social scientists contributed to the development and implementation of antipoverty programs. Psychologists contributed much of the thinking behind the Head Start program, sociologists and political scientists contributed to the Community Action Program, and economists formulated proposals to reform income maintenance programs to raise the incomes of the poor.

In a paper delivered at the 1964 meeting of the American Economic Association, Robert Lampman presented the poverty problem as multi-causal, deriving from some combination of events external to individuals (such as illness or disability, family dissolution, the death of the family breadwinner, unemployment), social barriers in the form of discrimination based on caste, class, or custom (racial and gender discrimination, employer hiring procedures, union rules), and limited ability to earn (for example, a lack of the skills needed for the labor market). According to this point of view, external events were a major culprit, and among them unemployment was chief. As a result, improved macroeconomic performance was the primary instrument. If cyclical unemployment could be abolished, poverty would be reduced and economic gains would be widely distributed. A second major problem was inadequate education, training, and labor force skills. An array of programs designed to increase human capital and reduce discrimination were to be put in place to ensure that the disadvantaged would not be left behind.

Those who were not expected to participate in the labor market and those who remained poor in a growing economy would need access to government assistance even in good economic times. To aid them, the President's Commission on Income Maintenance Programs in 1969 recommended "a universal income supplement program to be administered by the federal government." Shortly thereafter, President Nixon proposed the Family Assistance Plan (FAP), a low-guarantee negative income tax.

The 1970s

In the early 1970s, academics and some federal agencies and policymakers continued to propose variations of a universal, comprehensive income transfer system as a replacement for the many separate welfare programs. The 1972 election campaign highlighted Democratic candidate George McGovern's proposed $1,000-per-person "demogrant" as a replacement for existing welfare programs. McGovern and his plan were roundly rejected, and Nixon's FAP failed in the Senate (having passed the House twice) because it was too conservative for liberals and too liberal for conservatives.

Senator Russell Long of Louisiana opposed income guarantees for all of the poor. He argued that public support should be given only to low-income *workers*. His proposal, the Earned Income Tax Credit (EITC), was adopted in 1973, and has enjoyed bipartisan support over the past quarter-century. By the late 1990s, EITC funding exceeded funding for cash welfare.

The idea of a minimum income guarantee was resurrected by President Carter in his 1977 Program for Better Jobs and Income (PBJI). While PBJI, like FAP, provided a universal income guarantee, it also made cash assistance dependent on work, guaranteeing a minimum-wage public-service job for poor welfare recipients who were able-bodied and expected to work.

Like FAP, it was not enacted by Congress. With the defeat of PBJI, federal discussion of a minimum income guarantee for the able-bodied poor ended.

The idea of a guaranteed income for all of the poor in the form of food stamps did take hold. By the end of the 1970s, the food stamp program—a small effort to stabilize and support farm prices in 1970—had grown to assist all low-income families regardless of their work or marital status. Congress also created the Supplemental Security Income (SSI) program, which provides a minimum annual income for the elderly, blind, and disabled poor. The coverage, benefits, and total spending on health care for the poor also expanded rapidly after the adoption of Medicaid in the mid-1960s.

The 1980s

By the late 1970s, the optimistic belief that government could solve most social problems had turned to the pessimistic attitude that "nothing works." Despite the increase in public spending, poverty rates for the nonelderly did not fall after the early 1970s, in large part because of adverse macroeconomic conditions—two oil price shocks, multiple recessions, and widespread industrial restructuring. Critiques of public redistribution and other social policy interventions took center stage after the election of President Reagan. His administration set out to cut back the scope of social programs, arguing that the social policies enacted in the 1960s and 1970s had undermined the functioning of the nation's basic institutions and, by encouraging permissiveness, nonwork, and welfare dependence, had led to marital breakup, nonmarital childbearing, and the erosion of individual initiative. Spending on employment programs was cut dramatically, and the Comprehensive Employment and Training Act (CETA), enacted in 1973 to provide public-service jobs and on-the-job training to disadvantaged workers, was replaced with a much smaller job training and job search assistance program, the Job Training Partnership Act (JTPA).

The Reagan administration set in motion a major change in welfare policy that would eventually radically alter the Aid to Families with Dependent Children (AFDC) program. In 1981 it proposed a program of mandated work for able-bodied welfare recipients. Although this was not legislated, the law that did pass encouraged states to establish work requirement programs and signaled new work expectations for single mothers with children. The generally positive experiences with these programs in many states in the mid-1980s influenced the Family Support Act of 1988 and culminated with the 1996 welfare reform bill. Other major changes in antipoverty policies in the 1980s included further expansion of the Earned Income Tax Credit and the Family Support Act of 1998. The latter required all states to implement welfare-to-work programs and offer a range of support services to increase the work effort of welfare recipients.

The Reagan philosophy was that tax cuts and spending cuts would increase the rate of economic growth, and that the poor would ultimately benefit through the increased employment and earnings that would follow such growth. However, a deep recession in the early 1980s increased poverty, and the subsequent economic growth did not "trickle down." Although the economy expanded for many years in the 1980s, the wage rates of low- and medium-skilled male workers did not. On the other hand, the earnings of those in the upper part of the income distribution grew rapidly.

The 1990s

As a presidential candidate, Bill Clinton emphasized the extent of poverty and economic hardship and promised that he "would make work pay" and "end welfare as we know it." In 1993 he delivered on the first part of the promise by promoting a large expansion of the Earned Income Tax Credit. Although his own welfare plan was set aside after Republicans took control of Congress in the 1994 elections, the Personal Responsibility and Work Opportunity Reconciliation Act of 1996 (PRWORA) ended welfare as we knew it by ending the entitlement to cash assistance, setting a time limit for the receipt of benefits, and mandating work.

Thus, by the end of the century, antipoverty policies had achieved one vision of the planners of the War on Poverty: a substantial set of income supports were in place for working poor families with children, regardless of where they lived or their marital status. As a result, a single mother with two children who worked full-time year-round at the minimum wage would receive an EITC that was about 40 percent of her earnings, bringing her gross income to just about the poverty line. She would also be eligible for increased child care subsidies, and her children would have greater access to subsidized medical care than in the past.

However, the vision of universal support for the nonworking poor had been rejected many times. Whereas President Nixon had proposed expanding cash assistance to all of the poor, under President Clinton PRWORA set strict limits on welfare receipt. As a result, cash support for the nonworking poor was less available and less generous in 2001 than it had been in 1969.

Trends in Poverty Since the War on Poverty

The declaration of the War on Poverty came during a long period of postwar economic growth, when both productivity and wages were rising. In its aftermath, much progress was quickly achieved—the official poverty rate for all persons fell from 17.3 percent in 1965 to 11.1 percent in 1973. The elderly poverty rate fell even more rapidly, from about 30 percent to 15 percent over the same period.

Since 1973, however, the official poverty rate for all persons has always exceeded 11 percent. Although the elderly poverty rate continued falling through the 1970s, the children's rate and that for prime-age adults drifted up over the period. In the early 1980s, the most severe recession since the 1930s raised the overall poverty rate to about 15 percent and the child poverty rate to more than 20 percent. Although the recovery of the 1980s was a long one, the real wages of low- and medium-skilled males continued the erosion that had begun in the mid-1970s, and inequality rose because only incomes at the top of the distribution increased. The poverty rate fell slowly, but it remained above 13 percent for the rest of the 1980s. The children's poverty rate remained stalled at over 20 percent until the mid-1990s.

During the recession of the early 1990s, the overall poverty rate rose, approaching 15 percent in 1993. By the mid-1990s, the elderly poverty rate had fallen to about 10 percent, below that of working-age people. During the prolonged expansion of the 1990s, the overall poverty rate declined, reaching 11.3 percent in 2000, the last year for which data are available, and the children's poverty rate fell to 16.2 percent. These declines were the first noticeable successes against poverty since the gains of the early 1970s.

Social and Economic Trends Since the War on Poverty

Trends in labor market outcomes, family structure, the diversity of the population, and government policies have affected trends in poverty over the past forty years. Here we introduce some of the major issues that are discussed in the chapters in this volume.

Growing Earnings Inequality and the Changing Nature of Work

Beginning in the early 1970s—and accelerating after 1980—inequality in male wage rates and earnings increased substantially. Changes in production technologies, the globalization of labor markets, the movement of jobs from central cities to suburbs, and other changes in the labor market made it harder for the less-skilled to earn their way out of poverty. The wage gap between workers with more and less education and skills increased, as did the gap between younger and older workers. Earnings for workers with few skills and little education deteriorated: from the early 1970s until the mid-1990s, the inflation-adjusted hourly wage rate for a man with only a high school degree fell by about 35 percent. In addition, there was a decline in labor force participation and an increase in joblessness, especially among African American men.

Increased "Atomization" of Households

Over the past forty years, living alone and in a family arrangement other than the two-parent family with children have become increasingly common; the growth of mother-only families with children has been a prominent aspect of this change. Apart from the effects of such change on people's well-being, this trend has a statistical effect that increases the overall poverty rate. Because the official family poverty line varies by family size and reflects economies of scale in living arrangements, it takes more income to support the same set of people if they live in two households than if they live in one. The atomization of households, then, is another factor that contributes to the failure of poverty to fall below the level of the early 1970s.

Increased Immigration and Population Diversity

The demographic composition of the population has also changed dramatically, primarily because of the rapid growth of the foreign-born population. Since 1970, the United States has admitted twenty million immigrants; in addition, several million more illegal immigrants have entered the country. On average, recent immigrants have less education and fewer skills than the native population and earlier immigrants, and a high proportion of them are officially poor. This trend has also contributed to slow progress against poverty since the early 1970s.

Shifts in Antipoverty Policies

As discussed earlier, periodic changes in our understanding of the causes and consequences of poverty led to public policy changes that also affected the official poverty trend. The rapid decrease in the poverty rate during the 1960s and early 1970s resulted from a series of policy changes that greatly increased the value of Social Security retirement benefits, access to cash income support for single parents, and aid to the poorest elderly through the passage of the SSI program. Social Security disability benefits were introduced in the 1950s, and both benefits and coverage from this source also expanded in the aftermath of the War on Poverty.

Although cash assistance for nonworking single mothers has actually eroded since the 1970s, spending on food stamps and Medicaid has continued to grow. However, because they provide in-kind, but not cash, benefits, they do not affect the official poverty rate. The substitution of in-kind for cash benefits to low-income families may not adversely affect their overall well-being, but this policy twist has contributed to the stickiness of the official poverty rate.

Analyzing the Causes and Extent of Poverty and the Nature of Antipoverty Policies

Trends in poverty and antipoverty policies, and the associated changes in thinking about the poverty problem, have been analyzed in four previous volumes that have been sponsored by the Institute for Research on Poverty over the past quarter-century: *Progress Against Poverty: A Review of the 1964–1974 Decade* by Robert Plotnick and Felicity Skidmore (1975); *A Decade of Federal Antipoverty Programs: Achievements, Failures, and Lessons,* edited by Robert H. Haveman (1977); *Fighting Poverty: What Works and What Doesn't,* edited by Sheldon H. Danziger and Daniel H. Weinberg (1986); and *Confronting Poverty: Prescriptions for Change,* edited by Sheldon H. Danziger, Gary Sandefur, and Daniel H. Weinberg (1994).

Each volume in this series presents detailed assessments of trends in poverty and the evolution of antipoverty policies based on the research that existed when they were written, and each contains suggestions for reforming antipoverty policies. Each addresses a common set of topics, including analyses of trends in the official poverty rate and the impact of income transfers on poverty, documentation of changes in the level and composition of expenditures on antipoverty programs, and assessment of changes in earnings and income inequality. The effects of macroeconomic changes on poverty are discussed in each volume, as are the special problems of racial-ethnic differences in poverty, education and training programs, health care, and employment policies.

All of the volumes address the major questions that persisted during each decade, though in different forms: Do public assistance programs create adverse incentives regarding work effort, marriage, or childbearing? How do demographic changes affect the poverty rates of specific groups and the composition of the poor population? Do antipoverty policy measures effectively reduce income poverty? What are the political constraints on the development of effective antipoverty policy? Although the empirical results presented in these volumes and the policy reforms they recommend have changed considerably, all of the questions they pose remain of scholarly interest even if their priority among policymakers and the public has waxed and waned.

Each volume also reflects the particular concerns of its time. For example, *A Decade of Federal Antipoverty Programs*, published in 1977 after the optimistic decade following the War on Poverty, which was marked by major reductions in the poverty rate, sought to identify themes other than income poverty on which public debate should focus in the future:

> In conclusion, then, the day of income poverty as a major public issue would appear to be past. . . . [F]ewer than 5 percent of the nation's households remain in income poverty when the value of in-kind transfers is taken into account. But serious income inequality remains. . . . Direct efforts to restructure or to supplement labor markets are likely to be increasingly proposed. . . . [T]hese include guaranteed and publicly subsidized employment, earnings supplements, and wage rate subsidies. (Haveman 1977, 18)

The 1986 volume, appearing after the Reagan retrenchment of social programs, sought to understand how poverty, an issue that had topped the nation's agenda two decades before, could have fallen so far down the list of national priorities. At that time, the environment was hostile not only to the new interventions proposed in the 1977 volume but also to existing policies. The Reagan administration "argued that social spending had grown too large and had become a drag on economic growth. Income poverty had been 'virtually eliminated,' but work incentives had been eroded for both the poor and the rich, and the incentive to save had been weakened. As a result, these programs should be scaled back or eliminated" (Danziger and Weinberg 1986, 2).

Nonetheless, the contributors offered a number of policy reforms, many of which are still relevant in 2001—such as continued experimentation with education, employment, and training programs, especially those that emphasize the integration of welfare and work, and expanded access to health insurance for those who lack coverage. They also proposed a reform that has long since been abandoned: a national minimum welfare benefit for all of the poor.

By contrast, *Confronting Poverty* conveys the impression that in the mid-1990s the poverty problem seemed to be edging its way back up the list of the nation's priorities:

> Thus, the United States is on the verge of another major shift in thinking about antipoverty policy. This new view is based on the research and policy lessons of the past three decades and can be characterized as reflecting realism, rather than either the optimism that characterized the war on poverty or the pessimism of the Reagan retrenchment. Rejected are the views that government can do almost anything *and* that government can do almost nothing. . . . [T]he goal of resolving the American paradox of "poverty amidst plenty" remains. (Danziger, Sandefur, and Weinberg 1994, 4)

In retrospect, the 1994 volume, like the 1986 volume, proved to be too optimistic: few antipoverty initiatives were undertaken in subsequent years.

Overview of the Volume

The chapters in this volume reflect both current U.S. attitudes toward domestic poverty and policies to combat it, and the experience of the prior volumes. The authors were asked to assess the progress that has been made over the last forty years in our understanding of the poverty problem and the potential of alternative approaches to it. They were to review past poverty research to establish what we know and do not know about the causes of poverty, and then to draw the policy implications of this improved understanding and to present their judgments regarding issues for further research. The volume reflects both the collective experience of the editors and the authors as poverty researchers and the current place of antipoverty policy on the national agenda. Hence, the emphasis of this volume on *under-standing* rather than on *fighting* poverty distinguishes it from some of its predecessors.

Part I: Trends and Determinants of Poverty, Inequality, and Mobility

The first part of this volume reviews important developments affecting the level and nature of poverty. Its chapters focus on trends in poverty, income inequality, and mobility in the United States and the roles played by demographic and economic changes. It also shows how poverty and antipoverty policies in the United States compare to those in other industrial countries.

In the first chapter, Gary Burtless and Timothy Smeeding discuss various concepts and measures of poverty—absolute and relative income standards, consumption versus income measures, and issues related to housing, spending on health care, and wealth. According to the official measure, the percentage of the population that is poor was about the same in 1998 (12.7 percent) as in 1968, but higher than the 11.1 percent rate of 1973. Under an alternative definition that does not subtract out-of-pocket medical spending, the 1998 rate was 12.0 percent. The two other series that use the official poverty measure, but with alternative price indices, have 1998 poverty rates of 11.3 and 10.5 percent and imply that poverty was not higher in 1998 than in the early 1970s. Burtless and Smeeding also document that the wide disparities by race-ethnicity are not artifacts of the choice of poverty measure. Using the alternative measure, the 1998 poverty rates for white non-Hispanics, African Americans, Asians and Pacific Islanders, and Hispanics are 7.9, 23.6, 12.8, and 24.0 percent, respectively.

Regardless of measure, however, Burtless and Smeeding point out that the lack of progress in reducing poverty should "be surprising in view of the large increase in national income per person that has occurred since 1979." Lack of progress against poverty is due largely to the increase in income inequality and the atomization of families, and this stagnation differs markedly from the record of the quarter-century following World War II, when poverty declined rapidly. The authors agree with Richard Freeman (chapter 3) that a healthy economy alone is not sufficient to reduce the American poverty rate substantially below the levels achieved two decades ago and to the lower levels maintained in northern Europe. They conclude that without reductions in income inequality or a reversal in family structure trends (discussed by Maria Cancian and Deborah Reed in chapter 2), improvements in health insurance coverage, income support to the indigent elderly and disabled, and supplements to work and earnings are necessary if poverty rates are to be reduced in the future.

In chapter 2, Maria Cancian and Deborah Reed ask: How have the changes in family structure and the employment of women over the past decades affected poverty? They document the increasing concentration of poor people in single-parent families and seek to unravel the reasons for this phenomenon.

Cancian and Reed document substantial declines over the past three decades in marriage rates and overall rates of childbearing and large increases in divorce, cohabitation, and nonmarital childbearing rates and the share of women who never marry. While some of these changes, such as declines in the number of children, decrease poverty, others, like higher rates of nonmarital childbearing, increase it. They also document increases in female labor force participation, work intensity, and earnings, especially among married women with children (primarily before 1990) and single mothers (after the mid-1990s).

After summarizing the literature that explores the labor market, demographic, and social causes of changed marriage and cohabitation patterns and women's labor force activity, Cancian and Reed examine the potential effects of policy measures on these changes, including changes in child support policy and expansion of the EITC and child care assistance. They conclude that while no single factor has played a substantial role in accounting for these changes, all of them have had some causal effect.

Cancian and Reed conclude by presenting a "counterfactual" analysis of the relative contributions of the changes in family structure and women's employment patterns to changes in poverty over the last three decades. They suggest that both for the entire population and for children the effect of changes in family structure (which worked to increase the poverty rate) dominated the effect of changes in the propensity of women to work, earn, and cohabit (which worked to reduce the poverty rate). They conclude that policy measures should recognize the increasing diversity among families. They see some potential in state measures to permit the full pass-through of child support payments without a reduction in cash assistance for the custodial parent and continued efforts to increase the payment of child support.

In chapter 3, Richard Freeman reviews the relationship between macroeconomic performance and the poverty rate since 1960 and assesses the potential of future economic growth to further reduce poverty. After the disappointing decade of the 1980s, in which macroeconomic performance lost much of its antipoverty bite, the 1990s again saw poverty fall with declining unemployment and economic growth.

Freeman shows that the antipoverty impact of growth was greatest in the 1960s; all subsequent periods experienced a reduced "bang" for the economic growth "buck." Combining the bell-shaped income distribution with the official absolute poverty definition has the unavoidable effect of making each additional unit of economic growth less effective in reducing poverty. This relationship, together with increased income inequality, reductions in government cash transfers, and the stagnation of real wage rates—all of which occurred during the 1970s and 1980s—accounts for the reduced antipoverty impact of macroeconomic performance.

Freeman's analyses show that the increased antipoverty impact of economic growth during the 1990s was due to the combination of rising real wages (especially among racial minorities, youths, and those with low levels of schooling), unexpectedly low unemployment, and the arrested trend toward increased inequality. However, he cautions, this rising economic tide must confront the unhappy fact that those who remained poor in the late 1990s were not as amenable to rising wages and low unemployment as those who had gone to work during the economic boom. Most of the remaining poor had serious barriers to employment—disabilities, retirement, lack of work experience. As a result, the economy now faces an asymmetry in that recession is likely to have a larger poverty effect than will a continuation of economic growth. In short, a rising tide will raise far fewer boats than the number that will sink with an ebbing tide. Freeman emphasizes that in the absence of changes that lead to less dispersion among incomes, social policy, if it is to further reduce poverty, will need to provide increased income support for some of the poor and recognize that the problems of other poor people (such as the homeless, substance abusers, and those with mental health problems) are unlikely to be resolved by economic growth. He also urges the nation's macroeconomic policymakers to view unemployment rates in the 4 to 5 percent range as sustainable, and hence to pursue maintenance of full employment.

In chapter 4, Mary Corcoran addresses the dynamic aspects of poverty, such as the possibility of moving up in economic position (mobility or "getting ahead") or the way the economic game is played (equal opportunity or "starting even"). Corcoran reviews evidence on a series of questions: Is poverty persistent, or is it transitory? Has long-term poverty increased over time? Is it concentrated among particular groups, such as racial and ethnic minorities? Are children who grew up in long-term poor families more likely to be poor themselves when they become adults (intergenerational poverty transmission)? If yes, how much more likely is it that they will be poor, and has this parent-to-child transmission of poverty been increasing or decreasing? To what extent do people move up (in, say, the income distribution) within their own lifetime (intragenerational mobility), and is this movement increasing or decreasing over time? Is it the lack of income in the families of poor children that causes this transmission of poverty, or is it caused by the other factors that tend to come "bundled" with low income— poor neighborhoods or schools, labor market discrimination associated with race, stress, or participation in public programs like welfare?

Corcoran points out that the intergenerational transmission of poverty is large; that intragenerational mobility is substantial; that the effect of income itself is relatively modest in explaining children's outcomes; that other factors associated with income, like having educated parents, are important; and that intragenerational mobility appears to be increasing.

Corcoran concludes that research has not uncovered whether increasing the money income of poor families will suffice, or whether other factors must also change—like the neighborhoods in which poor children grow up, or the quality of their schools, or the way employers treat people of their race, or the structure of the families in which they are raised. For this reason, her policy recommendations are cautious. She supports expansion of earnings supplementation policies (like the EITC and refundable child care tax credits), employment policies (including affirmative action and equal employment opportunity programs), and in-kind programs such as food stamps and Medicaid for families with children, so as to help them defray the costs of basic necessities.

In chapter 5, Timothy Smeeding, Lee Rainwater, and Gary Burtless contrast the trend in U.S. poverty and the antipoverty effects of the American safety net with those of other industrialized countries, using comparable data sets compiled by the Luxembourg Income Study. They compute a poverty measure for eleven countries for the mid-1990s that uses the official dollar values for the U.S. poverty lines; income amounts in the other ten countries are converted into dollars using purchasing power parities. They find that the U.S. poverty rate, 13.6 percent, is the third highest (Australia, at 17.6 percent, and the United Kingdom, at 15.7 percent, have the highest rates), whereas Canada, Germany, the Netherlands, Sweden, Finland, Norway, and Luxembourg all have a poverty rate below 7.4 percent. When they measure poverty relatively, using a standard of 40 percent of each country's median adjusted disposable income, the United States has the highest poverty rate, 10.7 percent, and eleven of seventeen countries have rates below 5 percent.

The authors document a strong association between the extent of low pay and national poverty rates, on the one hand, and the percentage of GNP devoted to social expenditures and the national child poverty rate, on the other. Their analysis of social policies in other countries leads them to advocate "an income package that mixes work and benefits so that unskilled and semi-skilled workers, including single parents, can support their families above the poverty level." They would expand the EITC, adopt refundable child and child care tax credits, provide guaranteed child support for single parents, set up programs to increase job access and skills (a "human capital strategy") for low-skilled, working-age people, and expand SSI benefits for the aged and disabled poor.

Part II: The Evolution of Antipoverty Policies

The chapters in this part of the volume address the evolution of understanding about a set of long-standing areas of relevance to the poverty problem. These include cash and in-kind transfers, the special case of welfare policies, the provision of health care for the poor, and policies to raise the education and skill levels of children and adults.

John Karl Scholz and Kara Levine begin chapter 6 by reminding the reader of Americans' long-standing ambivalence toward antipoverty policies: many simultaneously believe that we are spending too much on welfare programs and giving too little assistance to the poor. These opinions constrain American antipoverty policies to a much greater extent than is the case in other countries.

Scholz and Levine document the growth in social insurance and means-tested transfers since 1970. Social insurance, the largest category, has grown more rapidly over this period owing to rapid increases in the real value of Social Security benefits and the introduction and rapid growth of Medicare. Cash means-tested transfers, excluding the Earned Income Tax Credit, have grown more slowly than social insurance spending since the mid-1970s. The EITC has grown rapidly, particularly in the 1990s.

They find that cash and in-kind income transfers fill about three-quarters of the pretransfer poverty gap and lower the monthly poverty rate from 29 to 10 percent. They also find that the antipoverty effects of transfers were re-markably similar in 1979, 1984, and 1997. The antipoverty effectiveness of transfers ranges from about 46 percent for nonelderly childless families and individuals to about 80 percent for nonelderly single-parent families and 99 percent for elderly families and individuals.

Scholz and Levine review evidence concerning the behavioral effects of transfers on work, savings, marriage, and fertility. They find that policies that make work pay, like the EITC, can increase labor force participation, but that other income transfers have small negative effects on savings and mar-riage. Taking the antipoverty effects and the behavioral responses into ac-count, they conclude that the "safety net needs shoring up," especially be-cause it now provides less than it did in the past for children whose parents are unable or unwilling to work. As examples, the authors cite increasing food stamp outreach efforts, expanding rental housing subsidies, and ensur-ing that states have sufficient resources to work with families who reach welfare's new time limit. They also suggest implementing or supplementing programs that increase the returns to work (such as the EITC or a variety of work supplementation demonstrations that have been favorably evaluated) to further reduce poverty. They note that part of the federal budget surplus could be spent on these efforts.

In chapter 7, LaDonna Pavetti describes how the Personal Responsibility and Work Opportunity Reconciliation Act of 1996 transformed the safety net for poor families. PRWORA eliminated Aid to Families with Depend-ent Children and replaced it with the Temporary Assistance for Needy Fam-ilies (TANF) program. Because PRWORA grants states much new authority, Pavetti reviews state policy choices. She shows that as of 2001 there had been "no race to the bottom"—that is, most states have the same welfare benefit levels they had in 1996. Most states had altered welfare rules and now disregard some earnings in the calculation of welfare benefits, there-fore increasing a recipient's ability to combine work and welfare. Pavetti also shows that most states have adopted "work first" or labor force attachment models, which are "changing the culture" of the welfare office. Declines in cash assistance have been rapid, with national welfare caseloads down by more than half between 1994 and the end of 1999.

Pavetti also reviews changes in the social contract for legal immigrants. For the first time, PRWORA made eligibility for federal public assistance conditional on citizenship. A number of states have responded by using their own funds to provide assistance to legal immigrants who were in the United States when the act was signed. Pavetti cites one study that found that, between 1994 and 1997, welfare use by noncitizen households fell by 35 percent, compared to a 14 percent decline among citizen households.

Pavetti concludes that the transition from AFDC's cash-based safety net to TANF's work-based assistance system will not be complete until further reforms are implemented. She emphasizes the development of strategies to help the hardest-to-employ move from welfare to work, such as integrating substance abuse, learning disability, and supported work measures into current welfare-to-work efforts. Because recipients who have found jobs often need help to retain them and advance to better ones, she suggests continued supplementation of wages and the provision of ongoing personal support for former recipients of cash assistance as they strive to meet family and workplace demands. Because it is now more difficult for working single-parent families to gain access to such services, TANF offices need to become more accessible in terms of hours, waiting times, and the complexity of application procedures.

Pavetti emphasizes that PRWORA made life more difficult for unskilled noncustodial parents. She advocates providing these fathers with employment services, such as public-service jobs and training opportunities. Finally, both state and federal government should seek ways of supporting marriage and creating two-parent families, directly through marriage training programs and indirectly by reducing the EITC's marriage penalty for low-income families. She cautions that the early implementation of TANF was facilitated by an extraordinary economic climate, and that it remains uncertain how states will respond—and how current and former welfare recipients will fare—during the next recession.

In chapter 8, John Mullahy and Barbara Wolfe analyze health care policy for the nonelderly population, emphasizing public interventions to provide health care services to poor people and special groups that are overrepresented among the poor. Because poor health and low earnings are so closely tied, it is not clear which causal factors account for the higher prevalence of health problems among the poor. A further complication is that differential access to medical care and the incidence of unhealthy behaviors (such as smoking and sedentary lifestyles) are also associated with both health and income, as is racial-ethnic background. Regardless of causality, two facts remain: poor families have a greater need for health care services than do nonpoor families, and a variety of barriers, such as lower rates of insurance coverage and higher costs of seeing providers, keep poor families from gaining access to health care services.

The authors explore the effect of the health care sector on the health status of the nonelderly poor and point out how market failures complicate public-sector involvement. This sector is marked by "market failures" that lead to an inefficient allocation of resources, including a lack of information, uncertainty in assessing health care needs, "spillovers" in people's behaviors (such as failing to be immunized or engaging in health-compromising acts), limits on entry into the health care sector, problems of "supplier-induced demands," and the costly and lumpy nature of medical research leading to new drugs or procedures.

Mullahy and Wolfe document the extensive involvement of government in health care, including the fact that the United States spends more per person on the provision of health care than any other nation—$4,500 per person per year. Yet gaps in coverage and high rates of people without health insurance have been increasing over time, primarily because the tax benefit to low-wage employees of employer-provided health insurance is far less than for other workers.

They review major government programs, including Medicaid and the State Children's Health Insurance Program (SCHIP). Because of limitations on access to providers and quality-of-care issues, even low-income families who are covered by public programs receive fewer, and lower-quality, health services. Although measures could be undertaken to equalize access to good health care, the authors point out that the health status of the poor and nonpoor would remain substantially different, in part because of differences across the population in propensities to engage in unhealthy behaviors.

Mullahy and Wolfe assess proposals for reform, from mandating employers to provide health insurance to expanding current programs, passing tax incentives, and nationalizing health insurance. They see potential gains from several reforms. Providing consumers with more information about the effects and costs of offering coverage to the uninsured, they note, would reveal that universal coverage is not as costly as many believe. They also suggest that attaining coverage through incremental expansions of income eligibility thresholds (as opposed to refundable health insurance tax credits) may lead to adverse labor supply effects. And, therefore efficiency gains from implementing means-tested coinsurance arrangements, despite their potential adverse financial and health care effects on the poor. They advocate imposing a cap on the existing tax subsidy for employer-provided insurance—designed to reflect the actuarial cost of insurance for those covered—and improving the incentives facing insurers, consumers, and providers. Finally, they propose a program of progressive and refundable tax credits for the purchase of a basic health insurance plan, together with state requirements that insurance companies join together to offer such basic-coverage insurance to all. Failing these, they advocate guaranteeing health care coverage for all children under a single-payer arrangement, along with expansion of the community health center network for adults.

Lynn Karoly, in chapter 9, reviews research on the antipoverty effectiveness of education and training programs. Many early intervention programs produce sizable cognitive benefits in children in the short term, but these benefits are often eroded once the children enter public schools. She speculates that this erosion may be due to the poor-quality schools that many poor children attend. Benefits from early interventions in other domains, however, such as increased educational attainment and lower crime delinquency, are long-lasting. Some successful programs have included continuing interventions that last into the early elementary school years, suggesting that disadvantaged children require more than a single intervention to achieve their full developmental potential.

Karoly finds little evidence that across-the-board spending increases on public schools help disadvantaged children, although increasing school resources for minority and disadvantaged students can improve outcomes. In her review of the research on school choice, she finds insufficient evidence to support either the view of supporters that vouchers improve educational quality or the view of critics that vouchers harm the students who are left behind in low-quality public schools.

Some programs seek to prevent students from dropping out of high school and to ease the transition from school to the workforce, whereas others, such as Job Corps, offer a second chance to those who have already dropped out. Except for Job Corps, most of these programs have not been effective. The same is true for job training programs for disadvantaged adult men. Documented benefits have exceeded program costs only in programs for disadvantaged women, particularly welfare mothers.

Karoly suggests a strategy based on optimal investment through the life course—that is, increasing investments in early childhood programs targeted at disadvantaged children and providing ongoing interventions for the most disadvantaged. She suggests the expansion of high-quality, center-based early childhood programs, home visiting services to young, high-risk, first-time mothers, reduced class sizes in early grades for schools serving disadvantaged children, Job Corps for school dropouts, and employment-focused welfare-to-work programs for single mothers.

Part III: Neighborhoods, Groups, and Communities

The chapters in the third part of the volume cover topics that were not widely discussed in the previous volumes. Whereas the chapters in parts I and II emphasize an individual's attributes and behaviors and labor market and family income outcomes, these chapters emphasize social and economic processes that affect groups, neighborhoods, and communities.

John Yinger examines housing discrimination and residential segregation in chapter 10. He argues that the housing market contributes to the poverty problem, and that ethnic and racial discrimination in housing markets magnifies the labor market problems of minorities. Given the increased earnings of the most educated and skilled over the past quarter-century, racial and ethnic minorities are doubly disadvantaged: on average they have less education and fewer job skills, and they continue to experience discrimination in employment and wages.

To begin with, the poor and minorities tend to live near central cities but pay more per unit of housing, live in small or poor-quality apartments or double up, and live in the least desirable neighborhoods. As a result, residents of central cities pay higher rents (relative to their incomes) than do suburban families; hence, financial strategies that might help them overcome poverty, such as owning their own home, are lost. Yinger points out that the official measure of poverty understates the extent of urban poverty by failing to account for the quality of the housing and the neighborhoods in which urban poor people live. Moreover, the urban poor have higher housing health risks (lead paint exposure and insect pests, for example) than other groups, and poorer access to neighborhood amenities (such as quality schools) and suburban labor markets where job growth has been most rapid.

Yinger also shows that past racial discrimination has a lasting effect on current poverty and contributes to persisting high levels of racial residential segregation. He documents current housing market discrimination, based on studies of "fair housing audits." Minority families are not told as often about housing opportunities and must work harder to complete a transaction. Discrimination by mortgage lenders and insurers compounds the problem. As a result, minority families pay higher rents and are less likely to own their own home than would be expected based on their income alone.

Finally, Yinger explores the potential of several housing policy options that might reduce high racial and ethnic poverty rates. He concludes that "a program to eliminate poverty differentials between ethnic groups should include federal policies to promote fair housing and fair lending, to support community activities that maintain neighborhood integration, to combine housing certificates with housing counseling, and to promote homeownership among low-income households."

Chapter 11, by Steven Durlauf, explores how group membership affects poverty. In Durlauf's memberships-based theory of poverty, an individual's well-being is influenced by the larger groups of which she is a member. He incorporates ideas from sociology and social psychology into economics and extends the traditional model of individual choice to include the influence of the characteristics and behaviors of the members of a group on a person's choices and outcomes.

Relevant groups include race, neighborhood, schools, and workplaces (through, for example, trade union membership). Such memberships may influence individual choices and outcomes through various channels, including the desire to emulate the behavior of other members ("peer group effects"), the influence of the choices and attitudes of respected group members ("role model effects"), and the instructional value of observing the choices made by other members and their consequences ("social learning"). If these influences are strong, then the sequence of group memberships over the lifetime and the interrelationship of these groups can have an important independent effect on an individual's poverty status.

Membership models in the literature have analyzed several aspects of the poverty problem, including the role of neighborhood or firm-based coworker feedbacks ("endogenous membership" cases) and racial-ethnic group effects (an "exogenous membership" case). Durlauf reviews the ethnographic, quantitative, social quasi-experimental, and psychological controlled-experiment literatures on these effects. He challenges the literature for its absence of "any deep causal analysis of why these effects exist" and notes the failure of researchers to distinguish exogenous from endogenous membership arrangements and to account for the problem of self-selection into groups. In particular, Durlauf explores the relationship of membership-based theories of poverty with those associated with the concept of social capital, and he cites ongoing research that promises to reliably identify membership effects.

Durlauf notes that the memberships framework has important implications for how we think about antipoverty policy, largely because of its emphasis on redistributing group memberships rather than income. Affirmative action, school busing, and charter schools are all examples of efforts to alter the pattern of social interactions by altering group composition. If we accept equality of opportunity as the goal of public policy, then "associational redistributive" policies like these may be the only way of attaining this goal. However, such measures may also have the serious negative side effect of violating certain freedoms (for example, the right to free private association). Durlauf concludes that there is a trade-off between the gains and losses of associational redistribution in terms of conflicts with other basic values. He concludes that the potential of such measures warrants the expansion of carefully designed neighborhood socioeconomic integration programs (such as an experiment with the objectives of the Moving to Opportunity program) and the extension of school or training vouchers to those with the most serious disadvantages.

Chapter 12, by Ronald Ferguson, reviews the long-standing debate about whether policies should focus primarily on helping people or on helping places. In the 1990s, the debate pitted enterprise zones, which bring jobs to poor areas, against policies that reduce spatial and skills mismatches by opening up suburban jobs to inner-city residents. Ferguson warns us to avoid concluding that we can pursue policies only on one front; he advocates both community revitalization and residential mobility strategies.

Ferguson begins by reviewing the literature on spatial mismatch and pointing out that both physical distance and lack of access to information, or social distance, contribute to the high unemployment rates of inner-city residents. He suggests that programs that simply provide transportation are not likely to be as effective as those that combine transportation with services for employers and workers that try to overcome misinformation on both sides of the labor market.

Ferguson then reviews the literature on enterprise zones and concludes that business financial incentives are unlikely to be a cost-effective way to increase the number of jobs going to the inner-city poor. He is more optimistic, however, that well-designed workforce development programs can help overcome the social isolation of the poor and expand the share of jobs that employ the poor. He also concludes that community development corporations can promote both business development and the quality of life in the inner city. The challenge is to combine policies that foster business-led economic revitalization and workforce development with programs that encourage some of the poor to leave the inner city and some middle-income people to return.

Part IV: Concluding Thoughts

The concluding part of the volume includes three brief contributions that offer thoughts on some key research and policy issues that cut across the issues covered in the other chapters.

Glenn Loury, in chapter 13, focuses on a variety of issues not fully addressed in the volume. He questions why the long history of poverty research has been so dominated by quantitative researchers, primarily from economics and sociology, and why ethnographers, developmental psychologists, social philosophers, and political analysts have not had greater influence. He also emphasizes the need to clarify the distinctions between "poverty," "disadvantage," "inequality," and "social exclusion," suggesting that most poverty research has focused on individual behavior and neglected normative issues concerning social values.

Loury reacts to the findings of the other chapters in this volume relating to race and social division by pointing out "that racial differences in the experience of poverty are large, intractable, and poorly understood." He suggests that we distinguish between "discrimination in contract" (such as in formal market transactions) and "discrimination in contact," which involves unequal treatment of persons on the basis of race in the informal, private spheres of life. The former type of discrimination has been greatly restrained by federal laws and policies since the civil rights revolution. According to Loury, the latter cannot be regulated by the state because "preserving the freedom of persons to practice this discrimination [in contact] . . . is essential to the maintenance of liberty [and] because the social exchanges from which such discrimination arises are so profoundly intimate and cut so closely to the core of our being." He concludes that, because educational, labor market, and other socioeconomic outcomes are affected by both "contract" and "contact," equality of opportunity is a goal unlikely to be attained, given the racial divisions that characterize contemporary American society.

David Harris, in chapter 14, also addresses an issue not considered by the other authors. He notes that the rapid technological changes of the past decade have the potential to either reduce or increase discrimination. The increased use of e-mail and online purchases of everything from books to cars to homes reduces face-to-face interaction and hence reduces the likelihood that an African American or other minority will be differentially treated by a nonminority real estate agent, homeowner, or firm otherwise inclined to be discriminatory. On the other hand, the "digital divide"—in which whites and the wealthy have greater computer access than minorities and the poor—puts these latter groups at a disadvantage in that they end up with less information about market possibilities than is available to the "connected." Harris suggests that closing the digital divide should become a high public policy priority.

Jane Waldfogel, in chapter 15, identifies four issues that warrant further research: group differences in poverty, particularly the experiences of recent immigrants; interactions between poverty and other socioeconomic disadvantages, such as living in poor neighborhoods, attending poor-quality schools, and not speaking English; parenting practices and child well-being; and the policies of other countries.

Waldfogel points out that Britain's New Labour government has launched a set of antipoverty policies designed to reduce "social exclusion," a concept broader than income poverty that extends to "nonparticipation in . . . important sectors of society or social life." The British policies have been influenced by U.S. experience but are much more expansive. They include a minimum wage and a working families tax credit that, like our Earned Income Tax Credit, are designed to "make work pay"; increased investments in children (for example, expanded early intervention programs, influenced by our Head Start program); and higher income support benefits for those who cannot work. Waldfogel suggests that the British experience should lead us to focus on both the question of why support for government programs is so much greater in Great Britain than in the United States and the likely success of this new round of policies in reducing poverty.

PART I

Trends and Determinants of Poverty, Inequality, and Mobility

CHAPTER 1

The Level, Trend, and Composition of Poverty

GARY BURTLESS AND TIMOTHY M. SMEEDING

The nature and prevalence of poverty have been topics of intense political debate since the concept was first officially defined and measured by the federal government in the early 1960s. Most of this debate has focused on the form and appropriate scale of government efforts to reduce poverty or ameliorate its effects. Some of the debate, less visible to the public, has focused on defining poverty and accurately tracking its level and trend in the population. Nearly everyone has a general idea of what it means to be poor, but even the most profound philosophers would have trouble deciding whether the problem is getting better or worse without first agreeing on a definition of who is poor. The keenest minds in philosophy and science unfortunately do not agree on the best approach to defining poverty. Their disagreement has led to a second and more troublesome controversy: Is poverty becoming a more or less serious problem in the United States?

In this chapter, we examine common definitions of poverty and present evidence about the level and trend in the number of poor under several definitions. Under almost any reasonable definition, the prevalence and intensity of American poverty fell during the first quarter-century after World War II. It is less certain whether poverty has declined in the past quarter-century. Many plausible statistics suggest that the poor have become more numerous, and their poverty more intense, since the 1970s. But this conclusion depends on how we measure changes in consumer prices and on our understanding of what it means to be poor. Under an optimistic view of price changes and improvements in the quality of goods and services, living standards have continued to rise, even among people with very low incomes. Under a pessimistic view, inflation-adjusted incomes are lower today than they were two decades ago, at least among people with the lowest incomes. If it is debatable whether low-income Americans enjoy higher or lower living standards than they did in the past, it is more certain that their incomes are a smaller percentage of the average income today than was the case twenty-five years ago. Income disparities have risen sharply since the late 1970s, and this has opened a wider gap between incomes at the bottom and incomes in the middle and at the top. If being poor means being a long way from the society-wide average (or median), the percentage of Americans who are poor has almost certainly risen over the past two decades.

This chapter is divided into four parts. The first considers alternative ways to define who is poor and to measure the resources and needs of people who are at risk of being poor. The second contains estimates of the level and trend of American poverty under alternative definitions, including the official government definition. The third section presents a statistical portrait of the nation's poor under alternative poverty definitions. And the fourth offers an assessment of poverty trends in important subgroups of the population. We conclude with a brief summary of the main conclusions.

Background: Concepts and Measures of Poverty

The measurement of poverty in rich nations involves the comparison of some index of household well-being or economic resources with household needs. When command over economic resources falls short of needs, a household (or person or family) is classified as poor. Economic well-being refers to the material resources available to a household.[1] The concern with these resources is not with material consumption per se, but rather with the capabilities such resources give to household members so that they can participate fully in society (Sen 1983, 1992). These capabilities are inputs to social activities, and participation in social activities gives rise to a particular level of well-being (Rainwater 1990; Coleman and Rainwater 1978). Methods for measuring a person's or household's capabilities differ according to the context in which one assesses them, either over time or across nations or among subpopulations within a nation.[2]

All advanced societies are highly stratified, with some individuals having more resources than others. The opportunities for social participation are affected by the resources that a household disposes, particularly in nations like the United States where there is heavy reliance on the market to provide such essential services as health care, postsecondary education, and child care. Money income is therefore a crucial resource. Of course, there are other important kinds of resources, such as social capital, noncash benefits, primary education, and access to basic health care, all of which add to human capabilities (Coleman 1988). These resources may be available more or less equally to all people in some societies, regardless of their money incomes.

Other factors besides the absence of money can reduce well-being by limiting capabilities for full participation in society, including racial discrimination, neighborhood violence, low-quality public schools, and job instability. In this chapter, we do not propose to examine these limiting forces or to investigate related topics, such as social exclusion. Rather, our purpose is to offer an economic definition of poverty, compare alternative ways of implementing such a definition, and provide a statistical portrait of poverty in the United States, both over time and across subpopulations.

Our task requires us to make important choices regarding the exact measures of resources and needs, the definition of the population to be studied, and the time frame in which poverty is measured. From a practical standpoint, these measures must be based on regularly available data of reasonable quality, and they must be available to document the level and trend in poverty across a wide range of policy-relevant subpopulations.

Absolute and Relative Income Poverty

An absolute poverty standard is defined in terms of a fixed level of purchasing power, one that is sufficient to buy a fixed bundle of basic necessities. A relative standard, on the other hand, is defined in terms of the typical income or consumption level in the wider society. The purchasing power of a relative poverty standard changes over time as societywide income or consumption levels change.

In one sense, all measures of poverty or economic need are relative (Fisher 1996). Context is important to the definition of needs. The World Bank uses poverty measures of $1 to $2 per person per day—or $1,095 to $2,190 per year for a family of three—in the developing nations of Africa or Latin America (Ravallion 1994, 1996). This standard for defining poverty would seem absurdly low if applied in a rich country such as the United States. The 1998 official U.S. poverty threshold was $13,003 for a family of three—six to twelve times the World Bank's poverty line.

Many social scientists believe the official absolute poverty line of the United States needs updating. Critics of the official threshold are skeptical that a poverty standard created in 1963 using 1955 consumption data and price-indexed since then can provide a valid starting point for assessing poverty today (Ruggles 1990; Citro and Michael 1995).[3] In 1963 the four-person-family poverty threshold adopted by the U.S. government was exactly 50 percent of median family income (before taxes), but by 1998 it had fallen to just 35 percent of median family income.[4]

The National Research Council (NRC) recently appointed the Panel on Poverty and Family Assistance to perform a thorough assessment of poverty statistics (Citro and Michael 1995). The panel recommended adoption of a poverty line based on median consumption levels in the U.S. population and regularly updated to reflect changes in median consumption. The panel proposed that the government use household consumption surveys to estimate the median consumption of food, clothing, and shelter for a reference family type, and then define the basic poverty line as a fixed percentage of this consumption level. (In the next two sections, we use versions of the proposed thresholds to estimate poverty rates in recent years.) In essence, the NRC panel suggested abandoning the absolute poverty thresholds embodied in the official U.S. poverty definition and replacing them with a relative poverty standard, one defined in terms of typical consumption patterns.[5]

To define which households are poor under either an absolute or relative poverty definition, it is necessary to measure available resources. The estimate of household resources should be comprehensive as well as appropriate given the way the thresholds are derived. The Census Bureau's principal measure of income for estimating poverty includes before-tax cash income from all sources except gains or losses on the sale of property. This definition includes gross wages and salaries, net income from the operation of a farm, business, or partnership, pensions, interest, dividends, and government transfer payments distributed in the form of cash, including Social Security and public assistance benefits. This measure of resources is not comprehensive; it ignores all sources of noncash income, including food stamps, housing subsidies, and government- and employer-provided health insurance. The resource measure is also inappropriate for measuring poverty because some of the noncash income sources that are ignored can be used to pay for basic necessities, such as food and shelter.

The NRC panel on poverty statistics recommended changing the census definition of income to include post-tax cash and near-cash income, while making an allowance for necessary work-related expenses. This definition subtracts income and payroll taxes and an estimate of work-related expenses from the Census Bureau's current income definition, but it adds near-cash benefits that can be used to pay for food, clothing, and shelter. Such transfers include food stamps, free school lunches, low-income energy assistance, and public housing subsidies. Near-cash benefits would not include employer- or government-provided health insurance because insurance coverage cannot directly pay for food, clothing, or shelter. The panel argued that out-of-pocket spending on medical benefits, including premium payments for insurance, should be subtracted from other household income in calculating the income available to pay for food, clothing, and shelter.

In this chapter, we measure poverty using three alternative measures of resources to determine whether a person, family, or household is poor under a particular standard. In examining trends, we use the Census Bureau's official income definition and two alternative definitions that are closely linked to the recent recommendations of the NRC panel on poverty statistics. Obviously, we could have used other measures of resources and other multidimensional measures of deprivation to estimate poverty. In the next section, we review some of these alternative measures and assess their advantages and disadvantages.

Other Measures of Poverty

There is no single way to measure poverty. Social scientists have proposed a variety of additional poverty measures that substitute for or complement income-based measures (see, for example, Haveman and Mullikin 1999; Ruggles 1990). Poverty is a multidimensional concept and should reflect several aspects of personal well-being. Forms of deprivation other than economic hardship are certainly relevant to policymaking. Even restricting consideration to economic poverty, measures other than annual income might be used to estimate household resources. In this section, we examine five alternative conceptions of poverty or deprivation: wealth-based poverty measures; consumption-based measures (including specific types of consumption such as housing and health care); measures of earnings capacity; social indicators of deprivation or affluence; and long-run poverty measures. Other conceptions of hardship, such as "subjective poverty," "time poverty," "social exclusion," and membership in an "underclass," are not treated here.

CONSUMPTION MEASURES OF POVERTY   For households with fluctuating incomes, annual income can provide a poor approximation of permanent or long-run average income. Some economists suggest that annual consumption represents a better proxy for permanent income and hence should be preferred over annual income for measuring household resources.[6] Analysts who have used consumption-based poverty measures have reached conflicting conclusions about recent trends in American poverty.[7]

A criticism of consumption-based poverty measures is that household consumption is difficult to measure. The Consumer Expenditure Survey (CEX) is the single source of nationally representative data that can be used to make such calculations. The main purpose of the CEX is to obtain the appropriate quantity weights for consumer purchases used in constructing and updating the Consumer Price Index. The goal of the survey is not to measure the distribution of household consumption. There are also problems in measuring the flow of consumption, even assuming that reliable household data are available. Consumption of durable goods needs to be prorated. Housing consumption and the costs of maintaining an owner-occupied home are difficult to estimate. Goods produced and consumed in the home are not included in most consumption surveys (or in income surveys). Finally, the consumption of some services, such as health care, is difficult to determine using respondents' reports of their spending on the service.[8]

HEALTH CARE POVERTY   A number of authors have suggested that separate measures of needs ought to be developed for different goods and services, such as housing and health care (Aaron 1985). The NRC panel recommended that family poverty thresholds reflect differences in housing costs across regions, an adjustment also suggested by other authors. The NRC panel's proposed housing cost adjustment was not intended to measure "housing poverty" per se, but rather to adjust for regional differences in the cost of a minimum consumption bundle. The panel noted that regional differences in the cost of other basic consumption items, such as food and clothing, are too small to affect measured poverty.

Health care is a special consumption good. Because of its peculiar nature, different levels, amounts, and types of health care consumption have very different welfare implications for different people. Neither social scientists nor policymakers have defined a basic bundle of health care "necessities" as opposed to less essential health care "luxuries." Essential life-saving medical procedures or drugs cannot be easily distinguished from interventions that greatly improve the quality of life but are not necessary to survival. In general, welfare evaluation of either medical consumption or medical need is very difficult. Some early researchers added the value of health insurance subsidies to other components of cash and noncash income to estimate total family resources (Smeeding 1977, 1982; U.S. Bureau of Census 1996). This procedure greatly reduced poverty in population groups, such as the elderly, that have both generous health insurance subsidies and heavy medical utilization. The procedure probably assumes, however, too great a substitutability between health insurance protection and ability to consume other necessities. If households cannot easily use their insurance coverage to help pay for nonmedical necessities, adding the cash value of health insurance subsidies to other household income surely overstates its value to most households (Smeeding 1977, 1982).

The NRC panel proposed that health care expenses be integrated into poverty measurement by subtracting out-of-pocket spending on medical care from household income. In effect, health care expenses, including those for health insurance premiums, would be treated as a tax on incomes. Under this procedure, health care expenses are treated as nonsubstitutable for other basic needs. We follow this approach in one of the alternative poverty measures we consider. However, subtracting health care expenses from other income produces a poverty measure that does not directly address the problem of households' differing health care needs. Actual expenses reflect differences in health status and insurance coverage to some extent, because out-of-pocket spending is higher for those who are seriously ill and lower for those who are covered by good insurance. But actual medical spending provides no clear measure of the adequacy of the health care available to individuals or households. A separate health care consumption standard or health care needs standard would allow us to measure health care poverty separately from income poverty (or from nonmedical poverty). A separate measure would require periodic assessment of households' health care needs compared with the health care services they actually consume. At this time, the data to perform such a periodic assessment are not available often enough for use in constructing an annual poverty index.[9]

WEALTH POVERTY   Most, but not all, people with low income have limited wealth (Ziliak 1999). Income-based measures of poverty include current interest, rent, and dividends in the definition of income, and a few also include net gains or losses on the sale of property. However, these are imperfect measures of the flow of income from wealth, and they do not reflect the household's ability to draw down assets when its income is low, nor do they include a measure of the value of service flows from nonfinancial wealth—for example, the flow of housing services from an owner-occupied home. Many government programs aimed at improving the well-being of the poor also impose an asset test, which discourages formal savings as well as accurate reporting of financial wealth in household surveys.

In a world with perfect data, most economists would prefer a poverty measure that reflects a household's ability to draw on wealth to sustain current consumption or to use nonfinancial wealth to substitute for current spending on necessities. Reliable wealth data, however, are rarely available in income surveys (but see Haveman and Wolff 2001). It is unclear whether the inclusion of financial wealth holdings would greatly affect our assessment of who is poor. Because low-income households have relatively little financial wealth, adding a financial wealth component would probably do little to reduce the income-based poverty rate. In fact, accounting for household debt might even lead to a net increase in estimated poverty rates.[10]

An accurate income imputation for the service flows from owner-occupied homes would have a larger effect on poverty, especially among the elderly. Over 90 percent of aged, married-couple families own their own homes, and most of their homes are fully paid for. In contrast, less than 40 percent of younger, single, female householders are homeowners, and a large majority have outstanding mortgages (U.S. Bureau of the Census 1999a). In our view, if net service flows from owner-occupied homes could be accurately measured, they should be added to other sources of income in order to calculate household resources.[11] Since reliable data on these service flows are not available, we do not include them in the estimates of poverty reported here.

SOCIAL INDICATORS   Researchers have a long tradition of using social indicators to measure both economic hardship and affluence. Analysts often define direct measures of deprivation, such as lack of food, heat, or access to health care, and measures of affluence, such as the fraction of low-income households with cars, color television sets, or video recorders (Baumann 1998; Mayer and Jencks 1993; Rector, O'Beirne, and McLaughlin 1990; Rector 1998). Because each household's need is imperfectly measured by a cash poverty threshold, many a household with an income above the threshold may still experience hardships such as hunger or face high rent payments or heavy medical expenses that prevent its members from buying enough food or fuel. Individual members of a household may suffer hardship because of unequal sharing of incomes within the household. In these cases, direct measures of material hardship might offer a useful indication of poverty. On the other hand, some income-poor households possess assets or other attributes that few of us associate with poverty. For example, a few own boats, expensive cars, or second homes.

The problem with indicators of hardship or affluence is that it is difficult to use them to distinguish true need from individual differences in the taste for different kinds of consumption. Low-quality housing or failure to pay rent on time may represent a hardship from one perspective. But they may also reflect a distinctive set of consumer preferences. Someone with a taste for good clothes or cars might choose to rent an inexpensive—and perhaps "inadequate"—apartment rather than devote a large part of his or her monthly income to rent. We consider measures of social indicators or hardship as complementary to other measures of poverty, not as substitutes for them.

EARNINGS CAPACITY   Self-reliance, or the ability to support oneself and one's dependents through one's own capabilities, represents another concept of poverty. This kind of measure recognizes that having the capacity to maintain an adequate income is a meaningful measure of full participation in a society. Sen (1992), Garfinkel and Haveman (1977), Haveman and Bershadker (2001), and others argue that this capacity should be nurtured through good public policy. A measure of economic independence does not substitute, however, for a measure of current economic need. A "capable" household may be income-poor by choice or as a result of circumstances beyond its control (circumstances that could include unmeasured needs or involuntary unemployment). Similarly, "incapable" breadwinners could earn incomes above the poverty line because they work exceptionally long hours or share living quarters with a large extended family. Although measures of earnings capacity are relevant to policy and can be measured with increasing accuracy, they too are complementary to measures of actual or income-based poverty rather than a good substitute for them.

MULTI-PERIOD POVERTY   There is nothing sacred about twelve months for purposes of measuring poverty. Assessing household incomes over shorter periods, such as a month, would show a higher poverty rate because of income variability within a year. If the poverty rate were reported more frequently than once every year, it might become a more important economic indicator, perhaps on a par with the unemployment or inflation rate. Measuring household incomes over a longer period, such as two or five years, would produce a lower poverty rate than a measure based on annual incomes. The longer-term measure of income would also provide a more reliable yardstick for identifying people exposed to truly serious deprivation.

SUMMARY   Researchers have used a variety of methods to define and measure poverty. Each approach has strengths, weaknesses, and distinctive policy relevance. Over the past few decades, however, income-based poverty measures using annual assessments of household income have provided the main statistics for tracking poverty over time, across nations, and across subpopulations within nations. They have also provided important tools for assessing the effectiveness of social policy.

Level and Trend of U.S. Poverty

Although poverty can be measured in a variety of ways, as just noted, the official measure of American poverty is defined in terms of personal or family income. Persons and families with incomes that are judged to be too low are classified as poor; those with incomes above official poverty thresholds are classified as nonpoor. Under this conception of poverty, a poor person is one whose income places him or her in the extreme lower tail of the overall income distribution.

Distribution of Cash Income

The government has tracked and published statistics on the distribution of cash income under the Census Bureau's standard income definition since shortly after World War II, even before there was a widely accepted definition of American poverty. Figure 1.1 shows how annual family cash income was distributed in 1998. The solid line represents the frequency distribution of pretax cash income from all sources except capital gains. A small percentage of families have incomes that are less than zero—someone in each of these families lost money on the operation of a farm or business. The lighter, broken line shows what the 1998 distribution of income would have looked like if families had received no government transfers. Not surprisingly, the elimination of transfer payments dramatically increases the percentage of families with extremely low incomes. If government benefits are included in income, just 6.4 percent of families had annual incomes below $10,000 in 1998. When government benefits are ignored, the fraction with an annual income below $10,000 more than doubles, rising to 14 percent of all families. Government benefits clearly reduce the percentage of families with very low cash incomes.

Given the income-based definition of poverty, the proportion of the population that is poor is closely linked to the amount of inequality in the income distribution. A common way to measure income inequality is to calculate the percentage of total income received by families in different parts of the distribution. The Census Bureau, for example, calculates the income rank of every family, ranks families from lowest to highest, and then divides families into five equal-sized groups. In 1998 the one-fifth of all families with the lowest incomes received 4.2 percent of total income. Families in the top one-fifth of the distribution received 47.3 percent of all income. Families in the other three-fifths received the remainder, or slightly less than half of total income. If incomes were distributed equally, of course, each fifth of the

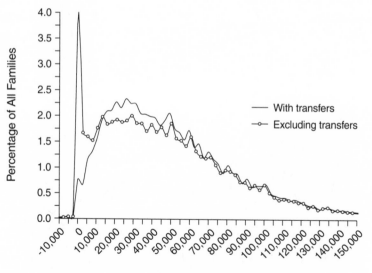

Figure 1.1 Distribution of 1998 Pretax Family Income, With and Without Government Transfers (*Source:* Authors' tabulations of March 1999 CPS files.)

distribution would receive exactly 20 percent of aggregate income. Families in the bottom one-fifth of the distribution would thus need to see their incomes rise about fivefold in order to obtain an equal share of aggregate cash income.

The top panel in figure 1.2 shows the trend in income inequality as reflected by the percentage of total cash income received by families in the top and bottom fifths of the annual income distribution. The two trend lines are almost mirror images of one another. From World War II until the middle of the 1970s, the share of income received by the bottom one-fifth of families increased while that of the top one-fifth fell. Inequality obviously declined as the relative position of families at the bottom of the income ladder improved while that of high-income families lagged. Since the 1970s, the share of cash income received by the bottom fifth of families has shrunk, while that of high-income families has grown.

The same general trends can be seen using another popular measure of inequality, the Gini coefficient, a statistic that ranges between 0 and 1, with 0

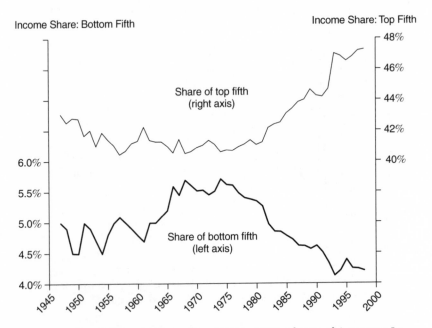

Figure 1.2 Family Income Inequality, 1947 to 1998: Shares of Aggregate Income Received by Top and Bottom Fifths of Family Income Distribution (*Source:* U.S. Bureau of the Census.)

indicating perfect equality (all families receive exactly the same income) and 1 indicating an extreme level of inequality (all income is obtained by a single family). Figure 1.3 shows the Census Bureau's estimates of the Gini coefficient over the postwar period. The estimates suggest that inequality fell in an erratic pattern until the end of the 1960s, and then began to grow. By the end of the 1990s, inequality was about one-quarter larger than it had been at the end of the 1960s.

Of course, statistics on the trend in inequality shed no direct light on the trend in real, or inflation-adjusted, income among families with the lowest incomes. Under the right circumstances, even a rise in inequality can be associated with an improvement in living standards at the bottom, assuming that overall income growth is strong enough. Conversely, a jump in the share of income going to the bottom fifth of families could be associated with falling real incomes at the bottom if average incomes in the population at large are shrinking.

Figure 1.3 Family Income Inequality, 1947 to 1998: Gini Coefficient of Family Income Inequality (*Source:* U.S. Bureau of the Census.)

Figure 1.4 shows the trend in inflation-adjusted family incomes over the postwar period, using the real income level in 1973 as a benchmark for measuring income levels in earlier and later years (that is, the income levels for every year are divided by the group's 1973 income). The solid line shows the trend in average family income over the period. Real income climbed rapidly from 1947 through 1973, growing 2.6 percent a year.[12] Income growth in the early postwar period was even faster among families at the bottom of the income distribution (see the line with squares in figure 1.4). Average income in the lowest one-fifth of families grew 3 percent a year after 1947, and it had more than doubled by 1973. Average income among the top one-fifth of families, indicated by the third line in the figure, grew more slowly than population-average incomes.

The income trends since 1973 stand in marked contrast to those before 1973. Overall family income growth fell sharply after 1973. It averaged about 1 percent a year, versus 2.6 percent in the earlier period. Income increases among families in the top one-fifth of the distribution, though slower than in the earlier postwar period, were significantly greater than they were among families with lower incomes. Income growth stopped alto-

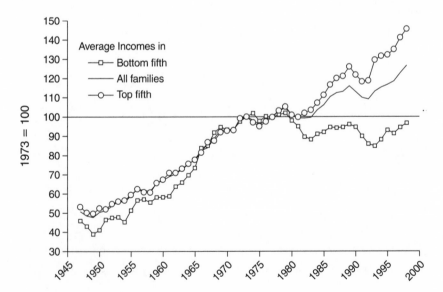

Figure 1.4 Trend in Real Average Family Income, by Rank in the Income Distribution, 1947 to 1998 (*Source:* U.S. Bureau of the Census.)

gether among families at the bottom of the income distribution. After adjustment for inflation, average income in the bottom one-fifth of families was about 3 percent lower in 1998 than it had been in 1973. Even if the incomes of low-income families had grown as fast as population-average family income after 1973, there would have been a sharp slowdown in the rate of gain in their incomes compared with their experience in the early postwar period. But the surge in inequality after 1973, and especially in the fifteen years after 1979, left low-income families with smaller incomes in 1998 than families in the same part of the distribution had received twenty-five years earlier.

INCOME-TO-POVERTY-LINE RATIO   The percentage of people or families who are poor cannot be calculated using family incomes alone. Incomes must be compared with appropriate poverty thresholds to determine whether families are poor. These thresholds provide estimates of the incomes necessary for persons or families in different circumstances to purchase a minimally adequate level of consumption. The most important circumstance affecting income needs is family size—larger families need higher incomes than smaller ones to achieve an adequate level of consumption. In 1998, for example, the weighted-average poverty threshold for a typical unrelated individual was $8,316. The poverty threshold for a family with four members was $16,660, almost exactly twice that for one person. The implicit equivalence scale in the poverty thresholds therefore implies that a quadrupling of unit size doubles the unit's income requirements. The official poverty thresholds also vary depending on the ages of family members.[13]

 The adjustments in the poverty threshold for differences in family size and composition were originally based on detailed estimates of the cost of a minimally adequate diet for different family sizes and family compositions. To derive specific poverty thresholds, estimates of the cost of a minimally adequate diet were multiplied by three. Using information collected in the 1955 Household Food Consumption Survey, government analysts observed that the average family containing three or more members spent one-third of its post-tax income on food.[14] The analysts therefore concluded it was appropriate to multiply the cost of an adequate diet by three to approximate the minimum income needed to meet a family's basic consumption requirements (Orshansky 1965, 3). Until 1969, the poverty thresholds were updated every year to reflect changes in the cost of the Department of Agriculture's Minimum Food Plan, but since that year the thresholds have been increased in line with changes in the Consumer Price Index for Urban Consumers (CPI-U) (Citro and Michael 1995, 124).

Assuming that the poverty thresholds accurately measure the differing consumption requirements associated with different family sizes and compositions, the thresholds offer a convenient benchmark for assessing a family's income. Each family's income can be divided by its poverty threshold to determine how far its income falls short of or exceeds minimum consumption requirements. Families with an income that is one-half the threshold must see their incomes double in order to pay for a minimum consumption basket. Families with incomes more than three times the poverty threshold can comfortably pay for their minimum consumption needs and still have money left over to buy other goods and services.

Dividing a family's income by its poverty threshold also offers an advantage for evaluating the distribution of incomes. Most income distribution statistics, including those displayed in figures 1.2, 1.3, and 1.4, refer to the unadjusted incomes received by families or households. This misrepresents the living standards enjoyed by families with different sizes and compositions. A large family with $20,000 in annual income is clearly in a worse economic position than a small family with the same income. In addition, each family enters into the standard income distribution statistics with an equal weight, regardless of whether the family contains ten members or just two. Unrelated individuals in households are excluded altogether from the family income statistics because they are not considered members of families. In assessing the prevalence and severity of poverty, it obviously matters whether the typical poor family contains more or fewer members than the average family, and it also matters whether poverty is common among unrelated individuals, especially since such individuals constitute a growing percentage of the nation's population.

Figures 1.5 and 1.6 show the distribution of the income-to-poverty-line (or income-to-needs) ratio in 1998. Figure 1.5 shows the frequency distribution of this ratio for all people except those in the top 2 percent of the distribution. We have converted all income-to-needs ratios that are negative into zeros, but otherwise the distribution pattern is broadly similar to that of pretax family income, as shown in figure 1.1. The median income-to-needs ratio in 1998 was 3.09. For a family containing three members, this was equivalent to an annual income of about $40,200. The inequality of the income-to-needs ratio distribution is somewhat greater than the inequality of family income.[15] This means that adjustments for differing consumption requirements across families, appropriate weighting of families to account for their size, and inclusion of unrelated individuals in the calculations tend to increase the measured amount of cash income inequality.

Figure 1.6 focuses on the lower part of the income-to-needs distribution. People with a ratio below 1.0 are poor; people with a ratio greater than 1.0 are not poor. The figure shows the 1998 distribution of the ratio among people with incomes around the poverty threshold. About 34.5 million people, or 12.7 percent of the population, were unrelated individuals or members of families with incomes below the official poverty thresholds. Another 48.9 million, or 18.0 percent, had pretax cash incomes between one and two times the poverty thresholds. Among people with pretax incomes below the poverty line, the average income was 54 percent of the poverty threshold; the implication is that their cash incomes would have to almost double for them to reach the poverty threshold. The average family or unrelated person who was poor under the official definition needed $5,350 in extra annual income to reach the poverty line. Because 7.2 million families and 8.5 million unrelated individuals were poor in 1998, it follows that about $83.8 billion—or 1 percent of national output—would have been needed to elimi-

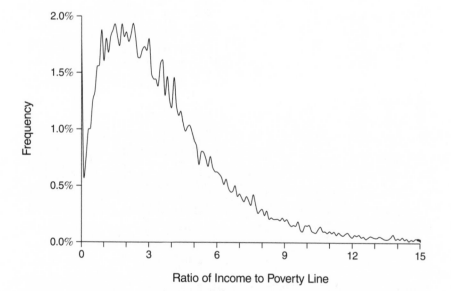

Figure 1.5 Distribution of Income-Poverty Ratio Among Persons, Entire Population, 1998 (*Source:* Authors' tabulations of March 1999 CPS files.)

nate cash poverty in the United States. This difference between poor families' actual incomes and the incomes needed for all of them to reach the poverty line is usually called the "poverty gap."

The trend in the official poverty rate is displayed in figure 1.7. The prevalence of poverty fell steeply in the decade after 1959, reached an all-time low in 1973, and then increased in the early 1980s and early 1990s. The sharp increases in poverty in the periods 1979 to 1983 and 1989 to 1993 were connected to the recessions in those years, but the magnitude of the increase was a surprise to most economists. Although the 1980 to 1982 recession produced the highest unemployment rate of the postwar period, the recession of 1974 to 1975 was almost as severe and did not cause the same dramatic rise in the poverty rate. In comparison with the recessions in 1974 to 1975 and 1980 to 1982, the 1990 to 1991 recession was comparatively brief and mild. (The peak monthly unemployment rate was 7.8 percent in the 1990s recession, compared with a peak rate of 9.0 percent in 1975 and 10.8 percent in 1982.) Even more surprising was the failure of the poverty rate to fall back to the level reached in the 1970s, even after prolonged eco-

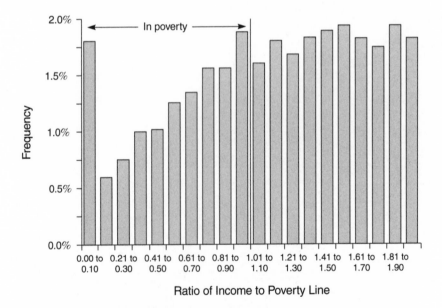

Figure 1.6 Distribution of Income-Poverty Ratio Among Persons with Income Below Twice the Poverty Level, 1998 (*Source:* Authors' tabulations of March 1999 CPS files.)

nomic expansions in the 1980s and 1990s. As illustrated in figures 1.2 and 1.3, the recessions of the 1980s and 1990s were accompanied or soon followed by large increases in income inequality. Even when average incomes rose in the 1980s and 1990s expansions, the share of income received by low-income households stagnated or even declined. Although the poverty rate dropped during the expansions, it did not fall far enough to offset the surge in poverty that took place during and immediately after the earlier recessions. The official statistics imply that poverty increased about one-tenth in the twenty years after 1978, climbing from 11.4 percent to 12.7 percent of the population.

Measuring Price Changes

Our interpretation of recent income and poverty trends is affected by the way the government measures price change. The official poverty estimates displayed in figure 1.7 are based on official poverty thresholds, which in turn are based on Bureau of Labor Statistics (BLS) estimates of changes

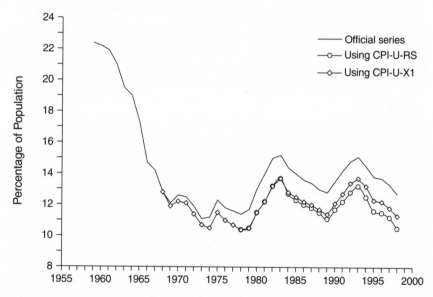

Figure 1.7 Percentage of Persons Who Are Poor Under Alternative Measures of Price Change, 1959 to 1998 (*Sources:* U.S. Bureau of the Census; authors' tabulations of March CPS files.)

in the Consumer Price Index for urban consumers. If the BLS measured price change inaccurately, the annual adjustments in the poverty thresholds would not reflect true changes in the cost of a minimum consumption bundle. Most economists believe BLS estimates of changes in the CPI-U overstated increases in consumer prices during many of the years after 1959. The BLS has reformed its methods for calculating price change, partly in response to economists' criticisms (Boskin et al. 1997; Stewart and Reed 1999). If the current methods used by the BLS to measure price change had been used in the past, the poverty thresholds would have increased more slowly and the number of Americans with incomes below the poverty line would have been smaller. Moreover, the real income trends displayed in figure 1.4 would appear far more favorable after 1973.[16]

Figure 1.7 also shows trends in poverty using two alternative price indexes. The first is the CPI-U-X1 series, which provides alternative (and lower) estimates of price change in most years between 1967 to 1983. The second alternative series is the CPI-U-RS, which implements all improvements in the measurement of price change that the BLS has adopted between 1978 and 1998.[17] Both alternatives to the standard price index imply there has been less inflation and therefore less absolute poverty since 1967. The difference between the poverty rates estimated using the CPI-U and the CPI-U-X1 grows progressively larger from 1968 through 1983, when the two price indexes start to show an identical rate of inflation. The gap between the official estimate of poverty and the estimate obtained using the CPI-U-RS continues to grow after 1983. By 1998 the poverty rate estimated using the CPI-U-X1 is about one-tenth lower than the official poverty rate (11.3 percent versus 12.7 percent), and the poverty rate using the CPI-U-RS is about one-sixth lower (10.5 percent versus 12.7 percent).

If we accept the estimates of price change implied by the CPI-U-RS series, the apparent increase in absolute poverty since the 1970s essentially disappears by 1998. Since 1979 there have been cyclical fluctuations in poverty linked to business-cycle contractions and expansions, but there has been no long-term change in the absolute poverty rate at the business-cycle peak. From a different viewpoint, even if we accept the CPI-U-RS inflation series, there has been no progress in reducing American poverty for more than two decades. The lack of progress should itself be surprising in view of the large increase in national income per person since 1979. This recent pattern stands in stark contrast to the progress against absolute poverty the nation achieved in the first quarter-century after World War II.

Alternative Measures of Income and Poverty

As noted earlier, the official measure of poverty is not the only yardstick for determining who is poor. Even if we restrict attention to measures of *income* poverty, the official U.S. definition has a number of deficiencies. It is based on a definition of income that ignores all noncash government transfers, even though many noncash transfers help pay for basic necessities, such as food, shelter, and medical care. The official income measure makes no allowance for income and payroll taxes, which reduce the household resources available to pay for necessities. For some families, ignoring the impact of the tax system leads to a serious understatement of income, because low-income working families with children are eligible for tax credits, such as the Earned Income Tax Credit (EITC), that can significantly boost family incomes. These credits are ignored in the official definition of poverty. The official definition also makes no distinction between sources of income that are costly to earn, such as wage income, and those that have little or no direct cost to the recipient, such as pensions and corporate dividends. The significant costs associated with getting to work and paying for child care when all adults in a household are employed are ignored in the official poverty definition when calculating the income produced by a job.

Some of the shortcomings in the official poverty definition lead to an overstatement of actual household income, while others yield an underestimate. On balance, the incomes available to low-income families are understated as a result of the omissions. Because noncash transfer benefits have been expanded over the past four decades, the understatement of household resources was larger in the late 1990s than it was when poverty estimates were first published in the 1960s. In 1998 the inclusion of capital gains and losses, the subtraction of income and payroll tax payments, and the addition of noncash income sources would have reduced the estimated poverty rate from 12.7 percent to less than 10.0 percent. And if the official thresholds had been updated after 1967 using the CPI-U-X1 instead of the CPI-U price index, the 1998 absolute poverty rate under an expanded definition of income would have fallen to 8 percent, about two-thirds the poverty rate calculated under the conventional definition and using the standard price index.[18]

As noted earlier, the 1995 NRC panel recommended changing the current definition of household income. Ignoring for a moment the panel's recommendations on the treatment of medical spending and work-related expenses, its proposals for broadening the definition of income would have reduced the poverty rate in 1997 from 13.3 percent under the official definition to 11.1 percent using the same thresholds but a broader definition of income. Subtracting an estimate of work-related expenses from countable income reduces measured income and thus increases the poverty rate, although the reduction in counted income does not wholly offset the impact of broadening the income definition to include near-cash benefits and refundable tax credits (Short et al. 1999, 9–10).

The panel's most controversial recommendation was to subtract out-of-pocket spending on medical care from household income. Because such spending is often burdensome, especially for the elderly and disabled, this procedure substantially increases the number of poor. The Census Bureau reckons that subtracting medical spending from the official definition of countable income would have increased the 1997 poverty rate from 13.3 percent to 16.3 percent (Short et al. 1999, 11).

The NRC panel also proposed important changes in determining poverty thresholds and calculating how the thresholds should be adjusted from one year to the next. Instead of updating the thresholds by the change in prices to ensure that a poverty-line income can purchase the same absolute standard of living each year, the panel proposed adjusting the thresholds in line with median consumption in the general population. If median consumption rises, as would be expected when real incomes improve, the real standard of living at the poverty thresholds would also improve. If adopted by the government, the NRC panel's suggested updating procedure could fundamentally change the U.S. poverty thresholds. In principle, the official thresholds have been updated to keep poverty-level living standards constant over time.

Although the NRC panel suggested a complete overhaul of the government's methods for determining poverty thresholds, its recommendations in that area have only a modest impact on the overall poverty rate. The panel's proposed thresholds are sometimes higher and sometimes lower than the existing official thresholds, depending on the circumstances of individual families, including the number and ages of family members. The principal effect of the panel's recommendations on thresholds is to change the composition of the population classified as poor. The panel's suggestions have a particularly large impact on the geographic distribution of poverty, because the panel proposed increasing thresholds in regions with high housing costs (mainly in large metropolitan areas on the East and West Coasts) and reducing them in regions where housing is inexpensive (mainly in less densely populated areas and in the middle of the country). The panel's recommendations on the measurement of household resources have far greater effects on the level and composition of poverty. On balance, they would increase poverty significantly, especially among low-income working families and among households that incur large medical bills (such as the elderly and disabled).

Trends Under Alternative Poverty Definitions

The NRC panel's recommendations have yet to be adopted, even in part, by the government. In this section, we adapt many of the panel's recommendations to define an alternative measure of poverty, one based on a broader definition of family resources than that used to estimate the official poverty rate. In particular, we include near-cash government transfers and net capital gains in our definition of gross family income; we subtract income and payroll taxes and add in the EITC; and we subtract estimated work-related expenses to determine net household income. We also follow the panel's recommendations with regard to establishing a poverty threshold based on a fixed percentage of median spending on food, clothing, and shelter. We have chosen a fixed percentage in the middle of the range recommended by the panel. For a family containing two adults and two children, the threshold in 1998 is 3 percent lower than the official poverty threshold for the same family. (Bear in mind that the alternative threshold, unlike the official poverty threshold, does not have to cover the cost of medical care or necessary work-related expenses, both of which are subtracted from income to determine a family's resources.) For other family sizes and compositions, the percentage difference between the official and alternative thresholds varies, because we also follow the panel's recommendation and adopt a more defensible equivalence scale than the one embodied in the official thresholds.[19]

In our tabulations, we do not adopt the NRC panel's method for annually updating the thresholds in line with recent changes in median consumption. Rather, we follow the government's current practice of updating the thresholds using the Consumer Price Index. Finally, we also follow the official practice of defining a single nationwide set of poverty thresholds. Because data on differences in local and regional housing costs are inadequate, we were not able to obtain consistent and reliable estimates of local and regional poverty thresholds.

The NRC panel's most controversial proposal was to subtract an estimate of household out-of-pocket medical spending from net household income in determining the resources each household has available to pay for the basic necessities of food, clothing, and shelter.[20] Many experts on poverty are not persuaded that this is the best approach for handling medical spending and health insurance in a poverty measure. Whether or not the panel's method is the best among feasible ways of calculating poverty, the lack of medical expenditure data makes it difficult to calculate historical poverty rates using its procedures. We have been able to include out-of-pocket medical spending in our estimate of household resources only for the 1990s. We therefore offer two alternative estimates of the trend in poverty, one that ignores medical out-of-pocket spending and a second that subtracts it in the definition of household net income.[21]

Estimates of the trend in the national poverty rate under the official definition and the two alternative definitions are displayed in figure 1.8, which shows the actual rates calculated under the three definitions for all

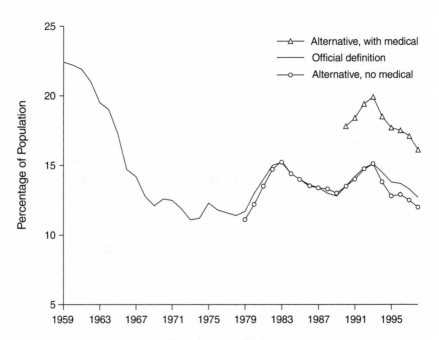

Figure 1.8 Poverty Rate Under Alternative Definitions of Poverty, 1959 to 1998 (*Sources:* U.S. Bureau of the Census; authors' tabulations of 1980 to 1999 March CPS files.)

years where a calculation of the rate is possible. If out-of-pocket medical spending is not subtracted from available resources, the poverty rates under the official definition and the alternative definitions are very close. The estimated poverty rate under the two definitions is within one percentage point over the entire period since 1979. After 1993 poverty declined somewhat faster under the alternative definition than under the official definition. The faster improvement in poverty under the alternative definition reflects the rapid expansion of the EITC in the 1990s, since the EITC is not counted in the official poverty definition. The most striking feature of figure 1.8 is the much higher rate of poverty if out-of-pocket medical expenses are subtracted from household resources. In comparison with a definition that ignores household medical spending, a definition that subtracts such spending adds about four and a half percentage points to the national poverty rate. As we shall see later, it also significantly changes the composition of poverty. Many of the people who are pushed into poverty have high medical expenses because they are old or chronically disabled.

The level and intensity of poverty under alternative poverty definitions are shown in table 1.1. The first two columns show the number of poor persons (in millions) and the poverty rate in selected years since 1968. The third column shows the average income of people below the poverty line measured as a percentage of the poverty threshold. The three poverty definitions imply that an average person who is poor received a 1998 income between about 53 percent and 61 percent of the poverty threshold. Americans who are poor have become increasingly impoverished over time under all three definitions. In 1968, for example, the 25.4 million people who were poor under the official definition received an annual before-tax cash income equal to 60 percent of the official poverty threshold; by 1998 this ratio for the 34.5 million officially poor at that time had fallen to 54 percent. The percentage of the population that is poor under the official definition was about the same in 1998 as in 1968, but the average income of the poor had dropped about one-tenth.[22] Under the alternative poverty definition that does not subtract out-of-pocket medical spending, the income-to-needs ratio has also fallen among the poor, but the decline has been more modest.

The last column in the table gives estimates of the poverty gap, defined as the amount of money needed to bring all poor Americans' incomes up to the poverty threshold. We measure the gap as a percentage of gross domestic product (GDP) to give readers a sense of the national effort required to eliminate poverty.[23] The poverty gap is roughly 1 percent of GDP under all three

Table 1.1 U.S. Poverty Under Alternative Income and Threshold
Definitions, 1968 to 1998

| | Poverty Population | | Average Income | Poverty Gap |
Year	(Millions)	Percentage of Population	of Poor (Percentage of Poverty Line)	(Percentage of GDP)
Under official poverty definition				
1968	25.4	12.8	60	1.14
1972	24.5	11.9	60	1.01
1976	25.0	11.8	60	0.96
1980	29.3	13.0	58	1.11
1984	33.7	14.4	56	1.19
1988	31.7	13.0	56	1.02
1992	38.0	14.8	55	1.18
1996	36.5	13.7	56	1.03
1998	34.5	12.7	54	0.96
Alternative poverty definition: not accounting for medical spending				
1979	24.7	11.1	64	0.79
1980	27.5	12.2	64	0.89
1981	30.7	13.5	64	0.97
1982	33.7	14.7	64	1.08
1983	35.5	15.3	64	1.08
1984	33.7	14.4	65	0.94
1985	33.1	14.0	65	0.91
1986	32.2	13.5	65	0.86
1987	32.3	13.4	65	0.84
1988	32.4	13.3	64	0.83
1989	32.0	13.0	64	0.79
1990	33.6	13.5	65	0.82
1991	35.2	14.0	64	0.88
1992	37.7	14.7	63	0.93
1993	39.2	15.1	62	0.99
1994	36.1	13.8	61	0.91
1995	33.8	12.8	64	0.79
1996	34.3	12.9	64	0.78
1997	33.6	12.5	62	0.79
1998	32.4	12.0	61	0.77

Table 1.1   (continued)

| Year | Poverty Population | | Average Income of Poor (Percentage of Poverty Line) | Poverty Gap (Percentage of GDP) |
	(Millions)	Percentage of Population		
Alternative poverty definition: subtracting medical spending from household income				
1990	44.3	17.8	58	1.32
1991	46.2	18.4	58	1.40
1992	49.8	19.4	56	1.50
1993	51.6	19.9	54	1.60
1994	48.4	18.5	54	1.48
1995	46.7	17.7	56	1.34
1996	46.6	17.5	57	1.30
1997	45.9	17.1	55	1.29
1998	43.6	16.1	53	1.24

Sources: U.S. Bureau of the Census; authors' tabulations of 1969 to 1999 March CPS files.

definitions of poverty. Measured as a share of GDP, it has fallen since 1968, though the rate of decline is neither impressive nor steady. Because the poverty rate has failed to decline since the 1970s while the average income of the poor has shrunk, it may seem surprising that the poverty gap was smaller in the late 1990s than in the late 1970s. The absolute size of the poverty gap has increased, but national income has increased even faster. The poverty gap thus represents a slowly and erratically shrinking share of GDP.

INCOME SOURCES OF THE POOR   Table 1.2 sheds light on the income sources of the poor. Each element of income is measured as a percentage of the person's poverty threshold. (The poverty lines used in these calculations are the alternative poverty thresholds based on median family consumption of food, clothing, and shelter.) We show the income sources of three groups of people. The first column displays average incomes of people who would be poor if only their pretax market incomes were counted in determining their poverty status. This group of people is often referred to as the "pretax and pretransfer poor." Market incomes include pretax wages, salaries, self-employment income, pensions (except Social Security), interest, dividends, and capital gains and losses. It also includes an adjustment to

Table 1.2. Sources of Net Income Among People with Income Below the Poverty Threshold, Under Alternative Concepts of Income, 1998

Income Concept or Component of Net Income	Counting Pre-tax Market Income (1)	Counting Post-tax Cash and Near-cash Income (2)	Subtracting Out-of-Pocket Medical Spending (3)
Market income	35%	33%	48%
Taxes (except EITC)	−3	−3	−5
Social insurance	50	9	16
Means-tested transfers (including EITC)	22	22	20
Out-of-pocket medical spending	−18	−13	−25
Total income, ignoring medical spending[a]	104	61	78
Total income, subtracting medical spending	86	48	53
People below poverty threshold (millions)	57.6	32.4	43.6

Source: Authors' tabulations of March 1999 CPS files.

Note: Average income of each type is measured as a percentage of the poverty threshold. The poverty thresholds are derived from the Census Bureau's estimates of the food, clothing, and shelter consumption patterns of the median reference family, updated to 1998 using the CPI-U and the three-parameter equivalence scale (Short et al. 1999, C-2). The computation of family poverty status in column 2 is identical to that in the middle panel of table 1.1; the computation of poverty status in column 3 is identical to that in the bottom panel of table 1.1.

a. Post-tax, post-transfer income, including near-cash transfer benefits.

reflect necessary work-related expenses of people who derive part of their incomes from employment. In 1998 the market incomes of 57.6 million Americans (21 percent of the population) fell below the poverty thresholds. The second column shows income sources of people who have post-tax and post-transfer incomes that are below the poverty threshold. In determining whether these people are in poverty, we added cash and near-cash government transfers to market income and subtracted income and payroll taxes. We did not make any adjustment for out-of-pocket medical spending. About 32 million people (12 percent of the population) are poor under this income definition. The third column shows the income sources of people who are poor after subtracting an estimate of their out-of-pocket medical expenses. Almost 44 million people (16.1 percent of the population) are poor under this concept of income.

The average market income of the poor is very low no matter which income concept is used to determine poverty. On average the people in the three groups derive only one-third to one-half of a poverty-line income from market income sources alone. Not surprisingly, the estimated taxes paid by poor people are also quite low. On average, tax payments (ignoring the EITC) amount to 3 to 5 percent of the poverty threshold and to less than 10 percent of household income. In contrast, social insurance benefits are quite large, especially among people who are poor on the basis of their market incomes alone. These people on average receive social insurance payments equal to one-half the poverty line (see table 1.2, column 1). Social insurance benefits are typically much smaller among people who are poor based on their post-tax and post-transfer incomes. From this it follows that social insurance removes many people with low market incomes from the ranks of the poor. Programs such as Social Security and workers' compensation were specifically designed to replace one kind of market income—wages—when it is temporarily or permanently reduced because of death, injury, or retirement. Means-tested benefits are an important source of income no matter which concept of income is used to determine poverty status. (Note that we include EITC payments among means-tested transfers rather than in taxes.) Poor people receive means-tested benefits that on average equal one-fifth of the poverty threshold.

A comparison of the first two columns in table 1.2 suggests that a large fraction of people who are poor on the basis of their pretax and pretransfer incomes are removed from poverty as a result of the combined impact of government tax and transfer policies. Column 1 shows that the average post-tax, post-transfer incomes of the pretax, pretransfer poor are three times larger than their market incomes. In fact, their average total income before subtraction of medical expenses is slightly higher than the poverty line. Americans with market incomes below the poverty threshold on average have post-tax, post-transfer incomes that are above the poverty line. The transfers received by people who are poor using a post-tax, post-transfer income definition are simply too small to remove them from poverty. In fact, the people who remain poor after taxes have been subtracted and transfer payments have been added to income derive most of their incomes from the market. Their market income is 33 percent of the poverty threshold, but their net income from taxes and transfers is just 28 percent of the threshold.

When out-of-pocket medical spending is subtracted from household income, the prevalence of poverty increases and the composition of the poor shifts toward an older and sicker population. Note that the average predicted medical expenditure of people who are poor after medical spending has been subtracted is 25 percent of the poverty threshold. This spending is equal to almost one-third of household income before medical outlays are subtracted (twenty-five divided by seventy-eight).[24] Predicted outlays on health insurance and medical care in the population at large are extremely unequal. Even middle-class households facing large medical bills can be pushed into poverty under the NRC panel's preferred definition of income. For families in modest circumstances, the risk of poverty is greater, because even average levels of health spending can severely deplete family finances.

Poverty Rates for Population Subgroups Under Alternative Definitions of Poverty

Poverty rates vary widely across different population groups, and many of these differences have persisted for decades. Differences in poverty rates by race, for example, have proved stubbornly resistant to policy remedies over the past generation. Figure 1.9 shows the trend in official poverty rates for groups of Americans defined on the basis of their race and ethnicity. White Americans have the lowest poverty rate, though the prevalence of poverty among Asians and Pacific Islanders is not much higher. African Americans have historically suffered the highest poverty rates, but in recent years the rate among people of Hispanic descent has been approximately as high. This is partly because of the noticeable decline in the black poverty rate in the 1990s. But it also can be traced to a long-term trend toward worsening poverty among people of Hispanic background. The rapid inflow of Hispanic immigrants with limited education and skills during the 1980s and 1990s contributed to this long-term trend. Much of the trend increase in white poverty rates is due to the trends among whites with Hispanic backgrounds. Aside from cyclical fluctuations, the official poverty rate among non-Hispanic whites has been essentially flat since the mid-1970s.

The differences in poverty rates across subpopulations are not the result of peculiarities in the official poverty measure. With a few exceptions, the differences are evident under any plausible definition of income poverty. Table 1.3 provides a statistical portrait of the poor in 1998 under the three definitions of poverty mentioned in table 1.1—the government's official poverty definition; one that uses the alternative poverty thresholds described in the previous section and a comprehensive definition of net cash and near-cash income after taxes and work expenses but ignores medical out-of-pocket spending; and one that starts with this alternative definition but then subtracts medical spending from household income.

The poverty rates of black and Hispanic Americans are significantly higher

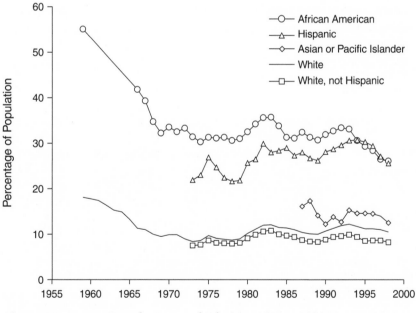

Figure 1.9 Poverty Rates by Race and Ethnicity, 1959 to 1998 (*Source:* U.S. Bureau of the Census.)

Table 1.3 Profile of the Poor Under Alternative Poverty Definitions, 1998

Group or Characteristic	Percentage of Group That Is Poor			Percentage of Poor in Group		
	(1)[a]	(2)[b]	(3)[c]	(1)	(2)	(3)
All persons	12.7	12.0	16.1	100	100	100
Race and ethnicity						
White	10.5	10.0	14.0	68	69	72
White, non-Hispanic	8.2	7.9	11.5	46	47	51
African American	26.1	23.6	28.8	26	25	23
Asian or Pacific Islander	12.5	12.8	16.3	4	4	4
Hispanic[d]	25.6	24.0	30.0	23	23	22
Member of immigrant household[e]						
Yes	21.9	21.1	27.1	20	20	20
No	11.5	10.8	14.6	80	80	80
Age group						
Children (under age eighteen)	18.9	17.0	21.2	39	38	35
Non-elderly adults (age eighteen to sixty-four)	10.5	10.4	13.5	51	54	52
Elderly (age sixty-five and older)	10.5	8.9	17.7	10	9	13
Family structure						
In all families	11.2	10.7	14.6	74	75	76
In married-couple families	6.2	6.0	9.3	32	33	38
In families with a female householder, no spouse present	33.1	31.1	37.4	37	38	34
Unrelated individuals	19.9	17.4	22.9	25	23	22
Residence						
In metropolitan areas	12.3	11.5	15.1	78	78	77
In central cities	18.5	17.0	21.6	43	42	40
In suburbs	8.7	8.2	11.3	35	35	36
Outside metropolitan areas	14.4	14.0	19.5	22	22	23
Region						
Northeast	12.3	10.7	14.6	18	17	17
Midwest	10.3	9.8	13.5	19	19	20
South	13.7	13.5	17.9	38	39	39
West	14.0	13.0	17.1	25	25	24
Head of family or spouse works						
Yes	8.7	8.6	11.9	57	59	61
No	31.6	28.0	35.9	43	41	39

Sources: U.S. Bureau of the Census; authors' tabulations of March 1999 CPS file.

a. Official poverty measure.

b. Alternative measure, ignoring the impact on net income of medical out-of-pocket spending.

c. Alternative measure, subtracting medical out-of-pocket spending from household income.

d. Persons of Hispanic origin may be of any race.

e. Member of a family headed by an immigrant or an unrelated individual who is an immigrant.

than those of Asian Americans and non-Hispanic whites. For example, under the official definition, the rates for the four groups were 26.1, 25.6, 12.5, and 8.2 percent, respectively. Taken together, slightly less than half of the nation's poor are of African American or Hispanic descent. The Hispanic poverty rate is affected by the large proportion of recent immigrants in the Latino population. (Thirty-five percent of Hispanic Americans are immigrants.) The prevalence of poverty in immigrant households is almost twice the rate in non-immigrant households under all three definitions of poverty.

Note that the differential between the poverty rate of whites and other groups is somewhat smaller under a broad definition of income that accounts for out-of-pocket spending on medical care. Although non-Hispanic whites have high rates of health insurance coverage and thus have a generous proportion of their medical consumption reimbursed by third-party payers, they are typically older than members of other racial or ethnic groups. With increased age comes a higher risk of serious illness and costly medical outlays. Hence, a larger percentage of whites than of other groups face high out-of-pocket medical bills, even when reimbursement from insurance providers is taken into account.

The choice of a poverty definition makes a significant difference in the relative poverty rates of different age groups. Under the official poverty definition, both elderly and non-elderly adults had the same poverty rates in 1998. The rate among children was 80 percent higher than that among adults (18.9 percent versus 10.5 percent). Under the second definition of poverty, the rate among children and the elderly falls while the rate among non-elderly adults is virtually unaffected (column 2). Under this definition, the elderly face the *lowest* risk of poverty (8.9 percent). Under the alternative definition that subtracts out-of-pocket medical spending, the poverty rate among the elderly almost doubles, rising to 17.7 percent (column 3). The rates among children and non-elderly adults rise more modestly, to 21.2 and 13.5 percent, respectively. Because the elderly face the highest medical bills, their relative income position suffers the most under the third poverty definition.

Of course, the heavy medical spending of the elderly also provides genuine enhancements to their well-being. As older Americans' spending has increased over time, their average health has improved and their risk of dying at a given age has declined (Wolfe and Smeeding 1999, table 2). Under a definition of income that subtracts medical spending from household income, the upward trend in out-of-pocket spending could yield an increase in measured poverty, even though it also produces a real improvement in health, especially among the people who are spending the greatest amounts. For this reason, social scientists are divided on how our poverty measures should account for health insurance and medical spending.

People who live with their relatives typically have lower poverty rates than people who live alone. Almost one-fifth of unrelated individuals were poor in 1998 under the official poverty threshold, whereas 11.2 percent of people who lived in families were poor. People in families headed by single, divorced, separated, or widowed women have even higher poverty rates than people who live alone (33.1 percent). These families typically contain only one potential breadwinner. If the potential breadwinner is a widow, she is usually too old to work. Single mothers who head families containing children must divide their time between working and rearing children. This leaves many single mothers with too little time or energy to earn a good living. In addition, a large percentage of single mothers, especially never-married mothers, have limited education and few labor-market skills. Even if less-skilled single mothers worked full-time, their low hourly wages would keep their annual incomes low.

In recent years, the government has expanded the range of public benefits available to low-income, working single mothers, even as it has reduced their access to cash welfare benefits. Expansions in child health insurance programs, subsidized child care, and the EITC have improved the situation of low-income working parents, but even under a broad definition of income, 31.1 percent of the people in female-headed households remain poor (column 2). In contrast, married-couple families enjoy major advantages in earning market incomes. The parents in such families are usually better educated and thus earn higher wages than single mothers, and they have more time to devote to paid employment. The official poverty rate for people in married-couple families in 1998 was just 6.2 percent.

If a family head does not work, the family's risk of being poor under all three poverty definitions is very high. A person who is a member of a family without a working head faces about three times the risk of poverty of a person who is a member of a family with a working head. Most U.S. families contain a working head, however, so about 60 percent of the poor live in families where the head works. Estimates in table 1.3 also show that poverty is more prevalent in the South and the West and in central cities than it is elsewhere. Under the broadest income definition, which accounts for medical spending, the poverty rate is almost as high outside of metropolitan areas as it is in the central cities. Residents of the nation's suburbs have roughly one-half the probability of being poor as residents of the central city or of nonmetropolitan areas.

Trends in Poverty Among Population Subgroups

Table 1.4 shows trends in the poverty rate among various subpopulations over the four-decade period after 1959. Many of the differences between groups have remained stable over time. For example, women have consistently faced a greater risk of poverty than men, and the poverty differential has changed only modestly since the mid-1960s. The most striking change in relative poverty rates has been among the nation's elderly. In 1959 older Americans faced a poverty rate that was 18.2 percentage points higher than that of non-elderly adults (35.2 versus 17.0 percent). In 1979 the differential had fallen to 6.3 percentage points, and by 1998 the elderly had the same poverty rate as non-elderly adults.

During the 1960s and early 1970s, the elderly benefited from the rapid expansion and increasing maturity of the Social Security and private pension systems. More retired workers had been covered by Social Security and an employer pension plan during lengthy parts of their careers, and thus they qualified for much better pensions when they stopped working than had retired workers in earlier generations. The elderly also benefited from the liberalization of cash public assistance benefits in the 1970s. None of the improvement in aged Americans' circumstances can be traced to improvements in their current earnings. The employment rate of the elderly fell significantly and almost without interruption between the 1950s and the mid-1980s (Burtless and Quinn 2000). The improvement in circumstances of the low-income elderly is almost entirely traceable to increases in government-financed transfer payments.

Non-elderly adults, with the exception of the disabled, have not benefited from an equivalent expansion in government benefits. Their poverty rate fell from 17.0 percent in 1959 to 8.9 percent in 1979, but rose to 10.5 percent in 1998. Nondisabled adults who lack job skills remain at high risk of poverty, especially if they have child dependents. This risk increased in the 1980s and early 1990s for families in which the main breadwinner was an unskilled or semiskilled male. In the decade and a half after 1979, real wages fell as much as 20 percent for men with hourly earnings in the bottom half of the male wage distribution. Younger workers suffered some of

Table 1.4 Composition of the Population in Poverty Under the Official Poverty
Definition, 1959 to 1998

	Percentage of Group′ That Is Poor			Percentage of Poor in Group		
	1959	1979	1998	1959	1979	1998
All persons	22.4	11.7	12.7	100	100	100
Gender						
Females	16.3[a]	13.2	14.3	57[a]	58	57
Males	13.0[a]	10.0	11.1	43[a]	42	43
Member of immigrant household[b]						
Yes	—	14.6	21.9	—	10	20
No	—	11.4	11.5	—	90	80
Age group						
Children (under age eighteen)	27.3	16.4	18.9	44	40	39
Nonelderly adults (age eighteen to sixty-four)	17.0	8.9	10.5	42	46	51
Elderly (age sixty-five and older)	35.2	15.2	10.5	14	14	10
Family structure						
In all families	20.8	10.2	11.2	88	77	74
In families with a female householder, no spouse present	49.4	34.9	33.1	18	36	37
Unrelated individuals	46.1	21.9	19.9	12	22	25
Residence						
In metropolitan areas	15.3	10.7	12.3	43	62	78
In central cities	18.3	15.7	18.5	26	37	43
In suburbs	12.2	7.2	8.7	17	25	35
Outside metropolitan areas	33.2	13.8	14.4	55	38	22
Region						
Northeast	—	10.4	12.3	—	19	18
Midwest	—	9.7	10.3	—	22	19
South	35.4	15.0	13.7	48	41	38
West	—	10.0	14.0	—	16	25
Head of family or spouse works						
Yes	—	7.1	8.7	—	49	57
No	—	32.0	31.6	—	51	43

Sources: U.S. Bureau of the Census, Camarota (1999, 21); and authors' tabulations of March
1980 and 1999 CPS files.

a. Data by gender are for 1966 rather than 1959.

b. Member of a family headed by an immigrant or an unrelated individual who is an
immigrant. Data for 1979 are based on 1980 decennial census data, with overall rate adjusted to
match the CPS poverty rate for 1979.

the worst losses in earning power. Workers in their twenties typically have the lowest skill levels because they have not yet accumulated much job experience. The wage differential for extra work experience increased substantially in the 1970s and 1980s, placing young workers at an even greater disadvantage relative to middle-aged and older workers.

Since workers in their twenties and thirties are the main breadwinners in many families containing children, especially young children, the erosion in unskilled young workers' real wages increased the risk that families containing children would be poor. To some extent, the erosion of entry-level male wages was offset by increased employment among young mothers. Married mothers' growing earnings supplemented the shrinking paychecks of less skilled husbands. The child poverty rate in 1998—18.9 percent—was lower than in 1959, but higher than in 1979.

A rising percentage of young families contain only one parent rather than two. The strategy of putting two parents rather than just one in the workforce is obviously not feasible for single-parent families. In 1959, 18 percent of all poor persons lived in female-headed families. The percentage had doubled by 1998. In a society that expects nondisabled working-age adults to be self-supporting, the adverse wage trends facing young, unskilled workers have placed large numbers of young adults and their children at increased risk of poverty. Although several safety net programs, such as Medicaid and the EITC, have been expanded or reformed to offer additional help to low-income parents, the extra aid has not been enough to offset the impact of lower real wages and higher rates of out-of-wedlock childbearing. Moreover, the expansion of these in-kind transfers and tax credit programs is not reflected in the government's main measure of family income, which includes only pretax cash income.

Table 1.4 also documents a shift in the geographical distribution of American poverty. In 1959 the poverty rate in the South (35.4 percent) was substantially higher than it was in the nation as a whole (22.4 percent). By 1998 the southern rate (13.7 percent) was much closer to the national poverty rate (12.7 percent). In contrast to the improving situation of the South is the declining relative position of the West. Partly because of a surge in immigration from low-income countries, the western states now contain a much larger concentration of the country's poorest residents.

There has also been a redistribution of poverty from rural toward urban areas and a trend toward greater concentration of poverty in central cities. In 1959, 55 percent of the nation's poor lived outside of metropolitan areas.

The risk of poverty outside of metropolitan areas at that time (33.2 percent) was much greater than it was inside major cities (18.3 percent) or their suburbs (12.2 percent). The incidence of poverty in central cities, though higher than in the suburbs, was below that in the nation at large (22.4 percent). By 1998 the poverty rate outside of metropolitan areas (14.4 percent) was only modestly greater than that in the nation as a whole, while the rate in central cities (18.5 percent) was much higher than the national average. Over time the poverty rate in the suburbs edged closer to that in the nation as a whole. This is hardly surprising. Suburbs contained only 31 percent of the nation's population in 1959; by 1998 a majority of the population lived in suburbs. The shift of the Americans out of central cities, and especially out of non-metropolitan areas, has brought a shift of the nation's poor population toward the suburbs as well. The poverty rate in the suburbs, however, remains substantially lower than it is in central cities and rural areas.

Summary and Outlook

After declining steeply between World War II and 1973, the official poverty rate increased by about one-seventh over the next quarter-century. The official rate increased sharply during and immediately after the recessions of 1980 to 1982 and 1990 to 1991. Although it eventually fell in the long expansions of the 1980s and 1990s, the official rate did not shrink enough to bring American poverty down to the levels observed in the 1970s. The unfavorable trend does not necessarily imply that absolute poverty has worsened since 1973. Shortcomings in the official definition mean that many kinds of income received by the poor are not counted when measuring the resources available to low-income households. Some types of uncounted income, such as food stamps and the Earned Income Tax Credit, have increased much more rapidly than the forms of income that are counted in the official poverty definition. In addition, deficiencies in the Consumer Price Index caused the official poverty thresholds to rise more rapidly than the true cost of a fixed poverty-line consumption bundle. If the poverty thresholds had been indexed to a better measure of consumer prices, the absolute poverty rate would have increased much more slowly (and may even have declined).

Even allowing for major defects in the official poverty statistics, however, the evidence powerfully suggests that progress against poverty has been slight since 1973. It is natural to ask why the trend in poverty was so different in the twenty-five years after 1973 compared with the trend in the twenty-five years before. One difference was the slower growth of productivity and, consequently, of average earnings. From 1947 through 1973, output per employed American increased at an average rate of 2.4 percent a year; between 1973 and 1998, it increased at an average rate of just 1.2 percent a year. The slower rate of improvement in average output meant that working Americans' incomes did not increase as fast in the 1980s and 1990s as they did in the 1950s and 1960s. Even if the distribution of income had remained unchanged, the nation's progress in reducing poverty would have slowed.

The distribution did not remain unchanged after 1973, however. It shifted in a way that hurt low-income Americans. The reasons for this shift are examined in detail elsewhere in this volume. Researchers agree that the growth in income inequality was linked to growing disparities in worker pay. Some, but not all, of the increase in wage differences was associated with growing pay differentials based on workers' education, job experience, and occupational skills. Workers with limited skills suffered declining real pay from 1980 through the mid-1990s; highly skilled workers—including superstars in sports, entertainment, management, and the professions—enjoyed rapid gains in pay. Researchers also agree that shifts in family composition reinforced the effects of widening wage disparities. The percentage of Americans living in single-parent families grew while the fraction in married-couple families declined. This trend increased the percentage of Americans, especially children, who faced a high risk of being poor, for single-parent families tend to have fewer wage earners and are thus much less likely to enjoy a middle-class income.

Shifts in the labor market and changes in family composition go only partway toward explaining the slower progress against poverty in the years after 1973. Much of the reduction in poverty during the 1950s and 1960s was caused by public policy reform. New or liberalized programs boosted the incomes of people whose situation was not directly affected by the state of the economy. The nonworking elderly, the disabled, and single mothers saw big improvements in their cash incomes between 1950 and 1973. Social Security benefits became much more generous and were provided to many more of the frail and elderly. Cash welfare benefits for single parents and the indigent aged and disabled were liberalized in the 1960s and early 1970s. The low-income elderly were much better off in the 1970s than they had been in the 1950s because the government provided larger transfer payments, not because a healthy economy and fatter paychecks gave them higher market incomes. The elderly and disabled actually *reduced* their employment rates over the whole period from the 1950s through the 1970s, partly in response to larger public transfers.

Policy reform did not produce equivalent income gains for the poor after the 1970s. The 1980s and 1990s saw major expansions in only two kinds of public programs—the Earned Income Tax Credit and public medical insurance for the indigent. Neither program directly affected the official poverty rate because neither provided benefits that added to families' pretax cash incomes. Even using an expanded definition of poverty, the higher benefits provided by these programs did not offset the adverse effects of family composition shifts and increased inequality in market incomes.

The healthy economy of the late 1990s helped push down the poverty rate under all three definitions we consider in this chapter. The nation's experience since 1979 suggests, however, that a healthy economy alone will never reduce the American poverty rate to the levels prevailing in northwestern Europe (see chapter 2). To achieve a much lower poverty rate without a major overhaul of public policy, the United States would need to experience a dramatic reduction in wage inequality or a sharp reversal in the family composition trends that have prevailed over the past four decades. Although such changes in the economic and social climate are possible, they are not very likely. Changes in public policy that provide good health insurance, better incomes to the indigent elderly and disabled, and supplements to the earned incomes of working-but-poor breadwinners represent the best hope for achieving large poverty reductions in the near term.

Appendix: Procedures for Estimating Poverty Under Alternative Experimental Measures

Both of our alternative measures of poverty follow the NRC panel's recommendations with respect to construction of the *basic poverty threshold*, although we did not follow the panel's recommendation in our method for annually adjusting the basic threshold. Instead, we followed the government's current practice of adjusting the thresholds to reflect annual changes in the CPI-U. We used a variant of the equivalence scale proposed by the

NRC panel to calculate the thresholds for families of different sizes and compositions. The differences between our procedures and those used to construct estimates of poverty under the official poverty guidelines are described in this appendix.

Procedures for Measuring Household Resources

Besides pretax cash income (the measure of income used in the official poverty definition), we used in-kind benefits, except health insurance (that is, food stamps, school lunches, energy assistance, housing subsidies), at market value and net capital gains. We subtracted federal and state income taxes and FICA contributions. We also added refundable tax credits (the EITC). We subtracted work-related expenses calculated using the SIPP (Survey of Income and Program Participation) median method (see Short et al. 1999, C-11–14). When we calculated household resources to reflect medical spending, we subtracted estimates of household out-of-pocket medical spending, including spending on insurance premiums. Estimates of out-of-pocket spending are derived using the medical out-of-pocket (MOOP) imputation method, as described by Short et al. (1999, C-16–19).

Threshold Changes

The NRC panel recommended that poverty thresholds provide enough income to cover the cost of food, clothing, shelter, and other common needs (except medical care). The basic threshold is calculated for a reference family consisting of two adults and two children. The panel proposed that the reference family's threshold be set equal to some plausible percentage of the median spending on food, clothing, and shelter of all families of that type, as measured in the Consumer Expenditure Survey. The panel suggested that a plausible range would be 89.7 to 103.75 percent of median spending on food, clothing, and shelter. Our basic threshold represents the midpoint of this range, or 96.725 percent of median spending. (For a more detailed discussion of how the basic threshold is estimated using the Consumer Expenditure Survey, see Short et al. 1999, pp. 4–5, C-2.)

To calculate poverty thresholds of families with different sizes and compositions, we used the three-parameter equivalence scale proposed by Betson (1996), as implemented by Short et al. (1999, C-1–3). In this scale, let A equal the number of adults in the family, and K equal the number of children in the family.

1. For single parents: $[A + .8 + .5*(K - 1)]^{.7}$
2. For all other families: $[A + .5*K]^{.7}$
3. The ratio of the scale for two adults compared with one adult is 1.41.

To adjust our alternative thresholds for successive years between 1979 and 1998, we increased the thresholds in line with the annual percentage change in the CPI-U. The same procedure is used to adjust the official poverty thresholds. We used a single set of poverty thresholds for the entire nation, the same procedure used to develop the official poverty thresholds.

CHAPTER 2

Changes in Family Structure: Implications for Poverty and Related Policy

MARIA CANCIAN AND DEBORAH REED

Changes in family structure are central to poverty policy discussions because marriage and fertility have undergone substantial changes recently and because poverty rates vary dramatically by family structure. In 1998 about 7 percent of married couples with children, 39 percent of single-mother families, and 15 percent of single-father families were poor.[1] The "typical" American family is harder to find today than it was in 1950. Not only is there greater variety in family forms, but the members of any given family are more likely to experience changes in household structure over time (Bumpass and Lu 2000).

In this chapter, we trace changes in family structure over the past thirty years and discuss the implications for poverty and income support policy. We review changes in marriage, childbearing, family living arrangements, and labor force participation. We document declines in marriage and increases in divorce, and we explain the trends behind the increasing proportion of children born outside of marriage. Increases in cohabitation are important to our understanding of these changes; we discuss family living arrangements, including cohabitation with an unmarried partner as well as the extent to which single parents live with other related adults.

We then review the changing relationship between women's labor force participation and their marital and maternal status. After exploring alternative explanations for these changes, we discuss their importance in accounting for changes in poverty rates and the composition of the poor. We find that changes in family structure alone would have led to a substantial increase in poverty, but that this effect was mitigated by the growth of women's labor force participation. We also show that considering cohabita-

69

tion reduces the importance of changes in family structure for explaining poverty trends.

In addition to its relationship to economic well-being, family structure is of particular interest because children living with only one parent may be more vulnerable to other risks, even after taking economic factors into account (McLanahan and Sandefur 1994; Cherlin, Kiernan, and Chase-Lansdale 1995; see also Corcoran, this volume). Poverty also creates challenges for families that may be particularly difficult to manage with only one available parent (Oliker 1995; Edin and Lein 1997). Thus, recent changes in family structure not only place more individuals at greater risk of poverty but also may increase their vulnerability to the challenges associated with poverty.

Changes in family behaviors are central to discussions of poverty *policy* because policies that treat different types of families differently may have unintended effects on family structure. The prototypical example is Aid to Families with Dependent Children (AFDC), which until 1996 was the primary income support program for poor families with children. AFDC benefits were largely limited to single-parent families and, as we discuss later, its critics have argued that AFDC benefits encouraged nonmarital fertility and may actually have increased poverty (Murray 1984).

Debates on income support policy and family structure also reflect changing definitions of gender roles, parental responsibility, and the family. For example, the employment emphasis of the 1996 welfare reform reflects growing acceptance of maternal employment, even in the case of mothers with young children (Cancian 2001). Reflecting concerns about the incentive effects of alternative policies, as well as changing expectations of parental roles, many recent income support policy reforms attempt to encourage certain family structures and to meet the challenges of others.

In this chapter, we analyze the importance of changes in family structure and family behavior for poverty. Our analysis largely focuses on *women's* marriage rates, fertility, living arrangements, and employment. This has been the conventional approach in this area in part because public concern has been for the "deserving poor"—those who tend to be seen as not personally responsible for their poverty. This includes children and, to a lesser extent, women. (It also includes older adults and individuals with disabilities.) The focus on women's behaviors follows from the concern for children, given contemporary assumptions about the primary responsibility of women for fertility decisions and child well-being, as well as the reality that most children live with their mother, and less often with their father. In the case of employment patterns, an explanation of changes in poverty naturally focuses on the labor force participation of women because it has grown dramatically during a period of relatively modest participation declines for men (Fullerton 1999).

Trends in Family Structure

The policy implications of current poverty patterns, as well as prospects for the future, depend on the interrelationships between poverty and marriage, childbearing, family living arrangements, and employment status. We review trends over the past thirty years, considering differences by race and ethnicity where the data permit.

Marriage, Divorce, and Cohabitation

The "Ozzie and Harriet" family, including an employed father, a homemaker mother, and children, may never have been as dominant empirically as it was in popular conceptions of the family. Nonetheless, in 1970, 42 percent of all families fit this general model, and thirty years later only 16 percent did (U.S. Department of Labor 2001). In fact, almost one-third of children were born to unmarried mothers in recent years, and research that follows families over time shows that half of all children will spend at least some portion of their childhood living with only one parent (Bumpass and Raley 1995).

Family composition changes reflect changes in the proportion of individuals who marry, the stability of those marriages, and for those who divorce, the probability of remarriage. Because of the increasing importance of cohabitation as a prelude to, or substitute for, marriage (Bumpass and Lu 2000; Seltzer 2000), we discuss the implications of cohabitation for the interpretation of marriage trends and related policy.

Figure 2.1 illustrates changes in the proportions of married individuals, by age.[2] It shows that the proportion of women who are currently married has declined substantially over the period. The first line shows that in 1970 almost 80 percent of women between the ages of twenty-five and twenty-nine were married, with the share married remaining fairly stable through the forty- to forty-four-year-old category. By 1999 only about 50 percent of women were married by age twenty-five to twenty-nine, and even by age forty to forty-four, only about two-thirds were married. The steepest declines in most age-specific marriage percentages occurred between 1970 and 1980, and between 1980 and 1990, with more modest declines in the 1990s.

The declining proportion of women who are currently married reflects a growth in the proportion of women who never marry, as well as changes in divorce, remarriage, and cohabitation. In 1970, 95 percent of women had been married by age forty to forty-four, a figure that had declined modestly to 90 percent in 1999. The proportion currently married fell more dramatically because of substantial increases in divorce rates over the past thirty years. In 1970 about 6 percent of women in their thirties and early forties were divorced. Just ten years later, the figure had doubled, to 12 percent. By 1999 the percentage of ever-married women who were divorced remained at 12 percent for women age thirty to thirty-four but had risen to 18 percent for women age forty to forty-four.[3]

Any discussion of trends in marital status for all women obscures substantial variation across racial and ethnic groups. Figure 2.2 shows the percentage of women married and cohabiting at age forty to forty-four for white non-Hispanics, black non-Hispanics, Hispanics, Asian and Pacific Islanders,

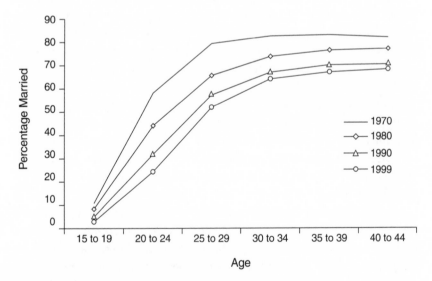

Figure 2.1 Married Women, by Age, 1970 to 1999 (*Sources:* Authors' calculations from the decennial census (1970, 1980, 1990) and CPS files (1998 and 1999 combined).)

and American Indians. First, consider marriage only. A relatively high proportion of white women were married, with the share declining moderately: between 1970 and 1999, the percentage of white women age forty to forty-four who were married declined from 85 to 72 percent. Over the same period, the proportion of black women who were married declined from 61 to 44 percent. The proportion married for Hispanic women declined from 78 to 67 percent, remained fairly stable for Asians and Pacific Islanders at about 80 percent, and declined more substantially, from 76 to 58 percent, for American Indians. The two groups with the lowest proportion married in 1970 (blacks and American Indians) also experienced the sharpest declines, such that differences in the proportion married by race and ethnicity increased over this period, at least through 1990.

Figure 2.2 also shows that rates of cohabitation have increased dramatically over time.[4] Calculations of the proportion of women who are married *or* cohabiting show a smaller decline than that shown in figure 2.1. For example, while the proportion of white women married at age forty to forty-four declined from 85 to 72 percent between 1970 and 1999, the proportion married or cohabiting fell only from 85 to 77 percent. Other evidence sug-

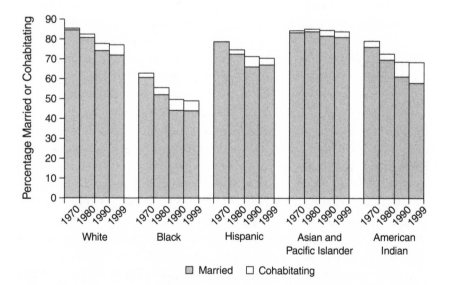

Figure 2.2 Married and Cohabiting Women, Age Forty to Forty-five, by Race and Ethnicity, 1970 to 1999 (*Source:* Authors' calculations from the decennial census (1970, 1980, 1990) and CPS files (1998 and 1999 combined).)

gests that increases in cohabitation account for an even greater part of the decline in marriage at younger ages (Bumpass, Sweet, and Cherlin 1991).

Differences in marriage patterns by race and ethnicity are also affected by the inclusion of cohabitation. As noted earlier, blacks and American Indians experienced large declines in the proportion of women married. For American Indians more than for blacks, this decline occurred during a period of substantial increases in cohabitation. The percentage of forty-year-old American Indian women who were married or cohabiting fell eleven percentage points, from 79 to 68 percent, between 1970 and 1999—compared with the eighteen-percentage-point decline in marriage alone, from 76 to 58 percent.

Childbearing

Declining marriage rates and increasing divorce rates have important implications for poverty rates for women and children because single women, especially single mothers, are more likely to be poor than their married counterparts. Changes in marriage patterns interact with changes in childbearing and affect both the prevalence of poverty and the composition of the poor.

Although increases in the proportion of children being born outside of marriage have been the focus of concern for academics, policymakers, and the public, the overall decline in childbearing also has important consequences for poverty. Figure 2.3 shows that the average number of children present in the household has declined over time, falling especially in the 1970s and 1980s.[5] For example, in 1972 women in their thirties had an average of about 2.5 children; by 1990 this figure had fallen to about 1.5 children. All else being equal, women are more likely to be poor the more children they have, both because larger families need more income to avoid poverty and because greater parenting responsibilities restrict women's ability to work in the paid labor market and earn wage income. Thus, the declining numbers of children per woman can be expected to reduce poverty.[6]

Although overall fertility declines can be expected to reduce poverty, changes in the proportion of children born outside of marriage have had the opposite effect. In 1960 only 5 percent of children were born to mothers who were not married. As shown by the dark line in figure 2.4, by 1997 the share had risen to about one-third of all births. A substantial academic literature, as well as popular debate, has focused on the social, economic, and policy changes responsible for these trends and on their implications (see, for example, Murray 1984; McLanahan and Sandefur 1994; Moffitt 1998). To understand the trends we must first recognize that the proportion of births to unmarried mothers depends on the marriage rate and the fertility patterns of all women, not just unmarried women. The tendency for married women to have children, the tendency for unmarried women to have children, and the proportion of women of childbearing age who are married—all determine the proportion of births to unmarried women.[7]

Figure 2.4 shows that the increase in the proportion of children born to unmarried mothers in the 1960s and early 1970s was the result of sharp declines in fertility among married women (solid line) rather than increases in the fertility of unmarried women (dotted line). The declining proportion of women who were married, shown in figure 2.1, also contributed. Since the 1970s, birth rates among married women have largely stabilized, but birth rates for unmarried women have increased, at the same time that the proportion of women who are not married (and are thus at risk for an unmarried birth) has continued to grow.

The proportion of children born to unmarried mothers varies substantially by race and ethnicity. In 1997 the lowest proportion was among Asians (16 percent), followed by whites (26 percent), Hispanics (41 percent), Ameri-

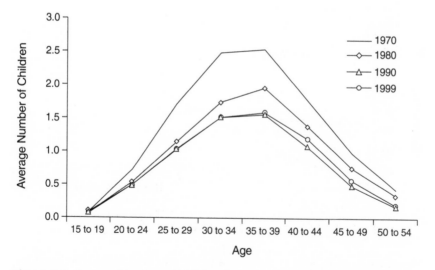

Figure 2.3 Average Number of Children by Age of Woman, 1972 to 1999 (*Source:* Authors' calculations from CPS files (1971 and 1972 combined, 1979 and 1980 combined, 1989 and 1990 combined, and 1998 and 1999 combined).)

can Indians (60 percent), and blacks (69 percent) (see U.S. Department of Health and Human Services 1999a, table 8). Trends in birth rates also vary substantially by race, though detailed time-series information is available principally for whites and blacks. Between 1970 and 1993, the marital birth rate fell by about 27 percent for white women and 43 percent for blacks (U.S. Department of Health and Human Services 1995, table III-7). Between 1970 and 1998, the nonmarital birth rate increased by 80 percent for whites while it fell by 23 percent for blacks (National Center for Health Statistics 2000a, 2000b, table 18). Thus, for blacks especially, increases in the proportion of children born to unmarried mothers are due to declines in marriage rates and in marital fertility rather than increases in the likelihood that an unmarried woman will have a baby. For whites, both the decline in marital fertility and the growth in nonmarital fertility contributed to the change.

Understanding the origins of the increase in the proportion of births to unmarried women is important in evaluating potential causes and policy responses. For example, though empirical evidence for a connection is mixed (Moffitt 1998), there are at least some theoretical reasons to expect that increased welfare benefits might increase nonmarital births. However, to the extent that the increased proportion of births to unmarried women is due to

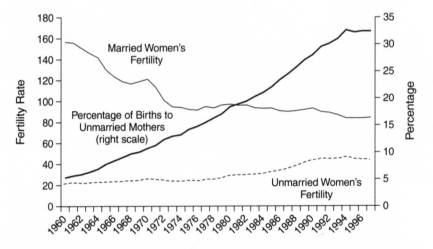

Figure 2.4 Fertility Rate by Marital Status, 1960 to 1997 (*Sources:* Measures for the period 1960 to 1993 from U.S. Department of Health and Human Services (1995); measures for 1994 to 1997 from National Center for Health Statistics (2000a).)

changes in *marital* fertility, a causal role for AFDC policy may be more difficult to argue.

Regardless of the causes, the increased percentage of births to single mothers contributes to children's vulnerability to poverty. All else being equal, the changes in the marital status of mothers have increased their economic vulnerability. But declines in the number of children per family have had a countervailing effect on the likelihood of poverty. Thus, contemporary women are less likely to have a husband on whom to rely for economic support, but they are also less likely to need to support large families.

Family Living Arrangements

The implications of marital status and fertility changes for children's living arrangements and poverty rates can be complex, especially when we consider the presence of unmarried partners or other adults. Figure 2.5 shows changes in the living arrangements of children over the past thirty years. The top panel shows that in 1972, 86 percent of all children lived in a mar-

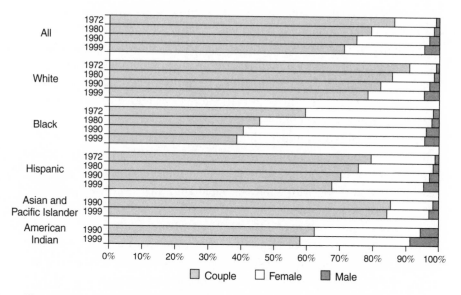

Figure 2.5 Family Structure for Families with Children, 1971 to 1999 (*Source:* Authors' calculations from CPS files (1971 and 1972 combined, 1979 and 1980 combined, 1989 and 1990 combined, and 1998 and 1999 combined).)

ried-couple family—though the couple may have included step- or adopted parents.[8] The share dropped consistently over this period, so that by 1999 only 71 percent of children lived in a family headed by a married couple. Most children living in a single-parent household lived with a single mother, though by 1999 one in six children not living with a married couple lived with their father.

Figure 2.5 also shows great variation in family structure across different racial and ethnic groups.[9] Living with a married couple was most common for white children (91 percent in 1972 and 78 percent in 1999) and Asian and Pacific Islander children (about 85 percent in 1990 and 1999; earlier figures not available). Black children were least likely to live in a married-couple family: only 39 percent lived with a married couple in 1999, a substantial decline from 59 percent in 1972. The proportion of Hispanic children living with a married couple fell from 79 to 68 percent between 1972 and 1999. The bottom panel shows that about 60 percent of American Indian children lived in married-couple households in 1999. A relatively high rate of single-father households (roughly 9 percent) is also evident for this group.[10]

When children live with an unmarried mother or unmarried father, they may still live with more than one adult, and increasingly they do. Figure 2.6 shows the living arrangements of single mothers, distinguishing those mothers who are cohabiting, living with relatives, living with other unrelated adults, or living alone. In the two later years shown, 1990 and 1999, we are able to distinguish grandparents from other adult relatives. From the top panel, we observe a substantial decline in the proportion of all single mothers who live alone; this is primarily due to increased cohabitation. In 1972, 2 percent of single mothers lived with a cohabiting male partner,[11] 34 percent lived with another adult relative, 2 percent lived with another nonrelative, and the remaining 62 percent did not live with another adult. By 1999, 12 percent were cohabiting, with a parallel decline in living alone. The proportion living with another related adult had decreased modestly. Half of those single mothers living with a relative were living with a parent (the maternal grandparent of their child) in 1990 and 1999.

The remaining panels of Figure 2.6 show differences by race. For most groups, single mothers were less likely to live alone over time. However, the proportion of black single mothers living alone increased over the past twenty years—reflecting the declining proportion living with their children's grandparents or other relatives. The greatest variation appears in changes in cohabitation rates. In 1972 cohabitation was rare for all groups for which we have data; 2 to 3 percent of white, black, and Hispanic single mothers were cohabiting. By 1999 cohabitation rates were higher for all groups and varied from lows of 7 and 8 percent for blacks and Asians to highs of 14 percent for American Indians and 16 percent for whites.

The living arrangements of single fathers are quite different from those of single mothers. In 1999 only 39 percent of single fathers (compared with 55 percent of single mothers) lived with no other adult. Thirty percent of single fathers cohabited, and an additional 25 percent lived with another relative. White single fathers were more likely to live alone (45 percent) than black (35 percent) and especially Hispanic (24 percent) fathers.[12]

The increasing tendency for single parents to live with an unmarried partner or related adult has consequences for the economic and social resources available to these parents and their children. In determining poverty status, official poverty statistics include both the income and the needs of related adults—that is, they include their income as part of total family income and include them as family members. In contrast, the income and needs of "unrelated" cohabitants are not considered. If an unrelated cohabitant is, in practice, part of the same economic unit, household income needs

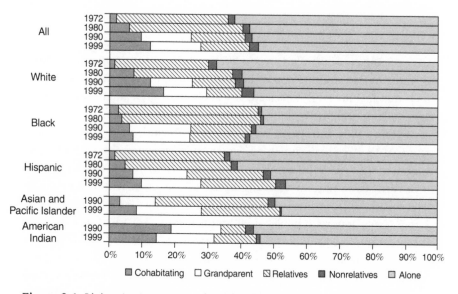

Figure 2.6 Living Arrangements of Single Mothers, 1971 to 1999 (*Source:* Authors' calculations from CPS files (1971 and 1972 combined, 1979 and 1980 combined, 1989 and 1990 combined, and 1998 and 1999 combined).)

are greater (given larger household size) and household resources may be greater as well (if the cohabiting adult has income).

The technical issues related to household membership and poverty measures are a manifestation of the importance and difficulty of defining economic units and assessing their resources and needs. Ideally, additional adults, such as grandparents, increase the financial and social resources available to vulnerable families. In addition to direct contributions to income, a grandparent or other adult may provide formal or informal child care and other supports. On the other hand, additional adults sometimes increase family stress and the responsibilities of a single parent. For example, an elderly parent may require care, or the potential for physical or emotional abuse from an additional adult may increase the need for the single parent to supervise the children (Oliker 1995). Even the assumption that parents and their biological children share resources to maximize some measure of family well-being is a simplification (Bergstrom 1997). The increasing proportion of children living without both biological parents and with other adults highlights the importance of understanding the implications of different household structures for the resources available to children.

Employment

All else being equal, families are less likely to be poor the greater the number of adults in the household and the fewer the number of children. Households that include adult males are less likely to be poor than those that include only adult females, both because men work more hours on average and because they earn more per hour on average. However, at the same time that the trends documented earlier have increased the proportion of women and children living in female-headed households, women's labor force participation has increased, especially for women with children, and gender gaps in labor market outcomes have declined (Blau 1998). These changes have important implications for the level and distribution of income among families headed by married couples as well as among families with single female heads (Blau 1998; Cancian and Reed 1999).

Figure 2.7 shows the proportion of men and women who worked at least one week in the previous year, by age, in 1970, 1980, 1990, and 1999. It shows substantial increases in female labor force participation, especially in the 1970s and 1980s. In the 1970s, women's labor force participation was lower during prime child-rearing ages, but by 1999 there was no longer a substantial shift in the proportion working between ages twenty and forty-five. In 1970 about 50 percent of all women age thirty-five to thirty-nine worked; by 1990 and 1999, almost 80 percent did.

Figure 2.8 shows the increases in the proportion of women age eighteen to sixty-four working at some point in the previous year, by marital status and the presence of preschool or school-age children. Although employment rates increased in almost every period for almost every group, the patterns of growth vary substantially. The increase was more pronounced for married than single women. Between 1972 and 1999, the percentage working at some point in the year grew from 54 to 74 percent for married women and from 74 to 79 percent for single women. Within these categories, employment increased most dramatically for mothers of children under age six, from 43 to 69 percent for married women and from 56 to 74 percent for single women. For married women, most of the change occurred before 1990. For single women, there is less consistency: the greatest increase for single mothers with young children occurred between 1990 and 1999, a period of

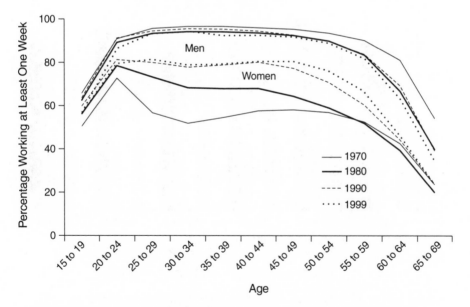

Figure 2.7 Annual Labor Force Participation Rates, by Gender and Age, 1970 to 1999 (*Source:* Authors' calculations from the decennial census (1970, 1980, 1990) and CPS files (1998 and 1999 combined).)

falling employment rates for single women without children. The increased employment for single mothers of young children is concentrated in the mid- to late 1990s, coinciding with more restrictive welfare policies that have reduced the availability of cash assistance. (Trends within the 1990s are not shown in the figure.)

Again, the trends differ substantially by racial and ethnic group. For example, of women age eighteen to sixty-four, the proportion who worked at some point in 1999 varied from a low of 64 percent for Hispanics to 70 percent for Asians and American Indians, 75 percent for blacks, and 78 percent for whites. Among whites and Hispanics, single mothers of young children were more likely to work in 1999 than their married counterparts. The opposite was true for blacks. Patterns of change over time also show substantial differences. Among single women with children under age six, employment increased by twenty-two percentage points for blacks (from 53 percent in 1990 to 75 percent in 1999) and by less than ten percentage points for whites (from 71 to 79 percent) and Hispanics (from 50 to 59 percent).

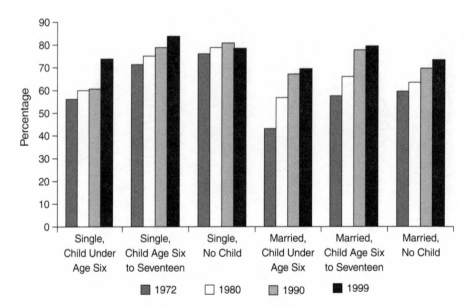

Figure 2.8 Women Age Eighteen to Sixty-four Who Worked During the Previous Year, by Marital Status and Motherhood, 1972 to 1999 (*Source:* Authors' calculations from CPS files (1971 and 1972 combined, 1979 and 1980 combined, 1989 and 1990 combined, and 1998 and 1999 combined).)

At the same time that single-mother families have become more prevalent, increases in women's earnings have made them less vulnerable to economic hardship. We consider explanations for these countervailing changes in the next section, and then turn to an assessment of their importance in explaining changes in the level of poverty over time.

Explaining Changes in Family Structure

Changes in women's marital, maternal, and employment status are interrelated. For example, delays in marriage may reduce fertility, thereby reducing demands for work within the home and facilitating women's market work. On the other hand, changes in women's employment opportunities may change the costs to women of leaving the labor market and thereby discourage some women from having children, or from having more children. We recognize that few factors can accurately be viewed as independent. Yet an assessment of the causes of family structure change is critical to policy discussions for several reasons. First, to the extent that social policy attempts to alter certain behavior—for example, to encourage employment—an understanding of the factors underlying current behavior is an important starting point. On a related note, concerns that current undesired patterns of behavior are the *result* of policy have been used to motivate policy change. For example, the emphasis of the 1996 welfare reform (the Personal Responsibility and Work Opportunity Reconciliation Act, or PRWORA) on reducing nonmarital childbearing reflected concerns that recent increases in the proportion of children born outside of marriage were the result of the incentives created by AFDC.

Changes in marriage patterns are a primary concern. The proportion of married individuals declines when people marry at older ages, or not at all. That decline also reflects higher rates of divorce, which are only somewhat offset by increases in remarriage. What accounts for these trends? One set of explanations stresses the impact of women's greater economic prospects on their incentive to marry. The standard economic model of marriage emphasizes the gains from a specialized division of labor in a context where one spouse (generally the husband) commands a substantially higher wage (Becker 1981/1991). In this case, marriage creates a context in which the lower-wage spouse can devote herself to the tasks of home production—raising children, preparing meals, and maintaining the home. This arrangement leaves the higher-wage spouse free to specialize in earning wages. As men's advantage in the labor market relative to women has declined (Blau 1998; Bowler 1999), however, so have the potential gains from specialization.[13]

Women's increasing relative market opportunities reduced gains from specialization at the same time that marital instability increased the risks to women of interrupting their wage employment. As divorce has become more common, the probability that a woman will have to be the primary provider for herself and her children has increased. At the same time, as women's labor force participation has increased, so has the feasibility of leaving an undesirable marriage. The extent to which women's increasing economic independence is a cause or consequence of greater marital instability is the subject of ongoing research (Cherlin 1992; Greenstein 1995; Dechter 1992).

Of particular relevance given our focus, the past two decades have seen increased inequality in the distribution of wages for men and stagnant or declining wages, especially for younger men with little education. Thus, men's labor market advantages, and the consequent potential gains from marriage, have been particularly eroded for low-income individuals. According to William Julius Wilson (1987), industrial restructuring and changes in the organization and location of jobs substantially reduced men's employment and earnings prospects, especially for urban black men with little education. He argues that the resulting decrease in the size of the pool of "marriageable" men with access to family-supporting employment contributes to the substantial decline in marriage among blacks.

Together with women's increased economic prospects and the availability of birth control, changes in social norms have made it easier to have sexual relationships outside of marriage, to establish households independent of parents or spouses, and to rear children outside of marriage. Thus, as the economic advantage of marriage has declined, so has the importance of marriage as a marker of adulthood and a precursor to parenthood. The independent causal role of social norms is difficult to disentangle. Nonetheless, cohabitation, nonmarital childbearing, and divorce are increasingly accepted (Bumpass 1990, 1995).

Many of the same factors that reduced the incentive to marry have contributed to increases in women's labor force participation. Increased marital instability has made it riskier for women to be out of the labor market, and with increases in female-headed households, more women of necessity rely principally on their own earnings. At the same time, relatively poor earnings prospects for men, especially young men with little education, have reduced the potential for growth in family income in families with only one earner (Cancian and Reed 1999). Changes in contraceptive technology and reduced fertility are also potentially important explanations for women's increased labor force participation. Of course, as with changes in family structure, it is difficult to distinguish cause and effect: mothers may be more likely to work in the market because they have fewer children, or they may be having fewer children because of the demands of greater labor force participation.

Another focus of public debate and research has been the role that policy plays in facilitating changes in marriage, childbearing, and employment among low-income women. This focus reflects the disincentives to work and marriage embedded in the welfare system. It also reflects the vulnerability of the low-income population, especially poor women of color, to policies aimed at altering family behaviors.

Charles Murray's (1984) classic discussion of the incentives that the welfare system creates for "Harold and Phyllis," a fictional young unmarried couple expecting a child, suggests that AFDC and related programs discouraged marriage and parental responsibility. The benefit structure of income support programs certainly cannot fully explain changes in marriage. AFDC benefits declined substantially and became a less attractive alternative after the mid-1970s, the same period when marriage rates declined. And the decline in marriage was not confined to those for whom the program was most relevant, that is, low-income or low-skill individuals. Some research suggests that welfare did discourage marriage, and early findings from some welfare reform efforts suggest that changes in policy may encourage marriage (Knox, Miller, and Gennetian 2000). However, estimates of the magnitude of any negative impact of welfare on marriage vary quite substantially (Moffitt 1998, 2000b), and the potential importance of welfare policy in explaining family structure changes remains a matter of debate.

In contrast to cash welfare, increased child support enforcement has been hailed as a policy promoting marriage and *decreasing* the incentives to nonmarital childbearing, at least for fathers. Policy changes over the past twenty years have substantially increased the proportion of nonmarital births for which paternity is established and have contributed to the increase in the number of fathers of children born to unmarried parents being ordered to pay child support and making payments (Garfinkel, Meyer, and Seltzer 1998). Although child support enforcement and paternity establishment are primarily aimed at increasing the formal economic support provided by nonresident fathers, improved enforcement may contribute to a reduction in nonmarital births (Plotnick et al. 1999).

The literature on the impact of child support on family structure is relatively new, and some recent research on the effects of welfare suggests that its impact is greater (Rosenzweig 1999); nevertheless, child support policy may have a clearer impact on family structure than AFDC. From some perspectives, the difference is not surprising. Even when they receive child support or cash welfare payments, single mothers typically bear most of the responsibility for raising their children. Changes in welfare benefit levels (or child support payments)[14] may thus have a relatively minor impact on the benefits and costs faced by a single woman considering motherhood. In contrast, in the absence of paternity establishment or child support enforcement efforts, a man who fathers a child outside of marriage does not necessarily face major long-term investments of financial or other resources. Many nonmarital fathers are very actively involved with their children, especially near the time of the child's birth (Garfinkel and McLanahan 2000). However, for some single men who might otherwise provide few resources to their children, increased child support enforcement may dramatically raise the expected costs of fatherhood.

A number of policy changes have been designed to encourage employment and "make work pay" for low-income parents. In addition to reducing the availability of cash welfare and stepping up child support enforcement efforts, these changes include expanded earnings subsidies (notably the Earned Income Tax Credit) and efforts to improve the availability of child care. As discussed elsewhere in this volume, the EITC provides a substantial earnings subsidy for low-income earners with children. Child care policy, including increased regulation, additional income tax adjustments, and recently expanded subsidies for some low-income families also facilitate employment for some families with children, though their effect on employment may be small (see Spain and Bianchi 1996; Blau 2000).

The Impact of Changes in Family Structure on Poverty

We now decompose changes in poverty over time, estimating the importance of changes in poverty within different demographic groups and of changes in the representation of those groups in the population. Table 2.1

reports poverty rates and population shares for five family types. The overall poverty rate (last row) differs slightly from the official poverty rate for all families because we focus on families headed by persons age eighteen to sixty-four.[15] The first column shows poverty rates in 1998. Families headed by single women raising children had the highest poverty rate, 38.7 percent. Married couples had the lowest poverty rates, 2.6 percent for those with no children and 6.6 percent for those with children. Most persons, 66 percent, lived in married-couple families (second column).[16] Poverty rates in 1969 showed the same pattern, with high rates for single mothers with children and low rates for married couples.

Over the period 1969 to 1998, the overall poverty rate grew by 0.9 percentage points, from 10.8 to 11.7 percent. However, the poverty rate within four of the five family types declined—the only exception was single males with children, who accounted for only 3 percent of persons in 1998. An important factor in the growth of the overall poverty rate was the shift away from married-couple families with children toward single-head families (see column 6). This was a shift away from a family type with relatively low poverty rates toward family types with higher poverty rates.

By how much would overall poverty have increased if there had been a change in family structure but no change in poverty rates for each type of family? To answer this question, we construct a counterfactual level of poverty using the 1998 shares of persons by family type and the 1969 poverty rates. We found that the poverty rate in 1998 would have been 14.4 percent. Therefore, if all else had remained as in 1969, the change in family structure would have led to an increase in the poverty rate of 3.6 percentage points, from 10.8 percent in 1969 to 14.4 percent in 1998.

The lower panel of table 2.1 reports the poverty rate and population share statistics when cohabiting adults are treated the same as married couples.[17] Including cohabiting adults and their income in calculating family size and total family income changes the patterns of poverty and family structure and leads to a lower estimate of the 1998 poverty rate and a very small estimated increase in poverty over time. With the cohabitation adjustment, there was a smaller decline in families headed by a couple and less growth in single-head families. All else being equal, the change in family structure between 1969 and 1998 would have produced an increase in poverty of 2.4 percentage points, from 10.7 percent to 13.1 percent (instead of a 3.6-percentage-point increase).

The counterfactual calculations based on table 2.1 suggest that, all else be-

Table 2.1 Poverty Rates and Population Shares by Family Type, 1969 to 1998

	1998		1969		Change	
	Poverty Rate	Population Share	Poverty Rate	Population Share	Poverty Rate	Population Share
Actual						
Single, no children	15.4%	18%	19.5%	7%	−4.1%	11%
Single female, with children	38.7	12	49.4	7	−10.7%	5
Single male, with children	15.3	3	14.6	1	0.7	2
Married couple, no children	2.6	19	3.5	17	−0.9	2
Married couple, with children	6.6	47	7.7	68	−1.1	−21
Overall	11.7	100	10.8	100	0.9	—
Adjusting for cohabitation						
Single, no children	14.8	15	19.0	7	−4.3	8
Single female, with children	38.3	11	49.1	7	−10.8	4
Single male, with children	12.1	2	13.2	1	−1.1	1
Couple, no children	2.8	22	3.5	17	−0.8	5
Couple, with children	7.1	50	7.7	68	−0.6	−18
Overall	10.8	100	10.7	100	0.1	—

Source: Authors' calculations from CPS files (1970 and 1999).

Note: Data include only persons in families in which the head is between eighteen and sixty-four.

ing equal, family structure changes would have increased poverty substantially. Figure 2.9 presents this same analysis for the last thirty years. The light solid line shows the actual poverty rate from 1967 to 1998. Most of the major movement in the poverty rate has followed the business cycle—rising during recessions and falling during recovery periods. Looking at business-cycle peak years allows us to focus on longer-run trends, as opposed to shorter-run fluctuations. The diamonds in the figure mark peak years in 1969, 1979, and 1989. Although 1998 was not at the height of the recent peak, data for that year are the most current available and should be roughly comparable to data for the previous peak years. The figure shows that from peak to peak, poverty declined over the 1970s, increased over the 1980s, and changed very little over the 1990s.[18]

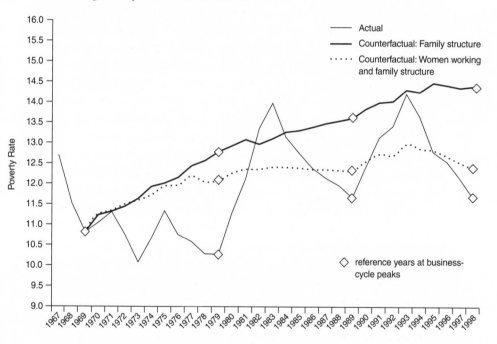

Figure 2.9 Poverty Rates, Actual and Counterfactual, 1967 to 1998 (*Source:* Authors' calculations from CPS Files (1968 to 1999).) *Note:* The solid line represents the expected trend in poverty rates based on changes in family structure holding poverty rates within family type at 1969 levels. The dotted line represents the expected trend in poverty rates based on changes in family structure and employment of female heads holding poverty rates at 1969 levels. Data include only persons in families headed by an adult between the ages of eighteen and sixty-four.

The dark solid line in figure 2.9 shows the expected trend in the poverty rate since 1969 based on the family structure in each year, all else being equal. The figure shows that the changes in family structure have not fluctuated with the business cycle. Rather, based on these changes, the poverty rate would have trended upward fairly consistently over the last three decades—reaching 14.4 percent in 1998. However, the actual poverty rate in 1998 was 11.7 percent.

Why did poverty rates rise less than expected given changes in family structure alone? Growth in female employment is one potential explanation. To calculate the impact of changes in female employment on poverty, we repeat the counterfactual calculations using the five types of families in table 2.1 interacted with five categories of work behavior for female family heads (no work; one to thirteen weeks of work; fourteen to twenty-six weeks of work; twenty-seven to thirty-nine weeks of work; and forty or more weeks of work). All else being equal, changes in family structure and female employment together would have led to a more moderate upward trend in poverty, reaching 12.4 percent in 1998 (see the dotted line in figure 2.9).

Figure 2.9 suggests that trends in family structure would have produced a substantial increase in poverty had it not been for increasing female employment. This result is summarized in the first row of table 2.2. Between 1969 and 1998, changes in family structure would have led to an increase in poverty of 3.6 percentage points, all else being equal. Changes in female employment would have reduced poverty by 2.0 percentage points. The total change resulting from family structure and female employment would have produced an increase of 1.6 percentage points.[19] By comparison, the actual change was an increase of 0.9 percentage points. The remaining rows of table 2.2 show that adjusting for cohabitation and measuring the poverty rate only among children does not change our conclusion that trends in family structure would have produced a substantial increase in poverty that was mitigated by growth in female employment.

Trends in family structure and behavior also affect the composition of people who are poor. Between 1969 and 1998, the proportion of the poor who were living in families headed by single women with children grew from 32 percent to 41 percent—an increase of nine percentage points (see table 2.3). Our counterfactual approach suggests that changes in family structure alone would have led to a thirteen-percentage-point increase in the proportion of the *poor* living in families headed by single mothers.

Changes in family structure and female employment together would have led to an increase of nine percentage points. Thus, trends in family structure would have led to an even greater concentration of the poor in single-mother households had the increased employment of single mothers not had a countervailing impact.

During the last three decades, the proportion of the poor who are children has declined (when we focus on households headed by persons age eighteen

Table 2.2   The Expected Impact of Changes in Family Structure and Female Employment on Poverty Rates, 1969 to 1998

	Expected Change			Actual Change
	Family Structure	Female Employment	Total	
Poverty rate	+3.6%	−2.0%	+1.6%	+0.9%
Poverty rate, adjusted for cohabitation	+2.4	−1.9	+0.5	+0.1
Child poverty rate	+6.1	−3.6	+2.6	+2.2
Child poverty rate, adjusted for cohabitation	+4.6	−3.3	+1.3	+1.3

Source: Authors' calculations from CPS files (1970 and 1999).
Note: Data include only persons in families where the head is age eighteen to sixty-four.

Table 2.3   The Expected Impact of Changes in Family Structure and Female Employment on the Composition of the Poor, 1969 to 1998

	Expected Change			Actual Change
	Family Structure	Female Employment	Total	
Single female, with children	+13%	−4%	+9%	+9%
Single female, with children, adjusted for cohabitation	+9	−1	+8	+7
Under age eighteen	−9	−2	−11	−9
Under age eighteen, adjusted for cohabitation	−9	−1	−10	−8

Source: Authors' calculations from CPS files (1970 and 1999).
Note: Data include only persons in families where the head is age eighteen to sixty-four.

to sixty-four). Despite the fact that the child poverty rate grew by more than the overall poverty rate, this decline occurred because of the large decrease in the proportion of the population under age eighteen—from 39 to 30 percent. Overall, the share of the poor who were children fell by nine percentage points, from 52 percent in 1969 to 43 percent in 1998. Our counterfactual calculation suggests that trends in family structure would have led to a decline of nine percentage points, all else being equal. Trends in female employment would have led to an additional fall of two percentage points. That is, the trends in family structure, particularly the decline in the share of families with children, brought about a substantial fall in the proportion of the poor who are children. The final row of table 2.3 confirms this result when family types are adjusted for cohabitation.

The results from our counterfactual calculations are suggestive of the impact of trends in family structure and female employment on poverty over the last thirty years. Because the analysis ignores the relationship between family behaviors and poverty rates, however, they do not measure how much changes in family behaviors have caused changes in poverty. The calculations rely on the unrealistic assumption that family structure and behaviors could change to 1998 levels while poverty rates within each type of family could remain at 1969 levels—in other words, the "all else being equal" assumption.[20]

Conclusions and Policy Implications

We have shown that the declining proportion of married-couple families reflects a variety of interrelated trends. Fewer people are marrying, and those who are married are on average older and more likely to divorce. Married couples are having fewer children, while birth rates for unmarried women have declined for blacks and increased for whites. Together, these trends result in a greater proportion of families headed by single mothers—both because of the higher proportion of births that take place outside of marriage and because of the growth in the proportion of children born within marriage whose parents divorce.

Because single-mother families are more than five times as likely to be poor as married-couple families, the change in family structure has increased poverty. However, a number of factors have had countervailing impacts. First, there has been a major increase in the labor force participation and earnings of women. Although fewer women and children can expect regular support from a husband or resident father, more women, especially mothers, are working and earning sufficient incomes to escape poverty.

A second important factor is the increase in cohabitation. Growth in cohabitation may substantially explain the delay in entry into marriage (Bumpass et al. 1991). Moreover, estimates suggest that almost half of recent nonmarital births are to cohabiting parents (Bumpass and Lu 2000).[21] When we treated cohabiting adults as partners and included their income, our estimates of the increase in poverty due to changes in family structure were substantially reduced.

There are effects of changes in employment and cohabitation that are not considered in our estimates. For example, though increased employment has made women less economically vulnerable, it has presumably come at the cost of (unpaid) time spent supporting their family and community (Waring 1999). In addition, the standard measure of income poverty used here neglects the nondiscretionary personal *costs* of employment, such as transportation and child care, and thus overstates the poverty-reducing effects of employment (Iceland and Kim 2000).

Similarly, while many unmarried mothers may live with the father of their children, cohabiting relationships provide less economic security than marriage, if for no other reason than their relative instability (Bumpass and Lu 2000). We know relatively little about the level and stability of economic support within cohabiting families and about the implications for child well-being.

How has public policy responded to changes in family structure? How should future policy development take into account the increased diversity and instability of family forms? Some critics of income support for low-income families contend that helping poor families may do more harm than good by encouraging more individuals to make the bad choices that result in dependence on public assistance. Welfare especially is seen as a potential *cause* of undesired family change. Some suggest that drastic reductions in the availability of public assistance are justified because, with fewer incentives to seek public assistance, future generations will be less likely to find themselves in similar situations.

In contrast, supporters of an expanded safety net emphasize that low-income families often face very few "good" choices. From this vantage point, poverty is less the product of individual choices than the result of the constraints posed by the structure of social and economic opportunity. As such, policy should improve the opportunities available to the poor and, through income support, reduce their material deprivation. Cash welfare is a minimal *response* to changes in family forms that make children particularly vulnerable given the current structure of opportunities.

There is only limited evidence that changes in public assistance policies have had important impacts on family structure, though a few studies suggest that changes in child support enforcement have been effective in reducing nonmarital fertility. In addition, the focus on altering the family structure decisions of poor families (through welfare policy) is troubling in the absence of parallel attention to policies that might have an impact on a broader population (for example, restrictions on divorce). In this context, policy changes that reduce economic support for poor families and children in the hope of reducing future nonmarital fertility are suspect. Ideally, public policies should respond to current needs and also create incentives for preferred family structures and employment behaviors. A policy designed to respond to one goal, however, often works against the other.

Certainly much of the recent policy debate can be characterized by its attention to changes in family structure and women's employment and the struggle to create public programs that support the poor while creating incentives for desired behaviors. Changes in welfare and related programs in the late 1990s include provisions that respond to greater instability in family structure (including increased efforts to establish paternity and enforce child support orders) and that increase incentives for single mothers, even those with very young children, to work for pay (for example, elimination of a federal exemption from work requirements for mothers of infants and greater subsidies for child care). The 1996 PRWORA and the state welfare programs that emerged in its wake also include provisions aimed at reducing nonmarital fertility and increasing the responsibility of nonmarital fathers. In addition to child support provisions, the PRWORA allows states to eliminate increases in cash benefits for families who have additional children, requires that minor parents live with their own parents or in another supervised setting, and provides cash bonuses to states that reduce nonmarital fertility without increasing abortions.

It is still early to assess the success of the PRWORA in altering family structures and employment patterns. Welfare reforms in the mid- and late 1990s coincided with dramatic declines in welfare caseloads, increases in employment—especially among women potentially eligible for benefits—and a decline in the rate of nonmarital births. Because the reforms took place during an exceptionally long economic expansion, distinguishing the impacts of policy changes, macroeconomic growth, and other factors is difficult (see Danziger 1999). A complete assessment of the long-run implications of these reforms requires that we consider a number of factors beyond current program participation and employment rates: the characteristics of women's employment and opportunities for advancement; the quality of child care and the ability of single parents to both work for pay and parent their children; and the ability of the new system to respond to periods of unemployment, whether related to macroeconomic changes or personal circumstances.

Even as policy changes "make work pay," there is a recognition that many single parents will not be able to provide for their children on their own. Paternity establishment and child support enforcement policies are one direct policy response to changes in family forms. Much remains to be done. Recent estimates suggest that only about 15 percent of mothers of children born outside of marriage regularly receive all the child support ordered by the courts to be paid on behalf of their children. Another 10 percent receive only partial support, while a similar proportion have a child support order but receive no support at all. Most children born outside of marriage are not eligible for child support because they do not have a legally established father (Freeman and Waldfogel 1997).

However, the potential for increasing child support payments is limited by the poor resources of many fathers. Moreover, the current system of paternity establishment and child support is not well adapted to the dynamic and complex arrangements between many unmarried parents. For example, paternity establishment procedures may unintentionally drive unmarried fathers away from their children (Pate and Johnson 2000; Waller and Plotnick 1999; Garfinkel and McLanahan 2000). In addition, under current policy, cooperating with the child support system does not "pay" for low-income families. In most states, when a father pays child support on behalf of a child receiving welfare, the government retains the payment to offset welfare costs. Thus, many fathers who follow the law and pay support through formal channels reduce their own resources without increasing the resources available to their children.[22]

The past thirty years have been a period of increasing diversity in family structures. Children are more likely to spend at least some time living outside a married-couple family. Children, especially young children, are also more likely to live with a mother who is working in the paid labor market. To reduce the economic vulnerability of children and families, public policy must respond to the diversity and instability of family forms and provide greater support for the growing proportion of mothers who must balance the demands of paid work and parenting.

CHAPTER 3

The Rising Tide Lifts . . .?

RICHARD B. FREEMAN

     That sustained economic growth can cure most economic ills is fundamental to the American view of how our market economy works. Americans give less support to policies that redistribute income outside the market than do the citizens of most other advanced democracies. Americans look more favorably on policies designed to produce equality of opportunity in schooling and in the job market than on policies that give citizens safety net insurance through the welfare state. President Johnson's War on Poverty of 1964 to 1968 exemplifies this assessment. The War on Poverty initially put resources into education and training to increase the marketable skills of the poor more than it redistributed money to bring them above the poverty line. The president explicitly rejected the notion of simply cutting bigger welfare checks to the poor because he believed that much more than handouts to needy citizens was needed to cure poverty.

Historically, economic growth has been highly efficacious in raising living standards. In 2000 the real wages of American workers were about five times their value in 1900, a fact that supports the view that over the long run the rising tide of economic progress lifts all boats. Simply by living in a wealthier society, today's poor have televisions, cars, and other consumer goods that did not exist years ago (Rector, Johnson, and Youssef 1999), though they still face material hardships—such as uncertain medical insurance and the risk of losing telephone service, electricity, or housing—that make their lives insecure and difficult (Federman et al. 1996).

Nevertheless, the traditional view that a growing economy benefits all citizens, including the poor, did not fare well in the 1980s. Economic developments from the mid-1970s to the early 1990s raised doubts about the ability of a growing economy to reduce poverty in a world of skill-biased technical change and globalization (Cutler and Katz 1993). In the 1980s, real gross domestic product (GDP) per capita grew by 20 percent while the official rate of poverty for all families rose from 9.2 percent in 1979 to 10.3 percent in 1989. The early 1990s recession brought the rate of poverty to 12.3 percent, the same as in the 1983 recession and above the rates that had prevailed from 1966 through 1983. National policymakers believed that any effort to lower the rate of unemployment below the "natural" rate of approximately 6 percent would generate accelerating inflation. Since unemployment is concentrated among the less-skilled, a 6 percent average rate of unemployment, which implies double-digit unemployment for the lowest-skilled and lowest-paid, seemed to doom them to a life of declining or stagnant real wages and continued poverty. Analysts feared that the "rising tide lifts all boats" view of growth and poverty had permanently broken down.

What a difference a decade of economic boom makes! The stellar performance of the U.S. economy in the late 1990s challenges the gloomy reading about the link between the labor market and poverty based on the experience of the 1970s to the 1980s. With an unemployment rate hovering around 4 percent in 2000, the real wages of low-skill workers increased noticeably and the unemployment of less-educated and low-skilled individuals fell to levels last seen in the 1960s. Welfare reforms moved many single mothers from dependence into the workforce, where some managed to earn above-poverty incomes. When Congress increased the minimum wage, the earnings of the low-paid were raised with minimal if any loss of employment, and when it increased the Earned Income Tax Credit (EITC), take-home income for low-wage workers was increased. The poverty rate fell rapidly enough in 1999 for President Clinton to declare in the fall of 2000 that under his administration "the rising tide of the economy is lifting all boats." Perhaps the 1980s were the exception rather than the new rule linking poverty to growth (Haveman and Schwabish 1999; Cain 2000). If the job market remains healthy and strong, perhaps the United States can win the War on Poverty by going with the flow of economic growth. But perhaps President Clinton and other optimists have made too much of the reduction in poverty at the peak of a long economic recovery. It would be weird indeed if poverty did not fall during the longest economic boom in U.S. history.

This chapter is motivated by the conflict between the pessimistic view of the ability of the labor market to reduce poverty that developed in the 1980s and early 1990s and the euphoria over the late 1990s boom. How much can the labor market reduce poverty in the twenty-first century? Will the rising tide of economic progress win the War on Poverty in the foreseeable future?

Or is something more needed to improve living standards at the bottom of the distribution?

I argue that continued full employment will reduce poverty in the next decade, but that the reduction will be less than needed to eliminate poverty. Indeed, the loss of full employment—a return of unemployment to the 6 percent rate that the Federal Reserve and others regarded as natural in the mid-1990s—will increase poverty substantively. The principal reason for this asymmetry is that with a poverty rate for individuals of 11.8 percent (the 1999 rate) and a poverty rate for families of 9.3 percent (the 1999 rate), it is clear that many of the residual poor have characteristics that prevent them from entering the labor market or that limits their wages and the hours they work. Many are disabled or must take care of disabled relatives or children; many are elderly retirees; many others are less-educated immigrants with very limited skills. I estimate that approximately 7 percent of the U.S. adult population fits into these categories. The vast bulk of these people would be unlikely to work, or to have the hourly pay to move them out of poverty if they were to work, even in an extended boom. This puts a lower bound on how far continued prosperity by itself can reduce measured poverty in the next decade. By contrast, if the economy turns down and unemployment rises to 6 to 7 percent, poverty will increase markedly, because the scaling back in the United States in the late 1990s of the safety net welfare system will have left many job losers with only modest access to non–labor market transfers.

Thus, in both a perpetual full-employment scenario and a return of the business-cycle scenario, something more than the labor market will be needed to bring incomes at the bottom to socially acceptable levels. Given the unwillingness in the United States to fund a European-style welfare state redistribution of income, full employment is necessary to lower poverty in the foreseeable future. But given the characteristics and situations of the residual poor, full employment is unlikely to be sufficient to reduce the family poverty rate below 6 to 7 percent or to reduce the individual rate (which historically has been two to three points higher) below 8 to 9 percent.

Economic Growth, Business Cycles, and Poverty

The natural starting point for any investigation of how the economy affects poverty is to examine the linkages between the secular growth of the economy and poverty and between the cyclical performance of the economy and poverty among families. Table 3.1 summarizes these relationships from 1959, when the U.S. census first measured poverty using an official poverty line for families, through 1999.[1] The upper panel of the table gives the rate of growth of GDP per capita and the level and change in poverty in each of the four decades covered. It shows that poverty fell rapidly in the 1960s when the economy grew rapidly and the nation began its War on Poverty (Anderson 1964). During this period, a 1.0-percentage-point increase in GDP per capita was associated with a 0.26-percentage-point reduction in the poverty rate. Measuring poverty reduction in percentage terms, the elasticity of the rate of poverty to GDP per capita was over 1.5. In the 1970s, by contrast, the 23.8 percent rate of growth of GDP per capita was associated with a fall in poverty of just 0.5 points, while in the 1980s, a 22.9 percent growth rate was accompanied by a *rise* in poverty of 1.1 points. The 1990s look more like the 1970s, with growth reducing poverty more modestly than in the 1960s, when growth reduced poverty massively. Taking the 1970s, 1980s, and 1990s together gives a depressing picture of the ability of economic growth to reduce poverty. Over those three decades, GDP per capita rose by 73 percent while the rate of poverty among families barely fell from 9.7 percent in 1969 to 9.3 percent in 1999.[2]

The bottom panel of table 3.1 organizes the 1959 to 1999 experience into periods of recession and recovery. It records the change in unemployment rate from peak to trough or trough to peak, as defined by the level of unemployment and the corresponding change in the poverty rate of families. The column to the far right gives a crude measure of the impact of unemployment on poverty within each period—the ratio of the changes in the poverty rate to the change in the unemployment rate. By this metric, the recessions and booms in the 1960s stand out as extraordinary: poverty fell modestly in the 1959 to 1961 recession and dropped sharply in the 1961 to 1969 recovery, giving an impact coefficient of 2.63. In succeeding recessions, poverty and unemployment rose together, and the impact coefficient rose until 1989 to 1992. In succeeding booms, however, declines in unemployment have been associated with falls in poverty smaller than in the 1960s. The 1992 to 1999 recovery was associated with a larger drop in poverty per percentage-point change in unemployment than were the 1982 to 1989 and 1975 to 1979 recoveries, but the latest poverty rate decline still falls short of the fall in the 1960s and early 1970s recoveries. Since poverty rates have hovered around 10 to 12 percent since the 1970s, this finding is not an artifact that results from using percentage points to measure changes in poverty rather than measuring changes in percentages or some other metric.

Table 3.1 Four Decades of Growth, Cyclical Swings, and the Family Poverty Rate

Decadal Patterns

Years	Percentage Change in GDP Growth Per Capita	Family Poverty		Change in Poverty Rate (in percentage points)
		Start	End	
1959 to 1969	34.6%	18.5%	9.7%	−8.8
1969 to 1979	23.8	9.7	9.2	−0.5
1979 to 1989	22.9	9.2	10.3	1.1
1989 to 1999	22.2	10.3	9.3	−1.0

Cyclical Patterns

	Change in Unemployment Rate	Change in Poverty Rate	Change in Poverty Rate / Change in Unemployment Rate
Recessions			
1959 to 1961	1.2	−0.4	—
1969 to 1971	2.4	0.3	.13
1973 to 1975	3.6	0.9	.25
1979 to 1982	3.9	3.0	.77
1989 to 1992	2.2	1.6	.73
Recoveries			
1961 to 1969	−3.2	−8.4	2.63
1971 to 1973	−1.0	−1.2	1.20
1975 to 1979	−2.3	−0.5	.22
1982 to 1989	−4.4	−1.9	.43
1992 to 1999	−3.3	−2.6	.79

Sources: Poverty rates: U.S. Bureau of the Census (2000, table B-3); GDP per capita: U.S. Council of Economic Advisers (2000, table B-31); Unemployment rates: U.S. Council of Economic Advisers (2000, table B-35).

All told, table 3.1 shows that, by itself, changes in macroeconomic performance do not predict well the magnitude of change in poverty. Other factors intervene between aggregate economic performance and the proportion of families or individuals who fall below the poverty line. What might these factors be? Why was the rising tide of growth associated with a great reduction in poverty in the 1960s, with little or no reduction in the 1970s and 1980s, and with a renewed but more modest reduction of poverty in the 1990s?

Four factors might explain the differing effect of economic growth on pov-

erty across the decades: demographic factors; the bell-curve shape of the income distribution; governmental policies; and labor market factors.

Demography

The principal demographic change that may have altered the relationship
between the aggregate economy and poverty is the increased proportion of
single-parent, female-headed families. Single-parent, female-headed households have rates of poverty three to four times those of all families, so that,
all else being equal, an increase in the single-parent share of families would
raise poverty independently of economic growth and thus weaken the
growth-poverty link over time. The increased proportion of lone-parent, female-headed families is one of the most widely documented and studied social phenomena in the latter part of the twentieth century (Cancian and
Reed, this volume). In 1959 the vast bulk of the poor lived in married-
couple households. In 1965, when Daniel Patrick Moynihan raised alarms
about the rise of female-headed households among blacks, the proportion of
female-headed households among whites was modest. By contrast, by 1999
the proportion of white families with female householders and no husband
present was on the same order of magnitude as the proportion among blacks
that had upset Moynihan, while the proportion among blacks was two and
half times that rate thirty years earlier. The absence of a male breadwinner
in families invariably increases poverty in a world where men earn more on
average than women and many families need two earners to achieve a reasonable level of income. In 1999, 49.6 percent of people in families who fell
below the poverty line were in families with female householders, no husband present, while 30.4 percent of female-headed households were poor
(U.S. Bureau of the Census 2000, table B-1).[3] Many of these families received welfare benefits, but cash welfare payments have been historically
insufficient to move families above the poverty line.

   The most direct way to estimate the contribution of changes in the family
composition to the rise and fall of poverty rates is to decompose changes in
poverty using a shift-share analysis. In such an exercise, the analyst assumes
that different types of families have constant rates of poverty and then calculates how changes in the distribution of the groups alter aggregate poverty. This exercise can also be done for other characteristics of families, such
as the age of heads of families, the education or occupation of heads of families, their immigrant status, and so on. The analyst can examine changes in
poverty among individuals in the same way.

Analysts who have examined the impact of changes in the composition of families on poverty have found that such changes have had only a modest role in explaining observed changes in poverty. Sheldon Danziger and Peter Gottschalk (1995) show that the decline in poverty from 1949 to 1969 was due entirely to economic changes, while changes in the composition of households worked in the opposite direction. They attribute the rise in poverty from 1973 to 1991 (the last year of their analysis) to economic factors rather than to the changed demographic composition of the population (Danziger and Gottschalk 1995, table 5.3) and identify sluggish growth in mean adjusted income as the principal cause for the weakened effect of the economy in reducing poverty. Similarly, Jared Bernstein, Lawrence Mishel, and John Schmitt (2001, table 5.12) report that changes in family structure were "quite unimportant" in accounting for the divergent pattern of poverty reduction among decades.

One reason why shifts in the composition of families contribute little to explaining changes in poverty is that the growth of female-headed families, though the largest demographic trend that acts to raise poverty, has not been the only important demographic development in the period. For example, the educational attainment of family heads increased over the period. Shift-share calculations show that this should have reduced poverty by about as much as the rising proportion of female-headed homes increased poverty. But even taken by itself, the change in the proportion of female-headed homes does not dominate the overall pattern of change in poverty rates. What dominates those movements are changes in income within given demographic groups.

By affecting the impact of any given change in growth or unemployment on poverty, however, changes in the family composition of the population could affect the growth-poverty relation in a way that the standard decomposition analysis of changes does not measure. Assume that the population consists of two groups: one made up largely of labor market participants whose incomes depend greatly on the state of the aggregate economy; and a second group made up largely of nonparticipants, such as retirees or people on welfare, whose incomes are largely independent of the aggregate economy. A shift in the share of the population near poverty from participants to nonparticipants would reduce the impact of economic growth on aggregate poverty. As the U.S. population has aged over time, it has shifted from one dominated by young persons whose poverty status depends greatly on the aggregate economy to one dominated by older persons whose poverty status does not depend so much on the aggregate economy.

But this change in the age structure also does not explain the changing re-lationship between the aggregate economy and poverty. The timing of the change in the age composition of the population is inconsistent with a great effect of aging on the link between growth or unemployment and pov-erty. The entrance of the baby boomers into the job market in large num-bers in the 1970s should have raised the impact of growth or unemployment on poverty, contrary to the observed weakening of the relationship. Simi-larly, the falling youth share of the population in the 1990s was associated with a stronger relationship between growth or unemployment and pov-erty, rather than with a weaker relationship. Finally, as we shall see, the 1990s boom was associated with a greater fall in poverty among individuals below age eighteen and individuals age sixty-five or older than among indi-viduals eighteen to sixty-four.

The Shape of the Income Distribution

A different compositional factor does help explain the changing extent to which the rising tide story fits the U.S. poverty experience. This is the single peaked or roughly bell-curve shape of the *distribution of incomes* around the mean value of income (see Burtless and Smeeding, this volume). Consider the normal distribution in figure 3.1 (upper left quadrant). When distribu-tion keeps its shape, shifts in the mean income shift the entire distribution in the same direction. Because the rate of poverty is defined in absolute terms, and because a larger proportion of people are found in the middle of the bell-curve distribution than in its tails, increases in income have larger ef-fects in reducing poverty when the average income is closer to the poverty line than when it is further away. The implication is that if the income distri-bution maintains the same shape, as the economy grows, any given increase in mean incomes necessarily reduces poverty by less at higher levels of in-come than at lower levels of income.[4] It takes a larger change in mean in-come to reduce poverty by one percentage point when the poverty rate is 10 percent than when it is 25 percent, simply because there are fewer people in the tail of the distribution.

To assess the magnitude of this effect, I calculated the effect of a change in mean income normalized by its standard deviation on the proportion of the population that falls below poverty. A change in income in this analysis is comparable to a change in the value of the standard normal variable (that is, in income relative to the standard deviation of income). The rate in poverty is the proportion of the population in the distribution below the specified poverty line. When 30 percent of the population is below the poverty line, the normal distribution table shows that an increase of 0.1 points in the standard normal variable would reduce poverty by 3.2 percentage points. When 20 percent of the population is in poverty, the same increase in in-

Growth Lowers Poverty with
Stable Distribution

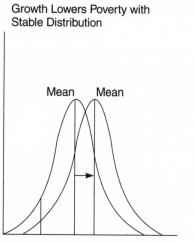

Growth Effects May Be Offset
by Rising Inequality

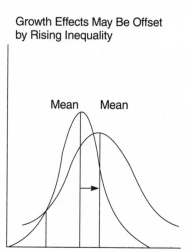

Growth Affects Few Persons in
the Tail of Distribution

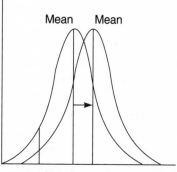

Growth Affects Many Persons
Near the Mean of Distribution

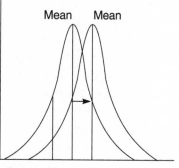

Figure 3.1 The Effect of Growth on Poverty

come would reduce poverty by 2.6 percentage points—0.6 points less. When 10 percent of the population is in poverty, an increase in income of 0.1 points would lower poverty by even less—a 1.6-percentage-point effect. Thus, the impact of an increase in income on poverty falls roughly in half as poverty drops from 30 percent to 10 percent, owing simply to the shape of the income distribution.

If the U.S. income distribution had the same shape over time, this distributional analysis would tell the entire story of the relationship between the growth of mean income and poverty. Growth would be associated with a falling impact on poverty dependent on the dispersion of the income distribution.[5] But such a story would never predict that increases in income would be associated with rising poverty rates, as occurred in the 1970s and 1980s, nor that economic growth would reduce poverty more in the 1990s than in the 1980s. Other factors are also at work.

Government Policies

Government policies affect the relation between economic growth and poverty and the impact of cyclical changes in unemployment on poverty. The most immediate way in which the government alters the rate of poverty is by direct transfers to citizens with below-poverty-level incomes. These transfers can take the form of money (a negative income tax for all individuals, or the Earned Income Tax Credit for those who work) or of specified goods or services (food stamps, health insurance, subsidized housing). The government can also affect poverty by intervening in wage determination in the labor market (setting minimum wages), by regulating the hiring and promotion policies of firms (promoting antidiscrimination policies), and in diverse other ways as well.

Ideally, measures of poverty would include all of the ways in which governments transfer resources to low-income individuals. In fact, because the official measure excludes many noncash transfers and even the cash EITC, it understates the contribution of government policies to reducing poverty. Still, we can use the pattern of change in the official poverty rate shown in table 3.1 to examine the potential explanatory impact of changes in governmental antipoverty and associated policies on the rate of poverty because, as noted, more refined measures of poverty seem to follow a time path similar to the official rate over the period under study.

The timing of federal government efforts to reduce poverty is broadly consistent with the decadal patterns of change in poverty. The 1960s were the heyday of the War on Poverty, while succeeding decades saw fewer anti-poverty initiatives. But the United States has never developed a European-style welfare state that would make poverty rates depend largely on government policy. Indeed, spending on AFDC and other transfer programs was never so large as to raise many families above the poverty line, so that by itself changes in those expenditures could not cause the poverty rate to fall by as much as 8.8 points, as it did in the 1960s, or to rise by as much as 3.0 points, as it did in the recession of 1979 to 1982.

The implication is that something beyond government policies explains the changing relationship between growth and poverty over time and can be used to assess the validity of the rising tide analogy. That something else is the labor market. Approximately three-fourths of family income comes from labor income, and even families in the lowest fifth of the income distribution, where government transfers are important, rely more on labor income than on any other source for their total family income.

Labor Market Forces: Real Wages and Wage Inequality

Perhaps the most striking difference between the economy in the 1960s and in ensuing periods is that 1960s economic growth was associated with large rises in the real wages of workers, whereas later growth was associated with only a modest increase in real wages. In the 1960s, when poverty fell substantially, the real average hourly earnings of nonsupervisory workers in the private sector increased by 19.3 percent. In the 1970s, when poverty barely dropped, real average hourly earnings rose by just 2.4 percent. In the 1980s, when poverty increased, real average hourly wages actually fell by 6.5 percent. Finally, in the 1990s, when poverty decreased modestly, growth was associated with a rise in real wages of 2.9 percent. Real average hourly earnings fell in the first part of the decade (1989 to 1995) by 3.3 percent, and then rose by 6.4 percent in the later part (1995 to 1999).[6] These data suggest that the major factor in the declining impact of economic growth on poverty is a change in the relationship between the growth of the economy and the growth of real wages.

Figures 3.2 and 3.3 examine the interrelationships between growth of GDP per capita, real wages, and poverty. Figure 3.2 graphs the growth of real wages against the growth of GDP per capita. It shows that the rate of increase in real wages associated with a given growth rate fell sharply between the 1960s and later periods, recovering only modestly in the 1990s. Figure 3.3 graphs the percentage-point reduction in the poverty rate against the growth of real wages. Here, the data fit a straight line, albeit with a drop in the slope as the rate of poverty fell from the high levels in the 1950s to the lower levels posted in the 1960s. The difference between the breakdown in

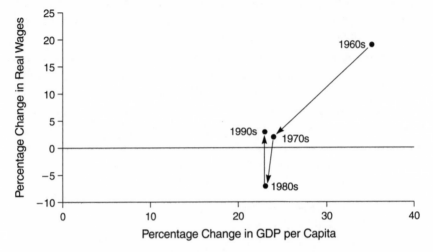

Figure 3.2   Rates of Growth, in GDP: Real Wages (*Sources:* Earnings: U.S. Council of Economic Advisers 2000, table B-45; GDP per capita: 1999a, table B-29.)

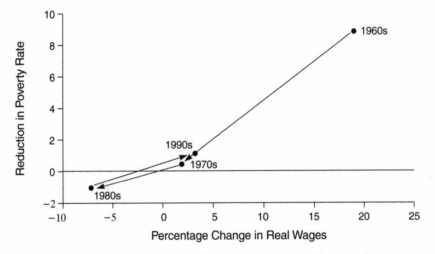

Figure 3.3   Rates of Growth, in GDP: Poverty (*Sources:* Earnings: U.S. Council of Economic Advisers 2000, table B-45; Poverty rates: U.S. Bureau of the Census 2000, table B-3.)

the link between the growth of GDP and of real hourly earnings in figure 3.2 and the continued relation between the growth of real earnings and changes in poverty in figure 3.3 suggests that the major contributing factor to the weakened impact of growth on poverty over time was the breakdown in the historic link between the growth of the economy and the growth of real wages.

One other labor market factor—the rise in wage inequality in the United States in the 1980s (for a summary, see Levy and Murnane 1992)—is also likely to have contributed significantly to the weakened link between economic growth and poverty. When the distribution of earnings is stable and real wages rise, growth lowers the rate of poverty, albeit with smaller impacts as poverty falls. In a period of rising inequality, the change in the shape of the income distribution can offset or overpower the effects of growth on poverty (see figure 3.1). If, for simplicity, we measure inequality as the ratio of the earnings of individuals with poverty-level incomes to mean earnings, rises in inequality at the same rate as mean earnings would produce rough stagnation in the rate of poverty, despite rises in overall income. Historically, real wages have grown pari passu throughout the income distribution, so that the distribution of wages was roughly unchanged or narrowed modestly. In the 1980s, however, the distribution of wages widened significantly as the earnings of low-paid workers fell in real terms while the wages of higher-paid workers rose or remained roughly constant. Declines in the earnings of low-paid workers due to falling mean wages and a widening income distribution will increase poverty, all else being equal.[7]

Regression Analysis of the Impact of Earnings and Inequality on Poverty

To measure the effect of the level of real earnings and the level of inequality in earnings on the official rate of poverty, I have undertaken two statistical analyses: a times-series analysis that links the national poverty rate for families to unemployment, to the level of earnings, and to earnings inequality; and a pooled, cross-section time-series analysis that does the same for individual states over time. In both cases, my dependent variable is the rate of poverty given by the incomes of families, which depends on public transfers and non–labor market income as well as on labor market earnings. Thus, the observed changes in poverty will depend on factors beyond the change in the mean and dispersion of the earnings distribution.

Table 3.2 shows the results of the time-series analysis. The dependent

Table 3.2 Time-Series Regressions Relating Poverty to Growth, Inequality, and the Labor Market, 1959 to 1999

Years	Constant	Ln Average Real Hourly Earnings	Gini Coefficient	Ln Median Family Income/Lowest Quintile	Unemployment	Time	R-squared
Family poverty as dependent variable							
1959 to 1999	2.07	−.32	.65	—	.44	−.0025	.97
		(.02)		(.11)	(.06)	(.0003)	
1959 to 1999	2.46	−.37	—	.22	.28	−.0019	.97
		(.02)		(.04)	(.06)	(.0001)	
1969 to 1999	1.67	−.25	.36	—	.42	−.0013	.89
		(.03)	(.12)		(.06)	(.0004)	
1969 to 1999	1.86	−.27	—	.09	.34	−.0007	.87
		(.03)		(.05)	(.06)	(.0003)	
Individual poverty rates as dependent variable							
1959 to 1999	1.74	−.27	.56	—	.41	−.0022	.97
		(.02)	(.09)		(.05)	(.0002)	
1959 to 1999	2.05	−.31	—	.19	.27	−.0016	.97
		(.02)		(.03)	(.05)	(.0001)	
1969 to 1999	1.44	−.22	.33	—	.38	−.0013	.88
		(.03)	(.11)		(.05)	(.0004)	
1969 to 1999	1.63	−.24	—	.09	.30	−.0008	.86
		(.03)		(.04)	(.05)	(.0003)	

Source: Tabulated from the series data in table 3A.1.

variable in the upper part of the table is the rate of poverty for families. The dependent variable in the lower part of the table is the rate of poverty for individuals. Real earnings are average hourly earnings for nonsupervisory workers in the private sector deflated by the Consumer Price Index. I measure inequality by the widely used Gini coefficient of family income, which reflects inequality in the entire distribution, and by the ratio of median family income to the income of families in the bottom quintile of the distribution—a measure of inequality for the lower half of the distribution. Unemployment is the national rate of unemployment for all individuals. Because the 1960s differed so much from ensuing decades in poverty reduction, I estimate the equations for the 1969 to 1999 period that exclude the 1960s as well as for the entire sample period.

The regressions show that regardless of how we measure poverty or the distribution of income, the three economic variables—real wages, inequality, and unemployment—have sizable and significant impacts on poverty. The coefficients on real wages and inequality (though not on unemployment) are smaller in the regressions that exclude the 1960s than in the regressions for the entire period, but the coefficients are still substantial in the post-1980s period.[8] This result is consistent with the explanation of the weakened impact of economic growth on poverty in the 1970s and 1980s as the consequence of the weakened impact of growth on real wages and the rise of inequality. Note, finally, that in all of these regressions the coefficient on the time trend term is negative. This could reflect the fact that the U.S. government had antipoverty programs in place over the entire period, though a simple time-series regression like this is hardly a way to demonstrate the effectiveness, if any, of antipoverty policies.

With just ten years of data for the 1990s, however, it is hard to reach reliable conclusions about the impact of that period's boom on poverty independently of other factors that might have affected the 1990s. Accordingly, I examine next the links between labor market factors and poverty across states in the 1990s. Poverty varies more across states than in the country as a whole and has changed differently among states as economic conditions have changed. With unemployment and real wages also varying considerably across states, the greater variation in both the independent and dependent variables should provide more reliable estimates of the effects of labor market factors on poverty. The data on poverty come in the form of three-year moving averages of poverty rates for all individuals in a state; I have centered these averages on the midyear for the analysis. Measures of real

Table 3.3 Estimates of the Impact of Labor Market Factors on Poverty of Persons, Cross-Section Time Series, State Data, 1989 to 1998

Constant	Unemployment	Ln Median Real Hourly Earnings	Ln "Inequality" (Median/Twentieth Percentile)	Ln Earnings, Twentieth Percentile	Year Dummies	State Dummies	R-squared
.46	1.01	−.21	.26	—	✓	—	.51
	(.10)	(.01)	(.03)				
.43	.37	−.16	.10	—	✓	✓	.92
	(.07)	(.02)	(.02)				
.48	1.08	—	—	−.21	✓	—	.52
	(.08)			(.01)			
.36	.37	—	—	−.13	✓	✓	.92
	(.07)			(.01)			

Source: Poverty rates: *www.census.gov/hhes/poverty/povanim/povmaptxt.html* (these poverty rates are for persons living in families below the poverty line); hourly wage rates: *epinet.org/datazone/medhrlywages.html*; wages for twentieth-percentile workers: *epinet.org/datazone/wrates_lowwagewkrs.html*; unemployment rates: U.S. Bureau of Labor Statistics, *Employment and Earnings* (May editions). Inequality is defined as the ratio of median hourly earnings to the earnings of workers at the twentieth decile.

Note: Number of observations: 510, with 51 state observations, including the District of Columbia, and ten years.

wages, inequality, and unemployment relate to the particular year rather than to a moving average. The real wage figures are the median hourly earnings of all workers in a state from the CPS files, as calculated by the Employment Policy Institute (EPI). Unemployment rates are the rate of unemployment for all workers, as reported in the U.S. Bureau of Labor Statistics' *Employment and Earnings*. To measure inequality, I have taken the ratio of the earnings of the median worker to the earnings of the bottom quintile worker, calculated by the EPI. With 51 state observations, including the District of Columbia, I have 510 observations with which to examine the association between earnings and inequality and poverty in the 1990s.

Table 3.3 presents the results of the state analysis. Line 1 gives regression coefficients for the effect of the ln of median hourly earnings in a state, of earnings inequality, and of unemployment on the rate of poverty. The regression includes year dummies, so that the coefficients reflect solely cross-section differences among states. All of the regression coefficients are highly significant and sizable. A 1.0-point change in unemployment changes poverty by 1.0 points, while a 1 percent change in ln median earnings reduces poverty by 0.21 percentage points. An increase in inequality has an offsetting 0.26 impact in the direction of raising poverty.

Line 2 gives the coefficients from an analysis in which I included state dummy variables. This removes the cross-section variation and thus focuses solely on how changes in unemployment and wages within a state affect poverty within that state. Because some of the variation in poverty with labor market factors occurs across states, the estimated coefficients fall, but they still remain substantial and significant. In these calculations, unemployment reduces poverty by over one-third of a point for each point reduction in the unemployment rate, while an increase in ln real earnings has a −0.16 impact on poverty.

Lines 3 and 4 replace the median earnings and inequality measures with the ln of earnings of workers in the twentieth percentile of the earnings distribution. Given the similar magnitude of the impact of real wages and inequality on poverty in the previous regressions, the estimated effect of ln earnings of low-paid workers of −0.21 (line 3) and −0.13 (line 4) is comparable to the estimated effect of the ln of median earnings, holding inequality fixed in the corresponding lines 1 and 2.

Since the unemployment rate cannot drop much below the 4 percent rate attained in early 2000, the effect of the labor market on poverty as time proceeds depends critically on how median real wages and inequality change or, what amounts to the same thing, on how the real wages of low-paid workers change. The coefficients of -0.16 or -0.13 from the regressions with state dummies suggest that even a booming labor market will not reduce the rate of poverty rapidly in the future. If real wages rose by, say, 2 percent in a year, these estimates indicate that poverty would fall by about 0.3 percentage points.[9] Thus, three years of solid real wage gains lower the poverty rate by one percentage point—a reasonably rapid (or sizable) reduction.

The Impact of Work Experience

The analysis thus far has inferred the effect of employment on poverty by estimating the impact of unemployment on poverty. But it is joblessness per se, rather than unemployment, that is most likely to contribute to poverty. Someone who lacks work because he or she is disabled and out of the labor force (and thus missing from the unemployment count) has the same zero earnings from the labor market as someone who is unemployed. To get a more accurate picture of the relationship between a person's employment experience and his or her poverty status, I have examined the poverty status of workers, differentiated by their work experience, for individuals (rather than for families) with different ages and with different gender and ethnicity, using the Current Population Survey.

Table 3.4 records the results for 1999; the pattern in other years is similar. The principal finding is that for all individuals, regardless of gender, ethnicity, and age, there is a massive difference in poverty rates between those who work *full-time year-round* and those who work less than that, and that poverty is endemic among individuals with no work experience. For the country as a whole, just 2.6 percent of all Americans who worked full-time year-round were in poverty in 1999, compared with 13.1 percent of those who worked either part-time or for only part of the year, and 19.9 percent of those who did not work at all. There is no noticeable gender difference in rates of poverty for individuals with the same work experience, but there is a marked difference in poverty among ethnic groups. Blacks and Hispanics who work year-round full-time have higher poverty rates at all levels of work experience than whites. But they also experience steep declines in poverty with work experience. Blacks who work full-time year-round have a poverty rate of 11.6 percent—25.3 percentage points less than for blacks with no work experience. Hispanics who work full-time year-round have a

Table 3.4   Poverty Rates by Age and Work Experience, 1999

	No Work Experience in Year	Worked, but Not Full-time, Year-round	Worked Full-time, Year Round
All	19.9	13.1	2.6
Men	19.2	12.4	2.4
Women	20.4	13.6	2.7
White	16.9	11.2	2.3
Black	36.9	26.0	11.6
Hispanic	33.5	12.4	7.0
Age sixteen to seventeen	20.4	8.8	4.0
Age eighteen to twenty-four	27.8	17.1	5.5
Age twenty-five to thirty-four	34.6	17.0	3.2
Age thirty-five to fifty-four	27.2	12.4	2.0
Age fifty-five to sixty-four	20.5	7.4	1.8
Age sixty-five or older	11.1	3.5	1.9

Source: U.S. Bureau of the Census (2000). These poverty rates are for persons living in families below the poverty line for families.

poverty rate of 7.0 percent, compared with 33.5 percent for those who do not work at all.

The pattern of markedly lower poverty among those who work full-time year-round compared with those who work less holds even for teenagers and the elderly, though here other sources of income (such as family support or Social Security) produce lower poverty rates for those with no work experience than for other age groups.

Poverty in the 1990s Boom

At the turn of the twenty-first century, the U.S. economy was the envy of the world, for one basic reason: the U.S. labor market had reached full employment, for the first time in decades. The employment population rate in the United States was at an all-time peak, and the unemployment rate had fallen to 4 to 5 percent without inflation—an event that the Federal Reserve Board and other experts had viewed as impossible as late as 1996.

Equally important in terms of poverty reduction, the boom of the late 1990s was associated with rising real wages for low-paid workers, who were likely to be on the margin of poverty. As documented in table 3.5, which records the change in real wages for low-wage workers categorized in various ways in the late 1990s economic boom, the usual weekly earnings of workers in the bottom decile of the wage distribution rose by about 10 percent from 1996 to 1999. The median earnings of men aged 16 to 24 rose by 8 percent after having fallen steadily since 1980. The earnings of workers in low-paid industries increased and the earnings of workers in low-paid occupations rose. Among ethnic groups, the usual earnings of blacks increased more rapidly than those of whites, so that the ratio of usual weekly median earnings of all black full-time male workers to white full-time male workers rose from 0.71 in 1996 to 0.76 in 1999. To be sure, the earnings of the low-

Table 3.5   Change in Real Wages for Selected Groups, 1996 to 1999

Group	Earnings	Change
Workers at tenth decile	Median hourly	+10.2%
Workers in low-pay industries, 1996 to 1999		
Retail	Hourly	+7.0
Services	Hourly	+6.8
Full-time workers in low-pay occupations, 1996 to 1999		
Information clerks	Median weekly	+7.2
Food preparation and service	Median weekly	+5.2
Handlers, cleaners, laborers	Median weekly	+3.3
Full-time workers		
White	Median hourly	+6.8
Black	Median hourly	+8.1
Hispanic	Median hourly	+6.9
Male	Median hourly	+6.0
Age sixteen to twenty-four	Median hourly	+9.2
Female	Median hourly	+6.8
Age sixteen to twenty-four	Median hourly	+7.1

Sources: Wages by decile: Bernstein and Mishel (1999, tables 1 and 3, updated); wages in low-pay industries and occupations: U.S. Bureau of Labor Statistics, *Employment and Earnings* (January 2000 and January 1997); median hourly earnings of full-time workers, 1996: U.S. Bureau of the Census (1998a); median hourly earnings of full-time workers, 1999: U.S. Bureau of Labor Statistics, *Employment and Earnings* (January 2000); Consumer Price Deflator: *ftp.bls.gov/pub/special.requests/cpi/cpiai.txt.*

paid and disadvantaged did not rise to their 1970s levels. Nor did the late 1990s gains reverse the long term increase in earnings inequality. What the boom did was to arrest the rising trend in inequality, so that economic expansion has once again improved the living standards of low-paid workers and distribute the fruits of economic growth more or less equally distributed among the working population. This in turn reduced poverty.

Table 3.6 examines the pattern of poverty reduction in the 1990s boom. It records rates of poverty for individuals and for families in 1992, when the

Table 3.6 Poverty Reduction in the 1990s Boom

	1992	1999	Change
Poverty of individuals	14.8%	11.8%	−3.0%
All			
White	11.9	9.8	−2.1
Black	33.4	23.6	−9.8
Hispanic	29.6	22.8	−8.6
Age			
Younger than eighteen	22.3	16.9	−5.4
Eighteen to sixty-four	11.9	10.0	−1.9
Sixty-five and older	12.9	9.7	−3.2
Poverty of families			
All	11.9	9.3	−2.6
With children under eighteen	18.0	13.8	−4.2
Married	8.3	6.3	−2.0
Single female parent	47.1	35.7	−11.4
White	9.1	7.3	−1.8
With children under eighteen	14.0	10.8	−3.2
Married	7.8	5.9	−1.9
Single female parent	28.5	22.5	−6.0
Black	31.1	21.9	−9.2
With children under eighteen	39.1	28.9	−10.2
Married	15.4	8.6	−6.4
Single female parent	57.4	46.1	−11.3
Hispanic	26.7	20.2	−6.5
With children under eighteen	32.9	25.0	−7.9
Married	22.9	16.8	−6.1
Single female parent	57.7	46.6	−11.1

Source: U.S. Bureau of the Census, *Historical Poverty Tables* (2000, table 4).

economy was at rock bottom, and in 1999, the latest year for which I have data on the boom; it also gives the change in poverty rates over the period. The table shows a sizable 3.0-percentage-point drop in the poverty rate for individuals and a 2.6-percentage-point drop in the rate for families. The declines in poverty for minority groups with exceptionally high poverty rates, blacks and Hispanics, are far greater: 9.8 points for black individuals, 9.2 points for black families, 8.6 points for Hispanic individuals, and 6.5 points for Hispanic families. Among the sizable drops in poverty for individuals in all age groups, the largest are for those younger than eighteen, presumably because their parents worked more at higher wages as the boom lengthened. Most striking are the double-digit declines in poverty among single-parent, female-headed homes. The United States has not seen drops of this magnitude since the 1960s.

In short, poverty reduction in the 1990s boom shows that when economic growth produces "genuine" full employment—that is, an increase in real wages as well as in employment—the rising tide of economic progress can indeed substantially cut into poverty, particularly among the demographic groups with the highest poverty rates.

How Far Can the Rising Tide Go?

How much further can the rising tide take the United States?

In 1999 the national rate of poverty for individuals was still in double digits, and even in the state with the lowest rate of poverty among individuals in 1998–99, Maryland, poverty was at 8 percent. The reduction in poverty among single-parent, female-headed homes still left over one-third of those families in poverty in 1999. If full employment were to continue, what are the prospects for reducing the rate of poverty among the "residual poor"?

One way to answer this question is to look at the characteristics of individuals in poverty in the boom year 1999 and to infer from those data the potential for full employment to improve their economic situation. Table 3.7 records the characteristics of adult individuals (those age sixteen or older) below the poverty line and shows their relationship to the labor market in 1999 or in March 2000 (on the assumption that this provides information on their 1999 status as well).

The main finding shown in this table is that a substantial proportion of individuals in poverty in 1999 have characteristics that will make it hard for them to benefit much from a booming labor market. The upper part of the table shows that only 42 percent of poor individuals age sixteen or older worked at all in 1999. Of those who did not work in 1999, 24 percent said that they could not work because they were disabled, 27 percent said they had retired, and 23 percent cited family responsibilities. Taking the poverty population age sixteen or older as a whole, 21 percent were disabled, and 15 percent were over age sixty-four—and thus unlikely to work. Another substantial proportion of poor individuals had relatively little education: 17.5 percent had completed only grade school or less, while 26.7 percent had between eight and twelve years of schooling. Twenty-three percent were immigrants, largely from less-developed Latin American and Caribbean countries, with limited job skills.[10] Adding together the "risk" factors of age, disability, immigrant status, and poor education, 53 percent of the adults in poor families in 1999 had at least one such difficulty.

Table 3.8 turns from all individuals age sixteen and older to individuals more likely to benefit from continued full employment: nonstudents age sixteen to sixty-four. Here too, however, the data show that relatively few of those in poverty in 1999 were in the job market. In March 2000, 44.5 percent were working, and 8.1 percent were unemployed. Nearly half of the

Table 3.7 Individuals Age Sixteen and Older in Poverty, 1999

Characteristics	Percentage
Worked in 1999	42.1
Did not work in 1999	57.9
Did not work because disabled	23.9
Did not work because retired	26.9
Did not work because of family obligations	23.4
Disabled	21.0
Over age sixty-four	15.0
Eight years of schooling or less	17.5
Nine to eleven years of schooling	26.7
Immigrant	24.9
Has at least one "risk" factor (disabled; over age sixty-four; eight years of schooling or less; or immigrant)	53.2

Source: Author's tabulations from March 2000 CPS files (individuals).

Note: These data relate to persons living in families with incomes below the official poverty line.

Table 3.8   Poor Nonstudents, Age Sixteen to Sixty-four

Characteristics	Percentage
Worked during survey week	44.5
Unemployed during survey week	8.1
Out of labor force	47.4
Disabled	14.8
Retired	6.1
Worked during 1999	42.9

Source: Author's tabulations from March 2000 CPS files (individuals).

Note: These data related to persons living in families with incomes below the official poverty line. Average weeks worked per year: 35.9; average hours worked per week: 36.0; average hourly earnings: $8.31.

nonstudent sixteen- to sixty-four-year-olds in poverty in 1999 were out of the labor force in the boom period and thus unlikely to benefit much from improved labor market conditions. Many said they were not looking for work because they were disabled or retired; relatively few said they were not looking because they could not find work. Those in poverty who had worked in 1999 had an average hourly wage considerably above the minimum wage, but they worked only thirty-six of fifty-two weeks and averaged thirty-six hours per week. These individuals had myriad reasons for working only part of the year, but if it at the peak of a long boom they could not manage to work more despite their family's fall into poverty, it is unlikely that a longer boom could greatly increase their work time.

All told, close to 60 percent of all adults in poverty and over 50 percent of those who were both below retirement age and not a student were unlikely to benefit much from the booming labor market.

To be sure, an extensive boom would bring more of the residual poor into the job market and improve their wages. But this group consists of persons who will benefit less than others, reducing the impact of full employment in lowering poverty, consistent with the bell-curve analysis given earlier.

Another way to assess how much poverty might drop with continued full employment and rising real wages is to examine the extent to which the current income of families in poverty falls short of the poverty line. Families whose income is close to the poverty level could arguably rise above that level if the wages or employment of family members improved moderately. Families with income far below the poverty line, by contrast, are likely to suffer from problems that limit their participation in the market. Data from the U.S. Bureau of the Census (2000, table D) show that most families in poverty have incomes that put them thousands of dollars below the poverty line. The average income deficit for poor families (the dollar amount needed to raise a poor family out of poverty) was $6,687 in 1999. The distribution of families by the level of deficit shows that increases in family income of even $1,000 per family would move only 9.2 percent of them above the poverty line—reducing poverty, in turn, by about one percentage point (U.S. Bureau of the Census 2000, table E). Increased incomes of this magnitude would greatly improve the well-being of those in poverty, but the poverty rate would not capture the true extent of the improvement because so many poor families are far below the poverty line.

Finally, scattered evidence on the extreme forms of poverty that grew in the wake of the recession of the 1980s—homelessness and hunger—supports the conclusion that even a strong boom will not raise all boats in the economy. Because the United States has no national data on homelessness, inferences about patterns of change in homelessness during the 1990s boom come from scattered reports. A 1997 National Coalition for the Homeless review of research conducted in eleven communities and four states found that shelter capacity more than doubled in nine communities and three states during the preceding decade, indicating greater demand on shelters at least through 1997. In its 2000 report, the U.S. Conference of Mayors also indicated that homelessness had not fallen in urban areas. Since these groups base their readings largely on use of shelters, they could be confusing shelter usage with increased homelessness, but the basic economics of homelessness suggests that they cannot be too far off base in their assessments. One contributing factor to homelessness is the price of rental housing, which has risen in the boom. Another factor is the prevalence of serious problems among a sizable proportion of the homeless population—mental illness, physical ailments, drug or alcohol addiction, or a history of crime. Because these problems reduce their employability, an economic boom is likely to help them less than other citizens.

As for hunger, the U.S. Department of Agriculture's study of food insecurity and hunger in the United States, derived from a special supplement to the Current Population Survey, shows little improvement through 1998. The government defines "food insecurity" as not simply outright hunger but also a lack of access to food to meet basic needs. Outright hunger is more severe. The 1998 study found that 36 million people, over one-third of them children, lived in households that were food-insecure. This is over 10 percent of American households! About 10 million persons lived in households suffering outright hunger in 1998—or about 4 percent of the population. The incidence of food insecurity was higher than average among households with children, especially those led by single women, minorities, and households with poverty-level income.

More important in inferring the effect of full employment, there appears to have been no change in the overall prevalence of food insecurity in the United States between 1995 and 1998. Additional evidence of the extent of hunger in the United States is the fact that emergency food shelters provided food to over 25 million people in 1998—again, with no evidence of declines in usage over time.

The implication of these data is that full employment and economic growth are unlikely by themselves to eliminate the problems of homelessness and hunger—two major elements of poverty.

Conclusion: Economic Boom and Behavior

The main finding of this study—that the 1990s economic growth was associated with reduced poverty—goes a long way to gainsaying the gloom that had developed from the 1980s. With unemployment rates of 4 to 5 percent, the rising tide of 1990s growth improved the wages as well as the employment of the poverty-prone individuals and groups whom the growth of the 1980s had bypassed.

Social science research is just beginning to focus on one additional piece of good news from the 1990s boom: many forms of socially deleterious behavior that threatened to lock individuals into a life of poverty also declined in the 1990s. Individuals in poverty-prone groups seem to have responded substantively to the employment and earnings opportunities that the boom offered them, taking advantage of newly available opportunities to work (Freeman and Rodgers 2000) and rejecting the "underclass" activities that many analysts had come to view as an intractable part of the U.S. social system.

The best-documented behavioral change is the drop in crime. Administrative data on crimes reported to police and citizens' survey-based reports of victimizations show a huge drop in crime in the 1990s. Although falling crime rates in New York City have been widely publicized around the world (and attributed to particular policing policies), in fact the drop is countrywide: crime is down in cities and towns with very different policing strategies, and the declines are greatest in the areas of the country with the best labor market conditions. Three econometric studies, covering somewhat different time periods and area groupings, have found that the change in crime is closely associated with labor market conditions (Gould, Mustard, and Weinberg 2000; Raphael and Winter-Ebmer 2000; Freeman and Rodgers 2000). Based on these findings, I estimate that about one-third of the 1990s drop in crime in the United States is attributable to the booming job market (Freeman 2001). The reduced supply of young, less-educated men to the criminal underclass, with its adverse effects on employment and earnings in the market, promises better lives and higher incomes in the future for persons from poor, largely inner-city backgrounds.

For disadvantaged women, the key indicator of underclass behavior, having children out of wedlock in their teens, has historically led them to rely on welfare for their later subsistence. In 1996 Congress enacted legislation designed to eliminate "welfare as we know it," by restricting the length of time individuals can be on welfare and encouraging states to get welfare mothers into work. Absent the late 1990s boom, the new welfare policies might have been a disaster. But in the strong labor market, they succeeded beyond anyone's expectation. There was a remarkable drop in the welfare population and an increase in the employment of former welfare recipients. In June 1999, 6.9 million individuals received welfare, in contrast to the 14.4 million who received welfare in 1993. The proportion of the U.S. population on welfare went down by more than half—from 5.5 percent to 2.5 percent. In a careful econometric analysis, the Council of Economic Advisers attributed part of this striking drop to full employment, part to the new welfare law, and part to the fact that the law operated in a full employment economy (an interaction effect).

Over the same period, the birth rate for teenage women fell sharply, owing in large part to a drop in the teen pregnancy rate. In 1991 the birth rate for women age fifteen to nineteen was 62.1 per 1,000 births. In 1998 the rate was 51.1. Among blacks, the teen birth rate fell from 116 per 1,000 to 85 per 1,000. The *New York Times* reported on October 27, 1999, that officials at the National Center for Health Statistics confirmed that for girls age fifteen to seventeen the birth rate had reached its lowest level since 1969. Since these drops occurred despite a decline in the abortion rate among teens, the implication is that the main cause was a drop in the teen pregnancy rate. I know of no estimates of the extent to which the booming job

Table 3A.1 Data for Time-Series Analysis

Year	Poverty Rate for Individuals	Poverty Rate for Families	Gini Coefficient for Family Income	Real Average Hourly Earnings, Private (Dollars per Hour)	Unemployment Rate (In Percentage Terms)	Income of Low-Quintile Family (Current Dollars)	Median Family Income (Current Dollars)
1959	22.4	18.5	.361	6.69	.055	2,677	5,417
1960	22.2	18.1	.364	6.79	.055	2,784	5,620
1961	21.9	18.1	.374	6.88	.067	2,800	5,735
1962	21.0	17.2	.362	7.07	.055	3,000	5,956
1963	19.5	15.9	.362	7.17	.057	3,096	6,249
1964	19.0	15.0	.361	7.33	.052	3,250	6,569
1965	17.3	13.9	.356	7.52	.045	3,500	6,957
1966	14.7	11.8	.349	7.62	.038	3,935	7,532
1967	14.2	11.4	.358	7.72	.038	4,109	7,933
1968	12.8	10.0	.348	7.89	.036	4,544	8,632
1969	12.1	9.7	.349	7.98	.035	5,000	9,433
1970	12.6	10.1	.353	8.03	.049	5,100	9,867
1971	12.5	10.0	.355	8.21	.059	5,211	10,285
1972	11.9	9.3	.359	8.53	.056	5,612	11,116
1973	11.1	8.8	.356	8.55	.049	6,081	12,051
1974	11.2	8.8	.355	8.28	.056	6,707	12,902
1975	12.3	9.7	.357	8.12	.085	6,987	13,719
1976	11.8	9.4	.358	8.24	.077	7,505	14,958
1977	11.6	9.3	.363	8.36	.071	8,000	16,009
1978	11.4	9.1	.363	8.40	.061	8,808	17,640
1979	11.7	9.2	.365	8.17	.058	9,861	19,587

1980	13.0	10.3	.365	7.78	.071	10,400	21,023
1981	14.0	11.2	.369	7.69	.076	11,015	22,388
1982	15.0	12.2	.380	7.68	.097	11,399	23,433
1983	15.2	12.3	.382	7.79	.096	11,835	24,580
1984	14.4	11.6	.383	7.80	.075	12,575	26,433
1985	14.0	11.4	.389	7.77	.072	13,285	27,735
1986	13.6	10.9	.392	7.81	.070	14,000	29,458
1987	13.4	10.7	.393	7.73	.062	14,598	30,970
1988	13.0	10.4	.395	7.69	.055	15,102	32,191
1989	12.8	10.3	.401	7.64	.053	16,003	34,213
1990	13.5	10.7	.396	7.52	.056	16,846	35,353
1991	14.2	11.5	.397	7.45	.068	17,000	35,939
1992	14.8	11.9	.404	7.41	.075	16,713	36,573
1993	15.1	12.3	.429	7.39	.069	16,970	36,959
1994	14.5	11.6	.426	7.40	.061	17,940	38,782
1995	13.8	10.8	.421	7.39	.056	19,070	40,611
1996	13.7	11.0	.425	7.43	.054	19,680	42,300
1997	13.3	10.3	.429	7.55	.049	20,586	45,262
1998	12.7	10.0	.430	7.75	.045	21,600	46,737
1999	11.8	9.3	.445	7.86	.042	20,599	48,950

Sources: Poverty rate for individuals: U.S. Bureau of the Census (2000, table B-1); poverty rate for families: U.S. Bureau of the Census (2000, table B-3); Gini coefficient: U.S. Bureau of the Census, *Historical Income Tables—Families* (table F-4); income of lowest quintile: U.S. Bureau of the Census, *Historical Income Tables—Families* (table F-1), where the figure refers to the upper limit of the lowest fifth, and 1999 was estimated by multiplying median family income by the ratio of the twentieth-percentile upper limit of household income to median household income; median family income: U.S. Bureau of the Census, *Historical Income Tables—Families* (table F-7); real hourly earnings, private: U.S. Council of Economic Advisers (1999b, table B-47); unemployment rate: U.S. Council of Economic Advisers (1999b, table B-42).

market contributed to this change in behavior, but certainly the better opportunities for young women and for the men in their lives must have led some to postpone having children until later in life.

The reduction in poverty and the improvement in behavior that accompanied the 1990s boom do not, however, mean that the United States can rely exclusively or even primarily on economic growth to achieve the goal of ending poverty. The shape of the income distribution and the characteristics of the residual poor suggest that the effect of full employment on poverty will weaken in the future. As noted, many of the residual poor have personal characteristics that keep them out of the job market and thus make it hard for them to benefit from full employment. Social policy, private or public, will be needed to bring their living standards above any measured poverty line. For some, ending poverty will simply require additional income transfers. Bringing others out of poverty, however, such as the homeless, the drug-addicted, and the mentally ill, will take more than money, since their problems, based in illness rather than simple lack of cash, are more extensive.

The experience of the 1990s boom raises caution in another area as well: the U.S. economy requires rates of unemployment of 4 to 5 percent to overpower the forces of inequality and improve the conditions of low-wage workers. Anything short of the 4 to 5 percent unemployment rates that the Federal Reserve and other macroeconomic policymakers once viewed as unsustainable will return the United States to a 1980s experience of economic growth without a reduction in poverty. The rising tide of economic progress can lift many boats, but the ebb tide of recession can sink many boats as well. The lesson of the 1990s is that the key indicator of the level of the tide is not 6 to 6.5 percent unemployment, but 4 to 5 percent unemployment. Even then, something more will be needed to improve the living standards of the poor who cannot benefit from a booming job market.

CHAPTER 4

Mobility, Persistence, and the Consequences of Poverty for Children: Child and Adult Outcomes

MARY CORCORAN

The United States has a much more unequal distribution of incomes than Canada and most Western European nations, and income inequality in the United States widened in the 1980s and early 1990s (see Burtless and Smeeding, this volume). But most U.S. residents are far less concerned about whether incomes are unequal than about mobility and equality of opportunity. According to Ralph Turner (1960), Americans view mobility as a race in which contestants compete on an equal basis for success, with the rewards going to the most talented, most enterprising, and hardest-working. As long as the race is fair, the resulting inequality is the price of living in an open and mobile society.

One way of assessing openness and fairness is to measure the degree of mobility—both within and across generations—and to see who succeeds and who does not. Annual data such as the census or Current Population Survey (CPS) files provide "snapshots" of the income distribution at a point in time, but longitudinal data are required to track the same individuals' and families' income trajectories and poverty status over time and across generations. This chapter reviews recent research that uses longitudinal data to delineate patterns of intragenerational and intergenerational economic mobility and to assess the consequences for children's future well-being of growing up poor and/or in a single-parent home.

I begin by examining the persistence of poverty. Although much poverty is transitory, about 5 percent of adults and children are poor for extended periods of time, and poor children are many times more likely than nonpoor children to be poor in their midtwenties. Long-term childhood poverty is unequally distributed: almost nine out of ten long-term poor children are African American, and more than six out of ten long-term poor children have spent time in single-parent families.

127

I next review studies that measure the extent of intragenerational and intergenerational mobility. There is considerable mobility and considerable persistence of income status. Rates of intragenerational income mobility have not increased over time in the United States, but rates of intergenerational income mobility have increased over time. A disturbing finding is that African Americans and single mothers and their children are less likely to be upwardly mobile.

The third section focuses on how childhood poverty shapes children's future attainments. Growing up in a poor family matters for a number of child outcomes—test scores, schooling, fertility choices, labor market outcomes, and incomes—even after controlling for background characteristics associated with child poverty, such as schooling, mother's cognitive test scores, whether raised in a single-parent family, and family size. The effects of parental income on economic outcomes typically are large in size, whereas effects on non-economic outcomes are modest in size. Children born to poor parents may not be competing on an equal footing with children born to rich parents.

The fourth section examines the extent to which growing up in a single-parent family diminishes future well-being. Growing up in a single-parent family is associated with less schooling, more male idleness, higher rates of teen births, and more psychological and behavioral problems. These negative associations are due in large part, though not exclusively, to the fact that single-parent families have fewer economic and community resources than do two-parent families. However, even after controlling for race, ethnicity, family size, parental schooling, and family income, growing up in a single-parent home matters for children's futures.

The fifth section summarizes the evidence of race differences from the previous sections. Race differences are striking. African Americans are many times more likely to be long-term poor than are whites, and they are much less likely to be upwardly mobile, either within or across generations.

The last section summarizes these results and discusses their policy implications.

Poverty Persistence

There has been considerable debate in both academic and policy circles over the extent of long-term poverty. Some argue that there is no long-term poverty problem—that most poverty is temporary and reflects short-run adjustment problems or life-cycle stages. For instance, an individual may lose a job, then go through a period of low income before getting a new job. When a family breaks up, the single-mother household may go through a period of low income before the mother increases her work or remarries. When young adults first leave home, their earnings and incomes are low as they acquire schooling, begin work at entry-level jobs, and begin their families. In the middle adult years, earnings and incomes peak, then decline during the retirement years. According to this view, most poverty is transitory and few individuals experience long-term economic distress.

Others argue that some individuals and families remain poor for long periods, perhaps over generations. One view blames poverty persistence on poor labor market opportunities, segregation, discrimination, inadequate and underfunded schools, and the lack of community resources in disadvantaged neighborhoods. Another points to the work and marriage disincentives in the welfare system, the increasing number of female-headed families, increases in teen pregnancy and illegitimacy, deviant subcultures, and the personal deficiencies of the poor.

Whatever the cause, the size and composition of the long-term poor are matters of concern for several reasons. First, the persistently poor consume disproportionately large percentages of the public dollars spent on antipoverty programs (Blank 1997). Second, the unequal distribution of persistent poverty across demographic groups violates norms of fairness, equal opportunity, and meritocracy. Third, growing up poor may have negative consequences for poor children's cognitive and social development and economic futures. If parental income is a major determinant of children's economic prospects, then society may not be as open as is commonly imagined. Finally, even if poverty has no effect on children's futures, there is a quality of life issue. For eighteen years, children's material well-being and access to resources, such as good schools and safe communities, depend in large part on their parents' incomes.

In this section, I address three questions about long-term poverty:

- How much long-term poverty is there, and are any demographic groups disproportionately likely to experience long-term poverty?
- What is the extent of intergenerational poverty? Do poor children escape poverty as adults?
- Has the incidence of long-term child poverty changed over time?

How Long Do People Stay Poor?

What percentage of people who are poor in a given year are trapped in long-term poverty? And what percentage are poor only temporarily? Rebecca Blank (1997) tracked the poverty experiences of adults and children over the thirteen-year period from 1979 to 1991 and reported that one in three people experienced at least one year of poverty over that period (see figure 4.1). Poverty was a widespread risk, but most people who became poor were not in long-term poverty: half of those experiencing poverty were poor for only one to three years over the thirteen-year period. Long-term poverty was rare—only 1.5 percent of the population were poor in all thirteen years, and 4.9 percent were poor in ten or more years.

Long-term poverty was not equally shared. African Americans, high school dropouts, individuals with health problems, and women and children living in single-mother families were more likely to be long-term poor. Race differences were striking: fewer than one in fifty whites were poor for ten or more years between 1979 and 1991, but one in six African Americans were poor for that many years.[1]

How Long Do Children Remain Poor?

The poverty experiences of children are of special concern because many suspect that growing up in poverty damages children's life prospects. Greg

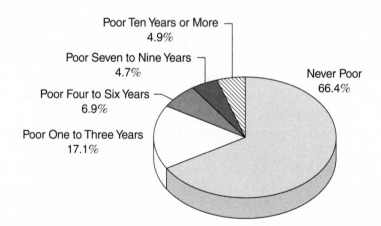

Figure 4.1 Poverty Among Americans, 1979 to 1991 (*Source:* Blank (1997, 23).

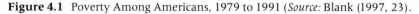

Duncan (1991) tracked the economic circumstances of a nationally representative sample of children who were between the ages of one and four in 1968 for fifteen years. Once again, poverty was widespread, but most poor children were only temporarily poor. One in three children spent at least one year in poverty; two-thirds of them spent fewer than five years in poverty as a child. But for 5 percent of all children and 15 percent of children who were ever poor, childhood poverty lasted ten years or more.

Differences between African American and white children in long-term poverty rates are even more striking than differences in annual rates (see figure 4.2). Long-term childhood poverty was rare among whites—fewer than 1 percent were poor for ten years or more—but common among African American children, 29 percent of whom were poor for ten years or more. Although white children constituted about 60 percent of all children who were poor in 1982, almost 90 percent of the long-term poor children were African American (Duncan 1991).

The duration of childhood poverty varied along other dimensions as well. Children who lived with a single parent throughout their childhood, who lived in the South, and whose parents were disabled were all poor for higher-than-average durations.

Analysts who have investigated the events associated with the beginnings and ends of spells of childhood poverty report that changes in the employment and wages of adults are at least as important, and often more important, than changes in family structure in accounting for these transitions (Duncan and Rodgers 1991; Stevens 1995). For instance, Ann Stevens (1995) found that 42 percent of children's poverty spells began with reductions in the earnings of an adult household member, and that 75 percent of childhood poverty spells ended because of increased earnings of household members.

Do Poor Children Remain Poor as Adults?

Table 4.1 compares poverty rates measured over ages twenty-five to twenty-seven for poor and nonpoor children for a sample of children age one to fifteen years in 1968.[2] Mobility was common: less than one in four poor children were still poor by their midtwenties. But poor African American children were less likely to escape poverty than poor whites. One in three poor African American children were still poor at age twenty-five to twenty-seven, compared with one in fourteen for whites. Nonpoor African Ameri-

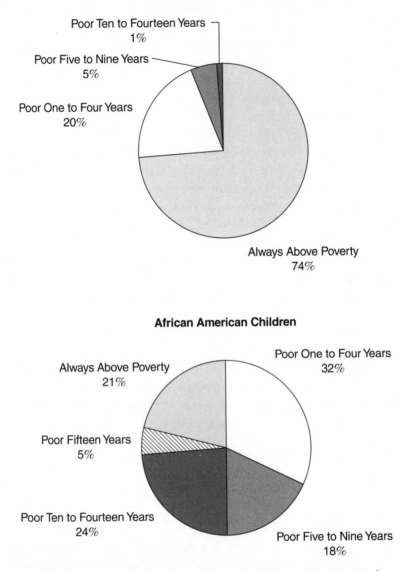

Figure 4.2 Fifteen-Year Poverty Experiences of Children Who Were Under Age Four in 1968 (*Source:* Duncan and Rodgers (1988).) *Note:* Data in this figure are from the PSID, which traced the experiences of a group of the same children over a fifteen-year period beginning in 1968 when they were under the age of four. Reprinted with permission from the *Journal of Marriage and the Family.*

Table 4.1 Transitions Between Childhood Poverty and Poverty at Age
Twenty-five to Twenty-seven, by Race

	Poverty Status at Age Twenty-five to Twenty-seven[b]	
Poverty Status During Childhood[a]	Poor	Not Poor
African American		
Poor	33.4	66.6
Not poor	14.9	85.1
White		
Poor	7.1	92.9
Not poor	2.7	97.3
All		
Poor	24.1	75.9
Not poor	3.8	96.2

Source: Computations by author.

Notes: Sample includes all respondents in the 1968 to 1993 Panel Study of Income
Dynamics (PSID) who were observed as children between age fifteen and seventeen
and as adults between age twenty-five and twenty-seven. All percentages are
weighted.

a. An individual is defined as poor as a child if the ratio of his or her family income
to the census poverty line averaged over all years observed as a child is less than 1.0.
Depending on the respondent's age in 1968, there are three to seventeen years of data
on childhood family income.

b. An individual is defined as poor as an adult if the ratio of his or her family
income to the census poverty line averaged over age twenty-five to twenty-seven is
less than 1.0.

can children were more than twice as likely to be poor at age twenty-five to
twenty-seven than were poor white children (14.9 versus 7.1 percent).

Is Long-term Childhood Poverty Becoming More Common?

Annual child poverty rates were higher in the 1980s than in the late 1960s
and early 1970s. In 1972 the poverty rate for children was less than 15
percent; by 1983 it was 22.3 percent. However, the rate of long-term childhood poverty did *not* increase between the late 1960s and mid-1980s. Greg
Duncan and William Rodgers (1991) compared children's poverty experiences during two six-year periods, 1967 to 1972 and 1981 to 1986, and

reported no consistent or significant trend in long-term childhood poverty. This stability in long-term childhood poverty was due to several offsetting economic and demographic trends. Increased economic inequality, increased numbers of single-parent families, and younger parents contributed to longer stays in poverty, but these were offset by reductions in stays in poverty due to declining family size and increased parental schooling.

We do not yet know whether long-term childhood poverty declined in the 1990s. Annual child poverty rates fell from 22.3 percent to 16.9 percent between 1992 and 1999, but longitudinal data from the 1990s are not yet available.

Income Mobility

This section examines patterns of intragenerational income mobility, changes in long-term income inequality, and intergenerational income inequality. I pose three questions:

- What is the extent of income mobility? Does it vary across demographic groups?
- Did income mobility increase in the 1980s and early 1990s? If so, did these increases in mobility counterbalance the increases in cross-sectional income inequality over this period?
- Is there greater income mobility in the United States than in other Western industrialized countries with lower rates of income inequality?

The Measurement of Mobility

Relative income mobility is measured by tracking the same individuals' incomes over time and estimating the extent to which their relative positions in the income distribution change over that period. Analysts typically divide incomes into five quintiles, and then measure the movement between quintiles between the first year and end year of the period examined (McMurrer and Sawhill 1998). Movements between quintiles in years other than the first and end years are ignored.

Studies typically focus on two aspects of mobility. First is the total *amount* of relative mobility: What proportions of individuals changed income quintiles between the first and end years? This tells us how much mobility there is but does not provide information about who moves. The second aspect is the *extent* of mobility out of the bottom quintile: What proportion of individuals in the bottom quintile experienced upward mobility? This tells us the extent to which individuals are "stuck" in a low-income situation.

How Much Intragenerational Mobility Is There?

Analysts who have tracked individuals' incomes over time agree that relative mobility is considerable, and that rates of relative mobility are higher the longer the period over which individuals' incomes are tracked. Depending on the study, 25 to 40 percent of individuals switched income quintiles over a two-year period; 40 to 50 percent switched quintiles over a five-year period; and 60 percent switched quintiles over a nine-year, seventeen-year, or twenty-three-year income period (Gottschalk 1997; Danziger and Gottschalk 1998; McMurrer and Sawhill 1998).

Although rates of relative mobility are high, there is considerable immobility as well. Sheldon Danziger and Peter Gottschalk (1998), for instance, tracked the incomes of a nationally representative sample of individuals age twenty-two to thirty-nine in 1968 over the twenty-three-year period 1968 to 1991. More than half of individuals who were in the bottom income quintile in the period 1968 to 1970 were still in the bottom in the period 1989 to 1991; one-quarter had moved up one quintile; and only 1.3 percent were in the top income quintile. Rates of upward mobility out of the bottom quintile were lower for nonwhites and for single mothers who received welfare: 72 percent of nonwhites and 78 percent of welfare recipients who were in the bottom quintile in 1968 to 1970 were still in that quintile over twenty years later. The comparable number for whites was 46 percent.

Does Intragenerational Mobility Increase over Time?

Long-run income inequality depends on two factors: the distribution of income at a point in time and income mobility over time. Income mobility over time can be further broken down into two components: mobility due to life-cycle stages and mobility due to short-term transitory fluctuations in income (Solon 1999b). Long-run income inequality need not have worsened in the 1980s if the increases in annual income inequality had been offset by increases in income mobility during the same period.

To understand this, consider the following. Joseph Schumpeter likened the long-run income distribution to hotel rooms (see Danziger and

Gottschalk 1998; McMurrer and Sawhill 1998). Room sizes in a hotel vary. On any day, the distribution of individuals across rooms is unequal: some have large rooms, and others have small rooms. If individuals never switch rooms, then long-run inequality will equal short-run inequality. If individuals switch rooms frequently, then the degree of long-run inequality will depend on both the distribution of rooms (short-run inequality) and the extent to which individuals move between small and large rooms (mobility). If the hotel owner increases the inequality in room size (for example, by combining some large rooms and splitting some small rooms into even smaller rooms), then long-run inequality will also increase unless this increased inequality in room size is offset by a comparable increase in the rate at which individuals switch between rooms of different sizes.

Relative mobility in the United States did not increase during the decades following the postwar boom (McMurrer and Sawhill 1998). Figure 4.3 reports the proportions of individuals who switched income quintiles in the 1970s and the 1980s. Rates of mobility were virtually the same in both decades. Thus, increased short-run economic inequality in the 1980s and early 1990s, as measured by annual statistics, was not canceled out by a corre-

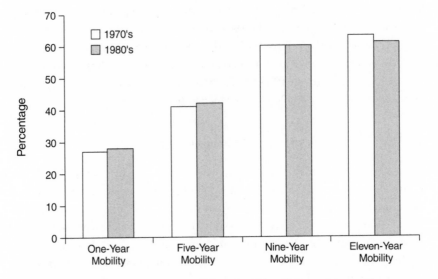

Figure 4.3 Mobility Rates in the 1970s and 1980s. (*Sources:* Adapted from McMurrer and Sawhill (1998; 35) and Gottschalk and Danziger (1998; 108, table 7).)

sponding increase in relative mobility. As a result, long-run economic inequality must also have widened—that is, the gap in incomes between those at the bottom of the income distribution and those at top grew in the 1980s and early 1990s.

Although overall relative mobility did not change over time, the extent to which relative mobility varies with schooling has changed. In the 1970s, rates of income growth were similar across education groups, but in the 1980s college graduates experienced considerably more income growth than did other individuals. Average rates of family income growth over the decade 1970 to 1979 were approximately 47 percent for high school dropouts, 45 percent for school graduates, and 55 percent for college graduates (Rose 1993, as cited in McMurrer and Sawhill 1998). Corresponding rates between 1980 and 1989 were only 18 percent for high school dropouts, 29 percent for high school graduates, and 57 percent for college graduates (Rose 1993, as cited in McMurrer and Sawhill 1998).

International Comparisons of Intragenerational Mobility

Economic inequality varies considerably across the Western industrialized nations, and the United States has a much more unequal distribution of income than do most European countries. But when analysts compare income mobility across Western industrialized countries, they found that U.S. rates of intragenerational mobility are no higher than those of the Nordic European states, Germany, France, Italy, and Great Britain (McMurrer and Sawhill 1998). It is sometimes asserted that greater economic inequality in the United States is the price of greater economic mobility. But the data contradict this assertion: rates of intragenerational mobility vary little across Western industrialized countries even though these countries have very different degrees of economic inequality, very different political structures, and very different economic structures.

To What Extent Is Income Inequality Transmitted Across Generations?

In the late 1980s and 1990s, researchers began to use longitudinal data to examine the persistence of economic inequality across generations. They constructed multi-year measures of fathers' and sons' incomes and earnings and estimated the correlations between fathers' and sons' long-run economic status. Estimates of father-son correlations in long-run earnings averaged above 0.4, and estimates of father-son correlations in long-run income ranged from 0.4 to over 0.5. (For excellent reviews of this research, see Solon 1999a, 1999b.) The size of father-son correlations in economic status grew with the son's age—from about .25 for sons in their midtwenties to about .5 for men in their late thirties (Solon 1999a). Paternal income was also strongly associated with daughters' adult economic status, and father-daughter income correlations are similar in magnitude to those reported for fathers and sons (Chadwick and Solon 1999). Apparently, at least 16 to 25 percent of the variance in children's long-run adult incomes is due to the intergenerational transmission of economic status (Solon 1999a).[3]

Has the Rate of Intergenerational Mobility Changed over Time?

The increase in returns to skill in the 1980s and early 1990s could have reduced intergenerational mobility, since one of the primary means by which affluent parents are hypothesized to influence children's adult incomes is by investing in their children's human capital. Robert Reville (1995) investigated the extent to which the association between fathers' and sons' earnings varied with the returns to schooling and found that the size of the association between fathers' and sons' earnings increases as returns to schooling increase. Gary Solon (1999b) cautions that Reville's model did not allow for the fact that increases in the perceived returns to children's schooling could eventually lead low-income parents to increase investments in their children's human capital.

Susan Mayer and L. Lopoo (2000), on the other hand, found that the associations between parental income and sons' annual earnings and family incomes have dropped over time. They report that the standardized regression coefficient for the effect of parental income on sons' family incomes at age thirty was above .36 for sons born between 1949 and 1957, .26 for sons born between 1958 and 1961, and .20 for sons born between 1962 and 1965.

Table 4.2 reports the correlations between parental income and sons' economic attainments for two cohorts of sons: sons age eight to fifteen in 1968 and sons age eight to fifteen in 1976. Sons in the earlier cohort would have turned twenty in the 1970s; sons in the second cohort would have turned twenty in the 1980s.

Like Mayer and Lopoo (2000), I found that men's intergenerational income mobility has increased over time. The correlation between parents'

Table 4.2   Correlations Between Parental Income and Sons' Earnings, Hourly Wages, and Family Incomes

	Correlations Between Parental Incomes and Sons' . . .		
	Labor Incomes	Hourly Wages	Family Incomes
Children who turned twenty in the 1970s[a]	.25	.29	.26
Children who turned twenty in the 1980s[b]	.20	.25	.18

Source: Computations by author.

Notes: All income, earnings, and wage measures are logged. Analyses are weighted. Family income is defined as the sum of family income plus the value of food stamps. Parental family income is averaged over all the years respondent has been observed since age eight. Thus, there are three to ten years of data on parental income. Sons' adult economic attainments are averaged over age twenty-five to twenty-seven.

a. Sample includes all PSID respondents age eight to fifteen in 1968 who were observed between age fifteen and twenty-seven. Parental family income is averaged over all the years from 1968 until the respondent is age seventeen.

b. Sample includes all PSID respondents age eight to fifteen in 1976 who were observed between age fifteen and twenty-seven. Parental family income is averaged over all the years from 1976 until the respondent is age seventeen.

and sons' incomes was .26 for children who turned twenty in the 1970s and .18 for children who turned twenty in the 1980s. The correlation between parents' incomes and sons' labor earnings was .25 for men who turned twenty in the 1970s and .20 for men who turned twenty in the 1980s.

Analysts who have tracked intergenerational occupational mobility over the 1960s, 1970s, and 1980s reach a similar conclusion: the association between fathers' and sons' occupational statuses declined over those decades (Biblarz, Bengslan, and Bucur 1996; Hauser 1998; Mare 1992).

International Comparisons of Intergenerational Economic Inequality

A number of analysts have estimated father-son correlations in earnings or incomes for countries outside the United States, the majority from northern and western Europe. These studies often use only single-year income or earnings measures and so may underestimate the degree to which income inequality persists across generations. Keeping that in mind, the United

States and the United Kingdom appear to have similar rates of intergenerational income mobility, while Sweden, Finland, Germany, Canada, and Malaysia appear to have higher rates of intergenerational mobility than does the United States. (For a review, see Solon 1999a.)

Does Growing up Poor Affect Children's Futures?

Explanations of Poverty Effects

What processes explain the transmission of income inequality across generations? Some analysts argue that a lack of parental economic resources restricts children's opportunities. Poor parents must devote all of their resources to meeting consumption needs and have little time, money, or energy left over to devote to improving their own and/or their children's education and skills (Becker 1981/1991; Haveman and Wolfe 1994, 1995). Similarly, the poor cannot afford to relocate to communities that are closer to available jobs, and they can afford housing only in disadvantaged neighborhoods that provide lower-quality schools, fewer good role models, less social control, and fewer job networks and are more likely to have teenage gangs and high crime rates (Jencks and Mayer 1990).

Others emphasize how economic and demographic factors—such as deindustrialization, globalization, residential segregation, labor market discrimination, and the migration of middle-class residents from inner cities—constrain economic opportunities and choices across generations. William Julius Wilson (1996) contends that globalization, technological upgrading, the decline of unions, and the shift of manufacturing employment from the cities to the suburbs caused a drop in the number of well-paid manufacturing jobs that were compatible with ghetto residents' skills and available to them. This shift increased male joblessness and contributed to and increased the number of children being raised in single-parent families. At the same time, the migration of middle-class residents out of the inner city left poor inner-city residents behind, weakened important socializing institutions, reduced the exposure of poverty-area residents to mainstream values and norms, reduced job-finding networks, and reduced the number of work role models. Ghettos became increasingly disorganized, and residents increasingly engaged in economic activity in the underground economy. All of these changes reduced the mobility prospects of the next generation.

Developmental psychologists argue that long-term poverty can hamper parents' abilities to raise their children effectively (Brooks-Gunn and Duncan 1997; Chase-Lansdale and Gordon 1996; McLoyd 1998). Poor parents are constantly stressed by the necessity to make ends meet and often must raise their children in unsafe neighborhoods with few community resources. These stresses can lead to mental health problems (such as depression) and harsh and inconsistent parenting practices and can make it difficult for parents to provide the emotional and cognitive environments that foster children's cognitive and emotional growth.

Still other analysts focus on the loss of "family values," the decline of the nuclear family, illegitimacy, teen births, and increased numbers of single mothers. According to Robert Rector (1995), teen childbearing and out-of-wedlock childbearing consign mothers and children to lives of poverty and dependency. Charles Murray (1995) claims that children raised by single mothers will grow up to be idle, unproductive, and poor adults. Sara McLanahan and Gary Sandefur (1994) agree that children raised in single-parent families fare poorly on many outcomes, but they argue that a large part of the reason for such outcomes is a lack of resources. Single parents have fewer economic resources, less time, and more stresses than two-parent families.

Lawrence Mead (1986, 1992) claims that when individuals use welfare heavily and work rarely or intermittently, the stigma associated with welfare diminishes, a "welfare culture" develops, and individuals develop self-defeating work attitudes and poor work ethics that are passed on to the children.

Finally, Susan Mayer (1997) asserts that many of the apparent negative associations between growing up poor and children's attainments reflect unmeasured parental advantages, such as abilities, good health, genetic endowments, values, and motivations, that positively affect both parents' incomes and children's attainments. One possible unmeasured parental characteristic is parental depression. Depression may lower both a parent's earnings potential and his or her parenting effectiveness. In this case, a positive correlation between parental income and child well-being is not a true income effect but instead reflects the fact that depression reduces both a parent's income and his or her parenting abilities.

Determining the appropriate policies for dealing with long-term childhood poverty and intergenerational economic inequality depends on which of the above views are correct. If a lack of resources and low skills inhibit the chances that poor individuals and their children will escape poverty, then policies that deliver resources to poor families and policies that raise the skill levels of poor children are appropriate. The Earned Income Tax Credit (EITC), refundable child care tax credits, and housing vouchers are ways to increase the economic resources of the poor. Policies targeted at improving skills include providing compensatory education and making more college scholarships available to the poor.

If economic, demographic, and cultural changes have socially isolated inner-city poor children and inhibited their chances of escaping poverty, then it will require both economic and social service strategies to reverse the factors that generated an urban underclass. If macroeconomic policies can provide jobs and social services policies can combat the effects of social isolation, then reductions in negative attitudes and behaviors will eventually result.

In the recent welfare reform debate, teen childbearing, out-of-wedlock births, and single parents were cited as major causes of poverty and welfare dependency for women and their children. To the extent that these assertions are correct, policies that encourage girls to delay pregnancy until they are married and in their twenties are the appropriate strategies. But if teen births and unwed births are not a cause of poor marriage and work opportunities but rather a response to that situation, then policies aimed at expanding the economic opportunities of disadvantaged girls might be more effective at preventing poverty (Hotz, McElroy, and Sanders 1996; Geronimus 1997). Similarly, if a lack of resources, not a deviant family structure, is the primary factor that inhibits the social and economic attainments of children raised by single mothers, then policies that deliver resources to single-parent families are the appropriate solution (for example, EITC, child allowances, counseling programs, federally guaranteed child support).

If it is not childhood poverty per se but parental disadvantages that are associated with or cause parental poverty and lead to negative associations between childhood poverty and child outcomes, then the policy solution is less obvious. We need to identify which parental disadvantages are the culprits and to target policies toward either changing these disadvantages or reducing their impact on children's futures.

Associations Between Childhood Poverty and Children's Attainments

Table 4.3 reports the associations between childhood poverty and children's educational, fertility, labor market, and income outcomes, measured at ages twenty-five to twenty-seven.[4] Childhood poverty status strongly predicts *all*

Table 4.3   Schooling, Fertility, Labor Market, and Income Outcomes, by Childhood Poverty Status

Outcomes	Childhood Poverty Status[a]	
	Poor	Nonpoor
Schooling outcomes		
Mean years of schooling	12.0	13.4
Percentage who did not complete high school	29.7	9.0
Fertility outcomes (women only)		
Percentage who had a teen birth	39.0	18.7
Percentage who had an unwed birth	24.6	9.4
Labor market outcomes at age twenty-five to twenty-seven (men only)		
Mean hours worked per year	1,744	2,100
Mean hourly wage	$8.51	$12.14
Mean annual earnings	$15,188	$25,246.7
Mean weeks idle between age twenty-five and twenty-seven[b]	11.8	4.7
Income outcomes at age twenty-five to twenty-seven		
Mean family income	$21,541	$36,003
Mean family income to needs ratio[c]	2.0	3.7
Percentage who are poor[d]	24.1	3.8

Source: Computations by author.
Notes: See table 4.1 note. All means are weighted.
a. See table 4.1, note a.
b. A man is defined as "idle" if he is not working and is not a full-time student.
c. "Needs" is the census poverty line.
d. See table 4.1, note b.

the outcomes in table 4.3. Poor children average 1.4 fewer years of schooling than do nonpoor children, and they are more than three times as likely to have dropped out of high school. Poor girls are more than twice as likely to have had a teen birth, and they are 2.6 times more likely to have had an out-of-wedlock birth than are nonpoor girls. Poor boys work fewer hours per year, have lower hourly wages, have lower annual earnings, and spend more weeks idle in their midtwenties than do nonpoor boys. Poor children have higher poverty rates (24 percent versus 4 percent) and lower incomes ($21,514 versus $36,003) in their midtwenties than do nonpoor children.

Poor children also fare worse than do nonpoor children on non-economic outcomes in addition to those examined in table 4.1. Poor children are roughly twice as likely as nonpoor children to be in fair or poor health, to die during infancy, or to have spent time in the hospital in the last year; they are approximately one and a half times as likely to have a learning disability or cognitive developmental deficit; and they are twice as likely to have repeated a grade or to have been expelled from school (Brooks-Gunn and Duncan 1997).

These statistics, however, do not tell us how much child poverty *itself* actually affects children's outcomes because poor and nonpoor families differ on many dimensions. Differences in family structure, parental education and behaviors, and other factors, not income per se, could be leading to undesirable outcomes for poor children. To the extent that this is true, previous studies have overestimated the effects of child poverty.

Also, studies that only estimate associations between child poverty and child outcomes do not tell us why and how child poverty affects children's development. Do poor children suffer developmental delays because of poor nutrition? Because their home environments are not stimulating? Because poor parents do not use effective parenting practices? Because poor parents are psychologically distressed? Because poor families reside in disorganized communities with poor schools? Or because of genetically based abilities that are transmitted from parents to children (Brooks-Gunn and Duncan 1997; Mayer 1997)?

New Longitudinal Research on the Effects of Child Poverty

In two recent books, *The Consequences of Growing up Poor* and *What Money Can't Buy*, the authors estimate income effects on a variety of child outcomes across several longitudinal data sets using similar methodologies. This research also allows us to examine the extent to which children's attainments are affected by measured family characteristics—such as family structure—which are thought to be important in the transmission of economic inequality. In this section, I will summarize the results of this research about the effects of child poverty on children's economic attainments, cognitive test scores, schooling, physical health, psychological functioning, and teenage pregnancy.

To compare the size of income effects across studies, I use the convention used by Greg Duncan and Jeanne Brooks-Gunn (1997). An income effect is defined as large if in the majority of studies reviewed the change in the child outcome amounted to at least one-third of a standard deviation and was associated with (1) an increase of $10,000 of income, (2) an increase in income from below the poverty line to between the poverty line and twice the poverty line, (3) a doubling of income, or (4) a change from persistent poverty to no poverty. An effect is defined as small/modest if most of the income coefficients across studies were significant but not large. An effect is defined as weak if some studies showed small, significant income coefficients and other studies found insignificant income coefficients. An effect is defined as "no effect" if few if any studies find significant income coefficients. Table 4.4 reports the size of childhood poverty effects on children's outcomes using this convention.

Children raised in long-term childhood poverty have lower wages, work hours, earnings, and family incomes and higher rates of idleness and poverty than do nonpoor children, even after controlling for family and neighborhood background disadvantages. The size of these estimated effects ranges from modest to large. In other research (Corcoran and Adams 1995, 1997a), I have found that growing up in a poor family rather than a middle-income family reduced men's hourly wages by more than 30 percent, men's annual earnings by more than 40 percent, and men's and women's income-to-needs ratios by more than 40 percent, even after controlling for family structure, number of siblings, mother's education, parental work hours, parental welfare use, and neighborhood poverty rate. Mayer (1997) reports

Table 4.4   Effects of Child Poverty (or Low Income) on Children's Outcomes, Controlling for Measured Parental Advantages

Outcome	Size of the Effect[a]
Adult earnings	Sizable
Adult income	Sizable
Adult idleness	Modest
Education	Modest
Fertility	Modest
Cognitive test scores	Modest or weak
Health outcomes	Weak
Behavioral and psychological outcomes	None

Source: Authors' compilation.

a. Sizable: doubling income increases outcome by one-third of a standard deviation or more; modest: effects are significant but not sizable; weak: effects are modest in size and sometimes insignificant; none: effects are not significant.

that doubling parental income from $15,000 to $30,000 was associated with an increase of 26 percent in men's annual earnings and an increase of 21 percent in men's hourly wages at age twenty-four. These effects are large. Elizabeth Peters and Natalie Mullis (1997), on the other hand, found that poverty during late adolescence has only modest effects on men's wages at ages twenty-six and twenty-seven. Most analysts have found that the effects of low income on male idleness and male work hours in early adulthood are modest in size (Haveman and Wolfe 1995; Corcoran and Adams 1995, 1997b; Corcoran and Kunz 1999; Mayer 1997).

Growing up poor is associated with cognitive deficits in early childhood. Differences in cognitive test scores between poor and nonpoor children are small, and sometimes significant, in studies that control for maternal test scores; they are larger and usually significant in studies that do not control for maternal test scores (Mayer 1997; Smith, Brooks-Gunn, and Klebanov 1997).

Growing up poor has modest effects on the number of years of schooling children acquire. A child who grows up in a poor or low-income household averages one-third to one-half year less schooling than a child who grows up in a middle-income household, once parental education, family structure, and race and ethnicity are controlled (Brooks-Gunn and Duncan 1997; Duncan and Brooks-Gunn 1997; Mayer 1997).[5]

Parental poverty is also associated with higher probabilities of dropping out of high school, but these associations are typically small in size once race, ethnicity, parental schooling, family structure, and neighborhood characteristics are controlled (see Brooks-Gunn and Duncan 1997; Teachman et al. 1997; Haveman and Wolfe 1994, 1995). Mayer (1997), on the other hand, estimates that doubling a five-year measure of average annual family income from $15,000 to $30,000 would reduce high school dropout rates by more than one-third. This discrepancy may be due to the fact that Mayer does not control for family structure.

Poor girls are almost three times more likely to have a teenage out-of-wedlock birth than are nonpoor girls. But growing up poor has small effects on girls' chances of having a teen birth or a nonmarital birth once parental schooling, family structure, parental AFDC receipt, and race and ethnicity are controlled (Duncan et al. 1998; Haveman and Wolfe 1995). Mayer (1997) reports larger associations between income and teen childbearing and between income and nonmarital childbearing, perhaps because, again, she does not control for family structure.

Researchers have examined only a few physical and psychological outcomes using longitudinal data, and the evidence here is mixed. According to Brooks-Gunn and Duncan (1997), poverty is associated with exposure to lead paint, with stunted growth (low height for age), and with behavioral problems in early adolescence. It is not associated, however, with motor and social development in early childhood, wasting (low weight for age), obesity, hyperactivity, or lack of self-esteem in children. Poverty is associated with low birthweights for white, but not African American, children. Some analysts have found that poverty is associated with higher rates of anxiety in children; others have found no such association (Brooks-Gunn and Duncan 1997).

Does Source of Income Matter?

Several analysts have investigated whether growing up in families that receive welfare diminishes children's attainments. Children whose parents received welfare acquire fewer years of schooling and are less likely to graduate from high school than children whose parents never received it (Duncan and Yeung 1994; Haveman and Wolfe 1994, 1995). Girls whose mothers received welfare are more likely to have a teen birth and to receive welfare themselves than girls whose mothers never received welfare (Gottschalk 1992; Haveman and Wolfe 1994). These effects are modest in size and significant even after adjusting for measured family and neighborhood background disadvantages. The evidence is mixed on whether growing up on welfare reduces sons' labor supply.

The research on welfare tells us very little about how parental welfare receipt under the new reformed welfare system will affect children. In the Temporary Assistance to Needy Families (TANF) program, unlike the old AFDC program, receipt of benefits is conditional on work and time-limited. Also, recipients can combine welfare and work in states with generous earnings disregards.

Why Does Childhood Poverty Lead to Diminished Life Chances?

The longitudinal research reviewed here has documented the effects of childhood poverty on a number of outcomes, but it has done little to clarify the processes by which child poverty influences these outcomes. There are a few clues. Up to half the association between parental poverty and children's test scores is due to the fact that nonpoor families provide richer and more stimulating home environments than do poor families (Brooks-Gunn and Duncan 1997; Duncan et al. 1998; McLoyd 1998). Part of the association between parental poverty and children's economic outcomes occurs because nonpoor children get more schooling. Some analysts have speculated that parental poverty affects children's attainments by increasing health risk factors (for example, low birthweight, exposure to lead paint), affecting parents' health, mental health, and parenting practices, or exposing children to dangerous or negative environments. The evidence on these avenues, however, is weak, descriptive, and inconclusive.

Does Money Itself Matter?

Although childhood poverty and low income are negatively associated with many outcomes, analysts differ over whether money *itself* matters for children's outcomes (for example, see Mayer 1997; McLoyd 1998; Duncan et al. 1998). Most studies can control only for a small, easily measured set of family background characteristics. It is possible that there is some unmeasured parental trait that is both responsible for children's negative outcomes and correlated with family poverty. If this is the case, then previous studies have overstated the effects of childhood income on future well-being, and government programs designed to increase the income of poor parents may do less to improve the life chances of children than their proponents assert.

Mayer (1997) contends that parental income is primarily a proxy for unmeasured attributes, such as parental values, expectations, talents, health problems, behavioral problems (such as drug problems), genetic endowments, and motivations, and that parents who are in poor health or who possess low expectations, few talents, or little motivation are less likely to succeed economically themselves and also less likely to raise successful children. She employs a variety of strategies to calculate what she refers to as "true" estimates of income effects—that is, estimates that control for *all* parental attributes that affect both parental income and children's attainments.

Mayer begins by calculating "conventional" estimates of parental income effects on a variety of childhood, adolescent, and adult outcomes. She estimates each outcome as a function of a multi-year measure of parental income plus a limited set of family background measures. Income effects on test scores and behavior are very small and often insignificant, while income effects on schooling, fertility, and economic outcomes range from modest to large. Mayer's conventional estimates of income effects on test scores and economic outcomes are similar in size to those reviewed earlier, but her conventional estimates of income effects on fertility and schooling are typically larger than the estimates reported in other studies.

Mayer contends that these conventional estimates are too large, because she has controlled only for a limited set of parental advantages. She employs two procedures to get "true" estimates of income—that is, estimates of income effects that control for *all* the possible advantages that are correlated with parental income and that also affect children's outcomes. Given that Mayer's conventional estimates of income effects on test scores and behavior are very small and often insignificant, I report only results of "true" estimates for the eight schooling, fertility, and economic outcomes that Mayer examined.

In one test, Mayer adds measures of income after an outcome has occurred to her statistical models and compares the effect of this income with the effect of income before the outcome occurs, arguing that if income measured after an outcome occurs has an effect on that outcome, it must be because that income is correlated with other parental characteristics that affect parental income both before and after the outcome. Results of this test are mixed. For four of the eight outcomes examined, adding future income to the model sharply reduces the effect of prior income, which she infers to mean that unmeasured parental traits have a greater effect on these outcomes than previously realized. However, for three of the remaining four outcomes, controlling for future income actually results in an *increase* in the effect of prior income.

This test assumes that income received after an outcome occurs cannot have caused the outcome.[6] Solon (1999a), Brooks-Gunn and Duncan (1997), and Duncan and his colleagues (1998) question this assumption, suggesting that parental investments in children are likely to depend on parents' expectations of future income. Solon (1999a, 37) further notes that measures of parental income after a child leaves home "may serve as a proxy for imperfectly measured income during the child's youth."

In a second test, Mayer uses income from sources other than earned income and government transfers to measure the true effect of income on childhood outcomes, arguing that "other income" is less likely than earned income or transfer income to be correlated with parental characteristics and thus provides a better measure of the true income effects.[7] For five of the eight outcomes she examined, the effects of other income were smaller than the effects of total income.

There are at least two potential problems with this analysis, both of which Mayer notes. First, if more mistakes are made in measuring other income than in measuring earned income and transfer income—and evidence from the census and the PSID suggests that this is indeed the case—then the effect of other income will tend to be biased toward zero. Second, not all families receive other income. In particular, low-income families are less likely to receive rents, interest, or dividends.

In both of Mayer's statistical tests, the sizes of her true estimates of income effects on high school dropout, teen births, and out-of-wedlock births were considerably smaller than the sizes of her conventional estimates of these effects. But her true estimates were similar in size to the conventional estimates of income effects on these outcomes obtained by other researchers. Results were less consistent when Mayer examined years of schooling, adult wages, and adult earnings. In one test, the true estimates of the associations between these outcomes and parental income were larger than the conventional estimates; in the second test, true estimates were smaller than conventional estimates.

Mayer further investigated income effects by directly testing what she refers to as the two major social science models of income effects: the "investment" model and the "good parent" model. According to the investment model, having access to more resources enables parents to improve children's human capital by helping them meet the family's basic material needs (food, shelter, health care) and purchase inputs (housing, good neighborhoods) that improve children's skills. Mayer examines families' consumption patterns to test whether the goods that affluent parents purchase in greater numbers lead to improved child outcomes. She reports: "Poor families spend less on food, and live in smaller homes that are in worse repair, spend less on eating out, and are less likely to have health insurance; but these differences in living conditions have small effects on child outcomes." The major shortcoming of this analysis is that her data sets do not measure the kinds of material hardships and parental expenditures that are more relevant, such as food insufficiency, evictions, homelessness, utility cutoffs, lack of medical care, neighborhood crime rate, and school quality.

The good parent model focuses on parental stress: poverty is stressful, stress reduces parents' abilities to be effective parents, and poor parenting in turn harms children's social, emotional, and cognitive development. Mayer tests this model by examining the relationships of income with the measures of parental psychological well-being and parenting practices available in her data sets. These associations are weak, and she concludes that income does not affect child outcomes through parental mental health or parenting practices. Unfortunately, many of the indices that Mayer uses to measure stress and measure parenting practices may be weak measures of these concepts. It would also be useful to examine the effects of disturbances in maternal psychological health, such as depression, post-traumatic stress syndrome, and domestic violence, dysfunctional states that occur disproportionately to poor women.

To sum up, even the new, improved studies of intergenerational income effects control only for a limited set of non-economic background advantages when estimating income effects. Mayer (1997) may be correct in arguing that such studies probably omit key parental advantages that make parents good earners and good parents. As a result, estimates of income effects are probably too high. Mayer uses several clever techniques to estimate the effects of childhood income on children's outcomes, controlling for previously unobserved parental traits. There are weaknesses with each technique, but Mayer argues that when all these techniques consistently show that true estimates of income effects are smaller than conventional estimates, then conventional estimates of income effects are probably too large. Since Mayer's techniques, as she herself points out, often rest on strong and not always persuasive assumptions, it is less clear what to conclude when results of various tests are not consistent. Results of Mayer's tests generally indicate that true effects of parental income are smaller for male idleness than are those obtained in standard multivariate analyses. Her estimates of the true effects of income on high school dropout, teen pregnancy, and out-of-wedlock birth rates are similar to those obtained in conventional multivariate analyses by other researchers. Her results are less consistent about the size of the true effects of parental income on children's years of schooling, adult wages, or earnings.

Genetic Explanations of Intergenerational Inequalities

Several analysts claim that intergenerational inequalities are primarily caused by genetically inherited traits that parents pass on to their children (Herrnstein and Murray 1994). This claim is based on studies that use twin data to separate nature from nurture. In one type of twin studies, researchers compare the correlations between fraternal twins' attainments to the correlations between identical twins' attainments. Correlations are typically much higher for identical twins. Since identical twins have identical genetic endowments, analysts conclude that differences between identical and fraternal twin correlations are entirely due to genetics.

A second type of twin studies, adopted twin studies, compares the correlations for identical twins reared in different families to the correlations for identical twins reared in the same family. Analysts contend that the difference between these correlations measures the impact of nurture (for example, nongenetic background characteristics) on children's attainments. Since twin correlations between test scores (and schooling) of twins reared apart are similar to those of twins reared together, analysts reason that nongenetic family background plays at best a minor role in the transmission of intergenerational inequalities.

The conclusion that genes matter more than nongenetic family background rests on some very strong assumptions. Arthur Goldberger (1979) argues that attributing all the difference between the correlations of identical and fraternal twins to genetic factors ignores the possibility that identical twins experience more similar environments than do non-identical twins. This argument is plausible. For instance, parents probably are more likely to dress identical twins in the same outfits. If Goldberger's reasoning is correct, then it is impossible to assess the relative contributions of environmental and genetic factors by comparing the earnings correlations of identical and fraternal twins.

Robert Haveman and Barbara Wolfe (1999) argue that selection issues strongly limit the usefulness of studies of adopted twins. They argue that three sources of selection—the families who adopt, the agencies that place the child, and the participants' willingness to be part of an adoption study—severely restrict the range of parental background variation in studies of adoptive families. This restriction probably leads to serious underestimates of the role of nongenetic background differences in the transmission of intergenerational inequality.

There are two other objections to using twin samples to make inferences about the population. Many twin samples tend to be small and/or unrepresentative, and twins may be treated differently from other children (Solon 1999a; Haveman and Wolfe 1999).

Family Structure, Teen Childbearing, and Out-of-Wedlock Childbearing

Women and children living in single-parent families are disproportionately represented among the long-term poor, and poor children living in single-parent homes are less likely to move out of poverty than are poor children in two-parent homes. With longitudinal data, analysts can track families as they change over time and test dynamic models of how family structure affects children's outcomes.

Does Growing up in a Single-Parent Family Hurt Children?

Being raised in a female-headed family doubles the risk that a child will drop out of high school, triples the risk that a girl will have a teenage out-of-wedlock birth, and raises by 40 percent the risks of young men being idle (McLanahan and Sandefur 1994). Growing up in a female-headed family is also associated with fewer years of schooling and higher risks of behavioral and psychological problems during childhood and adolescence (McLanahan 1997).

One reason children raised in single-parent homes fare worse than children raised in intact families may be that children in single-parent families have many fewer resources: lower incomes, fewer parental, non-economic resources, such as time and attention from the parent and fewer community resources than do children in married-couple families (McLanahan and Sandefur 1994; Gottschalk, McLanahan, and Sandefur 1994). This story holds true for some outcomes. When McLanahan and Sandefur (1994) re-estimated the risks of high-school dropout, teenage premarital births, and idleness, after controlling for resource differences between single-parent and two-parent homes, they found that resource differences accounted for much, *but not all*, of the risks associated with being raised in a single-parent home. Controlling for income also sharply reduces but does not eliminate the strong negative association between growing up in a single-parent home and years of schooling. (For a review, see McLanahan 1997.) A primary reason that being raised outside an intact family was associated with diminished outcomes was that children in non-intact families had less access to parental economic resources, parental non-economic resources, and community resources. Still, being raised in a non-intact family significantly and negatively affected high school graduation, years of schooling, teenage fertility, and male idleness, even after resources were controlled.

On the other hand, access to fewer economic resources does not appear to account for many of the higher risks of behavioral and psychological problems associated with spending time in a non-intact home during childhood. When parental income (or poverty) was controlled, the associations between family structure and behavioral and psychological problems changed very little. This is hardly surprising, since family structure effects on behavioral and psychological outcomes were usually stronger than income effects (McLanahan 1997).

The same caveat that Mayer (1997) notes about income effects also applies to the research on the effects of being raised in a single-parent home. It is likely that some of the characteristics that lead parents to divorce or not to marry in the first place also affect their parenting abilities. As a result, past research may overstate the magnitude of family structure effects.

The Effects of Teenage Births on Girls' Economic Futures

Until the 1990s, academics and policymakers agreed that teenage births damaged the prospects of young women. This consensus was based on cross-sectional studies that showed that women who had their first child as a teenager were less likely to graduate from high school, earned less, had lower family incomes, were more likely to be poor, and were more likely to receive welfare than women who avoided teen births, even after controlling for differences in measures of background characteristics such as parental schooling and family income. This consensus was challenged by Arline Geronimus and Sanders Korenman (1992), who contended that cross-sectional studies did not control for all possible background differences between teen mothers and girls who avoided a teen birth (for example, parental values, school quality, neighborhood resources) and, as a result, had overstated the negative economic consequences of teen childbearing.

To control for unmeasured background differences between teens who did and did not have a birth, one set of studies compared outcomes for samples of sister pairs from the same family where one sister had a teen birth and one did not (Geronimus and Korenman 1992; Hoffman, Foster, and Furstenberg 1993; Corcoran and Kunz 1997). The logic runs as follows. Sisters are typically reared in the same families, grow up in the same neighborhoods, and attend the same schools. When researchers compare a woman with her own sisters, they "hold constant" the background factors (for example, parental resources, school quality, and neighborhood safety) that sisters have in common. Thus, sister comparisons provide more precise estimates of the effects of teen parenthood, independent of background, than do studies that control only measured background. A second strategy was to compare adult outcomes of pregnant teenagers who miscarried to the outcomes of teens who had a live birth in order to control for girls' propensities to become pregnant as teenagers (Hotz et al. 1996).

Both sets of studies found that teen parenting was associated with lower high school graduation rates. Studies further found that the effects of teen parenting on women's earnings, labor force participation, and incomes were smaller (sometimes nonexistent) than had been indicated by the cross-sectional research. The size of the effect of a teen birth on income varied from very small to large across these sisters' studies; the modal finding was that a teen birth reduced girls' adult incomes by about 20 percent. Joseph Hotz and his colleagues (1996) found no effect of teen parenting on girls' earnings or labor force participation in their late twenties.

Does Being Born to a Teen Mother Hurt Children's Life Chances?

Children born to mothers under age eighteen have modestly lower cognitive test scores and much higher risks of dropping out of school, having a child before age eighteen (girls), and being idle as a young adult (boys) than do children born to mothers age twenty to twenty-one (Haveman, Wolff, and Peterson 1996; Moore, Morrison, and Green 1996). Health and psychological well-being are similar for children born to women under age eighteen and for children born to women age twenty to twenty-one (Moore et al. 1996).

When measured family background and community characteristics are controlled, the differential risks of high school dropout, teen births, and idleness associated with a teen birth drop substantially but still remain significant. Haveman and his colleagues (1996, 269–73) estimate that if a woman who had a child at age sixteen or seventeen had delayed childbearing until age twenty to twenty-one, the probability that her child would complete high school would increase by five percentage points, the probability that her daughter would have a teen birth would drop by three percentage points, and the estimated probability that her son would be idle in his midtwenties would drop by five percentage points.

Controlling for measured background characteristics does not reduce the effects of being born to a teen mother on children's cognitive test scores (Moore et al. 1996). However, when Geronimus, Korenman, and Hillemeier (1994) controlled for unmeasured background characteristics by comparing the cognitive test scores of first cousins born to sisters, one of whom had a teen birth and one of whom did not, they did not find that children born to a teen mother had lower cognitive test scores than children born to an older mother.

The Effects of Out-of-Wedlock Births on Girls' Economic Futures

Increasing numbers of children are being born to unwed mothers. In 1940, only 4 percent of all births were to unmarried women; by 1996, 32 percent of all births were to unmarried women (Ventura et al. 1997). Public discussions of unwed births often assume that most unwed mothers are teen mothers. This is not the case: about 70 percent of all unwed births in 1996 were to women age twenty or older (Ventura et al. 1997).

Many policy analysts suggest that unwed births are a major source of societal problems. Charles Murray (1993, 14), for instance, states: "Illegitimacy is the single most important social problem of our time—more important than drugs, poverty, crime, welfare, or homelessness because it drives everything else." Given the prominence of unwed births in policy discussions, surprisingly little is known about the consequences of unwed births for women's incomes and earnings (McLanahan 1995). A notable exception is Corcoran and Kunz (1997); we used sister samples to estimate the effects of nonmarital births on women's adult incomes. We report that nonmarital births substantially lowered women's future incomes, even after controlling for age at first birth and for unmeasured background characteristics shared by sisters.

Race and Economic Inequality

African Americans are in radically different economic situations than whites. Table 4.5 compares the incidence of long-term poverty and upward mobility by race. About one in six African Americans in the general population were poor ten or more years between 1979 and 1991; only one in fifty whites were poor ten or more years. Almost three in ten African American children will spend ten or more of their first fifteen years living in a poor

Table 4.5   African American–White Differences in Persistence of Poverty, Intragenerational Mobility, and Intergenerational Mobility

	African American	White	Difference
Adults and children who were poor ten or more years between 1979 and 1991[a]	17%	2%	15%
Children age zero to four in 1968 who were poor in ten or more years 1968 to 1983[b]	29	1	28
Adults age twenty-three to thirty-nine in 1968 in the bottom quintile of the income distribution between 1968 and 1970 who where still there 1989 to 1991[c]	72	46	26
Poor children who remained poor in their mid-twenties[d]	33	7	26

a. *Source:* Blank (1997).
b. *Source:* Duncan (1991).
c. *Source:* Gottschalk and Danziger (1998).
d. See table 4.1.

household; fewer than one in one hundred white children will be poor ten or more years as a child. One in three African American poor children were still poor in their midtwenties; only one in fourteen white poor children remained poor in their midtwenties. Almost three in four African Americans age twenty-two to thirty-eight years in 1968 who were in the bottom income quintile remained in the bottom income quintile over twenty years later; the comparable figure for whites is fewer than one in two. These large differences suggest that race differences in opportunities are still alive and well in U.S. society.

Conclusion

Summary of Results

Snapshots of the annual income distribution or of poverty rates mask the degree to which there is mobility into and out of low income or poverty. In this chapter, I reviewed longitudinal evidence on the persistence of childhood poverty, on intra- and intergenerational mobility, on the consequences of growing up poor and growing up in non-intact families for children's non-economic and economic attainments, and on race differences in intra-generational and intergenerational poverty. To summarize these findings on the persistence of poverty:

- Poverty is widespread: one in three adults and children will be poor at least once over a thirteen-year period.
- Most poverty is transitory, but 5 percent of the population and 5 percent of children are poor for extended periods.
- Long-term poverty is unequally shared: African American children constitute almost 90 percent of long-term poor children, and children in single-parent homes constitute over 60 percent of long-term poor children.
- Most poor children escape poverty as adults, but poor children are many times more likely to be poor as adults than are nonpoor children.
- The incidence of long-term childhood poverty did not change from the late 1960s to the mid-1980s.
- The research on the persistence of child poverty is dated and badly needs updating.

The findings on mobility include the following:

- There is both considerable mobility and considerable persistence of economic status.
- Rates of mobility are no higher in the United States than in Western European countries, despite the lower rates of inequality in these countries.
- There is no evidence that intragenerational mobility increased in the 1980s. Thus, long-term income inequality must have widened in the 1980s.
- The intergenerational income mobility of men has increased.

Persistent childhood poverty has the following effects on children's life chances:

- Growing up poor has modest effects on childhood test scores, schooling, teen fertility, unwed births, and male idleness and sizable effects on adult earnings and incomes when *measured* parental advantages are controlled.
- It is not yet known whether these income effects are inflated because they serve as proxies for unmeasured parental advantages.

Family structure has the following effects on children's life chances:

- Growing up in a female-headed family has modest effects on schooling, male idleness, teen births, behavioral problems, and psychological problems, even after parental income and other measured background factors are controlled.
- Teen pregnancy is associated with a higher risk of dropping out of high school and lower future income, even after controlling for unmeasured background characteristics shared by sisters.
- Out-of-wedlock births are associated with lower incomes even when age at first birth and unmeasured background characteristics shared by sisters are controlled.

Race is associated with the following differences in long-term poverty:

- African Americans are many times more likely than whites to experience long-term poverty.
- Low-income African American adults are much less likely to be upwardly mobile than are low-income white adults.
- Poor African American children are less likely to escape from poverty as adults than are poor white children.

What Should We Do?

Long-term poverty is a serious issue. Although most poverty in the United States is temporary, 5 percent of adults and children are poor for prolonged periods. In other words, many millions of individuals are experiencing chronic economic distress. Also, the chronically poor are not a representative cross-section of the population: African Americans and individuals in female-headed families are disproportionately likely to be poor. Being born to an African American mother and/or to a single mother dramatically increases a child's chances of being poor throughout his or her childhood. Furthermore, long-term childhood poverty appears to have negative consequences for children's development and economic life chances. These findings suggest that our society may be less open than we would like it to be.

What can be done to help? Providing economic resources to poor families, especially poor single-parent families could help since both childhood poverty and growing up in a single-parent family matter for children's futures. This could be accomplished through tax policies, health policies, welfare policies, housing policies, and employment policies. Such policies must be carefully designed, however, so that they do not have undesirable side effects that hurt children. In particular, we want to avoid policies that provide incentives for parents to split up or not marry in the first place.

A major advantage of the tax system is that policies can be easily targeted to the poor, to parents, and to workers and that money (that is, credits) can be delivered directly to parents. The Earned Income Tax Credit is one of the best antipoverty policies. This credit is available to low-income working parents. Each dollar earned is matched by an additional benefit up to a designated maximum. Since low-income families generally pay little or no federal income tax, these credits, or "refunds," are not reductions in taxes owed (since no taxes are owed) but represent real increases in income. The maximum credit available to a single working mother with two children in 1998 was $3,756.

Another tax policy that could increase the incomes of working-poor parents, especially single mothers, is raising the child care tax credits and refunding them to working parents whose incomes are so low that they do not pay taxes. In theory, the child care tax credit is progressive since the proportion of child care costs returned as a credit decreases as income increases, from 30 percent in low-income households to 20 percent in high-income households. But since child care tax credits can be used only to reduce the federal taxes owed by low-income parents, and since low-income parents pay very little in taxes, few low-income parents actually benefit from these credits. Danziger and Gottschalk (1995) advocate raising the proportion of child care costs covered from 30 percent to 80 percent for poor families and making the credit fully refundable.

Policies that help defray the costs of basic necessities provide another way to increase the disposable income of poor families. Such policies include food stamps and housing vouchers, the extension of Medicaid coverage to all low-income parents and children, and state welfare programs that provide generous earning disregards.

Many persistently poor children live in single-mother families. Such families are doubly disadvantaged. There is only one adult breadwinner, and women typically earn less than men (McLanahan and Sandefur 1994). Employment policies that improve women's relative earnings, such as equal opportunity policies and affirmative action, may also benefit poor children living in mother-only families.

Policies that deliver economic resources to poor families can provide immediate economic relief and may well lead to small improvements in a number of poor children's future attainments. But as Mayer (1997) cautions, raising the incomes of poor families is unlikely to make dramatic improvements in poor children's future prospects since most income effects on child outcomes are small in size.

More important, we still do not understand why growing up poor hurts children. What are the intervening processes by which parental poverty affects children's life chances? McLoyd (1998) and Brooks-Gunn and Duncan (1997) speculate that higher rates of perinatal complications, reduced access to prenatal care, children's exposure to lead paint, less home-based cognitive stimulation, harsh and inconsistent parenting, unsafe neighborhoods, and exposure to acute and chronic stressors may be the pathways by which childhood poverty affects children's cognitive and educational outcomes. Mayer (1997) argues that many of the apparent effects of poverty on child outcomes may be due to omitted parental characteristics, such as poor parental health, parental depression, or domestic violence. Both arguments are plausible but as yet mostly unproven. We need to know more about why poverty matters for children's attainments if we are to improve poor children's futures.

Finally, this review shows that children born to African American parents can expect to experience very different economic trajectories than children born to white parents. African American children are many times more likely to be poor throughout their childhood. Poor African American children are more than four times as likely to be poor in their midtwenties as poor white children. Indeed, nonpoor African American children are more than twice as likely to be poor in their midtwenties than are poor white children. Low-income African American adults are less likely to be upwardly mobile than are low-income white adults. It is premature to pull back from race-conscious policies. African American children are not yet on an equal footing with white children in the race for success.

CHAPTER 5

U.S. Poverty in a Cross-national Context

TIMOTHY M. SMEEDING, LEE RAINWATER, AND GARY BURTLESS

The United States has a long tradition of measuring income poverty and weighing the effectiveness of government policies aimed at poverty reduction. Although this analysis has been valuable to policy-makers, it rests on an inherently parochial foundation, for it is based on the experiences of only one nation. The estimation of cross-nationally equivalent measures of poverty provides an opportunity to compare U.S. poverty rates and the effectiveness of American antipoverty policy with the experiences of other nations. The Luxembourg Income Study (LIS) database contains the information needed to construct comparable poverty measures for about two dozen countries. It provides data that allow a comparison of the level and trend of poverty across several nations. In this chapter, we use the cross-national comparisons made possible by the LIS to examine America's experience in maintaining a low poverty rate. We compare the effectiveness of U.S. antipoverty policies to that of similar policies elsewhere in the industrialized world.

If lessons can be learned from cross-national comparisons, there is much that can be learned about antipoverty policy by American voters and policy-makers. The United States has one of the highest poverty rates of all the countries participating in the LIS, whether poverty is measured using comparable absolute or relative standards for determining who is poor. Although the high rate of relative poverty in the United States is no surprise, given the country's well-known tolerance of wide economic disparities, the lofty rate of absolute poverty is much more troubling. After Luxembourg, the United States has the highest average income in the industrialized world. Our analysis of absolute poverty rates provides poverty estimates for eleven industrialized countries. The United States ranks second among the eleven in per capita income, yet it ranks third in the percentage of its population with an absolute income below the U.S. official poverty line. The per capita income of the United States is more than 30 percent higher, on average, than in the other ten countries of our survey. Yet the absolute poverty rate in the United States, at 13.6 percent, is five and a half percentage points higher than the average rate in the other ten countries—just 8.1 percent. This chapter suggests some reasons for this pattern.

We begin by reviewing international concepts and measures of poverty as they relate to the main measures of income and poverty used in other chapters of this book. Next, we present cross-national estimates of both absolute and relative poverty, concentrating on the latter measures. After examining the level and trend in these rates, we explore some of the factors that are correlated with national poverty rates and examine the antipoverty effectiveness of government programs aimed at reducing poverty. We conclude with a discussion of the relationship between policy differences and outcome differences among the several countries, and we consider the implications of our analysis for antipoverty policy in the United States.

Cross-national Comparisons of Poverty: Measurement and Data

The different national experiences in designing and implementing antipoverty programs provide a rich source of information for evaluating the effectiveness of alternative policies. Policymakers in most of the industrialized countries share common concerns about social problems such as population aging, widening wage disparities, family dissolution, and poverty. The availability of information from a number of countries makes it possible for us to compare the experience of one country to the experiences of others. This comparison can shed light on our own situation and help us understand the successes and failures of U.S. policy.

Poverty measurement may be an exercise that is particularly popular in the English-speaking countries, but most rich nations share the Anglo-Saxon concern over distributional outcomes and the well-being of the low-income population. Few Western European nations routinely calculate low-income or poverty rates, however. Most recognize that their social programs ensure a low poverty rate under any reasonable set of measurement standards (Björklund and Freeman 1997).[1] Although there is no international consensus on guidelines for measuring poverty, international bodies such as the United Nations Children's Fund (UNICEF) (UNICEF 2000; Bradbury and Jäntti 1999); the United Nations Human Development Report (UNHDR) (UN Development Programme 1998, 1999); the Organization for Economic Cooperation and Development (OECD) (Förster 1993, 2000); the European Statistical Office (Eurostat) (Eurostat 1998; Hagenaars, de Vos, and Zaidi 1994); and the Luxembourg Income Study (LIS) (Jäntti and Danziger 2000; Smeeding 1997; Kim 2000; Kenworthy 1998; Smeeding, O'Higgins, and Rainwater 1990) have published several cross-national studies of the incidence of poverty in recent years. The large majority of these are based on LIS data.

Measurement

There is considerable informal agreement on the appropriate measurement of poverty in a cross-national context. Most of the available studies share many similarities that help guide our research strategy here.

For purposes of international comparisons, poverty is almost always a relative concept. A majority of cross-national studies define the poverty threshold as one-half of national median income. In this study, we use both 40 and 50 percent of median income to establish our national poverty lines. We select 40 percent of national median income as our relative poverty threshold because it is closest to the ratio of the official U.S. poverty line to median U.S. household (pretax) cash income (42 to 43 percent in 1998 and 1994).[2]

Only a handful of cross-national studies use an absolute poverty line, but to permit comparisons with other chapters in this volume, we begin with one such definition. To estimate absolute poverty rates in different countries, researchers must convert national currencies into units of equal purchasing power or purchasing power parity (PPP) exchange rates for the currencies (Summers and Heston 1991). Construction of an absolute poverty threshold that is consistent across countries is problematic because national poverty rates are sensitive to the PPP exchange rate that is chosen. Moreover, PPP exchange rates were developed to permit accurate comparison of gross domestic product (GDP) across countries rather than the incomes or consumption of lower-income households. Thus, even though PPPs are appropriate for comparing national output or output per capita, they are less appropriate for establishing consistent income cutoff points for measuring poverty.[3]

Poverty measurement is based on the broadest income definition that still preserves comparability across nations. The best current definition is disposable cash and noncash income (that is, money income minus direct income and payroll taxes, and including all cash and near-cash transfers, such as food stamps and cash housing allowances, and refundable tax credits, such as the Earned Income Tax Credit).[4]

For international comparisons of poverty, the household is the single best unit for income aggregation. It is the only comparable income-sharing unit available for most nations. While the household is the unit used for aggregating income, the person is the unit of analysis. Household income is assumed to be equally shared among individuals within a household. Poverty rates are calculated as the percentage of all persons who are members of households with incomes below the poverty line.

A variety of equivalence scales have been used in cross-national comparisons in order to make comparisons of well-being between households with differing compositions. Equivalence scales are used to adjust household income for differences in needs related to household size and other factors, such as the ages of household members (see Corcoran, this volume). In the U.S. poverty literature, a set of equivalence scales is implicit in the official poverty lines. The official poverty threshold for a four-person family is twice as high as the poverty line for a single person who lives alone. To make our cross-national *absolute* poverty estimates consistent with the official U.S. poverty rate, we use the official American poverty line scales in these analyses. For the cross-national analysis of *relative* poverty rates, however, we use a different scale that is much more commonly used in international analyses. After adjusting household incomes to reflect differences in household size, we compare the resulting adjusted incomes to the figure for either 40 or 50 percent of the median poverty line. The equivalence scale used for this purpose, as in most cross-national studies, is a single parameter scale with a square-root-of-household-size scale factor.[5]

The Database

The data we use for this analysis are from the Luxembourg Income Study database, which now contains almost one hundred household income data files for twenty-five nations, covering the period 1967 to 1997 (Luxembourg Income Study 2000a). We can analyze both the level and trend in poverty and low incomes for a considerable period across a wide range of nations. In computing the trend of relative poverty, we have selected nineteen nations for which at least two years of observations are available for the period from 1979 to 1997.[6] The nineteen countries are the largest and richest in the world and include all of the G-7 nations, Scandinavia, Canada, Australia, and most of Europe.[7] We also include all of Germany, including the eastern states of the former German Democratic Republic (GDR), in many of our analyses.[8]

Results: Cross-national Levels and Trends in Poverty

We have calculated three sets of poverty rates, one absolute and two relative. In addition to overall poverty rates, we separately estimated poverty among two vulnerable populations, children and the aged.[9] Finally, we tabulated the trends in relative poverty for as many rich nations as the data permit.

Absolute Poverty

All poverty measures are in some sense relative and must be chosen as appropriate for the context in which they are used. The World Bank defines poverty in Africa and Latin America using an income threshold of $1 or $2 per person per day, and in Central and Eastern Europe a threshold of $2 or $3 per day (Ravallion 1994, 1996). In contrast, the absolute U.S. poverty line is six to twelve times higher than these standards. The World Bank poverty thresholds are obviously too low to be used in OECD countries. Scandinavian countries and Eurostat have "minimum income standards" that are as high as 60 percent of median national incomes in Europe. This would translate into a poverty standard that is roughly 25 to 30 percent higher than the official U.S. poverty line, depending on the average standard of living of a particular European country (European Community 2000; Eurostat 2000).

We begin our analysis by comparing the U.S. household poverty rate to absolute poverty rates in other nations using the U.S. poverty line, which is now about 42 percent of U.S. median household income. For a variety of reasons, the number of countries for which we can estimate absolute poverty rates is smaller than the number for which we can estimate relative poverty rates.

One limitation in estimating cross-national absolute poverty rates is that incomes in each country must be translated into a common currency using PPP-based exchange rates. Our estimates of absolute poverty are based on a single set of PPP exchange rates, those developed by the OECD for 1994 or 1995. These are close to the most recent OECD base year (1996) for estimating such exchange rates (OECD 2001). This limits our calculations to those OECD nations for which we have 1994 or 1995 LIS data.[10] We use the OECD estimates of PPP exchange rates to translate household incomes in each country into U.S. dollars. The measure of household income we use is LIS-adjusted disposable income, which includes cash and some near-cash income (including food stamps and the EITC) but subtracts income and payroll taxes. We also use the equivalence scale implicit in the official U.S. poverty thresholds. Because our definition of income differs from that used by the U.S. Bureau of the Census, the absolute poverty rate we calculate for the United States in 1994 (13.6 percent) is somewhat below the bureau's estimate of the official poverty rate in that year (14.5 percent).

The OECD's estimates of PPP exchange rates are far from ideal for comparing the well-being of low-income households in different countries. In principle, the PPPs permit us to calculate the amount of money needed in country A to purchase the same bundle of consumption items in country B. If relative prices on different consumption items differ widely between the two countries, however, the PPP exchange rate may be correct for only one particular collection of items. The exchange rates calculated by the OECD are accurate for overall national aggregate consumption (Castles 1996). Thus, the exchange rates are appropriate for comparing market baskets of all final consumption, including government-provided health care, education, and housing. These goods are paid for in different ways, however, in different nations. In most countries, health care and some forms of rental housing, child care, and education are subsidized more generously by the government than is the case in the United States. Thus, disposable incomes in countries with publicly financed health and higher education systems reflect the fact that health and education costs have already been subtracted from households' incomes (in the form of tax payments to the government). One implication is that in countries where in-kind benefits are larger than average, real incomes may be understated, and therefore absolute poverty rates may be overstated because citizens actually face a lower effective price level than is reflected by the OECD's estimates of the PPP exchange rate. The opposite is true for those counties whose citizens must pay larger amounts for health care and education out of their disposable incomes. Since the United States provides lower-than-average amounts of noncash benefits, U.S. absolute poverty rates are probably understated.[11] In contrast, northern European countries provide high levels of tax-financed health care and education benefits, and their absolute poverty rates are probably overstated. However, the extent of these differences is unknown at this time.[12]

Another problem in comparing poverty rates across countries arises because of differences in the quality of the household income survey data used to measure poverty. For example, the LIS survey for the United States is the Current Population Survey (CPS). The CPS captures about 89 percent of the total household incomes that are estimated from other sources (national income accounts data and agency administrative records). Most, but not all, of the other surveys used by LIS capture approximately the same percentage of total income (Atkinson, Rainwater, and Smeeding 1995). The household surveys of the Scandinavian countries capture between 93 and 94 percent of the incomes reflected in the aggregate statistical sources, while the Australian survey captures just 83 percent of the total. Unfortunately, not all countries have performed the calculations that would allow us to determine the overall quality of their household survey data. We used a rough methodology to compare the quality of survey data for the different LIS countries. Only those countries with LIS household surveys that captured a large percentage of national income are included in our comparisons of absolute poverty rates.[13]

Assuming that the household surveys from different countries yield information about disposable incomes with comparable reliability, we should expect that once incomes are converted into a common currency unit, those countries with higher average incomes will have lower absolute poverty rates. This expectation is based, of course, on the presumption that income inequality is approximately the same across all countries. If income inequality differs significantly, countries with higher average incomes but greater income disparities may have higher poverty rates than low-income countries, and indeed this is the case.

The results in table 5.1 indicate a wide range of absolute poverty rates across the eleven nations, ranging from a low of 0.3 percent in Luxembourg to a high of 17.6 percent in Australia. The unweighted average poverty rate for the eleven countries is 8.6 percent. The United States has the third-highest poverty rate (13.6 percent), ranking behind only Australia and the

Table 5.1 Absolute Poverty Rates for OECD Nations in 1994 and 1995, Using the U.S. Poverty Line

Nation	LIS Data Year	Poverty Rate	GDP per Capita in 1995 Amount[a]	Index[b]
Australia	1994	17.6%	$21,459	77
United Kingdom	1995	15.7	18,743	67
United States	1994	13.6	27,895	100
France	1994	9.9	20,192	72
Canada	1994	7.4	22,951	82
Germany[c]	1994	7.3	21,357	77
Netherlands	1994	7.1	21,222	76
Sweden	1995	6.3	19,949	72
Finland	1995	4.8	18,861	68
Norway	1995	4.3	23,316	84
Luxembourg	1994	0.3	36,570	131
Overall average		8.6	22,956	82.4

Sources: Authors' calculations from LIS, OECD (2001), and Smeeding and Rainwater (2001).

Notes: Poverty is measured using the official U.S. poverty line and equivalence scales. OECD (1999) PPPs are used to convert the U.S. poverty line.

a. Amount in 1995 U.S. dollars, using OECD PPPs.

b. Index with United States = 100.

c. Includes all of Germany, including the eastern states of the former GDR.

United Kingdom. The table also shows real PPP-adjusted GDP per capita for 1995. Since Australia and the United Kingdom have per capita aggregate incomes that are, respectively, about 23 and 33 percent below that of the United States, the higher absolute poverty rates in those two countries should hardly be surprising. However, nearly all of the countries in table 5.1 have a per capita income level that is below that of the United States, ranging from 67 percent of the U.S. level (in the United Kingdom) to 84 percent (in Norway). Only tiny Luxembourg has an average aggregate income per capita of 31 percent above that in the United States (OECD 2001). And as expected, Luxembourg has the lowest absolute poverty rate. Most of the other countries have absolute poverty rates substantially below that in the United States, despite their lower real per capita incomes.

Based on this table, it seems clear that among these rich nations, the distribution of income is as important as average absolute income in determining the level of poverty. Poor countries can have lower poverty rates than rich ones if their income distributions are compressed; rich countries can have higher poverty rates than poor ones if their incomes are very unequally distributed.[14]

While acknowledging that the United States has greater inequality than other industrialized nations, many defenders of American economic and political institutions argue that inequality plays a crucial role in creating incentives for people to improve their situations through saving, hard work, and investment in education and training. Without the powerful signals provided by large disparities in pay and incomes, the economy would operate less efficiently, and average incomes would grow less rapidly. In the long run, poor people might enjoy higher absolute incomes in a society where wide income disparities are tolerated than in one where law and social convention keep income differentials small. According to this line of argument, wide income disparities may be in the best long-term interest of the poor themselves. (For a lucid presentation and analysis of this viewpoint, see Okun 1975; Welch 1999.)

In recent years, the U.S. economy especially and also the Australian and British economies have in fact performed better than other economies in which income disparities are smaller. Employment growth has been faster, joblessness lower, and economic growth higher than in many other OECD countries where public policy and social convention have kept income disparities low. For low-income residents in these three countries, however, the theoretical advantages of greater inequality have failed to produce rapidly growing incomes over the past couple of decades. Their absolute incomes are below the incomes that poor people receive in other rich countries that have less inequality. As a result, the absolute poverty rates in these three countries are substantially higher than they are in other OECD countries. The supposed efficiency advantages of high inequality have not accrued to low-income residents of the United States, at least so far. To the extent that such advantages exist, they have been captured by Americans much further up the income scale, producing a conspicuously wide gap between the incomes of the nation's rich and poor.

Relative Poverty

To broaden the range of countries in our analysis and compare poverty as it is commonly measured in cross-national studies, we now examine relative poverty rates. A range of relative poverty standards is used in cross-national comparisons. One-half of national median adjusted income is the most commonly used poverty threshold for international comparisons. In fact, it is hard to find a study that does *not* use this standard. But other standards are also used, if for no other reason than to test sensitivity. In Europe, the European Statistical Office has recommended a standard of 60 percent of median income for measuring poverty and social exclusion (Eurostat 2000). In this chapter, we concentrate mainly on the 40-percent-of-median line because of its proximity to the U.S. poverty line, though we also provide poverty estimates using a threshold of 50 percent of national median income (see table 5A.1).

Relative poverty rates in nineteen nations, using both thresholds, are displayed in figure 5.1. All poverty rates are from the early to the middle 1990s. The poverty rate using the lower poverty threshold varies between 1.3 percent in Luxembourg and 10.7 percent in the United States, with an average rate of 4.8 percent across the nineteen countries. The fraction of people with incomes below the poverty line is obviously sensitive to where the line is drawn. Even though national poverty rates are sensitive to the level of the threshold, the ranking of the nineteen countries is affected only modestly by the change in the relative poverty threshold. However, extreme poverty in the United States stands out very clearly even when the poverty threshold is set at 40 percent of median income. At this threshold, almost 11 percent of the U.S. population is poor, more than are below the 50 percent threshold in thirteen of the other nations shown. More poor people in the United States suffer from extreme relative poverty than is the case in other high-income countries (see table 5A.1).

Overall national poverty rates using the 40-percent-of-median-income standard fall into several distinct categories (see table 5.2). The U.S. rate is clearly the highest, at 10.7 percent in 1997. Two anglophone nations—Australia and Canada—plus Italy and Japan, have somewhat lower rates, ranging between 6.6 and 8.9 percent. Three other nations—the United Kingdom, Spain, and Israel—have still lower rates. The remaining eleven nations—most of Central Europe and all of Scandinavia—have the lowest poverty rates, below the 4.8 percent overall average rate.

Higher poverty rates are found in countries with a high level of overall inequality (the United States, Italy), in geographically large and diverse countries (the United States, Canada, Australia), and in countries with less-developed national welfare states (Spain, Japan). Low poverty rates are

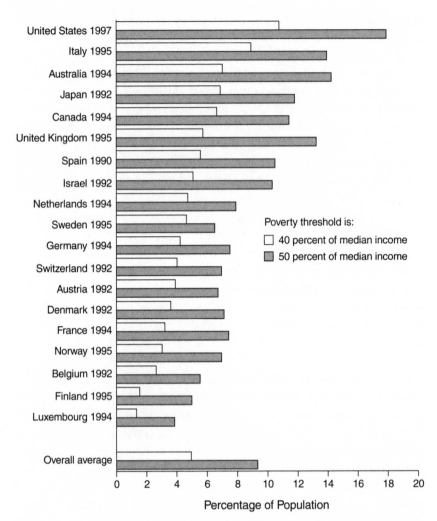

Figure 5.1 Relative Poverty Rates of Industrial Nations in the 1990s (*Source:* Authors' tabulations of LIS files; see table 5A.1 for exact values.) *Note:* Poverty is measured as a percentage of median adjusted disposable personal income (ADPI) for individuals. Incomes are adjusted by E = 0.5 where adjusted DPI equals actual DPI divided by household size (S) to the power E: ADPI = DPI/S^E.

Table 5.2. Poverty Rates in Nineteen Rich Countries, by Age Group, in the 1990s

Country	Year	Poverty Rate (Percentage of Population)[a]			Rank of Country		
		Overall	Children[b]	Aged[c]	Overall	Children[b]	Aged[c]
United States	1997	10.7	14.7	12.0	1	1	2
Italy	1995	8.9	14.1	4.7	2	2	5
Australia	1994	7.0	7.4	12.2	3	5	1
Japan[d]	1992	6.9	NA	NA	4	NA	NA
Canada	1994	6.6	8.5	1.2	5	3	14
United Kingdom	1995	5.7	8.3	4.0	6	4	7
Israel	1992	5.2	4.8	11.2	7	8	3
Spain	1990	5.1	7.0	3.9	8	6	9
Netherlands	1994	4.7	4.6	3.1	9	9	12
Sweden	1995	4.6	1.3	0.7	10	18	17
Germany[e]	1994	4.2	6.0	4.0	11	7	7
Switzerland	1992	4.0	4.4	3.1	12	10	12
Denmark	1992	3.6	2.1	3.7	13	15	10
France	1994	3.2	2.6	3.6	14	11	11
Norway	1995	3.0	2.2	0.7	15	13	17
Austria	1992	2.8	2.6	6.8	16	11	4
Finland	1995	2.1	1.5	0.9	17	17	15
Belgium	1992	1.9	1.6	4.2	18	16	6
Luxembourg	1994	1.3	2.2	0.9	19	13	15
Overall average		4.8	5.3	4.5			

Source: Authors' tabulations of LIS files, except for Japan.

a. Poverty is measured at 40 percent of median ADPI for individuals. Incomes are adjusted by E = 0.5 where ADPI equals unadjusted DPI divided by household size (S) to the power E: ADPI = DPI/S^E.

b. Children are under age eighteen.

c. Adults age sixty-five or older.

d. Japanese data runs were made for LIS by Professor Tsuneo Ishikawa.

e. Includes all of Germany, including the eastern states of the former GDR.

more common in smaller, well-developed, and high-spending welfare states (the European Community, Scandinavia) and in countries where unemployment compensation is more generous, social policies provide more generous support to single mothers and working women (through paid family leave, for example), and social assistance minimums are high.

Poverty rates computed using pretax and pretransfer household income do not differ among countries as much as those calculated with post-tax and post-transfer income. This finding implies that different levels and mixes of government spending on the poor have sizable effects on national poverty rates (Smeeding 1997). In fact, detailed analysis shows that higher levels of government spending (as in Scandinavia and northern Europe) and more careful targeting of government transfers at the poor (as in Canada) produce lower poverty rates (Kenworthy 1998; Kim 2000), a finding that we verify later in the chapter. Earnings and wage disparities are also important in determining poverty rates, especially among families with children (Jäntti and Danziger 2000; Bradbury and Jäntti 1999; Smeeding 1997). Countries with an egalitarian wage structure tend to have lower child poverty rates, in part because the relative poverty rate among working-age adults is lower when wage disparities are small.

Child poverty rates are half a percentage point higher on average than overall relative poverty rates (table 5.2). But child poverty rates are 4.0 to 5.2 percent higher than overall poverty rates in the two countries with the highest child poverty rates (the United States and Italy). Child poverty is also 2.6 points higher than overall poverty in the United Kingdom, and 2.9 points higher in Spain. If poverty is measured using a poverty standard equal to 50 percent of median national income, Canada also has a notable gap of 3.9 percentage points between child poverty and the overall poverty rate (see table 5A.1). In contrast, child poverty rates in the low-poverty countries of the European Community and Scandinavia are usually less than or equal to overall poverty rates. Using the 40-percent-of-median-income poverty threshold, child poverty in the United States is 14.7 percent, and 14.1 percent in Italy (table 5.2). Using the same threshold, child poverty rates in Scandinavia range between 1.3 and 2.2 percent, while they are below 5 percent everywhere else in Europe except the United Kingdom (8 percent), Germany (6 percent), and Spain (7 percent).

Child poverty and overall poverty rankings are more similar across countries than are rankings of poverty among the elderly (see the right-hand columns of table 5.2). As a group, the aged stand in greatest contrast to other groups. Using a poverty threshold of 40 percent of median national income, the elderly on average have a lower poverty rate than other age groups. A poverty rate for older people above 10 percent is found only in the United States, Israel, and Australia. Only one other country, Austria, has an aged poverty rate that exceeds 5 percent. Canada has achieved one of the lowest aged poverty rates, 1.2 percent, which is far below the rates for Canadian children and working-age adults.

However, the poverty rate of the elderly is particularly sensitive to the income cutoff used to determine poverty. Although aged poverty rates are on average below the overall national poverty rate when poverty is measured using the 40-percent-of-median-income standard, they average 3.0 percentage points higher than the overall poverty rate, and 1.7 points above the child poverty rate, when the higher income standard (50 percent of median) is used. Raising the poverty threshold from 40 to 50 percent of national median income increases the unweighted poverty rate of the elderly from 4.5 to 11.6 percent in the nineteen countries (see table 5A.1). This increase, the largest of any age group, suggests that social protection systems for the elderly often provide income guarantees that are no more than between 40 and 50 percent of median national income.

Relative poverty rates can vary across age groups within a nation as much as they do across nations. Comparing poverty among children and the elderly (table 5.2), we found large imbalances in several nations. Elderly poverty greatly exceeds child poverty in Australia, Israel, and Austria, while the reverse is true in Canada, Spain, Italy, and the United Kingdom. Poverty is high among both the young and the old only in the United States, at 14.7 and 12.0 percent, respectively. Child and aged poverty rates are approximately equal in the other eleven countries, at below 6 percent.

Poverty Trends

Evidence on the trend in relative poverty across nations is mixed (see table 5.3). The LIS data set contains different years of data for different nations over different periods. To determine poverty trends, we measure changes in poverty rates from a base year (between 1979 and 1981 in most cases) to a recent year (usually between 1994 and 1997), using the 40-percent-of-median-income poverty threshold. The table presents the actual change in poverty rates from the first to the last year. We also rank nations in table 5.3 according to their most recent poverty rate (table 5.2) so that we can look for changes in poverty in high- and low-poverty nations.[15]

If we regard a change of 2.0 points or more in either direction as significant, relative poverty rates rose significantly between the 1980s and 1990s in Italy, the United Kingdom, and the Netherlands. Four other coun-

Table 5.3   Changes in Poverty Rates in Seventeen Rich Countries, by Age Group

Country	Years	Overall	Children	Aged
United States	1979 to 1997	0.7	1.5	−4.2
Italy	1986 to 1995	4.9	4.6	−0.6
Australia	1981 to 1994	1.8	0.5	6.0
Canada	1981 to 1994	−0.2	0.0	−5.3
United Kingdom	1979 to 1995	2.4	3.7	0.5
Israel	1978 to 1992	0.1	0.6	−2.3
Spain	1980 to 1990	−1.5	−0.5	−4.4
Netherlands	1983 to 1994	2.3	3.8	0.5
Sweden	1981 to 1995	1.7	−1.0	0.7
Germany[a]	1984 to 1994	1.3	3.3	−0.6
Switzerland	1982 to 1992	1.5	4.1	−4.3
Denmark	1987 to 1992	−0.3	−0.2	−1.5
France	1979 to 1994	−0.8	−0.8	−3.5
Norway	1979 to 1995	0.5	0.1	−3.3
Finland	1987 to 1995	−0.4	0.2	−1.6
Belgium	1985 to 1992	−0.1	−0.3	−0.1
Luxembourg	1985 to 1994	−0.4	0.7	−2.8

Source: Authors' calculations with LIS files based on 40-percent-of-median-income poverty thresholds. Numbers show actual change in poverty rates at 40-percent-of-median income (in each year) calculated as the change from the initial year.

a. Only West Germany is included.

tries saw increases of 1.0 to 1.8 points in their relative poverty rates over the period; only one country, Spain, experienced a modest decline of 1.5 percentage points. Overall poverty rates changed by less than 1.0 percentage point in the other nine nations. On balance overall, relative poverty rates did not change much between the early 1980s and the early to middle 1990s. Even in the Netherlands, poverty rates rose by 2.3 points to peak at just 4.7 percent in 1994. In some nations, such as the United States, our selection of beginning and end dates for measuring the trend makes a difference. For instance, in 1979 the relative U.S. poverty rate was 10.0 percent, and in 1997 it was 10.7 percent. The rate rose sharply in the early 1980s, however, and again in the early 1990s, before falling later in the 1990s.

Different poverty trends are evident for the aged and for children. Among the elderly, significant declines in poverty rates are evident in eight of the nations studied here, including the United States. Modest declines can be seen in two other countries (Denmark and Finland). The poverty rate of the elderly increased significantly only in Australia, while it remained essentially unchanged in five other countries.

Among children, significant increases in the poverty rate were observed more frequently. Big increases occurred in Italy (4.6 percentage points), Switzerland (4.1), the United Kingdom (3.7), the Netherlands (3.8), and Germany (3.3). In the United States, the child poverty rate rose from 13.2 percent to 14.7 percent, though the latter rate represents a steep decline from 1986, when the child poverty rate was 18.6 percent in the LIS data set. Child poverty remained largely unchanged in the other eleven countries. Interestingly, child poverty did not fall by a noticeable amount in any of the nations studied here; the largest decline was 1.0 percentage point in Sweden.

It is important to recognize that widening income inequality does not always translate directly into increases in relative poverty rates. In the 1980s and 1990s, income inequality rose dramatically in the United Kingdom and somewhat less so in Italy and the United States. Relative poverty rose at the same time in all three countries. But overall income inequality also increased moderately in Norway, Finland, and Israel over this period with no appreciable effect on the overall poverty rates of these nations (Gottschalk and Smeeding 2000; Smeeding 2000).

Antipoverty Effectiveness of Social Spending for Working-Age Households

There are striking differences across countries in the level and configuration of their social safety nets. It is natural to ask whether differences in social policy lead to systematic differences in poverty, labor market performance, or income inequality. Table 5.4 summarizes market poverty rates and the effects of the transfer and tax system on poverty rates in seven OECD countries among working-age households.[16] The pretax and pretransfer poverty rate for household heads age twenty-five to sixty-four is displayed in the second column. Poverty is measured here by comparing the household's adjusted market income to a poverty cutoff equal to 40 percent of each country's median adjusted disposable income. The "market income" poverty rates range from a low of 14.9 percent in Germany to 25.0 percent in the United Kingdom. The next three columns show the effects of social in-

Table 5.4. Household Poverty Rates, with Household Head Age Twenty-five to Sixty-four, by Income Source

Country	Year	Market Income Poverty Rate	Poverty Rate After Universal Transfers	Poverty Rate After Taxes	Poverty Rate After Social Assistance[a]	Total Percentage Change
Australia	1994	19.1	17.9	18.1	6.3	−67.0
Canada	1994	18.4	9.4	9.8	6.9	−62.5
Germany[b]	1994	14.9	5.5	6.3	3.5	−76.5
Netherlands	1991	21.1	6.5	7.7	3.6	−82.9
Sweden	1992	15.8	3.1	4.1	1.8	−88.6
United Kingdom	1995	25.0	14.4	15.1	5.9	−76.4
United States	1994	17.2	11.7	12.9	10.9	−36.6

Source: Smeeding and Ross Phillips (2001, table A-2) and authors' calculations.

Note: Poverty rates are for persons living in households with incomes below 40 percent of median ADPI.

a. Refunds from the Earned Income Tax Credit (U.S.) and the Family Tax Credit (U.K.) are treated as social assistance.

b. Only West Germany is considered here.

surance, direct taxes, and antipoverty transfers on household poverty. In combination, these government interventions reduce relative income poverty rates for prime-age families by 76.4 to 88.6 percent in the four European countries (see the last column). That is, the poverty rate measured after tax payments are subtracted and transfer benefits are included is 76.4 to 88.6 percent lower than it is when only gross market incomes are included in household incomes. Market poverty rates are reduced by 67.0 percent and 62.5 percent, respectively, in Australia and Canada. The tax and transfer system reduces poverty rates for prime-age households by just 36.6 percent in the United States. Both social insurance and targeted social assistance contributed to this decline in all of the nations studied (with the exception of Australia, which has only a targeted social assistance system).

Timothy Smeeding and Katherin Ross Phillips (2001) note that there is a positive relationship between the percentage of GDP spent on social spending and poverty reduction. Sweden and the Netherlands reduced market poverty rates by more than 82 percent. Both countries devoted about 14 percent of GDP to social spending in the years observed here (table 5A.2). The United Kingdom and Germany eliminated more than three-quarters of pretax and pretransfer poverty through their tax and transfer systems, while devoting about 8 to 9 percent of GDP to social spending. Canada and Australia both reduced poverty by about 67 percent through their tax and transfer systems and spent 6.2 and 8.0 percent of GDP, respectively, on social transfers for the non-aged. The United States spent less than 4 percent of GDP on these programs, and it reduced pretax and pretransfer poverty by the least amount proportionally.

Summary

Both absolute and relative poverty rankings suggest that U.S. poverty rates are in the upper end of the range compared with poverty rates in other LIS member countries. The U.S. child poverty rates seem particularly troublesome. In most rich countries, the child poverty rate is 8 percent or less; in the United States, it is 14.7 percent. Part, though not all, of the explanation is that the United States devotes a relatively small share of its national income to social transfers for families with a non-aged head.

The trend in overall poverty between the 1980s and middle 1990s was typically flat, except in Italy, the United Kingdom, and the Netherlands. No country in our tabulations experienced a sizable decline in relative poverty over the period examined. The trend in aged poverty rates was generally down, but child poverty rates often rose, with significant increases in five nations.

Poverty Correlates and Some Policy Lessons for the United States

Poverty and inequality are higher in the United States than in other countries with similar (and indeed much lower) average incomes (table 5.1). American inequality differs noticeably from that in other rich countries, primarily because of differences in relative income levels in the lower tail of the American income distribution. An American citizen at the tenth percentile of U.S. income distribution has an adjusted disposable income that is just 34 to 38 percent of U.S. median income (Smeeding 2000; Gottschalk and Smeeding 2000). Although the tenth-percentile income level has drawn closer to the median during the 1990s, it is still five to seven points lower than in any other nation.[17] Poverty is also higher in the United States than in other nations. However, owing mainly to the continued strong economy in the 1990s, absolute poverty rates in the United States are falling back to levels last seen in the 1970s (see also Freeman, this volume).

The relative size of the low-income population in the United States is larger than in other rich countries for two main reasons: low market wages for those with few skills, and limited public benefits. The relationship between the prevalence of workers with low wages and poverty is highlighted in figure 5.2, which shows cross-national estimates of the incidence of overall poverty and the prevalence of low-paid employment in fourteen OECD countries (OECD 1996).[18] The estimates of low-paid employment reflect the percentage of a nation's full-time workers earning less than 65 percent of national median earnings on full-time jobs. These estimates refer to the period 1993 to 1995 for most nations. The estimates of the overall poverty rate are based on the 40-percent-of-median-income threshold and are taken from the second column of table 5.2.

Figure 5.2 shows a strong association between low pay and national poverty rates. The straight line shows the predictions from the regression line of the overall poverty rates on the incidence of low-paid employment.[19] Countries with values above the line have higher poverty rates than are predicted by the incidence of low relative wages; countries below the line have lower poverty rates. A substantial fraction of the variance in cross-national poverty rates appears to be accounted for by the cross-national variation in the incidence of low pay. Because the United States has the highest proportion of workers in relatively poorly paid full-time jobs, it also has the highest poverty rate. On the other hand, Canada has a lower poverty rate than its unequal wage distribution would lead one to expect. Other countries have a significantly lower incidence of low-paid employment and also have significantly lower poverty rates than the United States.

The prevalence of low-paid workers, however, is not the only reliable predictor of poverty rates. Although low pay is a good predictor of the Dutch and Norwegian poverty rates, other nations with similar overall poverty rates (Canada, the United Kingdom, Austria) lie further from the prediction line. Other factors, such as government antipoverty efforts, are also important predictors of the poverty rate.

Social spending clearly affects the prevalence of poverty. To measure each country's antipoverty efforts, we collected OECD statistics on the fraction of GDP spent on cash and near-cash social transfers for the non-aged (including refundable tax relief, such as the EITC). Measured in this way, social spending is negatively correlated with national child poverty rates. Figure

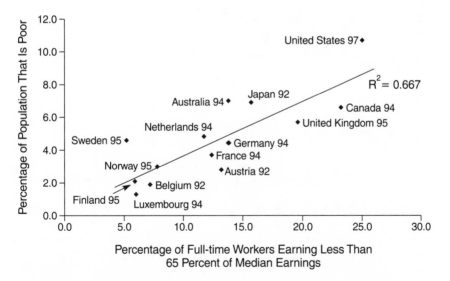

Figure 5.2 Relationship Between Low Pay and Poverty Rates in Fourteen Industrialized Countries in the 1990s (*Sources:* OECD (1996) and authors' tabulations of the LIS data files; see table 5A.2 for values.)

5.3 displays the cross-national relationship between social expenditures and child poverty rates.[20] The solid line in figure 5.3 shows the predicted line from a linear regression of child poverty rates on social spending. As a result of its low level of spending on social transfers to the non-aged, the United States has a very high child poverty rate, even higher than predicted by the regression. As in Italy, the United Kingdom, and the Netherlands, the United States has more child poverty than predicted by the cross-national regression equation. Nearly all of the high-spending nations in northern Europe and Scandinavia have child poverty rates of 5 percent or less.

Even though social spending in general has an inverse correlation with poverty rates, different patterns of social spending can produce different effects on national poverty rates. Antipoverty and social insurance programs

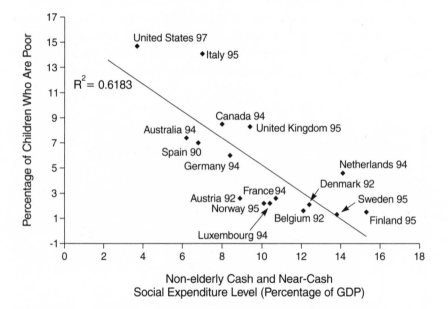

Figure 5.3 Relationship Between Cash Social Expenditures and Child Poverty Rates in Sixteen Industrialized Countries in the 1990s (*Sources:* OECD (1999) and authors' tabulations of the LIS data files; see table 5A.2 for values. Cash and near-cash social expenditures exclude health, education, and social services, but include all forms of cash benefits and near-cash housing subsidies, active labor market program subsidies, and other contingent cash and near-cash benefits. Non-elderly benefits include only those accruing to household heads under age sixty-five.)

are in many respects unique to each country. There is no one kind of program or set of programs that is conspicuously successful in all countries that use them. Social insurance, universal benefits (such as child allowances), and social assistance transfer programs targeted on low-income populations are mixed in different ways in different countries (see table 5.4). So too are minimum wages, worker preparation and training programs, work-related benefits (such as child care and family leave), and other social benefits. The United States differs from most nations that achieve lower poverty rates in its emphasis on work and self-reliance for working-age adults, regardless of the wages that workers must accept. For over a decade U.S. unemployment has been well below the OECD average, and for almost three decades American job growth has been much faster than the OECD average. The strong economy coupled with a few specific antipoverty devices (like the expanded EITC) has produced most of the U.S. poverty reduction in recent years.

As long as the United States relies almost exclusively on the job market to generate incomes for working-age families, changes in the wage distribution that affect the earnings of less-skilled workers will inevitably have a large effect on poverty among children and prime-age adults. Reductions in wages at the bottom of the earnings distribution between 1979 and 1993 eroded the living standards of a large and vulnerable population, just as real wage gains among these families since 1995 have reversed some of the previous trend. Improvements in the social safety net for these families were too small to offset the adverse effects of wage developments from 1979 to 1993, although the recent expansion of the EITC has greatly increased the effectiveness of U.S. antipoverty policy (see also Scholz and Levine, this volume).

Conclusion

The international comparisons in this chapter contain important lessons for understanding the high poverty rate in the United States. Clearly, both the wage distribution and the generosity of social benefits strongly affect poverty. The relationship between low wages and poverty is direct and obvious. Continued tight labor markets in the United States can help reduce poverty as the wages received by less-skilled workers are bid up. There are two important limits, however, to this effect. Not all of the poor can be expected to "earn" their way out of poverty. Single parents with young children, disabled workers, and the unskilled will all face significant challenges earning a comfortable income, no matter how low the unemployment rate falls.

A second, more uncertain limit on the benefits of low unemployment is the possibility of a recession. The poverty rate, especially among children, may go up in a future recession because declines in employment and hourly wages are likely to be particularly severe for low-income breadwinners. Building a stronger safety net in anticipation of the next recession could significantly improve the fortunes of low-wage breadwinners and their families. For example, many single mothers have become breadwinners as a result of welfare reform. One consequence of reform is that many single mothers who lose their jobs in the next recession will be ineligible for cash public assistance, and most will be ineligible for unemployment compensation. To prevent these mothers from falling into destitution, it may be necessary to create a new cash supplement or public jobs program for unemployed parents or to strengthen significantly the unemployment compensation system as it applies to low-wage workers.

The relationship between antipoverty spending and poverty rates is complicated, so the simple correlations discussed in the previous section are at best suggestive. U.S. poverty rates among children and the aged are high compared with those in other industrialized countries. Yet U.S. economic performance has also been outstanding compared with that of other rich countries. Carefully crafted public policy can certainly reduce American poverty. Implementing the policies that lower poverty rates would also have costs. A higher unemployment rate and slower economic growth might be two of the indirect effects of a more generous antipoverty policy. Of course, the direct and indirect costs of antipoverty programs are now widely recognized (and frequently overstated) in public debate. The wisdom of expanding programs targeted at children and poor families depends on one's values and subjective views about the economic, political, and moral trade-offs of poverty alleviation. For many critics of public spending on the poor, it also depends on a calculation of the potential economic efficiency losses associated with a larger government budget. In the strong American economy of the late 1990s and early 2000s, however, it is hard to argue that the United States cannot afford to do more to help the poor, particularly those who are working in the labor market.

A partial solution to the poverty problem that is consistent with American values lies in creating an income package that mixes work and benefits so that unskilled and semi-skilled workers, including single parents, can support their families above the poverty level. Such a package could include more generous earnings supplements under the EITC, refundable child and day care tax credits, and the public guarantee of assured child support for single parents with an absent partner who cannot or will not provide income to their children. Targeted programs to increase job access and skills for less-skilled workers could also help meet the booming labor demand in the U.S. economy. In the long run, a human capital strategy that focuses on improving the education and marketable job skills of disadvantaged future workers, particularly younger ones, is the approach likely to have the biggest payoff. If the nation is to be successful in reducing poverty, it will need to do a better job of combining work and benefits targeted to low-wage workers in low-income families (see, for example, Ellwood 2000).

An expanded Supplemental Security Income (SSI) program with a higher benefit guarantee for the aged and disabled who also receive Social Security could go a long way toward reducing poverty among these groups to levels that are common in northern Europe. Canada achieved a major reduction in poverty when it implemented a targeted expansion of its social assistance plan in the 1980s (Smeeding and Sullivan 1998).

A prolonged economic expansion and modest improvements in income supplements for low-wage breadwinners (through the expansion of the EITC) have recently pushed the U.S. poverty rate in the right direction. Given the political disposition of the American public, a near-zero percent poverty rate is not a plausible goal. A gradual reduction in the overall poverty rate to 8 percent, however, using the 40 percent standard or the absolute U.S. poverty line, is certainly feasible. Although this rate would represent a considerable achievement by the standards of the United States, it is worth remembering that an 8 percent poverty rate is higher than the rate in all but one of the eighteen other countries we have considered here.

Table 5A.1. Poverty Rates for All Persons, Children (Persons Under Eighteen), and Elderly (Persons over Sixty-five)

Country	Year	40 Percent Level of Poverty		50 Percent Level of Poverty	
		Rate	Rank	Rate	Rank
All					
United States	1997	10.7	1	17.8	1
Italy	1995	8.9	2	13.9	2
Australia	1994	7.0	3	6.7	13
Canada	1994	6.6	4	11.4	4
United Kingdom	1995	5.7	5	13.2	3
Spain	1990	5.2	6	10.4	5
Israel	1992	5.2	6	10.2	6
Netherlands	1994	4.7	8	7.9	7
Sweden	1992	4.6	9	6.5	15
Germany	1994	4.2	10	7.5	8
Switzerland	1992	4.0	11	6.9	11
Denmark	1992	3.6	12	7.1	10
France	1994	3.2	13	7.4	9
Norway	1995	3.0	14	6.9	11
Austria	1992	2.8	15	6.7	13
Finland	1995	2.1	16	5	17
Belgium	1992	1.9	17	5.5	16
Luxembourg	1994	1.3	18	3.9	18
Overall average		4.7		8.6	
Children					
United States	1997	14.7	1	22.3	1
Italy	1995	14.1	2	18.9	3
Canada	1994	8.5	3	15.3	4
United Kingdom	1995	8.3	4	20.1	2
Australia	1994	7.4	5	15.0	5
Spain	1990	7.0	6	12.8	6
Germany	1994	6.0	7	10.6	8
Israel	1992	4.8	8	11.6	7
Netherlands	1994	4.6	9	7.9	9
Switzerland	1992	4.4	10	7.5	10
France	1994	2.6	11	6.7	11
Austria	1992	2.6	11	5.9	12
Luxembourg	1994	2.2	13	4.4	14
Norway	1995	2.2	13	3.9	17

Table 5A.1. (continued)

Country	Year	40 Percent Level of Poverty		50 Percent Level of Poverty	
		Rate	Rank	Rate	Rank
Denmark	1992	2.1	15	4.8	13
Belgium	1992	1.6	16	4.4	14
Finland	1995	1.5	17	4.1	16
Sweden	1992	1.3	18	2.6	18
Overall average		5.3		9.9	
Elderly					
Australia	1994	12.2	1	28.9	1
United States	1997	12.0	2	20.7	2
Israel	1992	11.2	3	17.2	4
Austria	1992	6.8	4	17.4	3
Italy	1995	4.7	5	12.4	7
Belgium	1992	4.2	6	11.9	8
United Kingdom	1995	4.0	7	13.9	6
Germany	1994	4.0	7	7.0	13
Spain	1990	3.9	9	11.4	9
Denmark	1992	3.7	10	11.1	10
France	1994	3.6	11	10.2	11
Netherlands	1994	3.1	12	6.2	15
Switzerland	1992	3.1	12	7.4	12
Canada	1994	1.2	14	4.7	17
Luxembourg	1994	0.9	15	6.7	14
Finland	1995	0.9	15	5.1	16
Norway	1995	0.7	17	14.5	5
Sweden	1992	0.7	17	2.6	18
Overall average		4.5		11.6	

Source: Authors' calculations from LIS database.

Table 5A.2 Low-Wage Workers and Social Transfers

| Country | Year | Poverty Rate | | Percentage Low-Wage Workers[a] | Percentage of Country's GDP Devoted to: | |
		All	Children		Cash and Near-cash Total Social Transfers[b]	Cash and Near-cash Non-aged Social Transfers[b]
Australia	1994	7.0	7.4	13.8	9.3	6.2
Austria	1992	2.8	2.6	13.2	18.6	8.9
Belgium	1992	1.9	1.6	7.2	19.3	12.1
Canada	1994	6.6	8.5	23.2	12.5	8.0
Denmark	1992	3.6	2.1	NA	18.9	12.4
Finland	1995	2.1	1.5	5.9	23.3	15.3
France	1994	3.2	2.6	13.3	21.0	10.7
Germany	1994	4.2	6.0	13.3	18.4	8.4
Israel	1992	5.2	4.8	NA	NA	NA
Italy	1995	8.9	14.1	NA[a]	18.0	7.0

Japan	1992	6.9	NA	15.7	6.9	1.9
Luxembourg[a]	1994	1.3	2.2	6.0[a]	17.2	10.4
Netherlands	1994	4.7	4.6	11.9	21.0	14.1
Norway[a]	1995	3.0	2.2	7.8[a]	15.9	10.1
Spain	1990	5.2	7.0	NA	14.1	6.8
Sweden	1995	4.6	1.3	5.2	22.0	13.8
United Kingdom	1995	5.7	8.3	19.6	16.0	9.4
United States	1997	10.7	14.7	25.0	9.2	3.7

Data source: Tables 5.2 and 5.3.

a. *Sources:* OECD (1996); for low wages, LIS database. Italian OECD estimate is inconsistent with other sources of Italian wage data.

b. *Source:* OECD (1999). Cash and near-cash social expenditures exclude health, education, and social services but include all forms of cash benefits and near-cash housing subsidies, active labor market program subsidies, and other contingent cash and near-cash benefits. Non-elderly benefits include only those accruing to household heads under age sixty-five.

PART II

The Evolution of
Antipoverty Policies

CHAPTER **6**

The Evolution of Income Support Policy in Recent Decades

JOHN KARL SCHOLZ AND KARA LEVINE

This chapter documents the evolution of antipoverty pro-
grams in the United States, focusing particularly on the 1990s.[1] Antipoverty
programs are designed to mitigate the most pernicious aspects of market-
based economic outcomes—unemployment and low earnings. These programs make up society's "safety net," and each has different eligibility standards and benefit formulas. Although they can be aggregated and categorized to summarize trends in coverage and generosity, a consequence of
their patchwork nature is that the safety net may appear very different to a
family in one set of circumstances than it does to a family in another. Thus,
we strike a balance between providing an overview of the evolution of public spending on the poor and highlighting the changes that have affected
families in specific circumstances.

The magnitude of pretax and pretransfer poverty in the United States is
striking. As shown in figure 6.1, since 1979, between 18.6 and 22.1 percent
of the population had pretax and pretransfer incomes below the poverty line
(see also Burtless and Smeeding, this volume).[2] Figure 6.1 also plots a post-
tax and post-transfer measure of poverty, which, when compared with the
pretax and pretransfer measure, reflects the overall effects of the tax and
transfer system on poverty. Taxes and transfers have a substantial effect, reducing poverty rates by 9.6 to 11.8 percentage points across the years. The
similarity of the time-series patterns of the two measures plotted in figure
6.1 is also striking, though the post-tax and post-transfer measure increased
less (by 1.8 fewer percentage points) during the recession of the early 1990s
than did the pretax and pretransfer measure. The consistency in the two series suggests that there have been few major changes in the taxes and trans-

fers that affect low-income families, but in fact, this consistency masks significant programmatic changes.

Before describing how the evolution of programs accounts for the reduction in poverty illustrated by these two series, we briefly discuss three factors that provide context—the economy, public opinion, and trends in poverty rates for subgroups in the population.

Poverty rates vary with economic performance. The sensitivity of market-based poverty to economic cycles is apparent in figure 6.1: the poverty rate rose 2.9 percentage points during the severe recession in the early 1980s, and 3.3 percentage points during the milder (in aggregate) recession in the early 1990s.[3] Over the last two decades, the relationship between aggregate economic performance and poverty has weakened as income inequality increased. However, this relationship remains strong.[4]

The antipoverty effects of the safety net vary with Americans' attitudes toward welfare and assistance to the poor, because attitudes influence the evolution of specific programs. Figure 6.2 plots the responses to two questions drawn from the General Social Survey (GSS), a personal interview of households conducted by the National Opinion Research Center (NORC) at the University of Chicago almost annually since 1973. The two questions start: "We are faced with many problems in this country, none of which can be solved easily or inexpensively. I'm going to name some of these problems,

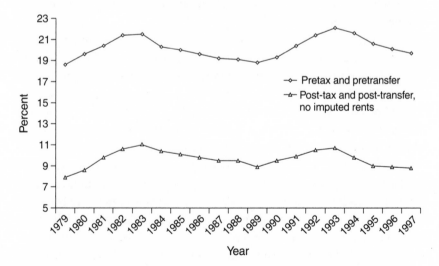

Figure 6.1 The Effect of the Tax and Transfer System on Poverty (*Source: www.census.gov/hhes/poverty/histpov/rdp06.html/*, definitions 2 and 14.)

and for each one, I'd like you to tell me whether we're spending too much money on it, too little money, or about the right amount. Are we spending too much money, too little money, or about the right amount on . . ." The two lines beginning in 1973 plot the percentage of respondents answering "too little on welfare" (the bottom series) and "too much on welfare" (the top series). In 1984 the GSS started asking an identical question on "assistance to the poor." The lowest line (which starts in 1984) shows the percentage who say we are spending "too much on assisting the poor." The highest line (which starts in 1984) shows the percentage who say we are spending "too little."

The GSS responses are striking.[5] First, a near-majority of respondents appear to simultaneously believe we are spending too much on welfare and too little on assisting the poor. The conflicting responses to welfare and assistance to the poor highlight the tensions that arise when crafting the safety net between an instinct to help disadvantaged families and an unwillingness to do so through welfare programs.

Second, there was a sharp increase, starting in 1993, in the percentage of respondents who said that spending on welfare was too high. The increase

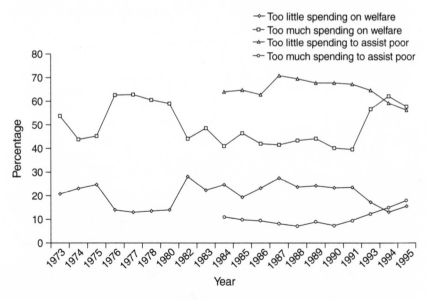

Figure 6.2 Public Attitudes on Welfare and Assistance to the Poor: GSS Data (*Source:* Authors' calculations from GSS data available at *www.icpsr.umich.edu/ GSS/.* variables NATFARE and NATFAREY.) *Note:* No GSS data were collected in 1979, 1981, 1992, and 1995.

coincides with President Clinton's 1992 campaign pledge to "end welfare as we know it" and the legislative deliberations that culminated in the Personal Responsibility and Work Opportunity Reconciliation Act (PRWORA), which eliminated the federal Aid to Families with Dependent Children (AFDC) program, the nation's basic welfare program at that time. There was a comparable decline in the percentage of respondents who said we were spending too little. These patterns both influence and are influenced by public debates, but they document Americans' long-standing antipathy toward welfare programs.

Because antipoverty programs target specific population subgroups, it is helpful to look at their poverty rates. Figure 6.3 shows trends in the conventional (cash income) measure of poverty for individuals older than sixty-four, children under eighteen, individuals eighteen to sixty-four, and for the full population. Two things stand out. Poverty rates for children are very high—nearly 20 percent of children are being raised in a poor family.[6] The 1998 child poverty rate (18.9 percent) is only 8.4 percentage points lower than the 1959 child poverty rate, and it is almost 5.0 percentage points *higher* than its lowest point in the late 1960s and early 1970s.

The second striking feature of figure 6.3 is the decline in poverty rates for the elderly. In 1959 the elderly poverty rate was 35.2 percent; by 1998 it was

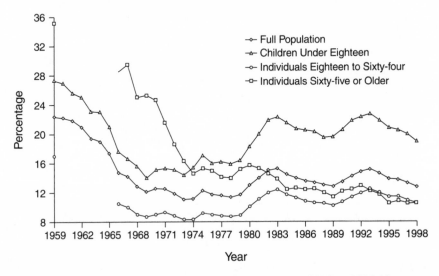

Figure 6.3 Child, Elderly, and Aggregate Poverty Rates, 1959 to 1998 (*Source:* U.S. Bureau of the Census 1999a, table B-2.)

10.5 percent, equal to the poverty rate for prime-age workers. A complete explanation for the strikingly different patterns of child and elderly poverty rates would require analysis of saving behavior of prime-age workers, retirement decisions of the elderly, marriage and fertility patterns of workers with low human capital (see Cancian and Reed, this volume), and the operation of low-wage labor markets. As we discuss later, however, many of the gains for the elderly can be traced to policy choices.

Antipoverty policy is conducted against this backdrop of economic performance and attitudes and beliefs. Many programs have resulted with different target groups and eligibility requirements. In our subsequent discussion, we separate these programs into "social insurance" and "means-tested transfers." Collectively, they compose the safety net.

Social Insurance

One distinguishing characteristic of social insurance programs is their universality: all individuals or their employers make contributions to finance the program, and all people can receive benefits when specific eligibility requirements are met. These programs also have dedicated funding mechanisms by which, at least in an accounting sense, social insurance taxes are remitted to trust funds from which benefits are paid.

Social Security and Medicare

The largest social insurance program is Social Security, formally known as the Old-Age, Survivors, and Disability Insurance (OASDI) program. Founded in 1935 as one of President Franklin Roosevelt's New Deal programs, Social Security was designed to meet the unmet social needs of older workers leaving the workforce without sufficient post-retirement income to be self-supporting.[7]

Figure 6.4 plots the time series of real (inflation-adjusted) Social Security (old-age and survivors insurance, or OASI) payments from 1959 to 1999. (Disability insurance benefits are not included in this series but are discussed later.) Real Social Security payments have grown sharply over the entire period, doubling between 1973 and 1999. Three factors are responsible for this increase. First, the number of retired workers covered by Social Security has steadily increased. Second, the Social Security taxable wage base grew steadily, as did real earnings. Third, legislated benefit increases frequently exceeded the cost of living into the early 1970s. Aggregate real Social Security benefits increased by roughly 170 percent between 1970 and 1998, while real benefits per recipient increased by 64 percent.

Social Security is a massive program, and pretax and pretransfer poor families receive half of its benefits. Consequently, it has a major effect on poverty rates among the elderly. Aggregate OASI payments were $334.4 billion in 1999. Average Social Security benefits (including survivors' benefits) were $9,689 in 1998, and average benefits for a retired worker exceeded $750 per month ($1,300 for couples). Thus, it is not surprising that poverty rates for the elderly are low, since the poverty line for a single elderly person in 1998 was $7,818, and $9,862 for an elderly couple.[8]

The elderly also receive substantial benefits from Medicare, which covers almost all people over age sixty-five and most people under sixty-five who are receiving Social Security Disability Insurance (DI) benefits. Medicare provides hospital insurance and, for some households, supplementary medical insurance.[9] Real Medicare outlays have increased more than tenfold, from $16.9 billion in 1967 (the year the program started) to $233.4 billion in 1999. Real expenditures per Medicare enrollee increased almost six times over the same time period, to $5,810 in 1998.

Fifty-two percent of Medicare benefits go to families whose pretransfer in-

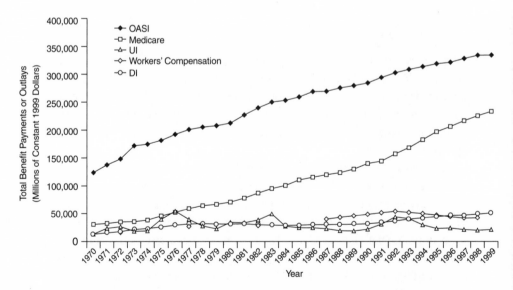

Figure 6.4 Total Benefit Payments on OASI, UI, DI, Workers' Compensation and Outlays for Medicare, 1970 to 1999 (*Sources:* See sources for table 6A.1.)

comes are below the poverty line. It is difficult to determine the specific antipoverty effectiveness of Medicare because it provides an in-kind benefit (medical care) and insurance. The official poverty measure does not account for Medicare benefits because they are in-kind rather than in the form of cash. There are several possible ways to value these benefits. We could value them at the cost to the government of their provision, the cost a recipient would have to pay to acquire comparable benefits, or the amount a person would be willing to pay for such benefits (which would be less than the cost to the government for many low-income recipients). (For a nice discussion of these issues, see Smeeding 1982.) When we assess the antipoverty effectiveness of spending on the poor in a later section, we make illustrative calculations of the degree to which Medicare reduces poverty.

Considerable attention has been given to the behavioral effects, and thus the lifetime distributional effects, of the annual $560 billion Social Security and Medicare expenditure. (For a discussion of Social Security and capital formation, see Feldstein 1996, and Bernheim 1987; for Social Security and retirement decisions, see Rust and Phelan 1997; for the Social Security and retirement decisions of the poor, see Kahn 1988; Medicare is discussed more extensively in Mullahy and Wolfe, this volume.) Despite these debates concerning the effects of Social Security on labor supply, capital formation, and retirement, the effect of Social Security and Medicare on poverty appears straightforward: the Social Security system redistributes a large amount of money from workers to retired families. As the Social Security system has matured, the poverty rates of the elderly have fallen precipitously.[10] The sharpest decline in elderly poverty rates occurred between 1959 and 1974 (see figure 6.3), a period that coincides with extremely rapid growth in Social Security spending.[11]

Social Insurance for Prime-Age Workers

Although Social Security and Medicare also provide benefits for non-elderly people through disability insurance and survivors' benefits, 87.1 percent of Medicare recipients were elderly in 1998, and 84.0 percent of Social Security recipients were elderly in 2000. In recent years, the elderly have typically received between 85 and 90 percent of all payments for both Medicare and Social Security.[12] Three smaller social insurance programs, unemployment insurance (UI), workers' compensation, and disability insurance (DI), target prime-age workers; real expenditures on these programs are also shown in figure 6.4.

Unemployment insurance provides temporary and partial wage replacement to recently employed workers who become involuntarily unemployed.[13] Unemployment insurance allows families to maintain their consumption during periods of involuntary layoffs (see, for example, Gruber 1997), but it has relatively minor antipoverty effects. Gustafson and Levine (1998), for example, suggest that only one-third of job separations for less-skilled men and fewer than 16 percent of job separations for less-skilled women meet the eligibility requirements for unemployment insurance.[14] Even fewer women who previously received welfare qualified. In 1992, a recession year, $43.9 billion in real unemployment insurance benefits were paid out, while real payments were $20.0 billion in the full employment year of 1998.

Workers' compensation provides cash and medical benefits to some persons with job-related disabilities or injuries and provides survivors' benefits to the dependents of those whose death resulted from a work-related accident or illness. Benefit levels vary widely across states. Workers' compensation payments are large, equaling $42.6 billion in real terms in 1998. Because there is little federal involvement in this system, it is difficult to find information on its antipoverty effects. We speculate that any such effects are likely to be small, however, for the same reasons that unemployment insurance has limited antipoverty effectiveness.

Disability insurance is part of the OASDI program. Disability benefits are drawn when a covered worker is unable to engage in "substantial gainful activity" by reason of a physical or mental impairment that is expected to last more than twelve months or result in death.[15] Workers must have a minimum period of covered employment before being eligible; depending on the age at which a disability occurs, this ranges from six to forty covered quarters. The disability insurance rules are stringent: fewer than 50 percent of all applicants are granted benefits; roughly 4.5 awards are made per 1,000 covered workers. Around 4.8 million disabled workers (or 6.5 million people when including spouses and children) receive disability benefits, which cost $51.3 billion in 1999. Most recipients of DI benefits are the pretax and pretransfer poor.

Summary of Social Insurance

Social Security, Medicare, unemployment insurance, workers' compensation, and disability insurance are the major social insurance programs in the United States. Over time the enormous increase in the value of their benefits has been driven largely by increases in Social Security and Medicare. The magnitude and growth of social insurance programs are not surprising, since their benefits are predicated on events that are salient for most Americans— retirement, unemployment, or a disability or work-related injury. Because they are universal for all contributors, receipt of benefits does not depend on an individual's income. All have dedicated financing mechanisms. And even though Social Security may reduce national saving and hasten retirement, and unemployment insurance may alter the intensity with which the unemployed search for jobs, there is no evidence that the social insurance programs encourage individuals not to marry, to have children out of wedlock, or not to work for extended periods in the paid labor market. (Unemployment insurance benefits are time-limited.) Thus, the rationale and incentives of the programs do not appear at odds with societal norms of personal responsibility. Social Security and Medicare have an added feature that is popular with both parents and children: lessening the caregiving responsibilities that children might have for their parents.

Means-Tested Transfers

A relatively small fraction of social insurance payments go to younger poor families. Many other programs target the non-elderly poor or otherwise disadvantaged. These programs are financed by general tax revenues rather than through dedicated financing mechanisms. Some are entitlements— that is, all who satisfy the stipulated eligibility requirements receive benefits, regardless of the total budgetary cost—and others are not. They all have income and asset tests that must be met, hence the label "means-tested transfers." The programs have explicit antipoverty goals. Together, they have a smaller budgetary cost than the social insurance programs.

Health Care and the Disabled

Medicaid, the largest means-tested transfer program (see also Mullahy and Wolfe, this volume), funds medical assistance to low-income persons who are aged, blind, disabled, members of families with dependent children, and certain other pregnant women and children. Asset and income tests, which vary across states, determine eligibility. All families who received AFDC benefits were statutorily covered under Medicaid. Recipients of Temporary Assistance for Needy Families (TANF) are not automatically eligible. States must cover families, however, who would have been eligible under the

AFDC rules in effect as of July 16, 1996, though states have the discretion to lower income eligibility standards to the levels in effect as early as May 1, 1988 (see also Pavetti, this volume).

More than 70 percent of all Medicaid recipients had income below the poverty line in 1997; just over 11 percent of Medicaid beneficiaries were sixty-five or older in 1995. Medicaid was expanded between 1986 and 1991 as Congress required states to cover pregnant women and children living in families with incomes up to 133 percent of poverty and allowed expanded coverage to families with incomes of up to 185 percent of poverty. These expansions led to a large increase in the total number of Medicaid recipients, to 40.6 million in 1998. Disabled and elderly families with little income and few assets also receive Medicaid, which, for example, often pays the nursing home costs of the low-income elderly.

The trend in Medicaid spending in constant dollars is shown in figure 6.5. After growing rapidly through the mid-1970s, Medicaid grew at annual rates between 0.6 and 9.7 percent between 1976 and 1989. The expansions to families with children and pregnant women in the late 1980s increased growth rates to 12.3, 21.1, and 25.3 percent in 1990, 1991, and 1992. Total real Medicaid spending increased from $20.8 billion in 1970 to $188.8 bil-

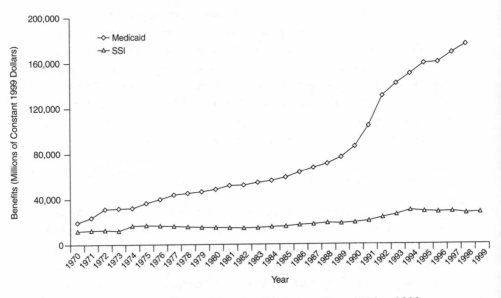

Figure 6.5 Total SSI Benefits and Medicaid Program Costs, 1970 to 1999 (*Sources:* See sources for table 6A.1.)

lion in 1998; it doubled in the 1990s. Attempts to assess the antipoverty effectiveness of Medicaid face the same difficulties that arise with valuing Medicare benefits. We briefly discuss the antipoverty effectiveness of Medicare and Medicaid in a later section.

Supplemental Security Income (SSI) is a means-tested safety net program for the aged, blind, and disabled. The disabled make up nearly 80 percent of SSI recipients. SSI is a federally administered cash transfer program that began in 1974 with the consolidation of several existing such programs.[16] Subject to meeting the income, asset, and categorical eligibility standards, an individual can receive a cash transfer of up to $500 per month, couples can receive up to one and a half times that amount, and children can receive $250, although states are allowed to supplement these amounts.

As shown in figure 6.5, SSI grew very slowly between 1974 and 1990, from $17.7 billion to $20.5 billion (in 1999 dollars). Between 1990 and 1994, program costs grew by 55 percent, making SSI one of the nation's fastest-growing entitlement programs. A major factor driving this growth was the Zebley decision, a Supreme Court case that revised the childhood mental health impairment eligibility criterion to be consistent with the criterion that applies to adults. The *Green Book* (U.S. House of Representatives 1998) reports that three groups accounted for nearly 90 percent of the program's growth during this time: adults with mental impairments, children, and noncitizens. Since the mid-1990s, SSI has actually shrunk in real terms as efforts have been made to reduce the growth rate of SSI payments to children and immigrants. SSI payments were $29.7 billion in 1999, benefiting 6.2 million recipients.

Cash Means-Tested Transfers for Able-bodied Families

Aid to Families with Dependent Children was the central safety net program for poor families with children from 1936 to 1996 (for more details, see Pavetti, this volume). This program was primarily directed at single-parent families, though some two-parent families with an unemployed parent also received benefits. The program was a means-tested entitlement: all applicants whose income and assets were below the stipulated levels could receive benefits. States determined benefit generosity that varied widely; funds were provided according to an uncapped federal matching formula.

PRWORA abolished AFDC and created Temporary Assistance for Needy Families, a set of block grants to states with few restrictions. States are required to spend at least 75 percent of their "historic" level of AFDC spend-ing; a five-year lifetime limit is imposed on receipt of federally supported as-sistance (though hardship exemptions are included in the law); and states have to meet certain targets in moving portions of their caseloads into spe-cific work activities. Whether through AFDC-TANF changes, the longest economic expansion in U.S. history, sharp increases in the Earned Income Tax Credit (EITC), or a combination of these and other factors, welfare case-loads have fallen precipitously. Between January 1993 and December 1999, welfare caseloads fell by 52 percent, to 2.4 million families from 5.0 million.

Several commentators feared that TANF might set off a "race to the bot-tom" in which states, fearful of attracting low-income families from other states, might lower benefits, causing other states in turn to lower theirs. Al-though there has been a sharp reduction in AFDC-TANF cash benefits, be-ginning in 1997 (see figure 6.6), the reductions are roughly proportional to the welfare caseload reduction. Furthermore, while cash benefits have de-creased, spending on other ancillary services (for example, child care and transportation) has increased, so that total spending under TANF has not fallen by as much as figure 6.6 would indicate. In fact, although spending categories before and after PRWORA are not directly comparable, in some

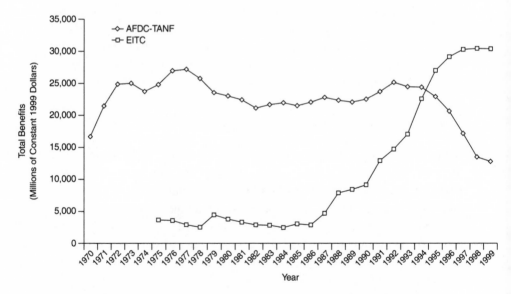

Figure 6.6 Total AFDC-TANF and EITC Benefits, 1970 to 1999 (*Sources:* See sources for table 6A.1.)

states—including Wisconsin, which was among the first states to sharply alter its welfare—total spending has actually increased since the 1996 reform.

Combined real spending on SSI and AFDC-TANF fell by roughly 2 percent in the last decade. In contrast, expenditures on the Earned Income Tax Credit grew sharply.[17] The EITC tax expenditure was $3.9 billion (in 1999 dollars) in 1975, the first year it was part of the tax code, and $31.9 billion in 1999. (For a detailed survey of the EITC, see Hotz and Scholz 2000.) Real EITC spending increased 232 percent in the 1990s. No other federal antipoverty program grew at a comparable rate. In 1999 the value of the EITC exceeded the *combined* federal spending on TANF and food stamps by several billion dollars.

The 1986 Tax Reform Act roughly doubled the total cost of the credit by increasing its size and extending its phase-out range. The credit rate, maximum credit, and spending increased every year from 1990 through 1996 as a consequence of the three-year phase-ins of legislative changes in 1990 and 1993. In 1999, 19.5 million taxpayers benefited from the EITC.

The incentives embedded in the EITC differ from those in AFDC-TANF. Historically, AFDC recipients with no earnings received the largest payments. In contrast, the EITC encourages low-skilled workers to enter the labor market, since earnings are needed to receive the credit and the benefit rises with earnings up to about the poverty line. Supporters of the credit among Republicans and Democrats have embraced its pro-work features.[18]

In-kind Means-Tested Transfers for Able-bodied People

The safety net for the poor includes a set of in-kind benefits, the largest of which are food stamps, housing assistance, Head Start, and two nutrition programs: school nutrition programs and the special supplemental nutrition program for women, infants, and children (WIC).[19] The evolution of expenditures for these programs is shown in figure 6.7.

Food stamps are designed to enable low-income households to purchase a nutritionally adequate, low-cost diet. The program is the country's single, almost universal entitlement for those with low income and assets.[20]

After food stamp benefits were made uniform across the country and indexed for inflation in 1972, real spending grew sharply. A set of legislative changes in 1981 and 1982 cut food stamp spending by nearly 13 percent ($7 billion) below what would have been spent under prior law between 1982 and 1985. The program was liberalized by a series of changes in 1985, 1986, and 1987; these changes, combined with the recession in the early 1990s, led to a sharp increase in total food stamp spending between 1988 and 1992.

Since 1994, real food stamp expenditures have fallen 38.3 percent. Although overall poverty rates and child poverty rates trended downward in recent years (see figure 6.3), they have not fallen as rapidly. According to the General Accounting Office (1999a, 4), food stamp participation fell 27 percent from 1996 to 1999, to 18.2 million people, and these declines were "faster than related economic indicators would predict." The GAO speculates that some people who are no longer eligible for cash assistance may think they are also no longer eligible for other benefits. The fraction of children living in families that have incomes below the poverty line and receive food stamps fell to 84 percent in 1997, from 94 percent in 1994, suggesting that new cracks in the safety net may be developing.

The Department of Housing and Urban Development and the Farmers Home Administration administer the housing assistance component of the safety net. Housing assistance has never been an entitlement. Rather, eligibility is based on family characteristics and income relative to 80 percent of the local median. Local public housing authorities allocate spaces to qualified applicants on a first-come, first-served basis, mediated by certain prefer-

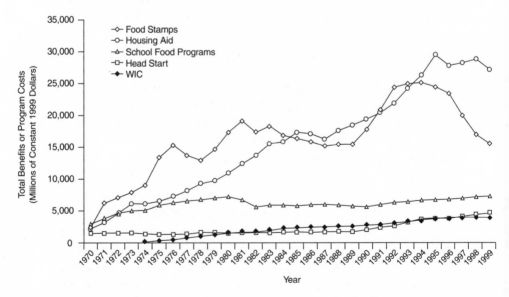

Figure 6.7 Total Benefits or Program Costs for Various In-kind Programs, 1970 to 1999 (*Sources:* See sources for table 6A.1.)

ences. Waiting lists are common. Aid comes in two principal forms: project-based aid (subsidies are tied to units specifically constructed for low-income households) and household-based subsidies (renters choose standard housing units in the existing private housing stock). Since 1982, project-based aid has been curtailed in favor of rental subsidies. Housing assistance grew from $2.2 billion in 1970 (in 1999 dollars) to nearly $30 billion in 1995, and fell modestly after that. The number of recipients followed a similar pattern: in 1977, 3.2 million renters and homeowners benefited from federal housing aid; after rising steadily to a peak of 5.8 million in 1995, this number has fallen slightly since then. Federal housing subsidies amount to roughly $5,000 in annual benefits per recipient.

The school lunch and breakfast program is an entitlement that provides federal support for meals served by public and private nonprofit elementary and secondary schools and residential child care institutions that enroll and guarantee to offer free or reduced-price meals to low-income children. Participation in the school breakfast program has grown from about 800,000 in 1971 to 7.4 million in 1999 (based on a nine-month average). The school lunch program is larger but has grown only gradually; participation was 24.1 million in 1971 and 27.0 million in 1999. Current expenditures on both programs (combined) are around $7.4 billion.

The Women, Infants, and Children Nutrition Program (WIC) provides food assistance, nutrition risk screening, and related nutrition-oriented services to low-income pregnant women and low-income women and their children (up to age five). WIC is not an entitlement. Participants receive vouchers for food purchase, supplemental food, and nutrition information. In 1999 roughly 7.3 million women, infants, and children received WIC benefits at a cost of nearly $4 billion.

Around 850,000 children are enrolled in Head Start, which provides a range of services to children under age five and their families. Its goals are to improve social competence, learning skills, health, and the nutrition status of low-income children so that they can begin school on an equal basis with their more advantaged peers. In real dollars, Head Start spending increased 136 percent between 1990 and 1999, to $4.7 billion.

Child Care

Several federal child care subsidy programs target low-income families. Many of these have been created since 1988. Since child care expenses are often seen as a deterrent to entering the workforce, the emergence of child care subsidy programs is part of the general trend noted here and elsewhere toward work-based assistance rather than welfare. (For further discussion of child care, see Blau 2000.)

In 1988 the Family Support Act created two programs: the Aid to Families with Dependent Children Child Care, and Transitional Child Care.[21] Two more new programs were implemented in 1990: the At-Risk Child Care, and the Child Care and Development Block Grant. The first three programs mentioned served, respectively, families on AFDC participating in a job training program, families who had recently moved off welfare, and families at risk of going on welfare. The fourth program, the Child Care and Development Block Grant, provided additional funds to low-income working families as well as funds to improve the quality of child care. In 1996 PRWORA consolidated these fragmented programs into the Child Care and Development Fund (CCDF).

In 1995 federal and state funding for all four programs totaled $3.4 billion (in 1999 dollars). In 1998 total spending through the CCDF was $5.5 billion. Despite increased spending on child care subsidies in the last few years, the number of recipient children has remained essentially unchanged: 1.4 million children were served in 1995 by one of the four programs. In 1998, 1.5 million were served by the CCDF. The antipoverty effects of subsidized child care are unknown.

Child Support

The Child Support Enforcement and Paternity Establishment Program (CSE) was established in 1975 to aid custodial parents in collecting child support payments from noncustodial parents.[22] Part of the impetus for the program was to replace public welfare benefits with parental support, although beneficiaries of the program are not limited to poor families; all custodial parents are entitled to assistance. Under the CSE, the federal government awards matching grants to the states that administer local programs. The role of the CSE is not to transfer money directly to custodial parents; instead, it provides a collection of services to custodial parents, including aid in establishing paternity, obtaining child support awards through a legal process, and collecting payments from noncustodial parents. The authority of the CSE has expanded continually over the years. In 1996 PRWORA consolidated federal child support funds into the TANF block grants. This legislation imposed more stringent requirements on the performance of state-run CSE programs in order for states to receive TANF funds. PRWORA also established a nationwide, integrated, automated network to improve states' ability to locate noncustodial parents.

Total child support collections rose from $2.7 billion in 1978 (in 1999 dollars) to $12.8 billion in 1996, while total federal and state administrative costs increased over the same time period from $797 million to $3.2 billion. Costs as a percentage of collections have fallen slightly, from around 24 percent in 1980 to 20 percent in 1996. The increases in collections are driven primarily by increases in the number of custodial parents served. In 1978 a collection was made in 707,000 cases. By 1996 this figure had risen to 3.5 million cases (U.S. House of Representatives 1998b). Average support payments per family have remained fairly constant. Between 1978 and 1995, the percentage of custodial mothers receiving child support increased from 34.6 percent to 37.4 percent. Greater progress was made among poor mothers: only 17.8 percent of these families received child support in 1978; by 1995, 26.5 percent of poor mothers were receiving support. However, this increase is primarily due to an increase in award rates rather than increased collection rates (Lerman and Sorensen 2000).

Child support appears to have small antipoverty effects. According to Daniel Meyer and Mei-Chen Hu (1999), child support payments in 1995 raised the incomes of between 6 and 7 percent of poor, female-headed families to a level above the poverty line. The authors suggest that the antipoverty effectiveness of child support has been growing over time.

Summary

Figure 6.8 summarizes the evolution of social insurance and antipoverty spending. Table 6A.1 provides a more detailed breakdown of spending by program, and table 6A.2 shows the numbers of recipients by program.

Social insurance—Social Security, Medicare, unemployment insurance, workers' compensation, and disability insurance—is by far the largest category of spending. The cost of social insurance has risen steadily because of rapid increases in the cost of Social Security and Medicare. Total social insurance expenditures (in real dollars, excluding workers' compensation because of data limitations) rose at an annual rate of 6.9 percent in the 1970s, 3.1 percent in the 1980s, and 4.0 percent in the 1990s (through 1998).

The bottom two lines of figure 6.8 show total spending on in-kind transfers (without Medicaid) and cash transfers. In-kind transfers—the sum of school nutrition programs, WIC, Head Start, housing subsidies, and food stamps—grew rapidly in the 1970s, at an annual rate (in real dollars) of 16.4

percent. This growth was driven primarily by food stamps and housing. In-kind transfers grew at an annual rate of 1.5 percent in the 1980s and 4.3 percent from 1990 to 1998.[23] Cash transfers—the sum of AFDC-TANF, the EITC, and SSI—grew at an annual rate of 4.7 percent in the 1970s, 1.8 percent in the 1980s, and 4.2 percent in the 1990s.

The growth rates of both cash and in-kind safety net spending have increased significantly in the 1990s relative to the 1980s. Spending on cash and in-kind antipoverty programs, excluding Medicaid, was around $134 billion in 1999. Medicaid spending was an additional $190 billion. In the following section, we present some illustrative calculations of the degree to which these programs alleviate poverty.

Effects of Antipoverty Policy

In this section, we address the complex question: How does this wide range of programs affect the poverty rate and the depth of poverty among poor people? The simple comparison of pre- and post-tax and -transfer poverty rates in figure 6.1 tells us the percentage of families and individuals who were raised above the poverty line by the tax and transfer system. However, this type of analysis ignores the degree to which poverty may have been al-

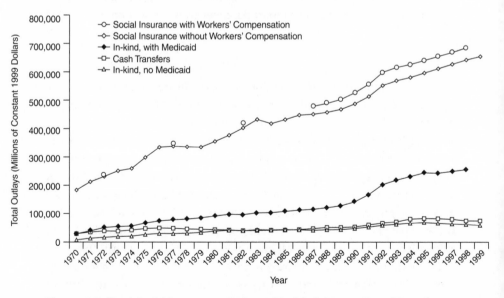

Figure 6.8 Total Social Insurance, Cash, and In-kind, Means-Tested Transfers (*Sources:* See sources for table 6A.1.)

leviated. An alternative way to examine the antipoverty effectiveness of tax and transfer programs is to look at the degree to which programs affect the poverty gap—the sum of the differences between market income and the poverty line for all families with incomes below the poverty line.

Our analysis of antipoverty effectiveness updates work by Daniel Weinberg (1985, 1987, and 1991), who measured the poverty gap using the Survey of Income and Program Participation (SIPP) and its predecessor, the Income Survey Development Program (ISDP), and then reported the degree to which antipoverty programs closed the poverty gap. His analysis does not take into account behavioral responses to different programs. In the absence of Social Security, for example, some elderly people would continue to work in the paid labor market, thus reducing the pretax and pretransfer poverty rate and the poverty gap. Hence, the calculations provide an *upper* bound on the magnitude of the poverty gap and the antipoverty effectiveness of different programs.

We address four questions. First, how large is the poverty gap, and how has it changed since 1979? Second, how effective are current programs in filling the poverty gap? Third, how has the antipoverty effectiveness of the tax and transfer system changed over time? Fourth, what are the differential effects of public policies across different demographic groups—the elderly, one- and two-parent families, and families without children? We conclude the section with a brief discussion of recent evidence about the effects of the tax and transfer system on labor supply, saving, and family formation.

The Poverty Gap, 1997

We draw data for all families and individuals in April 1997 from waves 4 and 5 of the 1996 Survey of Income and Program Participation. Because most programs determine eligibility on a monthly basis, we measure the poverty gap for a single month.[24] We do not consider the effects of the individual income tax, aside from the Earned Income Tax Credit. This omission has little consequence. Families with children who have income below the poverty line do not pay positive income taxes (even excluding the EITC), owing to personal and child exemptions, the standard deduction, and the $500 child credit. Low-income taxpayers without children and incomes near the poverty line pay small amounts of federal income taxes. Payroll taxes are more important, as all families pay the employee share of payroll taxes (7.65 percent) regardless of income. To account for this in table 6.1, we reduce wage

Table 6.1 Effect of Transfers on Poverty, April 1997: All Families and Individuals

	Total Transfers (Millions of Dollars)	Average Monthly Transfer per Recipient Family	Total Transfers To Pretransfer Poor	Total Transfers Used to Alleviate Poverty	Poverty Gap Filled	Poverty Gap, Post-transfer (Billions of Dollars)	Poor, Post-transfer[a]
No transfers	$0	—	—	—	—	$19.6	29.0%
All transfers	59,044	$1,104	55.3%	24.0%	72.4%	5.4	10.0
All cash transfers	34,133	687	53.1	32.5	56.5	8.5	16.7
All in-kind transfers	24,911	620	58.2	43.3	55.0	8.8	19.7
All income-conditioned transfers	8,196	478	77.0	64.3	26.9	14.3	26.1
Social insurance							
Social Security (OASDI)	25,396	868	49.0	28.0	36.3	12.5	19.8
Medicare	18,573	655	52.0	36.2	34.3	12.9	22.4
Unemployment insurance	1,015	703	50.4	37.4	1.9	19.2	28.7
Workers' compensation	918	1,107	57.9	26.6	1.2	19.4	28.8
Black lung compensation	37	438	84.5	69.1	0.1	19.6	29.0
Veterans' benefits	1,058	457	41.3	27.9	1.5	19.3	28.8

Means-tested transfers

Medicaid	3,729	72.7	65.7	12.5	17.2	28.0
SSI	2,280	76.9	69.3	8.1	18.0	28.5
AFDC-TANF	1,111	87.4	83.9	4.8	18.7	28.9
EITC	1,893	61.0	53.9	5.2	18.6	27.8
General assistance	202	85.4	83.1	0.9	19.4	29.0
Other welfare	100	66.4	61.1	0.3	19.5	29.0
Foster child payments	123	41.9	24.1	0.2	19.6	29.0
Food stamps	1,304	85.3	83.4	5.5	18.5	28.8
Housing assistance	1,130	81.3	77.8	4.5	18.7	28.8
WIC	175	62.6	62.0	0.6	19.5	29.0

Source: Authors' calculations from the 1997 SIPP (waves 4 and 5).

Note: Number of families: 111,375,693.

a. This poverty rate is for families and unrelated individuals: it reflects the fraction of families (including single-person "families") in poverty rather than the fraction of the total population in poverty; the latter is the more traditional measure, emphasized in other chapters of this volume. Also note that this is the poverty rate for a single month and thus is likely to show more families in poverty than an annual measure. Furthermore, annual underreporting of wages and salaries in the SIPP may contribute to a higher poverty rate measure than measures that rely on the CPS.

and salary income reported in SIPP by 7.65 percent (the employee Old Age, Survivors, Disability, and Health Insurance [OASDHI] tax rate, referred to as the payroll tax) and self-employment income by 15.3 percent.

A challenging part of this exercise is the valuation of noncash benefits. Because the value of food stamps does not exceed the food needs of the typical family, we value them at the cost to the government. Medicare and Medicaid are more difficult, since not all families consume health services. We assume that for most families Medicaid is worth about the cost of a typical HMO policy; for elderly or disabled families, we increase this by a factor of 2.5 to account for the greater medical needs of these groups.[25] (For a discussion of ways in which Medicaid is more valuable than private insurance and ways in which Medicaid is less valuable, see Gruber 2000.) We value Medicare using two and a half times the average cost of a fee-for-service plan, adjusting for regional cost differences (Kaiser Family Foundation 1999).

We use fair market rent (FMR) data from the Department of Housing and Urban Development to estimate the value of in-kind housing benefits. Specifically, housing benefits are assumed to be the difference between population-weighted, average, state-level (or major-metropolitan-area-level) FMRs, adjusted by the number of bedrooms needed to accommodate families of different sizes and the rents paid directly by families.

Table 6.1 summarizes our results. The first row indicates that the total pretax and pretransfer poverty gap was $19.6 billion in April 1997, and that 29.0 percent of families (including unrelated individuals) had pretax and pretransfer incomes below the poverty line.[26] The other entries of table 6.1 show the antipoverty effectiveness of the tax and transfer system. Reading across the "all transfers" row, the first column shows $59.0 billion of benefits, or $1,104 per recipient family. Of these payments, 55.3 percent went to families with pretransfer incomes below the poverty line, and 24.0 percent of total program dollars closed the poverty gap.[27] These transfers fill 72.4 percent of the total poverty gap, which resulted in a post-tax and post-transfer poverty rate of 10.0 percent and a poverty gap of $5.4 billion.

As expected given their universality, the major social insurance programs—Social Security (including DI), Medicare, unemployment insurance, and workers' compensation—are the least well targeted programs: roughly half the recipients (58 percent for workers' compensation) have incomes below the poverty line. Anywhere from 27 to 37 percent of total benefits directly close the poverty gap. Given the size of the programs, however, they have a very large effect on poverty rates, particularly Social Security and Medicare.

Of the other major programs (exceeding $1 billion), food stamps, AFDC, and housing assistance are the most tightly targeted toward the poor, with more than 78 percent of benefits directly reducing the poverty gap. Medicaid, SSI, and the EITC also have large antipoverty effects.

We now focus on how the effects of the tax and transfer system have evolved over time. Table 6.2 compares our results for 1997 with Weinberg's estimates for 1979 and 1984. First note that the poverty gap estimates (adjusted by number of families) are strikingly similar: $19.7 billion, $19.0 billion, and $19.1 billion for 1979, 1984, and 1997.[28] This result is consistent with the stubborn persistence of poverty rates over time documented in this chapter and elsewhere. Furthermore, the aggregate antipoverty effects of the tax and transfer system seem to be extraordinarily stable: in each year, a little more than 70 percent of the poverty gap is filled. That stability reflects stagnant real incomes over this period and stable trends in antipoverty spending. However, if society's goal is the elimination of income poverty, the lack of progress over the past eighteen years is unsettling.

Table 6.3 highlights gaps in the safety net by focusing on four types of families: elderly, non-elderly single-parent, non-elderly two-parent, and non-elderly childless families. The top row shows that $35.6 billion in transfers per month, primarily Social Security benefits, fill over 99 percent of the poverty gap of the elderly.[29]

Transfers appear well targeted to non-elderly single-parent families: 77 percent go to poor families, and 49 percent of the total dollars fill the poverty gap. Although these transfers fill 79 percent of the poverty gap, 17.5 percent of non-elderly single-parent families remain poor. Transfers are somewhat less well targeted to two-parent families: 49 percent of transfers to this group go to poor families, but their overall poverty rate is nevertheless low (6.5 percent).

Table 6.3 calls attention to possible cracks in the safety net for two groups. First, the tax and transfer system fills only 45.9 percent of the poverty gap for non-elderly childless families. Other than food stamps, these families, in the absence of a disability, have few sources of public assistance. Strengthening their safety net, however, runs the risk of creating incentives to not work or not invest in skills that could lead to future self-sufficiency. Second, post-transfer poverty rates remain very high for single-parent families with children.

Table 6.2 Comparison of Antipoverty Effectiveness of Taxes and Transfers, April 1997, 1984 and 1979 (Real Dollars)

	Total Transfers (Millions of Dollars)	Average Monthly Transfer per Recipient	Total to Pretransfer Poor	Used to Alleviate Poverty Gap	Poverty Gap Filled	Poor, Post-transfer[a]	Poverty Gap (Billions of Dollars)	Poverty Gap, Adjusted (Billions of Dollars)[b]
1997	$59,044	$1,104	54.3%	23.5%	72.7%	9.3%	$19.1	$19.1
1984	36,938	1,027	57.1	31.1	73.6	10.9	15.6	19.0
1979	29,774	893	65.4	38.0	73.6	11.7	15.4	19.7

Sources: 1997: Authors' calculations from the 1997 SIPP (waves 4 and 5); 1984: Weinberg (1987); 1979: Weinberg (1985).

Note: To maintain comparability with Weinberg (1985, 1987), we exclude payroll taxes from our calculations of the effects of the tax and transfer system. (They are included in table 6.1.) Dollar amounts are in 1997 dollars.

a. This poverty rate is for families and unrelated individuals: it reflects the fraction of families (including single-person "families") in poverty rather than the fraction of the total population in poverty; the latter is the more traditional measure, emphasized in other chapters of this volume. Also note that this is the poverty rate for a single month and thus is likely to show more families in poverty than an annual measure. Furthermore, annual underreporting of wages and salaries in the SIPP may contribute to a higher poverty rate measure than measures that rely on the CPS.

b. This poverty gap measure is adjusted for number of families: there were 111.38 million families and unrelated individuals in 1997, 91.39 million in 1984, and 87.07 million in 1979.

Table 6.3 Antipoverty Effectiveness of the Transfer System for Different Family Types, April 1997

	Number of Families (Millions)	Poverty Gap (Millions of Dollars)	Poverty Gap per Family	Total Transfers (Millions of Dollars)	Average Monthly Transfer per Recipient Family	Total to Pretransfer Poor	Total Used to Alleviate Poverty	Poverty Gap Filled	Poor, Post-transfer[a]
Elderly families and individuals	21.9	$6,275	$286	$35,616	$1,645	53.2%	17.5%	99.1%	1.0%
Non-elderly single-parent families	11.3	4,308	380	6,894	776	76.6	49.2	78.8	17.5
Non-elderly two-parent families	26.0	2,638	101	5,603	624	49.1	29.3	62.2	6.5
Non-elderly childless families and individuals	52.1	6,389	123	10,930	783	51.8	26.9	45.9	13.8

Source: Authors' calculations from the 1997 SIPP (waves 4 and 5).

a. This poverty rate is for families and unrelated individuals: it reflects the fraction of families (including single-person "families") in poverty rather than the fraction of the total population in poverty; the latter is the more traditional measure, emphasized in other chapters of this volume. Also note that this is the poverty rate for a single month and thus is likely to show more families in poverty than an annual measure. Furthermore, annual underreporting of wages and salaries in the SIPP may contribute to a higher poverty rate measure than measures that rely on the CPS.

Transfers and Behavior

The behavioral responses to changes in the tax and transfer system have been at the heart of the policy debates shaping the evolution of antipoverty policy. The rapid increase in the Earned Income Tax Credit since 1986, for example, reflects the fact that the credit is widely perceived as "pro-work." The momentum to "end welfare as we know it" in the early 1990s was fueled by a concern that AFDC had created a cycle of dependency, encouraging some women to not work and to have children.

These concerns have received considerable attention in the academic literature.[30] Here we briefly outline the issues and describe recent evidence on three topics: labor markets, saving, and family formation.

LABOR MARKETS   As the generosity of the safety net increases, work incentives are likely to decrease. Two distinct issues arise. First, with greater total resources, people are likely to consume more of everything they like, including leisure. Second, transfer program benefits are typically reduced as income increases, imposing high implicit tax rates on work. Stacy Dickert, Scott Houser, and John Karl Scholz (1995), for example, show that cumulative *average* tax rates exceeded 85 percent for some low-wage, single-parent families from New York working anywhere from eight to thirty-five hours per week in 1990. If the marginal return to taking a full-time job for a single parent is only fifteen cents per dollar of earnings, one might expect to see low levels of labor force participation.

Dickert, Houser, and Scholz found wide variation across states in work incentives. In high-benefit states (like New York at the time), the post-tax return to work is fairly low, as substantial benefits are scaled back, while in low-benefit states (like Texas at the time), the post-tax return to work is high, since there are few benefits to lose. Thus, if labor market participation decisions are sensitive to the post-tax returns to work, more single mothers would be expected to work in low-benefit states than in high-benefit states, all else being equal. In fact, Dickert, Houser, and Scholz found that a 10 percent increase in the post-tax wage results in a 2.0-percentage-point (or 3.5 percent) increase in labor market participation among single parents.

Bruce Meyer and Dan Rosenbaum (2001) seek to explain the factors driving the recent increase in labor force participation among single mothers. They found that EITC changes account for 61 percent of the increase in their employment rate from 1984 to 1996, and for 27 to 35 percent of the increase

from 1992 to 1996. Changes in maximum state welfare benefits, benefit reduction rates and Medicaid expansions account for 8 to 16 percent of the
change in labor force participation in both parties; and state welfare changes
have a slightly larger effect than Medicaid expansions. The effects of job
training and child care subsidies appear to be small. Other factors—the most
important of which is the performance of the economy—account for the remainder of the changes.[31]

Over the last decade, there has been extensive experimentation in welfare
program design. Gordon Berlin (2000a) discusses short-term results from
three recent social experiments: Project New Hope in Milwaukee, Wisconsin; the Minnesota Family Investment Program (MFIP); and the Self-Sufficiency Project (SSP) implemented in Vancouver, British Columbia, and
parts of New Brunswick. Each evaluation was designed as a randomized
social experiment. Each made work financially more rewarding for treatments relative to controls, and each offered incentives to hold full-time (or
near full-time) employment. Although results naturally differ across experiments, they provide additional evidence that work incentives can increase
employment, earnings, and total (earned plus transfer) income of families,
particularly for single-parent, long-term welfare recipients.

Across non-experimental and experimental studies, we see a growing
body of evidence that policies that increase post-tax wages have positive,
significant effects on labor market participation. Both the older and recent
studies found less evidence that changes in benefit rules in AFDC-TANF or
food stamps have labor market effects of an economically important magnitude.

SAVING   Many antipoverty programs have means and asset tests. Glenn
Hubbard, Jonathan Skinner, and Steven Zeldes (1995) construct a simulation model that predicts, in the absence of asset testing, that low-income
families would save considerably more than they actually do. They suggest
that families recognize that antipoverty programs could provide an alternative income source if needed, and so they save less than they otherwise
would, regardless of whether they ever draw program benefits.

Jonathan Gruber and Aaron Yelowitz (1999) found that among the eligible population, Medicaid lowered wealth holdings by between $1,293 and
$1,645 in 1993, and that the expansions in Medicaid from 1984 to 1993
lowered wealth holdings by about 7.2 percent. David Neumark and Elizabeth Powers (1998) found mixed evidence that SSI affects wealth and saving

but conclude that SSI reduces the saving of men who are nearing retirement. Powers (1998) found modest, negative effects on wealth accumulation of AFDC asset tests.

Taken together, there is some evidence, albeit far from definitive, that antipoverty programs reduce the asset accumulation of low-income families, although the magnitudes of the effects appear to be small. The welfare and policy implications of these results, however, are not clear. If reduced asset accumulation prevents families from making investments that would allow them to enhance their living standards, such as in cars or safe neighborhoods, then policymakers should be concerned about these negative effects on wealth accumulation. Alternatively, suppose that a primary motive for wealth accumulation is precautionary: to ensure against future contingencies. Then the presence of these means-tested programs might make families better off by allowing them to spend resources rather than save them. Consequently, the asset response to antipoverty programs *could* be indicative of the welfare-enhancing properties of social insurance.

FAMILY FORMATION   Antipoverty programs provide a safety net and hence, at the margin, encourage independence. AFDC-TANF, Medicaid, and housing assistance provide greater resources to single-parent families than they do to two-parent families, and so they may provide incentives to delay marriage, to divorce, or to not marry. Program benefits and the EITC also generally increase with family size and hence provide incentives to have children. Many studies have addressed the question of whether antipoverty programs affect behavior in the ways just described. Robert Moffitt (1998, 75) surveys studies of the effects of welfare on marriage and fertility and concludes: "A neutral weighing of the evidence still leads to the conclusion that welfare has incentive effects on marriage and fertility." These incentive effects are small, although Moffitt notes that results tend to vary significantly depending on the methodology used and other specification differences.

Summary

We conclude that the tax and transfer system has measurable effects on the behavior of low-income families. The strongest result appears to be the positive relationship between changes in the post-tax wage rates and labor force participation. This relationship suggests that economic growth and policies like the Earned Income Tax Credit can increase the labor force participation rates of those not currently working. Although programs appear to have measurable, negative effects on asset accumulation, the magnitudes are generally small. This is perhaps not surprising, given the low levels of financial wealth accumulated by typical (not poor or working-poor) families in the United States. Moreover, it is not clear from a policy perspective whether the asset response to transfers is a good or bad result. Finally, much of the existing literature tends to find, at most, modest effects of antipoverty programs on marriage and fertility. Interest in these areas, however, will remain high, and new developments could alter policymakers' (and our) views on these issues.

The Future of Antipoverty Policy

Predicting developments in any policy runs the risk of putting too much emphasis on recent events. Antipoverty policy is no exception. Nevertheless, we believe that the lessons drawn from welfare reform, rightly or wrongly, will dominate antipoverty policy discussions for the foreseeable future.

These lessons come in several pieces. First, benefits will continue to be linked with responsibility. This link is a natural consequence of the evidence (and perceptions of the evidence) on behavioral responses to antipoverty programs. Many of the incentives inherent in transfer programs—to have children, to not marry or divorce, to work less—are undesirable. Whether or not people respond to these incentives in an economically significant way is a topic of considerable research and debate. Policy debates, however, are often not settled on the basis of the best empirical evidence. Indeed, the mere existence of an adverse incentive can shape these debates, particularly when coupled with the apparent lack of progress in eliminating poverty in the United States.[32] Thus, a considerable amount of momentum has developed around policies that emphasize "personal responsibility." These include expanding the EITC, increasing child support enforcement, and making nascent efforts to enhance asset accumulation (through individual development accounts and Social Security privatization proposals). An interesting question associated with these developments is whether changes in administrative culture that emphasize work and personal responsibility can mitigate undesirable program incentives.

Second, we are unlikely to see a diminution of support for social insurance and the disabled. Leading Social Security privatization proposals now have "hold harmless" provisions in which families can choose to stay with the current, unchanged system. Social insurance continues to be popular. There seems to be little effort to reduce benefits targeted toward the disabled.

Third, large deficits throughout the 1980s and early 1990s led to budget rules that made it extremely difficult to initiate or expand existing spending programs. One result of this change was to put selected items into the tax code, where policy initiatives can be characterized as "tax cuts" rather than new spending. In the second half of the 1990s, we experienced a remarkable change in the fiscal condition of the federal government. With changes in fiscal climate, new debates will develop over the evolution of antipoverty spending.

We have clear *opinions* about how this debate should proceed. We start with a set of facts. First, between 1971 and 1998, total spending on all cash and in-kind transfers (excluding social insurance and Medicaid) ranged between 1.3 and 1.9 percent of GDP. It is currently 1.52 percent of GDP, 0.24 percentage points lower than the fraction of GDP devoted to antipoverty spending in 1975, the last year of the Ford administration. As shown in figure 6.3, poverty rates were somewhat lower in 1975 than they were in 1998. Second, as discussed earlier, the $19.6 billion estimate of the poverty gap for April 1997 is nearly identical to estimates of the poverty gap in 1979 and 1984, after adjusting for the overall size of the population (Weinberg 1985, 1987). Third, as shown in table 6.2, the aggregate effect of the tax and transfer system on the poverty gap appears almost unchanged between 1979 and 1997: policy continues to reduce the poverty gap by roughly 73 percent. Although there have been changes in the antipoverty policy mix and changes in the composition of the poor, there has been very little change in aggregate antipoverty spending over the last thirty years (other than Medicaid, which has experienced the same rapid price inflation as other health-related activities), little change in the apparent antipoverty effectiveness of that spending, and little diminution of the poverty problem.

We offer three possible reasons for the apparent stability of antipoverty spending over the last twenty to thirty years in the face of persistent and high poverty rates, at least by international standards. First, the public and consequently politicians are indifferent about the poverty problem. Second, there was a perception that policymakers, analysts, and poverty experts had little sense of what works and considerable concern that some well-intentioned policies may have counterproductive consequences. Third, the fiscal policy climate over much of the previous thirty years has been difficult.

The 1970s were characterized by "stagflation," the simultaneous problem of high rates of unemployment and inflation. Economic policy in the 1980s and early 1990s was dominated by enormous, seemingly perpetual budget deficits.

The public opinion results shown in figure 6.2 contradict the first possible explanation—public indifference—for persistent poverty. The majority of Americans, when asked their opinion, consistently state that we are spending too little on assisting the poor. We think the second explanation—the perception that we do not really know what is effective antipoverty policy—has been very important. There was widespread lack of support for the old AFDC program, and other than possibly Head Start, there were no large-scale programs over which there was widespread approval and evidence of success. The third explanation describes forces—first stagflation and then the fiscal straitjacket of deficits—that have also had an enormous impact on antipoverty policy.

Several fundamental factors underlying the second and third of these explanations have changed. Current budget estimates forecast government surpluses in the future. There is a large and growing body of evidence that work-based antipoverty strategies, like the Earned Income Tax Credit, the Canadian Self-Sufficiency Project, the Wisconsin TANF program (W-2) and the Minnesota Family Investment Program, can have positive effects on labor market participation and increase the post-tax incomes of families in poverty. Essential features of these policies are the requirement that people work to receive benefits and the idea that, at least to a point, greater work effort increases the disposable income available to families. Although these programs are not a panacea, there is consistent evidence from a number of studies with different methodological approaches that increasing the returns to work increases labor force participation. We would like to see programs like these aggressively expanded and evaluated.

At the same time, the safety net needs shoring up. Benefits (and consequently, living standards) are lower now than they have been for decades for families with children who, for one reason or another, are unable or unwilling to work. TANF now has a five-year time limit. Food stamp participation by eligible families has plummeted in recent years. The consequences of these two changes have not yet been widely visible, since few families have reached time limits and the economy has been very strong. In contrast to observed political reality, we think that ensuring a minimal standard of living for families and individuals, with or without children, is a federal func-

Table 6A.1 Social Insurance and Antipoverty Spending by Program, 1970 to 1999 (in Millions of Constant 1999 Dollars)

| | Social Insurance | | | | | Means-Tested Transfers | | | | | | | | |
Year	OASI	Medicare	UI	Workers' Compensation	DI	Medicaid	SSI	AFDC-TANF	EITC	Food Stamps	Housing Aid	School Food Programs	WIC	Head Start
1970	$123,645	$30,696	$13,199	—	$13,169	$20,834	$12,620	$17,527	—	$2,360	$2,164	$2,917	—	$1,398
1971	137,447	32,394	23,649	—	15,459	25,405	13,188	22,530	—	6,264	3,151	3,785	—	1,481
1972	147,955	35,153	26,465	$16,186	17,828	33,615	13,519	26,122	—	7,163	4,607	4,647	—	1,500
1973	171,632	35,568	18,337	—	21,455	34,187	12,825	26,277	—	7,998	6,195	5,022	—	1,504
1974	174,433	38,348	18,887	—	23,327	34,567	17,728	24,909	—	9,186	6,164	5,102	$35	1,365
1975	181,182	45,775	39,656	—	26,055	39,132	18,202	26,049	$3,871	13,580	6,587	5,950	277	1,251
1976	192,363	52,056	54,357	—	29,180	42,877	17,761	28,331	3,792	15,596	7,332	6,331	418	1,291
1977	201,000	59,242	39,398	23,725	31,514	47,019	17,336	28,558	3,098	13,930	8,267	6,625	704	1,306
1978	205,317	64,422	27,816	—	31,973	48,419	16,742	27,062	2,678	13,132	9,401	6,817	970	1,597
1979	207,805	66,888	22,574	—	31,457	49,923	16,235	24,735	4,709	14,871	9,877	7,098	1,206	1,560
1980	212,443	70,833	34,147	—	31,211	52,125	16,055	24,173	4,015	17,632	11,080	7,313	1,471	1,486
1981	226,889	77,871	33,575	—	31,522	55,674	15,749	23,542	3,504	19,482	12,575	6,797	1,597	1,501
1982	239,628	87,052	38,461	28,325	29,933	56,016	15,505	22,197	3,064	17,624	13,922	5,659	1,638	1,574
1983	250,071	95,123	49,458	—	29,322	58,471	15,730	22,760	3,002	18,654	15,805	5,961	1,883	1,525
1984	253,126	100,488	27,289	—	28,702	60,241	16,631	23,043	2,626	17,151	16,112	5,957	2,226	1,597
1985	259,128	110,546	24,532	—	29,164	63,353	17,125	22,575	3,233	16,635	17,654	5,845	2,306	1,664
1986	268,817	115,377	24,526	—	30,169	68,177	18,364	23,158	3,054	16,121	17,391	6,017	2,406	1,581

Year	OASI	Medicare	UI	Workers' comp.	DI	Medicaid	AFDC-TANF	Food stamps	EITC	SSI	Housing aid	WIC	School food	Head Start
1987	269,323	119,729	22,695	40,062	30,082	72,365	18,993	23,938	4,973	15,399	16,540	6,083	2,463	1,658
1988	275,351	123,474	19,210	43,239	30,549	76,211	20,244	23,466	8,303	15,701	17,923	5,958	2,531	1,699
1989	279,427	129,725	18,729	46,105	30,731	82,287	19,760	23,163	8,861	15,720	18,781	5,779	2,567	1,659
1990	284,244	139,843	21,833	48,740	31,616	92,404	20,516	23,631	9,614	18,083	19,733	5,671	2,705	1,978
1991	294,102	144,048	30,717	51,582	33,836	111,946	21,992	24,899	13,584	21,209	20,743	6,029	2,815	2,387
1992	302,729	157,048	43,935	54,229	36,919	140,317	25,243	26,421	15,470	24,825	22,296	6,377	3,083	2,615
1993	308,762	168,166	40,884	52,263	39,889	151,929	27,870	25,694	17,913	25,372	24,669	6,499	3,258	3,201
1994	313,772	182,669	29,723	50,122	42,400	160,984	31,800	25,627	23,725	25,573	26,759	6,737	3,563	3,739
1995	318,860	196,877	23,290	47,414	44,709	170,967	30,744	24,085	28,374	24,885	29,995	6,805	3,762	3,863
1996	321,641	206,255	23,979	44,666	46,905	171,976	30,187	21,673	30,607	23,829	28,308	6,891	3,924	3,790
1997	328,333	216,736	21,378	42,129	47,394	180,935	30,571	18,038	31,800	20,293	28,746	7,043	3,990	4,132
1998	334,035	225,574	20,019	42,614	49,237	188,792	29,073	14,191	31,959	17,262	29,320	7,275	3,976	4,443
1999	334,437	233,400	21,356	—	51,331	—	29,749	13,449	31,900	15,766	27,645	7,379	3,939	4,660

Sources: OASI: *www.ssa.gov/OACT/STATS/table4a5.html*, total annual benefits paid from OASI trust fund (all types of benefits); Medicare: U.S. House of Representatives 1998, table 2.1, total Medicare outlays; UI: US Budget Historical Tables, table 8.5, available at *w3.access.gpo.gov/usbudget/fy2002/hist.htm*, outlays for mandatory and related programs: unemployment compensation; workers' compensation: *www.nasi.org/WorkComp/1997-98Data/wc97-98rpt.htm* and *www.nasi.org/WorkComp/1994-95Data/wc94rpt.htm*, cash plus medical benefits; DI: *www.ssa.gov/OACT/STATS/table4a6.html*, annual benefits paid from DI trust fund, by type of benefit, 1957 to 1999; Medicaid: U.S. House of Representatives 1998, table 15.13, history of Medicaid program costs (total dollars, federal plus state); SSI: U.S. House of Representatives 1998, table 7.4, total federal and state benefit payments; AFDC-TANF: 1970 to 1996: U.S. House of Representatives, 1998, table 7.4, total federal and state benefits (excludes administrative costs); 1997 and 1998: *aspe.hhs.gov/hsp/indicators00/T_A_3.PDF* (cash and work-based activities only); 1999: *www.acf.dhhs.gov/programs/ofs/data.iq499/table-f.htm*; EITC: Hotz and Scholz (2000); food stamps: *www.fns.usda.gov/pd/fssummar.htm*, total benefits; housing aid: US Budget Historical Tables, table 8.7, available at *w3.access.gpo.gov/usbudget/fy2002/hist.htm*, outlays for discretionary programs: housing assistance; school food programs: *www.fns.usda.gov/pd/cncosts.htm*, total federal costs (sum of cash payments and commodity costs); WIC: *www.fns.usda.gov/pd/wisummary.htm*, total program costs (food, Nutrition Services and Administrative Costs, includes administrative, preventative services, nutrition education); Head Start: 1999 Head Start fact sheet, at *www2.acf.dhhs.gov/programs/hsb/research/99 hsfs.htm*, congressional appropriations.

Table 6A.2 Recipients by Program, 1970 to 1999 (Thousands)

| | Social Insurance | | | | | | Means-Tested Transfers | | | | | | | |
Year	OASI	Medicare	UI	DI	Medicaid	SSI	AFDC-TANF[a]	EITC	Food Stamps[a]	Housing Aid	School Breakfast[b]	School Lunch[b]	WIC	Head Start
1970	23,035	20,491	—	2,666	—	3,098	8,466	—	4,340	—	—	22,400	—	477
1971	23,888	20,915	—	2,930	—	3,172	10,241	—	9,368	—	800	24,100	—	398
1972	24,804	21,332	—	3,271	17,606	3,182	10,947	—	11,109	—	1,040	24,400	—	379
1973	25,953	23,545	—	3,561	19,622	3,173	10,949	—	12,166	—	1,190	24,700	—	379
1974	26,664	24,201	—	3,912	21,462	3,996	10,864	—	12,862	—	1,370	24,600	88	353
1975	27,509	24,959	—	4,352	22,007	4,314	11,165	6,215	17,064	—	1,820	24,900	344	349
1976	28,212	25,663	—	4,624	22,815	4,236	11,386	6,473	18,549	—	2,200	25,600	520	349
1977	29,069	26,458	—	4,854	22,832	4,238	11,130	5,627	17,077	3,164	2,490	26,200	848	333
1978	29,584	27,164	—	4,869	21,965	4,217	10,672	5,192	16,001	3,482	2,800	26,700	1,181	391
1979	30,236	27,859	—	4,777	21,520	4,150	10,318	7,135	17,653	3,749	3,320	27,000	1,483	388
1980	30,844	28,478	—	4,682	21,605	4,142	10,597	6,954	21,082	4,007	3,600	26,600	1,914	376
1981	31,474	29,010	—	4,456	21,980	4,019	11,160	6,717	22,430	4,139	3,810	25,800	2,119	387
1982	31,804	29,494	—	3,973	21,603	3,858	10,431	6,395	21,717	4,411	3,320	22,900	2,189	396
1983	32,221	30,026	—	3,813	21,554	3,901	10,659	7,368	21,625	4,668	3,360	23,000	2,537	415
1984	32,617	30,455	—	3,822	21,607	4,029	10,866	6,376	20,854	4,920	3,430	23,400	3,045	442
1985	33,120	31,083	—	3,907	21,814	4,138	10,813	7,432	19,899	5,080	3,440	23,600	3,138	452
1986	33,690	31,750	—	3,993	22,515	4,269	10,997	7,156	19,429	5,174	3,500	23,700	3,312	452
1987	34,126	32,411	7,500	4,045	23,109	4,385	11,065	8,738	19,113	5,301	3,610	23,900	3,429	447

Year													
1988	34,539	32,980	6,800	4,074	22,907	4,464	10,920	11,148	18,645	5,213	3,680	24,200	3,593	448
1989	35,012	33,579	7,000	4,129	23,511	4,593	10,934	11,696	18,806	5,295	3,810	24,300	4,118	451
1990	35,559	34,203	8,100	4,266	25,255	4,817	11,460	12,542	20,067	5,390	4,070	24,100	4,517	548
1991	36,074	34,870	10,200	4,513	28,280	5,118	12,592	13,665	22,624	5,465	4,440	24,200	4,893	583
1992	36,614	35,579	9,600	4,890	30,926	5,566	13,625	14,097	25,406	5,506	4,920	24,600	5,403	621
1993	36,990	36,306	7,800	5,254	33,432	5,984	14,143	15,117	26,982	5,625	5,360	24,900	5,921	714
1994	37,298	36,935	8,200	5,584	35,053	6,296	14,226	19,017	27,468	5,714	5,830	25,300	6,477	740
1995	37,529	37,535	7,900	5,858	36,282	6,514	13,652	19,334	26,619	5,792	6,320	25,700	6,894	751
1996	37,664	38,064	8,100	6,072	36,118	6,614	12,649	19,464	25,542	5,748	6,580	25,900	7,188	752
1997	37,818	38,445	7,500	6,153	34,872	6,140	10,936	19,490	22,858	5,751	6,920	26,300	7,407	794
1998	37,911	38,825	7,300	6,335	40,649	6,161	8,770	19,516	19,788	—	7,150	26,600	7,367	822
1999	38,072	—	7,400	6,524	—	6,221	7,203	19,542	18,188	—	7,400	27,000	7,311	—

Sources: OASI: *www.ssa.gov/OACT/STATS/OASDIbenies.html,* number of beneficiaries receiving benefits on December 31, 1970, through 1999; Medicare: HCFA, Center for Medicaid and State Operations, Health Care Financing Administration-2082 report, Medicare aged and disabled enrollees as of July 1, Hospital Insurance and/or Supplemental Medical Insurance; UI: U.S. House of Representatives 1998, table 4.1, unemployment compensation program data, beneficiaries, and *UI Outlook,* at *www.itsc.state.md.us/ui manage/Outlook/mid2000/sum.htm#hist;* workers' compensation: national beneficiary information not available; DI: *www.ssa.gov/OACT/STATS/OASDIbenies.html,* number of beneficiaries receiving benefits on December 31, 1970, through 1999; Medicaid: U.S. House of Representatives 1998, table 15.14, unduplicated number of recipients, all eligibility categories, and *www.hcfa.gov/medicaid/mstats.htm;* SSI: U.S. House of Representatives 1998, table 3.20, number of persons receiving federally administered SSI payments; AFDC-TANF: *www.acf.dhhs.gov/news/stats/3697.htm,* U.S. welfare caseloads information, recipients and families, 1936 to 1999, average monthly recipients; EITC: Hotz and Scholz (2000); food stamps: *www.frs.usda.gov/pd/fssummar.htm,* average monthly participation; housing aid: U.S. House of Representatives 1998, table 15.26, total households receiving assistance by type of subsidy: total assisted renters and homeowners; school food programs: *www.frs.usda.gov/pd/slsummar.htm, www.frs.usda.gov/pd/sbsummar.htm,* average participation (nine-month average); WIC: *www.frs.usda.gov/pd/wisummary.htm,* total participation; Head Start: 1999 Head Start fact sheet, at *www2.acf.dhhs.gov/programs/hsb/research/99 hsfs.htm,* enrollment.

a. Average monthly number of recipients.

b. Average monthly number of recipients, based on nine-month averages.

tion. But if states are ceded this authority, they must be given the resources to care for their most disadvantaged citizens who are unable or unwilling to work. So far the TANF block grants appear large enough to meet that challenge. Ensuring that this remains so during periods of weaker economic performance is imperative.

Major changes in poverty will not be achieved by simply reshuffling the 1.5 percent of GDP that is spent on cash and in-kind means-tested transfers (again, excluding Medicaid). If antipoverty spending as a fraction of GDP simply increased to its highest fraction over the last thirty years, 1.91 percent, there would be an additional $34 billion for new initiatives. Considerably more could reasonably be spent. The money could sensibly be used in two ways: expanding and exporting innovative, successful, state-level welfare reforms and providing new funding sources for ancillary child care and health insurance benefits that increase the attractiveness of work; and augmenting the safety net by increasing food stamp outreach, expanding rental housing subsidies, and ensuring that states have sufficient resources to handle families affected by TANF time limits in the way they see fit.[33]

In this time of unprecedented prosperity, a failure to make new investments will result in large numbers of children growing up in households unable to afford adequate food, housing, shelter, and activities that can enrich their lives. The consequences could be dire: an erosion of social cohesion, a waste of the human capital of a portion of our citizenry, and the moral discomfort of condoning poverty amid affluence.

CHAPTER 7

Welfare Policy in Transition: Redefining the Social Contract for Poor Citizen Families With Children and for Immigrants

LADONNA A. PAVETTI

The Personal Responsibility and Work Opportunity Reconciliation Act (PRWORA) of 1996 significantly altered the safety net for poor families. The most significant changes in the social contract have affected poor citizen families with children in need of cash assistance and noncitizen legal immigrants. For both groups, PRWORA changed the conditions under which individuals who were previously eligible for various forms of government assistance can continue to receive assistance.

Citizens who were entitled to receive cash assistance through the Aid to Families with Dependent Children (AFDC) program for as long as they met the eligibility criteria now must apply for such assistance through a state or local Temporary Assistance for Needy Families (TANF) program. To be eligible for TANF, families must comply with work mandates and satisfy other requirements as well, such as cooperating with all efforts to obtain child support from noncustodial parents. Some families are prohibited from receiving TANF-funded benefits, such as teen mothers who are not living with a parent or in a supervised living arrangement or are not attending school and parents who have been convicted of some drug felonies.[1] Families who do qualify are subject to time limits on the number of months they can receive assistance. Noncitizen legal immigrants have faced even more sweeping changes; some have been barred from receiving needs-based government assistance, including cash assistance, Medicaid, and food stamps.

The magnitude of these changes is reflected in the substantial reduction in the cash assistance caseload. In 1994, AFDC reached its peak: an average of 14.2 million individuals, most of them children, received benefits. By August 1996, when PRWORA was signed into law, the number of AFDC recipients had already declined by 14 percent to 12.2 million recipients (U.S. De-

229

partment of Health and Human Services 1998a). Between August 1996 and June 2000, cash assistance recipients declined by an additional 52 percent, to just 5.8 million recipients (U.S. Department of Health and Human Services 1999b). Caseload reductions ranged from a low of 22 percent in Rhode Island to a high of 90 percent in Wyoming (see table 7.1). In June 2000, only 2.1 percent of the U.S. population received cash assistance, the lowest fraction since 1964 (U.S. Department of Health and Human Services 1999c).

Because this decline in participation in the nation's primary safety net programs for poor families and children has occurred during a period of unprecedented economic growth, it is impossible to attribute all of the decline to welfare reform. However, several recent studies indicate that the policy changes resulting from PRWORA and reforms put into place prior to the passage of PRWORA have played a significant role in reducing the number of families receiving cash assistance (Blank and Schmidt 2001).

In this chapter, I start with a discussion of how the safety net was altered for poor families with children and then discuss the changes affecting immigrants. For both groups, I present the context for reform, the federal policy framework created through PRWORA, and any relevant subsequent legislation, and I describe how this framework has been implemented at the state or local level. I assess how individuals and families are faring under this new social contract and conclude with a discussion of the future of the social contract and my views on how the safety net can be strengthened.

Creating a New Social Contract for Poor Families with Children Seeking Income Support

The Context for Reform

PRWORA represented the culmination of nearly three decades of a social policy debate over how AFDC should be reformed. At the heart of this debate were differing views over how broad the coverage should be and how the program should balance the dual goals of providing a cash safety net for families with children and requiring families to work or look for work. The large number of single-parent families also raised important questions about how to require absent parents to make financial contributions to the care of their children. A separate, but equally important, debate focused on how responsibility for policy development and program oversight should be allocated between the federal and state governments.

Table 7.1   AFDC-TANF Recipients Prior to and After the Passage of PRWORA (Thousands)

State	Monthly Average 1994	August 1996	June 2000	Change 1994 to 1996	Change August 1996 to June 2000
United States	14,032	12,077	5,816	−13.9%	−51.8%
Alabama	132	101	55	−23.8	−45.2
Alaska	38	36	24	−6.5	−31.4
Arizona	201	169	84	−15.6	−50.3
Arkansas	69	56	28	−18.7	−50.1
California	2,639	2,582	1,272	−2.2	−50.7
Colorado	119	96	28	−19.5	−71.1
Connecticut	166	159	64	−4.0	−60.1
Delaware	28	24	17	−14.0	−27.0
District of Columbia	74	69	46	−6.4	−33.7
Florida	669	534	136	−20.3	−74.5
Georgia	394	330	135	−16.1	−59.0
Hawaii	62	66	43	7.2	−35.6
Idaho	23	22	2	−6.1	−89.1
Illinois	712	643	259	−9.8	−59.7
Indiana	216	143	97	−34.0	−32.1
Iowa	110	86	52	−21.9	−39.5
Kansas	87	64	37	−26.4	−42.7
Kentucky	208	172	86	−17.2	−50.2
Louisiana	248	228	79	−8.1	−65.4
Maine	64	54	27	−16.2	−49.3
Maryland	222	194	71	−12.5	−63.5
Massachusetts	307	226	94	−26.4	−58.5
Michigan	666	502	195	−24.5	−61.2
Minnesota	187	170	117	−9.2	−31.3
Mississippi	159	124	34	−22.0	−72.7
Missouri	264	223	123	−15.4	−44.8
Montana	35	29	14	−16.5	−51.9
Nebraska	45	39	27	−14.8	−30.4
Nevada	38	34	16	−10.1	−51.9
New Hampshire	30	23	14	−24.3	−39.6
New Jersey	335	276	125	−17.8	−54.6
New Mexico	102	100	68	−2.5	−31.8
New York	1,255	1,144	693	−8.8	−39.4
North Carolina	333	267	96	−19.6	−64.0
North Dakota	17	13	9	−20.3	−33.9

(Table continues on p. 232.)

Table 7.1   (continued)

State	Monthly Average 1994	August 1996	June 2000	Change 1994 to 1996	Change August 1996 to June 2000
Ohio	685	549	238	−19.7	−56.6
Oklahoma	131	96	33	−26.7	−65.7
Oregon	114	78	42	−31.2	−46.0
Pennsylvania	620	531	233	−14.3	−56.1
Rhode Island	63	57	44	−9.9	−21.8
South Carolina	140	114	36	−18.2	−68.7
South Dakota	19	16	7	−16.8	−57.8
Tennessee	300	255	144	−15.0	−43.6
Texas	788	649	343	−17.6	−47.1
Utah	50	39	24	−21.7	−38.3
Vermont	28	24	16	−12.5	−36.2
Virginia	195	153	68	−21.5	−55.5
Washington	292	269	146	−7.7	−45.6
West Virginia	114	89	32	−22.1	−64.6
Wisconsin	226	149	38	−34.2	−74.4
Wyoming	16	11	1	−30.5	−90.3

Sources: U.S. Department of Health and Human Services (1998a, 1999b).

Efforts to encourage recipients to leave welfare for work were first made at the federal level in the late 1960s when caseloads surged in the aftermath of the War on Poverty (see figure 7.1). However, the most sweeping changes were implemented much later, primarily in the early 1990s, and were initiated at the state, rather than federal, level. Together, these ongoing debates and programmatic changes paved the way for a major transformation in our cash safety net.

FEDERAL CONTROL OVER RULES AND STATE CONTROL OVER BEN-EFIT LEVELS   AFDC provided a safety net from 1936 to 1996 for poor families with little or no income. The program guaranteed ongoing income support to needy children who were deprived of parental support or care because their father or mother was continuously absent from the home, incapacitated, deceased, or unemployed. Eligibility was based on a number of factors, the most important being the family's income and assets (for example, a car or a savings account). As long as families met the eligibility criteria, they were entitled to receive benefits; a family could not be denied benefits because a state or county had already spent all of the funds they had allocated to the program for the year.

The rules guiding eligibility for AFDC were determined at the federal level; however, states were free to determine the maximum amount of benefits a family could receive. At the time PRWORA was implemented, benefits for one parent and two children with no income ranged from a low of $120 in Mississippi (11.5 percent of the poverty line), to a high of $923 in Alaska (70.8 percent of the poverty line). Over time the value of cash benefits began to erode substantially. Between 1970 and 1996, across the fifty states and the District of Columbia, the real value of the cash benefits provided to families declined by 42 percent (see table 7.2).

INCOME MAINTENANCE OR WORK PREPARATION AND SUPPORT? Although AFDC was initially created solely as an income maintenance program, over time the program sought to provide income support while promoting work. However, there was never consensus on how to do this, or on the extent to which working families should also be eligible for assistance

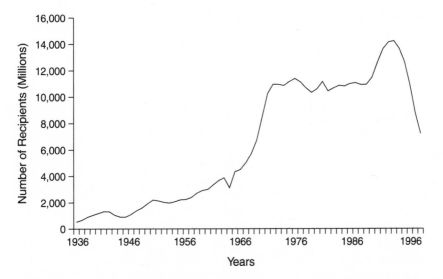

Figure 7.1 Cash Assistance Recipients over Time (*Source:* U.S. Department of Health and Human Services 1998a.)

Table 7.2 AFDC Maximum Benefit for a Family of Three, 1996

State	Maximum Monthly AFDC Benefit Level[a]	Maximum AFDC Benefit as a Percentage of Poverty[b]	Change in Real Value of Cash Benefits 1970 to 1996
Alabama	$164	15.7%	−35%
Alaska	923	70.8	−28
Arizona	347	33.3	−35
Arkansas	204	19.6	−41
California	596	58.2	−16
Colorado	356	40.4	−44
Connecticut	636	61.0	−42
Delaware	338	32.4	−46
District of Columbia	415	40.3	−45
Florida	303	29.1	−32
Georgia	280	26.8	−33
Hawaii (non-exempt)	712	59.4	−19
Idaho	317	30.4	−61
Illinois	377	36.1	−58
Indiana	288	27.6	−38
Iowa	426	40.8	−45
Kansas	429	41.1	−50
Kentucky	262	25.1	−54
Louisiana	190	18.2	−44
Maine	418	40.1	−20
Maryland	373	35.8	−41
Massachusetts (non-exempt)	565	54.2	−46
Michigan (Wayne County)	459	44.0	−46
Minnesota	532	51.0	−47
Mississippi	120	11.5	−45
Missouri	292	28.0	−28
Montana	438	40.7	−46
Nebraska	364	34.9	−45
Nevada	348	33.4	−26
New Hampshire	550	52.7	−46
New Jersey	424	40.7	−64
New Mexico	389	37.3	−33
New York (New York City)	703	55.3	−47
North Carolina	272	26.1	−52
North Dakota	431	41.3	−48

Table 7.2   (continued)

State	Maximum Monthly AFDC Benefit Level[a]	Maximum AFDC Benefit as a Percentage of Poverty[b]	Change in Real Value of Cash Benefits 1970 to 1996
Ohio	341	32.7	−45
Oklahoma	307	29.4	−48
Oregon	460	44.1	−36
Pennsylvania	421	40.4	−59
Rhode Island	554	53.1	−38
South Carolina	200	19.2	−39
South Dakota	430	41.2	−58
Tennessee	185	17.7	−57
Texas	188	18.0	−67
Utah	416	40.8	−37
Vermont	633	62.9	−37
Virginia	354	33.9	−60
Washington	546	52.3	−46
West Virginia	253	24.3	−43
Wisconsin	517	49.6	−28
Wyoming	360	34.5	−57
Median state	415	40.8	—

Source: U.S. Department of Health and Human Services (1998a).

a. Data are for July 1996 (USDHHS 1998a, table 5.7).

b. Data are for January 1996 (USDHHS 1998a, table 5.9).

(cash and services). Efforts to promote work included a mix of financial incentives and more service-oriented approaches to help recipients find paid employment.

The first significant policy initiatives to foster work among welfare recipients were initiated in 1967 when Congress enacted "earned income disregards" and created the Work Incentive (WIN) program. Prior to 1967, women who went to work lost one dollar of their AFDC benefits for every dollar they earned. With the earned income disregard in place, the first thirty dollars and one-third of a recipient's remaining earnings were disregarded when her eligibility for benefits was determined.

Under the WIN program, all employable recipients over the age of sixteen, and with no children under the age of six, were required to sign up for job training or work as a condition of eligibility. However, owing to limited resources, the program never amounted to more than a work registration requirement in most places.

The next major work-related reforms did not occur until 1981, when Congress significantly restricted the work incentive provisions that had been implemented in 1967, permitted states to require work in exchange for their benefits, and gave states the option to restructure their WIN programs by becoming WIN demonstration states. These changes had both short- and long-term effects on the relationship between welfare and work. The earned income disregards were limited to a four-month period, reducing the number of working families who could qualify for benefits. This had the effect of creating a program that served primarily nonworking families during a time of heightened concern about long-term welfare dependence. By 1989 the percentage of cases with earned income had dropped to 9 percent, down from 13 percent in 1979 (U.S. House of Representatives 1992).

State efforts to redesign their WIN programs had a substantial long-term impact on the design of welfare-to-work policies. Under the WIN demonstration option, states were given broad flexibility to design employment and training programs that would best meet the needs of their recipient populations. Rigorous evaluations of these efforts established that a variety of welfare-to-work programs had at least a modest impact on increasing the labor force participation and/or wages of welfare recipients (Gueron and Pauly 1991).

The positive results from these efforts, along with research by Mary Jo Bane and David Ellwood (1983) establishing that a large percentage of the AFDC caseload would spend long periods of time on the AFDC rolls, laid the groundwork for the passage of the Family Support Act (FSA) of 1988. This welfare reform legislation was celebrated by many as a major step forward in an effort to help women on welfare achieve self-sufficiency. Unlike earlier reforms, the FSA focused primarily on a service strategy to increase employment among welfare recipients.

The Job Opportunities and Basic Skills (JOBS) program, the cornerstone of this legislation, differed from earlier welfare-to-work programs in several important ways. First, it targeted substantial employment and training resources at recipients with a high probability of long-term welfare receipt—teenage mothers, young high school dropouts, and recipients with no recent labor market experience. Second, it emphasized placement in education and training programs to help welfare recipients increase their human capital. Third, it provided resources to fund transitional child care and Medicaid to support families in their transition to employment. Fourth, it extended mandatory participation to families whose youngest child was over the age of three or age one, at state option. Finally, recipients who were required to participate in JOBS but failed to do so could be sanctioned for noncompliance by removing the adult's needs from the grant for a minimum period of time or until compliance (U.S. House of Representatives 1998a).

By the time AFDC and JOBS were eliminated in 1996, work requirements had become a more important, but still small, aspect of AFDC. In fiscal year 1996, the last full year the programs operated, a total of $18.1 billion in state and federal funds was spent to provide cash assistance to recipients. In stark contrast, $1 billion in federal funds was authorized for JOBS; however, states spent only $684.5 million. (States were required to spend about an additional $76 million to draw down these funds, bringing total state and federal spending for the JOBS program to roughly $760 million.) In fiscal year 1995, only 11 percent of adult AFDC recipients participated in JOBS at the level expected of them. Although 42.6 percent of adult AFDC recipients were required to participate in JOBS, only 33.9 percent of all mandatory recipients were active in the program, and only 26.8 percent participated for a sufficient number of hours to meet the minimum federal participation requirement (U.S. House of Representatives 1998a).

EXPERIMENTATION AT THE STATE LEVEL   By the time PRWORA was enacted, the U.S. Department of Health and Human Services (HHS) had approved waivers from federal law allowing forty-three states to implement welfare reform demonstration projects (U.S. Department of Health and Human Services 1997). Waivers allowed states to deviate from federal law and implement changes they believed would better serve the needs of poor families. Most waivers were aimed at shifting the focus of AFDC from providing ongoing income maintenance to mandating and supporting recipients' efforts to become self-sufficient.

At the time PRWORA was passed, only a few states were operating welfare reform demonstration programs for their entire caseload. Nonetheless, because states had already been experimenting with significant policy changes through waivers, in many respects the policy changes enacted through PRWORA are best characterized as accelerating these changes rather than imposing an entirely new policy framework on the states.

Still, the passage of PRWORA signaled a break with the past—a program that provided income support was eliminated and replaced by a program that emphasized employment. A program with a rigid set of federally prescribed rules and regulations was replaced with a flexible block grant to the states. When AFDC and JOBS were eliminated, states were free to develop entirely new approaches to providing assistance to poor families with children. However, the legacy of AFDC and JOBS is still evident in most states' TANF programs.

The Federal Policy Framework After Reform

TANF was created to achieve four key goals: to provide assistance to needy families; to end the dependence of needy families by promoting job preparation, work, and marriage; to prevent and reduce out-of-wedlock pregnancies; and to encourage the formation and maintenance of two-parent families.

Although these goals cover several broad areas, the federal policy framework for TANF emphasizes the creation of a work-based assistance system through several key elements: explicit work participation requirements and penalties for noncompliance; time limits; a narrow definition of "assistance"; and continued eligibility for other safety net programs, especially Medicaid but also food stamps. In addition, PRWORA strengthened the emphasis on requiring both parents to contribute to the support of their children, primarily by strengthening child support cooperation and collection requirements.

TANF WORK REQUIREMENTS AND PENALTIES FOR NONCOMPLIANCE   PRWORA imposes explicit and steadily increasing work participation rate goals on the states; failure to meet them can result in substantial financial penalties that increase with repeated failure to meet performance expectations. Mandatory participation in work and work-related activities is expected of all families, except those with a child under the age of one if the state chooses to exempt such families from this requirement.

The share of the caseload required to participate in program activities and the intensity of participation increases over time. In fiscal year 1997, states were required to have 25 percent of recipient families participating in work activities for a minimum of twenty hours per week; by fiscal year 2002, these requirements will increase to 50 percent of the caseload working a minimum of thirty hours per week. A state's participation rate can be reduced if its AFDC-TANF caseload declines, as long as the reduction is not based on changes in the eligibility criteria for benefits. The participation rate reduction for a year is the number of percentage points the caseload has been reduced since 1995.

PRWORA specifies which recipients must be engaged in work activities and defines what constitutes participation. In contrast to JOBS, which emphasized placement in long-term education and training activities, allowable activities under TANF focus on work and include activities such as unsubsidized or subsidized private- or public-sector employment, work experience, and job search and job readiness assistance for up to six weeks. Participation in education programs is limited to single household heads under the age of twenty. Other parents may participate in job skills training or education directly related to employment, a GED program, or high school only if they are already participating in work activities for twenty hours per week.

States failing to meet work participation rates are subject to a financial penalty equal to 5 percent of their TANF grant. This amount can be increased by up to two percentage points for each subsequent year of noncompliance, subject to a maximum penalty of 21 percent. HHS has the authority to enter into a corrective action plan with a state that has failed to meet its work participation requirements and can do so in lieu of levying a penalty.

Federal law also requires states to impose a pro-rata (partial) benefit reduction for families who do not satisfy work and child support enforcement compliance requirements. States have the option to impose more stringent penalties but face penalties if they do not pose at least a partial sanction on noncompliant families. The sanction must remain in place until the family complies with the requirement. States also have the option to deny Medicaid benefits to nonpregnant adults in sanctioned families, but not to the children in those families. A state may also reduce or eliminate a family's food stamp allotment for noncompliance with work requirements. If a state exercises the most stringent options available to it, a family in which the head of household is noncompliant with a work requirement could lose all of its public benefits except Medicaid coverage for the children in the household.

TIME LIMITS   AFDC provided cash assistance for as long as a family met the eligibility criteria, but PRWORA limits the extent to which states can use federal TANF block grant funds to provide assistance to a family for more than sixty months. States can exempt up to 20 percent of the caseload from this limit based on "hardship," with hardship being left to the states to define. With a few minor exceptions, all cases that include an adult are subject to the federal time limit. States are free to use TANF funds to provide supportive services to all families who reach the time limit, as long as these services are not intended to help the families meet their basic needs. And states can use their own state funds, if they choose, to provide assistance to those reaching the sixty-month limit.

A NARROW DEFINITION OF "ASSISTANCE" Implementation of TANF's work and time limit provisions rests heavily on the definition of "assistance." In particular, work participation requirements, federal time limits, child support requirements, eligibility prohibitions, and data collection requirements apply only to families who receive assistance. Since states have broad discretion to decide how to use their TANF funds, the definition of assistance is not as straightforward as it was when families were entitled to a cash grant.

Only cash and cash-like programs (vouchers, for example) that provide ongoing support to families to allow them to meet their basic needs (food, shelter, clothing, utilities), benefits conditioned on participation in work experience and other similar programs, and the supportive services provided to unemployed recipients, like child care and transportation, meet the definition of assistance. Non-assistance includes supportive services such as child care and transportation for employed families; nonrecurring assistance lasting for no more than four months; wage subsidies paid directly to an employer; the refundable portion of state Earned Income Tax Credits and supportive services that do not provide income support (such as counseling, case management, peer support, and child care information and referral) for unemployed or employed individuals. By narrowly defining assistance, HHS has made it easier for states to use TANF funds to provide services or supplemental income support to working families and to those who might not otherwise be eligible for assistance as they look for or try to maintain employment (Greenberg and Savner 1999).

CONTINUED ELIGIBILITY FOR OTHER SAFETY NET PROGRAMS PROWRA was not designed to restrict the access to other key safety net programs of poor citizen families with children. Significant changes were made to the Food Stamp Program (FSP), but these changes were targeted primar-

ily at noncitizen legal immigrants and able-bodied adults without dependents, not at citizen families with children. PRWORA also included provisions ensuring that families who had previously been eligible for Medicaid would continue to be eligible.

Regardless of the employment status of household members, households that do not include a disabled or elderly member, have an income below 130 percent of the federal poverty level, and meet asset tests and other procedural requirements are eligible for food stamps. Prior to PRWORA, most AFDC recipients were eligible for and actively participated in FSP. States have little discretion over the rules for the Food Stamp Program. Thus, there was little concern that families might be denied food stamp benefits because of the elimination of the AFDC program.

In contrast, states have considerable flexibility in determining eligibility for Medicaid. Prior to the passage of PRWORA, AFDC recipients were categorically eligible for Medicaid; they did not have to meet additional eligibility criteria. For adults, receipt of AFDC was the only real pathway to obtain Medicaid benefits. To ensure continued Medicaid eligibility, PRWORA created a new category of Medicaid eligibility; known as "Section 1931," it allows families to qualify for Medicaid based on pre–welfare reform eligibility criteria. This requirement essentially "delinked" eligibility for Medicaid from eligibility for cash assistance. Regardless of how a state shaped its TANF program, Medicaid eligibility was to be determined separately, using pre-PRWORA criteria. States were also given several new options for extending Medicaid coverage to working-poor families who were unlikely to qualify for benefits using the AFDC income and resource standards in place prior to the passage of welfare reform.

INCREASED EMPHASIS ON CHILD SUPPORT ENFORCEMENT
PRWORA significantly altered the design and structure of the child support enforcement system for both welfare recipients and nonrecipients. Broad changes include: expanded and simplified paternity establishment procedures; enhanced access to information and mass data collection through a requirement that employers report all newly hired workers within twenty days to the state child support enforcement program, which then passes them along to the Federal Registry of New Hires; and increased use of administrative processes to establish child support awards.

States must operate a child support enforcement program that meets federal guidelines in order to receive TANF funding. TANF recipients are required to assign their child support rights to the state and are required to co-operate with all efforts to collect child support. States are required to reduce a family's cash assistance grant by at least 25 percent for failure to cooperate with child support activities, and they have the option to eliminate the entire grant. PRWORA also eliminated a provision that required states to "pass through" to welfare families the first fifty dollars of child support paid on their behalf by nonresident parents. States can continue to pass through a portion of the child support collected but must pay for the disregard out of their share of child support collections. As long as states reimburse the federal government for their share of child support collections, states also can choose to pass through to a family the full amount of child support collected on its behalf.

A New Administrative Framework for Providing Cash Assistance

PRWORA granted states considerable flexibility to design new approaches to providing assistance that would allow them to achieve the purposes of the legislation. The legislation greatly reduced the federal government's role in designing and regulating the provision of assistance. The greater decision-making role that states were given was accompanied by a more flexible, but fixed, funding stream. Instead of maintaining a federal-state cost-sharing arrangement that rose and fell with actual expenditures, PRWORA provided a family assistance block grant to states to establish a TANF program and imposed the so-called maintenance of effort (MOE) requirement that they maintain their state spending at 75 to 80 percent of current levels.[2]

This block grant structure represented a significant departure from the structure of the AFDC and JOBS programs. By ending the individual entitlement to benefits, PRWORA made it possible for states to deny assistance to families even if they met all eligibility criteria. Critics of the legislation were especially concerned about how states would respond if the number of families seeking assistance from the fixed block grant increased during an economic downturn.

Block grants to the states were set at the higher level of AFDC and AFDC-related[3] spending for fiscal years 1994 and 1995 or the 1992 to 1994 average. The size of a state's block grant reflected three elements: the number of people receiving assistance during this period; the rate at which the federal government matched the state's AFDC expenditures; and the state's past generosity. Thus, even though the number of families receiving cash assistance in Kentucky and Maryland in August 1996 was almost identical (71,300 and 70,700 families, respectively), Maryland's block grant was 26 percent higher than Kentucky's (see table 7.3). In addition, because Maryland had historically spent more on its AFDC program, it was required to continue to do so—Maryland's MOE requirement was 2.6 times greater than Kentucky's. Assuming that both states continued to assist the same number of families as they had in August 1996, Kentucky had an average of $291 ($212 in federal and $79 in state funds) to spend per family, whereas Maryland had $479 ($270 in federal and $209 in state funds) (U.S. House of Representatives 1998a).

All TANF and MOE funds must be used to accomplish one of TANF's four purposes, but states have considerable flexibility to decide how they will spend their TANF and MOE dollars, with fewer constraints on spending MOE dollars. States also have the option to transfer a total of 30 percent of TANF funds to their social services block grant (SSBG) programs and/or the child care and development block grant (CCDBG) programs. When funds are transferred to these programs, they are not subject to TANF requirements. Funds transferred to the SSBG program must be targeted to families with incomes below 200 percent of the poverty line; otherwise, the rules of the programs to which the funds are transferred apply (U.S. Department of Health and Human Services 1999c).

Because the purposes for which federal TANF and MOE funds can be used are broad, states have many options for how they use these funds. They can continue to provide cash assistance and employment-related services, but they can also provide a broader array of services. For example, they can use the funds to provide services through the child welfare system or to provide services and/or income supplements to working families (Sweeney et al. 2000). They can use TANF and MOE funds to fill gaps in the availability of affordable housing or health insurance coverage or to address the needs of specific populations, such as parents with disabilities, legal immigrants, victims of domestic violence, and low-income noncustodial parents (Sard and Kubell 2000). Importantly, states need not establish consistent eligibility criteria for each program or service provided. They can target employment-related services, such as job retention services to working-poor families with incomes below the poverty line (or some other state-defined standard), or they can target services for at-risk youth to a much broader pool of young

Table 7.3   Annual State Family Assistance Grants and State Maintenance of Effort Requirements

State	AFDC Caseload (Thousands of Families) August 1996	Federal Family Assistance (TANF) Grant (Thousands of Dollars)	State MOE Requirement (75 Percent Level) (Thousands of Dollars)	Minimum Available Funding per Family per Month[a]
Alabama	41.0	$93,315	$39,214	$269
Alaska	12.2	63,609	48,942	769
Arizona	62.4	222,420	95,028	424
Arkansas	22.1	56,733	20,839	293
California	880.4	3,733,818	2,732,406	612
Colorado	34.5	136,057	82,871	529
Connecticut	57.3	266,788	183,421	655
Delaware	10.6	32,291	21,771	425
District of Columbia	25.4	92,610	70,449	535
Florida	209.9	562,340	370,919	371
Georgia	123.3	330,742	173,369	341
Hawaii	21.9	98,905	72,981	654
Idaho	8.6	31,938	13,679	442
Illinois	220.3	585,057	429,021	384
Indiana	51.4	206,799	113,525	519
Iowa	31.6	131,525	61,963	510
Kansas	23.8	101,931	61,750	573
Kentucky	71.3	181,288	67,418	291
Louisiana	67.5	163,972	55,415	271
Maine	20.0	78,121	37,778	483
Maryland	70.7	229,098	176,965	479
Massachusetts	84.7	459,371	358,948	805
Michigan	170.0	775,353	468,518	610
Minnesota	57.7	267,985	179,745	647
Mississippi	46.4	86,768	21,724	195
Missouri	80.1	217,052	120,121	351
Montana	10.1	45,534	15,689	505
Nebraska	14.1	58,029	28,971	514
Nevada	13.7	43,977	25,489	423
New Hampshire	9.1	38,521	32,115	647
New Jersey	108.4	404,035	303,956	544
New Mexico	33.4	126,103	37,450	408
New York	418.3	2,442,931	1,710,795	828

Table 7.3   (continued)

State	AFDC Caseload (Thousands of Families) August 1996	Federal Family Assistance (TANF) Grant (Thousands of Dollars)	State MOE Requirement (75 Percent Level) (Thousands of Dollars)	Minimum Available Funding per Family per Month[a]
North Carolina	110.1	302,240	154,176	345
North Dakota	4.8	26,400	9,069	616
Ohio	204.2	727,968	390,551	456
Oklahoma	36.0	148,014	61,250	484
Oregon	29.9	167,925	92,255	725
Pennsylvania	186.3	719,499	407,126	504
Rhode Island	20.7	95,022	60,367	626
South Carolina	44.1	99,968	35,839	257
South Dakota	5.8	21,894	8,774	441
Tennessee	97.2	191,524	82,810	235
Texas	243.5	486,257	235,725	247
Utah	14.2	76,829	25,291	599
Vermont	8.8	47,353	25,653	691
Virginia	61.9	158,285	128,173	386
Washington	97.5	404,332	272,061	578
West Virginia	37.0	110,176	32,701	322
Wisconsin	51.9	318,188	169,229	783
Wyoming	4.3	21,781	10,665	629
United States	4370.4	16,488,671	10,434,960	513

Source: U.S. House of Representatives 1998a.

a. Assumes caseload remains at the August 1996 level.

people. One important constraint is that TANF funds cannot be used to provide medical services, except for prepregnancy family planning services (U.S. Department of Health and Human Services 1999d).

State Policy Choices

Although they have considerable flexibility, states have primarily shifted during the early stages of the implementation of TANF to a short-term, work-oriented assistance system. As these programs become more established and states become more comfortable with the considerable flexibility they have been given, the focus of these efforts is likely to broaden. If this happens, it will become increasingly difficult to compare state and local TANF programs using a consistent framework. In the short term, however, key state policy choices have revolved around how to restructure cash assistance programs, mandate work, impose time limits on the receipt of assistance, and support families in their transition to employment.

MAINTENANCE AND EXPANSION OF CASH ASSISTANCE PAYMENTS
Although states now have the option to determine eligibility for cash assistance differently than they did under AFDC, or to provide services instead of cash assistance, nearly all states have maintained a cash benefit structure and benefit levels for nonworking families that are comparable to those that were in place prior to 1996. Most states have expanded eligibility to working families, resulting in a larger share of employed families receiving cash assistance than prior to TANF.

These choices contradict what some experts predicted. A chief criticism of the TANF block grant was that states would engage in a "race to the bottom"—states lowering their cash benefits so as to not become a magnet for needy families from other states (Peterson 1995; Chernick and McGuire 1999). There also was concern that states would eliminate the entitlement to benefits, denying benefits to some families who requested them.

In contrast to these expectations, the majority of states (thirty-three of them) have opted to include explicit language stating that cash assistance benefits will be provided to all families who are eligible in their state policies. Only seventeen states have language explicitly stating that there is no entitlement to cash assistance (State Policy Documentation Project 2000a).

Only Idaho and Wisconsin have implemented benefit structures that differ greatly from their former AFDC programs. Both states shifted to a flat grant: all families with no earnings receive the same amount regardless of household size. In Wisconsin, the grant amount was increased for most families, while in Idaho it was reduced.

The most common state change was to extend eligibility to more working families. All states except Wisconsin disregard a portion of a family's earnings when determining eligibility. Most states have made the earned income disregard more generous than it was under AFDC rules (see table 7.4). In thirty-seven states, during the first month of employment, the TANF earnings eligibility limit is higher than the AFDC limit. After a year of employment, it is higher in forty-three states. Eight states lowered the earnings eli-

gibility limit during the first few months of employment but expand
limit during later months of employment, providing families with lo\._ _
comes with a longer transition period. In several states, families are eligible
for benefits until their income reaches or exceeds the poverty line (State
Policy Documentation Project 2000a).

MANDATING "WORK FIRST" The federal work participation requirements were intended to encourage states to shift away from placing recipients in education and training programs and toward promoting "work first"
models that emphasize quick labor market entry. PRWORA did, however,
provide states with the flexibility to continue to place some recipients in vocational training programs. Although a few states have taken advantage of
this flexibility, most have shifted almost entirely to a "work first" approach
built on a philosophy that any job is a good job. Most program efforts are
geared toward helping recipients look for jobs for which they are currently
qualified (Brown 1997).

In most states, recipients must look for work long before the twenty-four
months specified in federal law. Twenty-one states now require *applicants* for
assistance to participate in a job search or other work-related activity as a
condition of eligibility (see table 7.5). In most remaining states, participation
is expected either soon after an application is approved or when an application is reconsidered (usually every twelve months or less).

The combination of a strong economy, job search programs that emphasize immediate employment, and policies promoting work has resulted in
large caseload reductions that have made it possible for many states to meet
their work participation requirements primarily through the pro-rata reduction in the participation rate (see table 7.5).[4] In fiscal year 1999, states
were required to have 35 percent of all families participating in work activities, less any caseload reduction credit. Because of large caseload declines,
twenty-three states were not required to have any, and only two states were
required to have 20 percent or more of their TANF caseload participating in
work activities (U.S. Department of Health and Human Services 2000a).

MORE STRINGENT SANCTIONS THAN REQUIRED BY FEDERAL LAW
Greater work participation expectations have resulted in a much greater reliance on more stringent enforcement mechanisms than was the case with
previous reforms. In particular, financial penalties for noncompliance (sanctions) have become central features of most TANF programs. Sanctions are

Table 7.4 Comparison of Maximum AFDC and TANF Benefit Levels and Earning Eligibility Limits

State	TANF Maximum Cash Grant for a Family of Three	Relationship to 1996 AFDC Grant Level	Earning Eligibility Limit: First Month of Earnings	Relationship to AFDC Earning Eligibility Limit (First Month)	Earning Eligibility Limit: Thirteenth Month of Earnings	Relationship to AFDC Earning Eligibility Limit (Thirteenth Month)
Alabama	$164	No change	Unlimited	Higher	$205	Lower
Alaska	923	No change	$1,767	Higher	1,587	Higher
Arizona	347	No change	586	Lower	586	Higher
Arkansas	204	No change	558	Higher	558	Higher
California	626	Increase	1,447	Higher	1447	Higher
Colorado	356	No change	752	No change	511	No change
Connecticut	543	No change	1,138	Higher	1138	Higher
Delaware	338	No change	1,400	Higher	943	Higher
District of Columbia	379	Decrease	858	Higher	858	Higher
Florida	303	No change	806	Higher	806	Higher
Georgia	280	No change	756	No change	514	No change
Hawaii (non-exempt)	570	Decrease	1,641	Higher	1,363	Higher
Idaho	276	Decrease	625	Higher	625	Higher
Illinois	377	No change	1,131	Higher	1,131	Higher
Indiana	288	No change	1,138	Higher	1,138	Higher
Iowa	426	No change	1,065	Higher	1,065	Higher
Kansas	403	No change	762	Higher	762	Higher
Kentucky	262	No change	Unlimited	Higher	646	Higher
Louisiana	190	No change	1,210	Higher	310	Higher
Maine	461	Increase	1,023	Higher	1,023	Higher
Maryland	399	Increase	539	Lower	539	Higher
Massachusetts	565	No change	1,045	Higher	1,045	Higher

Michigan	459	No change	774	Higher	774	Higher
Minnesota	532	No change	1,311	Higher	1,311	Higher
Mississippi	170	Increase	Unlimited	Higher	458	No change
Missouri	292	No change	558	No change	382	No change
Montana	468	Increase	815	Higher	815	Higher
Nebraska	364	No change	669	Lower	669	Higher
Nevada	348	No change	Unlimited	Higher	438	No change
New Hampshire	550	No change	1,100	Higher	1,100	Higher
New Jersey	424	No change	Unlimited	Higher	848	Higher
New Mexico	439	Increase	1,128	Higher	1,128	Higher
New York	577	No change	1,138	Higher	1,138	Higher
North Carolina	272	No change	936	No change	634	No change
North Dakota	457	No change	784	Higher	1,014	Higher
Ohio	362	Increase	974	Higher	974	Higher
Oklahoma	292	Decrease	704	Higher	704	Higher
Oregon	460	No change	616	Lower	616	Higher
Pennsylvania	403	No change	806	Higher	806	Higher
Rhode Island	554	No change	1,278	Higher	1,278	Higher
South Carolina	201	No change	1,136	Higher	668	Higher
South Dakota	430	No change	628	Lower	628	Higher
Tennessee	232	Increase	921	Higher	921	Higher
Texas	197	Increase	402	No change	278	No change
Utah	451	Increase	1,002	Higher	1,002	Higher
Vermont	656	Increase	973	Lower	973	Higher
Virginia	291	No change	1,157	Higher	1,157	Higher
Washington	546	No change	1,092	Higher	1,092	Higher
West Virginia	303	Increase	422	Lower	422	Higher
Wisconsin	673	Increase	673	Lower	673	Higher
Wyoming	340	Decrease	540	Lower	540	Lower

Source: State Policy Documentation Project (2000a).

Table 7.5 Work Requirements and Work Participation Rates

State	Work Requirement at Application	All Family Work Participation Rates	
		Rate	Adjusted Standard[a]
Alabama	Y	37.4	0.0%
Alaska	N	46.0	16.8
Arizona	N	32.1	0.0
Arkansas	Y	23.7	6.0
California	N	42.2	8.5
Colorado	N	36.4	0.0
Connecticut	N	47.4	19.7
Delaware	N	24.9	0.0
District of Columbia	Y	26.7	13.9
Florida	Y	31.6	0.0
Georgia	Y	17.6	0.0
Hawaii	N	41.1	0.0
Idaho	Y	43.7	0.0
Illinois	Y	60.4	6.1
Indiana	Y	33.3	0.0
Iowa	N	54.8	4.7
Kansas	Y	57.3	3.9
Kentucky	N	38.1	5.8
Louisiana	N	29.4	0.0
Maine	N	54.9	5.9
Maryland	Y	11.2	7.2
Massachusetts	Y	27.8	0.9
Michigan	Y	43.8	0.0
Minnesota	N	36.9	13.7
Mississippi	N	27.0	0.0
Missouri	Y	28.2	2.2
Montana	N	92.3	0.0
Nebraska	N	34.7	19.7
Nevada	Y	34.8	1.1
New Hampshire	Y	29.9	0.0
New Jersey	Y	30.3	7.1
New Mexico	N	27.6	0.0
New York	N	36.3	8.3
North Carolina	N	16.0	0.0
North Dakota	N	31.7	0.8
Ohio	N	53.7	1.4

Table 7.5 (continued)

State	Work Requirement at Application	All Family Work Participation Rates	
		Rate	Adjusted Standard[a]
Oklahoma	Y	42.9	0.0
Oregon	N	96.7	0.0
Pennsylvania	N	16.2	0.9
Rhode Island	N	28.8	22.0
South Carolina	Y	44.7	6.7
South Dakota	N	46.5	1.6
Tennessee	N	41.1	23.1
Texas	N	27.3	0.0
Utah	N	44.0	2.2
Vermont[b]	Y	—	—
Virginia	N	41.1	0.0
Washington	N	40.3	12.9
West Virginia	N	25.6	0.0
Wisconsin	Y	80.1	0.0
Wyoming	Y	57.7	0.0

Sources: State Policy Documentation Project. 2000a; U.S. Department of Health and Human Services 2000a.

a. The work participation rate standard before the application of the state's caseload.

b. Vermont claims that waiver inconsistencies exempt all cases from participation rates.

designed to demonstrate to clients that there are consequences for not following program rules. Thirty-seven states have chosen to implement "full-family" sanctions for noncompliance with work or other personal responsibility requirements (see table 7.6). A full-family sanction makes the entire family ineligible to receive cash assistance. In fifteen of these states, a full-family sanction is imposed immediately, while in twenty-two states the grant is initially reduced to send a warning signal to the family that cooperation is expected. Only six states still use the sanctions that were in place under the JOBS program. The remaining ten states that have not implemented full-family sanctions have strengthened penalties for noncompliance by increasing the financial penalty or providing assistance to families only in the form of vendor payments. In nearly all types of sanctions cases, the sanction remains in effect until compliance is achieved, although the definition of

Table 7.6   Sanction Policies for Noncompliance with Work Requirements

State	Type of Sanction	Effect on Food Stamp Benefit	Adult Loses Medicaid Eligibility
Alabama	Gradual full-family	Reduced 100 percent	Y
Alaska	Partial	Partial reduction	N
Arizona	Gradual full-family	Partial reduction initially[a]	N
Arkansas	Partial	Partial reduction	N
California	Partial	Partial reduction	N
Colorado	Gradual full-family	Partial reduction	N
Connecticut	Gradual full-family	Partial reduction	N
Delaware	Gradual full-family	Reduced 100 percent	N
District of Columbia	Partial	Partial reduction	N
Florida	Immediate full-family	Reduced 100 percent	N
Georgia	Gradual full-family	Reduced 100 percent	N
Hawaii	Immediate full-family	Partial reduction	N
Idaho	Immediate full-family	Partial reduction	Y
Illinois	Gradual full-family	Partial reduction	N
Indiana	Partial	Partial reduction	Y
Iowa	Immediate full-family	Partial reduction initially[b]	N
Kansas	Immediate full-family	Reduced 100 percent	Y
Kentucky	Gradual full-family	Partial reduction	N
Louisiana	Gradual full-family	Reduced 100 percent	Y
Maine	Partial	Partial reduction	N
Maryland	Immediate full-family	Partial reduction	N
Massachusetts	Gradual full-family	Reduced 100 percent	N
Michigan	Gradual full-family	Partial reduction	Y
Minnesota	Partial	Partial reduction	N
Mississippi	Immediate full-family	Partial reduction initially[b]	Y
Missouri	Partial	Partial reduction	N
Montana	Partial	Partial reduction	N
Nebraska	Immediate full-family	Partial reduction initially[b]	Y
Nevada	Gradual full-family	Partial reduction	Y
New Hampshire	Partial	Partial reduction	N
New Jersey	Gradual full-family	Reduced 100 percent	N
New Mexico	Gradual full-family	Partial reduction	Y
New York	Partial	Partial reduction	N
North Carolina	Gradual full-family	Partial reduction	N
North Dakota	Gradual full-family	Reduced 100 percent	N
Ohio	Immediate full-family	Reduced 100 percent	Y
Oklahoma	Immediate full-family	Reduced 100 percent	N

Table 7.6 (continued)

State	Type of Sanction	Effect on Food Stamp Benefit	Adult Loses Medicaid Eligibility
Oregon	Gradual full-family	Partial reduction	N
Pennsylvania	Gradual full-family	Partial reduction	N
Rhode Island	Partial	Partial reduction	N
South Carolina	Immediate full-family	Partial reduction	Y
South Dakota	Gradual full-family	Reduced 100 percent	N
Tennessee	Immediate full-family	Partial reduction	N
Texas	Partial	Reduced 100 percent	N
Utah	Gradual full-family	Reduced 100 percent	N
Vermont	Gradual full-family	Partial reduction	N
Virginia	Immediate full-family	Reduced 100 percent	N
Washington	Partial	Partial reduction	N
West Virginia	Gradual full-family	Partial reduction	N
Wisconsin	Immediate full-family	Partial reduction	N
Wyoming	Immediate full-family	Partial reduction	Y

Sources: State Policy Documentation Project (2000b, table 8); U.S. General Accounting Office 2000; Pavetti and Bloom 2001.

a. Reduced 100 percent on third instance of noncompliance.

b. Reduced 100 percent for repeated or prolonged noncompliance.

what constitutes compliance varies from state to state. In seven states (Delaware, Georgia, Idaho, Mississippi, Nevada, Pennsylvania, and Wisconsin), continued or repeated noncompliance may result in a lifetime bar from receiving cash assistance (Pavetti and Bloom 2001).

To increase the severity of a sanction, states also can eliminate a noncompliant adult's food stamp benefits and eligibility for Medicaid. A total of nineteen states have chosen to eliminate a family's food stamp benefit if the household head does not comply with work requirements. Fifteen of them eliminate food stamps whenever a sanction is imposed; four do so after repeated or prolonged compliance (U.S. General Accounting Office 2000). Twelve states render the noncompliant adult ineligible for Medicaid benefits (State Policy Documentation Project 2000b, table 8).

Available evidence on the implementation of sanctions suggests that many families have lost benefits owing to sanctions, although there does appear to be considerable variation across the states.[5] Only a few studies look at *rates* of sanctioning. However, those that did find high rates of sanction-

ing, ranging from 26 to 45 percent of families subject to the work requirement (Pavetti and Bloom 2001). Because the largest states are not among
those that have implemented a full-family sanction, more than half of all
TANF recipients are not subject to them.

A RANGE OF APPROACHES TO TIME LIMITS   TANF's time limits offer
a distinctly different approach to reforming the welfare system. In deciding how to structure their time limit policies, states face three key design
choices: the length of the time limit, the period of the time limit, and the
consequence of reaching the time limit. All else being equal, the shorter the
time limit, the more likely that recipients will reach it. "Fixed-period" time
limits restrict recipients to a maximum number of months within a longer
calendar period (for example, twenty-four months within any sixty-month
period). "Lifetime" time limits restrict recipients to a maximum number of
months of benefits in their lifetime. Under a "termination" time limit, the
entire cash assistance case is closed when the family reaches the time limit.
Under a benefit reduction time limit, the adult is removed from the grant
calculation when the family reaches the limit, resulting in a lower benefit
amount (Pavetti and Bloom 2001).

As of early 1999, six states had implemented a lifetime termination time
limit of less than sixty months; eleven had set a fixed-period termination
time limit of less than sixty months; twenty-seven had set a lifetime termination limit of sixty months; and seven had gone with a benefit reduction
time limit (see table 7.7). As is the case with sanction policies, states with the
largest caseloads have less restrictive policies. For example, California, New
York, Texas, and Michigan account for 45 percent of the national assistance
caseload. With the exception of New York, all of these states either have no
time limit or have only a benefit reduction time limit. New York has a sixty-
month termination limit, but families who reach that point will be eligible
for vouchers or other restrictive payments in the same amount as a welfare
grant.

The length of the time limit and the consequence of reaching it do not
fully characterize a state's approach to time limits, primarily because states
also have the option to implement extensions to and exemptions from the
time limit. Extensions allow families to continue to receive benefits once
they reach the time limit under criteria specified by the state or locality.
For example, Connecticut grants renewable six-month extensions to clients

who make a good-faith effort to find employment but have family income below the welfare payment standard when they reach the time limit, or at any point thereafter. Since few states have had clients reach their time limit, it remains to be seen how expansive or limited these extensions may be. States also have the option to exempt families from the time limit: no clock is ticking while they receive assistance. The most common exemptions are for families with a disabled household head or other family member (State Policy Documentation Project 1999).

Over time several factors will shape the size and composition of the families who reach a time limit. Of particular importance are a state's welfare grant level, earned income disregard policy, work requirement, use of full-family sanctions, and exemption policies. In states with higher benefit levels and generous income disregards, many working families are likely to be affected. In states that impose significant numbers of full-family sanctions, the total number of families affected by the time limit will be reduced because some families who might have been affected by it will have already lost their benefits owing to noncompliance with program requirements.

INCREASED EMPHASIS ON WORK SUPPORTS   The emphasis on supporting families' efforts to find employment is most evident in the dramatic increases in child care spending. As cash assistance caseloads have declined, many states have shifted resources from cash grants to child care funding. In the first two quarters of fiscal year 1999, states spent $248 million of federal TANF funds and over $578 million of their own funds for child care. In addition, states transferred $736 million in TANF funds to the child care block grant to provide child care assistance to working-poor families (U.S. Department of Health and Human Services 1998b). Although child care funding has increased, in some states the increase in spending for child care has not kept pace with the demand, leaving substantial gaps in coverage.

Besides child care, another significant barrier to employment for many families leaving welfare is transportation. The flexibility provided to states makes it possible for them to use federal TANF funds or their state MOE dollars to provide transportation subsidies directly to program participants or to address systemic transportation issues. States or localities can address transportation issues in a variety of ways, including: contracting for shuttles, buses, and car pools; purchasing vans, shuttles, and minibuses; purchasing rider slots, passes, or vouchers; facilitating the donation and repair of older

Table 7.7   State Time Limit Policies

State	Type of Time Limit	Action at the End of the Time Limit	Length of the Time Limit (Months)	Date First Families Reach the Limit
Alabama	Lifetime	Termination	60	December 2001
Alaska	Lifetime	Termination	60	July 2002
Arizona	Fixed-period	Reduction	24 in 60	November 1997
Arkansas	Lifetime	Termination	24	July 2000
California	Lifetime	Reduction	60	January 2003
Colorado	Lifetime	Termination	60	July 2002
Connecticut	Lifetime	Termination	21	November 1997
Delaware	Fixed-period	Termination	48 on, 96 off	October 1999
District of Columbia	Lifetime	Termination	60	March 2002
Florida	Fixed-period	Termination	24 or 36 in 60	October 1998
Georgia	Lifetime	Termination	48	January 2001
Hawaii	Lifetime	Termination	60	December 2001
Idaho	Lifetime	Termination	24	July 1999
Illinois	Lifetime	Termination	60	July 2002
Indiana	Lifetime	Reduction	24	August 1997
Iowa	Lifetime	Termination	60	January 2002
Kansas	Lifetime	Termination	60	October 2001
Kentucky	Lifetime	Termination	60	November 2001
Louisiana	Fixed-period	Termination	24 in 60	January 1999
Maine	Lifetime	Reduction	60	November 2001
Maryland	Lifetime	Reduction	60	January 2002
Massachusetts	Fixed-period	Termination	24 in 60	December 1998
Michigan	No time limit	—	—	—
Minnesota	Lifetime	Termination	60	July 2002
Mississippi	Lifetime	Termination	60	October 2001

State	Type	Action	Limit	Date
Missouri	Lifetime	Termination	60	July 2002
Montana	Lifetime	Termination	60	February 2002
Nebraska	Fixed-period	Termination	24 in 48	December 1998
Nevada	Fixed-period	Termination	24 on, 12 off	January 2000
New Hampshire	Lifetime	Termination	60	October 2001
New Jersey	Lifetime	Termination	60	April 2002
New Mexico	Lifetime	Termination	60	July 2002
New York	Lifetime	Termination	60	December 2001
North Carolina	Fixed-period	Termination	24 on, 36 off	August 1998
North Dakota	Lifetime	Termination	60	July 2002
Ohio	Fixed-period	Termination	36 on, 24 off	October 2000
Oklahoma	Lifetime	Termination	60	October 2001
Oregon	Fixed-period	Termination	24 in 84	July 1998
Pennsylvania	Lifetime	Termination	60	March 2002
Rhode Island	Lifetime	Reduction	60	May 2002
South Carolina	Fixed-period	Termination	24 in 120	October 1998
South Dakota	Lifetime	Termination	60	December 2001
Tennessee	Fixed-period	Termination	18 on, 3 off	April 1998
Texas	Fixed-period	Reduction	24 or 36 on, 24 off	January 1998
Utah	Lifetime	Termination	36	January 2000
Vermont	No time limit	—	—	—
Virginia	Fixed-period	Termination	24 on, 24 off	October 1999
Washington	Lifetime	Termination	60	August 2002
West Virginia	Lifetime	Termination	60	January 2002
Wisconsin	Lifetime	Termination	60	October 2001
Wyoming	Lifetime	Termination	60	January 1999

Source: State Policy Documentation Project (1999).

vehicles; providing loans to eligible individuals to lease or purchase vehicles; and making onetime or short-term payments for repairs or maintenance (Kaplan 1998).

Creating a New Infrastructure to Support Welfare Reform

PRWORA also has given states and localities considerable flexibility to decide how to administer their programs. For example, the state could have the agency historically responsible for management of AFDC and JOBS administer the TANF program, or it could delegate this responsibility to another agency, such as the Department of Labor or another agency that is part of the workforce development system. It could also decide to develop state policies that would be implemented in all local offices, or it could allow counties or other local governments to develop their own policies. State and local welfare offices also were given the option to turn over full operation of their TANF programs to a private-sector entity and to contract directly with faith-based organizations to provide services.

States have made a wide range of choices about their infrastructure for supporting the transition to a work-based assistance system. Some continue to rely on the pre-1996 infrastructure, while others have shifted more responsibility to the workforce development system or to a broad range of private-sector organizations. Regardless of whether a state created an entirely new infrastructure or modified or maintained its current one, all welfare offices had to develop strategies for making employment a more integral part of their assistance programs.

CHANGING THE CULTURE OF THE WELFARE OFFICE   Historically, the primary work of local welfare offices was determining eligibility for benefits. High-performing offices were those that provided benefits accurately and in a timely manner. Because the JOBS program reached a relatively small share of the caseload, its existence never changed the primary focus of the welfare office. In contrast, the shift to a work-oriented temporary assistance system has required welfare offices to retrain eligibility workers and provide them with the skills to perform tasks that they had not performed in the past. It also has required that offices send a new message to both workers and clients. AFDC's message was that the agency would support families as long as they met the eligibility criteria. TANF's message, however, is that the agency is there to help families gain a foothold in the labor market so that they can eventually make it on their own.

DEVELOPING NEW ADMINISTRATIVE ARRANGEMENTS Broadly speaking, states have adopted one of four different administrative arrangements to implement their TANF programs (Pavetti et al. 2000). Under the most common structure, the welfare office acts as the sole administrative agency and has responsibility for determining eligibility for assistance and managing all work-related activities. In a modified version, the welfare office shares administrative responsibility with an agency from the workforce development system, with the welfare office determining eligibility for cash assistance and the workforce development system developing and managing all employment and training activities. In a third arrangement, administrative responsibility is shared between the welfare office and a newly created community-based entity. The final arrangement involves a merger between the welfare and workforce development systems; responsibility for determining eligibility for assistance and the management of employment and training activities (including those outside of the TANF system) are housed within one agency, generally a redefined workforce development agency. Regardless of the choice of administrative structure, most local TANF agencies work with intermediaries—organizations that act as brokers between the welfare system and employers—to help clients find employment.

CHANGING RELATIONSHIPS BETWEEN STATE ADMINISTRATIVE ENTITIES AND LOCAL WELFARE OFFICES The majority of states operated their AFDC program through a state policy and administrative framework; some, including several with the largest caseloads, operated their programs through a state-supervised, county-administered system. Regardless of the nature of the state and local relationship, except when demonstration projects were implemented, all local areas within a state operated under the same policies. The primary difference between state-administered and state-supervised systems was in the amount of local flexibility granted to administer the programs and define staff roles and responsibilities. With the implementation of TANF, several states (such as Colorado, North Carolina, and Ohio) have provided local welfare offices with substantial flexibility to develop their own TANF policies. As state-administered systems begin to provide local offices with more discretion, the distinction between state-administered and state-supervised, county-administered welfare systems is becoming blurred.

ADJUSTING TO NEW FINANCING ARRANGEMENTS   In the first few post-PRWORA years, the change from open-ended entitlement funding to block grants has not had as much impact on the program as one might expect. Owing to declining caseloads, states have far more money per recipient than they have had in the past. A recent General Accounting Office (1998) study found that the state TANF funds in 1997 were $4.7 billion larger than would have been the case under the AFDC formula. The median increase for states was 22 percent, with forty-six states having more money than they would have had under the AFDC formula. States also have achieved budgetary savings by reducing state expenditures on welfare programs to the 75 or 80 percent MOE required by federal law. Even with these state budgetary savings, twenty-one states are spending more per recipient than they were prior to TANF (U.S. General Accounting Office 1998).

Although states can spend their block grant funds on many services for TANF recipients or other poor families, they have been slow to do so. A number of factors may be holding them back: considerable uncertainty about how much flexibility they really have; a wariness about creating new programs that they may not be able to sustain over the long term; and start-up issues related to mounting new programs. States receive their block grant funds in an annual allocation; however, unspent funds can be saved for future use, with some restrictions.[6]

Nonetheless, preliminary evidence suggests that states are spending those funds differently: spending on cash assistance has declined while spending on child care and child development programs has increased. For example, in Wisconsin spending on cash assistance declined by 77 percent, while spending on child care and child development programs increased by 168 percent. Still, the increase in child care and child development spending accounted for only 37 percent of the reduction in spending for cash assistance (Ellwood and Boyd 2000).

Good States, Bad States?

The shift to a work-oriented assistance system has broadened the goals of state TANF programs, making it complicated to evaluate the extent to which states are providing an adequate safety net to poor families with children. Under AFDC, a state's benefit level was generally used as a measure of a state's commitment to poor families. Now that state TANF programs differ on so many dimensions, evaluating their responsiveness to the needs of poor families has become a much more complicated endeavor.

One way to assess the strength of the safety net is to examine it on three different dimensions. To what extent does it provide adequate income to families who are unable to work or need more time to make the transition to work? How well does it support families once they find employment, especially those who are only able to work part-time or at low wages? And does it balance the need to set clear expectations for parents while protecting the needs of children? Agreement on whether these three dimensions are the most important ones is not likely to be widespread. Some people might place more emphasis on providing cash assistance for nonworking families, while others might emphasize the level of support provided for working families. Others would argue that because providing government support to any families, working or nonworking, creates dependency, support should be limited, regardless of a family's circumstances or employment status. Regardless of how one defines a strong safety net, the process of classifying state approaches to providing a safety net is a complex undertaking.

Redefining the Social Contract for Immigrants

At the same time states were given more responsibility for determining how to provide assistance to working-poor families with children, they were also given more responsibility to decide what assistance should be provided to noncitizen legal immigrant families. Although states had significant experience designing safety net programs and making decisions for citizen families with children, most of them had limited experience, if any at all, in making decisions regarding benefits for immigrant families. Even though immigrants are concentrated in a few states, all states had to address these issues.

The Context for Reform

For citizen families with children, PRWORA codified into federal law changes that many states had been experimenting with for a number of years. In contrast, the immigrant provisions reflected an entirely new policy direction. This direction was influenced by concerns among some members of Congress that welfare use by immigrants was widespread, growing rapidly, and concentrated among the undeserving. Concerns were especially strong about growth in immigrant participation in the Supplemental Security Income (SSI) program: the participation of immigrants in the program doubled between 1989 and 1995. Although several groups (most notably the Urban Institute and the Center on Budget and Policy Priorities) tried to educate key congressional proponents about the program and the demographic factors contributing to this growth, they were not successful in stopping the momentum to restrict legal immigrants' access to public benefit programs (Fix, Passel, and Zimmerman 1996a).

THE SIZE AND COMPOSITION OF THE IMMIGRANT POPULATION IN THE UNITED STATES   Researchers estimate that by late 1993, the foreign-born population of the United States probably had reached 22 million—almost 10 percent of the population. The majority of the foreign-born, over 85 percent, are living in the United States legally. One-third are naturalized citizens, and nearly half are legal permanent residents (Fix and Passel 1994). PRWORA's policy changes were primarily directed at legal permanent residents—almost 11 million people. Given that illegal immigrants try to stay hidden from public view, estimating their numbers is extremely difficult. The Immigration and Naturalization Service (INS) estimated that in October 1996, 4.6 to 5.4 million undocumented residents lived in the United States (U.S. Department of Justice 1999).

Both legal and illegal immigrants are concentrated in just a few states. Of all legal immigrants entering between 1988 and 1994, 34 percent indicated that their intended destination was California. Another 44 percent were headed to one of five states: New York, Texas, Florida, Illinois, or New Jersey. Illegal immigrants are concentrated in the same states. The seven states with the largest undocumented population (California, Texas, New York, Florida, Illinois, New Jersey, and Arizona) accounted for 83 percent of the total in October 1996 (U.S. Department of Justice 1999).

IMMIGRANT PARTICIPATION IN PUBLIC BENEFIT PROGRAMS PRIOR TO THE PASSAGE OF PRWORA   In 1993 a small proportion of immigrants (6.6 percent) participated in the country's cash welfare programs—AFDC, SSI, and GA (general assistance). Among all U.S. residents, the rate of participation was somewhat higher among foreign-born residents than among natives (6.6 versus 4.9 percent). However, among the poor, immigrants were less likely to receive cash assistance than natives (16 versus 25 percent). The greatest concentration of benefit receipt among immigrants was in the Supplemental Security Income program, which is targeted to the poor elderly and disabled. In 1993 elderly immigrants made up 28 percent of elderly SSI recipients, but they accounted for only 9 percent of the total elderly population (Fix, Passel, and Zimmerman 1996b). This heavy immigrant reliance on SSI reflects a number of different factors. Many elderly immigrants who come to the United States in their later years have not worked enough to qualify for Social Security benefits. The SSI program acts as a replacement for Social Security benefits and also makes them eligible for Medicaid to cover their health expenses. The increase in immigrant reliance on SSI also reflects the growth in the immigrant population.

The Federal Policy Framework After Reform

PRWORA changed immigrant policy in several important ways. For the first time in history, eligibility for public benefits became conditional on citizenship. Second, PRWORA distinguished between immigrants who were in the country when the bill was passed on August 22, 1996, and those who arrived after that date. Third, it gave states the authority to decide whether some immigrants would be eligible for several federally funded benefit programs. Fourth, it strengthened and expanded "deeming" requirements: the expectation that family members' income will be taken into account when eligibility for public benefits is decided. Finally, it required states to report any information on illegal immigrants to the INS.

Table 7.8 outlines legal immigrants' current eligibility for public benefit programs, taking into account both changes enacted through PRWORA and subsequent revisions. As this table shows, the federal government guarantees access to public benefits only for immigrant groups that are considered especially vulnerable. Legal immigrants who were receiving SSI and those who were in the country when PRWORA was signed and became disabled later are eligible for SSI benefits. The elderly, disabled, and children who were in the United States on August 22, 1996, also are eligible for food stamps. Except for SSI recipients who remain categorically eligible for Medicaid, it is up to states to decide whether legal immigrants who were in the country on August 22, 1996, are eligible to participate in the Medicaid pro-

Table 7.8 Overview of Legal Noncitizens' Benefit Eligibility

Immigrant Status	TANF	Medicaid	Food Stamps	SSI	Title XX (SSBG)	Other Federal Means-Tested Benefits[a]	State/Local Public Benefits
Immigrants arriving before August 23, 1996							
Legal permanent residents	State option	State option, except SSI recipients			State option	Y	State option
Elderly (over sixty-five)[b]			Y	Y			
Disabled[c]			Y	Y			
Children			Y	Y			
Able-bodied adults			N[d]	—			
Refugees and asylees	Eligible for first five years	Eligible for first seven years	Eligible for first five years	Eligible for first seven years	Eligible for five years	Eligible for five years	Eligible for five years

Immigrants arriving after August 22, 1996

Legal permanent residents	Barred for five years, then state option	Barred for five years, then state option	N	N	Barred for five years	Barred for first five years; then state option	State option
Elderly							
Disabled							
Children							
Able-bodied adults							
Refugees and asylees	Eligible for first five years	Eligible for first seven years	Eligible for first five years	Eligible for first seven years	Eligible for first five years	Eligible for first five years	Eligible for first five years

Sources: Fix and Tumlin (1997); Health Policy Tracking Service (1999).

a. Programs include: emergency medical assistance, emergency disaster relief, school lunch program, child nutrition programs, public health assistance for immunizations, testing and treatment of symptoms of communicable diseases, foster care and adoption assistance, higher education, means-tested programs under the Elementary and Secondary Education Act, Head Start, and Job Training Partnership Act/Workforce Investment Act.

b. Legal immigrants over the age of sixty-five are eligible for SSI only if they were receiving SSI on August 22, 1996.

c. Those who become disabled in the future are eligible for benefits.

d. States can purchase food stamps to provide food assistance to legal immigrants.

gram. States also have the option to decide whether legal immigrants are eligible for TANF and the social services block grant (used by states to fund a variety of services, including child care and home health services).

Immigrants who have entered the country since August 22, 1996, are far more dependent on states' decisions and experience greater restrictions on their eligibility for benefits. In general, immigrants who have arrived post-PRWORA are restricted from receiving most public benefits for five years; they are barred from receiving food stamps and SSI benefits unless they accumulate ten quarters of work. States decide whether legal immigrants will be eligible for Medicaid, TANF, and SSBG after the five-year bar. For all programs, deeming applies after an immigrant has been in the United States for five years: that is, the income of the immigrant's sponsor is counted when determining eligibility for benefits. Deeming has the effect of making most legal immigrants ineligible for benefits.

The Congressional Budget Office (CBO) estimated that the largest source of federal savings resulting from PRWORA—44 percent, or $1.2 billion, in fiscal year 1997, and $23.8 billion between fiscal years 1997 and 2002—would come from the reduction in benefits to noncitizen legal immigrants. However, these estimates proved to be overstated because some benefits were restored for noncitizen legal immigrants who had been in the country prior to the signing of PRWORA. For example, the 1997 supplemental appropriation extended SSI eligibility through that fiscal year, and SSI and Medicaid benefits were later restored for disabled legal immigrants who had entered the country before August 22, 1996. In 1998 food stamp benefits were restored to immigrant children, elderly, and disabled.

STATE CHOICES States have been quite generous in their treatment of legal immigrants who were in the country when PRWORA was signed, but less so with new immigrants (see table 7.9). Among the six states with the largest numbers of immigrants, all have extended eligibility for TANF and created a state-funded food assistance program, and all except Illinois have extended eligibility for Medicaid to pre-enactment immigrants. Only California now provides a substitute for the SSI program and state-funded TANF assistance during the five-year ban for post-enactment immigrants. California and Illinois are the only two states to provide Medicaid during the five-year bar, but all of the states, except Texas, have decided to provide eligibility for Medicaid after that time period has elapsed.

Many of the substitute programs created by the states reach limited numbers of immigrants. Consequently, the social safety net for immigrants has weakened since the implementation of welfare reform. Many states target their replacement programs at limited groups, such as children or the elderly, leaving out the largest group—working-age adults. Most states also apply sponsor deeming rules. And finally, states have restricted eligibility by imposing residency requirements and mandating that immigrants apply for citizenship in order to receive assistance (Zimmerman and Tumlin 1999).

How Families Are Faring Under Welfare Reform

Although it is difficult to sort out how much of the dramatic caseload decline is due to welfare reform and how much is due to the economy and other policy changes, recent studies have found that welfare reform has played a significant role (Blank and Schmidt 2001). However, the fact that caseloads have declined provides little insight into how families are faring under welfare reform. It will be some time before sufficient information is available to examine fully the effects of welfare reform. In the interim, numerous studies provide some insights into how families are faring during the early stages of implementation. The findings from these studies are complex. Welfare reform seems to have helped some families gain a foothold in the labor market and is helping to raise their standard of living, if only by a small margin; for other families, the story is less clear. Some families who are no longer receiving welfare are not working and report little or no income; not much else is known about these families, and so it is difficult to determine whether their quality of life has declined, remained the same, or somehow improved. The rates of child support collection are still quite low; however, child support does seem to make a substantial difference for families who receive such payments. Even though it appears that many families who have left the welfare rolls—both citizen families and noncitizen legal immigrant families—should still be eligible for food stamps and Medicaid programs, many of these families are not participating in them to the degree one might expect.

Increased Employment, but at Low Wages

Some fifty "leaver" studies have examined how families who left the welfare rolls are faring. The early studies indicate that between one-half and

Table 7.9 State Immigrant Policy Choices: States with Largest Immigrant Populations

	California	Florida	Illinois	New Jersey	New York	Texas
Cash assistance						
TANF to pre-enactment immigrants	Y	Y	Y	Y	Y	Y
TANF (state-funded) during five-year bar	Y[a]	N	N	N	N	N
TANF following five-year bar	Y	Y	Y	Y	Y	N
SSI substitute program	Y	N	Y[b]	N	N	N
General assistance	Y[b]	N	Y[b]	Y[b]	Y[b]	N
Food assistance						
State-funded program for pre-enactment	Y[a]	Y[b]	Y	Y	Y[b]	Y[b]
State-funded program for post-enactment	Y[a]	N	Y[b]	N	N	N
Health care						
Medicaid to pre-enactment immigrants	Y	Y	Y	Y	Y	Y
Medicaid (state-funded) during five-year bar	Y	N	Y	N	N	N
Medicaid following five-year bar	Y	Y	Y	Y	Y	Undecided
Medicaid to certain unqualified immigrants	Y	N	N	Y	Y	N
State health insurance program	Y[b]	Y[b]	Y[b]	Y	Y	N
Naturalization initiative	Y	Y	Y	Y	Y	N

Source: Tumlin, Zimmerman, and Ost (1999).
a. Sponsor deeming applies.
b. Eligibility restricted to specific groups (for example, children).

three-fourths of parents are employed shortly after leaving the welfare rolls (Acs and Loprest 2000; Tweedie 1999), and that as many as 87 percent have been employed at some point (U.S. General Accounting Office 1999b). However, the earnings of welfare leavers are generally not sufficient to bring them up to the poverty line. Former recipients typically work more than thirty hours during the weeks in which they are employed; average reported annual earnings range from as low as $8,000 to as high as $15,144, leaving many families below the poverty line (Acs and Loprest 2000; Parrott 1998; U.S. General Accounting Office 1999b). In addition to low wages, most working recipients do not receive paid vacations, sick leave, or employer-sponsored health insurance (Parrott 1998).

For Some Families, Less Welfare and Increasing Poverty

All studies of welfare leavers have found that some leavers do not report working. Rates of non-employment are especially high among families who have left because of a sanction; studies focused on sanctioned cases have found employment ranging from only 20 to 50 percent (Tweedie 1999). So far there is limited information on how these families make ends meet and whether their disconnection from the labor market and TANF is temporary or permanent.

One study found that between 1993 and 1995 the average earnings and income of all single-mother families increased substantially. However, between 1995 and 1997 the poorest single mothers experienced a significant decline in their average disposable incomes, largely owing to sizable decreases from means-tested programs and a small decrease in earnings (Primus et al. 1999). A second study found that the poverty gap among children remained relatively constant between 1995 and 1998, after declining by 17 percent between 1993 and 1995. This stagnation occurred primarily because the children who remained poor became poorer. In addition, because fewer children received cash assistance or food stamps, these programs played a smaller role in reducing the poverty gap than they have in the past (Porter and Primus 1999).

A Modest Reduction in Child Poverty from Child Support Collections

Increased child support collections have the potential to improve the standard of living for poor single-parent families who leave welfare for work.

Since most child support collected on behalf of TANF recipients is returned to the state or federal government as reimbursement for the support they provide to families, families leaving welfare for work stand the most to gain from improved collections. In spite of concerted efforts to increase the receipt of child support, only about half of those with an order to receive it regularly receive some financial support. For those who receive it, child support is a substantial source of income. Among all children, child support accounts for 16 percent of their household's income; among poor children, child support accounts for 26 percent of their household income. Poor families who were formerly on welfare are more likely to receive child support than those who have never been on welfare, possibly owing to the child support cooperation requirements. Data from the NSAF indicate that child support reduces poverty by two percentage points, lifting about 500,000 children out of poverty; child support reduces the poverty gap by $2.5 billion, or 8 percent (Sorensen and Zibman 2000).

Declining Participation in the Food Stamp and Medicaid Programs

The number of people participating in two other key safety net programs, the food stamp and Medicaid programs, have declined substantially in recent years. Some food stamp policy changes reduced the caseload, but they do not explain the majority of the declines. The number of people receiving food stamps declined by 27 percent between fiscal year 1996 and the first half of fiscal year 1999 (Dion and Pavetti 2000). Like the decline in cash assistance caseloads, there is considerable variation among the states, ranging from 48 percent in Vermont to 5 percent in Nebraska (U.S. General Accounting Office 1999c).

Medicaid enrollment for children and their parents began to decline in 1996 for the first time in almost a decade (Ellwood and Ku 1998) and has declined steadily each year since (Ku and Bruen 1999). Between 1995 and 1997, enrollment among non-elderly, non-disabled adults and children declined by 5.3 percent nationwide. While some states witnessed increases in their Medicaid enrollment, others faced substantial declines. For example, in Oregon, Medicaid enrollment increased by 29.5 percent, while in West Virginia enrollment declined by 21 percent (Ku and Bruen 1999).

Although there are no definitive studies on the reasons for these declines, they appear to be linked, at least in part, to the implementation of welfare reform. Diversion programs that discourage families from applying for assistance, stringent work requirements, sanctions, and time limits are all likely to play a part (Dion and Pavetti 2000).

Declining Program Participation by Eligible Immigrants

Early information on noncitizen legal immigrants' receipt of public benefits indicates that the number of noncitizen families applying for and receiving TANF and Medicaid benefits in Los Angeles has declined substantially. The number of assistance applications fell by about half following welfare reform, while citizen applications remained about the same (Zimmerman and Fix 1998). These declines have occurred even though California decided to provide these benefits to noncitizen legal immigrants.

A second study that looks at national trends found that the use of public benefits among noncitizen households fell by 35 percent, compared with a 14 percent decline among citizen households. Consequently, noncitizens accounted for a disproportionately large share of the overall decline in welfare caseloads that occurred between 1994 and 1997 (Fix and Passel 1999). The researchers conducting these two studies indicate that neither naturalization nor rising incomes accounted for these declines. Other potential factors include concern about requirements that state agencies verify citizenship and immigration status and report undocumented immigrants to the INS, confusion about eligibility, and concern about becoming a "public charge."

LIMITED EVIDENCE OF SEVERE AND PERSISTENT ECONOMIC HARDSHIP   When PRWORA was enacted, opponents of the legislation expressed concern that its provisions (like sanctions and time limits) would result in large numbers of families turning to shelters and food pantries to meet their basic needs. Although some families currently on welfare and some of those who have left the welfare rolls clearly experience hardship, it does not appear to have reached the levels that some anticipated (Tweedie 1999). Because similar information was not collected prior to the implementation of welfare reform, it is impossible to determine how much of the hardship that families are currently experiencing would have occurred even in the absence of welfare reform and how much might be directly related to welfare reform. A review of selected studies of welfare leavers finds that between 9.4 and 27 percent of welfare leavers report having problems providing enough food for their families, and that 15.9 to 21.7 percent report difficulty paying utility bills (Acs and Loprest 2000).

The Challenges Ahead

The current public welfare system differs from the AFDC and JOBS programs in significant ways, and families are subject to a new social contract. States and local welfare offices have made substantial progress in shifting from a welfare system that provides ongoing income maintenance to one that helps families find employment as quickly as possible, but the transition is incomplete. Key remaining challenges include developing strategies to help the hardest-to-employ move from welfare to work; helping recipients who have found jobs retain them and advance to better ones; strengthening the safety net for working-poor families; providing more opportunities to help fathers find employment; and identifying strategies to encourage and support marriage.

Addressing the Needs of the Hard-to-Employ

Concerns about long-term welfare dependency provided the catalyst for PRWORA's dramatic changes in the purpose and structure of the safety net. However, most states have not yet focused their job search programs on the hardest-to-employ. Prior to the current round of reform, many hard-to-employ recipients were exempt from participating in welfare-to-work activities; others who were not exempt languished in a holding status because workers had neither the time nor the resources to work with them. The current resource-rich environment provides states and localities with an unprecedented opportunity to identify promising strategies for working with this group of families. However, there is little knowledge on how to help this group of families make the transition to employment, and states so far have seemed reluctant to take on the challenge of addressing some of these issues.

To address the needs of this group of families, states will need to overcome four key challenges. First, they will need to develop a programmatic framework that acknowledges the greater need for assistance among some families in making the transition to paid employment. Examples of such activities include substance abuse and mental health treatment, or job search programs that last longer than six weeks. Second, state and local welfare offices will need to forge partnerships with other agencies that have an expertise in helping families with significant employment barriers make the transition to work. Among these agencies are substance abuse treatment programs, community-based mental health centers, and vocational rehabilitation agencies. Third, the welfare offices will have to develop staff expertise in identifying recipients who need additional assistance to make the transition to employment and helping them to gain access to appropriate resources. Finally, they will need to consider options for providing long-term assistance to families who may be unable to find or maintain employment. Public-sector jobs, ongoing income support, and long-term supported work programs are among the options that program administrators might consider (Pavetti and Strong 2001).

Promoting Job Retention and Advancement

Now that many welfare recipients have made the transition from welfare to work, some welfare offices are turning their attention to developing strategies to help recipients keep their jobs or move to better jobs. About one-quarter of welfare recipients who go to work stop working within three months, and at least half are no longer working within a year (Hershey and Pavetti 1997; Rangarajan, Schochet, and Chu 1998). In addition, most parents who have left welfare for work earn low wages, and their wages increase little despite years of work. Earnings increase over time primarily because parents work more hours, not because their wages increase (Strawn and Martinson 2000). Unlike programs to help recipients find employment, programs to promote job retention and advancement are in their infancy. An experiment to extend case management services to welfare recipients who had become employed found that providing these services had a limited impact on helping recipients stay employed (Rangarajan and Novak 1999).

There is an increasing realization that strategies to promote job retention and advancement need to include options that can be integrated into programs to help recipients find employment as well as options targeted at employed recipients. Strategies for increasing job retention and advancement also may be targeted at employers. Strategies targeted at recipients include helping them move to better jobs initially and providing wage supplements and other work supports to help ease the transition to employment. Strategies targeted at workers include providing ongoing financial assistance to low-wage earners to help them make ends meet and personal support to help families cope with balancing the competing demands of parenting and working. Strategies targeted at employers include training supervisors to increase their skills at helping welfare recipients address some of the personal, family, and workplace challenges that often lead to job loss and helping employers to create career paths for the individuals who work for them.

Strengthening the Safety Net for Working-Poor Families

Even though most welfare offices have changed their cultures to emphasize the importance of work, few have made it easier for working families to gain access to the available services. Most TANF offices are open during daylight business hours only, making it very difficult for some working families to apply for the benefits to which they are entitled. For some welfare leavers, the stigma associated with participating in the program is so great that they prefer not to have any contact with the welfare office. As more families enter the paid labor market, there is likely to be an increased effort to get welfare agencies to redefine their mission and to identify specific changes they can make to address the needs of families not only while they are looking for work but also after they find employment.

One alternative is to deliver more work supports through community-based agencies or through the employment services system. A second alternative is to eliminate the cumbersome procedures for applying for some benefits, such as food stamps. A third, longer-term alternative is to identify strategies for changing the public's image of the welfare office and for changing the way welfare offices operate. Offices that acknowledge that many of their clients are working may begin to put a greater emphasis on customer service, focusing on changes such as seeing clients by appointment or instituting procedures that guarantee that clients do not spend hours waiting to apply for the benefits to which they are entitled. Finally, welfare offices may explore options for implementing some of the approaches used by the unemployment insurance system to streamline the application for benefits. In some states, nearly all unemployment insurance transactions occur over the phone.

Providing More Assistance to Noncustodial Fathers

Historically, the AFDC and JOBS programs provided assistance to single-mother families, while the child support system targeted its enforcement efforts at the absent fathers. It is becoming increasingly clear that the success of child support enforcement efforts will be limited if new opportunities are not provided to fathers to help them find and sustain employment. However, the results from the Parents' Fair Share (PFS) demonstration illustrate how difficult it may be to improve the economic circumstances of noncustodial fathers. PFS, a demonstration program implemented in seven urban areas, provided noncustodial fathers with opportunities to meet their child support obligations. In exchange for fathers' cooperation with the child support system, PFS offered services to help them find more stable and higher-paid work and become better parents. PFS was moderately successful in improving employment and earnings among the less-employable fathers—those without a high school diploma and little recent work experience. It had no effect, however, on the earnings of the more employable fathers (Martinez and Miller 2000).

Although these results are not as promising as one might hope, there is clearly a need to continue to provide employment services to noncustodial fathers. Alternative strategies that might be worth considering include offering them public-sector jobs or helping them to gain access to training programs that will help them meet the qualifications for higher-paying jobs.

Encouraging Marriage

One of the purposes of TANF is to support and encourage the creation of two-parent families. However, thus far it appears that few TANF offices have developed specific strategies aimed at achieving this goal. It is possible that some states will begin to focus resources on promoting marriage or examining existing policies and programs to determine whether they discriminate against two-parent families. These efforts are likely to take on many different forms. For example, the governor of Oklahoma proposed a statewide marriage training program that would be partially funded with TANF funds. The program would try to reduce the state's divorce rate. Some legislators in Arizona proposed spending TANF funds for marriage training, character education, and sexual abstinence programs, but the governor threatened to veto the bill (State Capitals Newsletters 2000).

At the federal level, there is interest in changing the EITC to enable more two-parent families to qualify for it. One way to restructure the credit to reduce the marriage penalty would be to base it on an individual's earnings rather than on the earnings of the household. To increase the target efficiency of the credit, eligibility could be restricted to families in which the earnings of no one individual exceed a specified threshold.

Increasing marriage rates is likely to be far more difficult and complex than increasing employment among TANF recipients. Although employment and training programs rarely produce stellar results, we have learned from a sufficient amount of experimentation what seems to work best and for whom. No such knowledge exists on how to promote marriage. In fact, there is very little information on why many poor women with children never marry. An additional hurdle is that an individual's decision to marry is perceived as a much more personal decision than his or her decision to seek employment. It has been difficult enough for some welfare workers to make the transition to promoting work; it is hard to imagine what it would take to expand the focus of welfare programs to promote marriage as well.

Conclusions

PRWORA significantly altered the safety net for poor families with children and for noncitizen legal immigrants. Poor families face a new social contract that expects able-bodied adults to work. Legal immigrants face a new social contract that expects them to become citizens as quickly as possible and expects families to assume greater responsibility for providing assistance during difficult times.

A system that once provided ongoing income maintenance to poor families with children now serves a dual purpose: providing cash assistance and helping families make the transition from welfare to work. Although states and localities had the option to create an entirely new service system, most have made incremental changes to the programs they already had in place. Over time it is likely that these programs will resemble the AFDC and JOBS programs far less than they do now.

The transition from a cash to a work-based assistance system will not be complete until states develop strategies for responding to the broad range of needs and circumstances that bring families to the welfare system for help. Families experiencing short-term crises or a disruption in employment are likely to need less assistance than families with limited skills who have experienced multiple personal and family challenges. A dilemma that most states have not yet resolved is how to create a work-based assistance system that provides families with just the amount of assistance they need to make the transition to employment.

As time limits approach, states are becoming increasingly concerned that narrowly defined "work first" programs will leave some families without a safety net when they exhaust their months on assistance. However, most states have been slow to move beyond "work first" programs and to offer alternatives to help families who remain on the TANF rolls make the transition to employment. A narrow definition of what constitutes acceptable work activities appears to be one factor that has hampered states' willingness to develop a service system that is flexible enough to respond to different needs and circumstances. States are also concerned about weakening the emphasis on work and incurring the cost of providing more extensive services to some families, especially when they do not know whether such services will have positive impacts.

Although states have made considerable progress in creating a new social contract for families with children, it is clear that the transformation of the safety net is far from complete. TANF has been implemented during extraordinary times. Low unemployment rates have made it far easier to place welfare recipients in jobs than anyone anticipated. Declining TANF caseloads and fixed levels of funding have provided states with significant resources to help families make the transition to work and to support them once they find work. However, until the country experiences a recession, no one will know whether the assistance system that is being established can be sustained over the long term.

CHAPTER 8

Health Policies for the Non-elderly Poor

JOHN MULLAHY AND BARBARA L. WOLFE

Health care reform, one of the important policy issues facing Congress, is often a topic of heated political debate. Health care ranked first among the issues that Americans believe the government should address (Harris Poll 1999), and third among the most critical issues facing the country today, according to the 1,001 respondents to the 1999 Health Confidence Survey (Employee Benefit Research Institute 1999). This chapter examines the particular problems of health care in the non-elderly poverty population. Improvements in the health of the non-elderly poor, we find, will require increased access to health care, but that access in itself will have only a limited impact in reducing the health disparities between the poor and the nonpoor.

Policymakers have begun to look at the relationship between income and health, including the U.S. Department of Health and Human Services (2000b), which recently set forth in *Healthy People 2010* two national goals:

- Increasing the quality and years of healthy life for all Americans
- Eliminating health disparities between Americans

The second objective recognizes that members of many socioeconomic groups—distinguished especially by income, education, and race—have distinctly poorer health on average than do members of other groups. These differences remain even after a variety of other factors associated with these groups are controlled for statistically.

Whether attainment of the second *Healthy People 2010* goal by the target date of 2010 is realistic, or whether the benefits associated with fully accomplishing the goal are worth the costs (Kenkel 2000), are open questions. Indisputable, however, are the data that point to significant variation in our population's health, much of it highly correlated with poverty.

This chapter summarizes the empirical evidence on the relationships between health and poverty, provides a basic overview of the health care market, and describes the U.S. health care system, emphasizing public and private insurance coverage. It then details the problems of the poor in obtaining coverage and care (many of these problems being related to the design of the system), discusses why changing the system is difficult, and offers some directions for reform.

Poor Health and Poverty

No matter how health is measured, low-income people are not as healthy as those with higher incomes. This disparity is shown in striking fashion in figure 8.1, which relates income to individuals' assessment of their own health. The negative relationship in the figure would appear even if we used

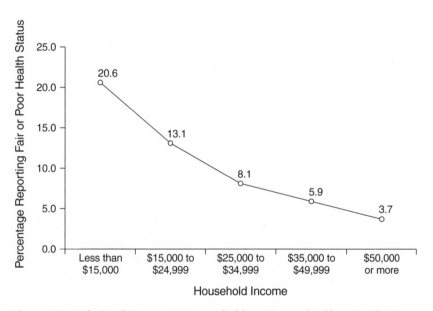

Figure 8.1 Relationship Between Household Income and Self-reported Fair or Poor Health Status, 1995 (*Source:* National Center for Health Statistics (1998, table 61).)

a variety of other health measures, such as age-adjusted mortality, the prevalence of various diseases or impairments, or unhealthy behaviors.

Poor health and poverty are strongly correlated. To some extent, poor health may cause poverty by restricting the hours an individual can work and the kinds of work he or she can perform, as well as by necessitating costly medical care and special equipment or services. On the other hand, as suggested by figure 8.2, limited resources, including lack of health insurance, the limited ability to pay the indirect and direct costs of medical care, inadequate housing, poor living conditions, and the unhealthy behavior associated with poverty, may cause health problems. Policies targeted at enhancing health, improving access to health services, and reducing unhealthy behaviors must necessarily address issues of causal direction. That is, those assessing the striking positive correlations between income and health need to acknowledge that over the life cycle, poverty may both influence health and be influenced by it. To the extent that such causal mechanisms are misunderstood, scarce resources may be squandered pursuing policies that have little or no causal impact on health.

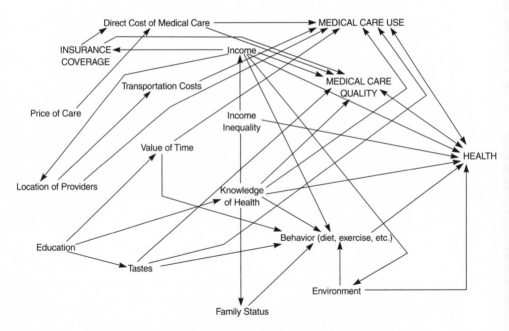

Figure 8.2 Determinants of Health (*Source:* Authors' compilation.)

Evidence of the association between poverty and poor health, however, seems clear (see figure 8.1). The National Center for Health Statistics (NCHS) (1999) reported that limitation of activity and self-reports of poor and fair health are higher among the low-income population than among those with higher incomes, and that these trends have intensified over time. In 1990, 22.9 percent of those with family incomes below $14,000 reported some limitations on activity, while 14.8 percent of those in families with incomes between $14,000 and $25,000 and 8.4 percent of those in families with more than $50,000 reported such limitations. In 1996, 26.4 percent of those with family income below $16,000 reported limitations on activity, and 15.7 percent of families with incomes between $16,000 and $25,000 reported such limitations, compared with 8.5 percent of those families with incomes of $50,000 or more (NCHS 1999, table 59). Similarly, 21.6 percent of poor white non-Hispanics reported fair or poor health in 1996, compared with 13.8 percent of the near-poor and 5.1 percent of the nonpoor. These percentages were 21.2, 12.9, and 5.2, respectively, in 1991, again suggesting some deterioration of the relative health of the lowest-income groups. Among black non-Hispanics, 26.9 percent of the poor, 16.6 percent of the near-poor, and 8.5 percent of the nonpoor reported fair or poor health in 1996. Five years earlier, these reported percentages were 24.9, 15.5, and 8.5, respectively. Only among Hispanics is there evidence of some improvement in health among all income groups and a reduction in the differential between those living in poverty and those not in poverty (NCHS 1999, table 60).

Consider some specific examples. One indicator of health, lead levels in the blood, also suggests a high correlation between poverty and poor health. The proportion of children age one to five with high levels of lead in the blood is far greater among the poor and near-poor than among children in higher-income families. Between 1988 and 1991, more than 16 percent of children in families with incomes below 130 percent of the poverty line had blood lead levels above ten micrograms per deciliter, compared with slightly more than 5 percent of children living in families with incomes at 130 to 299 percent of the poverty line, and 4 percent among children in higher-income families (U.S. Department of Health and Human Services 1998c).[1] Untreated dental caries convey a similar picture. Among young children (age two to five), untreated dental caries was reported for 28.8 percent of poor children; among children who were not poor, the percentage was 9.7 as of 1996.

From 1971 to 1974, 30.7 percent of poor young children were reported to have an untreated caries, compared with 17.5 percent of nonpoor children. Thus, from 1988 to 1994, the ratio was nearly three to one, while from 1971 to 1974, the ratio was less than two to one. The dental health of nonpoor children has improved, but the same cannot be said for poor children (NCHS 1999, table 72).

Additional evidence comes from the association between environmental pollution and health. Kenneth Chay and Michael Greenstone (1999, ii), for example, found evidence of a link between the presence of air particulates and "deaths occurring within one month and one day of birth, suggesting that fetal exposure to pollution has adverse health consequences. The estimated effects of the pollution reductions on infant birth weight provide evidence consistent with this potential pathophysiologic mechanism." Poor people living in urban areas are more likely than others to be exposed to such pollution.

Another avenue by which income and health are associated may be through neighborhood characteristics. Some researchers have asked whether neighborhood socioeconomic context is linked to individual health, apart from the individual's own income, and evidence of an association has been found (see Robert 1998, 1999), even after controlling for individual socioeconomic status. In these studies, living in a poor neighborhood is associated with poorer health and earlier death, regardless of an individual's own socioeconomic circumstances. Individual socioeconomic status, however, is found to be far more important than the neighborhood socioeconomic level.[2]

The overlap of risk factors may be especially troublesome for access to care and resulting health. Daniel Miller and Elizabeth Lin (1988), for example, studied a set of particularly vulnerable children: 158 children age seventeen days to seventeen years living in emergency shelters in the state of Washington. They reported that nearly half of these children had a wide variety of reported acute and chronic health problems.

When compared with the U.S. general pediatric population, the proportion of homeless children reported to be in "fair" or "poor" health was four times higher (13 percent vs. 3.2 percent). Thirty-five percent of the children had no health insurance, and 59 percent of the children had no regular health care provider . . . [and received] little preventive care; these children were twice as likely to lack measles immunization (21 percent vs. 9.0 percent), and twice as likely to never have had a tuberculosis skin test (48 percent vs. 27 percent). (668)

In the United States, there is a clear correlation between various measures of mental health and poverty. Individuals occupying the lowest rungs of the socioeconomic ladder are on the order of two and a half times more likely to have mental disorders than those in the highest socioeconomic group. Children in families characterized by multigenerational experiences with poverty are at extraordinary risk for the development of mental illnesses (U.S. Surgeon General 1999). The causal character of such associations is not well understood; it may be that the living circumstances of poor individuals lead to greater stress and vulnerability, and it may also be the case that mental illness is itself a determinant of reduced socioeconomic status. It is plausible that mental health is related to labor market outcomes, and some of the relevant studies in the economics literature (Ettner, Frank, and Kessler 1997; Frank and Gertler 1991; Mullahy and Sindelar 1990), based on measures of mental illness diagnosed in community surveys, have found generally negative labor market associations. Access to care in the form of appropriate mental health services is particularly problematic for the poor.

Probably the starkest tie between poverty and health is among those who are severely mentally ill and homeless. One-quarter to one-third of the adult homeless are estimated to suffer from severe mental illnesses (U.S. Department of Housing and Urban Development 1994).[3] They tend to suffer from other health problems as well, such as HIV/AIDS, resurgent tuberculosis, and alcohol abuse or dependence (U.S. Department of Housing and Urban Development 1994). About half of the homeless population have a history of alcohol abuse or dependence, and about one-third have a history of drug abuse or dependence.

Alcoholism tends to be common among only certain groups of homeless: younger members of minority groups and those with mental illness. Perhaps half of the homeless with serious mental illness also have substance abuse disorders. The rates of mental illness and mortality rates among the homeless are also about double those for comparable poor people who have a severe mental illness but are housed (Kasprow and Rosenheck 2000).

Ill health may be the cause of homelessness if the illness or disability leads to loss of income and housing. Homelessness itself can lead to malnutrition and exposure to infectious disease. But what may contribute most to the ill health of the homeless is the fact that being homeless makes medical treatment difficult. Without a permanent residence, the homeless are difficult for health care providers to contact, and living on the street or in a shelter is not conducive to rest and recuperation. Even sticking to a medication regimen may be difficult when an individual has nowhere to store the medication.

The overlap of poverty and minority social status creates additional health problems. A greater proportion of blacks than nonblacks are poor. Poor blacks seem to suffer inordinately from a number of health problems: high blood pressure; coronary heart disease; diabetes and its complications, such as blindness, kidney failure, stroke, and heart disease; and sudden infant death syndrome (SIDS).[4] The higher rate of teen out-of-wedlock births among blacks and Hispanics increases the risk of infant mortality and low birthweight, and it may also perpetuate the relationship between poverty and poor health.

Unhealthy Behavior and Poverty

Figure 8.3 displays the ten leading causes of death in the United States based on data from 1997. To some degree, all the processes and diseases underlying these causes of death are amenable to prevention or modification

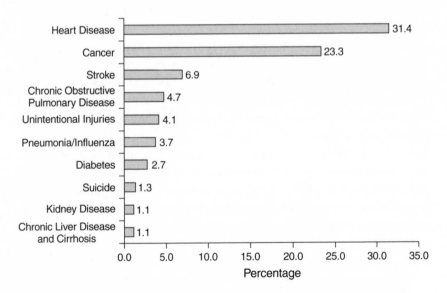

Figure 8.3 Ten Leading Causes of Death, 1997 (*Source:* U.S. Department of Health and Human Services (2000b).)

through changes in behavior (such as quitting smoking, or exercising) and enhanced access to health care services (for example, screening for hypertension and diabetes, serum cholesterol reduction through pharmacotherapies, immunization against pneumonia and influenza). Understanding why poor people tend to engage in unhealthy behaviors more than the nonpoor and to use health services less than the nonpoor is a prerequisite to improving the health of the poor.

Unhealthy behaviors range from poor diets to tobacco use to alcohol misuse to illicit drug abuse to a panoply of behaviors among poor individuals that tend to make them the victims of violence and injury more often than is the case among the nonpoor. The ten leading *Healthy People 2010* health indicators are physical activity, being overweight or obese, tobacco use, substance abuse, responsible sexual behavior, mental health, injury and violence, environmental quality, immunization, and access to health care. The majority of these indicators entail some degree of individual choice.[5]

But how do we encourage the poor to make healthy choices? Higher prices—which can be induced by the policy instrument of higher excise taxes—are often advanced as an attractive mechanism to reduce unhealthy behaviors like tobacco use and alcohol abuse and to correct the harmful externalities associated with them. It is generally, but not universally, assumed that higher prices will cut down use by youths but not by adults. If such a policy fails, then there will be increased public revenue flows; this outcome is not often emphasized in discussions of "corrective" excise taxes, apart from the recognition that such taxes tend to be regressive. In the context of the unhealthy behaviors of the poor, however, it is essential to recognize that higher prices in the presence of inelastic demands result in an increased budget share dedicated to the pricier commodity and therefore reduced expenditure on all other commodities. The prospect of higher prices on tobacco and alcohol resulting in reduced consumption of food, shelter, and clothing is sometimes articulated explicitly in discussions of tax policy in other industrialized nations, but it is much more rarely considered in policy deliberations in the United States. Yet it is clearly worth bearing in mind in such deliberations that a low-income individual who spends $6 each day on tobacco (for two packs of cigarettes) or alcohol has more than $2,000 less to spend each year on food, shelter, and other commodities than would have been the case in the absence of such unhealthy consumption. In the face of inelastic demands, higher prices on tobacco and alcohol induced by excise tax increases may exacerbate poor people's problems with having the resources to consume food and shelter more than they mitigate the problems associated with unhealthy behaviors.

Nutritional risk—malnutrition or obesity—is itself a measure of poverty. Food insecurity and inadequate nutritional intake have been combined into an index that is clearly tied to very low income (see, for example, Frongillo et al. 1997; and Gundersen and Gruber, in press). Obesity also carries nutritional risk. The proportion of overweight and obese individuals is disproportionately high in subpopulations of poor adolescents and poor adult females (U.S. Department of Health and Human Services 2000b). Some recent work finds that poverty and female household headship are key determinants of vitamin deficiencies, anemia, and food insecurity (Bhattacharya and Currie 2001).

Poor people are subject to much higher levels of violent crime and its associated incidence of injury and premature death than others. In a recent analysis of premature mortality from homicide, other injuries, and other causes of death, Jens Ludwig and his colleagues (1998) found enormous racial and ethnic differences in homicide rates, as well as in rates of premature mortality from other injuries and other non-injury causes of death. This analysis provides novel findings that permit racial and ethnic factors to be disentangled from socioeconomic factors. Using 1993 data on males age eighteen to forty-four, the authors found homicide mortality rates per 100,000 of 9.8 for whites, 50.0 for Hispanics, and 129.2 for blacks. Yet equally striking are the authors' findings with respect to the marginal association between family income and mortality rates, as reproduced in table 8.1. In multivariate analyses, the authors found that the racial and ethnic differences far outweigh standard measures of socioeconomic status in accounting for these differential rates.

Table 8.1   Causes of Death Among Males Age Eighteen to Forty-four, by Family Income, 1993 (per 100,000)

Family Income	Homicide	Other Injuries	Other Causes
Less than $14,000	110.8	191.3	376.3
$14,000 to $24,999	41.7	120.6	229.0
$25,000 to $49,999	15.2	64.6	113.2
$50,000 or more	3.6	12.4	11.4

Source: Ludwig et al. (1998).

Overall, then, health problems are greater for the poor than the nonpoor, leading to a greater need by the poor for medical care.

Access to Health Care

Market Failures in the Provision of Health Care

The market for health care has a number of special characteristics that complicate the provision of care to the poor. First, unlike many other markets for services, the health care market fails to secure an efficient allocation of resources. Why is this? Probably the central problem in the health care market is the nature of the "demand" for health care services. Individuals tend to be poor judges of the care they need, and if they do obtain care, they are often poor judges of the quality of that care. Numerous government policies have been designed to either correct or offset this information problem. These include the licensing of medical providers and the provision of subsidies both for certain types of care and for the purchase of health insurance.

A second source of market failure is the uncertainty that people face in their need for care. To avoid the enormous costs associated with a major health problem, they seek insurance coverage. Once a person is covered, however, there is a radical change in his or her incentives for choosing to seek care, or in seeking more or less care. With insurance, the price of the consumer's medical care is subsidized, and the consumer's price is below the real resource costs of providing the service. This subsidy leads to "moral hazard"—the inclination of the consumer to demand more care than would be the case if he or she were facing the full cost. Overprovision of health care services is the result.

Externalities (or "spillovers") are a third problem affecting health care markets. Spillovers occur when one individual's action or lack of action imposes costs or creates benefits for others, and these costs or benefits are not tied to some compensation. An individual's preventive actions—for example, getting vaccinations—reduce the probability of illness for that person and others. Sanitation and insect control reduce the spread of disease; driving while drunk places the individual and others at risk. To the extent that the spillover costs or benefits are not fully borne by those who create them, resources are misallocated.

The supply side of the health care market is also a source of market failure. Limits on entry (through licensing, for example) have created market power. Moreover, given the information problem mentioned earlier, health care providers stand to profit from the advice they give. Providers are often paid a fee for the services they provide, while the consumer of the service pays only a small fraction of this fee (because of insurance). One result is supplier-induced demand: prescribing more care than is optimal can lead to greater profits for the provider without imposing a direct cost on the patient.[6]

A fourth factor also affects the efficiency of the health care market. Medical research is a risky undertaking. Huge amounts can be spent with no assurance of a payoff. As a result, too little investment in medical care research is made if the market is left to operate on its own. Indeed, this problem is made worse if the knowledge from research is available to all at no cost after it has been developed—another case of a spillover. This situation presents a strong case for having a patent system or for subsidizing medical research.[7]

These market failures have led to numerous policies and other public interventions, chief among them being the subsidization of the purchase of health insurance. Individuals are permitted to purchase insurance with pretax dollars instead of their post-tax income, which has to be used to purchase almost everything else. Because health insurance is thus "on sale" relative to other purchases that people might make, some people may demand more health insurance coverage than they would if they had to pay the full cost of providing it. Moreover, this subsidy is regressive, since it helps persons with higher incomes more than it helps the poor, who pay low taxes.[8] In addition to this general subsidy, two main groups are provided with health care coverage directly through the public sector. Those sixty-five and over (and some severely disabled persons) receive insurance through the Medicare program, and a limited set of those with very low incomes (including pregnant women and children) are covered by the Medicaid program.

Multiple market failures have also led to a great deal of regulation of the health care sector. These regulations run the gamut from licensing requirements for all health professionals and institutions (physicians, hospitals, nursing homes, immediate care facilities, and so on) to Food and Drug Administration (FDA) regulatory oversight of the marketing of pharmaceuticals and medical devices, to mandates on the coverage that insurance companies must provide in order to be eligible for tax subsidies. Regulations have also led to subsidies for the provision of care and research.

In spite of all these interventions, the nation's health care system leaves many of our poor and near-poor with limited access to care. They find themselves with either no subsidy or very small subsidies, as well as little coverage despite the enormously complex public programs put in place to address their health needs.

Coverage within the Public System

The United States spends more per capita on health care than any other country. In 1998 we spent $1.1491 trillion on health care.[9] Table 8.2 presents an overview of the total costs, per capita costs, and share of the gross domestic product (GDP) spent on medical care over the last four decades. It documents the substantial increase in resources devoted to health care, from $779 per person in 1960 to $4,094 per person in 1998 (both in 1998 dollars).

Medical care is financed by several sources. As of 1998, 17.4 percent was financed by private sources (the consumer directly); about one-third by private health insurance—largely subsidized through tax expenditures—and 45.5 percent by direct public spending, including 19 percent by Medicare and 14.8 percent by Medicaid (Levit et al. 2000). About 10 percent of the nominal private share in fact takes the form of federal and state tax subsidies toward the purchase of insurance. The principal health care programs for the poor are Medicaid, the State Children's Health Insurance Program (SCHIP), and Medicare.

MEDICAID Medicaid is the primary public program providing health care coverage to the low-income, non-aged population. It was first established under Title XIX of the Social Security Act of 1965. Until then, most poor persons could not afford medical care and many went without. Eligibility for the program depends on income, age, and severe disability status.[10] Low-income pregnant women and infants are categorically eligible, as are poor children, though eligibility standards differ across states. The program is a jointly funded cooperative venture between the federal and state governments, and states have substantial leeway in determining who is eligible, what care is covered, and reimbursement formulas and amounts. As of 1997, 36 million low-income persons were covered (11 percent of the population and 44.6 percent of those with incomes below the federal poverty line), including 18 million children; total expenditures were $160 billion. Child and adult nondisabled recipients have far lower Medicaid expenditures per capita than other persons covered by Medicaid. In 1998

Table 8.2 National Health Expenditures, 1960 to 1998

	1960	1970	1980	1990	1998
National health expenditures (billions of dollars)	$148.0	$307.7	$489.1	$872.2	$1,149.1
Per capita amount	$779.0	$1,433.0	$2,080.0	$3,353.0	$4,094.0
Share of personal health care expenditures covered by private insurance	21.0%	23.4%	29.7%	31.8%	32.6%
Share of personal health care expenditures covered by public insurance	21.4%	34.6%	39.7%	41.3%	45.5%
Share of personal health care expenditures covered by out-of-pocket dollars	55.9%	39.5%	27.1%	23.3%	17.4%
Health care spending as a share of GDP	5.1%	7.1%	8.9%	12.2%	13.5%
Percentage of population uninsured	—	—	14.6%[a]	15.7%	—

Sources: Health Care Financing Administration (2000b); U.S. House of Representatives (2000).

Note: Constant 1998 dollars adjusted using the CPI-U-XI.

a. In 1979.

Medicaid payments averaged about $1,000 per child, as compared to $3,400 for all recipients. Yet the majority of poor and near-poor are not covered by Medicaid.

Mandatory coverage includes the following groups (U.S. House of Representatives 1998b; Health Care Financing Administration 2000a):

- Children under age six whose family income is at or below 133 percent of the federal poverty line (FPL)
- Pregnant women whose family income is below 133 percent of the FPL (services to women are limited to those related to pregnancy, complications of pregnancy, delivery, and postpartum care)
- SSI recipients in most states (some states use more restrictive Medicaid eligibility requirements that predate SSI)
- Recipients of adoption or foster care assistance under Title IV of the Social Security Act
- Special protected groups (typically individuals who lose their cash assistance owing to earnings from work or increased Social Security benefits but keep their Medicaid coverage for a period of time)
- All children born after September 30, 1983, who are under age nineteen, in families with incomes at or below the FPL (thus by the year 2002 all such poor children under age nineteen will be covered)
- Certain Medicare beneficiaries (described later)

Optional "categorically related" groups include:

- Infants up to age one and pregnant women not already covered, whose family income is no more than 185 percent of the FPL (the percentage amount is set by each state)
- Children under age twenty-one who meet what were the AFDC income and resources requirements in effect in their state on July 16, 1996 (even though they do not meet the mandatory eligibility requirements)
- Institutionalized individuals eligible under a "special income level" set by each state (up to 300 percent of the SSI federal benefits rate)
- Individuals who would be eligible if institutionalized, but who are receiving care under home and community-based services waivers
- Certain aged, blind, or disabled adults who have incomes above those requiring mandatory coverage, but below the FPL
- Recipients of state supplementary income payments

- Certain working and disabled persons with family income less than 250 percent of FPL who would qualify for SSI if they did not work
- Tuberculosis-infected persons who would be financially eligible for Medicaid at the SSI income level if they were within a Medicaid-covered category (coverage is limited, however, to TB-related ambulatory services and TB drugs)
- The medically needy—persons who meet the nonfinancial standards for inclusion in one of the groups covered under Medicaid but do not meet the applicable income or resource requirements (states may establish higher income or resource standards for them)

States are required to offer the following services to those covered under Medicaid: inpatient and outpatient hospital services; laboratory and X-ray services; nursing facility services for those over age twenty-one; home health services; prenatal care; vaccines for children; physician services; family planning services; rural health clinic services; pediatric and family nurse practitioner services; diagnosis and treatment for those under age twenty-one; nurse-midwife services; and ambulatory services by federally qualified health centers. States may also receive matching funds for providing optional services such as drugs, eyeglasses, and inpatient psychiatric care for individuals under age twenty-one or over sixty-five, diagnostic services, clinic services, transportation services, rehabilitation and physical therapy services, and home and community-based care to certain persons with chronic impairments.

The federal government helps states pay the cost of Medicaid services by means of a variable matching formula that is adjusted annually. This share is known as the federal medical assistance percentage (FMAP). A matching rate inversely related to a state's per capita income, the FMAP can range between 50 to 83 percent. In 1997 the highest rate was 77.22 percent, while eleven states and the District of Columbia received the minimum match of 50 percent. The federal share of administrative costs is 50 percent for all states.

Medicaid operates as a vendor payment program. Within federal guidelines, states have broad discretion in determining payment methodology and rates. States have the option of paying providers directly or paying for Medicaid services through various prepayment arrangements, such as health maintenance organizations (HMOs). Payments must be sufficient to enlist enough providers so that covered services are available at least to the extent that comparable care and services are available to the general population within the geographic area. Providers participating in Medicaid must accept Medicaid payment rates as payment in full, except where nominal cost-sharing charges may be required. States may impose nominal deductibles, coinsurance, or copayments on some Medicaid recipients for certain services. Some, however, must be excluded from cost-sharing: pregnant women, children under age eighteen, and hospital or nursing home patients, who are expected to contribute most of their income to the cost of institutional care. In addition, all Medicaid recipients must be exempt from copayments for emergency services and family planning services.

STATE CHILDREN'S HEALTH INSURANCE PROGRAM   Medicaid has been expanded in a piecemeal fashion to provide coverage to needy people —especially children—who do not fit into categories in which they would automatically be covered. A new program, the State Children's Health Insurance Program, was created under Title XXI of the Social Security Act with the goal of increasing health care coverage to uninsured children whose families have low income but earn too much for the children to be eligible for Medicaid. States were given the option of expanding coverage through Medicaid or establishing a separate program.[11] Under SCHIP, states may cover children in families whose incomes are either above the Medicaid eligibility threshold but less than 200 percent of poverty or up to fifty percentage points over the state's Medicaid income limit for children, as of the date of implementation. Nominal premiums and copayments are allowed only under separate (non-Medicaid) plans. In all cases, the annual total, out-of-pocket maximum for a family's children is not to exceed 5 percent of its income. As of mid-2000, all but one state had implemented a SCHIP program, and nearly 2.3 million children had been enrolled.

MEDICARE   Medicare is the largest public program that provides health insurance. It is of considerable value to the non-elderly poor it helps, but it chiefly provides coverage to those sixty-five and over.[12] Nearly all persons sixty-five and older in the United States are covered by Medicare. Expenditures for total benefits reached $209 billion in 1999; 39.1 million were enrolled, though not all in both parts of Medicare—part A, which is automatic and covers hospital costs, and part B, which is voluntary and covers non-institutional costs such as doctor costs.

ADDITIONAL PROGRAMS THAT SERVE THE UNINSURED POOR   A number of federal grant programs, as well as state programs, provide some access to care for those without other means. Among them are block grants for maternal and child health services, which provide care to low-income women and children; community health centers (CHCs), which provide primary care on a sliding-fee schedule to low-income populations (and coverage to others as well in underserved areas); migrant health centers, which provide care to seasonal and migrant workers; the Indian Health Service, which provides care to Native Americans; remaining obligations to provide care to indigents under the Hill-Burton Act, which funded the building of many hospitals; and a variety of other specially targeted programs. Hospitals provide care to the poor—some $19 billion worth in 1998, according to the American Hospital Association. Most of these "uncompensated care" programs face declining resources, however; under pressure to not shift the cost of this care to private and public insurers, hospitals may soon have to withhold such services. In an attempt to counter this pressure, Congress passed the disproportionate share reimbursement (DSR) payment-adjustment mechanism in 1980 and 1981. Conceived of as a way to compensate hospitals for providing care to the poor, the DSR may improve access. (Figure 8.4 shows DSR expenditures for 1990 to 1997.) Unfortunately, there is some evidence that its design leads hospitals to find it more desirable to provide

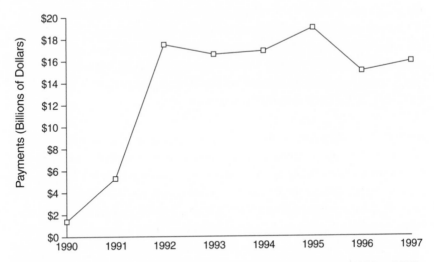

Figure 8.4 Medicaid Disproportionate Share Hospital Payments, 1990 to 1997 (*Sources:*1990 to 1993: Urban Institute (1997), 1994 to 1997: Health Care Financing Administration (2000a, 2000b).)

care for the insured poor (those on Medicaid) than for the uninsured poor (Nicholson 1997).[13]

Not directly related to the delivery of health care, but of paramount importance to the health of the poor, are a number of income-tested programs that address nutritional risks, including food stamps and the Women, Infants, and Children Nutrition Program (WIC).

Food stamps are available to all families whose monthly gross income is below 130 percent of the federal poverty line and who meet cash asset limits and work requirements. In 1999 the federal government spent approximately $19 billion on food stamps, which benefited 18 million participants each month on average.

WIC serves pregnant women and women whose children are under five years old, as well as their children, in families with incomes at or below 185 percent of the federal poverty line. In 1999 the federal government spent nearly $4 billion on WIC and served 7.3 million participants. Such programs are more successful in remedying nutritional problems (as opposed to providing general support) the more sharply they target specific nutritional risks (Rossi 1998). For example, the WIC subprogram for pregnant women tends to be a successful nutrition-enhancing program because it is targeted toward the specific nutritional problems experienced in the low-income segment of this particular population.

The National School Lunch Program, School Breakfast Program, Special Milk Program, Summer Food Service, and Child and Adult Care are additional nutrition programs aimed at poor children.

Private Coverage

Approximately three-quarters of the population is covered by private health care plans, and two-thirds of the population is covered through a plan offered at their place of employment (or that of a family member)—so-called employer-based plans. These now largely (86 percent) take the form of managed care (Levit et al. 2000). The tax system encourages the employer-provided arrangement, since the contribution of employers to health insurance is not counted as part of an employee's taxable income.[14] As of 1999, these employer contributions were 5.8 percent of wages and salaries (U.S. Department of Labor 2000, table 1). The value of the federal tax subsidies for the year 2000 is estimated to be $86.4 billion by the U.S. Treasury, but $125.6 billion by Lewin researchers. The difference is that the Lewin esti-

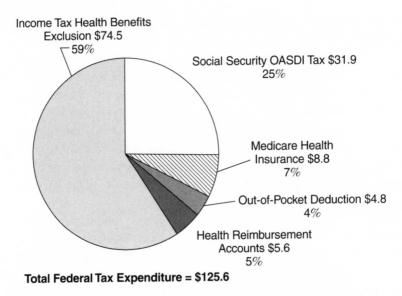

Figure 8.5 Federal Tax Expenditures for Health Benefits, 2000 (Billions of Dollars) (*Source:* Lewin Group estimates using the Health Benefits Simulation Model (Sheils et al. 1999).)

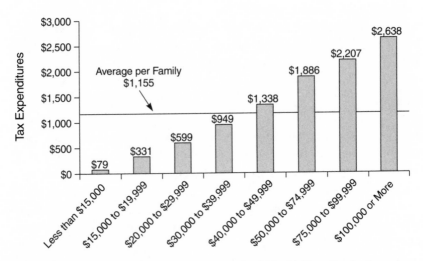

Figure 8.6 Tax Expenditures for Average Federal Health Benefits, by Income Level, 2000 (*Source:* Lewin Group estimates using the Health Benefits Simulation Model (Sheils et al. 1999).) *Note:* Estimates for families with a family head under age sixty-five.

mate includes the value of Social Security and Medicare health insurance payroll tax expenditures, while the Treasury estimates do not. On a per capita basis, this is $1,155 over all families, including an expected tax expenditure of $2,638 for families with incomes in excess of $100,000 per year, but $79 per family for those with incomes of less than $15,000 per year (see figures 8.5 and 8.6) (based on Lewin Group estimates using the Health Benefits Simulation Model [HBSM]; Sheils, Hogan, and Haught 1999). This reflects the fact that families with relatively higher incomes are in higher tax brackets and face a higher marginal tax rate, resulting in a large tax expenditure, as well as the fact that higher-income workers are more likely to have employer-sponsored coverage.

Problems of the Poor and Near-Poor in Obtaining Adequate Health Care

The Lack of Coverage

The most troublesome aspect of the current U.S. health care system is the very large and increasing number of individuals without health insurance. According to data from the National Health Interview Study, 41 million U.S. citizens have no health insurance coverage at any given point in time, including nearly one-third of those with family income below the poverty line and nearly 35 percent of those with incomes from one to one and a half times the poverty line. These numbers and the percentage of the population without coverage have been increasing since 1995 even as the economy performed at very high levels (see table 8.3). The proportion of the near-poor population without coverage has also increased since the mid-1980s. Perhaps another 20 million have too little health insurance to protect them from the financial burdens of a major illness.[15]

Data from the Current Population Survey (CPS) indicate that 44.3 million people, or 16.3 percent of the population, were uninsured all year in 1998; this includes 32.3 percent of the poor. Young poor adults are the least likely to have coverage: among the poor, 46.7 percent of eighteen- to twenty-four-year-olds, 49.2 percent of twenty-five- to thirty-four-year-olds, and 43.5 percent of thirty-five- to forty-four-year-olds had no coverage all year in 1998. Table 8.3 and figure 8.7 present the incidence of lack of insurance by age, race, and income group, as well as the distribution of the uninsured across these groups. Moreover, many low-income people, including adults

Table 8.3   Who Are the Uninsured?

	Incidence: Percentage Uninsured All Year	Composition: Percentage of Uninsured All Year
Age		
Less than six	15.5	8.4
Six to eleven	14.6	8.2
Twelve to seventeen	16.0	8.7
Eighteen to twenty-four	30.0	17.7
Twenty-five to thirty-four	23.7	20.8
Thirty-five to forty-four	17.2	17.5
Forty-five to sixty-four	14.2	18.6
All ages under sixty-five	16.2	100.0
Household income		
Less than $25,000	25.2	38.9
$25,000 to $49,999	18.8	33.4
$50,000 to $74,999	11.7	15.1
$75,000 or more	8.3	12.0
Ethnic-racial group		
Non-Hispanic White	11.9	51.7
Black	22.2	17.6
Asian or Pacific Islander	21.1	5.2
Hispanic	35.3	25.3

Source: Campbell (1999, tables 2 and 5).

in two-parent families, couples, and single men, are generally not covered by Medicaid.

Persistent lack of coverage is far more common among those with low income than among others in the population. About 10 percent of the near-poor, 9.3 percent of the poor, and 6.4 percent of those with incomes 150 to 200 percent of the poverty line had no coverage in a recent thirty-six-month period (1993 to 1996); in contrast, fewer than 1 percent of those with incomes four or more times the poverty line had no coverage over this time period (Bennefield 1998, 5). "Part-time, full-period workers were twice as likely [as] their full-time counterparts to lack continuous health insurance coverage—30 percent, compared with 15 percent." All of these statistics indicate that poverty and the probability of not being insured are strongly linked.[16]

Lack of coverage matters. Those with insurance use more care, controlling for health, age, and location, than those without coverage; those with more extensive coverage use more care (at least outpatient care) than those with less coverage. Is there evidence that coverage makes a difference? Table 8.4 presents the proportion of children who had no contact with a physician over two twelve-month periods—1993 to 1994 and 1995 to 1996—by income and insurance coverage. It shows that for every group, regardless of income, there is a very large difference in access to medical care depending on whether the child is insured (as measured by one or more provider contacts). Further, it shows that the differential increases over time, and that the differential probability of not using any care is far greater among the poor than among the near-poor or the nonpoor. In the first twelve-month period, 1993 to 1994, 21.7 percent of uninsured poor children did not see a provider, compared to 7.9 percent of poor insured—a two-to-seven ratio. Within one year, the ratio had climbed to two to eight: 22.1 percent of poor uninsured children had not seen a provider in twelve months.

Researchers have studied the link between insurance coverage and utili-

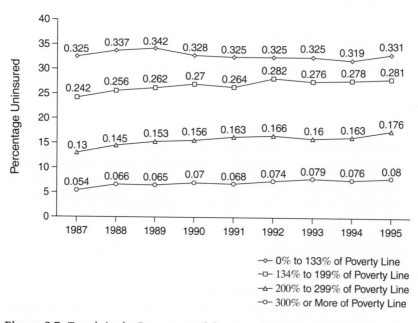

Figure 8.7 Trends in the Percentage of the Non-elderly Who Are Uninsured, by Poverty Level, 1987 to 1995 (*Source:* O'Brien and Feder (1999).)

Table 8.4   No Physician Contact within the Past Twelve Months Among
Children Under Age Six, According to Selected Characteristics:
Average Annual

Characteristics	1993 to 1994	1995 to 1996
All Children	8.3%	9.2%
Poverty status[a]		
Poor	10.6	11.6
Near-poor	9.9	10.7
Nonpoor	5.0	6.2
Poverty status and health insurance status		
Poor		
Insured	7.9	9.3
Uninsured	21.7	22.1
Near-poor		
Insured	8.6	8.9
Uninsured	13.7	18.4
Nonpoor		
Insured	4.8	5.5
Uninsured	8.7	15.2

Source: National Center for Health Statistics (1999).

a. Poverty status is based on family income and family size using U.S. Bureau of the
Census poverty thresholds. Poor persons are defined as below the poverty threshold.
Near-poor persons have incomes of 100 percent to 200 percent of the poverty
threshold. Nonpoor persons have incomes of 200 percent of the poverty threshold or
greater.

zation of care using a variety of approaches. Barbara Wolfe and David Vanness (1999) explore the potential role of insurance in reducing inequality in utilization of medical care using a simulation model built on nonparametric estimates.[17] The results suggest that if currently uninsured adults were insured, their expenditures would increase two-and-a-half-fold on average. Those in poor health would experience a nearly quadrupled increase in their expenditures, while those in good to excellent health would experience a smaller increase. If copayments were required, those with the highest income would be expected to have greater medical expenditures than those with less income. Howard Freeman and his colleagues (1990) found that low-income people without insurance had on average half as many physician contacts in 1986 as those who were insured. A Kaiser/Commonwealth survey in 1999 found that 49 percent of the uninsured had gone without needed medical care compared with 18 percent of those with coverage, including not filling a prescription and skipping a medical test or treatments owing to cost consideration (Burdetti and Shickles 1999). A study in New Jersey found that uninsured breast cancer patients were likely to have more advanced disease at the time of diagnosis than those who were insured, and that they were 1.4 to 1.6 times more likely than those with insurance to die from the disease (Ayanian et al. 1993). The Pepper Commission (1990, 34) report cites evidence that among persons with serious illnesses, the uninsured saw physicians only half as often as the insured, and that cancer treatments differed for persons with and without insurance. And a study on mental health treatment in one county found that the insured were nearly twice as likely to have had mental health treatment prior to their first psychiatric hospitalization than were those without coverage (Rabinowitz et al. 1998).

The uninsured are also less likely to have a regular source of care. A study in two states found that the uninsured were 1.5 to 1.7 times more likely to have a hospital admission for a condition that, if previously treated, would not have led to a hospitalization (Weissman, Gastonis, and Epstein 1992). In addition to delayed and forgone medical care,[18] the lack of coverage causes financial insecurity, inequitable burdens across communities, and increased costs for businesses owing to the shifting of the costs of care for uninsured and underinsured persons.[19]

Turning to evidence linking coverage to health, Janet Currie and Jonathan Gruber (1995, 1996) found that an expansion of Medicaid reduced infant mortality rates, especially among African American infants. An epidemiological study of nearly seven thousand adults from 1971 to 1987 reported a 25 percent higher risk of mortality for uninsured patients than for the privately insured (Franks, Clancy, and Gold 1993), while a study using hospital discharge data from 1987 reported that the uninsured had a threefold higher probability of dying in the hospital than did comparable patients with insurance (Hadley, Steinberg, and Feder 1991).

The Inadequacies of Public Programs

Although they are better off than the uninsured, Medicaid recipients face a number of difficulties obtaining care. They may be required to change providers, as they often find that their coverage is limited to a specific provider, usually an HMO, which may or may not have a facility nearby. That facility may not be open when the adults in the family are not working, and it may require long delays to get an appointment or long waits at the time of the appointment. Furthermore, access problems have become worse. Some children in a family may be covered while others are not. Recent evidence suggests that welfare reform, which broke the tie between Medicaid and other programs, has reduced the take-up of Medicaid coverage.

With the "all or nothing" nature of Medicaid (Moffitt and Wolfe 1992), either individuals are eligible or they are not. If the family income goes up by one dollar, Medicaid eligibility is lost. This "notch effect" creates an incentive to become eligible and stay on Medicaid. The effect is stronger for women who are less likely to receive private insurance at their workplace. Robert Moffitt and Barbara Wolfe (1992) found that Medicaid did keep some women on AFDC and out of the labor force, but that the impact was likely to be large only for women whose families had high expected medical care expenditures. This "notch" problem has been reduced somewhat by mandating the coverage of poor pregnant women and young children below 185 percent of the poverty line.

Medicaid coverage is inequitable. The eligibility income level—the income cutoff—varies considerably by state. States also differ in the service limitations they impose. Some states, for example, have limits on the number of inpatient days covered; some states require a second opinion for certain surgeries; many states have limits on the quantity of any prescription; and a few states have a limit on the number of physician office visits. Thus, a poor single mother with income at 75 percent of the poverty line may receive no coverage in one state, be fully covered with few constraints in a second, and experience limited benefits and difficulty in finding a provider in a third state. Average expenditures per AFDC-TANF (Aid to Families with Dependent Children and Temporary Assistance for Needy Families) child and adult reflect these differences: as of 1997, average expenditures for eligible non-SSI children varied from $641 in Alabama to $1,708 in New York and $2,397 in Alaska.[20]

Going beyond Medicaid, our entire medical welfare system (Medicaid, general assistance, other public medical service delivery programs, and charity care) functions as a *substitute* for private health insurance. This structure forces consumers to face an either-or situation: either rely completely on the medical welfare system or rely completely on privately purchased medical care and health insurance. There is little incentive for low-income consumers to contribute in part toward the cost of their coverage.

Inherent Drawbacks of Being Poor

Even those with apparently adequate coverage may fail to receive adequate care. Areas with heavy concentrations of the poor have difficulty attracting physicians. These include both inner-city and rural areas. This shortage reflects the financial differences between practicing in an area in which most people have private insurance or Medicare coverage and practicing in an area whose residents have Medicaid coverage and large numbers are uninsured. It also reflects the perceived differences in working conditions: fewer physicians are willing to work in the higher-crime areas where the urban poor live (see Kindig et al. 1987). In rural counties, the ratio of generalist physicians to population size has decreased since 1990 (Rivo and Kindig 1996).

The total cost of care and the location of care are significant barriers to the poor. Many poor persons do not have cars and must rely on public transportation. Residential location and health problems may require an individual to take a cab ride to obtain care.

Substandard care is more common for the poor. Issues ranging from inefficient and costly use of alternative health care venues (for example, emergency rooms to treat non-life-threatening acute illnesses); barriers to access to specialist care or particular medical procedures; lack of a "usual source of care"; and poor adherence to preventive and routine-care schedules may all be construed as components of low-quality health care for low-income individuals. Among children under age six and those age six to seventeen, the ratio of poor to nonpoor children who had no contact with a physician in 1996 was nearly 4 to 1 and 3.3 to 1, respectively. In 1994 a far lower percentage of low-income women over forty had had a mammogram in the last two years compared with other women—44 percent versus 65 percent.

The level of reimbursement is another factor that influences access to quality care. In a study of childbirths, physician reimbursement policies were found to influence physicians' choices of treatment modalities: relatively low reimbursement rates (specifically, Medicaid reimbursement rates) reduce the intensity with which patients under the care of low-reimbursement providers are treated (Gruber, Kim, and Mayzlin 1999).

The reasons for these quality problems are complex. Some problems are attributable to lack of health insurance or low-quality insurance (Lave et al. 1999). Some may be attributable to the effects of low income—such as reduced access to convenient transportation—holding constant health insurance coverage. Household- and work-related structural impediments (such as difficulties with time management in single-parent household, or night-shift work schedules) may underlie some of these problems. Others may be traceable to language barriers, cultural differences, or provider discrimination. And finally, some of the problems with the quality of care available to the poor may stem from a constellation of incentive- and preference-related factors that differ by poverty status.

Gaining assistance in addressing unhealthy behaviors is yet another area in which the poor are inadequately served. Some unhealthy behaviors are amenable to change if appropriate clinical services are made available and utilized. For instance, Donald Kenkel (1991) shows that individuals' knowledge of the health consequences of particular behaviors was an important determinant of certain health-influencing behaviors (specifically tobacco and alcohol use and exercise). Similarly, a small randomized trial of smoking cessation among pregnant women found that an intervention program reduced cigarette consumption by half and led to a reduction in low-birth-weight infants (Hebel, Nowicki, and Sexton 1985). Michael Fleming and his colleagues (2000) demonstrated in a randomized trial that brief provider counseling intervention strategies targeted at problem drinkers had significant salutary impacts on problem drinking behaviors. To the extent that a good deal of specific health information (for example, information on healthy prenatal maternal behaviors, the dangers of smoking and alcohol use, or screening for hypertension) is transacted in clinical settings, access to the health services that provide such information is likely to be an important determinant of individuals' health. Reduction in unhealthy behaviors requires enhanced access to clinical services as well as pharmacotherapies (nicotine replacement, antidepressants) (Jorenby et al. 1999), and pharmacotherapies are of increasing interest in efforts to curtail problem alcohol use. At present, however, health insurance coverage of such pharmacotherapies is not widespread.

The Inadequacies of Private Coverage

As mentioned earlier, private health insurance is subsidized by the federal government by means of a tax expenditure: the contribution of the employer to health insurance is not counted as part of the employee's taxable income. The higher the employee's income (and therefore marginal tax rate), the greater will be the benefit obtained from an employer-based plan. Because low-wage workers have low marginal tax rates (for workers earning very low wages, these rates may be limited to the Social Security payroll and Medicare taxes), the gain to them of acquiring employer-based coverage will be lower than it is for higher-wage workers. Indeed, the subsidy provides virtually no benefit to the poor. Moreover, many low-wage individuals may be unable to appreciate the value of the health insurance package at its full cost because they have greater immediate demands on their wages (see Wolfe, Wolaver, and McBride 1998).

Not surprisingly, then, a far smaller percentage of the poor are covered through employer-based private insurance. Indeed, in 1998 only 17.4 percent of persons below the poverty line obtained health insurance at their place of employment; in comparison, 62 percent of all individuals were insured through an employer. Adding to this difference is the growth in premiums and the employee share of premiums: over the 1988 through 1996 period, real average employee contributions for health benefits increased by 189.4 percent (14.2 percent annually) for employee-only coverage and by 85.1 percent (8.0 percent annually) for family coverage. This higher cost for coverage seems to be correlated with the lower take-up rate of employer-sponsored health insurance. Therefore, low-income workers, who frequently are not eligible for Medicaid, find themselves among the uninsured, with all the problems faced by that group.

Reforming the Health Care Sector

The realm of health, perhaps as much as any other, gives rise to the view that the private market should not be left to itself to determine such outcomes as health status, access to health care, or the use of care. The various failures of the market detailed earlier—lack of consumer information, the uncertainty that people face in their need for care, externalities, the market power of providers—provide the rationale for public intervention in the health care sector. Yet as this chapter demonstrates, the U.S. health care system provides little protection to the non-elderly poor. What should be the goals of the current system? In much of the discussion about the non-elderly poor, the stated goal of reducing barriers or eliminating barriers to utilization of care among this population is most often expressed in terms of reducing or eliminating the proportion without insurance. Underlying the debate on reform is the belief that equalizing access to health care will improve health, equalize opportunity, increase human capital (and hence productivity), and reduce unnecessary pain and suffering. It is not clear that a policy insuring all the non-elderly poor would successfully accomplish these broader goals, but it surely would decrease inequality in access.

Major Restructuring

Many economists, policy analysts, and politicians have proposed alternative health care plans. These plans can be classified into four categories. The first is the employer mandate, which would require employers to provide some minimum level of coverage to all employees and their dependents. Employers would either provide insurance to employees directly, following set specifications on both the breadth and depth of insurance coverage and the "proportion of the premium paid for by the employer,"[21] or they would give employees a voucher toward coverage.

The Pepper Commission proposed this type of plan that is generous to the poor (Pepper Commission 1990). Under this plan, any firm with more than twenty-five employees must eventually participate. Covered firms must provide certain minimum benefits. Medicaid would become a federal program, operating uniformly across all states, and open to those not otherwise covered—the self-employed, those working for small firms, those working for firms that decide not to contribute, and the unemployed. The poor would be covered without required premiums, while the near-poor would pay a premium of no more than 3 percent of their income.

Employer mandates do not generate any government budgetary costs (but do lead to tax expenditures—forgone taxes—under the current tax subsidies to insurance). They are thus seen as more politically attractive than plans that increase government spending. There is a crucial trade-off, however: to the extent that the pay component—the special payroll tax—covers the full cost of premiums for employees and contributes to the coverage of the low-income uninsured in general, the payroll taxes required would be substantial. If the special payroll taxes are low (and hence more politically acceptable), employers now providing insurance might stop and instead join the plan—giving the public sector a far larger role and creating the need for raising additional revenues as well.

The second set of reform plans expands the current public programs—Medicaid, Medicare, SCHIP (or only one of these)—by expanding eligibility or by allowing those without insurance to buy into these plans under an income-conditioned payment scheme. For example, individuals could "buy into" Medicaid, with the price of the buy-in determined by family income.

Such a plan would eliminate Medicaid's categorical eligibility requirements and vastly increase the number of participants. Medicaid would be a mechanism to distribute an income-related subsidy for the purpose of purchasing the covered services. More modest versions would restrict the extensions to particular groups: all pregnant women, infants, and young children; those with incomes less than twice the poverty line; disabled persons; adults under age sixty-five with family incomes below the poverty line; and those who retire before age sixty-five (the current age for eligibility for Medicare).[22] There are drawbacks, however, in relying on the expansion of Medicaid as presently structured to solve the problems of the uninsured. This plan provides extensive benefits and hence may be more expensive than necessary; it is horizontally inequitable if applied only to certain targeted groups; and it may contribute to the size of the uninsured population at the same time that it attempts to reduce it.[23] This phenomenon is called "crowd-out": a consumer chooses to drop private insurance if he or she becomes eligible for Medicaid, or firms drop their coverage as public coverage is expanded.

A third set of plans modifies the tax incentives currently in place regarding health insurance by reducing or modifying the federal tax subsidies of health insurance. Rather than the current subsidies, which are worth more to higher-income individuals, the proposed modifications would provide refundable tax credits to low-income families;[24] permit tax-free accounts for health insurance and health care expenditures (Pauly et al. 1991); or set a maximum on the amount of the employer-based premium that can be excluded from the employee's tax base.[25] This maximum could be based on the actuarial cost of a basic insurance plan for families of specified sizes and ages (with an adjustment for disability).[26]

A number of recent proposals attempt to make the tax subsidy for employer-provided insurance more progressive. Many make the credit refundable for low-income workers. The proposals differ largely in how the credit is calculated. The American Medical Association (AMA) plan would replace the current system with a refundable tax credit equal to a percentage of individuals' or families' insurance expenditures. The percentage would be inversely related to income (American Medical Association 1999). Representative Jim McDermott's plan, the Working Uninsured Tax Equity Act of 1999, provides a refundable tax credit for 30 percent of a family's health insurance spending.

The fourth set of policies being discussed, some form of nationalized health insurance, ranges from the expansion of current public programs to full-blown "single-payer" systems like those of Germany or Canada. Providers remain private, but the financing is public. These plans seek to eliminate the high cost of "overhead" due to the duplication of forms, administration, and so on, of multiple payers.[27] Another advantage is uniformity of benefits across all individuals, regardless of income.[28] A national plan like Germany's covers most individuals through their place of employment using nonprofit insurers, called "sickness funds." These sickness funds are heavily regulated: they must offer a minimum plan; employees and the self-employed (except those with high incomes) must enroll in a plan; dependents must be covered; unemployed and retired individuals and their dependents must be covered by the sickness fund that covered the individual while employed; no deductibles are permitted; and there is cost sharing only for hospital care and prescription drugs. Low-income individuals are protected from cost sharing. The funds are financed through mandatory payroll contributions that cover the entire cost.[29]

Why Change Is Difficult

Proposed reforms of health care are more likely to be small than large, even if they do not solve (and might exacerbate) the problems of the current system.

Those who see changes as threatening to their well-being are bound to oppose them. Individuals with private coverage are concerned about the increasing share they must pay and about the restrictions on care provided through managed care. These interests are likely to lead to public requirements of minimum packages of care and more choices of providers. These changes will increase the cost of medical care.

Entrenched interest groups wish to avoid any change that might penalize them. For example, the private insurance sector, including its employees, would fight against the shift to public provision of health coverage or mandated private coverage of high-risk individuals. Private health providers (depending on the proposed plan) may fear reduced compensation and further regulation of their services. Suppliers of prescription drugs and medical equipment also fear loss of business and price regulation. Employees and their dependents who currently have broad coverage provided by their employers with limited cost sharing required of them also prefer the status quo, as do employees who lack employer-provided coverage of their own but are covered by the policy of another family member. Employees in firms that do not offer insurance, or offer only limited coverage, may fear the increase in costs, as do high-salaried workers. And low-income earners may place a value on health insurance smaller than its actual cost under the proposed plans.

Parties who might gain tend to be more diffuse and may not coalesce to lobby for a proposed change. These groups include employers who now provide extensive coverage; providers who primarily serve low-income populations, especially uninsured populations; individuals who are not covered at their job or who are not covered because they are high-risk; employees who see their wages eroding as the cost of insurance coverage takes a larger and larger share of total compensation; former welfare recipients who are now working and whose young children are eligible for Medicaid or SCHIP; and finally, employees who fear the loss of coverage either because of anticipated reductions in the breadth of coverage or loss of their jobs.

Mandating coverage may increase unemployment, particularly among low-skilled workers or workers with chronically ill family members, and it may force some small businesses into bankruptcy. This is a problem primarily for employer-mandated plans (see Wolfe, Wolaver, and McBride 1998). Some reorganization of the labor market might also occur under such a plan (see Steuerle 1991).

Many citizens (employers, employees, and others with private income) fear that these plans will lead to higher taxes. On the surface, most of the new plans seem to be more costly to employees than the current system because few employees fully understand that they are now paying (albeit with pretax dollars) for most of their health insurance. Furthermore, employees are not likely, at least immediately, to gain the full value of their current contribution to health insurance (this refers to the component now known as the employer's contribution) in their paychecks if coverage is removed from their place of employment.[30] And it is likely, under any scenario, that some individuals will lose (pay more, get less coverage) and others will gain (obtain coverage, pay less). But it is difficult to predict accurately what sort of redistribution of costs and benefits will occur.

Finally, there is little willingness to provide the highest-quality care to the publicly insured (for example, to those on Medicaid or to those currently uninsured), but there is also an unwillingness to "bite the bullet" and establish explicit rationing or set up clearly defined dual standards of care.

Major change will continue to be difficult in the next several years, but realistic attitudes toward medical care, based on accurate information, could increase the probability of change. If people had an accurate picture of the likely cost of covering the uninsured and of how much they are now paying—and for what—they could better assess the proposed changes. The general assumption that covering the uninsured will substantially increase the costs of medical care may not in fact be true. About half of those who are uninsured at any point in time will have coverage within about eight months, and their utilization of the system is unlikely to increase substantially if they have coverage all of the time rather than intermittently. In addition, most people without insurance already receive care when they are seriously ill. Although included in medical care expenditure averages, the distribution of the costs associated with such care is undoubtedly not the same as that which would arise if these individuals were seeking care with rather than without insurance. The lack of coverage is tied to some postponement of care, particularly preventive care. But preventive care tends to be cost-effective, so an increase in early screening may reduce medical care costs rather than increase them. Overall, full coverage should be expected to lead to some increase in expenditures, at least in the initial period in which coverage is extended, but the total cost may be small—and smaller than is publicly perceived. The current piecemeal approach to broadening coverage has not led to the hoped-for decrease in the number of uninsured. And this piecemeal approach has added disincentives toward higher earnings. Simply moving eligibility for coverage to higher income levels is not effective at reducing the number of uninsured, though it helps those targeted.

Incremental Change

Steps can be taken to patch the current health care system, improve the position of those in poverty, and bring about a more efficient allocation of resources. Copayments should be part of *all* health insurance to prevent consumers from using too much care, as they are now encouraged to do under many existing plans.[31] With coinsurance, consumers pay a part of the cost of their medical care and hence are expected to act more like consumers of traditional retail goods and services; that is, they are expected to "shop" for medical care selectively, to not buy more than they need, and to look for a good value. Small, required copayments, however, may create substantial financial hardship among the poor and a much greater response among low- than among higher-income persons. To prevent this, copayments could be structured to be income-conditioned: smaller copayments or a lower percentage for children and pregnant women of lower-income families, and greater copayments (or a higher percentage) for children and pregnant women of higher-income families. The practical implementation of such means-tested copayments is, however, not entirely straightforward (for example, what elements of income should be counted or excluded), and the administrative costs might be quite high. Exclusion from copayment of certain types of care, such as vaccines, that are viewed as particularly cost-effective might be a simpler way to structure copayments.

We would also propose a cap (a maximum amount that is not subject to taxes) on the tax subsidy on employer-based health insurance.[32] This would be imposed on individual employees, who would have to pay taxes on any employer contribution above the cap. The cap should be designed to reflect the actuarial cost of insurance for those covered under the plan. These savings in tax expenditures could be used to provide the basis of some of the financial coverage for the low-income population. In addition, such a cap could improve upon our current system to the extent that it induces a redesign of policies to provide protection for major health problems—rather than first-dollar coverage. Insurers would have an incentive to design policies that provide full coverage for care that is cost-effective (immunizations, certain screening programs) but to require significant copayments for other care. Faced with a new incentive—to provide coverage such that the premium is not much beyond the cap—insurers would be motivated to redesign policies in order to reduce the costs of the plan. Employees would have a greater concern with the cost of their insurance, for they would directly pay any amount over the cap with post-tax dollars. And new copayments would increase consumers' concern about the cost of medical care.

To cover some of the individuals not currently covered and to make our current tax subsidy system more progressive, refundable tax credits—essentially vouchers—whose value depends on a family's income would be created. These would have to be sufficiently generous to allow low-income families to buy a basic plan that covered non-elective hospital care and physician care. Families with incomes beyond some substantial multiple of the poverty line would receive a reduced credit along a graduated schedule, much in the spirit of the Earned Income Tax Credit.[33] A reduced credit, which would substitute for the present employer subsidy, could be made available at all income levels.[34] States would be mandated to require insurance companies operating in the state to join a pool that offered such basic coverage to all who wanted it.[35] Geographic differences should be based on true underlying cost differences, such as differential rent and the competitive wage for nurses and other assistants, rather than on a historical basis, and further adjustments should be made on the basis of preexisting conditions, such as disability status, that affect the true cost of care. The disadvantage of this approach is the higher marginal tax rate, which may have negative labor market consequences.

If our preferred plan based on a substantial refundable credit and reduction of the employer-based tax subsidy is not feasible, clearly a substantial part of the population would remain without coverage. Two options seem possible: to provide coverage for all children under a single-payer arrangement; or to expand the community health center network. Under the first alternative, *all* children under the age of nineteen, as well as pregnant women, would be eligible for coverage for a specific set of services. This "Healthy Kid" program would provide primary care in centers where parents and children would learn to go for children's care (and for prenatal care). Further medical care would be referred to other private providers, but with the community care center as the manager of the care for all children who live in the area.[36] Certain basic care would be provided to all children and pregnant women without charge; specific additional care would require copayments that would be income-conditioned and would rise with family income. Medicaid for children and pregnant women and SCHIP would be replaced by the Healthy Kid program.[37] Providing coverage for all children and all pregnant women has a number of advantages. It would increase the use of preventive care, such as immunizations, among all children, especially those in low-income areas. It would provide a place to go for continuing care, a place that is known to teens, particularly to those at risk, so that family planning could be made available in a "safe" environment. It would eliminate the need for a number of programs that provide either limited services or services to a limited set of individuals and hence potentially create savings.[38] Two additional implications of such a plan are that tax subsidies could be reduced and the cost of private coverage would be reduced (since less coverage for children would be provided under family plans).

A second alternative is expanding the network of community health centers for low-income populations, with centers using a sliding scale, as many currently do. The federal government would forgive or pay off 10 percent of a doctor's medical school loans (or a fixed dollar amount) for each year he or she worked in these centers, while paying him or her a salary perhaps equal to the median income of doctors in that urban area or state. To improve access in underserved rural areas, we would use similar subsidies to encourage providers to locate in these areas. Additional financing of each center would come from Medicaid to cover the cost of services provided to Medicaid-covered individuals; private insurance to cover the cost of services rendered to its participants; and general revenue to cover any remaining gaps, which should be small. There are two disadvantages to this proposal: it is likely to lead to dual-quality care, since chiefly low-income individuals would use a community health care system, and it would provide access only to those who lived in a community served by a center.

Incremental changes that would improve the equity and efficiency of our current health care system include: a cap on the tax subsidy for health insurance; a generous refundable tax credit targeted at the poor and near-poor but available to anyone who does not receive other public subsidies (Medicaid, Medicare, or employer-based tax subsidies); and a requirement that insurance coverage have copayments. Among the alternative approaches to providing access for at least some of our population without coverage, or with limited access to care, would be a universal program for children and pregnant women (Healthy Kid), subsidies to health care professionals who locate in areas of limited supply of medical care, and an expansion of community health care centers. Such plans should lead to an increase in the proportion of the U.S. population covered by health insurance, moving in the direction of equal access. However, as we have pointed out throughout this chapter, access and indeed utilization are but limited inputs into health status. Public policies that equalize schooling, reduce poverty, reduce risky behavior, improve housing quality for the poor, and upgrade neighborhoods, in addition to policies that lead to a more equitable distribution of medical providers across communities, are all approaches that are likely to lead to some improvement in the health of the poor and near-poor.

CHAPTER 9

Investing in the Future: Reducing Poverty Through Human Capital Investments

LYNN A. KAROLY

Antipoverty programs that offer "a hand up, not a handout," have long been attractive as a way of improving the economic well-being of the least advantaged. Since the War on Poverty began, for example, programs have targeted poor children prior to school entry and during the school-age years; other programs have served younger and older adults at the bottom of the economic ladder in need of further education or training. The shift in welfare policy that culminated in the 1996 Personal Responsibility and Work Opportunity Reconciliation Act (PRWORA) has moved antipoverty policy even further away from traditional income support (the handout) and toward policies that stress responsibility and self-sufficiency (the hand up). Although much of current policy focuses on raising the skills and labor market prospects of adults, there is also an interest in promoting the development of children so that they can avoid a cycle of poverty. Thus, instead of reducing poverty immediately, these programs make investments today with the expectation that the payoff of poverty alleviation will occur in the future.

The goal of this chapter is to explore the role that policies aimed at human capital investments through education and training have played in poverty alleviation in the past, and their potential for further poverty reduction in the future.[1] I look at evidence on successful programs designed to increase human capital through education and training, as well as on those strategies that appear not to be so successful. Where possible, I also highlight evidence of the cost-effectiveness of specific program strategies. The chapter focuses on human capital investments more narrowly defined to include early care and education, K-12 schooling, and adult education and training. Other human capital investment strategies aimed at work experience, health care, and investments in communities and neighborhoods are covered in other chapters (Mullahy and Wolfe, Pavetti, Ferguson, all this volume).

The chapter examines human capital investment strategies chronologically through the life course. Consideration is given in the first section to programs aimed at at-risk children age zero to five, an increasingly popular investment approach with policymakers and the public. The next section focuses on programs aimed at disadvantaged children during the school-age years, including strategies that focus on school resources and school access. For older youth, strategies designed to prevent school dropout or promote the school-to-work transition are discussed. The following section reviews what is known about the benefits of raising the human capital of disadvantaged adults through remedial education, formal classroom training, and on-the-job training. The final section concludes with a discussion of the evidence regarding the trade-offs associated with different investment strategies and the implications for poverty reduction in the future.

Investing in Children Prior to School Entry

Child development experts have known for some time that the early years of a child's life are critical for the child's cognitive, emotional, social, and physical development. In recent years, there has been renewed interest in the potential for early childhood programs to improve child outcomes in general, and specifically for children at risk of developmental delays.[2] These programs aim to raise human capital during the preschool years by promoting cognitive development, social development, and emotional regulation, along with other dimensions of well-being such as health and nutrition. With improvements in these domains, children are expected to enter school "ready to learn" and thus more likely to have better outcomes during the school-age years and beyond. This enthusiasm for programs targeted at young children is countered by some who argue that early childhood programs do not work, and that resources spent on preschool-age children are not justified in cost-benefit terms. In this section, I look at programs that incorporate parenting classes, home visiting, center-based educational day care, and related services and review the evidence that such programs can improve short-run and long-run outcomes for participating children and their families and are a worthwhile investment.

Strategies for Intervention with At-risk Children

Given the likely importance of the first years of life, a number of early childhood intervention programs have been designed and tested with the aim of overcoming the biological or environmental stressors that might otherwise compromise a child's healthy development. Perhaps the best-known large-scale program is Head Start, implemented in 1965 as one early effort in the War on Poverty. Head Start was begun at a time when there were few paradigms for early childhood programs in the United States, although various developmental theories pointed to the potential benefits of inoculating children in the preschool period against the detrimental effects of poverty (Zigler and Muenchow 1992). The program was initially viewed as a possible way to raise IQ scores, even though it was designed with broader goals in mind. The program evolved from an initial eight-week pilot project to the current format: in most cases, part-time or full-time operation during the school year. Today about 800,000 children participate in Head Start annually, at a total cost of $4.5 billion (U.S. Department of Health and Human Services 2000c). With the growing attention to the importance of the first few years of life, the 1994 reauthorization of Head Start established the new Early Head Start program, which now annually serves about 35,000 children under the age of three (U.S. Department of Health and Human Services 2000c).

It may be the best-known program, but the Head Start model is not the only approach to early intervention. Recent reviews of the literature have identified a diverse array of program models (see, for example, Barnett 1995; Currie, in press; Karoly et al. 1998; Reynolds et al. 1997). Table 9.1 summarizes key features of some of the better-known intervention programs beyond Head Start that have been implemented and evaluated over the past three decades, often with experimental designs that randomly assign participants to treatment and control groups. (For brief descriptions of these programs, see Karoly et al. 1998.) The programs listed include small-scale demonstration studies as well as large-scale programs like the Chicago Child-Parent Center (CPC), a publicly funded, school-based preschool and follow-on program that continues to operate.

These programs illustrate the range of strategies used to intervene with at-risk children and their families. For example, different criteria are used to target disadvantaged children, such as the family's income or socioeconomic status, or the child's health or cognitive development. Some programs intervene before or soon after a child's birth, while other interventions begin later in infancy or early childhood, up to age three. These programs focus on the child, the parent (typically the mother), or both depending on their objectives and designs, such as strengthening the parent-child relationship, improving child health and nutrition, or enhancing school readiness. Services are delivered in center-based settings or in homes, and sometimes services are provided in both venues.

Do Early Intervention Programs Work?

The early intervention programs listed in table 9.1, as well as many others, have been evaluated to assess their effect on participating children and families. With the exception of Head Start, most of the model programs (including those summarized in table 9.1) are typically implemented among relatively small populations; correspondingly small samples are associated with any formal evaluation. Thus, the evaluation literature is riddled with concerns about the validity of inferences drawn from studies that were based on small samples, had high rates of attrition over time, or were limited to specialized populations (for example, specific geographic locations or demographic subgroups). Nevertheless, several comprehensive literature reviews have suggested that broader conclusions can be drawn from the most rigorous of these studies (see, for example, Barnett 1995; Currie, in press; Karoly et al. 1998; Lazar and Darlington 1982; Reynolds et al. 1997; White 1985).

Consider first the evidence for the effectiveness of the Head Start program. Evaluations of Head Start have been limited by the absence of a national randomized trial in which children are randomly assigned to treatment and control groups. Comprehensive reviews of studies of specific Head Start programs in given geographic locations suggest that it is difficult to draw inferences about the national program from smaller-scale studies (Barnett 1995; McKey et al. 1985). In a series of papers, Janet Currie and Duncan Thomas (Currie and Thomas 1995, 1998, 2000) have used non-experimental evaluation techniques and nationally representative surveys to assess the impact of Head Start on a number of child outcomes in both the short run and the long run. For white and Latino children, they found, Head Start has significantly favorable and lasting effects on test scores and school attainment relative to these outcomes for children who participate in other preschool programs or in no program at all. In contrast, the significant initial gains for black children eventually disappear. Head Start appears to produce

Table 9.1 Features of Selected Targeted Early Intervention Programs

Program (Years of Operation)	Site	Target	Ages of Participants	Intervention		Evaluation (Sample Size)
				Focus/Mode	Content	
Early Training Project (1962 to 1965)	Murfreesboro, Tennessee	Low SES	Entry: four to five years Exit: six years	Child Center/home	Summer part-day preschool program; home visits	Experimental (E = 44, C = 21)
High/Scope Perry Preschool Project (1962 to 1967)	Ypsilanti, Michigan	Low SES and low IQ scores	Entry: three to four years Exit: five years	Child Center/home	School-year part-day preschool program; home visits	Experimental (E = 58, C = 65)
Chicago Child-Parent Center (CPC) (1967 to present)	Chicago, Illinois	Low SES	Entry: three to four years Exit: six to nine years	Child/parent Center	Preschool: half-day school-year program School-age: kindergarten and primary (to third grade) programs	Quasi-experimental (E = 1,150, C = 389)
Houston Parent-Child Development Center (PCDC) (1970 to 1980)	Houston, Texas	Low SES	Entry: one year (HV); two years (center) Exit: three years	Child/parent Home/center	Home visits; part-day child care; center-based program for parents	Experimental (E = 90, C = 201)
Syracuse Family Development Research Program (FDRP) (1969 to 1975)	Syracuse, New York	Low SES	Entry: last trimester (HV); six months (center) Exit: five years	Child/parent Home/center	Home visits; part-day (six to fifteen months) to full-day (fifteen to sixty months), year-round, family-style day care	Experimental (E = 108, C = 108)

Program	Site	Target population	Entry/Exit	Focus/Setting	Services	Design
Carolina Abecedarian (1972 to 1985)	one North Carolina site	High score on high-risk index	Entry: six weeks to three months; Exit: five to eight years	Child/parent Center	Preschool: full-day, year-round, center-based, educational day care; School-age: parent program	Experimental (E = 57, C = 54)
Project CARE (Carolina Approach to Responsive Education) (1978 to 1984)	one North Carolina site	High score on high-risk index	Entry: four weeks (HV); six weeks to three months (center); Exit: five years	Child/parent Home/center	E1: Home visits and full-day, year-round, center-based, educational day care; E2: Home visits only	Experimental (E1 = 17, E2 = 25, C = 23)
Infant Health and Development Program (IHDP) (1985 to 1988)	Eight sites	Premature and low birthweight	Entry: birth (HV); one year (center); Exit: thirty-six months (adjusted for prematurity)	Child/parent Home/center	Home visits; full-day, year-round, center-based, educational day care	Experimental (E = 377, C = 608)
Elmira Prenatal/ Early Infancy Project (PEIP) (1978 to 1982)	Elmira, New York	First births to young, single, or low-SES mothers	Entry: up to thirtieth week gestation; Exit: two years	Parent Home	Home visits by trained nurses	Experimental (E = 116, C = 184)

Source: Karoly et al. (1998).

Note: HV = home visits; E1, E2 = first and second experimental (treatment) groups; E = experimental group; C = control group.

other benefits as well, consistent with the program's broader goals. For example, both black and white Head Start children show higher rates of immunization, although there are no significant differences in long-run nutritional status. The fade-out effects of Head Start for measures of cognition are often cited as evidence that the program does not work. This issue is addressed later in the chapter in the discussion of the long-term effects of other programs. Currie and Thomas (1998) have suggested, however, that part of the blame rests with the poor quality of the schools that black children in particular attend after they complete the Head Start program.

Several comprehensive reviews of other program models suggest that other inferences about early intervention programs can be gleaned from the literature. Drawing largely on results summarized in Karoly et al. (1998), table 9.2 provides additional perspective on the benefits of early intervention programs for participating children. For the programs listed in table 9.1, table 9.2 shows the relevant follow-up age and statistically significant program impacts in three broad domains: cognition (as measured by IQ tests), educational outcomes (as measured by grade repetition, use of special education, and school attainment), and economic outcomes (including employment, earnings, welfare use, and criminal behavior).[3] Not all outcomes are measured for each study, and in some studies that measure outcomes, effects are never statistically significant.

As seen in the first panel of table 9.2, with one exception, the statistically significant gains in cognition from early intervention are not observed much beyond the early primary grades (age six to eight), and for some programs the gains are no longer registered after age two or three. The one exception to the pattern of cognitive gains fading out is the Carolina Abecedarian program—a full-day, year-round, center-based early intervention program from birth to age five: that program produced a significant IQ difference for treatment versus control groups through age twelve. This promising result suggests a role for programs of very high quality and intensive interventions. Although the IQ gains may attenuate over time, studies with longer-term follow-up have demonstrated that there are lasting effects in other domains. For example, educational outcomes by the teenage years or later are significantly better for program participants, with differences in rates of special education, grade retention, and high school completion differing by twenty percentage points or more. Many of the studies summarized in table 9.2, as well as others, also find significant and long-lasting differences in achievement test scores after participation in early intervention programs.

For example, such gains are evident through age fourteen or fifteen for the Perry Preschool Project, the Chicago child parent centers, and the Carolina Abecedarian program (Karoly et al. 1998).

The Perry Preschool Project, a high-quality, part-day, center-based preschool program implemented in Ypsilanti, Michigan, from 1962 to 1967, has one of the longest follow-up periods as part of its experimental evaluation. Table 9.2 shows that the educational gains for Perry Preschool participants translated into better economic outcomes in young adulthood. For example, earnings by age twenty-seven were 59 percent higher for the Perry Preschool children compared with earnings rates for the control group. Employment rates were also higher, and welfare utilization was lower. The Perry Preschool Project and three others also demonstrate that participants in early intervention programs are less prone to involvement in delinquent or criminal activity during adolescence and the transition to adulthood. Finally, there is some evidence that early intervention programs can also change other life-course decisions, such as rates of teen pregnancy and the timing and spacing of births (Carolina Abecedarian Project 1999; Karoly et al. 1998).[4] By improving educational outcomes, adult earnings, and family formation decisions, early intervention programs have the potential to reduce poverty among their participants when they reach adulthood.

When programs are also designed to promote human capital accumulation and economic self-sufficiency among participating parents (typically the mother), there may be parenting, educational, economic, and health benefits for those parents (see Brooks-Gunn, Berlin, and Fuligni, in press; Karoly et al. 1998). For example, the Prenatal/Early Infancy Project (PEIP) provided nurse home visits to first-time mothers in Elmira, New York, beginning in the prenatal period and continuing until the child turned two. The program's rigorous curriculum aimed to improve pregnancy outcomes and, once the child was born, the parenting skills of the mother and her economic self-sufficiency. The program targeted higher-risk women who were teenage mothers, of low socioeconomic status, or single parents, although both the program and the accompanying experimental evaluation were open to all first-time mothers who asked to participate. For a higher-risk subsample of mothers, those who were unmarried and had low socioeconomic status, there was a significant reduction in the time spent receiving AFDC benefits and food stamps—by thirty months and thirty-seven months, respectively—through age fifteen of the child. The time the mother spent working before her child turned fifteen was also higher by sixteen

Table 9.2 Outcomes for Participating Children in Selected Targeted Early Intervention Programs

			Statistically Significant Program Effects			
Program (Years of Operation)	Age at Last Follow-up	Outcome	Age When Last Significant	Control Group	Change in Treatment Group	Percentage Change in Treatment Group
Cognition						
Early Training Project (1962 to 1965)	16 to 20	IQ	6	82.8	+12.2	+15
Perry Preschool Project (1962 to 1967)	27	IQ	7	87.1	+4.0	+5
Houston PCDC (1970 to 1980)	8 to 11	IQ	2	90.8	+8.0	+9
Syracuse FDRP (1969 to 1975)	15	IQ	3	90.6	+19.7	+22
Carolina Abecedarian (1972 to 1985)	15	IQ	12	88.4	+5.3	+6
Project CARE (1978 to 1984)	4.5	IQ	3	92.9	+11.6	+12
IHDP (1985 to 1988)	8	IQ (HLBW sample)	8	92.1	+4.4	+5
Educational outcomes						
Early Training Project (1962 to 1965)	16 to 20	Special education	18	29%	−26%	—
Perry Preschool Project (1962 to 1967)	27	Special education	19	28%	−12%	—
		High school graduation	27	45%	+21%	—
Chicago CPC (1967 to present)[a]	20	Special education	18	25%	−10%	—
		Grade retention	15	38%	−15%	—
		High school graduation	20	39%	+11%	—
Carolina Abecedarian (1972 to 1985)	15	Special education	15	48%	−23%	—
		Grade retention	15	55%	−24%	—

Economic outcomes

Perry Preschool Project (1962 to 1967)	27				
Arrest rate		27	69%	-12%	—
Employment rate		27	32%	+18%	—
Monthly earnings		27	$766	+$453	+59
Welfare use		27	32%	-17%	—
Chicago CPC (1967 to present)[a]	20				
Juvenile arrests		18	25%	-8%	—
Syracuse FDRP (1969 to 1975)	15				
Probation referral		15	22%	-16%	—
Elmira PEIP (1978 to 1982)	15				
Arrests (HR sample)		15	0.53	-0.29	-45

Sources: Chicago CPC: Reynolds et al. (2001); all other programs: Karoly et al. (1998).

Note: For full program names, see table 9.1. All results are significant at the .05 level or higher. HLBW = heavier low-birthweight sample; HR = high-risk sample.

a. Results for preschool treatment group versus no preschool comparison group.

months, although this employment effect was not significantly different from the control group. Subsequent pregnancies and births were lower for participating higher-risk mothers, and the number of months between the first and second pregnancies was higher by more than two years (twenty-eight months).[5] Other early intervention programs, by providing high-quality day care, may promote greater work effort on the part of mothers, especially single mothers.

Overall, the results from the early intervention evaluation literature suggest that small-scale demonstration programs and some larger-scale, publicly funded programs can provide lasting benefits in a wide array of domains. It is true that early IQ gains are more likely to fade with time. But benefits in other domains (such as educational achievement and attainment, crime and delinquency, and measures of economic success) are less prone to a fade-out effect; measurable and often sizable improvements for program participants last into adolescence and young adulthood.

At the same time, it is less clear that early intervention programs change the developmental trajectory for program participants, with benefits that accelerate over time, compared with nonparticipants. Although many of the program evaluations show significant and lasting improvements for participating children, there often remains a persistent gap between the achievement levels of the disadvantaged children in the intervention program and those of their more advantaged peers. Thus, while the gap may be narrowed, the programs do not compensate for all the sources of disadvantage facing these children.

A related inference from this literature is that the booster effect of early intervention can be enhanced, or at least sustained, by continued intervention beyond the preschool years. The Abecedarian and Chicago CPC programs, each of which include post-school follow-on components, suggest that continued program services during the early elementary school years produce stronger effects than what is observed when the treatment services end prior to school entry. In the Abecedarian program, this is especially true for the long-term gains in achievement test scores and other school performance measures (but not for the IQ effects, which are largely attributable to the preschool intervention) (Campbell and Ramey 1994, 1995). The long-term Chicago CPC evaluation also shows that benefits in terms of school achievement and need for remedial services (for example, grade repetition and special education) are larger for those who participate in the extended school-age intervention compared with those who stop after receiving preschool or kindergarten services (Reynolds et al. 2001).

Moreover, the CPC results indicate that there may be a threshold effect: program gains in some domains—specifically, educational attainment—are not linearly related to time spent in the program but instead are relatively flat until program participation reaches five or six years (Reynolds et al. 2000). Unfortunately, the ability to examine the effects of program intensity within the same program model—whether measured by time in the program or by intensity of service delivery in a given time period—is rather limited; most experimental studies do not contain such variation. Although the CPC results are based on a quasi-experimental design, they should raise concerns among those who would consider implementing less intensive versions of the early intervention programs reviewed here. If the threshold effects evident for the CPC program can be generalized to other intervention designs, programs that attempt to deliver less intensive services compared with those of proven model programs, whether at a given point in time or over time, will generate not necessarily proportionally lower effects, but perhaps no effects at all.

The early intervention studies reviewed here are promising as a whole, but several caveats should be kept in mind (Karoly et al. 1998). First, the programs in table 9.2 are designed to serve particular groups of at-risk children. Often the results for more advantaged children, as might be expected, are considerably less pronounced or even nonexistent. In other cases, like the Infant Health and Development Program (IHDP), the stronger results were found for the more advantaged children in the group of at-risk children.[6] Second, the results for the studies summarized in table 9.2 may not be readily generalizable. Most of these programs were implemented on a small scale, for specialized populations, during the 1960s, 1970s, and 1980s. Thus, there is considerable uncertainty as to whether similar results could be obtained for full-scale versions of these programs, implemented in diverse communities, with a vastly different set of issues facing families and communities today compared with the past.

Third, for each of the successful programs in table 9.2, there are other examples in the literature of programs that fail to produce even short-term gains for participating children. For example, a recent review of the home visiting programs embodied in six program models that received careful evaluation through randomized trials (including the Elmira PEIP) concluded that the studies collectively provided mixed results. Even when positive, results were modest in size and concentrated among subgroups with no consistent pattern. The reviewers' (Gomby 1999, 15) bottom-line assessment was that the home visit evaluation literature offers a "tale of improvements as exceptions rather than the rule."

Across the range of early intervention models, there are several features that appear to differentiate the successful and unsuccessful programs, including earlier and more sustained intervention (even into the school-age years) and an intensive set of services delivered by high-quality professionals following a rigorously developed curriculum. Even so, one lesson from this literature is that while there is strong evidence that programs *can* work, there is no assurance that every program *will* work, with benefits generated in the domains and at the magnitudes shown in table 9.2.

Cost-Benefit Analysis of Early Intervention Programs

Although the early intervention literature has largely concentrated on reporting program benefits in terms of child and parent outcomes, a few studies have been analyzed in terms of program benefits versus program costs. Table 9.3 summarizes the results of cost-benefit analyses of three of the programs cited in tables 9.1 and 9.2: the Perry Preschool Project, the Elmira PEIP, and the Chicago CPC (Karoly et al. 1998; Reynolds et al. 2000).[7] This perspective is relevant given the sizable costs of many early intervention programs, especially those that are intensive and operate over several years. For example, the Perry Preschool Project cost, in 1996 dollars, about $12,000 per child over the service delivery period, which averaged somewhat less than two years. The Elmira program cost $6,000 per child for about two and a half years of program services. The Chicago CPC program falls in between with a weighted average cost of $6,933 for the preschool component (about one and a half years) and $2,998 for the average participant in the follow-on program (a total of $9,931, all in 1998 dollars).

Although program costs are fairly well known, one issue for any cost-benefit analysis of early intervention programs (compared with, for example, similar assessments of the training programs discussed later in the chapter) is that many of the benefits that can be readily expressed in dollar terms are not observed until years after the intervention ends and the participating children reach adolescence and young adulthood. One advantage of the Perry Preschool, Elmira, and Chicago CPC evaluations is the relatively long

Table 9.3   Net Present Value of Benefits Minus Costs for Selected Early Childhood
Intervention Programs

Program (Cohort, N)	Program Costs (in 1996 Dollars)	Net Present Value in 1996 Dollars of Benefits Minus Costs for:		
		Program Participants	Rest of Society	Society
Elmira PEIP–lower-risk (1978 to 1982, N = 145)	$6,083	$1,622	−$993	$630
Elmira PEIP–higher-risk (1978 to 1982, N = 100)	$6,083	$1,010	$23,673	$24,683
High/Scope Perry Preschool (1962 to 1967, N = 121)	$12,148	$13,846	$23,979	$37,824
Chicago Child-Parent Center (1967 to present, N = 1,281)[a]	$9,931[b]	$11,784[b]	$14,898[b]	$26,682[b]

Sources: Elmira PEIP and Perry Preschool: Karoly et al. (1998), tables 3.3, 3.4, and 3.7; Chicago CPC: Reynolds et al. (2000), figure 6.
    a. Results for total CPC participation, which combines any preschool participation with any follow-on participation. Most of the cost savings result from the period of preschool participation.
    b. 1998 dollars.

period of follow-up (twenty-seven, fifteen, and twenty years, respectively); these evaluations give us the opportunity to observe outcomes that produce measurable economic benefits to the government (that is, to taxpayers) and the rest of society. These benefits include reduced education costs (due to less grade repetition and use of special education), reduced costs associated with the criminal justice system (due to lower rates of crime and delinquency), reduced social welfare costs (due to lower rates of welfare utilization by both parents of participants and the children themselves once they reach adulthood), and greater income for program participants and tax revenues for government coffers. Such benefits can be compared with program costs to arrive at the net present value of the benefits to program participants or society as a whole, compared with program costs.

As seen in table 9.3, the net benefits of successful early intervention programs can be sizable, especially when services are targeted at those who can benefit the most. In the case of the Elmira higher-risk sample (single, low-SES mothers), the program returns a net benefit to society as a whole of over $24,000, or four times the program cost. Most of the benefit accrues to the rest of society in the form of savings on government programs (special services, welfare) and reduced tangible crime costs. Program participants (mothers and children combined) experience modest gains, reflecting the increase in the mother's labor income net of reduced welfare payments. Other gains to participants, particularly children, may be evident as they age and potentially become higher-paid workers than members of the control group. Since many of the savings to government arise from changes in the parents' behavior, cumulative savings to government exceeded cost after only three years (Karoly et al. 1998).

In other cases, the savings to government take time to accumulate, particularly from programs that primarily generate improved outcomes in adulthood for children. The Perry Preschool Project, also shown in table 9.3, does not break even (that is, cumulative savings to government begin to exceed cumulative program costs) until the participating children reach about age twenty. Eventually, the benefits to society as a whole reach over $38,000, more than three times the program costs.[8] Compared with the Elmira estimates, for which the length of the follow-up period did not permit projections of lifetime earnings gains, the participating Perry Preschool children reap even larger benefits owing to their projected higher earnings in adulthood based on the observed gain through age twenty-seven.

The Chicago CPC program produces similar results, with net savings of over $26,000, or nearly three times the program costs (Reynolds et al. 2000).[9] The greatest share of the benefits stems from the preschool component of the program, which generates $32,667 in total benefits compared with $6,993 in costs (in 1998 dollars). As with the estimates for the Elmira PEIP and Perry Preschool programs, these estimates are likely to be conservative, since many of the benefits of these programs (such as potential gains in health, changes in fertility behavior, and other life-course changes) have not been monetized.

The lower-risk group served by the Elmira program generates savings of a much smaller magnitude (see table 9.3). Since program participants were not that much better off than the control group, the net benefits to society as a whole are only just above zero.[10] Thus, on pure economic grounds, an argument can be made for targeting program services to those who will benefit the most, especially when resources for such a program are scarce.

Investing in School-Age Children and Youth

The quality of the U.S. workforce depends in large part on the quantity and quality of the human capital investment made in current and future generations of children. Beyond the window of opportunity in the preschool years considered in the previous section, the school-age years are the traditional period for investing in the knowledge and skills of the future workforce. During the elementary school years, there is near-universal concern over the quality of the schools that students attend and the content of the educational curriculum, particularly for youth who come from disadvantaged backgrounds or live in poor neighborhoods. In light of signs that the U.S. educational system has serious problems, including evidence that U.S. youth score poorly on tests of basic knowledge and skills compared with students in other countries (Lynch 2000), the spotlight has been turned on the need for reform of that system. The period of adolescence and the transition to adulthood are marked by similar concerns: Will these young people actually complete high school? Will they experience a successful transition to the labor market or post-secondary schooling?

In this section, I first review evidence that investments focused on schools themselves, in terms of quality and access, can have an impact on outcomes for children and youth.[11] The discussion continues with an examination of other strategies designed to promote better educational attainment and other measures of success as children age. These include programs designed to work with youth at risk of dropout or poor educational performance, as well as models for promoting the school-to-work transition. Youth education and training programs are also considered.

Investments Focused on School Quality and Access

SCHOOL QUALITY   There has been considerable controversy in the recent literature about the importance of school resources for educational outcomes. The perspective on the effectiveness of school resources has been shaped by a series of influential literature reviews conducted by Eric Hanushek (1986, 1989, 1994, 1996a, 1996b, 1996c, 1997). Hanushek's (1986, 1162) compilation of the literature prior to the 1990s found little evidence for a "strong or systematic relationship between school expenditures and student performance." At the same time, several other literature reviews based on other methods and focusing on different studies suggested that particular school resources may matter more than others. For example, a meta-analysis by Larry Hedges, Richard Laine, and Rob Greenwald (1994) for a subset of the studies included in Hanushek's reviews, using alternative methods to combine results across studies and account for statistical power, provided support for the view that some resources do matter—specifically, per-pupil expenditures and teacher experience. Weaker effects were found for the pupil-teacher ratio, teacher salary, and teacher education. Alan Krueger (1999a) likewise reanalyzed studies included in Hanushek (1997) and applied another strategy for weighting the results from different studies. In particular, when studies, not estimates, are given equal weight in Krueger's reanalysis, class size is systematically related to student performance.

The mixed evidence in the literature of a relationship between school spending and student or post-schooling outcomes indicates that simply devoting more resources to the educational process does not necessarily guarantee a better outcome. Rather, how the resources are spent (for example, on lowering class size, raising teacher salaries, or improving teacher training), and for which groups (on younger versus older students, on minority or disadvantaged students versus more affluent students), is likely to determine whether there are returns to greater school spending. This perspective is consistent with that of several newer experimental evaluations that consider the impact of investing in particular types of school resources.

Project STAR (Student/Teacher Achievement Ratio) in Tennessee is among the better known of these educational experiments. To test the impact of class size on student achievement, approximately six thousand disproportionately minority and low-income kindergarten students within seventy-nine schools were randomly assigned to three class-size configurations: small (thirteen to seventeen students), regular-size (twenty-two to twenty-five students), and regular-size with a full-time teacher's aide. (Teachers were also randomly assigned to classrooms of different sizes.) The class-size assignments were made in the 1985–86 school year and were essentially maintained for four years through third grade. Students who entered the schools after kindergarten were also randomized into the different classes; the experimental sample eventually included a total of nearly twelve thousand students.

Analyses of the experimental data consistently show statistically significant and positive effects from smaller class sizes at the end of kindergarten through eighth grade in each subject tested (Finn and Achilles 1999; Krueger 1999b; Nye, Hedges, and Konstantopoulos 1999). Moreover, the estimated effects are sizable. For example, Krueger (1999b) reports that students in smaller classes score an average of five to seven percentage points higher on standardized tests compared with those in a regular-size class, depending on the grade. The measured class-size effect for kindergarten is about 64 percent as large as the white-black test score gap, and the effect in third grade is about 82 percent as large. At both the kindergarten and third-grade levels, the class-size effect is about 40 percent as large as the gap between students who qualify for free lunch versus those who do not. In addition, the initial gain and cumulative advantage of small class size is larger for black students, for those receiving free lunch, and for students in inner-city schools. These findings appear to be robust to efforts to account for the inevitable deviations from ideal experimental conditions (Krueger 1999b).[12] The Tennessee findings are also replicated in a somewhat different quasi-experimental evaluation in Wisconsin (Molnar et al. 1999).

The strong findings from the Tennessee experiment and related quasi-experimental studies lend additional support to the view that school resources are likely to matter most for minority and disadvantaged students and may matter less, if at all, for more advantaged students. The Tennessee results suggest that lower class size has a significant impact; other non-experimental evaluations also indicate a positive impact of some aspects of teacher characteristics, particularly teacher cognitive and verbal ability, teaching style, and expectations (Grissmer et al. 2000). The class-size effects are stronger when the reductions take place in earlier grades and are sustained over several years. This assessment parallels the findings for the early childhood intervention literature discussed in the previous section.

SCHOOL ACCESS To the extent that school quality matters, access to high-quality schools has important implications for student outcomes and subsequent adult attainments. Disparities in school quality, especially the lower levels often experienced by inner-city schools serving poor and minority students, have lent support to alternative approaches to determining the quality of the schools that students attend. While one approach would require increased spending to raise the quality of schooling provided for disadvantaged students (for example, by lowering class size), another strategy calls for schools to be more efficient in their use of existing resources. The supporters of the school-choice movement argue that if schools had to compete for students—because students would have more say in which school they attend—poorly performing schools would be forced to raise quality. The school-choice movement thus aims to give students and their families more and better schooling options, and its proponents often promote a voucher system to accomplish this goal. Vouchers would either allow students to choose among a greater number of schools in the public system or subsidize students who attend public schools in other districts or private schools. Opponents of school choice argue that such programs would further drain resources and motivated students from public schools, thus decreasing the chances of improving them.

Across the country, at all levels of government, there is growing interest in implementing voucher programs. In 1990 Wisconsin became the first state to implement a publicly funded school voucher program enabling low-income students to attend nonsectarian private schools. The Wisconsin voucher program, implemented in Milwaukee, is the oldest and largest, serving about six thousand students per year with vouchers worth about $5,000. The program has been upheld by Wisconsin's highest court. Called the Milwaukee Parental Choice Program, it has also received the most study. Cecelia Rouse's (1997) analysis of the Milwaukee program used administrative and survey data for the low-income, largely minority population that participated in the first four years of the program, in kindergarten through eighth grade. The results of the quasi-experimental evaluation indicate that the program raised math scores by one to two percentage points a year (or 0.05 to 0.11 standard deviation units) for participating students, compared with a comparison group of students who applied for the program but were not selected in the random lottery. Reading test scores showed less evidence of a strong, systematically positive effect of the school-choice program.

Although these results are suggestive, much more evidence is needed to confirm the effectiveness, and cost-effectiveness, of voucher or school-choice programs as a mechanism to raise the achievement of disadvantaged students, both those who transfer to new schools using the vouchers as well as those who remain in the public school system. How the latter group fares is particularly relevant and as yet relatively unexplored in the literature. Voucher supporters claim that the increased competition brought about by vouchers will improve the quality of the education received by those who remain in their local public schools. Critics, on the other hand, contend that voucher systems will cause public schools actually to lose resources and more motivated students, making reform difficult and the prospects for improved outcomes poor. Any future assessment of the cost-effectiveness of voucher programs will be incomplete without information as to the impact on students in the public school system.

Other Direct Strategies for Improving Youth Outcomes

While improving the quality of schools that students attend is one strategy for promoting better attainments, an alternative is to invest directly in children and youth through programs targeted at those at risk of poor out-comes. For example, despite the future rewards to obtaining more educa-tion, dropout rates among today's youth remain high, especially for some minority youth. For the cohort age twenty-five to twenty-nine in March 1998, 37.2 percent of Hispanics had not completed high school, compared with 12.4 percent of blacks and 11.9 percent of whites (U.S. Bureau of the Census 1998b). At the same time, while 28.4 percent of whites had completed at least a college degree in that age group, only 15.8 percent of blacks and 10.4 percent of Hispanics had done so (U.S. Bureau of the Census 1998c).

For non-college-bound youth, the transition to the labor market is an-other passage of the teenage years. Yet evidence for recent youth cohorts that have made the transition indicates that the transition to stable employ-ment—defined by the age at which the first job of one, two, and three years of tenure is held—takes even longer for high school dropouts (despite their earlier labor market entry) and for the most disadvantaged minorities (Ahituv et al. 1994; Klerman and Karoly 1995). The remainder of this sec-tion considers evidence that approaches aimed at preventing dropout and easing the school-to-work transition can be effective in closing the human capital gap.

DROPOUT PREVENTION   I look first at programs that target youth in school who are at risk of poor outcomes, such as dropout or low achieve-ment. One approach to increasing youth's attachment to school and ability to resist the antisocial behaviors pursued by delinquent peers is to provide incentives to stay in school. One such program, called the Quantum Oppor-tunity Program, was first implemented from 1989 to 1994 in five sites (Mil-waukee, Oklahoma City, Philadelphia, San Antonio, and Saginaw, Michi-gan) and has produced some promising results. (For a discussion of related programs, including Ohio's LEAP [Learning, Earning, and Parenting] pro-gram, the Teenage Parent Demonstration, and the New Chance program, see Heckman and Lochner 2000.) The program offered learning, develop-ment, and service opportunities along with modest cash and scholarship incentives to minority youth in families who were receiving welfare and lived in poor neighborhoods (Hahn, Leavitt, and Aaron 1994; Taggart 1995). The services began in ninth grade and continued for the four years of high school. The original demonstration randomly assigned fifty students in each site to the program or to a control group. Participants and controls were evaluated through time, with information collected on high school graduation rates, postsecondary enrollment, childbearing, and arrest records. After four years, the demonstration revealed that program participants were more likely to be high school graduates (63 versus 42 percent), enrolled in postsecondary schools (42 versus 16 percent), and enrolled in a four-year college (18 versus 5 percent), and less likely to have ever been arrested (7 versus 13 percent). The program is currently being replicated in half a dozen additional sites around the country.

Also available are myriad other programs and services, provided largely by the private sector and designed to promote positive schooling and other positive outcomes for youth. However, there is a paucity of evidence on the effectiveness of most of these programs. Although there is some promising quasi-experimental evidence of the effectiveness of mentoring programs such as Big Brothers/Big Sisters (Sipe 1996; Tierney, Grossman, and Resch 1995), the follow-up periods have been relatively short, so it is difficult to determine whether the near-term benefits of participation will persist. Unfortunately, the formal evaluation of an intervention like the Quantum Opportunity Program is the exception rather than the rule. Consequently, cross-sectional or longitudinal studies of youth outcomes have made relatively few assessments of the impact of programs and services made available through local churches, YMCAs or YWCAs, Boy Scouts and Girl Scouts, and so on.

SCHOOL-TO-WORK TRANSITION PROGRAMS   There has been a renewed interest in strategies for promoting the school-to-work transition for students who remain in school, particularly those who are not college-bound. The 1990 Carl Perkins Act and the 1994 School-to-Work Opportunities Act symbolize the effort to reinvigorate the school-to-work movement. Together, these two pieces of legislation aim to integrate vocational and academic education and to create a school-to-work transition infrastructure that involves cooperation between employers, organized labor, public agencies, community groups, and schools (Donahoe and Tienda 2000). This strategy is based on the premise that efforts to promote the school-to-work transition can be successful for a diverse array of youth.

Debra Donahoe and Marta Tienda (2000) reviewed the strategies for facilitating the transition from school to work and the available evidence of the effectiveness of such programs. Among the approaches they considered were traditional vocational education, cooperative ("co-op") education, career academies, technical preparation ("tech-prep"), and apprenticeships. The evidence on vocational education is both mixed and dependent on the population being served: minority youth and women are more likely to benefit. However, with fewer than one-third of participants in vocational education programs actually placed in a job in the field of their training, it is not surprising that program outcomes are not more widely successful. For co-op programs, a variant of the vocational track with more intensive part-time work effort during high school, there has been even less favorable evidence in support of improved labor market outcomes. Although there is some evidence that career academies and tech-prep programs improve student motivation and school attachment, these programs have yet to be systematically evaluated in terms of their impact on postschooling labor market outcomes.[13] Finally, the youth apprentice model, arguably the most radical in its movement away from the current, less-structured school-to-work transition approach in the United States, is also understudied in its potential effectiveness. Even so, the youth apprenticeship model invites both strong supporters and detractors based on its perceived effectiveness in other settings (such as Germany) and the question of whether the benefits in those settings are transferable to the U.S. labor market context and the needs of disadvantaged youth in this country.

Youth Employment and Training Programs

The school-to-work movement seeks to serve the non-college-bound population while they are still in school. By contrast, a series of youth employment programs have been implemented since the 1960s to promote improved labor market outcomes for youth who are already disconnected from the educational system and the labor market. The programs have included Job Corps, in operation since 1964; the federal programs that evolved during the 1970s (the 1973 Comprehensive Employment and Training Act [CETA]) and the 1980s (the 1982 Job Training Partnership Act [JTPA]); and other smaller-scale demonstration projects such as JOBSTART (Grubb 1996).

During the nearly four decades of federal job training programs for disadvantaged youth, a variety of programs have been implemented, and in some cases evaluated. Job Corps offers an intensive mix of training and counseling services in a residential environment to highly disadvantaged youth between the ages of sixteen and twenty-four. This program is among the most comprehensive and expensive: about $17,000 per year per participant (in today's dollars) for the 60,000 primarily urban high school dropouts served annually (LaLonde 1995; Schochet, Burghardt, and Glazerman 2000). The program's services include academic education, vocational training, counseling, health care and health education, and job placement, delivered in one of 116 residential campuses in 46 states, for an average period of eight months. A related nonresidential program, JOBSTART, begun in 1985 on an experimental basis, was less intensive than Job Corps (Grubb 1996). The JOBSTART programs, tested in thirteen sites, provided over seven hundred hours of basic education and job training, using several models that varied in the sequencing and provision of the services. Programs for disadvantaged youth under JTPA are much less intensive than these other models; they typically combine remedial classroom education (possibly leading to a GED) with work experience (for example, a short-term job in the public or nonprofit sector).

In contrast to the school-to-work transition programs already discussed, these targeted "second-chance" programs have been extensively studied (see reviews by Grubb 1996; LaLonde 1995), although non-experimental evaluations largely prevailed until the 1980s, when a number of experimental evaluations were implemented. The widely held consensus of this literature is that these programs, particularly those that are not very intensive, have failed to produce economically meaningful improvements in employment or earnings for program participants and so have not been very successful at moving youth out of poverty. Table 9.4 summarizes quasi-experimental and experimental results from evaluations of Job Corps, JOBSTART, and JTPA.[14] For the two less-intensive programs, JOBSTART and JTPA, experimental evaluations produced no evidence of significant earnings gains for up to four years after services ended. For those two programs, participation did produce beneficial effects on educational attainment, as measured by the fraction receiving a GED or high school diploma (although the effect was very small for male non-arrestees in the JTPA program).[15] More disappointing is the result for JOBSTART and JTPA: mothers who entered JOBSTART experienced higher pregnancy and birth rates than controls, and males who entered JTPA with no arrest record had a higher arrest rate than the control group.

This overall bleak assessment is countered by the largely positive results for the more intensive Job Corps program, including the earlier quasi-experimental evaluation of the 1977 cohort and the more recent experimental evaluation of a cohort that entered the program between 1994 and 1996. The results of the national randomized control trial of the Job Corps program, based on results through thirty months, provides the most favorable assessment of the program to date (Schochet et al. 2000).[16] The evaluation compares outcomes for ninety-five hundred applicants who were randomly assigned to receive program services with outcomes for six thousand randomly assigned controls. A comparison of self-reported employment, earnings, and criminal activities shows favorable program benefits on each front. For example, participants were more likely to earn a GED (40 versus 17 percent), and their earnings were higher by 11 percent (or by about $1,000 per year). The earnings differential is equivalent to the expected earnings gain from an additional year of schooling, an outcome consistent with the one thousand hours of training received by program participants (about the same number of instructional hours as they would have received during a year of school). In addition, participants had lower welfare use and were 22 percent (or six percentage points) less likely to be arrested. Other indicators showed no differences between treatment and controls, including the rates of college attendance, use of alcohol and illegal drugs, and childbearing. Those in the nonresidential component of the program, with the exception of women with children, showed no gain from participation compared with the controls.

Given the overall weakness of the results for youth training programs, it is not surprising that cost-benefit analyses tend to show little or even negative benefits for participants, and negative benefits for society as a whole. In calculating the net present value of benefits and costs, researchers consider costs and benefits for both program participants and the rest of society. Program benefits for participants include the earnings gains net of any welfare loss and the opportunity cost of lost wages while in training. The rest of society (the taxpayer) bears the cost of publicly provided programs but also gains from higher taxes, lower welfare utilization and utilization of other public programs, the output produced by trainees while in training, and reduced costs of crime.

Table 9.5 summarizes the results from cost-benefit analyses of the Job Corps, JOBSTART, and JTPA programs. Again, with the exception of the 1977 Job Corps evaluation, the youth training programs do not appear to be a good investment. In each case shown, the net benefits to the rest of society are negative, since the areas of savings are not large enough to offset the program costs. For the JTPA program, in which earnings gains were nonex-

Table 9.4   Outcomes of Selected Youth Training Programs

Program (Cohort)	Design	Follow-up Period	Outcomes				Other
			Earnings			Percentage Difference	
			Treatment	Controls	Difference		
Job Corps (1977)	QE	Twenty-four months	$82.76/wk	$73.73/wk	$9.03	12%	Employment rate: up*** Earnings/hour: down Crime rate: down**
Job Corps (1994 to 1996)	E	Thirty months	181.00/wk[a]	168.00/wk	13.00[b]***	8[b] 11[c]	GED rate: up** Arrest rate: down*** Welfare use: down** Drug use: no change Childbearing: no change
JOBSTART (1985 to 1987)	E	Forty-eight months	5,592/yr	5,182/yr	410.00	8	GED or high school diploma rate: up*** Number of custodial mothers ever or gave birth: up** Other women: welfare use: down Number of men ever arrested: down

| JTPA—Females (1987 to 1989) | E | Thirty months | 10,241 over two and a half years[a] | 10,106 over two and a half years | 135.00[b] 210.00[c] | 1[b] 2[c] | GED or high school diploma rate: up* Welfare use: no change |
| JTPA—Male arrestees (1987 to 1989) | E | Thirty months | 15,786 over two and a half years[a] | 16,375 over two and a half years | −589.00[b] −868.00[c] | −4[b] −5[c] | GED or high school diploma rate: no change Welfare use: no change Arrest rate: up** |

Sources: Job Corps: Grubb (1996, table 4.3); JOBSTART: Grubb (1996, table 4.14); JTPA: Grubb (1996, tables 4.4, 4.5, 4.6); Job Corps, 1994 to 1996: Schochet, Burghardt, and Glazerman (2000, table 3).

Notes: E = experimental; QE = quasi-experimental; GED = general equivalency diploma.

a. Assignees and enrollees.

b. Impact per assignee.

c. Impact per enrollee.

* Statistically significant at the 10 percent level

** Statistically significant at the 5 percent level

*** Statistically significant at the 1 percent level

Table 9.5   Net Present Value of Benefits Minus Costs for Selected Youth Training
Programs

| Program (Cohort) | Program Costs | Net Present Value for Benefits Minus Costs for: | | |
		Program Participants	Rest of Society	Society
Job Corps (1977)	$5,070[a]	$2,485[a]	−$214[a]	$2,271[a]
JOBSTART (1985 to 1987)	$4,431[b]	$254[b]	−$4,540[b]	−$4,286[b]
JTPA—Females (1987 to 1989)	$1,392[c]	−$83[c]	−$1,087[c]	−$1,170[c]
JTPA—Males nonarrestees (1987 to 1989)	$2,065[c]	−$620[c]	−$2,284[c]	−$2,904[c]

Sources: Job Corps: Grubb (1996, table 5.6); JOBSTART: Grubb (1996, table 5.11); JTPA: Grubb (1996, table 5.8).
a. 1977 dollars.
b. 1986 dollars.
c. 1988 dollars.

istent (females) or even negative (males), participants actually lose as well. The 1977 Job Corps evaluation is the only one to show sizable benefits to program participants that are large enough to offset the small net negative benefits to taxpayers. However, it is important to note that the positive net benefits of the Job Corps program for society as a whole do not arise exclusively from the earnings gains to participants (LaLonde 1995). Rather, program costs are offset in part by the estimated savings from reduced criminal activity and reduced use of welfare programs, where the estimate of the former has a large confidence interval. The ongoing assessment of the national Job Corps evaluation, which will include a cost-benefit analysis with forty-eight months of follow-up data, will determine whether the earlier cost-benefit assessment from the 1970s remains valid.

W. Norton Grubb (1996) identifies several factors as possible explanations for the ineffectiveness of most youth second-chance training programs. First, the nature of labor markets is such that, unless those markets are especially tight, employers are more reluctant to hire young people, especially those without a high school diploma. Second, job training programs may suffer from the features of the youth culture that reject school, discipline, and strong labor force attachment. In addition, youth may be adversely influenced by their family environments, which, in all likelihood, have failed to provide a supportive environment through their childhood and adolescent years. Third, the programs themselves may not be sufficiently tailored to meet the complex needs of adolescents compared with adults; they may lack a sufficiently broad array of support services regarding other life-course issues such as substance abuse, sexuality, and reproductive health. Besides these three strikes against youth training programs, several other factors cited by Grubb plague second-chance training programs more generally, such as their limited scope and time frame, misplaced assumption that the problem is lack of job placement rather than lack of job skills, lack of serious job training, and use of ineffective pedagogical techniques.

Investing in Adults

Whether measured by formal schooling or measures of skill, sizable numbers of young adults enter the labor market without sufficient skills to command a wage that will provide themselves or their family with a standard of living above the poverty line. This skill deficit may follow them throughout their labor market career. For example, by age twenty-seven, 45 percent of young mothers who have ever received welfare have less than a high school education, and 55 percent score in the bottom quartile of a test of basic skills (Pavetti 1999). These women are further disadvantaged in their effort to find good jobs by their need to find adequate child care, and many of them must overcome other barriers as well, such as a lack of transportation or a history of drug or alcohol use, mental illness, or domestic violence (Danziger et al. 1999). Likewise, there is a segment of the male adult population that is disconnected from the world of work or lacks the basic skills necessary to provide for a decent standard of living (Besharov and Gardiner 1999).

One solution for addressing the skills gap in these adults is further education and training. Given the inability of employers to fully reap the benefits of additional skills training, however, especially more general workplace skills, employers are likely to underinvest in such individuals. With imperfect capital markets, workers themselves are not able to finance their own training by borrowing against future earnings. The resulting market failure has been the motivation for publicly provided training programs to upgrade the skills of disadvantaged adults. In the remainder of this section, I consider evidence of the effectiveness of training programs for disadvantaged adults in terms of raising earnings and achieving other positive economic outcomes.[17]

Strategies for Raising the Human Capital of Disadvantaged Adults

In addition to the youth-focused training programs discussed in the previous section, public-sector job training programs focus primarily on two groups of disadvantaged adults: disadvantaged adults voluntarily seeking employment services, and welfare recipients (Reville and Klerman 1996).[18] In serving these groups, the history of publicly funded training programs is one of consolidation and devolution.[19] In the earliest efforts, the 1960s saw the creation of the Manpower Development and Training Act (1962) for displaced workers and disadvantaged adults, and the Work Incentive (WIN) program (1967) for the training of welfare recipients. These and other federally administered programs established in the 1960s were consolidated in the 1973 Comprehensive Employment and Training Act, which devolved responsibility for program administration and operation to the state and local levels. This transfer from federal to local authority continued with the 1982 Job Training Partnership Act, which placed greater authority for program oversight with the states and enhanced the private-sector role. Over this same period, welfare-to-work programs also devolved as the federally administered WIN program was replaced by the state-administered 1998 Job Opportunities and Basic Skills (JOBS) program. With implementation of the 1998 Workforce Investment Act, which provides for vouchers to be used by disadvantaged workers to purchase training services, public-sector training programs are being further consolidated (Lynch 2000).

Under JTPA, disadvantaged adults who seek job training assistance typically receive one or more services in the following four areas: job search assistance, classroom training, on-the-job training, and work experience (LaLonde 1995). The mix of services received depends in part on the demographic characteristics of the group served. For example, adult women are most likely to participate in classroom training that provides vocation-related instruction. On-the-job training is typically provided to men with some employment skills, while work experience programs are designed for those with a limited or nonexistent employment history.

In contrast to the voluntary programs for disadvantaged adults, programs for welfare recipients who meet certain criteria (for example, age of the youngest child) require that participants be enrolled in employment and training programs. The orientation of these mandatory programs has been more dramatically transformed over the last two decades. Under WIN, services consisted primarily of job search assistance, although short-term work experience components were added early in the 1980s. Welfare recipients whose youngest child was six or older were required to participate. In practice, however, only a small fraction of the caseload enrolled in WIN, owing to limited funding. Under the JOBS program, the age limit for the youngest child was reduced from six to three (or one as a state option). The program combined job search assistance with more formal classroom training that provided either remedial education or vocational training, although many communities lacked sufficient funds to fully implement this range of services. This "human capital" approach can be contrasted with the earlier "work first" orientation.

With the passage of the 1996 Personal Responsibility and Work Opportunity Reconciliation Act and the replacement of Aid to Families with Dependent Children with Temporary Assistance to Needy Families, an even larger fraction of welfare recipients are now required to work (50 percent of all single-parent families and 90 percent of all two-parent families by 2002). This orientation toward greater work effort has shifted many states and localities back to a "work first" approach: efforts are first made at job placement and retention, with formal classroom or on-the-job training pursued only if employment cannot be secured. Wisconsin's New Hope demonstration project and W-2 (Wisconsin Works) program, implemented in 1992 and 1994–95, respectively, exemplify this new approach (Kaplan and Rothe 1999). At the outset, both programs minimized formal training and instead emphasized community service jobs and aggressive case management. Although the programs have added more formal training components, such training is still tied to community service jobs and the number of hours in training is limited. Other aspects of the programs address other employment-related needs, such as child care, health insurance, and transportation.

Evidence That Programs Work or Do Not Work

An extensive literature evaluates the success of adult education and training programs and welfare-to-work programs using both non-experimental and experimental methods, each with its own limitations. Several recent reviews provide the basis for a consensus from both the non-experimental and experimental evaluations: job training programs appear to be most effective for disadvantaged women but show small or nonexistent benefits for adult men (see, for example, Grubb 1996; LaLonde 1995). These conclusions rest, however, on a literature with considerable variability in estimates across programs or for different cohorts or subgroups of program participants, and even for analyses of the same programs (especially for the non-experimental evaluations). In contrast, welfare-to-work programs tend to provide greater promise in terms of raising earnings of program participants and lowering welfare dependency and show more consistent results across subgroups (Michalopoulos, Schwartz, and Adams-Ciardullo 2000).

Table 9.6 summarizes the results of a selected number of evaluations of welfare-to-work programs for welfare recipients (under JOBS) and training programs serving disadvantaged adults (under JTPA). California's Greater Avenues for Independence (GAIN) program was evaluated in six county sites during the late 1980s using random assignment methods. Program services differed across sites and ranged from a "work first" orientation in Riverside County to a more "human capital" approach in the other five counties. The overall impacts were modest but significant, with earnings gains averaging $471 per year for single-parent household heads and $370 for two-parent household heads. Although welfare payments decreased for both household types, the fraction on welfare dropped only three percentage points for single parents, and there was no difference for two-parent households. The earnings gains for single-parent heads did exceed the drop in welfare income (by about $500 over three years), but there was no real gain in net income for two-parent heads.

The average effects mask considerable differences across the GAIN sites. Indeed, in Riverside County the results were dramatic: program participants increased earnings by an average of 50 percent compared with the control group. The earnings gains were also large enough to offset the decline in welfare payments by more than $1,000 over three years. These effects stand in contrast to the absence of any earnings effect in the worst-performing county of the six, Los Angeles County (see table 9.6). The results in Riverside have been cited by some as evidence that a "work first" approach, which is part of the philosophy now embedded in the post-PRWORA welfare-to-work environment, is the most effective.

Florida's Project Independence, implemented for AFDC recipients under JOBS, was a more modest program that, like the Riverside GAIN program, also primarily provided job search assistance. In this case, the earnings gains were even smaller ($114 on average per year), and not enough to offset the decline in welfare payments ($133 on average per year). A comparison of outcomes for subgroups showed that effects were stronger for mothers with older children ($237 per year for mothers whose youngest child was age six or older versus $10 per year for mothers whose youngest child was three to five), for whom the transition to work was expected to be easier. A worsening economy during the course of the program resulted in reduced program funding for later cohorts, which consequently demonstrated smaller gains than the earlier cohort (Grubb 1996).

Beginning in 1995, Los Angeles County modified its GAIN program to incorporate a mandatory welfare-to-work program with a strong focus on employment. A two-year evaluation of the revamped "work-first" program known as Jobs-First GAIN provides results nearly as strong as those for Riverside's GAIN program (Freedman et al. 2000). In particular, as seen in table 9.6 for the single-parent sample in Jobs-First GAIN, earnings gains for program participants exceeded $1,600 over two years, an increase of 26 percent over the control group. Significant and favorable effects were also found for employment rates, welfare use, and the amount of welfare payments. Although there was no gain in total income in the second year of follow-up, a larger increase was evident in the last month of the follow-up period. The results were similar for most subgroups of single parents, and even stronger for the two-parent sample. These effects are considerably more favorable than what was found for the county's earlier GAIN program implemented in the late 1980s, which focused on basic education (discussed earlier in the chapter).

Table 9.6 also summarizes the results of the JTPA evaluation for adult women and men. The earnings impacts over two and a half years are up to two times as large for women compared with men, but the earnings gains are still modest when annualized ($470/$735 per year per assignee/enrollee for women; $391/$640 per year per assignee/enrollee for men) and hold out little opportunity for moving out of poverty or off welfare. There is also some evidence of an increase in educational attainment, particularly for women. While adult women showed no change in welfare use, adult men actually showed an increase in welfare utilization.

Most government training programs represent only a small investment in human capital acquisition, costing less than one year of school and requiring far fewer hours of formal or informal training input. Consequently, even at their best, these programs raise earnings only $1,000 to $2,000 per year (LaLonde 1995). Grubb (1996) notes that it is difficult to draw solid conclusions from the wide-ranging results in the adult training literature. Some evaluations suggest that those individuals with the greatest barriers to employment benefit the most from training programs, while other studies find that it is the most job-ready who gain the most. Likewise, the literature is not uniform in identifying the training program components or services that

Table 9.6 Outcomes of Selected Training Programs for Welfare Participants and Disadvantaged Adults

Program (Cohort)	Design	Follow-up Period	Outcomes				Other
			Earnings				
			Treatment	Controls	Difference	Percentage Difference	
GAIN—All single heads (1988 to 1990)	E	Thirty-six months	$7,781 over three years	$6,367 over three years	$1,414[b]***	22	Welfare use: down*** Welfare payment: down*** Employment rate: up*** GED rate: up***
GAIN-Riverside— Single heads (1988 to 1990)	E	Thirty-six months	9,448 over three years	6,335 over three years	3,113***	49	Welfare use: down*** Welfare payment: down*** Employment rate: up***
GAIN-Los Angeles— Single heads (1988 to 1990)	E	Thirty-six months	4,943 over three years	4,683 over three years	260	6	Welfare use: down** Welfare payment: down*** Employment rate: up***
GAIN—Two-parent heads (1988 to 1990)	E	Thirty-six months	10,156 over three years	9,045 over three years	1,111	12	Welfare use: no change*** Welfare payment: down*** Employment rate: up***
Project Independence (1990 to 1991)	E	Twenty-four months	5,766 over two years	5,539 over two years	227	4	Welfare use: down*** Welfare payment: down*** Employment rate: up***

Jobs-First GAIN–Los Angeles— Single heads (1996)	E	Twenty-four months	8,012 over two years	6,385 over two years	1,627	26	Welfare use: down*** Welfare payment: down*** Employment rate: up***
JTPA—Adult females (1987 to 1989)	E	Thirty months	13,417 over two and a half years[a]	12,241 over two and a half years	1,176[b]*** 1,837[c]***	10[b] 15[c]	Welfare use: no change GED or high school diploma rate: up**
JTPA—Adult males (1987 to 1989)	E	Thirty months	19,474 over two and a half years[a]	18,496 over two and a half years	978[b]* 1,599[c]**	5[b] 9[c]	Welfare use: up** GED or high school diploma rate: up

Sources: GAIN: Grubb (1996, tables 4.9 and 5.5); Project Independence: Grubb (1996, table 4.10); JTPA: Grubb (1996, tables 4.4 and 4.5); Jobs-First GAIN: Freedman et al. (2000, table 2).

Notes: E = experimental; QE = quasi-experimental; GED = general equivalency diploma.

a. Assignees and enrollees.

b. Impact per assignee.

c. Impact per enrollee.

* Statistically significant at the 10 percent level

** Statistically significant at the 5 percent level

*** Statistically significant at the 1 percent level

are most effective, nor does it appear to be the case that more intensively provided services are necessarily more effective. Rather, the literature suggests, different components may be more effective for different subgroups, and different combinations of services may be equally effective.

A recent review of twenty welfare-to-work programs suggests that there is greater uniformity in the employment and economic impacts across the evaluations focused on welfare-to-work programs, especially those implemented since the mid-1980s under JOBS (Michalopoulos, Schwartz, and Adams-Ciardullo 2000).[20] The synthesis concluded that most of the welfare-to-work programs increased earnings and reduced welfare overall over the three-year follow-up period, but that there was no effect on combined income from work, welfare, and food stamps. Moreover, the welfare-to-work programs as a whole increased earnings about as much for more disadvantaged groups (for example, long-term welfare recipients, those without a high school diploma or GED, or those with no earnings in the year prior to random assignment) as for the less disadvantaged groups. Thus, most subgroups gained, but those with the lowest earnings did not gain disproportionately more, so that the gap in earnings between more advantaged and less advantaged participants was not closed. One group that had the smallest gains were those who were at risk of depression at the time of program entry. There is also evidence that, among the most disadvantaged groups, employment-focused programs tend to be more effective than education-focused programs, at least over the time horizon covered by the studies.

For both job training and welfare-to-work programs, the lack of follow-up much beyond three or four years post-training makes it difficult to ascertain whether even these modest benefits persist over a longer time horizon. Most training programs appear to be effective in increasing earnings by raising employment rates rather than raising wages, a finding that suggests that the long-term benefits may be smaller. Indeed, there is some evidence from welfare-to-work studies with longer periods of follow-up that earnings gains tend to fade over time, although there are certainly exceptions to this inference.[21] Given that welfare payments usually also decline, the modest earnings gains are not sufficient to raise family income above the poverty line.

Cost-Benefit Analyses of Adult Human Capital Investment Programs

Many evaluations of adult training and welfare-to-work programs have been accompanied by cost-benefit analyses to compare the net present value of program costs with the short-term and long-term benefits. The methodology is comparable to that described earlier for youth training programs. Table 9.7 summarizes the results for the programs listed in table 9.6. What is quite evident from the table is that despite the existence of even modest effects in terms of earnings and other outcomes, when those benefits are monetized and compared with program costs, most programs do not appear to be a very worthwhile investment.

Among the welfare-to-work programs summarized in the table, only the Riverside GAIN and Los Angeles Jobs-First GAIN programs show any sizable net benefit to society as a whole or positive benefits for both program participants and the rest of society. Project Independence stands out for its small

Table 9.7 Net Present Value of Benefits Minus Costs for Selected Training Programs for Welfare Participants and Disadvantaged Adults

Program (cohort)	Program Costs (in 1993 Dollars)	Net Present Value in 1993 Dollars of Benefits Minus Costs for:		
		Program Participants	Rest of Society	Society
GAIN—All single heads (1988 to 1990)	$3,442	$923	−$990	−$67
GAIN-Riverside—Single heads (1988 to 1990)	$1,597	$1,900	$2,559	$4,458
GAIN-Los Angeles—Single heads (1988 to 1990)	$5,789	−$1,561	−$3,485	−$5,046
GAIN—Two parent heads (1988 to 1990)	$2,917	−$186	−$652	−$838
Project Independence (1990 to 1991)	$1,150	−$369	$26	−$343
Jobs-First GAIN-Los Angeles— Single heads (1996)[a]	$1,392[c]	$572[c]	$1,698[c]	$2,270[c]
JTPA—Adult females (1987 to 1989)	$1,227[b]	$1,678[b]	−$1,146[b]	$532[b]
JTPA—Adult males (1987 to 1989)	$931[b]	$2,079[b]	−$1,509[b]	$570[b]

Sources: GAIN: Grubb (1996, table 5.9); Project Independence: Grubb (1996, table 5.10); JTPA: Grubb (1996, table 5.8); Jobs-First GAIN: Freedman et al. (2000, tables 8.2 and 8.3).

a. Assumes straight-line decay of impacts of five-year horizon.

b. 1988 dollars.

c. 1998 dollars.

net gains to taxpayers (the rest of society) but net losses for program participants (because reductions in welfare benefits were not offset by higher earnings). The poorly performing Los Angeles GAIN program resulted in net losses to both program participants and the rest of society. But these results were reversed when the program was revamped into the "work first"-oriented Jobs-First GAIN. The JTPA cost-benefit analysis shows positive benefits to program participants (in the form of higher earnings that more than offset lower welfare benefits), just offsetting the net negative benefits to the rest of society. Thus, although the JTPA program meets a strict standard of benefits that exceed costs, it does so at taxpayer expense.

Policy Issues Relevant for Future Poverty Alleviation

In this chapter, I have reviewed various strategies for investing in the human capital of disadvantaged populations throughout the life course, from the prenatal period through adulthood. Human capital investment programs aim to reduce poverty by improving individuals' underlying skills and competencies so that they become more productive workers and more responsible members of society in both the short run and the long run. This review suggests that some strategies along the continuum of the life course show great promise, while others have failed to pass the test of effectiveness or cost-effectiveness.

There is compelling evidence from a number of rigorously evaluated smaller-scale and larger-scale programs that intervention in the lives of disadvantaged children during the years prior to school entry can dramatically improve their outcomes in several domains. There is also evidence that parents sometimes benefit, especially when programs are designed to promote their well-being as well as their children's. Moreover, programs that support cost-benefit analysis demonstrate sizable returns for each dollar invested, in contrast to investment strategies that focus on disadvantaged youth and adults. When early intervention programs are effective, they may reduce rates of poverty and dependency during the early years by improving the economic outcomes of the parents, and may continue that trajectory as the children age and attain higher educational and economic status in adulthood. During the school-age years, human capital investment strategies revolve around improvements to school quality or access to quality schools and efforts to intervene directly with disadvantaged children and youth to help them achieve higher educational status and make the transition to the labor market. In terms of school quality, there has been considerable controversy in the literature about the most effective use of additional spending to improve student performance. As a result of new experimental results combined with earlier non-experimental evaluations, a new consensus is emerging that improvements in school quality appear to be most effective for disadvantaged children, especially when those investments are made and sustained during the primary grades. In contrast to the vast literature on school quality, there is a limited base of knowledge on the short- and long-term impacts on students of promoting better educational and economic outcomes through school choice, even though enthusiasm for the school-choice approach is growing.

Strategies to intervene directly with youth include efforts to promote staying in school and the school-to-work transition, as well as programs designed to raise the skills of youth through remedial education, counseling, and training. Although some smaller-scale dropout prevention programs suggest that this strategy may be promising, the literature is sparse, and evaluations are not always rigorous. Likewise, there has been little experimentation with different school-to-work transition models, although that is beginning to change. A great deal of experimentation on youth training programs indicates that, unless interventions are intensive and costly, they are unlikely to produce even small benefits for program participants, much less the rest of society.

Finally, the extensive literature on the benefits of investing in the human capital of disadvantaged adults is mostly discouraging. Job training programs appear to benefit adult women the most, and to a lesser extent adult men. More promising are the results from some of the recent evaluations of welfare-to-work programs, which tend to show short-term earnings gains and reduced welfare dependency. However, most programs produce only modest gains and demonstrate only marginal benefits (if any at all) to society and participants that exceed program costs. Even when cost-benefit analysis is favorable, the modest improvements in participants' earnings are typically not sufficient to reduce poverty rates, especially after accounting for the loss of welfare income. Some emerging evidence suggests that welfare-to-work programs may have beneficial but modest impacts on child well-being. In terms of both economic outcomes and non-economic benefits, however, it is essential to have more long-term follow-up of the populations served by these programs.

Research and Policy Issues That Affect Human Capital Investment Strategies Across the Life Course

Human capital investment strategies differ with the stage of the life cycle, but there are some common issues that confront researchers and policy-makers interested in making sound decisions about publicly sponsored investment programs. In the remainder of this section, I briefly review three of these issues: program targeting, optimal program design, and the implementation of effective, large-scale, publicly supported programs.

PROGRAM TARGETING   Across the stages of the life course, this chapter has provided a number of examples in which the benefits of human capital investment strategies are greater when the resources are targeted at the group that can benefit most. Properly targeted programs can generate better returns for each dollar invested, a relevant consideration especially when resources are tight. Although targeting may produce better returns, it can also serve to stigmatize and isolate disadvantaged children, youth, and adults. Disadvantaged children and youth may benefit from participating in programs with lower-risk peers who can provide role models and positive reinforcement for improved performance. Moreover, the public and politicians often demonstrate greater support for programs that are more universal rather than limited to subgroups of disadvantaged individuals. Targeted programs must also overcome the difficulty of defining and identifying the targeted population, especially if the goal is to maximize the returns from a given investment. Often the existing research is not sufficient to pinpoint which groups will benefit most from a given program.

OPTIMAL PROGRAM DESIGN   Many of the investment strategies discussed in this chapter have been assessed using specific program models, but in most cases we are quite far from fully understanding how to design optimal programs to serve a given population subgroup. This is true for subgroups broadly defined, such as the poor or the near-poor, as well as for more specific groups, such as children and adults with disabilities, immigrant children and adults, and so on. Additional research is needed to help identify the optimal mix, intensity, and timing of services to program participants, depending on the stage of the life course and the individual's own needs at the time of the intervention. Likewise, to the extent that there is value in integrating investment strategies across the stages of the life course—for instance, from the preschool to the school-age years—we need to learn more about the best ways to achieve such integration across programs and service providers. Our understanding of these issues will benefit from studies that focus on particular disadvantaged groups of children and adults, as well as from larger sample sizes that permit disaggregation of results by population subgroup. Evaluations that consider variation in the mix, intensity, and timing of services will also provide important information for future program design.

IMPLEMENTING LARGE-SCALE PROGRAMS   Many of the most promising investment strategies reviewed in this chapter have been implemented only in single sites or in a small number of sites. For example, many early childhood programs with demonstrated benefits have been implemented only on a small scale or in a limited geographic location. Likewise, the school-age interventions that show merit, such as the Tennessee STAR experiment reviewed here and youth mentoring programs, have been tested in only one state or a limited number of localities. Some of the programs that have been evaluated were implemented by the private or nonprofit sector but promoted as potential programs for public-sector sponsorship and funding. Consequently, there is considerable uncertainty regarding the ability to replicate the results of the specific model programs reported in the literature when those programs are implemented more broadly by public agencies. At the same time, the effects of these programs might be even larger when the programs are implemented on a larger scale, owing to social multipliers that amplify behavioral changes beyond those observed for program participants (Durlauf, this volume).

Optimal Investment Throughout the Life Course

Abstracting from these concerns, a question emerges: is there an optimal investment strategy to promote poverty reduction among disadvantaged populations? At first blush, it might appear that early childhood intervention programs are the best investment in terms of return for each dollar invested—such programs return three or four dollars for each dollar invested—compared, for example, with job training programs for adults, which typically fail to even return the original investment. Heckman and Lochner (2000) have recently argued in favor of early intervention strategies as the best use of the marginal investment dollar; in their view, the evidence of beneficial effects from investments during middle childhood and adulthood is weak at best.

On the basis of the early childhood intervention literature, I believe there is a foundation of solid research to support increasing investments in early childhood programs focused on disadvantaged children from birth through the preschool years. It is critical, however, that new resources be deployed effectively. Policymakers would be well served by drawing on proven model programs and by preserving the intensity of the program services already demonstrated to be effective. This may mean serving, at least initially, smaller population groups than would be ideal, with the goal of broadening program coverage over time as resources allow. Variations in proven program models should be rigorously evaluated to help address some of the research and policy issues discussed here. The implementation of proven designs can benefit, at a minimum, from process evaluations that assess fidelity to the original program model.

Although there is merit in efforts to start early to make up the skills gap, it is important not to completely abandon efforts to raise human capital for those at risk of poor outcomes beyond the preschool years. There are several reasons to continue to invest in effective, publicly provided human capital investment strategies for the least advantaged throughout the life course. First, to the extent that scarce resources require targeted expenditures, even during the early years not all children will be identified as being at risk of poor outcomes during the first few years of life. The individual-, family-, and community-level factors that place children and adults at risk of poor outcomes are not static but change over time. Thus, some children may appear well off in the early years, but new stressors may appear later in childhood that threaten their continued healthy development. Likewise, individuals may be at different levels of risk at different stages of development during the periods of middle childhood, adolescence, and the transition to adulthood. If programs are available only during certain windows of opportunity in the life cycle, some individuals will fall through the cracks.

Second, the most disadvantaged children, youth, and adults may require ongoing intervention to promote continued human capital investments. For example, evidence cited earlier suggests that part of the reason for the fade-out of the beneficial effects of Head Start for minority children is that they subsequently attend poor-quality schools. Without further investments in their schools, the value of the early investment is likely to erode over time. In his assessment of the poor performance of most youth and adult job training programs, Grubb (1996) concludes that the solution is to create a more coherent system of comprehensive education and training services instead of the "one-shot" efforts now in place. It is also worth noting that the favorable effects measured for some programs are averages: while some participants gain more than the average level of benefits, others do not benefit at all from the program. Thus, for some individuals a one-time inoculation will not be adequate and further investment may be required.

Third, by providing a continuum of human capital investment opportunities, it is possible that synergies will develop that generate an even greater cumulative impact over time than what would be predicted based on each stage of investment over the life course. If learning begets learning, for example, human capital investments in the early years may allow children to take better advantage of educational resources during the school-age years. Some earlier investments, if successful, may reduce the need for later investments or allow the resources available to be better targeted to a population that can benefit most from them. If group-level influences are tied to changes in individual behavior, there may also be social multipliers that amplify the effects of a given investment to produce broader social and behavioral changes among highly interdependent individuals (Durlauf, this volume). Yet another potential synergy comes from considering two-generation investment strategies: combining programs designed to promote economic self-sufficiency among adults with programs that provide effective intervention services for their children (McLanahan 1998). The hope is that addressing the needs of both generations simultaneously will produce interactions not yet measured by existing program evaluations.

If these arguments are valid, the optimal investment strategy through the life course will involve a continuum of services, potentially integrated over time to serve the needs of children, youth, and adults who continue to face disadvantages that place them at risk of low economic attainment. Based on my reading of the evidence from rigorous evaluations and cost-benefit assessments, the following approaches would appear to have the most merit:

- High-quality, intensive, center-based early childhood programs, with curricula designed to promote cognitive and social development and behavioral competence and transitional services that continue in the early grades (for example, models such as the Perry Preschool, Abecedarian, and Chicago CPC programs and larger-scale programs like Head Start)

- Proven home visiting programs that provide services to young, high-risk, first-time mothers beginning in the prenatal period and continuing through the first few years of life (for example, models such as the Elmira Prenatal/Early Infancy Project)
- Reduced class sizes in the early grades for schools serving disadvantaged children
- Job Corps for school dropouts
- Employment-focused welfare-to-work programs for single mothers (for example, Riverside GAIN and Jobs-First GAIN-Los Angeles)

Other programs that should be given consideration, but for which the evidence base is not as strong, include other school-based reforms targeted at disadvantaged children to raise quality and improve educational outcomes and dropout prevention programs for at-risk youth.

To alleviate poverty, is the best approach a hand up or a handout? If the former, should the offer be made to an infant or young child who has many years to reap the rewards, or to an adult in need of remedial education and job training? Effective poverty reduction strategies probably need to rely on traditional income transfers and other direct assistance programs combined with the human capital investment strategies reviewed here. In addition, while investments in the earliest years show tremendous promise, especially compared with the track record of investments later in the life course, it would be premature to abandon publicly provided programs to promote human capital investments among the least advantaged children and adults in favor of very young children. The menu of programs delineated in this chapter offers a starting point for such a life-course investment strategy. As we go forward along this path, we need to continue to invest in research that will shed more light on the optimal continuum of services to promote poverty reduction through human capital investment during early and middle childhood, adolescence, and the transition to adulthood.

PART III

Neighborhoods, Groups, and Communities

CHAPTER **10**

Housing Discrimination and Residential Segregation as Causes of Poverty

JOHN YINGER

Everyone knows that poor people have a hard time finding decent, affordable housing. What is not so well known is that the housing market helps to push people into poverty and to keep them there. Moreover, ethnic discrimination in housing markets, past and present, magnifies these forces for blacks and Hispanics and therefore helps to explain why people in these groups face higher poverty rates than do non-Hispanic whites. This chapter explains the role of housing markets in promoting poverty, reviews the evidence on discrimination and segregation in housing, and shows how they contribute to the relatively high poverty rates for blacks and Hispanics.[1]

Differences in poverty rates across groups are striking (U.S. Bureau of the Census 2001). Except for two years in the early 1980s, the white poverty rate has been below 10 percent since 1973, whereas the black poverty rate exceeded 30 percent from 1973 to 1994 and was 23.6 percent in 1999. The poverty rate for Hispanics was below the rate for blacks throughout much of this period but grew to equal the black rate in 1994; it stood at 22.8 percent in 1999. Although the gap between the black and white poverty rates in 1999, 15.9 percentage points, was disturbingly high, it was smaller than the gap in 1973, 23.9 points. The 1999 Hispanic-white gap, 15.1 percentage points, was about the same as the black-white gap, but it was somewhat larger than the Hispanic-white gap in 1973.

A hint about the role of housing in these outcomes can be found in homeownership rates (U.S. Bureau of the Census 2001). The rate for whites has been close to 70 percent since 1983, and it reached 74.0 percent in the first quarter of 2001. In contrast, the homeownership rates for blacks and Hispanics have never made it to 50 percent. Moreover, the black-white and Hispanic-white homeownership rate gaps both now stand at about 27 percent, close to their 1983 levels. Most poor households cannot, of course, afford to buy a house. As we will see, however, homeownership is a source of insurance against poverty, and these figures demonstrate just how little of this insurance is held by black and Hispanic families.

This chapter begins with a section on the link between poverty and housing. After presenting some basic principles of housing market analysis, I explore the channels through which housing markets influence poverty. In the next section, I turn to the linkages between poverty and both ethnic discrimination and segregation in housing. This section explores the legacy of past discrimination and the evidence of current discrimination, and it shows how segregation and discrimination magnify the impact of housing markets on poverty for blacks and Hispanics and thereby contribute to the relatively high poverty rates for these groups. The final section examines the potential of various housing policies to reduce these disparities.

Poverty and Housing

Many scholars have pointed out that poor people tend to live in neighborhoods where many other poor people live. It is not widely recognized, however, that this concentrated poverty is a housing market phenomenon; after all, any statement about where poor people live is a statement about the location of their housing. As a result, one cannot understand why poverty is often concentrated—or indeed, why urban poverty has many other features—without understanding something about urban housing markets. This chapter begins therefore with an overview of some basic housing market principles.[2] Ultimately, these principles shed light on several key dimensions of urban poverty, including the relatively high poverty rates for certain ethnic groups.

Basic Housing Market Analysis

BIDDING   The first step in analyzing urban housing markets is to determine how the price of housing varies within an urban area. All else being equal, a household will not live farther from its work site than similar households that work at the same location unless it is compensated through a lower price per unit of housing. The required compensation depends on its commuting costs and on the amount of housing it consumes, say in square feet. If one more mile of commuting costs fifty dollars per month, and a household lives in a one-thousand-square-foot apartment, then the price per square foot must drop by five cents per month (fifty divided by one thousand) as compensation for living one mile farther away. Thus, the amount of compensation depends on the ratio of per-mile commuting costs to housing consumption. The price that compensates a group for its commuting cost is called its "bid" for housing at that location. This analysis predicts that the price per unit of housing declines with distance from a work site. This prediction is strongly supported by a large empirical literature (Coulson 1991).

To add realism, housing can be measured in units of quality-adjusted square feet; after all, people care about not only the size of their house or apartment but also the number of rooms, the presence of animal pests, and so on. Because the demand for housing, like the demand for anything else, declines as price increases, the relatively high price of housing near work sites implies that people who live near work sites demand a relatively low quantity of housing. In other words, people who live near work sites will live in units that deliver relatively few quality-adjusted square feet, and they will pay a relatively high price per unit of housing (but will be compensated relative to similar people who live far from work sites by having lower commuting costs). Thus, one cannot fully compare the situations of households in different locations without considering both their housing and commuting costs, as well as their employment situation.

This bidding framework also predicts that the schedule of housing prices throughout an urban area will rise with the area's population. As more people compete for housing, the housing price schedule shifts upward, and all households, except those at the outer edge of the urban area, must pay more for housing. This upward price shift results, of course, in substitution away from housing, so this analysis also predicts that people will consume less housing, as indicated by smaller or lower-quality units, in larger urban areas, all else being equal.

SORTING   What happens when an urban area contains households with different incomes? Consider two income classes competing with each other for housing around a work site. Housing suppliers will sell or rent to the class bidding the most per unit of housing. The class that needs more compensation, in the form of a larger drop in the price of housing, to live farther from a work site will not bid as much for housing at distant locations and will lose out to the other class there—but will win close to the work site. Following the logic of bidding, the class that needs more compensation is the one with a higher ratio of per-mile commuting costs to housing consumption.

As it turns out, the ratio of per-mile commuting costs to housing consumption tends to decline as income goes up.[3] Higher-income people consume more housing than lower-income people and also tend to have higher commuting costs, largely in the form of a higher opportunity cost of their time. However, the operating costs of commuting increase slowly, if at all, as income increases, so income tends to have a smaller proportional impact on total commuting costs (time plus operating) than it has on housing consumption. It follows that high-income households tend to win the competition for housing at distant locations, whereas low-income households tend to win the competition close to a work site. Thus, it is the basic operation of the housing market, not zoning or some other government policy, that results in the concentration of poor people, and of low-income people in general, in central locations in U.S. urban areas.

Low-income households do not win the competition near work sites by paying more than high-income households for the same units. Instead, they bid a higher price per square foot while consuming less housing, that is, while accepting small or low-quality apartments or by doubling up. Landlords near work sites can make more money by providing many small or low-quality apartments to low-income tenants than by providing a few large or high-quality apartments to high-income tenants. Thus, spatial competition between income classes not only concentrates low-income people in central locations (and in other locations near their work sites) but also requires them to pay a high price per unit of housing for units that deliver few quality-adjusted square feet. Moreover, the larger the low-income population, the higher their housing bids must be to compete for housing with higher-income households.

NEIGHBORHOOD AMENITIES Now consider neighborhood amenities, such as the quality of surrounding houses, the neighborhood's social networks, air pollution, the crime rate, the quality of local public schools, and so on. Within a household type, households must be compensated for living in a neighborhood with poor amenities. Hence, housing bids depend on both neighborhood amenities and access to employment. The better the amenities, the more people will bid for housing in a neighborhood, all else being equal. This application of bidding concepts to neighborhood amenities is strongly supported by empirical work. The price of housing, controlling for structural housing characteristics, is higher in neighborhoods with more desirable amenities (Bartik and Smith 1987; Ross and Yinger 1999).

Neighborhood amenities also influence household sorting. People in different income classes compete for entry into high-amenity neighborhoods. In most cases, high-income people win this competition because as the amenity level rises, the amount they will pay per unit of housing increases more than does the amount that low-income people will pay. In other words, high-income people will pay more for an *increment* in the amenity, so they tend to sort into locations with better amenities (Ross and Yinger 1999).

This result reinforces the basic sorting result presented earlier. Because suburbs tend to have better amenities than central cities, the sorting based on access to employment alone is reinforced and magnified by the sorting based on amenities. Competition in the housing market therefore sorts lower-income households into less desirable neighborhoods, which tend to be close to employment concentrations and are often in the central city.

One way to summarize this analysis is to say that low-income households have two ways to win the spatial competition for housing: at any given level of neighborhood quality, they can double up or accept low housing quality; at any given level of housing quality, they can choose neighborhoods with poor amenities. In short, low-income people cannot win the spatial competition for housing without accepting either low housing quality or low neighborhood quality, or both.

COMPLEXITIES   Actual housing markets are more complicated, of course, than this stylized model. People decide where to live on the basis not only of access to employment and neighborhood amenities but also of other factors that are hard to quantify, such as distance from family or friends or from valued community organizations. Incomes also vary over time, and people typically make housing decisions based on expectations about future income.

Despite this complexity, however, the logic of sorting can be observed in urban areas. In 1999 the poverty rate was 16.4 percent in central cities compared to only 8.3 percent in suburbs (U.S. Bureau of the Census 2001). Moreover, John Kasarda (1993) documents that in the one hundred largest cities in 1990, 68.8 percent (28.2 percent) of poor people lived in census tracts in which at least 20 percent (40 percent) of the population was poor. Paul Jargowsky (1997) shows that poverty concentration is increasing nationwide: 17.9 percent of poor people lived in high-poverty tracts in 1990 (those in which at least 40 percent of the residents were poor), compared to just 12.4 percent in 1970.

Housing markets also are not static. The long-standing trend of suburbanizing employment lowers the desirability of central residential locations and boosts the desirability of suburban locations. Interregional and international job movements also alter the relative desirability of housing in various locations. New sorting outcomes emerge as households alter their housing choices in response to these job changes.

Housing and Poverty

Housing markets contribute to poverty through at least five channels: high rent burdens, housing health risks, lack of access to housing wealth, neighborhood effects, and spatial mismatch.

HIGH RENT BURDENS   A household's rent burden is defined as its rent (or equivalent ownership costs) plus utilities as a share of its income. A high rent burden limits a poor household's ability to use financial strategies that might overcome its poverty. To be specific, poor people may find it impossible to make needed investments in health care, education, or job-related expenses, such as child care, if they must devote a high share of their income to rent.

The evidence on rent burdens is staggering. Almost three-quarters (72.6 percent) of poor households spend more than 30 percent of their income on rent and utilities, and over half (54.9 percent, or almost 9 million households) spend more than 50 percent (U.S. Bureau of the Census 2001).[4] Among the nonpoor, housing costs exceed the 30 percent threshold for only 22.3 percent of households, and only 7.1 percent pass the 50 percent threshold. Moreover, a recent report (HUD 2000) finds that for every one hundred households with incomes below 30 percent of the area median—roughly the poverty line—there are only thirty-six available housing units with rents less than 30 percent of their income. The Department of Housing and Urban Development also reports that this number has been declining since 1991.

The relationship between rent burden and income depends primarily on two factors.[5] The first is the extent to which housing demand increases with income. If this income elasticity of demand for housing is less than one, as most research finds (Goodman 1988), then rent burdens are higher at lower incomes. The second factor, which reflects the role of housing prices, has two parts: the extent to which housing demand decreases with price, summarized by the price elasticity of demand, and whether housing prices decrease as income increases. Most studies find that the price elasticity is less than one in absolute value (Goodman 1988), but the analysis of housing bids presented earlier indicates that housing prices could increase or decrease with income. Holding neighborhood amenities constant, low-income households win the spatial competition for housing by living where the price of housing is relatively high, but low-income households also end up in poor neighborhoods, where the price of housing is relatively low, all else being equal. No study provides clear evidence on the net impact of these two effects. If the first dominates, so that housing prices decrease with income, then a price elasticity below one implies that this second factor also results in higher rent burdens at lower incomes. In short, the high rent burdens facing poor households arise because of the small income elasticity of demand for housing, perhaps combined with the impact on housing consumption of the relatively high housing prices that poor households must pay in large cities.

The true magnitude of this problem is masked because the official poverty lines do not recognize that the price of housing is higher in some places than in others. Housing prices show up in the poverty line only to the extent that they affect the national consumer price index. The housing component of the price index should reflect the fact that low-income households must pay more than high-income households per quality-adjusted square foot. Moreover, it should hold neighborhood amenities constant so that, unlike a rent burden calculation, it will not reflect the lower housing prices associated with living in an amenity-poor neighborhood. As a result, the current official poverty measure counts too many people as poor in rural and some suburban areas and counts too few people as poor in cities and large urban areas.

Most scholars agree that poverty lines should reflect geographic variation in the cost of housing, and perhaps of other items purchased by poor households. For example, according to a panel convened by the National Research Council, "The poverty thresholds should be adjusted for differences in the cost of housing across geographic areas of the country" (Citro and Michael 1995, 183). This panel also implemented a correction for geographic housing price variation. However, they had so little information to work with that their correction dramatically understated housing price differences. Consequently, we do not know how many people would be poor or how the geographic distribution of poverty would change with a poverty line that reflected actual housing costs. It seems likely, however, that an accurate adjustment would boost the poverty rate and the extent of concentrated poverty in large cities. It might also reveal that existing evidence significantly understates the number of poor households whose options for escaping poverty are severely limited by the share of their income they must devote to housing.

POOR-QUALITY HOUSING AND HOUSING HEALTH RISKS As explained earlier, one way for poor people to win the spatial competition for housing is to rent small or low-quality apartments, paying more per unit of housing than higher-income households. In 1997, for example, 13.7 percent of poor households, compared with 5.8 percent of nonpoor households, lived in houses with moderate or severe physical problems (U.S. Bureau of the Census 2001). In addition, 7.0 percent of poor households, compared with 2.0 percent of nonpoor households, lived in overcrowded conditions. Two features of low quality, the presence of lead paint and animal pests, are linked to poverty because they can have serious health consequences. Poor health contributes to poverty in the short run by requiring additional spending out of stressed budgets, and in the long run by interfering with education, sapping strength and energy, and ultimately lowering wages (Mullahy and Wolfe, this volume).

Paint containing lead was outlawed in 1978, but it remains on the walls of many old apartments. "Lead is dangerous for small children because it can lead to lowered intelligence. Elevated blood lead among children in the United States most often results from residence in an older house that has lead paint, which may flake or peel, causing lead dust to be distributed in the house. Young children may eat paint chips or inadvertently take in lead by tasting dusty objects" (Pamuk et al. 1998,62). The link between poverty and elevated blood levels of lead is strong for children between ages one and five. Over the 1988 to 1994 period, "about 12% of children living in poor families had an elevated lead level, compared with about 2% of children in high-income families" (Pamuk et al. 1998, 62). Although no direct measure of exposure to lead paint is available, the 1997 American Housing Survey (AHS) reveals that poor households are twice as likely as nonpoor households (5.2 percent versus 2.5 percent) to have broken plaster or interior peeling paint; (U.S. Bureau of the Census 2001).

Asthma is "the most common chronic disease in childhood" (Pamuk et al. 1998, 82) and "the most common cause of hospitalization among American children" (Noble 1999). Moreover, this condition is much more common among poor children than among other children. In 1996, 6.3 percent of the children in the country had asthma, whereas some poor elementary schools in the Bronx have rates over 20 percent (Bernstein 1999). Although asthma can be treated, severe, even life-threatening episodes can arise if it is not managed properly.[6] One measure of the incidence of severe episodes— namely, trips to the hospital to treat an asthma attack—shows a clear link to poverty. Between 1989 and 1991, children between ages one and fourteen "living in communities with a median family income below $20,000 were 2.4 times as likely to be hospitalized with asthma as those living in neighborhoods with an income of at least $40,000" (Pamuk et al. 1998, 82). Moreover, the annual hospitalization rate in very poor neighborhoods in New York City was 228 children per 10,000, compared with a rate of zero in rich neighborhoods (Noble 1999).

Asthma attacks are associated with indicators of poor housing quality, including the presence of cockroaches or mice (Associated Press 2000; Leary 1997). Also associated with asthma are dust, dust mites, mold, and mildew, all of which are more likely to occur in low-quality housing (Stolberg 1999). There is no direct measure of the extent to which poor households are exposed to these factors, but one hint comes from the 1997 AHS: poor households are almost twice as likely as nonpoor households (13.1 percent compared with 7.0 percent) to live in units with signs of rats or mice (U.S. Bureau of the Census 2001).

LACK OF ACCESS TO HOUSING WEALTH   Barriers to homeownership prevent poor people from gaining access to the most widely used method for obtaining wealth. Wealth is, of course, a buffer against income fluctuations and therefore provides insurance against falling into poverty. When a job loss or a bout of illness occurs, the owner of a house may be able to borrow against it, or even sell it, to obtain needed resources.

According to one recent estimate, most households hold the vast majority of their nonpension wealth in the form of home equity, and over one-third of total household nonpension wealth is in housing (Hurst et al. 1998). In the early years of a mortgage, the vast majority of the mortgage payment goes to paying interest and therefore does not add to wealth. Over time, however, both house values and the share of mortgage payments going toward principal tend to grow, so that long-term owners often accumulate substantial equity in their homes.

Homeownership may also have nonfinancial consequences that help protect homeowners and their children from poverty. Homeowners may learn home repair and management skills, for example, and pass them on to their children. Richard Green and Michele White (1997) find some evidence for such mechanisms. All else being equal, the children of homeowners are less likely to drop out of high school or to have children of their own while still teenagers. For example, the probability that a high school student in a low-income family will stay in school is nineteen percentage points higher if the student's parents are homeowners instead of renters. Because a high school degree has a large impact on a person's earnings potential (Karoly, this volume), homeownership serves as insurance against poverty in the next generation, even without considering its direct financial consequences.

Credit constraints appear to limit homeownership for low-income people. Recent research by John Duca and Stuart Rosenthal (1994) and Peter Linneman and his colleagues (1997), for example, shows that the down payment requirement poses a larger barrier to homeownership for most low-income households than does their low income. This constraint is not binding for low-income families who obtain funds from their parents or from a government-insured mortgage with a minimal down payment requirement. Kerwin Charles and Erik Hurst (in press) find, for example, that among households of white renters who became owners between 1991 and 1995, 15 percent received the funds for their down payment entirely from their extended families, and 27 percent received some family funds.

NEIGHBORHOOD EFFECTS   As shown earlier, poor people are concentrated in neighborhoods where poverty is relatively high. This income sorting is important because, according to a large literature, growing up in a high-poverty neighborhood may have a negative impact on many social and economic outcomes (Briggs 1997; Durlauf, this volume; Ellen and Turner 1997; Ginther, Haveman, and Wolfe, 2000). Although many studies find that growing up in a high-poverty neighborhood influences social and economic outcomes, there is no consensus about which outcomes are influenced by growing up in a distressed neighborhood or about the magnitude of these effects. Outcomes that show up in one or more studies include educational attainment, employment, teenage childbearing, and criminal activity. Different studies also use different variables to indicate neighborhood distress, and the literature does not determine exactly what mechanisms provide the link from poverty to outcomes.

In contrast, many studies find evidence that concentrated poverty has a negative impact on educational performance (Duncombe and Yinger 1998; Ferguson and Ladd 1996). Because an elementary school draws on a neighborhood, concentrated poverty in a neighborhood is the main explanation for concentrated poverty in a school. The exact nature of the causal mechanism is not well known, but schools with high poverty concentrations must spend more time dealing their students' family problems, and poor children receive relatively little reinforcement of school lessons at home. As a result, living in a neighborhood with concentrated poverty tends to lower a child's performance on standardized tests, all else being equal, and hence contributes to lower earnings potential and ultimately to poverty.

SPATIAL MISMATCH   As explained earlier, sorting outcomes change as job locations and other factors change. When low-skill jobs move to a new location, housing markets may adjust by providing housing nearby for low-income households. However, housing markets may not fully adjust to these trends. When low-skill jobs move to the suburbs, for example, established suburban neighborhoods may have such high levels of amenities that low-income households cannot compete for entry into them, even if they are willing to double up. Moreover, zoning restrictions and building codes may make it impossible to build low-income housing. Indeed, some of these types of policies may be selected by high-income communities as insurance against future housing market changes (Ross and Yinger 1999). Finally, adjustments in job and residential locations may be slowed by high search costs, which are made higher by the physical distance between existing residential locations and new job opportunities.

The result of these limits on adjustment may be a "mismatch" between residential locations and job locations. Because of restrictions posed by the high cost of housing in amenity-rich suburban neighborhoods, zoning constraints, and high search costs, housing markets may not adjust to the movement of low-skill jobs to the suburbs. As a result, low-income households may be stuck in the central city with poor access to low-skill jobs (Kasarda and Ting 1996).

Housing Discrimination, Segregation, and Poverty

As noted earlier, the poverty rates for blacks and Hispanics are much greater than the poverty rate for non-Hispanic whites. This section explores the role that housing markets play in maintaining these poverty differentials.

The Legacy of Past Discrimination

Discrimination is unfavorable treatment of an individual based on his membership in a particular group instead of on his relevant, observable social or economic characteristics. Even if there were no more discrimination in housing and mortgage markets (and that, as we will see, is not yet the case), the legacy of past discrimination would continue to affect housing market outcomes—and poverty. This section shows how three elements of this legacy—namely, income disparities, wealth disparities, and residential segregation—contribute to relatively high poverty rates for blacks and Hispanics.

INCOME DISPARITIES   Past discrimination in education, labor markets, and housing markets has resulted in lower education, fewer skills, and poorer job opportunities, and hence in lower incomes, for blacks and Hispanics than for whites. The relatively low incomes of Hispanics also reflect the fact that many Hispanics are recent immigrants who came to this country with little education and few skills. These income disparities continue to be large. In 1999, for example, median household income was $44,366 for non-Hispanic whites, $30,735 for Hispanics, and $27,910 for blacks (U.S. Bureau of the Census 2001).

Income disparities obviously make a direct contribution to the relatively high poverty rates of blacks and Hispanics. These disparities also have an important indirect impact on intergroup poverty differentials through all of the housing channels described earlier. A group with relatively low incomes faces relatively high rent burdens and can win the spatial competition for housing only by accepting low-quality housing, poor neighborhoods, or both. This low-income group also will find it harder to qualify for mortgages and will have poor access to suburban jobs.

WEALTH DISPARITIES   Intergroup wealth disparities are far larger than intergroup income disparities. Melvin Oliver and Thomas Shapiro (1995) find, for example, that in 1988 the ratio of black to white median household income was 0.62, but that the ratio of black to white median net worth was only 0.08. Moreover, the share of households with zero or negative net financial assets was much higher for blacks (60.9 percent) and Hispanics (54.0 percent) than for whites (25.3 percent). Erik Hurst, Ming Ching Luoh, and Frank Stafford (1998) find similar patterns for 1994. The median wealth of black households was $37,457, compared with a median of $177,952 for all other households. Even after controlling for permanent income and family characteristics, these authors find that blacks have $27,400 less wealth, on average, than other households.

Intergroup wealth disparities make it relatively difficult for low-income minority households to buy a house. Joseph Gyourko, Peter Linneman, and Susan Wachter (1999) find that blacks are more likely than whites to face a down payment constraint and that the existence of such a constraint has a larger impact on the likelihood of homeownership for black than for white households. The latter effect may reflect the intergenerational nature of wealth differences. As pointed out earlier, over 25 percent of whites receive family help with a down payment. In contrast, almost 90 percent of black home buyers come up with the entire down payment themselves, and only 6 percent receive the entire down payment from family (Charles and Hurst, in press).

RESIDENTIAL SEGREGATION Residential segregation, which is the physical separation of the residential locations of two groups, also contributes to intergroup poverty differentials (Massey and Denton 1993; Galster 1991, 1998; Yinger 1995).[7] The most widely used measure of segregation is the dissimilarity index, which indicates the extent to which the distribution of two groups across neighborhoods diverges from an even distribution, in which every location has the same group composition. According to this index, segregation between blacks and whites has been declining slowly since 1970 (Cutler et al. 1999; Massey and Denton 1993; Mumford Center for Comparative Urban and Regional Research 2001). In the twenty-three metropolitan areas with the largest black populations, for example, the average value of this index dropped from 78.8 in 1980 to 68.8 in 2000. The declines are largest in the areas with the fewest blacks, however, and blacks and whites are still far more segregated from each other than are other groups. Segregation between Hispanics and non-Hispanic whites is also relatively high. The average dissimilarity index in the twenty urban areas with at least two hundred thousand Hispanics was 48.0 in 1980 and increased slightly to 51.8 in 2000. This increase appears to be associated with extensive Hispanic immigration into these areas.

Evenness is only one dimension of residential segregation. Other dimensions include isolation, clustering, concentration, and centralization (Massey and Denton 1993). In a study of sixteen highly segregated urban areas (Denton 1994), black-white segregation increased between 1980 and

1990 on three of these five dimensions and decreased on two others (evenness and centralization). This study defines a "hypersegregated" metropolitan area as one with segregation indexes above 60.0 on at least four of these five dimensions. The number of hypersegregated areas increased from sixteen to nineteen between 1980 and 1990.

Segregation influences poverty in several ways. First, as explained by Douglas Massey (1990), it interacts with the high poverty rates among blacks and Hispanics to magnify concentrated black and Hispanic poverty—and hence to magnify the disadvantages that blacks and Hispanics face from living in high-poverty neighborhoods.

Another impact of segregation operates through the labor market (Kain 1968). Firms whose customers are mostly prejudiced whites may discriminate against black or Hispanic job applicants to avoid losing customers, particularly if the jobs involve face-to-face contact with customers. Because segregation results in many locations where most of the residents, and hence customers, are white, it also results in many locations where firms have an incentive to discriminate against black and Hispanic applicants. Harry Holzer and Keith Ihlanfeldt (1998, 862) uncover clear support for this hypothesis. They find that "the larger the fraction of minority customers, the higher is the probability that workers from that minority group will be hired. These results are apparent even in models with detailed controls for skill requirements on jobs and establishment location."

Cutler and Glaeser (1997) estimate the overall impact of segregation on social and economic outcomes for minorities. They find that, in 1990, blacks between the ages of twenty and thirty were less likely to have graduated from high school or college, less likely to have a job, more likely to have relatively low earnings, and more likely to be a single mother if they lived in a highly segregated metropolitan area instead of a less segregated area.

The Role of Current Discrimination

No one doubts that blacks and Hispanics have faced discrimination in the past, but many people assert that discrimination is no longer a problem. This section explores the evidence concerning the persistence of discrimination in housing and its impacts on poverty for blacks and Hispanics.

HOW MUCH DISCRIMINATION STILL EXISTS IN HOUSING MAR-KETS? The best recent evidence about the extent of discrimination in housing comes from studies based on a technique called a fair housing audit

(Fix and Struyk 1993; Yinger 1995).[8] An audit makes it possible to compare the way housing agents treat people in a historically disadvantaged group with the way they treat equally qualified people in the majority group. Auditors are carefully selected and trained and then assigned to teams consisting of one person from each group. These procedures are designed to ensure that teammates are equally qualified to rent an apartment or buy a house. Teammates are sent out successively to visit a housing agent and to inquire about an advertised housing unit, and each auditor independently records how he or she was treated. Discrimination is said to exist if auditors in the disadvantaged group systematically receive less favorable treatment than do their teammates.

Most audit studies focus on the *incidence* of discrimination, using one of two simple measures. The gross incidence of unfavorable treatment, or the "gross measure" for short, is the share of audits in which the minority auditor is treated less favorably than his or her teammate. The net incidence of unfavorable treatment, or the "net measure," equals the gross measure minus the share of audits in which the minority auditor is treated more favorably. This "netting-out" is designed to account for random factors that might lead to unfavorable treatment of the minority auditor. In practice, the net and gross measures are often far apart. Some scholars favor the net measure because it is a lower bound and therefore will not overstate discrimination. Other scholars favor the gross measure because, in the spirit of the Fair Housing Act, it identifies all cases in which a minority auditor was treated less favorably, for whatever reasons. Another approach is to estimate formally the role of random factors and then explicitly to remove them when calculating the incidence of discrimination (Ondrich et al. 2000). This approach tends to yield estimates of discrimination that fall between the simple net and gross measures.

A national audit study, the Housing Discrimination Study (HDS), was conducted in 1989 (Yinger 1995). It examined discrimination against blacks and Hispanics in twenty-five metropolitan areas with significant minority populations and was designed to yield nationally representative results. Each audit was based on a housing advertisement randomly selected from the weekend edition of the major newspaper in the area. Almost four thousand audits were conducted in all. Table 10.1 presents a few of the incidence results from the HDS.[9] Using the net measure, for example, black renters faced a 10.7 percent chance of being totally excluded from housing made available to comparable white renters, and a 23.3 percent chance of learning about fewer apartments.

Table 10.1   Incidence of Discrimination in Housing: 1989 Housing Discrimination
             Study

	Black-White Audits		Hispanic–Non-Hispanic Audits	
	Net	Gross	Net	Gross
Sales audits				
Excluded from all available units	6.3*	7.6	14.5[+]	7.5
Advertised unit inspected	5.6*	13.3	4.2*	13.2
Number of houses made available	19.4*	44.1	16.5*	43.6
Auditor asked to call back	3.3*	25.9	11.5*	30.4
Auditor received follow-up call	7.7*	18.5	5.5*	16.4
Auditor received positive comments on house	12.5*	47.9	7.5*	47.5
Agent offered to help auditor find financing	11.3*	24.4	4.4[+]	22.1
Overall treatment[a]	30.1*	50.4	23.9*	44.6
Rental audits				
Excluded from all available units	10.7*	15.1	6.5*	12.1
Advertised unit inspected	12.5*	23.0	5.1	17.6
Number of apartments made available	23.3*	41.4	9.8	17.6
Auditor asked to call back	15.8*	30.5	8.6*	28.5
Auditor received special rental incentives	5.4*	10.3	5.1*	12.6
Auditor received positive comments on apartment	16.8*	48.4	14.6*	46.4
Overall treatment[a]	27.8*	45.7	22.3*	42.7

Sources: Yinger (1995, tables 3.1, 3.3, 3.5) and calculations by the author.

a. Overall treatment is measured with an index covering housing availability, efforts to complete a transaction, credit, and steering.

* Statistically significant at the 5 percent two-tailed level based on a fixed-effects logit procedure (net measure only).

[+] Statistically significant at the 5 percent one-tailed level based on a fixed-effects logit procedure (net measure only).

There is no evidence of a trend in the incidence of discrimination over the last twenty years. The results of a 1977 national study (Wienk et al. 1979) were similar to those of the 1989 HDS (Yinger 1995). Moreover, fair housing groups conducted both black-white and Hispanic-white audits in several metropolitan areas during the 1990s and found incidence measures that are roughly comparable to the HDS results (Yinger 1998).

Some types of agent behavior, such as the number of houses shown to a customer, are a matter of degree. In these cases, audits can explore the *severity* of discrimination, defined as the magnitude of treatment differences between groups (Page 1995; Roychoudhry and Goodman 1996; Yinger 1995). According to the HDS data, black home buyers learn about 23.7 percent fewer houses than do their white teammates. The comparable measure of severity is 24.5 percent for black renters, 25.6 percent for Hispanic home buyers, and 10.9 percent for Hispanic renters (Yinger 1995).

HOW MUCH DISCRIMINATION STILL EXISTS IN MORTGAGE MARKETS?   A study of discrimination in the approval of mortgage loans, based on 1990 data from Boston, found that black and Hispanic customers were 82 percent more likely to be turned down for a loan than were white customers, even after controlling for credit qualifications and loan type (Munnell, Browne, et al. 1996).[10] Although this study, which is known as the Boston Fed Study, has been criticized by many observers, several independent investigations have confirmed the original study's findings (see Ladd 1998 and Ross and Yinger, forthcoming, and the studies cited therein).

Audit studies of preapplication behavior by lenders have also found evidence of discrimination. Recent audit data from eight major urban areas indicate, for example, that whites were more likely than blacks or Hispanics to receive an estimate of mortgage payments and of closing costs, and in some cities whites were also quoted lower interest rates and were less likely to be steered toward Federal Housing Administration (FHA) loans (Smith and DeLair 1999).

THE IMPACT OF DISCRIMINATION ON HOUSING MARKETS   Households find housing through a complicated search process, which is initiated whenever some change in their circumstances, such as a change in employment or the arrival of a new child, significantly alters their demand for housing (Yinger 1997). Housing discrimination affects this search process in several different ways. First, it prevents blacks and Hispanics from learning about some available housing units. Second, discrimination makes the search process both less pleasant and more costly for blacks and Hispanics than for whites.

According to the HDS, blacks and Hispanics encounter discrimination in both the sales and rental markets (Yinger 1995). Compared to whites, blacks and Hispanics are quoted higher rents for advertised housing units; are less likely to be offered special rental incentives, such as a free month's rent or free parking; and are given less information and assistance in finding a mortgage. This discrimination by real estate agents is accompanied, of course, by lending discrimination.

The net impact of this discrimination is that black and Hispanic households cannot expect to gain as much as white households do from a housing search. As a result, black and Hispanic households are less likely than white households to move. One estimate finds that discrimination at the levels currently observed could discourage as many as 20 percent of the moves that would otherwise be made by black households (Yinger 1997). Moreover, Charles and Hurst (in press) find that black renters are significantly less likely than whites to apply for a mortgage, even controlling for age, income, family composition, and a variety of other factors. In addition, when black and Hispanic families do move, they can expect to find houses that have a poorer match to their preferences than the matches obtained by whites.

Overall, therefore, black and Hispanic households must pay higher search costs, accept lower-quality housing, and live in lower-quality neighborhoods than comparable white households. These three possibilities are directly related to poverty. Higher search costs represent higher housing costs; living in lower-quality housing carries a higher risk of exposure to lead paint and asthma-inducing conditions; and living in lower-quality neighborhoods results in poorer social and economic outcomes. One study estimates that to avoid these discrimination-imposed constraints, an average household would be willing to pay roughly $4,000 every time some change in circumstances gives it an incentive to search for a new home (Yinger 1997).

Continuing discrimination obviously reduces the homeownership rate of blacks and Hispanics. Several studies find that blacks and Hispanics still have lower homeownership rates than whites even after controlling for factors that reflect past discrimination or immigration status, such as income, down payment capacity, and family structure—a sign that housing discrimination is still at work (Gyourko and Linneman 1997; Painter, Gabriel, and Myers 2001).

Segregation, Discrimination, and Poverty

The combined impact of past and current discrimination on poverty can be seen in four of the five channels through which housing affects poverty.

HIGH RENT BURDENS   Black and Hispanic poor people are affected by the high rent burdens that face all poor people. However, segregation and discrimination do not appear to boost the role of housing costs for these groups. First, the most recent studies of intergroup price differentials in housing find no evidence that blacks pay more than whites at any income level, after controlling for housing and neighborhood characteristics (Chambers 1992; Harris 1999; Kiel and Zabel 1996). Second, rent burdens in 1997 are virtually the same for black, Hispanic, and white poor households: 68.2 percent of poor blacks, 74.0 percent of poor nonblacks, 75.8 percent of poor Hispanics, and 72.1 percent of poor non-Hispanics pay more than 30 percent of their income for housing. Moreover, rent burdens exceed 50 percent for close to half of the poor people in each of these four groups (U.S. Bureau of the Census 2001).

These results might change if poverty lines were revised to account for geographic variation in housing costs. Black and Hispanic poor people are more likely than white poor people to live in central cities, where the cost of housing is relatively high. As a result, revising the poverty lines would probably increase the number of black and Hispanic poor people relative to the number of white poor people, and it might also increase the share of black and Hispanic poor people with high housing costs relative to the comparable share of white poor people.

POOR-QUALITY HOUSING AND HOUSING HEALTH RISKS   The impacts of segregation and discrimination on housing quality can be seen in the incidence of housing problems. In 1997 moderate or severe housing problems were experienced by 20.1 percent of poor blacks, 11.8 percent of poor nonblacks, 19.6 percent of poor Hispanics, and 12.7 percent of nonpoor Hispanics (U.S. Bureau of the Census 2001). The rough indicators of health problems mentioned earlier also vary across groups: 8.3 percent of poor blacks and 4.2 percent of poor nonblacks lived in housing with evidence of rodents, and 20.7 percent of poor blacks, compared with 10.9 percent of poor nonblacks, lived in housing with chipped plaster or peeling paint. These figures are virtually the same for poor Hispanics compared to poor non-Hispanics. Thus, segregation and discrimination concentrate low-income blacks and Hispanics in poor, even health-threatening housing, adding another barrier to escaping poverty.

LACK OF ACCESS TO HOUSING WEALTH   Income and wealth differentials, along with segregation and discrimination, combine to produce large, long-standing intergroup differences in homeownership. Homeownership is obviously less common among poor than among nonpoor households.

However, the homeownership of poor nonblacks is greater than the home-ownership rate of all blacks, and the rate of poor non-Hispanics is greater than the rate of all Hispanics (U.S. Bureau of the Census 2001). Thus, segregation and discrimination constitute severe barriers to homeownership for all black and Hispanic households, especially poor ones. The resulting low homeownership rates for blacks and Hispanics imply that these groups have limited access to the "insurance" against poverty that homeownership represents.

NEIGHBORHOOD EFFECTS Segregation and discrimination magnify concentrated poverty. In large cities in 1990, 83.2 percent of black poor people (compared with 58.2 percent of poor nonblacks) and 77.0 percent of Hispanic poor people (compared with 66.1 percent of poor non-Hispanics) lived in neighborhoods where more than 20 percent of the residents were poor (Kasarda 1993). For blacks, these disparities were even more striking for residence in neighborhoods where the poverty rate exceeded 40 percent. The share of poor blacks who lived in these neighborhoods, 41.6 percent, was more than two and a quarter times the share of poor nonblacks, 18.3 percent. This share also appears to be increasing. For the nation as a whole, not just in large cities, the share of poor blacks in high-poverty tracts increased from 26.1 percent in 1970 to 33.5 percent in 1990 (Jargowsky 1997).

Not surprisingly, black and Hispanic poor households also tend to live in neighborhoods that experience relatively high distress on other indicators. According to the 1997 American Housing Survey, for example, 12.9 percent of poor blacks, compared with 5.8 percent of poor nonblacks, live in neighborhoods where crime is so bothersome that they would like to move (U.S. Bureau of the Census 2001). Overall, therefore, the negative impact of harsh neighborhood conditions on social and economic outcomes, and hence on poverty, is more likely to be experienced by poor people who are black or Hispanic than by poor people who are white.

The impact of segregation and discrimination on the school environment for black and Hispanic children is also dramatic. Two-thirds of black students and almost three-quarters of Hispanic students in 1990–91 attended schools in which most of the students were black or Hispanic (Orfield et al. 1993). In large cities, 92.4 percent of black children and 93.8 percent of Hispanic children attend predominantly minority schools, and a majority of black and Hispanic children attend largely minority schools even in the suburbs of large cities.

School segregation is driven largely by segregation across school districts, not by segregation within school districts (Clotfelter 1999). Thus, intergroup disparities in income and wealth and current discrimination in housing continue to play important roles in maintaining school segregation. In the South, where school districts tend to be relatively large, residential segregation within districts used to play a major role in school segregation. This within-district segregation was reduced dramatically by school district desegregation orders issued by federal courts and upheld by the U.S. Supreme Court in the 1970s. However, the Supreme Court is now repealing these orders (Orfield and Eaton 1996), and within-district segregation may once again become an important phenomenon.

Gary Orfield and his colleagues (1993) show that 60.2 percent of schools in which fewer than 10 percent of the students are black or Hispanic have poverty rates below 10 percent. In contrast, 56.5 percent of largely minority schools have poverty rates above 50 percent. Thus, segregation and discrimination in housing serve to separate black and Hispanic children into schools where poverty rates are relatively high and, as a result, student performance is relatively low. The ensuing educational disparities translate into earnings disparities, and hence into higher poverty for blacks and Hispanics.

SPATIAL MISMATCH   Residential discrimination and segregation play an important role in the well-known spatial mismatch hypothesis (Kain 1968). Segregated housing patterns keep blacks far from suburbanizing jobs and associated job information networks, and housing discrimination makes it difficult for blacks to adjust to suburbanizing jobs by moving. Because of this limited residential mobility, blacks have less information about jobs than whites do and will not receive as much benefit from the suburban jobs they do find owing to the long commuting distance from their central locations. Thus, segregation, suburbanizing employment, and continuing housing discrimination together result in higher unemployment and lower wages for blacks than for whites.

Because it brings together two well-known and widespread urban phenomena, namely, residential segregation and job suburbanization, this hypothesis has been extensively studied (Ihlanfeldt and Sjoquist 1998; Kain 1992, Ferguson, this volume). Because it is so complicated, however, the spatial mismatch hypothesis has proven to be difficult to test. As shown by a basic analysis of urban housing markets, for example, one cannot compare the real incomes of two groups simply by looking at their employment outcomes but instead must also consider how much the two groups pay for housing and how far they have to commute. A full test of the spatial mismatch therefore requires a simultaneous examination of job, housing, and commuting outcomes.

Perhaps the most compelling evidence for the spatial mismatch hypothesis comes from the employment situation of teenagers, who for the most part do not make their own housing decisions. Ihlanfeldt and Sjoquist (1990) and Ihlanfeldt (1993) find that access to jobs heavily influences employment for both minority and white youth; that average access to jobs is much higher for whites than for blacks or Hispanics; and that differences in job access explain a large portion of the unemployment gap between white and minority youth. The spatial mismatch for adults is harder to study because it requires comparisons of housing prices, commuting distances, and employment outcomes. One study examines unique data on the racial composition of the workforce and the geographical location of firms in Chicago and Los Angeles in 1974 and 1980 (Leonard 1987). In both cities, the share of workers who were black fell steadily with distance from largely black neighborhoods. This finding is consistent with the spatial mismatch hypothesis, but it does not indicate the precise mechanism at work or the role of housing discrimination.

Evidence about spatial mismatch is also provided by studies of the Gautreaux Program, which helps public housing residents in Chicago find housing throughout the metropolitan area, including in largely white suburbs. Since it began in 1976, this program has helped over six thousand families, mostly headed by black single women, by giving them rent subsidies and housing counseling. Roughly half of the participating families moved to the suburbs; the other half moved to noncentral parts of Chicago. Susan Popkin, James Rosenbaum, and Patricia Meaden (1993) find that participants who moved to the suburbs were more likely to have a job than participants who stayed in the central city. Rosenbaum and his colleagues (1993) find that children in participating families had a higher likelihood of attending college or, for those not attending college, higher employment rates, higher wages, and higher job benefits if their family moved to the suburbs instead of staying in the city. This evidence supports the spatial mismatch hypothesis because it indicates that employment outcomes for blacks and outcomes for their children improve when barriers that keep them from finding suburban jobs, such as housing discrimination, are broken.

In 1994 the federal government implemented a Gautreaux-type program called Moving To Opportunity (MTO) in five urban areas (Turner 1998). This program is distinguished by the random assignment of applicants to treatment and control groups. Evidence on the employment impacts of MTO is not yet available, so it does not yet shed much light on the spatial mismatch hypothesis. However, early MTO evidence highlights two of the other channels through which housing markets influence poverty, namely, housing quality and neighborhood effects. Using Boston MTO data through 1998, Lawrence Katz, Jeffrey Kling, and Jeffrey Liebman (2001) find that the participating families had better neighborhood outcomes than families in the control group, particularly in terms of safety.[11] In addition, children in the participating families had better outcomes than children in control families on a variety of indicators, including the prevalence of behavioral problems, injuries, and asthma attacks. For example, participation resulted in a 65 percent decline in the probability of an asthma attack requiring medical attention. Thus, MTO clearly leads to a significant improvement in neighborhood quality. The result for asthma also could reflect an improvement in housing quality. In principle, these improvements in neighborhood and housing quality result in lower poverty for participating families and for their children when they form families of their own, but the MTO studies do not directly test this prediction.

Housing Policies to Reduce Ethnic Poverty Disparities

This section explores some of the federal housing policies that might be able to lessen ethnic poverty disparities. Other chapters in this volume explore relevant policies in other markets.

Antidiscrimination Legislation and Enforcement

The most direct way to combat discrimination is through antidiscrimination legislation and enforcement.

FAIR HOUSING ENFORCEMENT   Discrimination in housing is prohibited by the Fair Housing Act of 1968.[12] However, the enforcement provisions of that act were limited, and the federal government did not obtain broad enforcement powers until the Fair Housing Amendments Act of 1988 established a system of administrative law judges (ALJs) with the power to hear cases brought to HUD and to levy fines, allowed HUD to initiate investigations independent of complaints, and authorized damages and civil penalties in cases brought by the Justice Department.

HUD now processes about ten thousand discrimination complaints per year (Schill and Friedman 1999). Most cases are settled out of court, some are dismissed by HUD, and others go to either an administrative law judge or the Justice Department for prosecution in federal court.[13] In many cases, discriminators have been required to pay large financial penalties. Moreover, both HUD and Justice have been using their investigative powers in recent years. For example, Justice has been using the auditing technique described earlier to determine whether various large landlords practice discrimination. Since this program was put into place in 1992, fifty-nine cases have been settled or adjudicated, all but three in favor of Justice, with total damages of $8.7 million.

State and local fair housing agencies, both public and private, are the federal government's partners in enforcing the Fair Housing Act. Public agencies operating under a fair housing law that is substantially equivalent to the federal act must process a complaint before it can be sent to HUD. Most states now have such a law. Moreover, private agencies can bring civil suits against alleged discriminators, and many such suits have brought relief for victims of discrimination. In recognition of these partnerships, the federal government passed the Fair Housing Assistance Program of 1984, which assists public agencies with their complaint-processing duties, and the Fair Housing Initiatives Program of 1986, which supports public and private fair housing agencies in their auditing programs and other activities. Since 1990, fair housing agencies supported by these programs have brought over one thousand lawsuits against alleged discriminators and obtained financial recovery totaling over $115 million (Fair Housing Center of Metropolitan Detroit 1999).

The main objective of fair housing policy should be to maintain and strengthen this enforcement system. However, some new policies may have to be designed. One example concerns the growing role of the Internet in housing sales and rentals.[14] In principle, this development could make it more difficult for housing agents to discriminate because they cannot identify a person's ethnicity based on an Internet inquiry. However, housing agents still might screen people once they make face-to-face contact, and access to the Internet appears to differ on the grounds of both income and ethnicity.

Another example of limits in the current fair housing enforcement system concerns the marketing of housing in largely black neighborhoods. The national housing audit studies conducted in both 1977 (Wienk et al. 1979) and 1989 (Turner 1992; Turner and Mickelsons 1992; Yinger 1995) found that houses in black neighborhoods were significantly underrepresented in a random sample of newspaper advertisements. To some degree, this outcome may reflect discrimination in real estate brokers' advertising practices (Newburger 1995; Turner 1992). However, this outcome also could reflect the fact that brokers do not seek, and prospective sellers do not offer, listings in some black neighborhoods, and may therefore not involve any discrimination. As a result, new policies may be needed to ensure that multiple listing services and other elements of the real estate brokerage network cover all neighborhoods in an urban area (Yinger 1995).

FAIR LENDING ENFORCEMENT   Discrimination in mortgage lending was made illegal by the Fair Housing Act of 1968 and by the Equal Credit Opportunity Act of 1974. In addition, the Community Reinvestment Act (CRA) of 1977 requires some lenders to meet the credit needs of all the neighborhoods in their lending territories. The main burden of enforcement falls on the federal financial regulatory institutions, such as the Federal Reserve Board and the Comptroller of the Currency, although HUD and Justice also play an important role (Yinger 1995). These institutions try to prevent discrimination with a variety of regulatory tools, but discrimination in mortgage lending is difficult to prove, and few cases of lending discrimination have made it into court or even into formal settlement discussions. In recent years, however, several high-profile settlements have been reached in cases involving lending discrimination (Yinger 1995).

The fair lending enforcement system faces several challenges. The first grows from the increasing use of credit scoring and other automated underwriting techniques. Credit scoring involves the calculation of an applicant's creditworthiness using a strict formula applied to her financial characteristics, such as her income or whether she has ever defaulted on a loan. An applicant's credit score may be combined with the characteristics of the property or other factors in another automated calculation to determine whether the loan should be approved.

The use of automated underwriting techniques has the potential to lessen discrimination because it leads to mortgage transactions that do not involve face-to-face contact. However, civil rights laws outlaw two different forms of discrimination. Disparate-treatment discrimination occurs when a lender uses different underwriting standards for blacks and Hispanics (or some other legally protected class) than for whites. Disparate-impact discrimination occurs when a lender uses underwriting standards that both have a disproportionate impact on a protected class and are not necessary to protect the lender's profits.[15] Even if automated underwriting techniques eliminate disparate-treatment discrimination, they may result in disparate-impact discrimination. Unfortunately, evidence on this possibility does not yet exist. Moreover, current far-lending enforcement procedures do not even look for disparate-impact discrimination, and they are in urgent need of revision (Ross and Yinger, forthcoming).

A second challenge grows out of the large role now played by non-depository lenders, called mortgage bankers, who arrived on the scene after the banking deregulation that started around 1980. They now make approximately half of all mortgage loans. Instead of raising money through deposits, these lenders finance their loans by selling them as income-producing assets to institutions in the secondary mortgage market. Mortgage bankers pose a challenge to the fair lending system for two reasons. First, they are not regulated by a federal financial regulatory agency but instead are covered by the Federal Trade Commission (FTC), which does not have the breadth of regulatory tools available to these other agencies. Second, mortgage bankers often specialize in relatively high-risk (and hence high-priced) lending but are not covered by the Community Reinvestment Act (Yinger 1995). As a result, low-income neighborhoods are increasingly served primarily by high-cost loans provided by mortgage bankers. In some cases, the higher rates charged in low-income neighborhoods might be justified by higher credit risk. In other cases, they could be the result of discrimination that is covered by existing legislation. According to existing fair lending legislation, however, it is not illegal for a mortgage bank to specialize in low-income, minority areas and to charge the same high interest rate to all its customers. If the residents of these areas do not learn about the lower-cost loan products provided by other lenders, they may end up paying higher-interest rates than other people with the same credit qualifications, without any discrimination. Programs to provide information about available loan products might help to avoid these problems, as would making mortgage bankers subject to CRA (Yinger 1995).

Programs to Support Neighborhood Integration

One way to help break the segregation-poverty link is to lessen segregation, or equivalently, to promote stable neighborhood integration. The evidence reviewed earlier indicates that there is more intergroup contact in neighborhoods than there used to be, but well-established and recognized integrated neighborhoods are still hard to find. Philip Nyden and his colleagues (1998) identify fourteen neighborhoods with significant integration between blacks and whites in both 1980 and 1990. Virtually all of these neighborhoods have public or private organizations to provide housing information, promote intergroup contact, or conciliate intergroup disputes. One approach to promoting integration, therefore, would be for the federal government to fund community-based integration efforts.

A program of this kind should not use discrimination to promote integration (Yinger 1995). In some circumstances, integrated neighborhoods are difficult to sustain because many more blacks or Hispanics than whites want to move in. It is tempting in this case to maintain integration by denying entry to some blacks or Hispanics. This approach was used, and eventually rejected, by the U.S. Supreme Court in Starrett City, a large housing development in New York City. The best way to avoid this dilemma is to inform people who want to move into an integrated neighborhood about alternative neighborhoods and to give them assistance in finding housing there. Some of the programs discussed in the next section could serve this purpose.

Another issue concerns the use of financial incentives that encourage individuals to move into integrated neighborhoods. Several communities have used incentives of this type. Shaker Heights, Ohio, offered subsidized second mortgages, and Oak Park, Illinois, implemented an equity assurance program to calm residents' fears about their property values (Galster 1990a). A problem with this approach is that these subsidies primarily go to white households, not to blacks or Hispanics, and they give the appearance of paying people for their prejudice.

Rental Housing Subsidies

The serious housing affordability problem faced by poor households is not eliminated by federal assistance; only 15.7 percent of poor households receive a federal housing subsidy (U.S. Bureau of the Census 2001).[16] Federal rental housing subsidies fall into three categories: project-based, household-based, and tax-based. This section discusses these categories of assistance and their potential for narrowing intergroup poverty differentials.

PROJECT-BASED SUBSIDIES   Project-based subsidies go to public housing and to the developers of low-income private housing. Public housing was the main form of federal housing assistance in the 1950s and early 1960s, and project-based subsidies were the main form in the late 1960s and 1970s (Quigley 2000).

Public housing is no longer being built by the federal government, but public housing projects exist throughout the country. Large public housing projects in large cities are the most segregated and distressed neighborhoods in the nation. In 1993, for example, 90 percent of the tenants in the projects operated by the largest public housing authorities were black or Hispanic, and most of the tenants were very poor single mothers (U.S. Department of Housing and Urban Development 1995). In addition, 36.5 percent of public housing units are in census tracts with a poverty rate above 40 percent, and 37.6 percent of these units are in tracts where blacks and Hispanics make up at least 80 percent of the population. The comparable figures for units inhabited by all households that receive welfare are only 11.6 and 17.8 percent, respectively (Newman and Schnare 1997). Moreover, most of these projects are now old, deteriorated, and expensive to maintain, and for many years HUD enforced a one-for-one rule that made it illegal to tear down a unit of public housing without building a replacement unit, even though no funding for replacement units was available. This situation is full of irony. A program designed to provide decent, affordable housing now traps poor black and Hispanic households in very low-quality housing with the nation's highest concentrations of poverty. To some degree, therefore, public housing contributes to intergroup poverty disparities through the housing quality and neighborhood channels described earlier.

In recent years, HUD has modified the one-for-one rule so that a tenant could be given a household-based subsidy instead of a new unit when her unit was demolished (Cuomo and Lucas 2000). HUD also has upgraded some projects, knocked down some of the worst projects, raised the income limits so that some projects will not have such concentrated poverty, and provided new household-based subsidies to allow some tenants to find alternative housing. The available evidence indicates, however, that public housing tenants who receive household-based subsidies move to neighborhoods that are higher in quality but no less segregated than the neighborhoods in which their projects were located (Varacy and Walker 2000). Moreover, HUD has not made much progress in integrating public housing projects.

In the 1980s, a consensus developed among scholars and policymakers that project-based subsidies were more expensive per household than household-based subsidies (McClure 1998; Quigley 2000). Moreover, most subsidized projects were built in low-income areas, so they did not improve neighborhood quality for tenants relative to unsubsidized households with the same income (Newman and Schnare 1997). As a result, the federal government no longer subsidizes new construction in this manner. However, hundreds of thousands of apartments built in the 1970s still receive project-based subsidies; the contracts on these developments are starting to run out, and some of the owners are converting them into market-rate projects. The federal government has responded to this loss of affordable housing by funding new household-based subsidies, but the net impact on the ability of low-income households to find affordable housing may still be negative.

HOUSEHOLD-BASED SUBSIDIES Household-based subsidies, also called certificates or vouchers, are now the only significant source of new housing assistance. The main program, Section 8, provides participating households in qualifying apartments with a certificate equal to the difference between their rent and 30 percent of their income.[17] HUD issued fifty thousand new Section 8 certificates in fiscal year 1999, and sixty thousand in fiscal year 2000. Housing certificates allow participants to move into higher-quality housing units, and they appear to have a larger impact on recipients' neighborhood quality and on segregation than do project-based subsidies (Newman and Schnare 1997; Turner 1998). For black and Hispanic households, however, anticipated discrimination constricts the range of housing search, so the origin and destination tracts of new Section 8 certificate holders have similar poverty rates and minority concentration (Turner 1998).[18]

The evidence from the Gautreaux and MTO programs indicates that the geographic range of a recipient household's housing search can be expanded by combining a housing certificate with housing counseling, including assistance in identifying available apartments (Turner 1998). These programs have potential for reducing intergroup poverty differentials by reducing rent burdens, improving housing quality, improving neighborhood quality, and lessening spatial mismatches.

TAX SUBSIDIES The current federal income tax subsidy program for rental housing, which was enacted in 1986, is called the Low-Income Housing Tax Credit. This program has helped subsidize the construction of roughly half a million apartments, mostly in ethnically homogeneous neighborhoods (Cummings and DiPasquale 1999; McClure 2000). Although many of these units have been built in relatively poor neighborhoods, their rents tend to be too high for poor households, despite the fact that the tax subsidy alone is estimated to be about $30,000 per unit. This subsidy is typically accompanied by other subsidies, including household-based subsidies, and most of the units are built by nonprofit developers.[19] Overall, therefore, this program appears to be a relatively expensive way to expand the supply of moderate-cost housing and to ease the neighborhood effect in some poor areas.

Support for Homeownership

DIRECT SUBSIDIES The federal government funds a variety of small programs designed to promote homeownership. The HOPE program, which began in 1992, helps nonprofit and city agencies purchase single-family homes, repair them, and sell them to low-income families. By the end of 1995, this program had provided homes for 1,234 families, one-third of whom were former tenants of public housing (U.S. Department of Housing and Urban Development 1996). The Home Investment Partnership Program, which also was started in 1992, provides about $1.5 billion per year to localities, both directly and through their states, for subsidizing low-income home buyers (Stegman and Luger 1993). Homeownership programs like these have a high cost per household and have never been a large part of the federal housing budget.

TAX SUBSIDIES The federal government provides extensive assistance to homeowners in the form of income tax deductions for property taxes and home mortgage interest. The official estimate of the cost of these deductions is about $75 billion, but a proper accounting, which recognizes that homeowners do not pay taxes on the implicit rental income from their houses, places the value of these tax breaks 80 percent higher (Follain, Ling, and McGill 1993). Since the total HUD budget is only $26 billion, these tax breaks obviously cost the federal government many times as much money as it spends on all its rental assistance programs.

For two reasons, these tax breaks are more valuable to high-income owners than to low-income owners. First, these deductions do not provide any benefit unless they total more than the standard deduction, which is now quite generous. Houses of lesser value are obviously less likely to generate deductions meeting this condition. Second, the value of the deductions depends on a homeowner's marginal tax bracket: a low-income family in the 15 percent bracket receives only half as much benefit per dollar of deduction as a family in the 30 percent bracket.

Alternative income tax provisions would be more powerful for promoting homeownership near the bottom of the income distribution. The most effective reform would change the deductions into a tax credit so that all taxpayers received the same benefit per dollar of mortgage interest or property tax payment, even if they used the standard deduction. A tax credit equal to 15 percent of mortgage interest plus property taxes would help low-income homeowners, while raising federal revenue by about $10 billion (Follain et al. 1993).

FEDERAL LENDING POLICIES   The federal government also supports homeownership through its activities in the mortgage market—for example, insuring mortgages through the Federal Housing Administration and maintaining oversight of the government-sponsored enterprises (GSEs) in the secondary mortgage market.

Each year eight hundred thousand families take out a mortgage insured by the FHA. Because of this insurance, the lenders must follow rules and procedures specified by the FHA, but they will not lose any money if the borrower defaults. Although these mortgages are somewhat more expensive than conventional mortgages and cannot exceed a specified maximum amount, they are attractive to many families because they have relatively loose underwriting standards and low down payment requirements, usually 3 percent. For many years, FHA mortgages have been the main source of housing credit for black and Hispanic families. In 1999 the share of one- to four-family, home-purchase mortgages insured by FHA was 42.6 percent for blacks, 43.3 percent for Hispanics, and 18.6 percent for whites (Federal Financial Institutions Examination Council 2000). These high shares for blacks and Hispanics reflect several factors, including the legacy of past discrimination (which leaves families in these groups with relatively poor credit histories on average) and the practice by real estate brokers and lenders of steering blacks and Hispanics toward FHA loans.

FHA mortgages have expanded homeownership opportunities for blacks and Hispanics, but not without costs. Unscrupulous lenders and real estate brokers have occasionally exploited FHA mortgages in ways that destroyed neighborhoods (Yinger 1995). Brokers identified neighborhoods near black concentrations, scared whites into selling with tales of "invasion" by blacks, then resold the houses to blacks at a profit. Lenders joined in by offering low-down-payment FHA mortgages to the new black homeowners without completing inspections of the houses, and therefore without telling the black families about necessary repairs, which sometimes proved too expensive for these families to complete. Because they had little or no equity in their new houses, these families then abandoned their houses and defaulted on their mortgages, and the lenders collected on the FHA insurance.

This is obviously a scenario for neighborhood decline. HUD has been struggling with the problem for decades and appears to have made progress. For example, HUD recently revised housing appraisal requirements to ensure that FHA mortgage holders receive good information on the fair market price and on necessary repairs for the house they are considering. Overall, FHA insurance continues to play an important role in providing mortgages to low- and middle-income families, particularly black families. Its role may change in the future as more lenders, particularly mortgage bankers, provide their own high-cost mortgages in low-income areas. For now, however, the federal government should continue to provide FHA insurance and to strengthen the consumer protection provided by the FHA's rules and procedures.

As discussed earlier, mortgage bankers sell their mortgages to institutions in the secondary mortgage market, and these institutions then sell the mortgages to investors. Commercial banks and savings and loans also sell mortgages on the secondary mortgage market. The largest institutions in this market are two GSEs, namely, the Federal National Mortgage Association (Fannie Mae) and the Federal Home Loan Mortgage Corporation (Freddie Mac). Another smaller GSE, the Government National Mortgage Association (Ginnie Mae), buys only FHA-insured loans. These institutions are influential in mortgage markets because they set loan standards that must be satisfied before they will purchase a loan.

The large GSEs are private corporations but were originally government institutions, and HUD retains some oversight responsibilities. The federal government has a strong interest in determining the extent to which the GSEs promote homeownership in low-income and minority neighborhoods. In recent years, Fannie Mae and Freddie Mac have developed new loan programs with relatively flexible underwriting standards designed to attract low-income borrowers. There is some evidence that these programs have expanded homeownership opportunities, but some elements of the GSEs' underwriting standards also may have a relatively severe impact on black and Hispanic applicants without a business justification—a sign of disparate-impact discrimination (Temkin et al. 1999).

Conclusion

The poverty disparities between whites and both blacks and Hispanics obviously have many causes and can be addressed through federal policies concerning employment, education, health, crime, and welfare. This chapter has shown that housing markets also contribute to poverty through several different channels and that these effects are magnified by ethnic discrimination and segregation in housing. As a result, housing policy should be an important element of any antipoverty program. A program to eliminate poverty differentials between ethnic groups should include federal policies to promote fair housing and fair lending, to support community activities that maintain neighborhood integration, to combine housing certificates with housing counseling, and to promote homeownership among low-income households.

CHAPTER 11

The Memberships Theory of Poverty: The Role of Group Affiliations in Determining Socioeconomic Outcomes

STEVEN N. DURLAUF

Social scientists have long been aware of the importance of group influences as a cause of socioeconomic deprivation. Nevertheless, research in economics has generally focused on individual and family explanations of poverty, for two main reasons. First, it has been difficult to model formally the sorts of interactions that are associated with group influences. Second, data have typically not existed to allow quantification of the insights that social approaches might provide.

Since the late 1980s, there has been a major change in thinking within the economics community about group-based explanations for poverty (see Manski, in press). Interest in group-level influences has been sparked by a growing sense within empirical economic research that individual-level explanations are inadequate for understanding cross-group patterns for a range of socioeconomic phenomena. A growing number of papers have established that knowledge of group characteristics is useful in predicting individual behavior. For example, in studying teenage sexual activity and fertility, Jonathan Crane (1991), Karin Brewster (1994a, 1994b), and others have shown that the accuracy in predicting such behaviors for a given individual is improved by knowledge of certain characteristics of the adults in the neighborhoods where the individuals reside.[1] The work of William Julius Wilson (1987, 1996) has sensitized social scientists to the causal role of social isolation in producing the large-scale socioeconomic problems commonly associated with ghettos. Similar conclusions may be drawn from recent ethnographies, such as Anderson (1999). My belief is that underlying the new interest in group memberships among economists is a feeling that one cannot explain the levels of socioeconomic deprivation and self-destructive behavior associated with inner cities in a framework that embodies the neoclassical assumptions of rationality, preferences defined exclusively over commodities, and complete markets for borrowing and lending. Put differently, the standard neoclassical assumptions seem better suited for explaining socioeconomic success than socioeconomic failure.

One important scientific aspect of this new research on group memberships, poverty, and inequality is that it attempts to integrate ideas from sociology and social psychology into economics. The traditional oppositions between economic and sociological approaches in explaining phenomena of common interest—oppositions that are often described in terms of rational choice versus social structural models—are being dissolved in this new paradigm.

In this chapter, I describe the basic ideas of the memberships theory of poverty, indicate the dimensions along which it has found empirical support, and discuss some of the implications for public policy. The links between theory, empirics, and policy are still relatively weak, reflecting the fact that this paradigm is still in its infancy. These weaknesses represent opportunities for new research, however, rather than fundamental weaknesses in the paradigm.

Theory

Basic Ideas

The central idea of the memberships theory of poverty is straightforward. Suppose that an individual's socioeconomic outcomes depend on the composition of the various groups of which he is a member over the course of his life. Such groups may in principle be defined along many dimensions, including ethnicity, residential neighborhood, schools, and workplace.[2] These memberships can exert causal influences on individual outcomes through a range of factors, which are assumed to include:

1. *Peer group effects:* The impact of the choices of some members of a group on the preferences of others in assessing those same choices. Standard contexts where peer group effects are thought to matter include juvenile crime (the appeal of participating in a crime may be higher when one's friends are involved) and cigarette smoking (which may be more appealing when one's friends smoke).

2. *Role model effects:* The influence of characteristics of older members of

a group over the preferences of younger members. If a typical student places a higher value on a college education when the percentage of adults in his community who attended college is high, then college attendance exhibits role model effects.

3. *Social learning:* The influences that the choices and outcomes experienced by some members of a group have on the subsequent choices of others, through the information that those choices and consequences impart. When a community contains only adults who attended college but have not succeeded economically, this information can influence how high school students assess the benefits of college.

4. *Social complementarities:* The influences that the choices of others have on the productivity of an individual's choices. A study group, in which hard work by some members makes the efforts of each member more productive, exhibits social complementarities.

Clearly, these types of group effects are not independent, and one could imagine alternative classifications.

Depending on a particular context, the group memberships themselves may or may not be choice variables. One often distinguishes endogenous memberships defined by residence, school, or firm from exogenous ones determined by ethnicity or gender.[3] When the memberships are endogenous, a complete theory of inequality needs to account for their determination. For example, a theory of the role of residential neighborhoods in perpetuating poverty needs to explain how families come to live in neighborhoods in addition to how neighborhood compositions affect individual families.

When group-level influences are powerful, socioeconomic success or failure is significantly causally influenced by the evolution of these memberships, as well as by the groups themselves. Suppose that an individual is a member of an ethnic group that suffers from discrimination, grows up in a poor community whose role models and peer groups militate against economic success, and subsequently finds himself in a series of poor schools and jobs. This sequence constitutes an explanation of why such an individual is in poverty. By the memberships theory of poverty, I refer to a perspective in which group influences play a primary role in understanding why this individual is poor for much of his life.

To understand how economists conceptualize this type of explanation I begin with a basic model of individual choice. Suppose we are interested in the outcomes ω_i for individuals in some population of size I. These outcomes are assumed to represent choices made by individuals in order to maximize a payoff function V subject to the requirement that the choices lie in the constraint set each individual faces; that constraint set can be denoted as Ω_i. In a standard formulation of these choices, both the payoffs to individuals and the constraint sets are assumed to depend on two types of factors: observable individual characteristics X_i and unobservable characteristics (to the modeler, but observable to agent i) ε_i. The observable vector can include elements such as family background and past behavior. Algebraically, the choice of each individual i represents the solution to:

$$\max_{\omega_i \in \Omega_i} V(\omega_i, \varepsilon_i)$$
$$\text{such that } \Omega_i = \Omega(X_i, \varepsilon_i)$$

The standard approach to characterizing the behavior of the population of choices is to make some assumption concerning the distribution of the ε_i's.

Memberships-based theories of behavior may be based on this same model, once explicit attention has been given to the influence of a group's characteristics and behaviors on its individual members. To formally incorporate these influences, I make several assumptions. First, each individual i is assumed to be a member of one neighborhood, denoted as n(i). Each neighborhood is associated with a set of observable group characteristics, $Y_{n(i)}$, as well as a set of beliefs the individual i possesses concerning the choices of others in that neighborhood; these beliefs may be expressed as a subjective probability measure $\mu_i^e(\omega_{-i})$ where $\omega_{-i} = (\omega_1, \dots \omega_{i-1}, \omega_{i+1}, \dots \omega_I)$ denotes the choices of others in I's neighborhood. Algebraically, an individual's choice is now described by

$$\max_{\omega_i \in \Omega_i} V(\omega_i, X_i, Y_{n(i)}, \mu_i^e(\omega_{-i}), \varepsilon_i)$$
$$\text{such that } \Omega_i = \Omega(X_i, Y_{n(i)}, \mu_i^e(\omega_{-i}), \varepsilon_i)$$

At this level of abstraction, the model simply says that individual behaviors are interpreted as choices determined by some combination of individual and group factors. Presumably, any observed behavior can be interpreted this way through suitable specification of the objective function and constraint set associated with a given agent. There is nothing in the introduction of group influences on individual outcomes that is inconsistent with the methodological individualism—or equivalently, the choice-based reasoning about individual behavior—that underlies economic theory. (For more on this issue, see Blume and Durlauf 2001; Durlauf 2000.)

The memberships theory differs from standard economic models in two respects. First, it shifts the emphasis in a causal explanation of poverty from individual characteristics as an explanation of the heterogeneity in behavior to memberships and group influences that constrain individual outcomes. Second, such theories highlight the role of externalities in producing poverty. Poverty is conceptualized not as a by-product of an efficient economy, but rather as a manifestation of various factors that are usually associated with economic inefficiency. Typically, role models and peer influences fulfill the standard conditions that characterize externalities in that each is an example of the choices of one group of individuals directly (that is, without market mediation) affecting others.

The presence of group-level externalities has important implications for the aggregate outcomes observed in these environments.[4] First, there can be multiple equilibria in the level of behavior within a group. This occurs because the strong interdependencies between the behaviors of individuals within a group provide no information as to what sorts of behaviors will be observed. Rather, these interdependencies imply only that whatever behaviors occur will be highly correlated with the group. When these interdependencies are strong enough, the private factors that lead to one choice versus another may be overwhelmed by the incentives to conform, so that more than one possible set of individual behaviors will be consistent with individual rationality. Operationally, this means that phenomena such as the levels of out-of-wedlock births, crime rates, and substance abuse within a group will not be uniquely determined by the microeconomic characteristics of the members of the group.

Second, the models can exhibit large "social multipliers." When individuals are highly interdependent, small changes in their individual incentives to make a particular choice (these are the X_i's in our choice problem) can create large changes in group-level behavior, because of the feedbacks induced. Such a property has important implications for policy. For example, a given level of resources allocated to fight poverty could have much larger effects if concentrated on individuals who interact rather than spread across individuals who do not.

Third, because these models are highly nonlinear, the effect of change in a particular individual or group characteristic on a group's behavioral outcomes generally differs according to the levels of the various variables involved. This is important because it means that the use of linear statistical methods to uncover the effect of some policy can be highly misleading.

Applications

This basic choice structure has been used to illuminate several aspects of the determination of poverty and inequality. Perhaps the most common application has been to the role of residential neighborhoods in transmitting poverty and inequality across generations. Models of this type have been developed by Roland Bénabou (1993, 1996a, 1996b), Suzanne Cooper (1998), and myself (Durlauf 1996a, 1996b). These models have a common structure. At a given point in time, families organize themselves into residential neighborhoods. Entry into particular neighborhoods may be restricted through rental or house prices or through overt discrimination. Each residential neighborhood influences children through some combination of peer groups, role models, and local determination of educational expenditures through taxes. As adults, the onetime offspring in various neighborhoods reorganize themselves into possibly new neighborhoods, and the cycle is repeated.

In these models, the incentives for stratification of neighborhoods are increased by the degree of cross-section inequality. Thus, as inequality at a point in time increases, social mobility can be reduced. In addition, phenomena such as uniformly poor neighborhoods can emerge endogenously as individual families desire affluent neighbors. Further, if one considers black ghettos, which historically were socioeconomically diverse, a reduction of barriers to social mobility can produce many forms of deprivation in residual communities. These dynamic models of neighborhood feedbacks and endogenous stratification represent a formalization of ideas of long-standing importance in sociology, such as William Julius Wilson's (1987, 8) analysis of the modern ghetto:

> Changes have taken place in ghetto neighborhoods, and the groups that have been left behind are collectively different than those that lived in these neighborhoods in earlier years. It is true that long-term welfare families and street criminals are distinct groups, but they live and interact in the same depressed community and they are part of the population that has, with the

exodus of the more stable working- and middle-class segments, become increasingly isolated socially from mainstream patterns and norms of behavior.

We can see strong similarities between this conclusion and one of the conclusions of Kenneth Clark's (1965/1982, 81) classic study of ghettos a generation earlier:

> Not only is the pathology of the ghetto self-perpetuating, but one kind of pathology breeds another. The child born in the ghetto is more likely to come into a world of broken homes and illegitimacy; and this family and social instability is conducive to delinquency, drug addiction and criminal violence. Neither instability nor crime can be controlled by police vigilance or by reliance on the alleged deterring forces of legal punishment, for the individual crimes are to be understood more as symptoms of the contagious sickness of the community itself than as the result of inherent criminal or deliberate viciousness.

Why do neighborhoods matter? Although most theoretical models of neighborhood effects make those effects a primitive modeling assumption, one can identify several structural reasons that would lead to neighborhood effects. First, there is the role of local public finance. Approximately 45 percent of all public revenues spent on primary and secondary education are generated through local sources. Jonathan Kozol (1991) provides a powerful description of the implication of this for disparities in school quality.

Second, peer group influences can create such effects. If the educational effort and aspirations of one child are influenced by the efforts of his friends and peers, then neighborhoods can create powerful forces promoting or retarding social mobility.

Third, role models can exert powerful influences. One reason for this is informational, as explored by Peter Streufert (1991) and by John Roemer and Roger Wets (1995). If children within a community employ the experiences of adults in assessing the economic payoff of education, children in poor communities observe biased outcomes in the sense that the observed payoff among adults in the community is lower than what the child should expect. This creates the possibility that poor children are systematically misinformed about the benefits of education and therefore make lower educational choices than are "objectively" appropriate for them.

Fourth, social networks may matter for labor market matching (Boorman

1975). It is well established that approximately 50 percent of all workers at a point in time knew someone at their current firm when they first took the job. As argued by James Montgomery (1992, 1994a), this suggests that poor communities are less able to generate the labor market information necessary for rapid and successful matching of community members to jobs.

A final reason why neighborhoods influence individuals falls under the rubric of social norms. Neighborhoods can represent the carriers of aspirations toward economic success and family responsibility, with attendant implications for the perpetuation of poverty. For example, George Akerlof and Rachel Kranton (2000) show how personal identity may be endogenized, and Montgomery (1994b) shows how adherence to norms concerning parental responsibility can, through cognitive dissonance, be weakened owing to the level of various behaviors within a neighborhood.

Another area where group effects have been studied is in terms of ethnicity. George Borjas (1992, 1995) has advocated this approach in understanding differences in socioeconomic outcomes for a wide range of ethnic groups. Glenn Loury (1977) provides a model to explain persistent black-white inequality. The complementarities associated with the ethnic-group income determination in Loury's model correspond to the memberships theory I have been describing, and indeed, his analysis should be considered a major progenitor of the current theoretical literature. From the perspective of theory and model construction, the key difference between neighborhood and ethnic notions of memberships is that neighborhood memberships are endogenous whereas ethnic group memberships are not. As suggested before, why ethnicity should be a salient membership is something we wish to explain.

A final area in which memberships-based theories have application is the allocation of workers across firms. Michael Kremer and Eric Maskin (1996) suggest that the productivity of a given worker is determined by the skills of his coworkers, implying that the degree of stratification of workers by skill can have large influences on the degree of inequality and poverty. Kremer and Maskin note that an economy in which the paradigmatic company is Microsoft, whose labor force consists almost exclusively of high-skilled, white-collar workers, is very different from one in which the paradigmatic firm is Ford, which links workers of different skills and occupation types in a common production process. This research suggests that an important causal factor in understanding persistent deprivation is the extent to which poor workers are decoupled from the rest of the economy. Relatively little work has been done on this question, and it is an important area for future research. It should be noted that for this case there are no externalities involved, as firms will, in the course of maximizing profits, account for interworker productivity effects in hiring.

Social Capital

Although interest in the influence of groups on individual outcomes has received increasing attention, this change is small compared to the explosion of interest in social capital. James Coleman, a pioneer in this regard, characterized the forms of social capital (1990, 300) as "the relations of authority and of trust and . . . [of] norms." "The value of the social capital concept," he continues, "lies primarily in the fact that it identifies certain aspects of social structure by their function. . . . The function identified by the 'social capital' is the value of those aspects of social structure to actors, as resources that can be used by the actors to realize their interests" (305). In the context of poverty, many authors have argued that the problems of the inner city may be interpreted as at least partially due to an absence of social capital of various types.

   In my judgment, the body of substantive ideas around social capital can all be subsumed within a general memberships theory of inequality. To the extent that social capital is a well-defined resource that members of some social network can access, then it is simply a version of a group influence. Its mathematical representation would therefore require that social capital be modeled as a group influence on individual decisionmaking that could be characterized by some collection of group-level variables of the type I described earlier. In fact, Loury (1977) used the term early on in precisely such a context. What perhaps creates the misimpression that social capital is an idea distinct from interaction effects is that Coleman and others have often defined it functionally, that is, in terms of what it does rather than in terms of what it is. As argued by Alejandro Portes (1998), defining social capital functionally renders the concept unfalsifiable and vague. (For additional criticisms of the social capital literature, see Durlauf 1999b, 2001, in press.)

Empirical Evidence

Empirical evidence on the role of memberships may be divided into four categories: ethnographic studies; regression analyses based on observational data; studies that attempt to evaluate the effects of government interventions in membership on individual outcomes; and controlled experiments from the social psychology literature. I also describe in this section the Project on Human Development in Chicago Neighborhoods, an ongoing research effort with important potential to elucidate the nature of group-level influences. Because there has yet to be any effort to estimate fully delineated, structural memberships-based models, the evidence concerning the theory is to some extent indirect.

Ethnographic Evidence

Ethnographic studies of poverty, such as Kenneth Clark's *Dark Ghetto* (1965/ 1982), provide a rich body of evidence on the ways in which community deprivation influences individual behavior. Much of this literature has focused on the emergence within inner cities of social norms that perpetuate deprivation across generations; classic examples include Oscar Lewis's *La Vida* (1966) and Elliott Liebow's *Tally's Corner* (1967). Carol Stack's *All Our Kin* (1974), an important study of the nature of social networks in poor, black communities, shows how strong, positive social networks militate against the effects of deprivation even within very deprived communities. Elijah Anderson's *Code of the Street* (1999, 9–10), an ethnographic study of inner-city Philadelphia, is primarily concerned with understanding the nature of violence in poor neighborhoods:

> In some of the most economically depressed and drug- and crime-ridden pockets of the city, the rules of civil law have been severely weakened, and in their stead a "code of the street" holds sway. At the heart of this code is a set of prescriptions and proscriptions, or informal rules, of behavior organized around a desperate search for respect that governs public social relations, especially violence. . . . In the social context of persistent poverty and deprivation, alienation from broader society's institutions, notably criminal justice, is widespread. The code of the street . . . involves a quite primitive form of social exchange that holds would-be perpetrators accountable by promising an "eye for an eye."

Although much of the ethnographic literature has tried to document the ways in which the socioeconomic problems of ghetto dwellers are reinforced, one should not conclude that ghetto life is a monolith devoid of positive social relations. Mitchell Duneier's brilliant *Slim's Table* (1992) is a useful corrective in this regard.

From the perspective of the memberships theory of poverty, these ethnographic studies provide examples of the rich social-context effects on which the theory relies. Further, the diversity of positive and negative interactions in poor communities, a diversity that is apparent from a juxtaposition of Anderson's and Duneier's work, for example, makes clear the need to interpret social pathologies as statistical regularities that emerge across purposeful agents. This is how the new theoretical models of social interactions study such phenomena (Brock and Durlauf 2000a). Ethnographic studies do not represent the sort of quantitative analyses that theoretical models of the memberships theory require for formal model evaluation. They are essential, however, in evaluating the substantive significance of these theories.

Regression Evidence

There is now a literature purporting to document the influence of group memberships on socioeconomic outcomes; a standard survey of older work is Jencks and Mayer (1990), and a valuable recent survey is Ginther, Haveman, and Wolfe (2000). This literature generally focuses on the role of residential neighborhoods on the future outcomes of children. A typical analysis in this literature computes a regression of the form

$$\omega_i = a + cX_i + dY_{n(i)} + \varepsilon_i$$

where, as before, individual characteristics and neighborhood characteristics are denoted by X_i and $Y_{n(i)}$, respectively. Acceptance of the null hypothesis that $d = 0$ is interpreted as meaning that no group influences exist. Individual outcomes that have been explored by this type of regression include years of schooling (Datcher 1982; Duncan 1994), wages and earnings (Corcoran et al. 1992; Corcoran and Adams 1997b), hours of work (Weinberg, Reagan, and Yankow 1999), and cognitive development (Brooks-Gunn et al. 1993; Duncan, Brooks-Gunn, and Klebanov 1994).

In addition to linear regression analysis, which presupposes that the outcome variable ω_i is continuous, some studies focus on binary choices in both static and dynamic environments. (In the latter case, the variables are allowed to vary across time.) Crane (1991), in a well-known early study, finds in a cross-sectional analysis that the percentage of professional workers among parents in a community reduces the probability of teenage pregnancy and high school dropout, once various individual characteristics are controlled for. Similar results are found by Brewster (1994a, 1994b), Sucoff and Upchurch (1998), and South and Crowder (1999).

These studies typically conclude that some combination of contextual variables are statistically significant, although there seems to be no consensus on which contextual effects are most robust. Efforts to show that these effects are robust with respect to individual characteristics suggest that the evidence of neighborhood effects is ambiguous. For example, by using sibling data for sibling pairs who were raised in different places (a method that presumably allows one to control for unobserved family characteristics), Aaronson (1998) finds strong evidence of neighborhood effects, whereas, Solon, Page, and Duncan (1999) and Page and Solon (2000) come to more skeptical conclusions.

Ginther, Haveman, and Wolfe (2000) thus make an important contribution to this literature by considering a wide range of alternative specifications of individual and neighborhood controls in assessing the role of neighborhood memberships for three youth outcomes: high school graduation, years of completed schooling, and nonmarital childbearing among teenagers. Their main finding is that richer individual controls systematically reduce the magnitude of estimated neighborhood influences, leading one to question whether findings of strong neighborhood effects in other studies are an artifact of a parsimonious choice of control variables. This work suggests that analyses of group effects need to explicitly account for model uncertainty, that is, the absence of any theory to guide the selection of control or neighborhood variables. In a different context, William Brock and I (Brock and Durlauf (2000b) discuss how to develop inferences that are robust to some forms of model specification. A valuable future exercise would be the construction of specification-robust neighborhood effects along the lines proposed in Brock and Durlauf (2000b).

Although this regression work is very suggestive, it is far from persuasive. To understand this, consider recent econometric work on the identification of interactions. This literature (see, for example, Manski 1993; Brock and Durlauf 2000a) has focused on the determination of conditions under which different types of interaction effects may be statistically identified. Following Manski (1993), it is typical to distinguish between two classes of interaction effects that influence individual decisions: endogenous effects and contextual effects.[5] Endogenous effects refer to the effects that one set of decisions has on others made contemporaneously. According to this terminology, peer group influences are endogenous. Contextual effects refer to feedbacks from predetermined (with respect to decisions) characteristics of a group to its individual decisions. Role model effects fall into this category.

Several main ideas emerge from this literature. (For a detailed survey of the econometric literature on interactions, see Brock and Durlauf 2000a.) First, linear models suffer from particular difficulties in terms of identification. Manski (1993) shows that for a particular linear class of models, these two effects cannot be distinguished. Brock and I (Brock and Durlauf 2000a) in turn show that for general linear models, identification of these two effects requires prior knowledge of the existence of some individual-level variable whose group average does not affect individuals causally. (For additional analysis, see Moffitt 2001.) Second, identification appears to be less problematic for models based on discrete or longitudinal data. Brock and I (Brock and Durlauf 2000a) have shown that the identification problem that arises in linear contexts does not arise in binary-choice and longitudinal data contexts. This is because the relationship between dependent and independent variables in these latter statistical models is nonlinear (in the sense that various control variables influence the probabilities of alternative behaviors), and that relationship is sufficient to break the collinearity between endogenous and contextual effects that can arise in linear models.

Two implications follow from this econometric literature. First, endogenous and contextual effects have not typically been distinguished in empirical studies; hence, it is unclear how to provide any causal interpretation of findings that group effects exist. Second, any attempt to do so needs an explicit analysis of what prior information concerning the statistical model under study is responsible for the identification of structural parameters. Put differently, the standard linear, binary-choice and longitudinal regressions that have appeared cannot be mapped into statements about the causal relationship between group influences and individual outcomes without first explicitly distinguishing between endogenous and contextual effects, and then showing that the statistical conditions under which they may be distinguished are plausible assumptions for the data under study.

The empirical literature on neighborhood effects is also plagued by another problem: self-selection. Individuals are not randomly assigned to neighborhoods; rather, they choose neighborhoods subject to prices and income. Thus, a group of individuals living in a "bad" neighborhood seem likely to have some unobserved characteristic in common. Thus, any group effect identified from data may be spurious. There are ways to deal with the effects of self-selection (see Brock and Durlauf 2000a) that paradoxically facilitate identification, but they have yet to be implemented in any empirical study.[6]

The major study that attempts to control for self-selection in neighborhoods is Evans, Oates, and Schwab (1992). Their analysis is concerned with identifying the role of neighborhood characteristics in the probability of teen pregnancy. Using a probit framework, this probability is assumed to depend on both a range of individual characteristics and a variable that is the logarithm of the percentage of other students in an individual's high school who are categorized as "disadvantaged" based on a federal government standard. In probit regressions that treat this measure as exogenous, this variable of disadvantaged schoolmates significantly increases the probability of a teen pregnancy.

To control for self-selection, Evans, Oates, and Schwab (1992) propose four metropolitan area instrumental variables for their neighborhood characteristics variable. Their identifying assumption is that the metropolitan area of residence is exogenous for families, although location within a metropolitan area is a choice variable. Employing these instruments, the contextual effect found in the univariate analysis disappears, both in terms of magnitude and in terms of statistical significance.

This result suggests caution in interpreting studies that do not deal with self-selection. However, the particular choice of instruments in Evans, Oates, and Schwab (1992) seems inappropriate if one thinks that memberships matter at a lower level of aggregation than metropolitan areas, since one could easily imagine it is that component of a neighborhood's characteristics relative to a metropolitan area's characteristics that ultimately produces a neighborhood effect. Also, a statistical procedure that explicitly models the group formation process seems more likely to produce accurate measures of neighborhood effects than one based on an ad hoc use of instruments.

Finally, there is a branch of the empirical literature that attempts to identify social interactions by examining group-level statistics. In one such approach, spatial correlations in average neighborhood behavior, once various within-neighborhood characteristics have been controlled for, are interpreted as social interaction effects. Giorgio Topa (1997), for example, finds such correlations for unemployment in the context of Chicago neighborhoods. Alternatively, one can ask whether intergroup behavioral averages vary too much to be explained by differences in intragroup individual characteristics. Edward Glaeser, Bruce Sacerdote, and José Scheinkman (1996) use this idea to identify social interactions in criminal behavior. This type of analysis seems promising as a complement to the individual-level structural modeling approach of Brock and Durlauf (2000a), Manski (1993), and Moffitt (2001).

Quasi-experiments

The concern over the possibility that self-selection can lead to spurious evidence of neighborhood effects is responsible for interest in "quasi-experiments." Researchers have sought out cases in which individuals have been reassigned to new groups (typically residential neighborhoods) owing to some exogenous event. By comparing individuals who have been reassigned to those who have not, one can in principle approximate a random experiment whereby those who are moved correspond to a "treatment" group and those who are not represent a "control" group.

The most prominent example of a quasi-experiment in the interactions literature is the Gautreaux Program, studied by James Rosenbaum and various coauthors (Popkin, Rosenbaum, and Meaden 1993; Rosenbaum 1995; and Rosenbaum and Popkin 1991). In 1966 the Chicago Housing Authority was sued for discrimination by public housing residents on the grounds that both the location of public housing sites and the allocation of slots in these sites intentionally placed minorities in isolated inner-city neighborhoods. In an agreement worked out between the plaintiffs and defendants, known as the Gautreaux Assisted Housing Program (Dorothy Gautreaux was the lead plaintiff), housing subsidies and placement services were established for public housing residents throughout Chicago. Families who applied for assistance were randomly given a single option of moving to another part of Chicago or moving to a suburb. (Families who declined the offered option were placed back in the pool of eligible families from which recipients of aid were drawn.) This body of work has found that along many dimensions, including high school dropout rates and postgraduation wages, children from families who were moved to suburbs did substantially better than their counterparts who moved within Chicago.

Although they are an important source of information on interactions effects, it is important to recognize that the Gautreaux data are not ideal.

Dropped from the program were applicants who either had poor rent-paying histories or failed a home inspection to determine whether they had mistreated their public housing. This prescreening eliminated approximately 30 percent of the program's applicants (Rosenbaum 1995). Hence, the Gautreaux families are not fully representative of the poor communities from which they were drawn. Further, the survey efforts conducted by Rosenbaum and his coauthors exhibit some sample selection problems. In particular, those families who moved to suburbs and then returned to Chicago could not be identified. Hence, the evidence of neighborhood effects obtained from the Gautreaux Program, while informative, is not decisive. That being said, recent work, such as Rosenbaum, DeLuca, and Miller (1999), links Gautreaux interview data to administrative data and thus should be able to partially address these concerns.

A second major quasi-experiment is the Moving To Opportunity (MTO) demonstration, currently being conducted by the U.S. Department of Housing and Urban Development to evaluate the effects of moving low-income families out of high-poverty neighborhoods. (For a detailed discussion of the program, see Goering 1996.) The demonstration randomly assigns a set of low-income families who apply to participate in the program to one of three groups: a group whose members are eligible for housing vouchers that provide a rent subsidy usable only in census tracts with less than 10 percent poverty; a group that is eligible for housing vouchers with no locational restrictions; or a group in which members are not eligible for housing vouchers but can still receive public housing assistance based on previous eligibility. The demonstration is being conducted in five metropolitan areas: Baltimore, Boston, Chicago, Los Angeles, and New York City.

Preliminary results on the various experiments are becoming available. In the most important study produced from the program, Lawrence Katz, Jeffrey Kling, and Jeffrey Liebman (2001) find improved behavior among boys as well as better household health among families who move to better neighborhoods.

The MTO demonstration is an important advance in the empirical study of neighborhood effects. At the same time, there are a number of caveats with respect to interpreting the findings about the program. One concern is self-selection. As mentioned before, participation in the program requires families to volunteer; further, many families who are eligible to move to more affluent communities apparently have not done so, at least by the time data were collected. Hence, it is difficult to extrapolate the asserted findings of neighborhood effects from the program to more systematic policy interventions.

Second, the findings of differential outcomes associated with residence in richer versus poorer neighborhoods cannot be interpreted causally without better efforts to control for individual-level effects, which may vary systematically with the neighborhoods. For example, the finding that there is a reduction in asthma attacks among MTO children who move to better neighborhoods (Katz, Kling, and Liebman 2001) is not decisive evidence of neighborhood effects without adequate controls for differences in the quality of housing for families in different neighborhoods.[7]

Third, the MTO data are associated with a sufficiently short time horizon that one must be worried about the distinction between transitory and permanent effects. It is possible that there could, over time, be regression toward the mean in the better outcomes associated with the movement of some families to richer communities. These concerns do not in any way diminish the importance of the research stemming from MTO, but they do point to its limits in terms of causal inference. And to be clear, Katz, Kling, and Liebman (2001) do an exemplary job of making clear that such limits exist. My own judgment is that the MTO demonstration complements the Gautreaux data but does not supplant it.

Controlled Experiments

The most persuasive evidence of group effects comes from the social psychology literature. Elliot Aronson (1999) reviews many controlled experiments that demonstrate a range of ways in which group influences matter. Indeed, a number of the classic experiments in social psychology illustrate group influences. One example is Stanley Milgram's (1974) work on obedience to authority. His experiments were designed to determine the conditions under which an individual, believing he was assisting psychological research, would be willing to obey instructions from an authority figure (literally a man in a white coat) to administer a sequence of increasingly powerful electrical shocks to a patient who began to protest that his health was in danger.[8] The most publicized result of this work was that 60 percent of the subjects continued to administer shocks even when the "victim" said that he had a heart condition. What is less well known is that when a second individual was present, if that person refused, the refusal rate by subjects increased dramatically. A key finding of this experiment is that the willingness of an individual to reject a behavior endorsed by an authority is a function of whether there is a peer who is willing to do the same.

Although this finding of a social interaction effect has no direct implications for thinking about the determination of poverty, it suggests why one might observe variations in social pathology rates across similar communities. One reason for this is that such pathologies are presumably "sanctioned" by social norms that are powerful in ways analogous to the power of authority figures. For one example of evidence of how large cross-sectional differences in behaviors cannot be accounted for without some sort of interactions-based explanation, see Glaeser, Sacerdote, and Scheinkman (1996).

Project on Human Development in Chicago Neighborhoods

The quantitative literature on membership effects is not based on any deep causal analysis of why these effects exist. Typically, measures of neighborhood-level characteristics, such as means of income or education, are added to a statistical model predicting individual outcomes. The statistical significance of these variables is interpreted as demonstrating that group effects matter. However, the finding of either contextual or endogenous effects does not provide guidance as to the actual causal mechanism through which these effects occur. Statistical evidence on group effects is by and large a black box.

An exception, the Project on Human Development in Chicago Neighborhoods, promises to provide not only important documentation of neighborhood effects but some insight into their structure. Among the studies generated by this project are Sampson, Raudenbush, and Earls (1997), Raudenbush and Sampson (1999), and Sampson, Morenoff, and Earls (1999). This project is designed to produce a rich data set on attitudes among Chicago residents for a wide range of issues. In 1995, for example, more than eight thousand individuals were surveyed across more than three hundred neighborhood clusters. The rich set of information that is being produced allows for the integration of information about individual characteristics with information on individual attitudes in order to study how these relate to neighborhood outcomes.

This data set has provided insights into a range of phenomena. For example, Robert Sampson, Jeffrey Morenoff, and Felton Earls (1999) make clear that a critical effect of concentrated poverty is to reduce the expectations by members of a community that others will assist parents in controlling children. Members of poor neighborhoods feel unable to rely on neighbors to report truancy or call the police when they observe illegal activity. These types of activity are standard examples of interaction effects that can produce multiple equilibria in community behaviors. By implication, therefore, these are the sorts of behavioral factors that can explain cross-community variation in school completion and crime rates and hence explain causally why poverty is perpetuated across generations. This sort of finding is very suggestive of the role of community institutions in ameliorating social problems and fulfills the authors' objective of moving beyond the typical vague formulations of social capital.

In my judgment, this project is an exemplar for the directions in which empirical work on group effects should proceed. This sort of microeconomic survey data is essential in understanding why and how group influences occur.

Implications for Policy

The memberships perspective has a number of implications for the conceptualization of antipoverty policies. A focus on group-level influences leads one to ask whether the government can and should intervene to alter how groups are formed in the economy and in the broader society. Elsewhere (Durlauf 1996c) I have used the term "associational redistribution" to distinguish those policies that redistribute group memberships rather than income (the more traditional objects of redistributive schemes).[9]

Although associational redistribution might appear to be a new and invasive form of government intervention, there are numerous examples of government policies of this type already in operation. The most obvious example is affirmative action, which is an intervention into the allocation of individuals into schools and firms that occurs in the society or economy. Similarly, programs of school desegregation through busing are examples of associational redistribution. Other examples include magnet and charter schools and the location of public housing projects. The latter has been shown by Douglas Massey and Shawn Kanaiaupuni (1993) to have had a major impact on residential segregation in large urban areas. What links these disparate types of programs is that each is designed to alter the social interactions experienced by individuals by altering the compositions of socioeconomic groups.

One implication of theoretical models of inequality is that, like income and wealth, group memberships may be appropriate objects of redistribution when the achievement of equality of opportunity is the policy goal. Following John Roemer (1993, 1998), I use "equality of opportunity" to refer to a situation in which an individual's expected life prospects are independent of factors for which he should not be held responsible. (For a definition of equality-of-life chances similar to this equality-of-opportunity notion, see Fishkin 1983.) As Roemer (1993, 147) states: "Society should indemnify people against poor outcomes that are consequences of causes that are beyond their control, but not against outcomes that are the consequences of causes that are within their control, and therefore for which they are personally responsible."

To be concrete, children are in no way individually responsible for the quality of their neighborhoods or schools, so equality of opportunity in employment would require that children's employment prospects as adults do not depend on any group effects that they experience in these contexts. Roemer's conceptualization also makes clear why it is misguided to criticize memberships-based theories of poverty on the grounds that they "blame the victim." One is not responsible for one's group memberships. And differences in group behaviors are not determined by anything intrinsic to the members of the groups.

With this notion of equality of opportunity as an objective of social policy, one can construct a justification for associational redistribution.[10] This justification for associational redistribution most clearly applies when there is no substitute for intragroup influences in equalizing expected life prospects that can be redistributed through income or similar transfers. More generally, the costs of achieving equality of opportunity without associational redistribution may prove to be prohibitive; that is one (speculative) way to interpret the finding of James Heckman, Anne Layne-Farrar, and Petra Todd (1996) that the effects of improvements in school quality appear to have weak effects on labor market outcomes ceteris paribus.

Associational redistribution can be justified in this way only when one considers how the political objective of equality of opportunity conflicts with and must therefore be traded off against any possible harms created by the policies required for its achievement. One possible argument is that associational redistribution violates some right to associations, a right presumably derived from some more general notion of a right to privacy. It is sometimes argued that antidiscrimination and affirmative action policies violate rights to free private association. Glenn Loury (1987, 257) remarks that "freedom to act on the prejudices and discriminations which induce each of us to seek out and make our lives among a specific, restricted set of our fellows, are for many if not most Americans among those inalienable rights . . . enshrined in the Declaration of Independence."

Loury is clearly right in some cases: for instance, an equality-of-opportunity argument cannot trump the right of parents to raise their own children. However, this does not seem germane to schools or businesses, in which group composition is instrumental to the group goals: provision of education in the one case and profit maximization in the other. For these two cases, one cannot invoke a separate right-to-privacy argument outside of the claim that the primary goals of these institutions are violated by policies that alter school enrollment or hiring decisions.

In the case of neighborhoods, which may form on the basis of the interaction effects associated with neighborhood composition, there is a stronger argument for respecting the right to engage in private association. However, in this case there is the question of whose rights are being protected. Parental preferences are not necessarily those that best serve children. To the extent that parental preferences for racial exclusivity are the source of segregated neighborhoods, for instance, a policymaker might reasonably reject those preferences as irrelevant because they impose segregation on children who cannot meaningfully assert that they share these preferences. Further, even if parents are acting as the agents for their children, it is unclear why a right to private association would justify their hurting other children through the choices they make, such as which neighborhood to live in.

Independent of privacy issues, such policies differ from income-based policies in how they alter individual opportunities, and in this respect, they have different ethical consequences. To see how this argument is constructed, consider two types of school-based associational redistribution. In the first case, children with different socioeconomic backgrounds but identical native abilities are randomly assigned to schools to eliminate a correlation that would otherwise exist between socioeconomic background and educational quality. In the second, suppose (following empirical work such as Henderson, Mieszkowski, and Sauvageau 1978) that average educational achievement is increased when students of different abilities are mixed in classes rather than segregated by ability, so that a school chooses to ban tracking in classes despite its adverse effect on higher-achieving students.

My claim is that this first case of associational redistribution is less ethically problematic than the second. Why? Because family background is not a component of a reasonable definition of what is "essential" about a person in the context of education (a concept found in Roemer's writings [1993, 1998], among other places), whereas innate intellectual ability is a component of what is essential in this context. Thus, in the case of ability tracking, it is the essential quality of ability itself that the more capable students would presumably not wish to pool (if given the choice) and whose development is reduced through ability integration, whereas in the former case it is the inessential quality of parental affluence that is responsible for the segregation of children into schools of different quality. If anything, in the former case the possibility that opportunities for gifted children to realize their potential are stifled if they come from a poor background makes economically induced segregation seem particularly unjust.

More generally, when group membership is determined by and in turn promotes the development of attributes we regard as essential to a person's self-realization, there can be compelling ethical objections to policies that promote associational redistribution. The fact that these objections can coexist with the equality-of-opportunity justification for associational redistribution reflects the complex interaction of our sense of justice, which requires that individual rewards correspond to individual responsibility, with our sense of the importance of self-fulfillment in making individual lives meaningful.

However, even if associational redistribution does generate conflicts with the rights that accrue to a person engaged in the actualization of his abilities, the memberships theory is still germane to public policy discussion and still speaks to the desirability of associational redistribution as a policy. So long as one's ethical position allows one to make trade-offs between equality of opportunity and other social goods that are reduced by associational redistribution, the presence and strength of interaction effects will be relevant to one's views on policy. Ethical judgments about associational redistribution may require adjudication between incommensurable goods in the sense analyzed in Berlin (1968, 1990), but this is the essence of politics. The development of the analytics and empirics of the memberships theory of inequality is therefore useful in ethical debates insofar as it elucidates the nature of the trade-offs between various social goods.

By itself, the presence of group effects does not logically entail any particular justification for a given social policy. As the discussion of empirical work indicated, the evidence on the relationship between group memberships and individual outcomes is strongest in precisely those contexts in which the implications for specific policies are weakest. Hence, though the ethnographic evidence that groups matter is especially compelling, this tells us little about the optimal design of affirmative action policies or the appropriate ways to draw school district boundaries and place magnet schools. I believe that the memberships theory naturally leads to new justifications for affirmative action, neighborhood socioeconomic integration, and related policies, but there are deep issues of policy design that the empirical literature has failed to address. For example, as I have argued elsewhere (Brock and Durlauf 2000a), if one were to expand Gautreaux- and MTO-type policies to attempt a massive movement of children out of inner cities—a policy advocated by Owen Fiss (2000) on the basis of an ingenuous reading of the evidence from these programs—one needs to account for the effects of large-scale programs on the composition of school student bodies and the attendant effects on the interaction structures within schools. This factor does not come into play when only a few students are involved, as is the case in current programs. Does one really think, for example, that adding two disadvantaged students to a school has the same average effect on the disadvantaged as replacing 20 percent of the students with their disadvantaged counterparts? Such an extrapolation requires very strong assumptions about the nature of friendship networks and peer group formation.

Further, one needs to recognize that individuals can adapt to these types of policies in ways that undermine them. Just as school desegregation problems reduced white enrollments in districts with those programs (Wilson 1985; Wilson and Smock 1991), one could easily imagine an abandonment of public schools in response to widespread socioeconomic integration. Acknowledging the likelihood of such a response of affluent families to efforts to economically integrate communities is not an attempt to justify that response; failing to do so, however, would be naive.

I therefore believe that an appropriate step in developing policies based on associational redistribution is to expand demonstrations such as MTO so as to trace the effects of alternative government policies, accounting for both scale effects and the rules by which memberships are redistributed. (In fact, a statistical literature on experimental design can be brought to bear on these issues.) Broad forms of associational redistribution of the type advocated by Fiss are, in my judgment, unwarranted by available empirical evidence on group effects. Moreover, they risk foundering, if the experience of previous efforts at associational redistribution such as school busing for desegregation is any guide. I am not giving up on associational redistribution as a practical guide to policy, but rather recognizing that important issues of policy design must be addressed if the desired outcomes of these policies are to be achieved.

Finally, let me suggest a reorientation in affirmative action, one that would achieve associational redistribution but encounter fewer of the objections associated with conventional affirmative action policies. Typical affirmative action policies may be thought of as "demand-side" policies that represent efforts to change the demand for students by schools and for workers by firms. An alternative policy approach could be called "supply-side" affirmative action; such policies are designed to alter the characteristics of students and workers in such a way that, given the demand schedules of schools and firms, an equilibrium redistribution of memberships takes place.[11]

What does this mean operationally? In the context of students, additional educational resources would be assigned to disadvantaged students. Programs such as Head Start or more intensive analogs, such as the Chicago Child-Parent Center and Expansion Program (Reynolds 1998) or the Perry Preschool Project (Schweinhart and Weikart 1998), if targeted at certain groups, can perform this role. One could even imagine an educational voucher system in which the amount a given student's enrollment brings to a school depends on some combination of his socioeconomic status and ethnicity and the composition of the school as a whole. Alternatively, one could envision forms of government subsidies for on-the-job training programs targeted at minority employees. While each of these possibilities targets resources on the basis of race, each is also a purely supply-side intervention, if the goal is to alter the distribution of groups across schools and jobs.

I do not take a stand here on the efficacy of such programs. Indeed, given the (at best) very mixed evidence of the efficacy of many current educational and training programs, especially for adults, this suggestion will neither serve as a panacea nor fully obviate the need for demand-side affirmative action policies. At the same time, there is evidence of how such programs can effectively deal with some of the hostility engendered by traditional affirmative action programs. George Moskos and John Sibley Butler (1996) provide a fascinating study of the treatment of blacks in the military. An important issue in the military has been the differential promotion rates between black and white soldiers. Moskos and Butler describe how this discrepancy has been addressed not through differential promotion criteria, an example of what I would call a demand-side policy, but rather through a supply-side policy of providing compensatory education targeted at the specific sources of the promotion differential. They argue that this supply-side strategy has minimized feelings of unfairness among white soldiers and avoided stigmatizing as unqualified those blacks who do receive promotions. More generally, this example is suggestive of how creativity in policy design may make some forms of associational redistribution relatively politically feasible.[12]

Conclusions

The memberships theory of poverty refers to a body of disparate theoretical and empirical studies, all of which point toward the same idea: the groups that define one's location in socioeconomic "space" (Akerlof 1997) play a crucial causal role in determining one's life prospects. As is true for any new research paradigm, there has yet to emerge a tight relationship between theoretical and empirical work. Hence, while there are many plausible theoretical arguments and empirical demonstrations that some sort of group influences matter, we are far from identifying many of the causal mechanisms that link individual outcomes to groups. Such mechanisms must be understood in order to construct policies that promote egalitarian objectives at a minimum cost in terms of economic efficiency or other social objectives. At the same time, the body of statistical evidence, when combined with ethnographic studies and social psychology experiments, strongly supports the view that group memberships play an important role in the determination of individual socioeconomic outcomes and hence are a significant causal factor in the generation and persistence of poverty. I therefore conclude that the memberships theory of poverty will prove to be an important approach for both the understanding of poverty and the design of efforts to achieve its amelioration.

CHAPTER **12**

Community Revitalization, Jobs, and the Well-being of the Inner-City Poor

RONALD F. FERGUSON

> Surely it's possible that poverty is not equivalent to blight, and that neighborhoods can improve without first becoming wealthier.
>
> Grogan and Proscio (2000, 45)

> But place-based policies suffer from several major problems. The biggest pitfall is their tendency to attract the poor to (or repel the rich from) areas of high poverty.
>
> Glaeser (2000a, 35)

The opening quotations exemplify a long-standing debate. Representing one side, Edward L. Glaeser believes it is counterproductive to give the poor incentives to concentrate in places where lots of poor people already live. He advocates spatially neutral antipoverty strategies—such as the federal Earned Income Tax Credit (EITC) and vouchers for housing, schooling, and training that can be used anywhere (Glaeser 2000a, 2000b). In contrast, Paul S. Grogan and Tony Proscio support revitalization of low-income neighborhoods and thus do not place a high priority on the spatial deconcentration of the poor. The work of neighborhood-level community development groups and their allies has helped many poor neighborhoods to become decent places to live, with housing, shopping, and services all tailored to the needs of residents—not imitations of well-off suburbs (Grogan and Proscio 2000).

A similar debate occurred in the late 1960s and early 1970s. It pitted ghetto community development against residential dispersal of the black poor to suburbs where jobs and opportunity were thought to be more plentiful. Central to the debate were competing claims about how best to improve the quality of life among the inner-city poor on dimensions of housing, schooling, social relations, and employment. I argue in this chapter that balanced support for both community revitalization and residential mobility, reinforced by spatially neutral income transfer policies, can promote vibrant, mixed-income, multiracial neighborhoods in all parts of a metropolitan region. Declining racial intolerance and rising interest in the vitality of cities make this ambitious aspiration increasingly appropriate and plausible.

A major goal of community revitalization *and* residential mobility strategies is to increase employment and raise earnings among the inner-city poor. A long-standing diagnosis for inner-city poverty is that even if jobs are plentiful at locations that are difficult for inner-city residents to reach, jobs are too scarce nearby (Kain 1968; Kasarda 1995; Wilson 1987, 1996). A second diagnosis is that many inner-city residents lack the skills and attitudes necessary to be good employees and, as a consequence, have difficulty holding jobs (Holzer 1996; Kirschenman and Neckerman 1991). A third is that the inner-city poor have isolated social networks. They lack well-connected associates who can inform them of job openings, advocate to get them hired, and then support them on the job (Dickens 1999; Melendez and Harrison 1998; Newman 1999; Tilly and Tilly 1994). Support is especially important when employers or coworkers are prone to discriminate on the basis of race, ethnicity, work experience, home address, age, or gender.

All three diagnoses—scarce or inaccessible jobs, worker deficiencies, and isolated social networks—have influenced community revitalization, residential mobility, and other antipoverty strategies, including job creation projects, transportation assistance programs, and workforce development initiatives. This chapter reviews evidence on the effectiveness of such interventions and considers the implications for twenty-first-century society.

Key Definitions

I use the words "neighborhood" and "community" interchangeably. Both connote a geographically contiguous residential area defined by geographic markers (for example, major roads or parks) or by a historical association with particular ethnic groups or institutions (such as churches) that is regarded (or could become regarded) as a distinct social or political entity within a city or town. There is no necessary assumption about the degree to which people identify with one another socially or politically, but there is the presumption that a sense of shared concern and collective efficacy regarding neighborhood affairs might exist or grow over time.[1]

By "inner city" I mean the central jurisdiction of a metropolitan region, including the central business district and its residential, commercial, and industrial areas. By "metropolitan region" I mean the broader geographic area, including the inner city and its inner and outer suburbs, across which adults routinely commute to work and shop.

Spatial Mismatch, Transportation, and Information

Unemployment levels are often higher in inner-city neighborhoods than one would predict based only on residents' personal characteristics, including measures of skill.[2] The spatial mismatch hypothesis is among the most popular explanations. Analysts who believe that spatial mismatch is important favor residential mobility programs that help the poor move to where jobs are more plentiful.[3] Others favor job creation. Historically, community leaders of racial and ethnic minorities have preferred local job creation over residential mobility strategies because it seemed more socially feasible in the face of prejudice and because political capital and social ties can be more easily preserved if the group stays together (Tate 1970). In addition, group members may have access to business ownership opportunities that come about as a result of group solidarity and concentrated purchasing power (Bailey 1971).

A third strategy is to provide transportation assistance that gives people access to jobs that might not be near the neighborhood but are within commuting distance. Its proponents favor this option because it does not depend on creating or relocating businesses or residences.

Physical Inaccessibility Versus Too Little Information

Many studies have examined whether spatial mismatch helps to explain why poor people in cities, especially minorities, have lower employment rates. John Kain's (1968) argument had three components. First, good jobs for low-skilled people were moving to the suburbs faster than the black population. Second, discrimination in housing restricted the ability of blacks from the inner city to follow the jobs to the suburbs. Third, distance and lack of transportation made it difficult for blacks to get to the places where the jobs were locating, and this exacerbated black unemployment. Studies generally support the first two points, but the third has been more controversial. Even Kain was less certain of this third proposition. Getting to jobs that are farther away can be a hardship, but it is difficult to determine just how much of the unemployment and poverty problem this distance effect explains.

It is difficult to distinguish the effect of physical inaccessibility, a problem of *physical* distance, from a lack of access to information about opportunities that are physically farther away, a problem of *social* distance. The problem of social distance is not to be underestimated. Residents of high-poverty neighborhoods get less than their proportionate share of even jobs that are nearby (Dickens 1999), owing possibly to discrimination, skill gaps, or a lack of the social contacts that would give them access.

Studies of spatial mismatch generally find either that blacks have longer commutes than whites or that there is no difference; estimated differences are almost never more than fifteen minutes (Dickens 1999). Dickens explains why simply showing that blacks have longer commutes is not sufficient to show that distance is a major problem. First, given what we know about labor supply behaviors (in other words, wage elasticities), having to travel an added fifteen minutes to work would not discourage enough people from working to account for large racial or neighborhood differences in employment levels.[4] Second, long commutes per se are not necessarily evidence that people live farther away on average from employment sites in the region; longer commutes for blacks than for whites could be due to discrimination, skill differences, or social isolation.

Dickens proposes the following thought experiment. Assume that workers and jobs are evenly distributed across the city. However, workers from disadvantaged neighborhoods get fewer job offers than do people from other neighborhoods (with the same intensity of job search), either because of discrimination or because residents of disadvantaged neighborhoods have fewer of the skills that employers are seeking. When do people decide to stop searching and accept an offer? Based on a standard economic search model, workers from the disadvantaged neighborhood will settle for a worse offer because their prospects of receiving a better one anytime soon are lower. A worse offer might pay a lower wage or require a longer commute.[5] Hence, longer average commuting times for blacks are not clear evidence of spatial mismatch.

Keith Ihlanfeldt (1999) points to two recent studies as the strongest evidence yet that spatial mismatch is important. One (Raphael 1998) seems to refute two of the most influential studies in the literature (Ellwood 1986;

Leonard 1987), each of which finds that racial differences in youth unemployment rates have little to do with job accessibility. For example, David Ellwood (1986) found large differences in employment rates for black and white youth living in contiguous areas and concluded, "The problem is race, not space."

Using 1990 census tract data for San Francisco, Steven Raphael (1998), argues that the number of job openings per worker within commuting distance is a better measure of employment opportunity than simply the number of jobs occupied. When Raphael replicates Ellwood's and Leonard's methods, by using only the number of jobs occupied as the measure of accessibility, his findings are the same as theirs: the relationship of accessibility to youth employment is statistically insignificant. However, when he uses job growth as the measure, he can explain between 30 and 50 percent of the average neighborhood employment differentials between black and white youth.

A similar study by Cynthia Rogers (1997) uses a sample of males, age eighteen to fifty-five, who submitted unemployment insurance claims in the Pittsburgh area. She examines whether residential location could help to predict which workers would become reemployed most quickly. Like Raphael, Rogers finds no effect of accessibility when using the number of jobs within commuting distance, but a strong positive effect when using the amount of job growth.

It seems quite plausible that Raphael and Rogers have captured the importance of information rather than physical accessibility. Specifically, in locales where employment is stable or growing slowly, a large percentage of jobs are likely to be filled by word of mouth; employees recruit friends and relatives, and employers use limited methods of outreach. People whose friends or relatives do not work at a site that is hiring will be relatively unlikely to learn of the openings. Indeed, there is some evidence that employers of unskilled workers are *especially* prone to hire through informal channels (Braddock and McPartland 1987; Tilly and Tilly 1994).

However, when rapid growth necessitates the use of recruitment methods other than word of mouth, either because the firms are new or because they are expanding quickly, then more publicly visible announcements give people outside the inner circle of friends and relatives better chances to learn about the openings. Also, employers who are expanding rapidly and need workers quickly might be less inclined to discriminate against youth or adults with poor work histories. Hence, people who are not well connected to people with jobs should fare better in environments where there is job growth, because information about job openings is more freely available. This could account for Raphael's and Rogers's results. Similar explanations may help to account for why more of the poor found jobs during the economic expansion of the late 1990s, when employment and earnings were rising among all segments of the society because labor demand was growing (see Freeman, this volume).

My general assessment is that studies that find evidence of spatial mismatch cannot distinguish whether information or the geographic accessibility of job openings is the key problem, and the studies by Raphael and Rogers are no exceptions. One exception, however, is a study by Holzer and Ihlanfeldt (1996), who studied representative samples of firms in Boston, Atlanta, Los Angeles, and Detroit and sought to explain the race of the most recently hired blue-collar employee. As expected, the farther the firm's location was from black residential concentrations, the less likely it was that the last person hired at the suburban firm was black. This finding seems consistent with spatial mismatch. When Holzer and Ihlanfeldt took into account the recruitment method that the firm had used, they found that the distance to black residential neighborhoods had a negative effect for three of the four methods—signs, walk-ins, and referrals. However, for the fourth method, newspaper advertisements, the distance from black neighborhoods did not affect the likelihood that the last person hired was black. Referring to the 1996 study, Ihlanfeldt (1999, 225) writes: "Since newspapers disseminate information over a wider geographical area than other methods, these results suggest that the distance effect may be attributable to central-city blacks possessing poor information about suburban job openings."[6]

Transportation Assistance Experiments

In response to the spatial mismatch hypothesis, there have been a number of efforts since the late 1960s to supply inner-city residents with transportation assistance. The results have not been encouraging for the idea that transportation is the key impediment to greater employment among the inner-city poor. Neither is the problem simply one of information.

The most recent major experiment to provide transportation services linking inner-city residents to suburban jobs is the Bridges to Work initiative, designed to serve 3,100 people over the four-year period from 1996 to 2000. To qualify, participants had to have a genuine transportation need and no access to a vehicle that could be used for commuting. The program used a random assignment design in four cities: Baltimore, Denver, Milwaukee, and St. Louis. In a fifth, Chicago, there was no random assignment, but the program tried to serve a larger number of participants in this city in order to test the feasibility of "going to scale."

The program designers assumed that plenty of work-ready applicants would be eager and able to participate (Elliot, Palubinsky, and Tierney 1999). They anticipated that the main problems would be in arranging and managing transportation services. To their surprise, it was much more difficult than expected to recruit and retain participants. Finding enough suburban employers to ensure a steady and substantial supply of jobs was not difficult. The midterm report explains that the difficulty in finding work-ready participants "was caused, in part, by the unwillingness of other training providers to refer good candidates to Bridges. It also may have been exacerbated by many job-ready people finding employment as a result of strong job growth. In any case, our experience is that most people participating in Bridges were not job-ready and needed assistance preparing for work" (Elliot, Palubinsky, and Tierney 1999, 8–9). Regarding the need for transportation, it is instructive that as of March 31, 1999, only 260 of the 1,050 participants who had been placed were still using the transportation service.

Bridges to Work employers have not been very concerned about whether participants have job-specific skills. Rather, they seek qualities such as dependability, willingness to take direction from a supervisor, and ability to maintain civil, if not cordial, relations with coworkers. Employers also place a premium on filing vacancies quickly. Over 70 percent say that they usually fill their openings within two weeks or less. Similarly, speed is important for participants: those not placed within two weeks of signing up with Bridges to Work tend to drop out of the program.

Bridges to Work has placed people in several hundred firms in a variety of industries. It is plausible that there will be positive outcome results from the random assignment evaluation, insofar as employment and retention rates among participants may turn out to be higher than among the control group. However, the treatment that the program has provided to participants is much more than simply information and transportation. Systematic differences compared to the control group's experience involve the total package of job information, transportation services, and job retention assistance.

The fact that more than transportation is needed is not a new lesson.

A survey of other transportation programs of the past few decades (Rosen-bloom 1992, 39; as quoted in Dickens 1999) concluded:

> Overall these experiences strongly suggest that projects providing transportation alone will not increase inner city employment unless they also (1) provide intensive training and skills enhancement, (2) offer a range of *continuing* support services, (3) ensure wages that more than compensate for both the loss of benefits and increased rent and employment expenses, (4) work with employers to overcome prejudice and stereotyping, (5) guarantee the worker meaningful on-the-job training and a real career ladder, and (6) keep travel times and distances reasonable (and in line with wage rates).

The timing of the Bridges to Work program, from 1996 through 2000, co-incided with a strong economic expansion in which many people with few skills or other resources were able to find jobs unassisted. Surely, recruitment for the program would have been easier if the economy had been weaker. In addition, transportation and information might have been sufficient for a larger percentage of program applicants.

Economic Development for Job Creation

Most references to economic development concern the birth, expansion, re-cruitment, or retention of businesses in order to increase the number of jobs in an area or to expand the area's tax base. Modifiers such as "state," "met-ropolitan," "city," or "neighborhood" describe the geographic area targeted. Typically, economists regard the metropolitan area as the relevant job market for adult workers, including the poor, who can commute. Concerns about job shortages for the poor lessened during the late 1990s because of the strong economy. However, when the economy weakens, there may be periods when concerns about job creation are widespread—especially because of time limits on the receipt of public welfare (Pavetti, this volume).

Weaknesses of Some Standard Approaches

Many government incentives for businesses aim to attract firms to locate in particular places. Most offer tax breaks or special regulatory exceptions aimed at lowering costs (Fisher and Peters 1997; Schweke, Rist, and Dabson 1994).[7] Though there is no consensus about the magnitude of the effects, economists believe that business financial incentives *can* affect the jurisdiction in which a business chooses to locate (Fisher and Peters 1997).[8] Whether such competition is a good idea from a social benefit–cost perspective depends on the details of the situation. The risk that development incentives will be of a zero-sum nature—in other words, one jurisdiction will gain jobs only at the expense of another—is one reason economists often say that such incentives are a bad idea.

Timothy Bartik (1994, 2000) has argued that shifting employers from labor-shortage areas to labor-surplus areas can be a net positive for society, especially for the poor and the unemployed, if moving costs do not use up too many resources. Rather than driving up wages in labor-shortage areas, if firms move instead to labor-surplus areas, they can have greater net impacts on employment, real earnings, and output. Peter Fisher and Alan Peters (1998) have measured the value of business incentives across 112 cities in the 24 most industrial states. Although Bartik's idea is correct in theory, Fisher and Peters find few indications that state and local business incentives are currently structured to favor labor-surplus areas.

The argument for steering firms to labor-surplus areas is sometimes used to justify subsidies for business development in the inner city. In this case, for adults who can commute, neighborhood business creation can be inefficient. Matching workers to openings in existing businesses at current business locations is likely to be faster and cheaper.[9] The strongest rationales for focusing on business growth in or near low- to moderate-income neighborhoods include supplying convenient shopping, increasing the leadership that local businesspeople often provide, making the community look better, and expanding employment options for youth and caretakers of young children who need to work near home (Gittell and Thompson 1999).

Similar concerns apply to subsidizing micro-enterprise and other small-business development programs. There are good reasons to favor them, other than job creation, including the value our society puts on giving people opportunities to own and operate their own businesses. However, start-up businesses require intensive technical assistance, their failure rates are high, and their employee numbers are small relative to the costs involved in helping them to succeed (Brown, Hamilton, and Medoff 1990). Subsidies for micro-enterprise or small-business development must be carefully targeted to help the poor in a cost-effective way (Servon and Bates 1998).

Economists concerned with economic efficiency advocate business incentives and assistance only when market failures justify them. Such failures are difficult to measure, however, and in any case, politicians make decisions that provide them with opportunities to score "wins" for their constituents (Eisinger 1995). A major win occurs when a large employer locates within the boundaries of the politician's jurisdiction. That the employer is lost to a competing jurisdiction may make it a zero-sum event for the region, but local politicians seldom take a regional perspective. When the opportunity arises, local leaders try hard to induce large businesses to locate in their jurisdictions, anticipating not only the new jobs but also customer-supplier linkages with other local businesses (Schweke, Dabson, and Rist 1996).[10]

Diminishing the benefits to local residents, however, is the fact that workers, like businesses, are mobile. Sometimes workers from other places migrate or commute to an area to take newly created jobs; as a result, the benefits for local workers, including the working poor, are smaller than expected.[11] Indeed, employers in low-income neighborhoods sometimes *prefer* to hire workers who commute into the area instead of people living nearby (Newman and Lennon 1995; Kasinitz and Rosenberg 1996).

Getting the Fundamentals Right

The most important policies affecting job growth are what I label the "fundamentals" of economic development: the public-sector functions that the government performs routinely. These are functions that society and markets depend on but that markets do inefficiently, if at all. The fundamentals include providing public physical infrastructure, administering broad-based tax and expenditure policies and business regulations that affect marginal incentives for investment across many types of investors, and funding public education. The fundamental priority in the provision of infrastructure is to construct streets, bridges, sewers, and utilities that are usable and well located, not to make a job creation strategy out of building them.

Also important are civic and elected leaders who cultivate a positive climate for new investment. This is more than a matter of maintaining low business costs. Although the cost of doing business remains a top consideration, location consultants who help companies find sites report that the quality of life—both business life and private life—affects final decisions about where to put new investment (Ady 1997). In addition to controlling the cost of doing business, local leaders should cultivate a civic culture and quality of life that investors will find attractive, even at the neighborhood level.[12]

Removing Barriers to Business Location and Growth

The most cost-effective and sensible economic development policies for the inner city often involve *removing barriers* to business location and growth. Such barriers include obsolete buildings that need to be demolished, soil pollution that needs to be removed, unnecessary zoning or building regulations, political disagreements about land uses, and inadequate public infrastructure (Blair 1995; Blakely 1994). Removing these barriers, even if doing so is costly, can foster the long-run economic vitality of the inner city.

Major disincentives to inner-city location also include fear of crime (INTERFACE 1985; Sampson 1999) and fear of social and political unrest (Schuchter 1971). Crime, riots, and physical deterioration have contributed to years of bad publicity for inner-city neighborhoods, reinforcing racial intolerance (Moore 1999) and deepening the negative stigma against inner-city locations.

Senator Robert Kennedy in 1966 touted the "untapped potential" of inner-city locations as both consumer and labor markets (Schuchter 1971). Twenty-nine years later, Professor Michael Porter (1995) made the same case. Bankers and businesspeople have told me that Porter's involvement has helped to lessen the stigma and to "give cover" to some who would like to invest in inner-city locations but might otherwise have trouble defending it to their peers. Regional organizations, businesses, local governments, nonprofit community-based organizations, and civic groups can all play a role in removing the barriers and disincentives that may discourage employment growth in disadvantaged areas.

State Enterprise Zones That Target Poor Areas

Some programs and policies explicitly target low-income places for job growth in the hope that new jobs will accrue disproportionately to low-income residents. Several questions should be asked about this type of targeting. First, do the programs succeed at creating jobs? Second, if jobs are created, do they employ neighborhood residents, particularly low-income and hard-to-employ residents? Finally, do the social benefits of these efforts exceed the costs? Are poverty levels affected? Unfortunately, the number of methodologically strong studies addressing these questions is small and the evidence is thin.

The concept of enterprise zones originated in England in the late 1970s as a way to induce businesses to develop vacant urban land. The focus was industrial development, not community revitalization or poverty alleviation. The British designated eleven zones in 1981 and another twenty-four in 1983, each for ten years. During those ten-year periods, businesses locating in the zones qualified for tax exemptions of various types and reductions in regulatory requirements. An early evaluation found that 86 percent of the firms relocating to the zones came from the same county as the zone (Tym et al. 1984).

In the United States, the enterprise zone concept was heavily promoted during Ronald Reagan's presidency by Congressman Jack Kemp, who in 1988 became secretary of Housing and Urban Development (HUD). However, as federal officials debated but did not implement the policy during the 1980s, state legislatures adopted their own versions of the enterprise zone model. By 1993, thirty-seven states and the District of Columbia had initiated zones targeted typically at depressed sections of their cities. According to Fisher and Peters (1997), the typical state zone includes investment tax credits, jobs tax credits, sales tax exemptions or credits, and property tax abatements.

Basic microeconomic concepts help us consider how the enterprise zones *could* affect business decisions. In theory, incentives affecting input prices can produce both output effects (how much firms produce) and factor substitution effects (what combinations of land, labor, and capital they use). Business incentives in state enterprise zone programs typically include property tax exemptions or abatements from city government that lower the cost of space and investment tax credits from state government that lower the cost of capital equipment. On the one hand, if such subsidies reduce the marginal cost of space or capital, they may tend to reduce employment by inducing firms to substitute away from labor and toward the inputs (land and capital) that the subsidies make cheaper. On the other hand, because the same subsidies reduce the marginal production cost for any given level of output, there is a positive output effect because it becomes profitable to increase output (assuming that demand is sufficiently elastic). The net effect of substitution and output effects on employment could be either positive or negative, depending on which is larger.

State enterprise zones often include training subsidies to help defray the costs of upgrading labor. Some also include wage subsidies (often tax credits) that pay a fraction of the wage for targeted categories of workers, especially zone residents. Measures that make labor cheaper can help to offset the ployment-reducing effects that land and capital subsidies may produce. As long as they are structured to affect the *marginal* cost of labor,[13] training and wage subsidies may produce a positive substitution effect toward labor and also a positive output effect.

A number of empirical studies of state enterprise zones and several reviews that critique this literature are available (Rubin and Richards 1992; Papke 1993; Ladd 1994; Wilder and Rubin 1996; for chapters on specific states, see Green 1991). The critiques explain why most studies are not useful for gauging impacts on employment, earnings, or poverty. The major methodological challenge is making a reliable estimate of the "counterfactual"—in other words, what would have happened if there had been no enterprise zone. Simple reports of job or earnings growth following zone designation can be misleading as impact estimates, since the same changes might have occurred even without the zone program, or the jobs may simply have moved from nearby areas that would still have been accessible by commute.[14]

I will briefly review the major studies. Leslie Papke (1994) studied the enterprise zone program that Indiana adopted in 1983. To qualify as a zone, an area had to have an unemployment rate at least one and a half times the statewide rate, a household poverty rate at least 25 percent above the national average, and a population between two thousand and eight thousand in an area not more than three square miles. As comparison places, she analyzed nonzone taxing districts and cities comparable to those that had zones.[15] She estimated whether areas with zones grew faster than areas without zones, controlling for how fast each area grew before the years in which zones were designated and for any constant unobserved differences (what econometricians call "fixed effects") that affected zone outcomes.

The main capital subsidy was an unusual 100 percent exemption from the property tax on total business inventory, not simply new additions. Most states do not impose taxes on inventories, so the opportunity to exempt firms from it is rare. However, when the tax exists, the exemption can be quite valuable to firms that store large amounts of inventory in warehouses. As theory would suggest, Papke finds that zone status increases business inventories by about 8 percent and reduces the value of manufacturing machinery and equipment (in other words, depreciable personal business property) by about 13 percent. Hence, the nature of the capital subsidy affected the mix of investment activity in the zones. The Indiana program also includes an employer tax credit for hiring zone residents equal to 10 percent of wages, up to a ceiling of $1,500 per qualified employee. Papke reports that only 3 percent of zone businesses claimed the wage credits.[16] Hence, it is doubtful that the wage credit made much difference.

Papke estimates that the typical city experienced a permanent 19 percent reduction in the annual number of unemployment claims following designation of an enterprise zone within its borders. These changes in unemployment claims pertained both to zone and nonzone residents. Zone residents did work in the zone, but whether the 19 percent reduction in unemployment claims reflects an improvement in *their* employment status is difficult to know. For example, in 1988, 2,779 zone residents were employed by 949 zone businesses (Papke 1993, n. 27). That same year, James Papke (1990) reports, zone residents got 14.7 percent of the new jobs. Further, in 1990 zone residents held 4.1 percent of all jobs in the zone and 19 percent of those that were new (though the average wage paid to zone residents was only about half that paid to nonresidents). These numbers make it seem quite plausible, or even likely, that zone residents were better off than they would have been without the zone program.

However, the budgetary cost per job was quite high. Leslie Papke (1994) reports that the *annual* direct budgetary cost of a zone job was $4,564, or $31,113 per zone resident job. This is a high cost for jobs that paid between $7,000 and $8,000 per year to the typical employed zone resident, especially if we assume that many would have been employed even without zone designation.

Papke later used data from the Census of Population and Housing for 1980 and 1990 to measure how employment and income among zone residents changed during the decade compared to similar places that did not have zones. She found that residents in the zones were hardly any better off economically in 1990 than in 1980. The per capita income gap between zone and nonzone residents was slightly larger in 1990 than in 1980, though the unemployment gap was slightly smaller, and the residential population had declined more in the zones than in the other areas. These findings provide no indication that zone designation appreciably helped zone residents, and they cast doubt on the possibility that the 19 percent drop in citywide unemployment claims estimated in Papke (1994) represented a major improvement for zone residents (compared with people from other parts of the city).

Daniele Bondonio and John Engberg (1999) analyze how zones have affected employment in California, Kentucky, New York, Pennsylvania, and

Virginia. Their units of analysis within states are U.S. postal zip code areas; zip codes that encompass any portion of an enterprise zone are treated as zone areas. The authors use predesignation data for income, percentage black or Hispanic, poverty, unemployment, and population density measures from the 1980 census, matched to the zip codes, to estimate the probabilities of zone designation for the areas in their analysis. These probability estimates, or "propensity scores," control for the fact that zone selection is not random. Controlling for propensity scores, for unobserved state-to-state variation in factors that may affect employment (using state-level indicator variables), and for unobserved year-to-year differences (using indicator variables for years), Bondonio and Engberg find no employment effects of enterprise zone designation. This is true in the aggregate and also for two-digit industries examined separately.[17] Thus, there is no confirmation that state-level enterprise zones consistently create jobs, that many jobs created go to needy residents and raise their incomes, or that the costs exceed the benefits. Evaluation reports from the federal empowerment zone program that began in 1994 will become available soon, and it remains plausible that the findings will be more encouraging. In addition to business incentives, the federal program involves a range of flexible supports for residents that, even without the incentives to businesses, could help.[18]

Whereas we have learned from numerous studies that business financial incentives are unlikely to be a *cost-effective* way of increasing employment for the poor, we lack evidence on the job creation impacts of attending to public policy fundamentals or of reducing unnecessary barriers to growth. The evidence would lead most economists to conclude that attending to fundamentals and reducing barriers are strategies that stand a better chance of making a positive difference. However, because these measures typically do not specifically target the poor, there is the possibility that new job openings will be filled by the nonpoor and by people who migrate or commute into an area. Therefore, the degree to which *poor residents* will benefit (and for how long) is always difficult to anticipate. It will depend on the tightness of the local job market, their skills and behaviors, and the structure of the social networks through which employment-related information and influence flow.

Businesses Helping Businesses

A number of projects and organizations, motivated primarily by profit, are attempting to have businesses help other businesses. Some are convened initially by governmental agencies (Sabel 1993), and others by civic groups or business organizations such as chambers of commerce (Berry 1998). The most visible of these is the nonprofit Initiative for a Competitive Inner City (ICIC), founded by Harvard Business School Professor Michael Porter.[19] These initiatives blend the concern for economic growth and job creation with an understanding that social and professional networks matter. ICIC, for example, heavily emphasizes that regional economies are made up of clusters of related businesses. Within clusters, there are bonds of professional understanding and trust among businesspeople, whose relationships are complex—for example, elements of competition and cooperation sometimes coexist within a single relationship (Powell 1990). Inner-city entrepreneurs are often isolated from these networks of relationships and the embedded flows of information that enable others to participate profitably in regional clusters.

ICIC connects inner-city businesses more extensively to regional clusters and informs businesspeople outside of the inner city about the advantages of locating stores and production facilities at inner-city sites. Instead of providing financial inducements, ICIC helps build professional networks and provides information regarding ways of making business more profitable at inner-city locations. For example, ICIC collects and disseminates information about training and managing workers who lack work experience or have poor work habits. The intention of these activities is to induce more businesses to locate at inner-city sites and employ inner-city residents.

Although there are stories of success,[20] I know of no formal evaluation studies to gauge the impact of these activities, on either business growth or the employment of the inner-city poor. However, the ideas make sense conceptually, and in my view, they have the potential to be effective.

Social Ties and Workforce Development Networks

The implicit question thus far has been whether there are effective ways of increasing the number of jobs in a neighborhood, city, or region so that employment of the inner-city poor increases. Now the question changes: are there ways in which the inner-city poor might get a larger share of existing jobs even if the aggregate number does not increase? The poor need opportunities to acquire competitive skills (see Karoly, this volume), and some also need help overcoming self-handicapping habits and lifestyles. In addition, because their informal social networks are prone to be isolated from mainstream work opportunities, many need supplemental supports to connect them with employers, to help negotiate hiring agreements, and to solve problems (both at home and on the job) that might otherwise lead to quits or dismissals. These supplemental supports augment workers' own informal social networks.

Isolated Social Networks

Labor economists have long recognized that norms and information transmitted through social ties with family, friends, and acquaintances affect a person's preparation for employment as well as access to particular jobs. The same social network relations that determine whether a person finds out about a job and gets hired into it can affect her prospects for learning how to do the job and retaining it. In short, social ties affect job preparation, job matching, and job retention. Dickens (1999) calls these "the three social network functions," because they are often performed for a person informally by unpaid family, friends, and acquaintances in her social network. Several studies emphasize how such phenomena determine labor market outcomes (Tilly and Tilly 1994; Harrison and Weiss 1998; Dickens 1999; Kirschenman and Neckerman 1991; Holzer 1996; Moss and Tilly 2001). These writers build on earlier works from the 1960s and 1970s (Rees 1966; Rees and Schultz 1970; Granovetter 1974). When a person's social networks are isolated from mainstream opportunities for work, local initiatives can supplement them in order to improve her employment outcomes.

The Center for Employment Training

The Center for Employment Training (CET) grew out of the Mexican farmworkers' movement in the 1960s.[21] It has become the leading exemplar among multi-site organizations that perform the three social network functions of helping poor people to prepare for jobs, to achieve good job matches, and to retain jobs once they have them.

When studied in relationship to similar programs, CET consistently rates as the most highly effective for both males and females who need help entering the mainstream labor market. The evaluation of the JOBSTART demonstration program in the early 1990s found that the sites operated by CET were the only ones that produced statistically significant gains in earnings for participants (seventeen- to twenty-one-year-old high school dropouts). Compared to nonparticipants who were randomly assigned to each site-specific control group, participants' earnings were higher by $7,000 per year for the first two years after training and by $6,000 per year in years three and four (Cave et al. 1993). CET also proved effective in a random assignment experimental evaluation called the Minority Female Single Parent Demonstration (Hollister 1990; Zabrowski and Gordon 1993; Kerachsky 1994).

The basic CET model uses contextual, hands-on learning. Students learn job skills along with basic academic skills in simulated job situations. The program is run so that a day in the program feels like a day at work. It is open-entry and open-exit, meaning that new people may come in at any time and trainees graduate when they and their supervisors determine that they are ready for a regular job. This point is reached, on average, after thirty weeks in the program (Melendez 1996). However, graduation is not the end of the CET connection: follow-up support is provided on an as-needed basis.

Although CET's basic design features are consistent with what many professionals regard as best practice in adult instruction, none is unique. Edwin Melendez and Bennett Harrison (Melendez 1996; Melendez and Harrison 1998) argue that two aspects of CET in addition to its design features account for its success. First, because CET is rooted in the Mexican farmworkers' political movement, it has a seriousness of purpose and is embedded within the extensive social networks of Chicanos in the western United States and northern Mexico. Second, CET is an especially trusted intermediary connecting Chicano workers with local employers. Employers trust the program in part because an extended informal network of community members enforces worker accountability for performance in the program, and later on the job. The trust that employers have in CET is a community resource. Members protect it by holding one another accountable.

Most analyses of employment and training programs neglect how they connect workers with jobs. In the standard analysis, workers move up in the hiring queue as their new skills or improved behaviors make them more attractive to potential employers. Discussion of "job development" or placement is typically perfunctory. Program managers understand that placement needs to be done, but the main work of the program is the training. For CET, working with employers is a critical prerequisite to working with trainees, because the needs of employers should guide what workers are trained to do.

CET embeds itself in recruitment channels using three methods. First, industrial advisory boards (IABs) give employers an opportunity to influence the design of training programs, including curriculum development, fund-raising, equipment donations, and other activities that support the organization. Second, technical advisory committees (TACs) advise CET training centers regarding curriculum and instruction for specific skills so that training does not become outdated. Along with the IABs, TACs help to identify equipment needs and may also help to supply them. Third, CET recruits instructors who typically have more than the minimum five years in the industry that CET requires.

The history of CET in the western United States is one of a gradual diffusion to sites away from San Jose, California, where the organization started.[22] However, the leaders at the western sites are typically people with strong ties to the San Jose headquarters who came up through the system.

The U.S. Department of Labor began a project in 1992 to replicate CET in other parts of the nation. An early evaluation concluded that sites had failed to implement the CET model by 1994 (Hershey and Rosemberg 1994). It appeared that sites had not been willing or able to take the details of implementation seriously.[23]

Clearly, replicating the political and social conditions that spawned and supported CET in California in the late 1960s is not a possibility. Still, to improve the quality of the replications, the intangible cultural and philosophical aspects of the program, including the accountability of trainees to the community, are important. There has been movement toward having the San Jose–based CET organization and its East Coast offices more directly involved in the management of the replication sites and toward having East Coast managers trained at well-established West Coast sites.

Growing Activity and Interest in Workforce Development

There is growing interest in workforce development organizations because of two recent changes in federal policy. First, Aid to Families with Dependent Children (AFDC) was replaced by the Temporary Assistance to Needy Families (TANF) program under the Personal Responsibility and Work Opportunity Act (PRWORA) of 1996 (see Pavetti, this volume). Second, the Workforce Investment Act (WIA) of 1998 replaced the federal Job Training Partnership Act (JTPA). TANF and WIA together are in the process of changing the nation's workforce development system. The change from JTPA to WIA was a four-year bipartisan effort on the part of the administration and the Congress. WIA's purpose is "to provide workforce investment activities, through statewide and local workforce investment systems, that increase the employment, retention, and earnings of participants, and increase occupational skill attainment by participants, and as a result, improve the quality of the workforce, reduce welfare dependency, and enhance the productivity and competitiveness of the Nation" (Geldhof 2000, 1).

Several recent publications analyze what is happening in the workforce development field (Elliot and King 1999; Stillman 1999; Lyall and Schweke 1996; Harrison and Weiss 1998; Giloth 1998; Berry 1998; Osterman and Lautsch 1996; Ma and Proscio 1998). There are several themes. One is the importance of serving employers' needs well *in order* to serve workers effectively. A second is that workers and employers need support after the match. A third is that roles and responsibilities can be divided up in many different ways among public-, private-, and nonprofit-sector organizations, but the basic issues and the types of tasks to be performed are very similar across initiatives.

Remaining unclear is the degree to which, and the conditions under which, preplacement job skills training produces worthwhile benefits. CET provides, on average, thirty weeks of training. However, other programs use a "work first" strategy, providing at most a few job-readiness skills. For example, America Works is a for-profit business that places low-skilled workers with employers and supports them after the placement, but without upfront skills training. In Dickens's (1999) view, the primary contribution of workforce development programs like CET and America Works is that they supplement workers' isolated social networks by matching them with employers, getting them hired, and supporting them after the placement.

Workforce development programs, as exemplified by CET, are a promising community-level strategy for connecting the isolated social networks of inner-city neighborhoods to the job recruitment and referral networks of the regional economy. However, more research is needed, because much of our current understanding is only impressionistic.

Jobs and Community Revitalization

The United States has a long history of "comprehensive" community development or revitalization strategies (Halpern 1995; O'Connor 1999; Perry 1987). They entail key roles for neighborhood residents in community-based organizations, an extensive list of quality-of-life ideals to which the community aspires, and assumed positive synergy between activities (Stoutland 1999; Briggs, Mueller, and Sullivan 1997; Bailey 1971). Promoted most recently in the form of the federal empowerment zone initiative, the idea is that outside resources combined with resident initiative can foster more employment, better housing, increased safety, less social isolation, more political influence, better schools, and so on.[24]

A new emphasis for these strategies is the view that jobs not only in the neighborhood but throughout the city and the region should be available to residents of the targeted communities. This regional perspective actually conflicts with the emphasis in the 1994 empowerment zone legislation, which gives wage subsidies and other benefits only to employers located within the zone. However, recent workforce development initiatives attempt to blend the community revitalization vision and the idea of regionalism (Harrison, Weiss, and Gant 1995; Harrison and Weiss 1998; Pastor et al. 2000).

Looking back, there were reasons in the 1960s and 1970s to focus on neighborhood business development and not on a more expansive regionalism. Active discussion of community revitalization was mostly a matter for black neighborhoods in older cities. Community development planners and activists at the time despaired of the possibility that blacks could successfully integrate into the regional economy and talked narrowly of building the ghetto economy (Harrison 1968, 1974; Vietorisz and Harrison 1970). Often their perspectives were informed by the "colonial analogy": the social, psychological, political, and economic relationship of black Americans to the United States was essentially similar to the relationship of African colonies to the European colonial powers (Blauner 1969; Bailey 1971). Without owning and controlling their own businesses in their own communities, there was no way, some argued, that blacks could overcome internal colonialism, develop a sense of collective pride, accumulate wealth and political power, or find enough jobs to employ all in the community who needed work (Tate 1970).

Reflecting separatist/integrationist tensions dating back to the nineteenth century (Du Bois 1899; Kinzer and Sagarin 1971), the racially separatist political emphasis of the ghetto development movement provoked an active debate. There were pro-ghetto development planners and activists on one side (Harrison 1968; Tate 1970; Bailey 1971) and, on the other side, people who warned that reinforcing the concentration of blacks in central cities was a mistake (Brimmer 1971; Kain and Persky 1969; Downs 1968). For example, John Kain and Joseph Persky (Bailey 1971, 315) asserted, "As between gilding the ghetto and dispersal, only the latter is consistent with the stated goals of American society." Anthony Downs (1968) also wrote perceptively about the drawbacks of a separatist ghetto development focus, emphasizing that separatism reinforced prejudice and discrimination, which were major barriers to fair treatment of blacks by employers. Downs advised a more mixed approach that would leave room for ghetto development by what he referred to as "black power" advocates, but he also encouraged residential integration of blacks into white suburbs along with various means of social and educational "enrichment" of the black poor.

The leading academic spokesman for the ghetto development perspective was Bennett Harrison, who believed that owing to racism and the poor preparation of blacks and whites to integrate socially with one another, blacks would be unable to follow jobs to suburban locations. Without ghetto development, he believed, large numbers of black males in particular would go jobless.

In the large cities of the Northeast and Midwest, there were efforts during the 1970s by community-based organizations called community development corporations (CDCs) to develop the ghetto economy. These efforts were supported financially by both foundation and federal dollars. Oversight on the use of federal dollars required annual reporting that was very burdensome.[25] Many of the people in key local positions were insufficiently experienced in business development.[26] Although the effort overall was not a complete failure, it was far from a complete success.[27] Given the poor record during the 1970s and the effect of such poor performance on prospects for continuing support, most CDCs gradually moved away from business development as a central focus.

At the same time, more blacks were achieving middle-income status and moving to the suburbs. David Cutler, Edward Glaeser, and Jacob Vigdor (1999) show that black segregation decreased somewhat between 1970 and 1990 because suburban communities gained black residents. However, the same study finds a larger number of heavily segregated black areas in 1990 than ever before.[28] Not only are these areas segregated, but they are also disproportionately low-income. Cities with the most segregation tend to be older ones in the Midwest and the Northeast; the ghetto development movement was strong in many of these cities in the 1960s and 1970s, and the community development movement that evolved from it remains strongest in these cities today (Vidal 1992). By the 1990s, after the community development movement had spread across the nation, white, Latino, Asian,

Native American, and ethnically mixed communities had become more active participants.

There are many ways to characterize the community development movement. A limited definition focuses on the community development corporations. The first major CDC was the Bedford-Stuyvesant Restoration Corporation in Brooklyn, New York, which was supported in the late 1960s and through the 1970s by the Ford Foundation and the federally sponsored Special Impact Program (SIP). SIP was an amendment to the Economic Opportunity Act of 1964; it was phased out beginning with Richard Nixon's presidency and ended early in the administration of Ronald Reagan. However, other sources of both governmental and foundation support remain available. The latest estimate from the National Congress for Community Economic Development (NCCED) is that over 3,400 CDCs existed in 1998.[29]

The largest CDC today, the New Communities Corporation in Newark, New Jersey, employs over 1,200 people and supplies a wide variety of services to Newark residents (including a site of the CET program). However, most CDCs are small, employing an average of six or seven employees. They tend to specialize in housing and commercial property development. The majority of CDCs list additional activities, such as planning and advocacy, youth programming, public safety, workforce development, and emergency food assistance, but given the scale of the organizations, the scope of these others is sometimes quite limited.[30]

Part of the vision in the late 1960s and early 1970s was that CDCs would create profitable new businesses to help support themselves and also to build the ghetto economy. However, as of 1994, only 8 percent of neighborhood-based CDCs listed "business owner and operator" among their activities (Ferguson and Dickens 1999, table 1.1).[31] Note that the "business owner and operator" category does not include housing and commercial property development, which CDCs do quite successfully as a primary specialization.

The failure of most community revitalization efforts in the 1970s and 1980s to successfully develop businesses to employ more than a few residents was the main point of Nicholas Lemann's (1994) attack in the *New York Times* on the Clinton administration's empowerment zone initiative. He accused the federal government of once again promising to revitalize the business environment of inner-city neighborhoods without much evidence from previous attempts that doing so was possible.

Lemann's article took a narrow view of what community development and the empowerment zone initiative were aiming to achieve. A broader view regards community development as all of the many types of activities, including but not limited to *economic* development, that expand the capacity of a community to support a decent quality of life for its residents. Under this conception, churches, public health agencies, precinct police stations, schools, CDCs, private housing rehabilitation firms, local banks, and a host of other actors all contribute to the community development process, whether they regard themselves as part of the community development field or not (see Ferguson and Stoutland 1999).

Lemann actually endorsed those aspects of this larger vision that did not involve business development, although he excluded these aspects from his definition of community development. This exclusion reflects standard practice among CDC activists, who distinguish business development, housing, and commercial development—all of which involve physical property development—from everything else, which they toss into an amorphous category called services. (For an extended discussion, see Ferguson and Dickens 1999.) This view, however, neglects the distinction between providing services and developing the capacity to do so. Developing capacity is development, from the perspective of microeconomics.

Lemann's article remains a sore spot for many in the CDC movement because of the headline that shouted community development was a myth. However, his aim was to shift the focus from what he saw as unrealistic aspirations for economic development to more realistic aspirations to improve the quality of life on other dimensions. His view in 1994 was very close to that of the community development experts Paul Grogan and Tony Proscio in their book *Comeback Cities* (2000).[32]

The quotation by Grogan and Proscio that opens this chapter is from *Comeback Cities*. The book lauds the progress achieved since 1970 among community-based organizations, especially CDCs. It emphasizes the importance of a growing national network of intermediary organizations that advocate for public support, organize private finance, and provide technical assistance. Grogan and Proscio write that while scholars have been wringing their hands about the intractability of urban problems, public officials, intermediaries, and community-level actors have been building the basis of a new urban revitalization. Although poverty is not being cured, communities are nonetheless becoming better places to live. Their favorite example is New York City's South Bronx, which in the past has been cited as the prime example of urban decline. Over the past twenty years, the city government demolished empty buildings and collaborated with CDCs to replace blight with homes that low-income people could own. Spurred by the federal Community Reinvestment Act (CRA), big banks that needed regulatory approvals for mergers in New York City went to the South Bronx seeking CDCs to help (Belsky, Lambert, and von Hoffman 2000). The financing that they supplied to the revitalization effort was critically important.

Edward L. Glaeser, also quoted at the opening of the chapter, argues that place-based strategies for helping the poor are usually a mistake. The examples of spatially targeted business development incentives that I have reviewed here provide some support for his perspective. To make policies to help the poor spatially neutral, he recommends putting more emphasis on earned income tax credits and transportable vouchers for housing and schooling.

CDCs do not understand their work simply as a strategy for helping the poor. Instead, they understand it as a strategy for making the community a better place to live. Grogan and Proscio (2000) point out that when communities become better places to live, land values and apartment rents often rise, and some of the poor cannot afford to stay without housing subsidies. Others who became homeowners have incentives to sell. Glaeser (2000a, 35) regards revitalization programs that cause rents to rise as a problem, because "landlords, not their tenants, get the benefits of the programs." In the case of communities like the South Bronx, however, low-income homeowners have benefited, and low-income tenants who have remained in the neighborhood like it better as well.

Perhaps the optimal combination of policies is a balanced blend of spatially neutral policies and spatially targeted community development strategies, complemented by programs that facilitate residential mobility between cities and suburbs. Pushing the balance too far in any one of these directions would probably be a mistake.

Conclusion: Many Communities to Develop

We have learned from experience that simply providing transportation assistance to the unemployed poor is unlikely, by itself, to make much difference in their lives. When the economy is near full employment, those who remain unemployed and poor need the types of job preparation, matching, and retention services that workforce development programs provide. Also, even though poor people get more jobs when the regional economy grows, subsidies aimed at inducing businesses to relocate or expand have not proven very effective as employment strategies, even when targeted to the areas where poor people live.[33] Further, subsidies to support micro-enterprise and small-business development programs are also not cost-effective as general employment strategies. If carefully targeted to people who can succeed, they can be defended on other grounds, such as giving people opportunities to participate in the free enterprise system. However, the main focus of local economic development strategies should be removing unnecessary barriers to business location and growth and getting the long-term fundamentals right with regard to infrastructure, taxation, regulation, and education.

Compared with the internally focused employment strategy that supporters of ghetto economic development thought was necessary in the 1960s and 1970s, today's discourse about employment and community revitalization is more regional and includes the private sector as a partner with non-profit and governmental organizations. The discourse is different today because the idea of an open, racially integrated society seems more plausible now than it did in 1970. Consequently, prospects have improved for integrationist options.

First, success is plausible now when the Initiative for a Competitive Inner City proposes to a mostly white business community that it should invest more in inner-city neighborhoods, sometimes with nonwhite business partners. Using the same language of "untapped markets" that Michael Porter uses today, Senator Robert Kennedy tried similar appeals in the late 1960s, but the racial climate was too hostile to permit progress in more than a few places.[34] Another difference is that there are more black MBAs now with the types of white-collar business experience that Andrew Brimmer (1971) proposed should be the foundation for mainstream black business development. Like Brimmer, Porter (1995) proposes key roles for such people in inner-city business revitalization.

Second, success is plausible when workforce development programs, such as CET and others, help both businesses and workers to make and sustain good employment matches involving inner-city workers in racially mixed workplaces, throughout the metropolitan region. Fears in 1970 that many employers would not have welcomed such relationships were among the reasons that regional *thinking* at the time did not produce more regional *action* to develop effective workforce development strategies.

Third, it is more plausible now than before (though still quite controversial) when advocates of vouchers for housing and education assert that low-income minorities will be accepted into middle-income communities and schools, using the purchasing power that vouchers can provide.

Finally, it is plausible that middle-income people of all races might move into a nontrivial number of inner-city neighborhoods as some of the poor leave, helping to make neighborhoods more mixed both racially and socio-economically.

Each of these strategies—business-led, inner-city economic revitalization, workforce development programs that go beyond training, vouchers of various types to give the poor mobility, and income mixing in the inner city—is being actively considered and acted upon by city leaders. Each has a better chance of succeeding in today's racial climate than it did thirty years ago. However, none is guaranteed to work every time or in every place. Each is more complex than the discussion here has indicated, and though race is less of a barrier than thirty years ago, it is still an impediment. Indeed, the interaction of race with poverty is increasingly complex as the nation moves beyond black and white to more fully incorporate Latinos, Asians, and American Indians.

If the poor of all racial and ethnic groups are to have access to jobs, assistance in acquiring skills, and adequate workforce development supports to help them succeed, the capacity of both the poor and the nonpoor to develop and manage diverse community relations in neighborhoods, schools, workplaces, and civic organizations will be critically important. Hence, there are many types of communities to develop in the twenty-first century. Ambitious visions for what might be achieved may help to organize and animate community-level initiatives in many types of settings, enhancing the quality of life along multiple dimensions for the poor as well as the rest of us.

PART IV

Concluding Thoughts

CHAPTER 13

Politics, Race, and
Poverty Research

GLENN C. LOURY

The great writer V. S. Naipaul once published a chronicle of his travels through the Islamic world called *Among the Believers*. Later, when commissioned by the *New York Review of Books* to write about the Republican National Convention, he produced a brilliantly satirical essay that ran under the title "Among the Republicans." And now, at this, my first poverty conference, I find myself "among the poverty nerds," so to speak. It has been an eye-opening experience. I've imagined myself these last days as an anthropologist in the field, or a travel writer wandering in a strange, exotic land. Don't misunderstand. I was pleased to have been asked by the organizers to take part in this conference. But of necessity I bring an outsider's perspective. Perhaps, then, I can be forgiven if some of my comments are uninformed or unconventional.

Although poverty research is not a field to which I have contributed, as a student of inequality in American society I have been an avid consumer of this work for some time now. One thing is immediately apparent. The field has progressed impressively over the last twenty-five years—with better data, more sophisticated analytic methods, and a growing number of creative scholars working on the problems. The quality of the papers presented at this conference, and the level of the discussion, reflect this progress. We have witnessed the professionalization and institutionalization of research in this field in the years since the War on Poverty. On balance, this is surely a good thing. Yet my sense of the matter is that it is also a mixed blessing. I will say more on this point in due course.

Stimulated by these goings-on, I would like to organize my remarks into three themes: conceptual issues in poverty research; politics and poverty research; and race and poverty research.

447

Conceptual Issues

Although some effort has obviously been taken here to gather an interdisciplinary group of scholars, the balance is still heavily weighted in favor of econometric analysis. There is nothing wrong with rigorous statistical inference from quantitative data—this activity is indispensable. But I'm moved to ask: Where are the ethnographers, developmental psychologists, social philosophers, and political analysts? These are vitally important areas of scholarship bearing directly on the issues under discussion. Yet few practitioners of these arts are in evidence here. I think this is too bad, because there are some puzzles raised by the poverty data that can only be illuminated, in my opinion, with cross-disciplinary collaboration. I know that effective scholarly exchanges across disciplinary boundaries are not easy. But a difficult thing becomes impossible when it is not tried.

I stress this because, as I see it, we will need to look beyond the conceptual resources of economics and quantitative sociology if we are to make progress on some of the crucial outstanding issues. Why, for example, does couching some interventions explicitly in terms of religious faith seem to matter for their success? How does a group of people (like welfare recipients living in cities and belonging to racial minority groups) come to be stigmatized, and what effect does the prospect of such stigmatization have on their behavior and their well-being? Where do ideas about identity (who am I?) and about social identification (who is essentially like me?) come from, and what role is played by people's ideas in this regard in producing or averting bad social outcomes? What can be said about the shaping of individual preferences—regarding work, sexuality and family formation, academic achievement, associational behaviors, and the like?

Social scientists have not made much progress toward answering such questions, but what progress there has been is the result mainly of qualitative investigations in the field. How can the insights from such qualitative inquiry be integrated with the knowledge produced from careful statistical analyses of nationally representative data sets? I urge that some consideration be given to this question at the next in-gathering of poverty researchers. The sociologist George Farkas, in his book *Human Capital or Cultural Capital* (1996), provides an apt illustration of the point I'm trying to make here. To paraphrase him, Farkas argues as follows: Here is a young man to whom one says, "Why don't you marry the girl you got pregnant? Why don't you work in a fast-food restaurant instead of standing on the street corner hustling? Why don't you go to community college and learn how to run one of the machines in the hospital?" And his answer is not, "I have done my sums, and the course you suggest has a negative net present value." Rather, his answer is, "Who, me?" He cannot see himself thus. Now, I ask, how are we to understand the people who answer us in this way? And how can we achieve a satisfactory grasp of the nature of poverty in American society in the absence of such an understanding?

On a different note, let me mention some other conceptual issues. There has been a huge change in the structure of our income maintenance/anti-poverty policy over the past decade, represented by the passage of federal welfare reform legislation in 1996. Much greater importance is now being placed on earnings relative to transfers. This is all well and good, but notice one thing. This policy shift implies a change in the allocation of business-cycle risks among income classes in the U.S. economy. I was surprised to see no discussion of this point here. Low-income American families would appear now to be much more vulnerable should we experience an upturn in unemployment. Moreover, it seems clear that one could assess quantitatively the consequences for well-being of this shift in the bearing of macroeconomic risks. This would be a worthwhile exercise at a time when so many people are trumpeting the decline of welfare rolls and the rise of job placements among recipients (which developments, needless to say, are most welcome).

As I listened to the discussion here, another area where my theorist's sensibility cried out for greater clarification involves the construction of the very concept of "poverty" itself. A clear distinction between "poverty," "disadvantage," "inequality," and "social exclusion" was often not drawn. Measurement of poverty involves imposing a binary categorization (poor/not poor) upon a continuous, multidimensional flux of social experience. There are two parts to this problem: to define a measure of well-being, and to define what about the distribution of well-being is normatively salient. Despite the disappointing (to me, anyway) results of efforts by axiomatic social choice theorists to deduce poverty measures from more primitive postulates about social values, the discussion here convinces me that this remains an area much in need of theoretical work. More generally, I think that there are both normative and positive issues raised by the problem of poverty (that is, issues of *social values* and of *individual behavior*), and judging by what I have seen at this conference, the former warrant more attention.

Politics and Poverty Research

At the conference, one participant commented that the discussion strikingly illustrates how dramatic has been the shift in the boundaries of legitimate discourse in the poverty research community in recent years. I am also struck by this fact. "Political correctness," if ever it held much sway in your tribe, is certainly dead now. Emphasis has been given to the possible disincentive effects of transfer payments, to the importance of maintaining reciprocity in relations with transfer recipients (expecting something from them in return for society's provision), to the value of paternalism in dealing with the poor, and even to the role of genetically transmitted influences in the study of the intergenerational transmission of poverty. Although neither is here, one can almost sense the ghostly presence of a Charles Murray or a Lawrence Mead in the room.

There is, of course, nothing wrong with open-mindedness and a willingness to consider seriously the views of more or less conservative writers where pertinent. But I detect something else here—something that illustrates one of the downsides to the professional institutionalization of poverty research. This is a tendency to accept without much critical examination in one's research the external constraints imposed on policymaking by prevailing political attitudes in the society as a whole—the tendency to limit one's work to technical exercises carried on within those constraints, hoping always to remain "relevant" to the policymaking process. Clearly, the political agenda in this area has shifted. (Witness the rightward drift in the welfare reform process between the presidential campaign of 1992 and the enactment of federal legislation four years later.) Much, perhaps most, of the electorate have moved "Beyond Entitlement" and suspect that we have indeed been "Losing Ground." These shifting public attitudes, of course, actively constrain policymaking, and politicians must take such constraints into account. But scholars ought not to have their horizons truncated by the shifting political fashions. Where, I would ask, is the *critique* of these public sentiments? I would even go so far as to ask: Where is the *radically progressive sensibility* in poverty research today? I would not, of course, expect scholarly papers to consist mainly of political advocacy, but the conventionality and timidity of the discussion here strikes me as regrettable.

What's to criticize, you ask? Well, how about the fact that changes in our welfare policy over the last decade have been driven, at least in part, by a "family values" politics rooted in reactionary sentiments that aims to impose upon those who happen to present themselves to the public for economic assistance a set of values about sexuality that are honored mainly in the breach elsewhere in our society? In the area of welfare (but also, I think, in drug enforcement policy), Americans seem to be trying to balance our cultural budget on the backs of our poorest, most vulnerable citizens. How can a discussion of poverty, such as was offered at this conference, omit to undertake any consideration of incarceration? (Prison populations have quadrupled over the last generation as a direct result of public policy, and those subject to being incarcerated are among the poorest of the poor.) How can the great disparity between our success in reducing poverty among the elderly and our relative failure in reducing poverty among children (a disparity emphasized fifteen years ago by Daniel Patrick Moynihan in his book *Family and Nation*) go virtually unremarked here? I wish not to be misunderstood. The tone of this conference has been admirably professional at the technical level, and that's great. My point, however, is that technical proficiency is not enough. More is required, because the subject of poverty raises more than technical problems, and the university (as distinct from the contract research-based consulting firm) is precisely the setting where one expects this broader context to be recognized. I saw too little of that recognition here.

Race and Poverty Research

As the director of an institute dedicated to the study of "race and social division," I would be remiss if I did not comment on this aspect of the poverty problem. Taking the papers presented here as a whole, in table after table and regression after regression, one encounters the disturbing evidence that racial differences in the experience of poverty are large, intractable, and poorly understood. Why are the extent, severity, and durability of impoverishment so much greater among blacks (and Hispanics) than whites and Asians? It is a failing of the poverty research tribe (though, of course, not yours alone) that so little can be said with confidence about this. I wish to use what remains of my claim on your attentions to offer two thoughts on this problem.

The first deals with the concept of racial discrimination. In the early days, discussions of race and poverty in the United States often entailed some consideration of discrimination. As a historical practice, this is appropriate and understandable. My current view, however, is that a focus on the discriminatory treatment of individuals is no longer adequate. To illustrate my position, consider an elemental distinction between two kinds of behavior—what I'll call discrimination in *contract* and discrimination in *contact.* By "discrimination in contract" I mean to invoke the unequal treatment of otherwise like persons based on race in the execution of formal transactions—the buying and selling of goods and services, or interactions with organized bureaucracies, for instance. By contrast, "discrimination in contact" refers to the unequal treatment of persons on the basis of race in the associations and relationships that are formed among individuals in social life, including the choice of social intimates, neighbors, friends, heroes, and villains. It involves discrimination in the informal, private spheres of life. An important difference is to be noted between these types of discrimination. Discrimination in contract occurs in settings over which a liberal state could, if it were to choose to do so, exercise review and restraint in pursuit of social justice. Precisely this has happened in the United States in the period since 1965, with significant if not complete success. Yet in any liberal political order, some forms of discrimination in contact (such as marriage, residence, or friendship networks) must remain a prerogative for autonomous individuals. Preserving the freedom of persons to practice this discrimination is essential to the maintenance of liberty, because the social exchanges from which such discrimination arises are so profoundly intimate and cut so close to the core of our being.

However, and this is my key point, mechanisms of status transmission and social mobility depend critically upon the nature of social interactions in both spheres—that is, on the patterns of contact as well as on the rules of contract. The provision of resources fundamental to the development of human beings is mediated both by formal and informal, by contractual and noncontractual, social relations. I have in mind here the roles played in the shaping of persons by the family, the social network, and (using the word advisedly) the "community." I am thinking about infant and early childhood development and about adolescent peer group influences. I mean to provoke some reflection on how people come to hold the ideas they in fact do hold concerning who they are (their identities), which other persons are essentially like them (their social identifications), and what goals in life are worth striving toward (their ideals). My fundamental empirical claim is this: In U.S. society, where of historical necessity patterns of social intercourse are structured by perceptions of race, it is inevitable that developmental processes operating at the individual level will also be conditioned by race.

From this it follows that, in a racially divided society like the United States, fighting discrimination in the sphere of contract while leaving it untouched in the sphere of contact will generally be insufficient to produce a baseline circumstance of equality of opportunity for all individuals. And yet a commitment to political liberalism would seem to require precisely this hands-off approach to one of the major spheres of discrimination—hence the dilemma, one that I believe is powerfully relevant to the study of racial disparities in the experience of poverty.

My second point has to do with the role of cultural explanations in accounting for racial disparities. I am deeply suspicious of the easy evocation of cultural arguments in this area, because these arguments typically neglect the crucial point that group identifications and racial self-understandings are endogenous. How are we to account for the ways in which, within a system of mutually susceptible individuals, each seeking approval or standing with the others, a normative type emerges that becomes the model for what "authentic" behavior represents within the (racial) group? The "peer effect" models typically posit a gravity-type idea: the norm (for a race-, class-, or neighborhood-based group) is the mean or median behavior found within the group, toward which individuals are pulled to some extent, contrary to their individual inclinations. But why? These are human beings, not celestial bodies. Why should criminal behavior, early unwed pregnancy, or hours spent studying be driven by the mean or median action within a peer group and not by the ninetieth- or tenth-percentile action? In other words, how does the group construct its notion of what constitutes a norm? I think this centrist-focused approach may be quite far off, and that examples can be found where the idealization of heroic, extreme behavior is more influential than "regression to mean" types of peer influence. For this reason, I am interested in how notions of stigma, shame, honor, and the rest arise as outcomes of intersubjective encounters among a group of people seeking to discover for themselves "who they really are"—both as individuals and collectively. And I am particularly concerned about such matters when the groups involved are defined in part on the basis of "race." Anyone who evokes notions like "black culture," "ghetto culture," or "underclass culture" in an effort to explain racial differences in poverty experience ought to be required to address such matters as well.

CHAPTER 14

Poverty Research and Antipoverty Policy After the Technological Revolution

DAVID R. HARRIS

In the middle and late nineteenth century, Karl Marx wrote about the relationship between expanding capitalism and the increasing exploitation of workers (Tucker 1978). As people moved from small towns and farms to take jobs in cities, there was a consequent change in the causes of poverty. Rather than blame bad weather for people's inability to feed their families, Marx argued that poverty was increasingly the result of workers being denied a fair share of the profits of their labor.

In the latter half of the twentieth century, numerous scholars (for example, Orfield and Eaton 1996; Wilson 1996) observed that space was playing an increasingly prominent role in poverty. The relative affordability of automobiles, as well as the construction of myriad highways and roads, allowed businesses and more affluent individuals to move away from central cities (Jackson 1985). The resulting loss of tax revenue in central cities and increasing spatial concentration of poverty dramatically worsened social and economic opportunities for poor central-city residents. Again, explanations for poverty and targets for antipoverty policy changed as researchers devoted greater attention to such concepts as spatial mismatch and social capital and the federal government sought to fight poverty by targeting communities (for example, enterprise zones) as well as individuals.

In this chapter, I argue that we are again at a critical transition point in our understanding of the causes of poverty. However, this time poverty is being transformed not by an industrial revolution or the spatial redistribution of jobs and people, but by a technological revolution. Computers in general and the Internet in particular are changing all aspects of American society. In the process, they are also changing the determinants of poverty. Although a full analysis of this transformation is beyond the scope of this chapter, I present a preliminary assessment of the potential for the Internet to narrow racial and economic gaps in social capital, education, employment, and housing and offer insights into how we might capitalize on this potential.

How the Internet Can Help Reduce Economic and Racial Inequality

In an earlier chapter in this volume, Steven Durlauf presents a detailed description of the memberships theory of poverty and its implications for antipoverty policy. Like recent social capital arguments (for example, Portes 1998), the theory maintains that poverty is affected by not only the human capital characteristics of individuals but also by the groups that individuals belong to and the characteristics of those groups. To illustrate his point, Durlauf observes that neighborhood effects (that is, the consequences of membership in residential groups) partially explain the intergenerational transmission of poverty. Neighborhoods affect school funding, available peer networks, adult role models, and the information people receive about educational and employment opportunities. Durlauf advocates combating the pernicious effects of group-level influences through "associational redistribution." He suggests that affirmative action, school desegregation, and programs like Moving To Opportunity could alter existing patterns of group formation and therefore lead to greater equality of opportunity.

Although I do not disagree with the logic of Durlauf's argument, I am concerned about the viability of his policy recommendations. As Durlauf acknowledges, public, political, and judicial support for explicitly redistributive policies has declined precipitously in recent years as opponents of these programs have succeeded in portraying them as unfair assaults on the individual rights of whites, males, and the affluent. Given this climate, it is unlikely that affirmative action or school desegregation will be expanded. For the same reasons, it is unclear that a large-scale implementation of Moving To Opportunity is viable. Are the forces that have aligned against affirmative action likely to sit idly by as large numbers of poor people and minorities receive assistance to move into economically advantaged neighborhoods?

If I am correct about the political fragility of redistributive policies, then we may be at a significant impasse: we have identified group membership as an important determinant of poverty but possess little ability to redistribute associations. However, I believe that there is another, more politically palatable way to respond to the memberships theory of poverty. The Internet offers the potential for limited associational redistribution by providing people with access to new groups. Furthermore, because these are new groups, advantaged members of society are less likely to see them as a direct challenge to existing groups. The haves are not required to forgo advantages so that the have-nots might benefit.

The potential of the Internet to reduce the effects of existing groups is clear if we again consider Durlauf's discussion of neighborhood effects. Neighborhood socioeconomic status affects youth outcomes in part because much funding for schools derives from local sources. As a result, children in poor communities often attend schools with fewer resources than do more affluent children. However, the Internet could reduce these gaps by providing poor children with access to an expansive virtual library. Like more affluent children, poor youth would be able to conduct in-depth research for school projects and follow their curiosity wherever it leads.

Second, Durlauf identifies peer effects on educational attainment and aspirations as an additional way in which neighborhoods affect youth outcomes. Again, the Internet has the potential to improve outcomes for poor youth. Signithia Fordham and John Ogbu (1986) discuss techniques used by intellectually curious students to excel at school while feigning disinterest in school to their friends. In addition to offering these students further intellectual resources, the many chat rooms on the Internet could give them the opportunity to interact with other students who are interested in doing well in school. Youth might use these alternative peer networks for help with school projects and as sources of information about educational and scholarship opportunities. Furthermore, because it would be easy to conceal interactions with these virtual peer groups from neighborhood peers, youth would not have to worry about being ridiculed by local youth for their intellectual pursuits.

Third, Durlauf identifies adult role models as an important component of neighborhood effects on youth outcomes. As William Julius Wilson (1996) and Elijah Anderson (1990) have argued, when children grow up in neighborhoods where a minority of adults are employed, it is more difficult to convince them that there are significant, positive returns to schooling. However, if these youth had access to the Internet, it is likely that the role model effects of local adults would be lessened. By interacting with advantaged members of their virtual peer networks and visiting sites that contain information about colleges and jobs, youth would be better able to see relationships between education and later success.

Last, Durlauf argues that neighborhoods affect poverty through job referral networks. In a survey of four large metropolitan areas, Harry Holzer (1996) found that 35 to 40 percent of new hires were generated through referrals from current employees and other informal sources. This finding suggests that in addition to one's human capital, having more contacts with people who hold desirable jobs is an important part of finding a good job. Although personal referrals will no doubt continue to be an important method for finding jobs, the Internet represents a new alternative to traditional job search methods. There are now numerous websites that provide career counseling, list jobs, and allow job seekers to post their résumés and apply for jobs online. One such site, *Monster.com*, currently boasts nearly five hundred thousand job postings, including many that require nothing more than a high school diploma or GED (for example, security guard, customer service representative, assembly-line worker). The site also provides useful tips about résumés and job interviews and hosts a series of chats and message boards that allow job searchers to get their questions answered and share experiences with one another. These represent powerful tools in the effort to combat the weak job referral networks found in many poor neighborhoods.

Housing

Thus far I have discussed the Internet's potential to achieve partial associational redistribution and, in the process, to promote greater equality of opportunity in education and employment. In addition, the Internet could also reduce levels of racial discrimination in housing markets. This is significant for poverty research because, as Douglas Massey and Nancy Denton (1993) have shown, there is a link between housing discrimination, racial residential segregation, and concentrated poverty.

The Internet's potential to reduce housing discrimination became clear to me as I compared my recent search for a new home with the search I had conducted in 1996. As an African American, I had been concerned about housing discrimination. As a producer and consumer of research on residential segregation, I knew my concerns were justified. Throughout the 1970s, 1980s, and early 1990s, numerous studies revealed substantial racial discrimination in the U.S. housing market. Some collected housing market data, checked for racial disparities, controlled for nonracial factors, and attributed residual race effects to discrimination (Munnell, Tootell, et al.

1996). Others interviewed blacks about their experiences in the housing market and took special note of reports of discrimination (Feagin 1994). Yet a third group of researchers uncovered evidence of antiblack sentiment in the neighborhood preferences of whites and used this finding to suggest that real estate agents, landlords, and lenders have reason to discriminate (Bobo and Zubrinsky 1996; Farley et al. 1978). A fourth body of work relied on housing audits (Yinger 1995). The basic idea was that if auditors were matched on relevant nonracial traits, any differences between the treatment of white auditors and their black or Latino partners would be due to racial discrimination. Although each of these studies has its own strengths and weaknesses, together they present compelling evidence that, in the mid-1990s, blacks and Latinos were less likely than comparable whites to be shown homes in thriving neighborhoods, less likely to be treated with respect by housing agents, and less likely to be approved for mortgages.

When I began looking for a new home in 2000, my earlier concerns about racial discrimination were only mildly aroused. It was not that I thought real estate agents had stopped discriminating against blacks, or even that my improved economic status shielded me from discrimination. Rather, my expectation that racial discrimination would play a smaller role in this search reflected my belief that the existing research on housing discrimination was dated. At issue was the technological revolution of the late 1990s. Whereas in 1995 I had obtained nearly all of my information about housing, neighborhoods, and mortgages from real estate professionals, I now made little use of these sources. Instead, I used the Internet to get detailed information about neighborhoods, search and tour homes, review the prices of recently sold homes, apply for a mortgage, obtain homeowner's insurance, and communicate with real estate agents and lenders. Moreover, because none of these sites ever asked for my race, either explicitly or implicitly, searching for a home in cyberspace granted me immunity from racial discrimination. Of course, at some point I did meet with real estate professionals, but even then there was less discrimination than there would have been if I had not used the Internet. Some agents were less motivated to discriminate because I had already established a relationship with them through e-mail; moreover, before all face-to-face meetings I had already gathered much of the information that agents traditionally provide, thus limiting their opportunity to discriminate.

This relationship between technology and housing discrimination is all the more important because evidence suggests that the Internet is playing an increasingly prominent role in the housing market. There are numerous sites that list homes for sale; *REALTOR.com* claims to list 90 percent of U.S. single-family homes that are for sale through real estate agents. According to a recent study, nearly two-thirds of real estate agents now use the Internet to supply potential buyers with information and to cultivate new business (Pafenberg and Roth 1999). In addition, most mortgage lenders have taken their business onto the Internet, and many now accept online loan applications. This combination of abundant information, extreme convenience, and free web sites has made the Internet an increasingly popular tool for many home buyers. A recent survey found that 37 percent of people who purchased a home in 1999 used the Internet to assist with some aspect of their search (Roth 2000).

How the Internet Exacerbates Racial and Economic Inequality

This potential for the Internet to affect associational redistribution and promote fairer housing markets should be welcome news to people who are concerned about racial and economic inequality, but thus far the Internet has done much more to widen racial and economic gaps than to close them. The problem is that there are significant racial differentials in Internet access. In a recent report on the "digital divide," the National Telecommunications and Information Administration (2000) found that Internet usage is growing rapidly among U.S. households, up from 26.2 to 41.5 percent from 1998 to 2000. The report also finds that Internet access is unevenly distributed. Fewer than 20 percent of households with an annual income below $20,000 use the Internet, compared with almost 80 percent of households with an annual income greater than $75,000. In addition to a digital divide by class, the report presents evidence of a digital divide by race and ethnicity (figure 14.1). While over 45 percent of Asian and white households use the Internet, fewer than 25 percent of African American and Latino households are online. Furthermore, there is evidence of an interaction between the racial and economic digital divides (Bikson and Panis 1999). Internet usage is somewhat more similar among households with similar incomes, but racial differences persist within income categories, especially among less affluent households (figure 14.2).

As a result of the digital divide, the advantages of the Internet discussed here disproportionately accrue to those who already enjoy economic and ra-

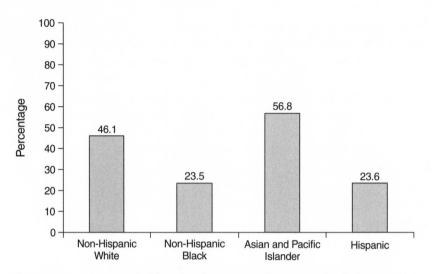

Figure 14.1 U.S. Households Using the Internet, by Race and Ethnicity (*Source:* National Telecommunications and Information Administration (2000).)

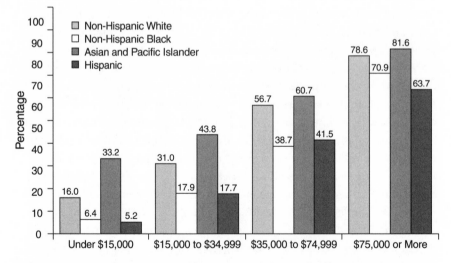

Figure 14.2 U.S. Households Using the Internet, by Annual Income, Race, and Ethnicity (*Source:* National Telecommunications and Information Administration (2000).)

cial privilege in our society. In the terms of the memberships theory of poverty, the Internet facilitates information sharing and reinforcement of norms among advantaged individuals, while the social networks of the disadvantaged remain dominated by local actors. Social network gaps in education are exacerbated by the differential access to reference materials that the Internet offers advantaged youth. While poor youth must use underfunded libraries to research school projects, their affluent peers benefit from superior school libraries and the Internet, which, unlike libraries, is open late at night and early in the morning. Similarly, labor market advantages accrue differentially to whites and the more affluent who use the Internet. These groups can use their referral networks and the resources of sites like Monster.com to increase the odds that they will be hired over similarly qualified blacks, Latinos, and poor individuals. Last, the benefits afforded whites by discriminatory real estate agents and lenders are compounded by the information advantage that whites gain from the Internet. In each of these ways, the Internet fails to level the playing field and instead exacerbates gaps between the haves and have-nots in our society.

How to Capitalize on the Potential of the Internet

Given the increasing prominence of the Internet in our society, its potential to reduce social inequality, and the digital divide, researchers and policymakers should make understanding these issues and their implications a top priority. Researchers need to ask about Internet use on surveys and to consider the digital divide when attempting to explain social inequalities. Policymakers must find ways to close the digital divide. This effort is already under way in the form of a partnership between government agencies, technology companies, and consumer advocates *(www.digitaldivide .gov)*, though it is unclear what form this partnership will take in the wake of recent Bush administration attacks on the initiative (Brindis 2001).

If we are to close the digital divide, three broad goals must be accomplished. First, we must make sure that everyone has access to the Internet. Computers and Internet access have declined dramatically in price, but many still find the cost of these resources prohibitive. One approach to broadening access has focused on equipping schools and public libraries with computers. This effort has largely been successful: today 98 percent of public schools and more than twenty thousand libraries and community centers offer Internet access (Weiner 2001). Despite this success, access might become more universal if the locations of public computers were diversified (Selwyn, Gorard, and Williams 2001). If people encountered public computers in the churches, shopping centers, grocery stores, fast-food restaurants, and other places they regularly visit, it is likely that Internet usage would increase.

Second, we need to give people reasons to use the Internet. A recent study found that 51 percent of people who are not online believe that the Internet has nothing significant to offer them (Lenhart 2000). For most people, this belief is probably misguided, but given the dearth of campaigns designed to inform people about the potential of the Internet to fight educational inequality, encourage employment, and reduce discrimination, it is not surprising that so many think this way.

Last, we must address the fears that keep people from going online. Chief among these concerns is the fear that the Internet is dangerous (Lenhart 2000). When a Baltimore housing project offered people Internet access in their homes, the acceptance rate was surprisingly low (Clines 2001). Some were concerned about what kind of information their children would find on the Internet, while for others issues of privacy were most salient. In addition to fears about the dangers of the Internet, many people stay offline because they fear that the Internet will be too complex for them to navigate (Lenhart 2000). These widespread fears about the Internet, as well as the all-too-common perception that the Internet has relevance only for a select subset of the population, suggest that more needs to be done to educate people about the Internet. Moreover, these fears suggest that although access is an important step toward closing the digital divide, unless we also give people reasons to use and trust the Internet, the potential of this new resource to narrow gaps between the haves and the have-nots will remain unrealized.

CHAPTER 15

Research on Poverty and Antipoverty Policies

JANE WALDFOGEL

The chapters in this volume raise four issues that should receive more attention in future research on poverty and antipoverty policies: group differences in poverty rates; interactions between poverty and other forms of disadvantage; the effect of poverty on child outcomes; and what we can learn about antipoverty policies from the experience of other countries.

Group Differences in Poverty

Several of the chapters effectively detail the differences in poverty between whites and African Americans. Much less attention, however, is paid to Hispanics (and the many subgroups that make up this group), immigrants, and other ethnic and racial minority groups (such as Asians and American Indians). I realize that data on these groups are sparse, but as the nonwhite share of the population grows and becomes more diverse, data on these groups are becoming increasingly available. As Mary Corcoran points out so effectively in her chapter, our attitudes about poverty tend to be affected by the extent to which it is inequitably distributed among groups, and thus it is important to document those differences wherever possible. In addition, group differences have implications for our understanding of poverty and how it might be most effectively addressed.

Research on the economic status of immigrants and the extent to which they have been disproportionately affected by recent policy reforms is particularly needed. LaDonna Pavetti addresses this issue in the context of welfare reform in her chapter, but the economic well-being of immigrants should receive more attention in future research.

Interactions Between Poverty and Other Forms of Disadvantage

The second issue concerns interactions between income poverty and other forms of disadvantage. For instance, children who grow up in poverty fare worse on a number of outcomes such as educational attainment and health, and children raised in single-mother families also fare worse on a number of outcomes (Duncan and Brooks-Gunn 1997; McLanahan and Sandefur 1994). However, we need additional research to determine whether there might also be interactions between poverty and single parenthood. Are children in single-parent families especially vulnerable to the adverse effects of poverty, whereas children in two-parent families are buffered from those effects? Or is the opposite true?

In a recent paper, Thomas Hanson, Sara McLanahan, and Elizabeth Thomson (1997) analyzed data from the National Survey of Families and Households and found that the adverse effects of low income on child outcomes differed by family structure: the effects of poverty were larger for children in single-parent families on five outcome measures (school performance, grade point average, and three measures of behavior problems) but were larger for children in two-parent families on three other measures of child well-being (sociability, initiative, and quality of life). However, a different pattern of interactions is found in the children of the National Longitudinal Survey of Youth. When I examined cognitive outcomes for children up to the age of eight, I found no significant negative interactions between poverty and single parenthood; even though growing up in poverty did have a significant negative effect, this effect was not greater for children in single-parent families. When I looked at behavioral outcomes, I found that, as expected, there were adverse effects of poverty on behavioral problems for young children, but that these effects were smaller for children in single-mother families than in two-parent families.

Thus, at this point the evidence is mixed as to the conjecture that children in single-parent families might be more vulnerable to the effects of growing up in poverty than children raised in two-parent families. It may be the case that children in single-parent families are more vulnerable on some outcomes, while children from two-parent families are more vulnerable on others. Or it may be that the correlates of poverty tend to be different in single-parent and two-parent families. For instance, poverty in two-parent families may be more strongly associated with unemployment, while poverty in single-parent families may be more strongly associated with early childbearing. Such differences, rather than differences in family structure per se, may account for the differential effects on outcomes.

Future research on the interaction of poverty with other types of disadvantage or risk factors might address whether the effects of growing up in poverty are different for:

- Children living in poor neighborhoods, segregated neighborhoods, or neighborhoods low in social cohesion (as suggested by Yinger and Durlauf, this volume)
- Children from immigrant families or children who do not speak English as a first language (several of the chapters suggest that immigrants or non-English speakers may be particularly at risk of poverty and particularly vulnerable to its effects)
- Children who attend poor-quality schools or have learning disabilities
- Children who have chronic health conditions or limitations
- Children who have experienced poor-quality child care or multiple child care transitions or who have a mother who worked early in their childhood

If the effects of growing up in poverty are more pronounced for children experiencing other types of disadvantage or risk factors, these interactions have implications for our understanding of those effects and also for our thinking about policy remedies. If, for instance, the effects of growing up in poverty are more severe for children from particular groups, estimating these effects across all groups will lead us to underestimate the impacts for these more vulnerable children. Moreover, understanding which children are more vulnerable can help us to target policy interventions at them and to design interventions that better address that vulnerability.

How Poverty Affects Child Outcomes

My third comment has to do with the consequences of poverty for children's later cognitive, behavioral, and economic outcomes. This is a hotly contested topic on which more research is needed. Mary Corcoran's chapter discusses the alternative hypotheses as to how and why poverty matters for child outcomes. Some insights from the literature on poverty and child maltreatment are relevant here.

Research has established that poor children, and children who live in poor communities, are more likely to be identified as abused or neglected and more likely than nonpoor children and those living in nonpoor areas to be placed in foster care (see, for instance, Pelton 1978; Garbarino and Sherman 1980; Garbarino and Kostelny 1992; Lindsey 1994; Coulton et al. 1995). At least four hypotheses have been put forward to explain this:

1. Individuals who report families to the child welfare agency are biased and more likely to report families if they are poor. If this hypothesis is true, we should see elevated rates of reports of *all types of maltreatment* among poor children.

2. Poor parents are under more stress and may therefore resort to harsher parenting. If so, we should see elevated rates of *physical abuse* among poor children.

3. Poor parents do not have the resources to provide adequate care for their children. If so, we should see elevated rates of *neglect* among poor children.

4. The connection between poverty and maltreatment is due to unob-served heterogeneity, that is, there may be underlying problems—such as substance abuse or mental health problems—that cause both the poverty and the abuse or neglect. Usually these underlying prob-lems are thought to lead to parents' failure to provide appropriate care for children (rather than actively maltreating their children), and thus this hypothesis predicts that we should see elevated rates of re-ported *neglect* among poor children.

We do not yet have enough evidence to document which of these hypoth-eses are valid, but what evidence we do have suggests that there is probably some truth to each one. In support of hypothesis 1, several studies have found that reporters are more likely to refer a family if they are told that the family is low-income (Hampton and Newberger 1985; Zellman 1992). In support of hypothesis 2, some work has suggested that economic shocks, such as losing a job, are associated with physical abuse (see, for instance, Trickett et al. 1991), while other studies have found an association between low income and harsh parenting (see, for instance, McLoyd 1990).

However, there is more evidence that poverty in the United States is most strongly related to neglect, rather than physical or sexual abuse (see, for in-stance, Lindsey 1994; Waldfogel 1998; and Paxson and Waldfogel 1999a, 1999b). Cross-country comparisons are also suggestive. The United States has a much higher rate of child maltreatment (nineteen cases per thousand children) than Canada (six and a half cases per thousand) or England (nine cases per thousand), as well as a higher rate of child poverty (Waldfogel 1998). The rates of physical and sexual abuse are not notably higher in the United States—the higher overall rate of maltreatment in the United States is driven almost entirely by the high rate of neglect, which is over nine cases per thousand children as compared with only two cases per thousand in both England and Canada. This finding, which suggests that the link between poverty and maltreatment has to do with poverty and neglect, not with poverty and other types of maltreatment, is consistent with hypotheses 3 and 4.

Thus, it probably is the case that poor parents either simply do not have the resources to provide adequate care for their children (hypothesis 3) or are affected by some underlying condition that explains both the poverty and the neglect (hypothesis 4). Differentiating between these hypotheses is difficult. Christina Paxson and I recently found that, in addition to the connection between poverty and neglect, there is a relationship between welfare benefits and neglect. Specifically, we found that in states and years in which welfare benefits were higher, fewer children were reported for neglect and fewer children were placed in foster care (Paxson and Waldfogel 1999b). These results suggest that when it comes to neglect, it is money, not just the unobserved characteristics of poor parents, that matters, since presumably the level of welfare benefits in a state and year is not determined by the unobserved characteristics of poor parents.

Focusing on how poverty affects children, like focusing on the interactions between poverty and other types of disadvantage, has implications for both our understanding of poverty and the design of policy responses. If poverty is related to child neglect, then that connection may help us understand the processes by which poverty leads to other adverse outcomes for children, and that understanding in turn may help us design interventions to ameliorate those outcomes.

What We Can Learn About Antipoverty Policies from the Experience of Other Countries

Through international comparisons, chapters 5 and 6 in this volume help us place the U.S. poverty rate in context. But we could go even further by looking at case studies that describe how other countries' policymakers approach the problem of poverty.

The antipoverty strategy of the New Labour government in Britain, under way since 1997, provides a particularly interesting example. The British government has broadened its conception of the problem from a narrow focus on income poverty to a more comprehensive concern with social exclusion. The government's Social Exclusion Unit (1997, quoted in Hills 1999, 3) uses the term as "a short-hand label for what can happen when individuals or areas suffer from a concentration of linked problems such as unemployment, poor skills, low income, poor housing, high crime, bad health and family breakdown." Others emphasize the notion of nonparticipation in one or more important sectors of society or social life. Researchers at the Centre for Analysis of Social Exclusion at the London School of Economics define an individual as socially excluded if "(a) he or she is geographically resident in a society and (b) he or she does not participate in the normal activities of citizens in that society" (Burchardt, Le Grand, and Piachaud 1999, 230). They have operationalized this definition along five dimensions—consumption, savings, production, political, and social.

Reframing "poverty" as "social exclusion" emphasizes inequality, relative standing, and the capacity of individuals to fully participate in society. This conceptualization leads us to think more about processes and dynamics than about populations and static conditions (Hills 1999; Atkinson 1999). Shifting the focus to social exclusion also changes the way we think about solutions.

With its explicit focus on social exclusion, the British government has put together a social policy agenda that combines an aggressive campaign to both end poverty and address the social problems that so often accompany it. The Social Exclusion Unit, established in 1997 when the New Labour government took office, reports directly to the prime minister and is charged with tackling the most difficult social problems, including homelessness, truancy, school expulsions, and teen parenthood.

In the spring of 1999, Prime Minister Tony Blair announced the goal of ending poverty in twenty years: "Our historic aim will be for ours to be the first generation to end child poverty, and it will take a generation. It is a 20-year mission but I believe it can be done" (Blair 1999, 21). He subsequently set an interim target of cutting child poverty in half within ten years. Although these deadlines will not occur until after Blair is out of office, it is still remarkable that he committed himself and his government to them. This is reminiscent of President Johnson's 1964 State of the Union message in which he declared "War on Poverty" (Katz 1996). Since then, no U.S. politician has taken up that challenge and made a specific commitment to end poverty. (Former Senator Bill Bradley of New Jersey came closest, in his pledge in the presidential primary campaign in 1999 to cut child poverty in half in ten years if elected.)

Each of the three components of Blair's (1999) antipoverty strategy is well grounded in research, much of it conducted in the United States. The first includes a series of investments in children, such as expanded early intervention programs, strengthened support for education, and increased efforts to help disadvantaged communities. These investments are designed to break the intergenerational cycle of poverty by preventing the current generation of poor children from growing up to be the next generation of poor adults. This strategy was influenced by a large body of primarily U.S.-based research that has documented the effectiveness of such investments in improving long-run outcomes for children. (For recent reviews, see Karoly et al. 1998; Danziger and Waldfogel 2000.) It is being implemented in Britain, however, as part of a strategy more comprehensive than any such program that has ever been undertaken in the United States (except perhaps during the 1960s War on Poverty).

The second element of the strategy is to ensure that all adults who are able to work do work and that they receive sufficient support from a combination of labor market policies (such as a recently introduced minimum wage) and social policies (such as the new Working Families Tax Credit and reforms to national insurance contributions) to raise them out of poverty. This element builds on American policies, like the Earned Income Tax Credit, that "make work pay" and are effective in moving adults into employment as well as raising their incomes (Berlin 2000a).

The third element of the British antipoverty initiative is quite different from the American experience of the past decades. The British government is raising benefit levels for those who cannot work, recognizing that even with policies to redress childhood disadvantage and policies to make work pay, some families must rely on benefits, even if only temporarily, and that their incomes too must be raised if poverty is to be eliminated.

Obtaining political support for this last component is challenging, even in New Labour Britain. Describing the challenge as "mak[ing] the welfare state popular again" (Blair 1999, 11), the prime minister noted that raising benefits would be possible only if the numbers of people who need support were reduced and government could increase the public perception that they are deserving of support.

The British case challenges us to further examine public perceptions about the poor and about antipoverty policies. Scholz and Levine (this volume) point out that public policies toward the poor are shaped by public attitudes, and vice versa, and that Americans are now much less supportive of aid to the poor in general, and of welfare in particular, than they were in the past. They note that nearly 60 percent of Americans think that we are spending too much on welfare, while only about 15 percent think we are spending too little. The levels of support for aid to the poor, rather than welfare, are higher, but they also show a downward trend over time (see also Wilson 1999).

The situation is quite different in Britain. Although some individual programs are unpopular there, overall levels of support are much higher (see Hills and Lelkes 1999; Hills, in press). When asked by the British Social Attitudes Survey whether the government should spend more money on welfare benefits for the poor, even if such spending might require higher taxes, 43 percent of the public agreed and only 26 percent disagreed. And for some specific population groups, support was considerably higher. Specifically, 82 percent favored more government spending on people who care for the sick or disabled; 72 percent favored more spending for the disabled who cannot work, 71 percent more spending for the retired, and 68 percent more spending for working parents with very low incomes. For only two groups did the support for raising benefits fall below a majority: only 34 percent favored more government spending on benefits for single parents, with 21 percent supporting less; and only 22 percent favored more spending for the unemployed, with 35 percent supporting less.

The British public is not just more supportive of aid to the poor than the American public. They are also more concerned about inequality—roughly 80 percent believe that the gap between those with high incomes and those with low incomes is too wide (Hills and Lelkes 1999; Hills, in press). When asked the same question, a much lower share of Americans, about 50 percent, agree that this gap is too wide (Hills, in press). Perhaps even more striking is the fact that 75 percent of the British public think that government should do something about inequality, with more than 50 percent agreeing that taxes on the better-off should be raised to spend more on the poor (Hills, in press).

The British case challenges us to think about where these attitudes come from and about the extent to which they may be shaped by research or policy. The British consider it reasonable that the government should strive to end child poverty (Walker 1999). As discussed earlier, they are also more concerned about inequality, a view shared by many other industrialized countries. Indeed, when the United States is compared with other countries (including Austria, Australia, West Germany, Hungary, the Netherlands, and Sweden as well as Britain), it stands out with the lowest share of the public agreeing that there is too much inequality (Evans 1993).

The British case also gives us a chance to see how effective a comprehensive antipoverty policy can be in a modern economy. The British government is making a substantial financial investment in poor families—an additional £6.7 billion in this parliament, which amounts to about 1 percent of GDP. What will the results be? Thus far, the reforms are projected to have moved about one-third of the poor children in Britain out of poverty, lowering the poverty rate from 26 percent to 17 percent (Piachaud and Sutherland 2000; HM Treasury 2000). At this rate, the reforms are on target to halve child poverty in ten years and eliminate it in twenty. But surely many challenges lie ahead. Maintaining political support for the reforms may be problematic, and keeping low-skilled adults in employment may prove difficult if the economy cools down or if employers' demands for skills continue to increase. The British reforms are off to a strong start, and it will be very interesting to see the results as the reforms proceed.

What lessons about antipoverty policies might we draw from the British case study? One lesson has to do with specific policies that we might adopt. The three key components of Britain's antipoverty strategy are expanding investments in children, making work pay, and raising benefits for those who cannot work. The United States is already doing a great deal to make work pay, but we could do more in the other two areas. As Isabel Sawhill (1999) and others have pointed out, expanding early childhood interventions would be a prudent use of the current budget surplus and would deliver services at a time when they are likely to be most effective. Raising public assistance benefits in the United States would be more challenging. A good first step toward raising incomes for those who cannot work would be to establish a universal benefit for children, whether through a child benefit or a child allowance, as is done in most industrialized countries (Kamerman and Kahn 1995), or through a refundable tax credit, as has been recommended by a number of analysts in the United States (see, for instance, the National Commission on Children 1991). About one-quarter of the additional benefits going to poor families with children in Britain are coming through increases in their universal child benefit, and further increases are likely to come through a new child tax credit. Like the U.S. Social Security program, the child benefit program is widely popular because it goes to all individuals.

A second lesson that can be drawn from the British case has to do with influencing public attitudes to be more supportive of antipoverty policies. Declaring a goal of ending child poverty and combating social exclusion shifts the debate from a focus on whether the government should do something about these problems to a discussion of the most appropriate strategies. Keeping the focus on children and using benefits that are seen as delivered to children are also ways to build public support. In much the same way that the United States has been more successful in delivering a national health insurance program for children than a national health insurance program for everyone, the lesson here is that in tackling poverty and social exclusion, policies that focus on child poverty and emphasize services to or benefits for children are likely to have the strongest public support and the greatest chance of being enacted.

Notes

Chapter 1: The Level, Trend, and Composition of Poverty

The authors are grateful to Patricia Powers of the Brookings Institution for superb assistance in preparing estimates of American poverty under alternative experimental definitions, and to Kati Foley, Esther Gray, and Ann Wicks of the Center for Policy Research and Sarah Siegel of Brookings for help in preparing the manuscript. The views expressed here are those of the authors and should not be attributed to the Brookings Institution, the Center for Policy Research, or the Institute for Research on Poverty.

1. We use the terms "household" and "family" interchangeably in the text. See note 3 and the section "Level and Trend of U.S. Poverty" for exact definitions.
2. The cross-national dimensions of poverty are explored more fully in Cancien and Reed (this volume).
3. The issue of the appropriateness of the Consumer Price Index (CPI) as an accurate cost of living deflator is addressed in the next section.
4. Between 1973 and 1994, mean U.S. income grew 15 percent faster than median income, implying that poverty measured relative to the mean grew faster than poverty measured relative to the median (Burtless 1996).
5. In contrast to the official U.S. poverty definition, cross-national comparisons of poverty in rich countries rely almost exclusively on a relative concept of poverty. Cross-national studies typically compare the percentage of persons living with income below some fraction, normally half, of the national median income. This kind of comparison is consistent with a well-established theoretical perspective on poverty (Sen 1983, 1992; Townsend 1979). Relative poverty measures are now calculated by the European Statistical Office (Hagenaars, deVos, and Zaidi 1994; Eurostat 1998), by the OECD (Förster 1993), and by other international groups such as the European Community (EC) (2000) and UNICEF (Bradbury and Jäntti 1999). The European Statistical Office Working Group on Poverty Measurement recently recommended using 60 percent of the

national median income as a common poverty threshold for EC poverty studies (Eurostat 2000).

6. Haveman and Mullikin (1999) offer an example of a wealthy family with substantial assets and adequate consumption, but a year of low income. We assess wealth-based poverty measures later in the chapter.

7. Cutler and Katz (1991) found that the level and trend in poverty based on consumption measures of household resources were broadly similar to those based on income measures through the 1980s. Under either approach to measuring poverty, the poverty rate has increased. Slesnick (1993), in contrast, found that poverty fell during the 1980s under a consumption-based measure. Triest (1998) and others have criticized Slesnick's adjustments for family size, which, by themselves, produce his result (see also Johnson and Smeeding 1997). Using a more plausible set of adjustment factors for differences in consumption requirements of different family sizes produces results different from those obtained by Slesnick. For additional studies of child poverty and consumption and comparison of income, poverty, and social indicators, see Mayer and Jencks (1993) and Jencks and Mayer (1996).

8. The CEX covers only about three thousand households in a rotating sample. In contrast, the March Current Population Survey (CPS), which is the main source of household income data, enrolls fifty-five thousand households. This is a large enough sample to provide accurate poverty estimates for many population subgroups of interest to voters and policymakers.

9. A social indicator approach that measures access to health care and aspects of the quality of care received is one possible alternative.

10. See Lupton and Stafford (2000) on recent changes in wealth and debt, both of which increased in the 1990s.

11. A proper measure of imputed rent includes the difference between the market rent that the house could command minus the costs of owning a house, including mortgage interest, depreciation, repairs, utilities, taxes, and so on. Thus, even though the elderly are by and large homeowners without mortgages, they may still be compelled by taxes and other housing and shelter costs to spend 30 percent or more of their incomes on housing.

12. To estimate real income levels over the postwar period, we use the CPI-U deflator, which is the deflator used to adjust the official poverty thresholds and, in turn, to estimate the prevalence of poverty under the official government definition of poverty (discussed later in the chapter).

13. Small families with an aged family head are assumed to have slightly smaller consumption needs than families with a non-elderly head, so they are assigned a lower poverty threshold. Families containing one or two children are assumed to have somewhat larger consumption requirements than families containing the same number of persons but no children. On the other hand, families with three or more children are assumed to have smaller consumption needs than families of the same size without children.

14. A slightly different procedure was used to estimate thresholds for families with

fewer than three members. See Citro and Michael (1995, 108–14). For a thorough review of the history of the official poverty thresholds, see Fisher (1992, 1997).

15. The Gini coefficient of the distribution of income-to-needs ratios is 0.412, while the Gini coefficient of the pretax family income distribution is 0.392. In both cases, we have converted negative values to 0 and ignored differences in income among people or families in the top 2 percent of the distribution. Since these procedures differ from those used by the Census Bureau, our estimates of the Gini coefficient also differ. To protect the confidentiality of respondents, the public-use CPS files contain less accurate reports of the incomes of people in the top 2 percent of the income distribution than the data available to Census Bureau statisticians. Consequently, our estimates of income inequality are lower than those published by the Census Bureau. These differences have no effect, however, on our estimates of poverty rates.

16. Although changes in the way we measure price inflation have an impact on the overall rate of growth of real income as displayed in figure 1.4, they probably have only a modest effect on the size of the *slowdown* in the rate of growth after 1973. Because the BLS has not used its new methods to recalculate inflation in the years before 1978, we cannot estimate a postwar series of real income using an up-to-date and consistent price index. It seems highly likely, however, that most of the biases identified in the years after 1978 were also present before 1978—and produced the same overstatement of annual price change. Errors in measuring inflation have no effect at all on the measured trend in inequality displayed in figures 1.2 and 1.3. Regardless of whether true price inflation averaged 4 percent a year or 3 percent a year, the Census Bureau's income surveys would show the same percentage division of total income between different income classes in a given year.

17. Beginning in 1983, the methods used to calculate the CPI-U-X1 index were also used to calculate the CPI-U index. The CPI-U-X1 and CPI-U-RS series show the same rate of inflation between 1967 and 1978. The BLS has not calculated the CPI-U-RS price series for the years before 1978.

18. According to estimates provided on the Census Bureau's web site (*www.census .gov/hhes/poverty/histpov/rdp05.html,* and *rdp06.html,* accessed on April 17, 2001), the 1998 poverty rate under an income definition that subtracts tax payments and includes the cash value of medical and nonmedical transfers was 9.5 percent. The 1998 poverty rate calculated using poverty thresholds updated using the CPI-U-X1 poverty thresholds under that same inclusive definition was 8.2 percent. It is important to note, however, that the trend in poverty after 1979 is generally similar under *all* of the Census Bureau's definitions of income. Only the level of poverty in a given year seems to vary systematically by definition. The choice of a price index for updating the poverty thresholds is much more important in determining the long-term trend in poverty, at least in the period after 1979. In the two decades *before* 1979, the definition of income was almost certainly more important. The government introduced and greatly ex-

panded a variety of noncash benefit programs in that period, though the effect of these programs on household resources was not systematically measured until 1979.

19. In particular, we use an equivalence scale proposed by David Betson (1996) that assumes that children have approximately one-half the consumption needs of adults, except in single-parent families, where the first child is assumed to have 80 percent of the consumption needs of an adult. Many specialists in household consumption believe Betson's three-parameter scale contains a more plausible representation of the differing consumption requirements of adults and children and of one-person and two-person households. For details and a comparison with other equivalence scales, including the official scale, see Short et al. (1999, C-2–3).

20. Details of the panel's recommendation can be found in Citro and Michael (1995, 223–37). Procedures for developing estimates of household medical spending are described in Betson (1997, 1998) and in Short et al. (1999, C-16–19).

21. Readers who are interested in the exact procedures we use to calculate net income and poverty thresholds are referred to an appendix available from the authors.

22. The amount of decline may be overstated because of errors in measuring price change. If the CPI-U-X1 price series had been used instead of the CPI-U to adjust the official poverty thresholds, those thresholds would have been 8 percent lower in 1998. If the CPI-U-RS price series had been used, the official thresholds would have been 12 percent lower.

23. The calculation is valid only under two assumptions. All money devoted to this effort must add only to the incomes of the people who are poor; none of the extra spending can be used to lift households' incomes above the poverty thresholds. Second, neither the poor nor the nonpoor can respond to the availability of the extra spending by reducing their own before-tax earned and unearned income. Neither assumption describes a plausible government policy or likely behavioral response to such a policy.

24. Estimates of the effect of medical spending on the number and composition of the poor are sensitive to the way medical expenditures are imputed to households. In this chapter, we use the imputation methods and results described by Short et al. (1999, C-16–20).

Chapter 2: Changes in Family Structure: Implications for Poverty and Related Policy

The authors gratefully acknowledge helpful discussions and comments on an earlier draft from the paper discussants, Sara McLanahan, Robert Plotnick, Aimee Dechter, Daniel Meyer, and Megan Sweeny, as well as from conference organizers and participants. Danielle Jones and Darin Renner provided research assistance.

1. These poverty measures are based on the authors' calculations from the 1999 March Current Population Survey for families with prime-age heads between the ages of eighteen and sixty-four.

2. Owing to the smaller sample size of the March Current Population Survey, calculations from the CPS are created from pooling two years of the survey. For ease of exposition, we refer to the pooled samples using the latter year. For example, marriage measures for 1999 are based on the combined 1998 and 1999 surveys.

   In figures 2.1, 2.2, and 2.7, we measure trends using data from the decennial census for 1970, 1980, and 1990 and data from the CPS for 1999. As a test of the potential impact of using two different data sources, we also calculated all measures for 1990 using the CPS. In 1990 the measures from the CPS closely matched those from the decennial census.

3. Divorce measures are based on the authors' calculations from the decennial census for 1970, 1980, and 1990 and the March CPS for 1999 (from combined 1998 and 1999 files).

4. Measures of cohabitation are difficult, both because, until recently, few surveys asked respondents about nonmarital partners and because social stigma and the lack of a formal legal status make self-reports of nonmarital partners more difficult to interpret. We use the adjusted Persons of Opposite Sex Sharing Living Quarters (POSSLQ) method developed by Lynne Casper, Philip Cohen, and Tavia Simmons (1999). Beginning with the 1990 census and the 1995 CPS, respondents were able to identify individuals as their "unmarried partner," providing a "direct" measure of partners. Casper and her colleagues compared their adjusted POSSLQ estimates with the direct measures from 1995 to 1998 and concluded that the adjusted POSSLQ population is quite similar to the "unmarried partner" population in terms of the distribution of observable characteristics. They found little evidence to suggest that estimates based on the adjusted POSSLQ would provide biased measures of the *composition* of the cohabiting population. The adjusted POSSLQ measure captured 95 percent of all self-identified "partners"; almost 40 percent of those identified by the adjusted POSSLQ measure, however, were not self-identified as partners. Casper and her colleagues reviewed alternative estimates from the National Survey of Families and Households and the National Survey of Family Growth and found that both surveys show substantially higher rates of cohabitation than even the adjusted POSSLQ.

5. For figures 2.3, 2.5, 2.6, and 2.8, we use CPS data instead of decennial census data in order to include "secondary families"—families not related to the household head. Household and family identifiers in the decennial census are not sufficient to link unrelated families together. For the measures in figures 2.5 and 2.6, the census and CPS do not agree in 1990, providing an additional reason to use CPS data to measure trends consistently. Before 1984, some children living with a parent in a household headed by the grandparent were coded in the March CPS as "other relative" instead of "child in subfamily." We correct for this

miscoding using the approach developed by Rebecca London (1998). The correction affects our estimates in figures 2.3, 2.5, 2.6, and 2.8.

6. The decline in the number of children is apparent for all racial and ethnic groups we consider. In particular, between 1972 and 1999 the number of coresident children of their own for women age thirty-five to thirty-nine declined from 2.5 to 1.5 for whites, from 2.7 to 1.5 for blacks, and from 2.9 to 1.9 for Hispanics. The sample size from the March CPS for 1999 is not sufficient to make an accurate measurement of this statistic for Asian and Pacific Islanders or for American Indians. Decennial census data for the period 1970 to 1990 shows a decline from 2.5 to 1.5 for whites, from 2.6 to 1.5 for blacks, from 2.8 to 2.0 for Hispanics, from 2.3 to 1.6 for Asian and Pacific Islanders, and from 3.3 to 1.7 for American Indians.

7. In particular, suppose that the only change between two periods was a decline in the portion of women who married—that is, that there were no changes in the likelihood that a married or single woman would have a child. In that instance, change in the relative number of married and unmarried women, by itself, would increase the proportion of births to unmarried women. Similarly, a decline in the fertility of married women, with no change in the fertility of unmarried women, would increase the proportion of births to unmarried women.

8. The calculations represented in figure 2.5 include only children under age eighteen living with at least one biological, step, or adopted parent. Persons under eighteen who are heads of families, not living with a parent, or in a foster home are not included in the figure. In 1971 this excludes 4.5 percent of persons under eighteen, and in 1999 it excludes 4.6 percent. The CPS survey does not cover institutionalized people.

9. Race and ethnicity are determined by the race and ethnicity of the female head, if present, and otherwise by the male head. For the first two years shown, we are able to distinguish only white, black, and Hispanic children. For the two later years, we also show estimates for Asian and Pacific Islander and American Indian children.

10. Owing to small sample sizes in the March CPS, statistics for Asians and Pacific Islanders and American Indians are measured imprecisely. The changes for these two groups between 1990 and 1999 in family types and living arrangements (figure 2.6) are not statistically significant.

11. Note that the data do not readily allow us to distinguish the relationship between the children of the household head and adults unrelated to the head. Thus, some of these "cohabiting male partners" may be the fathers of children in the household, and some of the children living with their unmarried mother may also be living with their (unmarried) father. The parallel situation exists in the case of single-father households and unmarried female partners.

12. The sample size from the March CPS in 1999 is not sufficient to make an accurate measurement of this statistic for Asians and Pacific Islanders and for American Indians. The 1990 decennial census shows that 38 percent of white single fathers lived alone compared to 18 percent of black fathers, 13 percent of His-

panic fathers, 22 percent of Asian and Pacific Islander fathers, and 22 percent of American Indian fathers.

13. Some explanations for the trend toward *delay* in marriage also emphasize changes in educational and labor market patterns. For example, see Bergstrom and Bagnoli (1993) and Oppenheimer (1988).

14. Note that for most of the past two decades the government retained all but the first fifty dollars per month of child support paid to welfare recipients to offset the costs of providing welfare. Thus, mothers receiving welfare could receive only very limited formal child support.

15. To calculate poverty rates we first adjust income to 1999 dollars and then use the CPI-U-X1 poverty lines for 1999. For families headed by couples, both heads are in the age range eighteen to sixty-four. As in the official poverty rate calculation, all related persons living in the same household are grouped as a single family. Families are classified into types based on the marital status of the family head(s). For example, a single woman heading a household that includes her married daughter, son-in-law, and grandchild is classified as "single female, with children."

16. Because married-couple families are relatively large, they include a proportion of all persons that is higher than their proportion of all families.

17. Cohabiting couples are identified as described in note 4.

18. In 1993 and 1994 the U.S. Bureau of the Census changed the processing of the CPS data and introduced new population weights based on the 1990 census. Therefore, yearly poverty rates from 1993 onward are not directly comparable with those in earlier years. For example, the official poverty rate for 1989 was 12.8 percent. However, using population weights from the 1990 census, the poverty rate would have been 13.1 percent (Census Bureau calculations). Therefore, the poverty rates reported in figure 2.9 for the late 1980s and early 1990s are probably too low. Taking this into account and considering the continued economic expansion over the 1990s, poverty was almost certainly lower in 1999 than in 1989.

19. The counterfactual results for female employment are based on estimates of the impact of family structure and female employment combined, less the impact of family structure alone.

20. One problem with the "all else being equal" assumption is that changes in family structure may actually bring about changes in poverty rates within family types. For example, if the shift from couple-headed families to single-head families occurred mainly among adults with high earnings, then this change in the marriage trend could help explain the decline in poverty rates for single-head families. Modeling family behavior choices based on observable personal characteristics such as education, age, and race-ethnicity partially addresses this limitation. Using a modeling approach does not change the basic conclusion that trends in family structure would have produced a substantial increase in poverty that was mitigated by growth in female employment (see Daly and Valletta 2000; Lerman 1996; Gottschalk and Danziger 1993). Modeling behavior is not a

complete solution, however, because many of the personal characteristics that affect family behavior choices are not measured in available surveys. In addition, even with the more detailed approach, we cannot account for the impact of changes that affect both family structure and poverty rates within given family types. For example, the growth in women's labor market opportunities may directly affect family structure (reducing marriage and fertility) and at the same time change vulnerability to poverty within, for example, single-mother families. In this case, it is not realistic to assume that the same changes in family structure would have occurred without changes in poverty by type.

21. Early evidence from the Fragile Families project—a new study of children born to low-income, primarily unmarried mothers—also suggests high levels of cohabitation among unmarried parents of newborns, as well as substantial emotional and financial involvement on the part of fathers (Garfinkel and McLanahan 2000).

22. Evidence from the Child Support Demonstration Evaluation suggests that policies that allow welfare recipients to receive child support paid on behalf of their children without reducing their welfare eligibility may increase child support payments (Meyer et al. 2001).

Chapter 3: The Rising Tide Lifts. . .?

1. The official poverty rate is an imperfect indicator. It is based largely on the relation between food expenditures and income and calculated without taking account of noncash benefits, such as food stamps, Medicaid, and public assistance, nor of the EITC money that workers receive when they have low incomes. See U.S. Bureau of the Census (1999b, table 770) for the poverty rates based on fourteen different definitions of incomes. Even these, however, ignore important aspects of life that affect the poor with particular harshness, such as crime. The alternative measures of poverty show a similar pattern of change over time and similar differences among groups. Thus, little is lost by using the official rate in analysis.

2. The rate of poverty among individuals shown in appendix 3.1 followed a similar pattern, falling from 12.1 percent in 1969 to 11.8 percent in 1999. The rates of poverty for individuals and families are highly correlated, so that it is largely a matter of convenience or taste as to which one uses in analysis.

3. Since a sizable number of poor persons do not live in families, the proportion of all people below the poverty line living in female-headed households is somewhat lower—36 percent in 1999 (U.S. Bureau of the Census 2000, table B-1).

4. This is true once the rate of poverty is below 50 percent.

5. In this calculation, I have used a standard normal table. Income distributions fit more closely lognormal distributions, so one could repeat the exercise for that distribution. But there are complications at the lower (and upper) part of the tail of the distribution that make neither of these distributions ideal. Simulation of the effects of changes in mean income on poverty using actual income distribu-

tions would give the most accurate measure of the declining effect of changes in income on poverty as poverty falls.

6. These data are for all private nonsupervisory workers, as reported by the U.S. Council of Economic Advisers (2000, table B-45).

7. This effect could be offset by increased employment by other family members, by governmental transfers, or by labor market policies.

8. I also estimated regressions in which I used the level of GDP per capita in place of the real wage as a right-hand-side variable. The R-squared in these regressions was lower than those in table 3.2, indicating that poverty is more closely linked to real wages than to the more aggregate real-GDP-per-capita measure of growth.

9. We multiply the real wage increase of 0.02 by −.16 or −.13 and get an expected decline in poverty of −.003 (rounded) in both cases, and thus a fall in poverty by 0.3 percentage points.

10. New immigrants are likely to rise in the U.S. earnings distribution as they assimilate over time, so that immigration is a very different condition from having little education or a disability. But because immigrants are also likely to be replaced at the bottom of the distribution by new immigrants, a constant in-flow of people into U.S. poverty is maintained. Many immigrants who come from poorer countries are likely, for some period of time, to make great improvements in their living standards while falling below the U.S. poverty line.

Chapter 4: Mobility, Persistence, and the Consequences of Poverty for Children: Child and Adult Outcomes

Sheldon Danziger, Peter Gottschalk, Robert Haveman, Christopher Jencks, Susan Mayer, and Gary Sandefur provided extensive comments and advice on this chapter. I thank the Russell Sage Foundation for funding the data set I used in my empirical analyses. I also thank Michael Hamner, James Kunz, and Mary Noonan for computing assistance. I especially thank Lee Ridley for typing this chapter. She is efficient, patient, and accurate.

1. There are no statistics on the incidence of long-term poverty among Latino groups or immigrant groups because no study has tracked the incomes of a nationally representative sample of immigrant or Latino families over a sufficiently long period of time. Given that annual poverty rates are extremely high for Puerto Rican families and immigrant families, it is likely that substantial minorities of these groups are stuck in long-term poverty.

2. A child is poor if the average ratio of his or her family's income to the poverty line during the years the child was observed living at home between 1968 and age seventeen was less than 1.0. Depending on the child's age in 1968, there are three to seventeen years of data on family income. An individual is defined to be

poor in his or her midtwenties if the average ratio of his or her family income to the poverty line over ages twenty-five to twenty-seven was less than 1.0.

3. Analysts typically measure the degree of intergenerational income inequality in a society by the correlation between parents' and children's economic statuses. The square of this correlation measures the proportion of variation in children's incomes that is accounted for by variation in parents' incomes.

4. See note 2 for the definition of childhood poverty.

5. Most studies of income effects on children's schooling measure income during the child's adolescence. Effects of family poverty on children's schooling outcomes are larger when income is measured during early childhood. Greg Duncan and his colleagues (1998), for instance, report that an increase in mean family income between a child's birth and age five was associated with nearly a full one-year increase in schooling—a much bigger effect.

6. Mayer (1997) tests this assumption by regressing measures of consumption on future income; she finds that future income is very weakly related to her consumption measures. However, her consumption measures are limited to the ones available in the National Longitudinal Survey of Youth (NLSY) and Panel Study of Income Dynamics (PSID) and provide at best a weak test of her hypothesis.

7. "Other income" has weaker associations with parental schooling and test scores than does total family income (Mayer 1997, 83). This supports Mayer's assumption.

Chapter 5: U.S. Poverty in a Cross-national Context

The authors would like to thank Martha Bonney, Kati Foley, David Jesuit, and Esther Gray for their help in preparing this manuscript. Also, thanks go to Sheldon Danziger, Robert Haveman, and the external referees for their comments on an earlier version of the manuscript. The authors thank the Institute for Research on Poverty and the Luxembourg Income Study sponsors for their assistance. The conclusions reached here are those of the authors and should not be seen as the official views of any of the institutions with which they are affiliated.

1. Poverty measurement began as an Anglo-American social indicator. In fact, "official" measures of poverty (or measures of "low-income" status) exist in very few nations. Only the United States (U.S. Bureau of the Census 1999a) and the United Kingdom (Department of Social Security 1993) have official poverty series. Statistics Canada publishes the number of households with incomes below a "low-income cutoff" on an irregular basis, as does Australia. In northern Europe and Scandinavia, the debate centers instead on the level of income at which minimum benefits for social programs should be set. In other words, their concept of insufficient or "low income" directly leads to programmatic responses.

2. In 1998 the ratio of the U.S. (four-person) poverty line to median *family* income was 35 percent, while the ratio to median *household* income was 42 percent. Median household income ($38,855) is far below median family income ($47,469) because single persons living alone (or with others to whom they are not directly related) are both numerous and have lower incomes than do families (U.S. Bureau of the Census 1999b). Families include all units with two or more persons related by blood, marriage, or adoption; single persons (unrelated individuals) are excluded. In contrast, households include all persons sharing common living arrangements, whether related or not, including single persons living alone. Different adjustments for family or household size might also make a difference in making such comparisons.

3. The Penn World Tables (Mark 5) PPPs were judged to be accurate and consistent for the early 1990s for all nations except Italy (Summers and Heston 1991). However, they have not been updated, and now the OECD and the World Bank have developed their own sets of PPPs. We do not present comparisons of real poverty rates over time, owing to the intertemporal inconsistency of PPPs dating back to the mid-1980s and earlier. For additional comments on PPPs and microdata-based comparisons of well-being, see Gottschalk and Smeeding (2000), Rainwater and Smeeding (1999), Smeeding and Rainwater (2001), Smeeding et al. (2000), Castles (1996), and Bradbury and Jäntti (1999, appendix).

4. For more on this income definition and its robustness across nations, see Atkinson, Rainwater, and Smeeding (1995). Note that the use of this disposable income concept is not unique to LIS. Eurostat and OECD have independently made comparisons of income poverty and inequality across nations using identical or very similar measures of net disposable income.

    This income definition differs from the broadest income definition used in Corcoran (this volume). The internationally comparable measure of income does not subtract work-related expenses or medical care spending, and it does not include noncash benefits provided in the form of public housing. The EITC and similar refundable tax credits and noncash benefits such as food stamps and cash housing allowances are included, however, in this income measure.

5. Formally, adjusted disposable personal income (ADPI) is equal to *un*adjusted disposable personal income (DPI) divided by household size (S) raised to an exponential value (E), $ADPI = DPI/S^E$. We assume the value of E is 0.5. To determine whether a household is poor under the relative poverty measure, we compare its ADPI to 40 or 50 percent of the national median ADPI. National median ADPI is calculated by converting all incomes into ADPI and then taking the median of this "adjusted" income distribution. To determine whether a household is poor under the absolute poverty measure, we first convert the official U.S. poverty thresholds for different household sizes into appropriate national currency units using PPP exchange rates, and then compare each household's DPI to the appropriate threshold.

6. We excluded Taiwan and the emerging nations of Central and Eastern Europe.

We also exclude Ireland because we currently have only one 1980s data set for that nation. We could not include New Zealand or Portugal because they are not members of LIS. We include Japan based on an exhaustive set of data runs completed under LIS supervision in 1996.

7. As LIS continues to add data sets, an even more complete picture of comparative national poverty incidence will emerge. Recent studies of poverty using the LIS database include Bradbury and Jäntti (1999), Jäntti and Danziger (2000), Kenworthy (1998), Smeeding (1997), Kim (2000), UNICEF (2000), and many others that can be found among the LIS working papers on the LIS web site *(www.lis.ceps.lu)*.

8. For the first time, we present LIS data on unified Germany for 1994. However, trend data for Germany are still restricted to West Germany. The LIS West German poverty rates tend to be 0.9 to 1.2 percentage points below those for all of Germany.

9. Children are defined as all persons under age eighteen, and the elderly as all persons age sixty-five or older. We do not include racial or ethnic breakdowns, since only five LIS nations have such variables. The poverty status of immigrants (that is, foreign-born citizens) can be studied in only four LIS countries.

10. The base year is important because PPPs are reconfigured with a different "base" market basket only every four to five years. Between base years, price indices are used to adjust base baskets for comparisons. These price indices may differ from the Consumer Price Index (CPI) used to adjust poverty lines within and across countries. As Corcoran (this volume) suggests, the choice of CPI may affect the results. Hence, we stick with 1995 base-year PPPs, adjusting back to 1994 PPPs and using the implicit OECD price index.

11. Smeeding and his colleagues (1993) find that countries that spend more on cash social expenditures also spend more on noncash subsidies. The largest differences between the United States and other nations are in the realm of health care costs. U.S. citizens spend roughly 15 percent of their disposable income on health care, compared to 5 percent in France, 2 percent in Canada, and 1 percent in the United Kingdom (Luxembourg Income Study 2000b).

12. Although the arguments tend to suggest that U.S. absolute poverty rates may be understated compared to those in other nations, some counterarguments can also be made. More than 85 percent of Americans are covered by health insurance. They do not pay for most of the health care they consume out of the disposable income measured on the Current Population Survey, though they do pay more for health care out-of-pocket on average (see note 10). In other words, the average insured American does not pay the full "price" of medical services reflected in the OECD's PPP estimates for the United States. For a large majority of low-income Americans, insurance is provided free through the Medicaid program or at reduced cost under Medicare. For others, it is subsidized by an employer's contribution to a company-sponsored health plan. Although low-income people in most, if not all, LIS nations pay lower net prices for medical care than do residents of the United States, the United States probably has

the highest final consumption prices for medical care of all OECD countries. The OECD's PPP estimates should therefore show that the United States has a high cost of living (at least for medical care). Second, Americans pay more for higher education (though not for primary and secondary schooling) than citizens in other OECD countries. Many Americans pay for college out of their disposable incomes. But low-income Americans can obtain a decent college education about as cheaply as most Europeans, so the difference in higher education costs may not be very relevant for comparing poverty market baskets across countries. Third, more than one-quarter of low-income Americans receive housing subsidies, either directly, through vouchers, or indirectly through below-market rents on publicly subsidized apartments. European subsidies for housing vary by country but are generally larger. Fourth, some consumption items that are more important to poor families than to the nonpoor are dramatically cheaper in the United States than they are in other OECD countries. Food is one such item. Because food consumption probably has a greater weight in the consumption of the poor than it does in aggregate consumption, the OECD's PPP exchange rates are biased against the United States. In summary, while we could develop better PPP exchange rates for purposes of comparing low-income families across OECD countries, it is not obvious that a superior set of PPPs would reveal a systematically higher absolute poverty rate in the United States and systematically lower rates in Europe. Hence, our comparisons in table 5.1 are about as good as any that could be done at this time.

13. We compared grossed-up LIS market incomes to OECD final domestic consumption aggregates. The one nation that differed most from the rest was Italy, which captured only about 47 percent of OECD gross final consumption in its LIS survey, compared to 86 percent for the United States. Most other nations were close to the U.S. level; a few were above it.

   Underreporting of income has a large impact in comparing absolute poverty rates across countries. The smaller the percentage of aggregate income reported in the household survey, the higher the measured poverty rate. Underreporting may also affect relative poverty comparisons if income at either the bottom or the top of the income distribution is differentially underreported. Unfortunately, we cannot currently assess the relative importance of income underreporting in different parts of the income distribution.

14. See also Rainwater and Smeeding (2000) and Smeeding and Rainwater (2001). To see where the countries with higher ratios of survey-reported income to OECD aggregate income than in the United States would be, we increased the poverty line from 43 percent of the U.S. 1994 median (the official poverty line) to 50 percent of the U.S. median in each of these nations. Poverty rates in Finland, Norway, and Sweden each rose by 2.7 to 3.8 percentage points but still remained below the average rate of 8.6 percent calculated at the bottom of table 5.1 in each country. For a similar result, see Bradbury and Jäntti (1999).

15. A similar type of comparison for poverty and inequality trends has been used by Smeeding (1997) and Gottschalk and Smeeding (2000), but others have used

different poverty measures and different methods of assessing trends (see, for example, Jäntti and Danziger 2000). The results of all of these studies and methods were based on trends in poverty rates measured at 50 percent of the median income, but they are also consistent with the 40-percent-of-median-income-based results in table 5.3.

16. Not all countries are included here. The ones that are included have been selected because of their 1990s data and because of the broad picture they provide of what is found in other similar countries. A similar analysis of changes in domestic poverty is found in Scholz and Levine (this volume; see also Smeeding and Ross Phillips 2001).

17. In 1986 the tenth-percentile point was 35 percent of the median; in 1991, 34 percent; in 1994, 36 percent; and in 1997, 38 percent (the same level as in 1979). For more on this point, see Atkinson, Rainwater, and Smeeding (1995), Gottschalk and Smeeding (1997), and Smeeding (2000). These adjusted income distributions are all measured using the same units, income definition, and equivalence scale as used elsewhere in this chapter.

18. The OECD reports on the prevalence of low wages for the early 1990s for twelve nations. We added low-wage workers from Luxembourg and Norway based on LIS-based tabulations of wages. Estimates were not possible for the other nations (Italy, Switzerland, Denmark, Israel, Spain) because neither the LIS nor the OECD had the requisite data. Table 5A.2 contains the raw data for both low wages and social spending.

19. A similar picture with an even stronger correlation (0.57) emerges for child poverty rates (not shown). Overall poverty rates are highly correlated with low wages because childless adults and the elderly are also more likely to be poor in low-wage countries.

20. A similar diagram for overall poverty rates and overall social spending (including elderly benefits) shows much the same result.

Chapter 6: The Evolution of Income Support Policy in Recent Decades

We are grateful to Jon Gruber, Scott Houser, the conference organizers, and other chapter authors for providing helpful advice.

1. In doing so, we update papers by Gary Burtless (1986, 1994) that document trends in public spending on the poor through 1986 and then through 1992.

2. Pretax and pretransfer poverty is based on market incomes, ignoring all taxes and transfers. It differs from the conventional measure of poverty, which takes income before taxes, adds government cash transfers, and compares this income measure with the poverty line. Freeman (this volume) discusses a similar pretax and pretransfer measure of poverty.

3. Real GDP (in 1996 dollars) fell 0.45 percent between the first and fourth quarters in 1980. It fell another 2.86 percent between the third quarter of 1981 and

the third quarter of 1982. Real GDP fell 1.49 percent between the second quarter in 1990 and the first quarter in 1991. Data are from the Bureau of Economic Analysis, Department of Commerce, available at *www.bea.doc.gov/bea/dn/gdplev.htm*. The difference in the apparent sensitivity of poverty rates to the business cycle in the 1980s and 1990s was due, at least in part, to the geographic dispersion of the 1990 recession. It was fairly light in the Midwest, which typically has somewhat lower poverty rates than the rest of the country, and it was more severe on the coasts. Los Angeles County, California, for example, had negative year-over-year job growth for three consecutive years, losing nearly 6 percent of its jobs between 1990 and 1991.

4. See Freeman (this volume) for further discussion of the relationship between the economy and poverty, which has been a topic of considerable interest. See also, for example, Blank and Blinder (1986), Cutler and Katz (1991), Blank and Card (1993), Haveman and Schwabish (2000), and Haveman (2000).

5. See Bobo and Smith (1994) and the citations therein for a more thorough discussion of these issues and public opinion on poverty and race.

6. Poverty rates are even higher for families with children under six: nearly one-quarter of the youngest U.S. children are being raised in poverty (U.S. House of Representatives 1998, 1293).

7. In 2000, the OASDI program was financed by a 6.2-percentage-point tax levied on employers and employees (for a combined 12.4 percent tax) on earnings up to $76,200. These tax receipts are credited to the Social Security trust fund. To receive benefits, a worker must have at least forty quarters of employment in jobs covered by the Social Security system (most jobs are now covered). Benefits are based on average indexed monthly earnings (AIME) for the highest thirty-five years of earnings (inserting zeroes for monthly earnings if workers had fewer than thirty-five years of positive earnings), using a formula that gives low-income workers a greater share of their AIME than high-income workers. Workers (who are not disabled) can begin drawing benefits as early as age sixty-two. Benefits payments increase (nonlinearly) as retirement is delayed until age seventy-two, at which point benefits no longer increase with age of retirement.

8. Recent work (see, for example, Coronado, Fullerton, and Glass 2000; Gustman and Steinmeier 2000) suggests that on a *lifetime* basis, Social Security does much less to redistribute resources from high- to low-income households than would be suggested by looking at the targeting of benefits in a single year. It is still useful to consider an annual time frame when considering poverty issues.

9. Medicare is financed by a 1.45 percent payroll tax on uncapped earnings levied on employers and employees (for a total tax of 2.9 percent).

10. Advocates of Social Security privatization (see, for example, Feldstein and Samwick 1998) suggest that we can do even better at a lower social cost, while others (see, for example, Aaron and Reischauer 1999) argue, among other things, that vulnerable low-income families may be harmed by privatization.

11. From 1959 to 1974, real Social Security spending increased 210 percent, a much sharper growth rate than in any other fifteen-year period. For example, real So-

cial Security spending increased 110 percent between 1970 and 1985, and 32 percent between 1984 and 1999. Since 1974, Social Security benefits have been indexed for inflation.

12. Authors' calculations from data provided by the Health Care Financing Administration and Social Security Administration.

13. The federal portion of unemployment insurance is financed by a 0.8 percent tax levied on employers on the first $7,000 of wages paid to each covered employee. The states levy modest additional taxes to finance their programs.

14. Although eligibility varies by state, typically one must have worked for at least two quarters of the previous year in covered employment, be actively seeking work, and have lost one's job through no fault of one's own. A worker can generally receive a maximum of twenty-six weeks of benefits, and these benefits generally replace between 50 and 70 percent of the individual's average weekly pretax wage up to some state-determined maximum.

15. "Substantial gainful activity" is defined as work activity that involves significant physical or mental effort and that is done for pay or profit (whether or not a profit is realized). Complex regulations promulgated by the commissioner of the Social Security Administration define disabilities and substantial gainful activity, though average monthly earnings above some threshold (currently $700) ordinarily demonstrate substantial gainful activity for people with an impairment other than blindness.

16. In addition to meeting program standards for being blind or disabled, or being over sixty-four, eligible people must meet income and asset tests. The income test restricts countable income to less than the 1999 federal benefit rate of $500 a month. Countable income excludes $20 a month, the first $65 a month from earnings, and 50 percent of earnings exceeding $65 per month, and food stamps. This implies that a person could have earned income of up to $1,085 per month and still be eligible for SSI. A couple with only wage income could have earnings of roughly $1,550. An individual also cannot have assets exceeding $2,000 ($3,000 for couples), though houses and generally automobiles do not count as assets. An applicant is expected to first file for all other available benefits, including disability insurance if he or she is eligible.

17. The EITC is a refundable credit that taxpayers receive after filing a tax return each year. It is essentially an earnings subsidy, intended to encourage individuals with low earnings to increase the number of hours they work. In 1999 taxpayers with two or more children could get a credit of 40 percent of income up to $9,540, for a maximum credit of $3,816. Taxpayers (with two or more children) with earnings between $9,540 and $12,460 receive the maximum credit. Their credit is reduced by 21.06 percent of earnings between $12,460 and $30,585. Taxpayers with one child could get a credit of 34 percent on income up to $6,800, for a maximum credit of $2,312. Childless taxpayers could get a credit of 7.65 percent on income up to $4,530, for a maximum credit of $347.

18. In his first State of the Union address, President Clinton said: "The new direction I propose will make this solemn, simple commitment: by expanding the refund-

able earned income tax credit, we will make history; we will reward the work of millions of working-poor Americans by realizing the principle that if you work forty hours a week and you've got a child in the house, you will no longer be in poverty."

19. This chapter does not discuss programs designed to enhance human capital; see Karoly (this volume) for more details.

20. Families receiving SSI or TANF payments are generally automatically eligible for food stamps. Roughly speaking, families not receiving SSI or TANF must have incomes below the poverty line after taking into account a modest ($134 per month) standard deduction; work, dependent care, and unusually large shelter expenses; and child support payments. Total income cannot exceed 133 percent of the poverty line. A family cannot have more than $2,000 in assets ($3,000 if the household contains an elderly member). Vehicles (under $5,000 in value) and houses do not count in the asset tests. Participating households are expected to devote roughly 20 to 25 percent of their total monthly income to food. Food stamps then make up the difference between the expected family contribution and the amount assumed to be needed to purchase an adequate low-cost diet. PRWORA retained the entitlement status of food stamps, but new restrictions disqualified most permanent resident aliens and mandated work activities for able-bodied adults without dependents, who are now generally eligible for only three months of benefits in a thirty-six-month period if they are not working.

21. One of the earliest major child care subsidies was the Dependent Care Tax Credit, enacted in 1954. Because it is a nonrefundable tax credit, however, it provides little or no benefit to families with incomes at or below the poverty line.

22. Child support is not a means-tested transfer program; however, 37 percent of custodial parents were poor in 1997, and 80 percent had incomes below 300 percent of the poverty line (Lerman and Sorensen 2000).

23. As is clear from figure 6.9, Medicaid is roughly the same size as the combined value of the other in-kind transfers. In-kind transfers including Medicaid grew at an annual rate of 12.3 percent in the 1970s, 3.7 percent in the 1980s, and 8.9 percent in the 1990s.

24. April is chosen to be consistent with Weinberg's analysis of April 1979, 1984, and 1986.

25. We have conducted a sensitivity analysis varying this factor from 1 to 5; our conclusions about the antipoverty effectiveness of Medicaid and Medicare remain essentially unchanged, despite variations in the dollar value of the program benefits.

26. This estimate of the poverty gap may differ from other estimates in this volume (for example, Freeman, Burtless and Smeeding), for several reasons. First, our measure is for a single month (April). Second, annual underreporting of wages and salaries in SIPP is larger than it is for the CPS, the source of the underlying data for figure 6.1. Hotz and Scholz (2001) note that in 1990 and 1996 the SIPP reported roughly 91 percent of the control total wages and salaries, while the

CPS reported 96 percent for 1990 and 102 percent for 1996. Third, varying definitions of income may contribute to different estimates of the poverty gap; ours, for example, excludes the payroll tax from wage income, while others' calculations may not. We also note that the reported 29.0 percent poverty rate is considerably higher than the 19.7 percent rate shown in figure 6.1 for the pretax and pretransfer poverty rate for all persons. The discrepancy arises because the family definition used here counts unrelated individuals as one-person families, and the pretax and pretransfer poverty rate of these families (many of whom are elderly) is higher than it is for other families in the population, in addition to the reasons already mentioned. The Weinberg (1985, 1987, and 1991) studies have very similar discrepancies between the poverty rates of all families and the CPS-based poverty rates of individuals.

27. If a family has a poverty gap of $1 and the program provides $1,000 of benefits, only $1 of benefits would be included in column 4.

28. Note that this poverty gap estimate for 1997 is smaller than the estimate in table 6.1. This is because the poverty gap in table 6.1 is based on a measure of income that excludes payroll taxes from wage income, thus widening the gap between the poverty line and income and yielding a larger poverty gap estimate. To maintain comparability with previous studies, table 6.2 does not exclude payroll taxes from wage income.

29. Robert Michael and Connie Citro (1995) develop—and the U.S. Bureau of the Census (1999c) implements—estimates of a new poverty measure that reflects a comprehensive measure of a family's access to resources, including work expenses and out-of-pocket medical expenses as well as taxes, cash, and in-kind transfers. The poverty thresholds (and implicit equivalence scales) are also altered to reflect the consumption needs of food, shelter, clothing, and a little bit more. Incorporating the effects of medical out-of-pocket expenditures would raise the post-tax and post-transfer poverty rate of the elderly and hence reduce the antipoverty effectiveness of the tax and transfer system.

30. In addition to the chapters in this volume, see, for example, reviews by Danziger, Haveman, and Plotnick (1981) and Moffitt (1992). Recent surveys on specific programs include Currie (2000) on food and nutrition programs, Gruber (2000) on Medicaid, Hotz and Scholz (2000) on the EITC, Moffitt (2000) on TANF, Olsen (2000) on housing assistance, Burkhauser and Daly (2000) on SSI, and Haveman and Wolfe (2000) on disability transfers.

31. David Ellwood (1999, 25) reaches broadly similar conclusions, finding for the period from 1990 to 1998 that roughly "20 percent of the growth in work can be traced to the economy, perhaps another 50 percent is linked to welfare reform and the remaining 30 percent can be traced to the EITC and other work supports."

32. Of course, antipoverty resources have not increased sharply over time, low-wage labor markets have not performed very well in recent decades, and the purpose of some programs is to blunt the effects of poverty rather than elimi-

nate it, so the persistence of poverty is perhaps not surprising (see Freeman, this volume).

33. As noted in Berlin (2000a), states get conflicting messages under TANF: they now have the flexibility to assist working-poor families with TANF funds, but doing so may keep the clock ticking on time limits. A breadwinner who becomes unemployed may not be able to access benefits in the future. Some states have designed their programs to mitigate this problem by using one pool of funds to support work and another to provide more traditional AFDC-like benefits.

Chapter 7: Welfare Policy in Transition: Redefining the Social Contract for Poor Citizen Families with Children and for Immigrants

1. States can provide assistance to felons, but they must explicitly decide to do so. Typically, a state must adopt legislation stating that convicted felons are eligible for assistance, requiring a majority of state legislators to support receipt of assistance by felons.

2. The federal government and the states (and in some cases, counties) shared responsibility for funding the AFDC and JOBS programs. Beginning in 1965, when the Medicaid program was established, states could receive federal matching funds for every dollar they spent on AFDC benefits. The Medicaid match rates used to determine how much a state would be reimbursed for its expenditures on benefits were inversely related to state per capita income. There was a statutory floor of 50 percent and a ceiling of 83 percent. In 1996, when the TANF program was created, twelve states had a Medicaid match rate of 50 percent; Mississippi had the top rate of 78.1 percent (U.S. Department of Health and Human Services 1998a). The JOBS program had a different funding structure; the federal government covered 90 percent of the cost of the program up to a maximum allocation, and states were required to cover the remaining 10 percent.

3. AFDC-related spending includes spending for the JOBS and Emergency Assistance Programs. Emergency Assistance was an optional program that states could operate to help families meet nonrecurring expenses to avert a crisis.

4. A state's participation rate is reduced one percentage point for every reduction in caseload since 1995. This caseload reduction credit does not apply to changes that result from changing the manner in which eligibility for benefits is determined. The purpose of the caseload reduction credit is to give states credit for moving TANF recipients from welfare to work. However, states do not have to show that families who left the welfare rolls went to work.

5. A recent study by the General Accounting Office (2000) suggests that in any given month only 5 percent of the TANF caseload is in a sanction status. However, given that states and clients have the option to close a client's case when a full-family sanction is imposed, this is likely to be a gross underestimate of the

number of families who have lost their TANF benefits because of such a sanction.

6. The HHS final regulations indicate that unspent reserves can be spent only on activities considered "assistance," defined as benefits and services that help families meet ongoing basic needs such as shelter or food, with some exceptions. However, states can designate funds during one year for other uses (such as child care, transportation, or employment and training services) during the next fiscal year.

Chapter 8: Health Policies for the Non-elderly Poor

1. A recently released report by the U.S. General Accounting Office (1999d) shows that children served by Medicaid remain at high risk of elevated blood lead levels and that the majority have not been screened, let alone treated.

2. A U.S. Bureau of the Census report (Short and Shea 1995) documents that there are more conditions that increase the risk of accidents, injury, and illness among the poor than among the nonpoor. Persons who are poor are about twice as likely as the nonpoor to have a leaking roof, a broken window, or exposed wiring, and they are nearly three times as likely to have rats, mice, or roaches, as well as plumbing that does not work. They are about twice as likely to report that they are afraid to go out; they view crime as a problem, and they report run-down or abandoned structures in their neighborhood. The poor are also nearly eight times as likely to report that they did not have enough food in the past four months. All of these conditions create a higher risk of disease and injury. See Massey (1996) and Waitzman and Smith (1998) for evidence on increasing concentrations of poor people in high-poverty, central-city, and rural areas where crime, poor nutrition, and bad living conditions are more likely to be found.

3. Estimates of the size of the homeless population vary from 2.3 percent to 4.4 percent of the adult population (Link et al. 1994). When the number of children is added, the range for the total population is 4.95 million to 9.32 million. The number of children is estimated at 15 percent of the total homeless population (Burt and Cohen 1989).

4. To the extent that some health problems are linked to poverty, and the research on them does not control for poverty, the link between race and health may really be between poverty and health (see Keil et al. 1992).

5. Such behaviors also tend to be associated with a variety of intrahousehold "externalities": secondhand tobacco smoke results in relatively greater risk of acute upper respiratory illness in the children of smokers; children of alcohol-abusing mothers may suffer from fetal alcohol syndrome/fetal alcohol effect (FAS/FAE); accidental-gunshot-related injuries and fatalities occur in households where firearms are present; and communicable disease spreads in families with substandard immunizations.

6. The reverse would be the case if a provider were paid a fixed fee for a specified

set of services. Then less care leads to greater profit for the provider, since the provider incurs lower costs. In either case, however, supplier-induced demand creates a market failure.

7. The long period of investment required to become a fully licensed health care provider presents a similar case for subsidization. The need to attract highly qualified individuals to the medical profession (and to biomedical research) has led to the subsidization of the extensive education and training of both providers and researchers.

8. For example, a high-income person who faces a marginal tax rate of approximately one-third is receiving what amounts to a 25 percent discount on the price of health insurance purchases.

9. According to recent Organization of Economic Cooperation and Development (OECD) data, the United States spends far more per person than any other OECD country—$3,912, as of 1997. The second highest was $2,611 in Switzerland, followed by $2,364 in Germany. Currency conversions to U.S. dollars use purchasing power parity (National Center for Health Statistics 2000c, table 114).

10. Traditionally, for the non-aged population, those eligible for federally assisted income maintenance payments must be covered, as well as those on Supplemental Security Income (SSI), a program for those with low income who are blind or severely disabled.

11. Sixteen states established Medicaid-only programs, seventeen states have both a Medicaid expansion and a separate program, while the remainder have separate state programs. About two-thirds of all children enrolled are in separate programs rather than Medicaid expansions (Kaiser Family Foundation 2001).

12. It also covers the disabled who qualify to receive Social Security based on their disability, and persons on end-stage renal dialysis. Aged and disabled persons with incomes below the poverty line (who meet an assets test) are eligible to have Medicaid pay their Medicare premiums, copayments, and deductibles.

13. DSR payments depend on the proportion of Medicaid-covered patients in a hospital rather than the proportion who are poor and uninsured. Hospitals can increase DSR revenue by serving more Medicaid patients rather than more who are poor and uninsured.

14. The portion of the health insurance premium paid by the employer is a deductible business expense for the employer and tax-free, in-kind income for the employee. Self-employed taxpayers may deduct a portion of their health insurance premium (60 percent in 1999). In addition, all taxpayers may deduct out-of-pocket health care expenditures in excess of 7.5 percent of adjusted gross income (AGI), and out-of-pocket expenditures for health care can be paid from funds set aside from pretax dollars in firms with tax-exempt reimbursement accounts.

15. The measure of inadequate coverage used in the literature is coverage that leaves a person at risk of spending more than 10 percent of his or her income on medical care in the event of a major illness. Using this definition, an estimated 20 million Americans had a 1 percent or greater risk of spending more than 10

percent of their income on health care in 1987 (Pepper Commission 1990, 23, 45). Most of these people have insurance plans with no caps on the amount that the insured pays in the event of high medical costs; these plans may also include exclusion waivers that omit prior conditions from coverage.

16. According to a survey on access to care (Donelan et al. 1996), 64 percent of those without insurance said that the main reason they had no coverage was that it was too expensive.

17. The data used are from a large national survey conducted in 1987, the National Medical Expenditure Survey, which covered about fourteen thousand households interviewed four times over a sixteen-month period. Subpopulations of special policy interest who were oversampled included poor and low-income families, the functionally impaired, and minorities. Total medical expenditures are the measure of utilization. (For more on the data set and the approach, see Vanness and Wolfe 1999.)

18. According to a survey by the Robert Wood Johnson Foundation (1987), in 1986, 1 million persons were turned away from hospitals because they could not pay.

19. Alternatively, patients without insurance are less likely to receive discretionary services that have no established medical protocol (Mort et al. 1996).

20. These figures were calculated using Health Care Financing Administration (2000a) data on Medicaid recipients and Medicaid medical vendor payments. They do not include administrative payments.

21. Most economists believe that, with the exception of workers at a mandated minimum wage, employees bear the bulk of the cost of insurance in terms of forgone earnings. However, if there is a sudden increase in coverage, it may take time for the full share to be shifted to employees, since wages tend to be sticky downward.

22. States may find the expansion of Medicaid preferable to state-based strategies, since the cost is shared with the federal government, an administrative structure is in place, and certain cost-containment strategies may be more easily employed than in alternative plans.

23. Extending a Medicaid buy-in to the seriously disabled population with special needs would represent an efficient as well as equitable arrangement, for special chronic care benefits are covered under Medicaid but not under most health insurance contracts. Private firms may be reluctant to hire the disabled if they must be included in the firm's health insurance policies, and private insurance often does not cover these special types of health-related expenses. Offering the disabled an option of buying into Medicaid would increase their employability and might also encourage firms to offer other employees coverage, since the average cost of covering the relatively healthier nondisabled employees would be smaller. Extending such benefits might increase employment—and reduce the need for other transfer payments. For example, people with a paralysis may need special equipment (such as a motorized wheelchair or a specially equipped vehicle) in order to function independently. With these aids, they can often be employed. The idea is that removing these costly employees might reduce insur-

ers' fear of adverse selection, and hence reduce the premiums offered to small firms. However, this effect is likely to be small.

24. The formation of risk pools is another alternative that is sometimes discussed in conjunction with refundable tax credits. Single individuals, families, and small firms generally must pay far more than individuals in large groups for the same insurance coverage. Risk pools combine groups of individuals or small groups of employees to reduce the surcharge that insurance companies charge small groups and individuals. (The surcharge reflects the higher costs of selling to small groups and the fear of adverse selection—that only those with the greatest expected medical expenditures will purchase individual policies.)

25. A proposal to reduce the tax subsidy to high-income persons is a more limited form of such policies.

26. A third alternative would combine employer-based insurance with a high deductible (say, $3,000 per family), with an employer contribution to a medical IRA (tax-free allowances) to cover deductibles and other health costs. The funds could be used for deductibles, for premiums should the individual not be employed, or for long-term care. The employee would keep any IRA amounts not spent, subject to certain limitations on withdrawals.

27. Patricia Danzon (1992) analyzes the difference in overhead in the United States and Canada and finds a far smaller difference than is commonly acknowledged.

28. Numerous studies of such systems, including Canada's and Great Britain's, find evidence of substantial differences in the care provided to those of differing income or socioeconomic groups. Those with more resources always appear favored.

29. These contributions have a ceiling. Furthermore, a small private-sector health system, used primarily by those with higher incomes, is growing alongside the national health system. Private insurance is primarily used for elective procedures for which there would be a wait within the national system.

30. This is likely to occur because firms will want to establish how much they will contribute under any new financing plan, and they may seek to offer alternative fringe benefits to enhance employee loyalty. Both of these will be viewed as part of employee compensation and will reduce the amount that firms are willing to offer employees as cash compensation.

31. This "moral hazard" also includes an incentive to take fewer precautions to avoid the need for medical care.

32. A related option is to substitute the refundable tax credit mechanism for the employer-based subsidy; under this plan, the "cap" on the employer tax subsidy is effectively set at zero.

33. This would be a refundable, family-size, income-conditioned tax credit for the working poor.

34. Those receiving other subsidies—such as Medicaid or Medicare—would not be eligible. Some adjustment for midyear changes might be included in this plan to provide a work incentive for Medicaid recipients or to reduce potential deterrents to job mobility.

35. HMOs would also be required to participate, offering a basic package to a speci-

fied minimum number of families set to reflect each HMO's share of the insurance market in the state in the prior year. The share of non-HMO-insurance companies would also be set according to their share of the health insurance market in the state for the prior year. New entry and exit of insurers would also influence the actual shares.

36. The providers in the community care center would be either private providers who contract to provide care at the center as well as manage all additional care for the children served by the center or, in certain limited cases, publicly employed providers.

37. This plan is similar in concept to one proposed by the American Academy of Pediatrics in 1998. Its proposed plan would cover children through age twenty-one, replace Medicaid and SCHIP, but maintain, and even encourage, private employer-based family coverage for children of employees. The academy estimated that its plan, which would allow choice of practitioners and access to specialists, would cost an average of $1,200 per year per child, or between $30 billion and $40 billion per year (American Academy of Pediatrics 1998).

38. For private insurance companies, Healthy Kid may represent a trade-off: a loss of the market for children and pregnant women, but an increase in the market for private coverage of adults.

Chapter 9: Investing in the Future: Reducing Poverty Through Human Capital Investments

1. In the introduction to the first edition of his classic monograph *Human Capital,* Gary Becker (1964/1993, 9) defined investments in human capital as those "activities that influence future monetary and psychic income by increasing the resources in people"; those resources include "skills, knowledge, or health." His initial focus was on human capital investments through education and training, although he also identified other forms of investment, including health care, migration, and searching for information about prices and income.

2. A related literature examines child care programs more generally for both preschool and school-age children, considering, for example, evidence that child care quality matters for children's outcomes (for recent reviews, see Vandell and Pierce, in press; Vandell and Shumow 1999; Vandell and Wolfe 2000).

3. There is also evidence of beneficial effects of early intervention programs in other domains, such as child behavior and emotional development (Karoly et al. 1998). For example, measures of behavior problems or socio-emotional development were significantly better for participants in the Houston Parent-Child Development Center (PCDC), the Syracuse Family Development Research Program (FDRP), and the Infant Health and Development Program (IHDP) when measured at ages ranging from four to seven.

4. For example, the Early Training Project and the Perry Preschool Project both found favorable program effects for rates of teen pregnancy, although the differences between the treatment and control groups are not statistically significant by ages eighteen and nineteen, respectively (Karoly et al. 1998). The recently

released age-twenty-one follow-up results for the Abecedarian program indicate that program participants were almost two years older, on average, when they had their first child compared with the control group (Carolina Abecedarian Project 1999).

5. Although these effects may be viewed as beneficial for the mother, it is possible that the child outcomes are worse, especially if total family income is lower or increased maternal employment is associated with poor-quality child care. However, the cost-benefit assessment presented later in the chapter indicates that participating mothers on average are calculated to have experienced a net income gain (Karoly et al. 1998). The issue of child care quality is not addressed in the Elmira PEIP evaluation.

6. IHDP selected children on the basis of biological risk measured by low birthweight. The intervention was more effective for the heavier low-birthweight children (more than two thousand grams), who were considered the more advantaged children in this group (McCarton et al. 1997).

7. Currie (in press) provides a "back-of-the-envelope" cost-benefit calculation for the Head Start program based on both the short-term and long-term benefits generated by the program. These calculations suggest that even considering only a subset of the short- and medium-term benefits, Head Start already pays back much of the program costs. With modest-sized long-term benefits, it is likely that the full benefits of Head Start would more than pay back the program costs, although more in-depth benefit and cost analysis is required to confirm this rough calculation.

8. Barnett (1993) estimated a higher benefit-cost ratio (about seven to one) as a result of including benefits to the rest of society from reduced intangible crime costs (for example, victim pain and suffering).

9. The methodology employed by Reynolds and his colleagues (2000) in the cost-benefit analysis of the Chicago CPC program is similar to that used by Karoly and her colleagues (1998) for the Elmira PEIP and Perry Preschool programs, with the exception that the former study includes the value of victim pain and suffering in the estimates of the benefits from reduced criminal activity. The break-even point for the Chicago CPC was not reported by Reynolds et al. (2000).

10. The lower-risk families in the control group had better outcomes than the higher-risk families in the control group. For example, in the first fifteen years of the child's life, the lower-risk control group used thirty months of welfare compared with ninety months for families in the higher-risk control group. Thus, there was less room for improvement with the lower-risk families.

11. The school reform movement that has been under way since the mid-1980s is considerably broader than the more limited set of interventions and strategies considered in the remainder of this section. Other approaches not discussed here include charter schools, contract schools, and other reforms to school organization; setting educational standards; testing and other accountability reforms; and home schooling and related movements (Grissmer et al. 2000).

12. Krueger (1999b) also reports a very rough cost-benefit calculation that suggests

that the STAR experiment could produce economic benefits (in the form of higher earnings) to students in smaller classes that outweigh the costs to the public sector of lowering class size. Future follow-up of students in the STAR experiment may demonstrate other domains of long-term benefits that would also produce public-sector savings or private benefits.

13. One exception is an experimental evaluation of the impact of career academies on student performance being performed by the Manpower Demonstration Research Corporation (MDRC) (Kemple and Snipes 2000).

14. In addition to the 1977 quasi-experimental Job Corps evaluation, Robert LaLonde (1995) has reviewed six other non-experimental studies of youth cohorts participating in job training programs from the late 1960s to the late 1970s. Excluding Job Corps, the other estimates range from negative annual earnings effects of about $1,000 per year to positive earnings gains of $1,200 per year (all in 1990 dollars).

15. Although the rates of attaining a GED or a high school diploma are reported as if they were equivalent, there is evidence to suggest that a GED has less value in the labor market than a high school diploma (Cameron and Heckman 1993).

16. A planned follow-up at forty-eight months will provide more evidence of the longer-term benefits of the program, as well as a cost-benefit assessment (Schochet et al. 2000).

17. There are other strategies for improving adult labor market and economic outcomes, although they largely fall outside of the realm of traditional human capital investment strategies. For example, among the models for promoting the transition from welfare to work are programs designed to "make work pay" by supplementing the earnings of low-wage workers (Berlin 2000b; Bos et al. 1999; Knox, Miller, and Gennetian 2000; Michalopoulos, Card, et al. 2000).

18. Since the 1960s, another target of publicly funded training programs has been dislocated workers, a less disadvantaged group than those considered here. (For a recent review of these programs, see Leigh 2000.)

19. In this section, the focus is on the major publicly funded training programs for adults. In reality, there is a much more diverse array of programs. A 1995 GAO report, for example, tallied 163 federally funded employment and training programs in 1995, with spending equal to $20 billion (General Accounting Office 1995).

20. Another recent synthesis considered the impact of eleven JOBS welfare-to-work programs on child outcomes based on two years of follow-up data (Hamilton, Freedman, and McGroder 2000). Although the programs did not target services to children and only limited information was collected about child outcomes, the review indicated that favorable effects were dominant for measures of cognitive development but not for academic achievement or health outcomes; results were mixed in terms of behavioral and emotional outcomes. Even when effects were favorable, however, they tended to be small in magnitude. A longer-term (five-year) follow-up is planned.

21. Daniel Friedlander and Gary Burtless (1995) have presented findings based on a

five-year follow-up of participants in four welfare-to-work programs implemented in the early 1980s. With one exception, the positive earnings gains of
the treatment group compared with the control group began to fade after three
to four years. Nevertheless, the experimental earnings gains remained significantly higher and demonstrate that program impacts can be sustained when
evaluated over a longer horizon.

Chapter 10: Housing Discrimination and Residential Segregation as Causes of Poverty

The author is grateful for helpful comments from Sheldon Danziger, David Harris, Robert Haveman, Jennifer Hochschild, and other conference participants.

1. In this chapter, "racial" and "ethnic" distinctions are considered equivalent (see
   Yinger 1995). For conciseness, the term "white" is used to mean "non-Hispanic
   white."
2. For alternative discussions, largely complementary to mine, see Brueckner
   (1987), O'Sullivan (2000), and Vandell (1995).
3. Edward Glaeser and his colleagues (2000) show that this claim clearly holds
   when the tendency of low-income households to use public transportation is
   considered.
4. I add the difference (if positive) between the number of people with zero or negative income and the number of people with no cash rent to the set of people
   with incomes above 30 percent of income.
5. In formal terms, let H = housing (quality-adjusted square feet), Y = income,
   P(Y) = price of housing (related to income), R = rent, and B = rent burden. By
   definition, R = (P)(H) and B = R/Y. A constant-elasticity demand function is H
   = $AY^\theta[P(Y)]^\mu$, where A is a constant, θ (> 0) is the income elasticity, and μ (< 0)
   is the price elasticity of demand for housing. Thus, B = $AY^{\theta-1}[P(Y)]^{\mu+1}$. Differ-
   entiation reveals that $(\partial B/\partial Y)(Y/B) = (\theta-1) + (\mu+1)(\partial P/\partial Y)(Y/P)$, which is the
   relationship in the text. Because θ and $|\mu|$ are both less than one, the left side
   of this equation is also less than one whenever $(\partial P/\partial Y)$ is negative.
6. Between 1995 and 1997, forty-four children under age nineteen died of asthma
   in New York City alone (Bernstein 1999).
7. For an analysis of the causes of segregation, see Galster (1991, 1998) and Yinger
   (1995), who argue that segregation reflects past discrimination (through its impact on intergroup income disparities and prejudice) and current discrimination.
   David Cutler, Edward Glaeser, and Jacob Vigdor (1999) claim that the key cause
   is now a white taste for segregation. This analysis misses the key conceptual
   point that prejudice is a product of past discrimination, and the empirical point
   that one cannot determine the impact of ethnic composition on housing prices
   without controls for neighborhood traits (Chambers 1992; Harris 1999; Kiel and
   Zabel 1996).
8. For studies of the causes of discrimination in housing, see Galster 1990b;

Ondrich, Stricker, and Yinger 1998; Page 1995; Roychoudhry and Goodman 1996; and Yinger 1995.

9. In addition, real estate brokers sometimes "steer" black and Hispanic customers toward black and Hispanic neighborhoods (Turner and Mickelsons 1992).

10. Home purchase also requires home insurance. Evidence on discrimination in home insurance is mixed. See Squires and Velez (1988) and Wissoker, Zimmerman, and Galster (1998).

11. The MTO program had two treatment groups. Both groups received housing subsidies, but one received assistance finding housing and faced constraints in the neighborhoods it could choose, and the other did not receive assistance but also faced no constraints (see Katz, Kling, and Liebman 2000). The results cited here involve the group that received assistance, but most results are similar for other comparisons.

12. A civil rights act passed in 1866 also has proven to be a powerful tool against racial discrimination in housing (see Yinger 1995).

13. Either party can elect to have the case handled by the Justice Department. Most of the cases that are not settled or dismissed end up in federal court, where they take longer and are more likely to be resolved in favor of the defendant. However, penalties imposed on defendants tend to be larger in federal court than in ALJ proceedings (see Schill and Friedman 1999).

14. I am grateful to David Harris for suggesting this example. See his comments in chapter 14 of this volume for further discussion.

15. Antidiscrimination legislation needs to cover both types of discrimination. Allowing disparate-impact discrimination would give economic agents a way to approximate the outcome of disparate-treatment discrimination by basing their business decisions on some observable characteristic that is highly correlated with membership in a protected class (see Ross and Yinger, forthcoming).

16. Subsidy data are not available for all housing units. Even if all cases of missing data are counted as subsidized housing, however, the total goes up only to 18.0 percent.

17. Strictly speaking, certificates and vouchers are different. A voucher pays the difference between *average* rent in qualifying apartments and 30 percent of a household's income. This difference has proved to have insignificant behavioral consequences.

18. In the past, the geographic scope of a recipient's housing search was also severely restricted by a certificate's lack of "portability" to jurisdictions other than the one that issued it. The Section 8 program has been revised, however, so that, at least in principle, Section 8 vouchers are fully portable.

19. With other supply-side subsidies added to the tax break, Jean Cummings and Denise DiPasquale (1999) find that the subsidy to a unit receiving the tax credit is about $45,000 (in 1996 dollars). This translates into an annual cost of about $4,850. Housing subsidies, which go to about 40 percent of tenants, add roughly $1,500 on average. Kirk McClure (1998) estimates that the annual cost of a Section 8 certificate is about $4,490 (also in 1996 dollars).

Chapter 11: The Memberships Theory of Poverty: The Role of Group Affiliations in Determining Socioeconomic Outcomes

I thank the John D. and Catherine T. MacArthur Foundation and the National Science Foundation for financial support, and Aimée Dechter, Mitchell Duneier, Elizabeth Evanson, Roberto Fernandez, Susan Nelson, Stephen Raudenbush, and especially Sheldon Danziger and Robert Haveman for valuable comments. As usual, Andros Kourtellos and Artur Minkin have provided outstanding research assistance.

1. This new empirical work, in turn, reflects the growing availability of neighborhood and school data. I thank Robert Haveman for this point.

2. One can also treat family formation in this group-membership framework. Raquel Fernandez and Richard Rogerson (1999) show the importance of this mechanism, through assortative mating, to an understanding of inequality.

3. The dichotomy between endogenous and exogenous groups is not entirely satisfactory, since we would in principle like to know why certain endogenous group memberships are salient. For example, we do not normally think of the set of bald, bearded professors as a salient source of role models for children the way we think of parents in a community as such a source.

4. In other work (Brock and Durlauf 1999, 2000a; Durlauf 1997), I have provided a general theoretical framework for studying models of this type. There is a very rich literature on models with interactions within the economics and sociology literatures. Schelling (1971) is an important precursor. See also Granovetter and Soong (1988) for an interesting example from sociology.

5. Notice that with reference to our baseline choice problem, endogenous effects are induced by $\mu_i^\varepsilon(\omega_{-i})$ and contextual effects are induced by $y_{n(i)}$.

6. Hauser's classic (1970) demonstration of how one can produce spurious evidence of contextual effects is actually a lovely example of what happens when self-selection is not properly accounted for when analyzing observational data.

7. John Yinger (this volume) states that "living in lower-quality housing carries a higher risk of exposure to lead paint or asthma inducing conditions." He goes on to argue that housing discrimination, by segregating the poor into low-quality housing, contributes to serious health risks for the disadvantaged. Hence, the question of whether housing quality is different across the groups in MTO is a serious caveat to the interpretation of health findings in general.

8. Participants in the experiment were told that the research was designed to explore the effects of punishment on learning.

9. This discussion borrows from my earlier work (Durlauf 1999a).

10. See Loury (1987) for a related set of arguments. On the other hand, these relatively similar general ethical considerations lead me to a view of affirmative ac-

tion much more sanguine than Loury's. I have enumerated some reasons for this elsewhere (Durlauf 1999a).

Notice that the full equality of opportunity need not be feasible through government policies; nor even desirable overall, owing to the costs of the necessary policies.

11. Loury (2000) draws a similar distinction between "preferential" affirmative action and "developmental" affirmative action.

12. Durlauf (1999a) and Loury (2000) also discuss the implications of the Moskos and Butler (1996) study for policy.

Chapter 12: Community Revitalization, Jobs, and the Well-being of the Inner-City Poor

I thank Sara Stoutland for helpful discussions and for assistance in gathering materials. I also thank Paul Jargowsky, Robert Haveman, and Sheldon Danziger for helpful suggestions. Special thanks to Sheldon Danziger for excellent suggestions that cut the paper's length and improved its readability.

1. This sense of concern and shared efficacy may encompass not only residents but also professionals in public, private, and nonprofit organizations who play important roles with residents in shaping their community's development and quality of life. Although the chapter emphasizes the significance of residential neighborhoods as communities, it also notes the critical importance of social ties and a sense of community in settings such as training programs and workplaces, both inside and outside the boundaries of the neighborhood. In addition, it appreciates that adult social networks span much wider geographic areas than residential neighborhoods (see Sampson 1999).

2. William Dickens (1999) used the Urban Institute's Underclass Data Base from the 1990 census to estimate the percentage of the differences in employment rates between distressed and other neighborhoods that could be explained by the observable characteristics of residents. He discovered that about half of the difference between average census tracts and the 10 percent with the lowest employment rates could be predicted by the census variables measuring age, education, marital status, and race.

3. John Yinger's chapter in this volume reviews evidence that small-scale residential mobility programs that help the poor move away from disadvantaged neighborhoods can result in better housing, better schooling, and sometimes even better jobs for those who move. However, as Steven Durlauf suggests in his chapter, results from small programs can be misleading. A massive migration of poor and near-poor people into nonpoor communities would cause changes in the receiving communities that many in those communities would find unacceptable. It seems highly unlikely that large-scale mobility programs would produce the benefits for movers that small-scale experiments have found.

4. Dickens (1999) argues that the size of the estimated effects of commuting time on employment that some authors find for what seem to be small differences in commuting times are implausibly large, considering what we know about labor supply elasticities, and therefore are very likely due to something other than the length of commutes.

5. Dickens (1999) also explains what would happen if workers from all neighborhoods received the same number of offers but workers from the disadvantaged neighborhood were offered lower wages. Under these conditions, workers from the disadvantaged neighborhood would not be willing to travel as far, and they would have both lower wages and shorter commutes.

6. Michael Stoll has pointed out in personal conversation that the employer's method of outreach may be related to his or her racial preferences. Employers willing to hire blacks may be the ones more likely to use newspaper advertisements. If this accounts for the difference in employment outcomes among employers using different methods, then the problem implicated by these results is discrimination rather than access to information or transportation.

7. In addition, incentives can include support for recruiting or training workers, for finding potential customers or collaborators, for financing new equipment, or for upgrading production or service-delivery methods in order to increase productivity (Blair 1995; Blakely 1994; Hatry et al. 1990). Findings are encouraging regarding the effectiveness of interventions to increase productivity, if they are well designed and matched with the needs of firms (see references in Bartik 1994).

8. The locality that wins a particular firm may think it is getting a good deal for its money because in most cases, businesses pay more in taxes (especially property taxes) than they use up in local public services (Blair 1995).

9. For example, the real estate developer James Rouse reported a simple formula that he said worked at the neighborhood-based Jubilee House in Washington, D.C.: thirty phone calls to employers equaled one new job for a neighborhood resident. Often volunteers made those calls. The example of Jubilee House may overstate the simplicity, but most economists agree that developing new businesses or expending more than minimal amounts to attract new businesses to the neighborhood is among the least cost-effective neighborhood *employment* strategies. Helping residents to connect to opportunities throughout the region (for example, within a thirty- or forty-minute commute) is more efficient.

10. See the online teaching case "North Carolina and the Battle for Business," John F. Kennedy School of Government, Harvard University.

11. Olivier Blanchard and Lawrence Katz (1992) conclude that the effects of employment growth on local employment rates are gone after five years. Timothy Bartik (1997, 70) reanalyzed the Blanchard and Katz data, however, and found that "the effect of local employment growth on labor force participation persists for at least 17 years."

12. A standard concern at the neighborhood level is that neighborhood-based

groups might put many demands on businesses, especially potentially large employers, and drive them away or keep them from locating in the area (see Porter 1995).

13. For example, lump sum subsidies or subsidies that are capped so that they do not affect decisions about the marginal worker hired or trained will not affect the marginal cost of labor.

14. The ideal experiment would be for a state to select a set of eligible areas and then randomly assign some to be zones and some to be in the control group. The impacts could be estimated by comparing the average employment or earnings gains in control areas (the counterfactual) with the average in the zones. However, this type of random assignment experiment has never been tried with enterprise zones, nor indeed with any major business incentive program that I know of. Instead, state zones are selected nonrandomly based on location, the economic status of residents, the quality of proposals (when required), and various political considerations.

15. According to Papke (1994), a taxing district is a geographic area within which property is taxed by the same taxing unit and at the same total rate. It is generally close to the size of an enterprise zone.

16. The wage credit offered in the current federal empowerment zone program is higher—up to $3,000 for each zone resident hired—so it is plausible that a larger percentage of zone firms use them than Papke found to be the case for Indiana. Upcoming evaluation reports will provide some indications.

17. See also Engberg and Greenbaum (1999), whose main finding is that zones do not on average increase house values (except in tight housing markets). Greenbaum and Engberg (1999) examine the effect of zones on manufacturing business activity and employment levels. They conclude that there is little net effect.

18. On the one hand, if the federal empowerment zones show larger drops in poverty and unemployment than their comparison areas that do not have zones, the coexistence of business incentives with political and social supports will make it difficult to untangle the reasons. On the other hand, the health of the economy is a reason to expect only weakly favorable findings; the macro economy has been increasingly healthy since 1994, the period during which the zones have operated. Hence, we should expect that both the zones and their nonzone comparison areas have shown improvements compared to their own past patterns. However, if the comparison areas improved as much as the zone areas did, then it will be reasonable to draw the conclusion that the zones would have done similarly well even if they had not been designated as zones. Hence, there may be a negative judgment about zone success even when it appears to observers that they did well.

19. Information on ICIC is available online at *www.ICIC.org.*

20. For example, see media reports available at *www.ICIC.org.*

21. The following description of CET is based on Melendez (1996) and Melendez and Harrison (1998) unless otherwise noted.

22. By 1981, CET had thirteen branch centers in California and at least one in Arizona, Nevada, Oregon, and Washington (Melendez 1996, 51).

23. Several reasons for this failure were discovered: sites were linked to private industry councils associated with the public job training system more than to indigenous community groups; they either had difficulty establishing standard CET links with employers or had not tried; they were missing the complementary services that disadvantaged workers often need and that CET routinely addressed; and as training sites, they did not simulate work settings.

24. Other federal programs that have targeted poor neighborhoods and communities include Urban Renewal in 1949, Community Action programs in 1964, Model Cities in 1966, Title VII of the Economic Opportunity Act in 1967 (to support community development corporations), community development block grants in 1974, and urban development action grants in 1977. The HOME program was enacted in 1990 to specifically focus on housing and to complement the community development block grant program. In addition, the Community Reinvestment Act (passed first in the 1970s and later revised) provides community investment incentives for banks, and the Low-Income Housing Tax Credit (first passed in the 1980s) provides tax credits for equity investments in low-income housing.

25. This statement is based on policy memos from federal officials that I had copies of during the 1970s, and on various reactions to those memos from people in the CDC field. CDCs were on annual funding cycles for their federal support and could not therefore do long-term planning. There was a great deal of confusion about whether CDCs should be trying to produce social or economic benefits and about the types of trade-offs that would be acceptable.

26. Many of these people were political activists who had been involved with creating the CDCs and then moved into leadership positions.

27. An early evaluation by Abt Associates (1973) produced a very negative assessment.

28. Their data begin with the U.S. decennial census of 1890 and include each census through 1990.

29. Information on the NCCED is available at *www.NCCED.org.*

30. Based on a national survey of CDCs conducted by the NCCED. For a table of CDC activities by size (full-time equivalent employees) based on an NCCED national survey, see Ferguson and Dickens (1999, ch. 1; see also chs. 2 and 5, and the works cited therein).

31. Eleven percent reported some business development role. Downey and Shabecoff (1996) present a number of case studies of successful businesses run by CDCs.

32. Paul Grogan was for many years the head of the Local Initiatives Support Corporation (LISC), a national organization with local branches that has contributed to much of the growth in the CDC field since 1980 and remains a major advocacy and technical assistance organization. Tony Proscio is a consultant and writer on community development and related issues.

33. Federal empowerment zone findings about employment impacts are not yet available and, even when available, are likely to be difficult to interpret because they mix business incentives with social supports for workers.
34. See the exchange between Senator Kennedy and Gerald L. Phillippe, chairman of the board of the General Electric Company, in the summer of 1966, reported in Schuchter (1971, 213–14). In one statement, Kennedy says that "you would have a market that really has been untapped as of the present time, first as far as workers is concerned, and, second, as far as purchasers are concerned."

References

Aaron, Henry. 1985. "Comments on Methods of Measuring Noncash Benefits." *Noncash Benefits: An Evaluation of the Census Bureau's Measurement Conference*, PEMD–86–8BR. Washington: U.S. General Accounting Office (April).

Aaron, Henry J., and Robert D. Reischauer. 1999. *Countdown to Reform: The Great Social Security Debate*. Washington, D.C.: Brookings Institution (January).

Aaronson, Daniel. 1998. "Using Sibling Data to Estimate the Impact of Neighborhoods on Children's Educational Outcomes." *Journal of Human Resources* 33(4): 915–46.

Abt Associates. 1973. *An Evaluation of the Special Impact Program: Final Report*. Cambridge, Mass.: Abt Associates.

Acs, Gregory, and Pamela Loprest. 2000. "Studies of Welfare Leavers: Methods, Findings, and Contributions to the Policy Process." Paper prepared for the National Research Council Panel on Data and Methods for Measuring the Effects of Changes in Social Welfare Programs. Washington, D.C.: Urban Institute.

Ady, Robert M. 1997. "Discussion [of business location decisionmaking]." *New England Economic Review* (March-April): 67–71.

Ahituv, Avner, Marta Tienda, Lixin Xu, and V. Joseph Hotz. 1994. "Initial Labor Market Experiences of Black, Hispanic, and White Men." Discussion Paper Series. Chicago: Population Research Center.

Akerlof, George. 1997. "Social Distance and Social Decisions." *Econometrica* 65(5): 1005–28.

Akerlof, George A., and Rachel E. Kranton. 2000. "Identity and Economics." *Quarterly Journal of Economics* 115(3): 719–53.

American Academy of Pediatrics. 1998. "An Analysis of the Costs to Provide Health Care Coverage to the Children and Adolescents Aged 0–21." Available at *www.aap.org/advocacy/towers/cstover.htm*.

American Medical Association. 1999. "Expanding Access to Insurance Coverage for Health Expenses: An AMA Proposal." Chicago: American Medical Association.

Anderson, Elijah. 1990. *Streetwise: Race, Class, and Change in an Urban Community*. Chicago: University of Chicago Press.

———. 1999. *Code of the Street*. New York: W. W. Norton.

Anderson, W. H. Locke. 1964. "Trickling Down: The Relationship Between Economic Growth and the Extent of Poverty among American Families." *Quarterly Journal of Economics* 78(4): 511—24.

Aronson, Elliot. 1999. *The Social Animal.* 8th ed. New York: W. H. Freeman.

Associated Press. 2000. "House Mice May Contribute to Asthma Attacks." *New York Times,* December 12.

Atkinson, Anthony B., Lee Rainwater, and Timothy M. Smeeding. 1995. "Income Distribution in OECD Countries: Evidence from the Luxembourg Income Study (LIS)." Social Policy Studies 18. Paris: Organization for Economic Cooperation and Development (October).

Atkinson, Tony. 1999. "Beveridge and the Twenty-first Century." Beveridge Lecture delivered at Toynbee Hall, London (March 18). Published in *Ending Child Poverty: Popular Welfare for the Twenty-first Century,* edited by Robert Walker. Bristol: Policy Press.

Ayanian, John Z., Betsy A. Kohler, Toshi Abe, and Arnold M. Epstein. 1993. "The Relation between Health Insurance Coverage and Clinical Outcomes among Women with Breast Cancer." *The New England Journal of Medicine* 329(5): 326–31.

Bailey, Ronald W., ed. 1971. *Black Business Enterprise.* New York: Basic Books.

Bane, Mary Jo, and David Ellwood. 1983. "The Dynamics of Dependence: The Routes to Self-sufficiency." Report prepared for the assistant secretary for planning and evaluation, Office of Evaluation and Technical Analysis, Office of Income Security Policy, U.S. Department of Health and Human Services. Cambridge, Mass.: Urban Systems Research and Engineering.

Barnett, Steven W. 1993. "Benefit-Cost Analysis of Preschool Education: Findings from a Twenty-five-year Follow-up." *American Journal of Orthopsychiatry* 63(4): 500–08.

———. 1995. "Long-term Effects of Early Childhood Programs on Cognitive and School Outcomes." *The Future of the Children* 5(3): 25–50.

Bartik, Timothy J. 1994. "What Should the Federal Government Be Doing About Urban Economic Development?" *Cityscape: A Journal of Policy Development Research* 1(August): 267–92.

———. 1997. "A Comment on Two Papers Concerning State and Local Development." *New England Economic Review* [Federal Reserve Bank of Boston] (March-April): 67–71.

———. 2000. "Group Wage Curves." Staff Working Paper. Kalamazoo, Mich.: W. E. Upjohn Institute for Employment Research (September).

Bartik, Timothy J., and V. Kerry Smith. 1987. "Urban Amenities and Public Policy." In *Handbook of Urban and Regional Economics,* vol. 2, edited by Edwin S. Mills. Amsterdam: North-Holland.

Baumann, K. 1998. "Direct Measures of Poverty as Indicators of Economic Need: Evidence from the SIPP." Technical Working Paper 30. Washington: U.S. Bureau of the Census, Population Division.

Becker, Gary S. 1991. *Treatise on the Family.* Cambridge, Mass.: Harvard University Press. (Originally published 1981).

————. 1993. *Human Capital*. Chicago: University of Chicago Press. (Originally published in 1964.)

Belsky, Eric S., Matthew Lambert, and Alexander von Hoffman. 2000. "Insights into the Practice of Community Reinvestment Act Lending: A Synthesis of CRA Discussion Groups." Working Paper CRA00–1. Cambridge, Mass.: Harvard Joint Center for Housing Studies (August).

Bénabou, Roland. 1993. "Workings of a City: Location, Education, and Production." *Quarterly Journal of Economics* 108(3): 619–52.

————. 1996a. "Equity and Efficiency in Human Capital Investment: The Local Connection." *Review of Economic Studies* 63(2): 237–64.

————. 1996b. "Heterogeneity, Stratification, and Growth: Macroeconomic Effects of Community Structure." *American Economic Review* 86(3): 584–609.

Bennefield, Robert L. 1998. *Dynamics of Economic Well-being: Health Insurance, 1993 to 1995: Who Loses Coverage and for How Long?* Current Population Reports Series P70, no. 64. Washington: U.S. Bureau of the Census.

Bergstrom, Theodore C. 1997. "A Survey of Theories of the Family." In *Handbook of Population and Family Economics,* edited by Mark R. Rosenzweig and Oded Stark. New York: Elsevier Science.

Bergstrom, Theodore C., and Mark Bagnoli. 1993. "Courtship as a Waiting Game." *Journal of Political Economy* 101(1): 185–202.

Berlin, Gordon L. 2000a. *Encouraging Work, Reducing Poverty: The Impact of Work Incentive Programs*. New York: Manpower Demonstration Research Corporation (March).

————. 2000b. "Welfare That Works." *The American Prospect Online* 11(15), available at: *www.prospect.org/archieves/v11–15/berlin-g.html.*

Berlin, Isaiah. 1968. *Four Essays on Liberty*. Oxford: Oxford University Press.

————. 1990. *The Crooked Timber of Humanity: Chapters in the History of Ideas*. London: John Murray.

Bernheim, Douglas. 1987. "The Economic Effects of Social Security: Towards a Reconciliation of Theory and Measurement." *Journal of Public Economics* 33(3): 273–304.

Bernstein, Jared, and Lawrence Mishel. 1999. "Wages Gain Ground." *Economic Policy Institute Issue Brief* 129(February).

Bernstein, Jared, Lawrence Mishel, and John Schmitt. 2001. *The State of Working America 2000–2001*. Ithaca, N.Y.: ILR Press.

Bernstein, Nina. 1999. "Asthma Is Found in 38 Percent of Children in City Shelters." *New York Times,* May 5.

Berry, Daniel E. 1998. "The Jobs and Workforce Initiative: Northeast Ohio Employers' Plan for Workforce Development." *Economic Development Quarterly* 12(1): 41–53.

Besharov, Douglas J., and Karen N. Gardiner. 1999. "Introduction: Preventing Youthful Disconnectedness." In *America's Disconnected Youth,* edited by Douglas J. Besharov. Washington, D.C.: American Enterprise Institute.

Betson, David M. 1996. "Is Everything Relative?: The Role of Equivalence Scales in

Poverty Measurement." Working Paper. South Bend, Ind.: Department of Economics, University of Notre Dame.

———. 1997. "In Search of an Elusive Truth: How Much Do Americans Spend on Their Health Care?" Working Paper. South Bend, Ind.: Department of Economics, University of Notre Dame.

———. 1998. "Imputation of Medical Out-of-Pocket (MOOP) Expenditures to CPS Analysis Files." Working Paper. South Bend, Ind.: Department of Economics, University of Notre Dame.

Bhattacharya, Jay, and Janet Currie. 2001. "Youths at Nutritional Risk: Malnourished or Misnourished?" In *An Economic Analysis of Risky Behavior Among Youths,* edited by Jonathan Gruber. Chicago: University of Chicago Press.

Biblarz, Timothy J., Vern L. Bengslan, and Alexander Bucur. 1996. "Social Mobility Across Three Generations." *Journal of Marriage and the Family* 58(1): 188–200.

Bikson, Tora K., and Constantijn W. A. Panis. 1999. "Citizens, Computers, and Connectivity: A Review of Trends." Working Paper. Santa Monica, Calif.: RAND Corporation.

Björklund, Anders, and Richard Freeman. 1997. "Generating Equality and Eliminating Poverty—The Swedish Way." In *The Welfare State in Transition: Reforming the Swedish Model,* edited by Richard B. Freeman, Robert Topel, and Birgitta Swedenborg. Chicago: University of Chicago Press.

Blair, John P. 1995. *Local Economic Development.* Thousand Oaks, Calif.: Sage Publications.

Blair, Tony. 1999. "Beveridge Revisited: A Welfare State for the Twenty-first Century." In *Ending Child Poverty: Popular Welfare for the Twenty-first Century,* edited by Robert Walker. Bristol, Eng.: Policy Press.

Blakely, Edward. 1994. *Planning Local Economic Development,* 2nd ed. Thousand Oaks, Calif.: Sage Publications.

Blanchard, Olivier Jean, and Lawrence F. Katz. 1992. "Regional Evolutions." *Brookings Papers on Economic Activity* 1: 1–61.

Blank, Rebecca. 1997. *It Takes a Nation.* Princeton, N.J.: Princeton University Press.

Blank, Rebecca M., and Alan S. Blinder. 1986. "Macroeconomics, Income Distribution, and Poverty." In *Fighting Poverty: What Works and What Doesn't,* edited by Sheldon Danziger and Daniel Weinberg. Cambridge, Mass.: Harvard University Press.

Blank, Rebecca M., and David Card. 1993. "Poverty, Income Distribution, and Growth: Are They Still Connected?" *Brookings Papers on Economic Activity* 2: 285–339.

Blank, Rebecca M., and Luci Schmidt. 2001. "Work, Wages, and Welfare Reform." In *New World of Welfare,* edited by Rebecca Blank and Ron Haskins. Washington, D.C.: Brookings Institution.

Blau, David M. 2000. "Child Care Subsidy Programs." Working Paper 7806. Cambridge, Mass.: National Bureau of Economic Research.

Blau, Francine. 1998. "Trends in the Well-being of American Women, 1970–1995." *Journal of Economic Literature* 36: 112–65.

Blauner, Rober. 1969. "Internal Colonialism and Ghetto Revolt." *Social Problems* 16(Spring): 393–408.

Blume, L., and Steven Durlauf. 2001. "The Interactions-Based Approach to Socio-economic Behavior." In *Social Dynamics,* edited by H. Peyton Young and Steven Durlauf. Cambridge, Mass.: MIT Press.

Bobo, Lawrence, and Ryan A. Smith. 1994. "Antipoverty Policy, Affirmative Action, and Racial Attitudes." In *Confronting Poverty,* edited by Sheldon Danziger, Gary Sandefur, and Daniel Weinberg. Cambridge, Mass.: Harvard University Press.

Bobo, Lawrence, and Camille L. Zubrinsky. 1996. "Attitudes on Residential Integration: Perceived Status Differences, Mere In-group Preference, or Racial Prejudice." *Social Forces* 74(3): 883–909.

Bondonio, Daniele, and John Engberg. 1999. "Enterprise Zones and Local Employment: Evidence from the States' Programs." H. John Heinz III School of Public Policy and Management, Carnegie Mellon University, Pittsburgh. Unpublished paper.

Boorman, Scott. 1975. "A Combinatorial Optimization Model for Transmission of Job Information Through Contact Networks." *Bell Journal of Economics* 6: 216–49.

Borjas, George. 1992. "Ethnic Capital and Intergenerational Income Mobility." *Quarterly Journal of Economics* 107(1): 123–50.

———. 1995. "Ethnicity, Neighborhoods, and Human-Capital Externalities." *American Economic Review* 85(3): 365–90.

Bos, Hans, Aletha Huston, Robert Granger, Greg Duncan, Tom Brock, and Vonnie McLoyd. 1999. *New Hope for People with Low Incomes: Two-Year Results of a Program to Reduce Poverty and Reform Welfare.* New York: Manpower Demonstration Research Corporation.

Boskin, Michael J., Ellen R. Dulemberger, Robert J. Gordon, Zvi Griliches, and Dale W. Jorgenson. 1997. "The CPI Commission: Findings and Recommendations." *American Economic Review: Papers and Proceedings* 87(2): 78–83.

Bowler, Mary. 1999. "Women's Earnings: An Overview." *Monthly Labor Review* 122(12): 13–21.

Bradbury, Bruce, and Markus Jäntti. 1999. "Child Poverty Across Industrialized Nations." Economic and Social Policy Series 71, Innocenti Occasional Papers. Florence: UNICEF International Child Development Centre (September). Available at *www.unicef-icdc.org/pdf/cps71.pdf.*

Braddock II, Jomills Henry, and James M. McPartland. 1987. "How Minorities Continue to Be Excluded from Equal Employment Opportunities: Research on Labor Market Institutional Barriers." *Journal of Social Issues* 43(1): 5–39.

Brewster, Karin. 1994a. "Race Differences in Sexual Activity Among Adolescent Women: The Role of Neighborhood Characteristics." *American Sociological Review* 59(3): 408–24.

———. 1994b. "Neighborhood Context and the Transition to Sexual Activity Among Black Women." *Demography* 31(4): 603–14.

Briggs, Xavier de Souza. 1997. "Moving up Versus Moving Out: Neighborhood Effects in Housing Mobility Programs." *Housing Policy Debate* 8(1): 195–234.

Briggs, Xavier de Souza, Elizabeth Mueller, and Mercer Sullivan. 1997. *From Neighborhood to Community: Evidence on the Social Effects of Community Development.* New York: Community Development Research Center, New School for Social Research.

Brimmer, Andrew F. 1971. "Small Business and Economic Development in the Negro Community." In *Black Business Enterprise,* edited by Ronald W. Bailey. New York: Basic Books.

Brindis, Ted. 2001. "Programs Set up to Close 'Digital Divide' May Be Cut Back." *Wall Street Journal,* February 15.

Brock, William, and Steven Durlauf. 1999. "Discrete Choice with Social Interactions." Department of Economics, University of Wisconsin. Unpublished paper.

———. 2000a. "Interactions-Based Models." University of Wisconsin. Unpublished paper.

———. 2000b. "Growth Empirics and Reality." University of Wisconsin. Unpublished paper.

Brooks-Gunn, Jeanne, Lisa Berlin, and Allison Fuligni. In press. "Early Childhood Intervention Programs: What About the Family?" In *Handbook of Early Childhood Intervention,* 2nd ed., edited by Jack P. Shonkoff and Samuel J. Meisels. New York: Cambridge University Press.

Brooks-Gunn, Jeanne, and Greg Duncan. 1997. "The Effects of Poverty on Children." *The Future of Children* 7(2): 55–71.

Brooks-Gunn, Jeanne, Greg Duncan, Paula Klebanov, and N. Sealand. 1993. "Do Neighborhoods Affect Child and Adolescent Development?" *American Journal of Sociology* 99: 353–95.

Brown, Amy. 1997. *Work First: How to Implement an Employment-Focused Approach to Welfare Reform.* New York: Manpower Demonstration Research Corporation.

Brown, Charles, James Hamilton, and James Medoff. 1990. *Employers Large and Small.* Cambridge, Mass.: Harvard University Press.

Brueckner, Jan K. 1987. "The Structure of Urban Equilibria: A Unified Treatment of the Muth-Mills Model." In *Handbook of Regional and Urban Economics,* vol. 2, edited by Edwin S. Mills. Amsterdam: North-Holland.

Bumpass, Larry L. 1990. "What's Happening to the Family?: Interactions Between Demographic and Institutional Change." *Demography* 27(4): 483–95.

———. 1995. "The Declining Significance of Marriage: Changing Family Life in the United States." National Survey of Families and Households Working Paper 66. Madison: University of Wisconsin, Madison Center for Demography and Ecology.

Bumpass, Larry L., and Hsien-Hen Lu. 2000. "Trends in Cohabitation and Implications for Children's Family Context in the United States." *Population Studies* 54(1): 29–41.

Bumpass, Larry L., and R. Kelly Raley. 1995. "Redefining Single-Parent Families: Cohabitation and Changing Family Reality." *Demography* 32(1): 97–109.

Bumpass, Larry L., James A. Sweet, and Andrew J. Cherlin. 1991. "The Role of Cohabitation in Declining Rates of Marriage." *Journal of Marriage and the Family* 53(4): 913–27.

Burchardt, Tania, Julian Le Grand, and David Piachaud. 1999. "Social Exclusion in Britain 1991–1995." *Social Policy and Administration* 33(4): 227–44.

Burdetti, John, and Janet Shickles. 1999. "Can't Afford to Get Sick." Available at: *www.cmwf.org/programs/insurance/budetti_sick_347.asp*.

Burkhauser, Richard, and Mary Daly. 2000. "SSI." Paper presented at "National Bureau of Economic Research Conference on Means-Tested Transfers," Cambridge, Mass.(May 11–12).

Burt, Martha, and Barbara Cohen. 1989. *America's Homeless: Numbers, Characteristics, and Programs That Serve Them.* Washington, D.C.: Urban Institute Press.

Burtless, Gary. 1986. "Public Spending for the Poor: Trends, Prospects, and Economic Limits." In *Fighting Poverty: What Works and What Doesn't,* edited by Sheldon Danziger and Daniel Weinberg. Cambridge, Mass.: Harvard University Press.

———. 1994. "Public Spending on the Poor: Historical Trends and Economic Limits." in *Confronting Poverty: Prescriptions for Change,* edited by Sheldon Danziger, Gary Sandefur, and Daniel Weinberg. Cambridge, Mass.: Harvard University Press.

———. 1996. "Trends in the Level and Distribution of U.S. Living Standards, 1973–1993." *Eastern Economic Journal* 22(3, Summer): 271–90.

Burtless, Gary, and J. Quinn. 2000. "Retirement Trends and Policies to Encourage Work Among Older Americans." Working Paper. Washington, D.C.: Brookings Institution (January).

Cain, Glen G. 2000. "The New Welfare Reform Law in the United States: Its Background and a Preliminary Appraisal." Paper presented at the Asia Pacific Economic Cooperation Forum on Shared Prosperity and Harmony. Seoul, Korea (March 30-April 1, 2000).

Camarota, Steven A. 1999. "Importing Poverty: Immigration's Impact on the Size and Growth of the Poor Population in the United States." Washington, D.C.: Center for Immigration Studies.

Cameron, Stephen, and James J. Heckman. 1993. "The Nonequivalence of High School Equivalents." *Journal of Labor Economics* 11(1): 1–47.

Campbell, Frances A., and Craig T. Ramey. 1994. "Effects of Early Intervention on Intellectual and Academic Achievement: A Follow-up Study of Children from Low-Income Families." *Child Development* 62(2): 684–89.

———. 1995. "Cognitive and School Outcomes for High-Risk African American Students at Middle Adolescence: Positive Effects of Early Intervention." *American Education Research Journal* 32(4): 743–72.

Campbell, Jennifer A. 1999. *Health Insurance Coverage: 1998.* Current Population Reports Series P60, no. 208. Washington: U.S. Bureau of the Census.

Cancian, Maria. 2001. "The Rhetoric and Reality of Work-Based Welfare Reform." *Social Work* 46(4): 309–14.

Cancian, Maria, and Deborah Reed. 1999. "The Impact of Wives' Earnings on Income Inequality: Issues and Estimates." *Demography* 36(3): 173–84.

Carolina Abecedarian Project. 1999. "Gains from High-Quality Child Care Persist into Adulthood." Available at: *www.fpg.edu/~abc/press_release.htm*.

Casper, Lynne M., Philip Cohen, and Tavia Simmons. 1999. "How Does POSSLQ Measure Up?: Historical Estimates of Cohabitation." Population Division Working Paper 36. Washington: U.S. Bureau of the Census.

Castles, Ian. 1996. "Review of the OECD-Eurostat PPP Program." STD/PPP(97)5. Paris: Economic Studies Branch, Organization for Economic Cooperation and Development.

Cave, George, Hans Bos, Fredrick Doolittle, and C. Toussant. 1993. *JOBSTART: Final Report on a Program for School Dropout.* New York: Manpower Demonstration Research Corporation.

Chadwick, L. N., and Gary Solon. 1999. "Intergenerational Income Mobility." Ann Arbor: Economics Department, University of Michigan. Unpublished paper.

Chambers, Daniel N. 1992. "The Racial Housing Price Differential and Racially Transitional Neighborhoods." *Journal of Urban Economics* 32(September): 214–32.

Charles, Kerwin K., and Erik Hurst. In press. "The Transition to Home Ownership and the Black-White Wealth Gap." *Review of Economics and Statistics.*

Chase-Lansdale, P. Lindsay, and R. A. Gordon. 1996. "Economic Hardship and the Development of Five- and Six-Year-Olds: Neighborhood and Regional Perspectives." *Child Development* 67(6): 3338–67.

Chay, Kenneth, and Michael Greenstone. 1999. "The Impact of Air Pollution on Infant Mortality: Evidence from Geographic Variation in Pollution Shocks Induced by a Recession." Working Paper 7442. Cambridge, Mass.: National Bureau of Economic Research (December).

Cherlin, Andrew. 1992. *Marriage, Divorce, Remarriage.* Cambridge, Mass: Harvard University Press.

Cherlin, Andrew, Kathleen Kiernan, and P. Lindsay Chase-Lansdale. 1995. "Parental Divorce in Childhood and Demographic Outcomes in Young Adulthood." *Demography* 32(3): 299–318.

Chernick, Howard, and Therese J. McGuire. 1999. "The States, Welfare Reform, and the Business Cycle." In *Economic Conditions and Welfare Reform,* edited by Sheldon Danziger. Kalamazoo, Mich.: W. E. Upjohn Institute for Employment Research.

Citro, Constance F., and Robert T. Michael. 1995. *Measuring Poverty: A New Approach.* Washington, D.C.: National Academy Press.

Clark, Kenneth. 1982. *Dark Ghetto.* Middletown, Conn.: Wesleyan University Press. (Originally published in 1965).

Clines, Francis X. 2001. "Wariness Leads to Motivation in Baltimore Free-Computer Experiment." *New York Times,* May 24.

Clotfelter, Charles T. 1999. "Public School Segregation." *Land Economics* 75(November): 487–504.

Coleman, James. 1988. "Social Capital in the Creation of Human Capital." *American Journal of Sociology* 94(Suppl.): S95–120.

———. 1990. *Foundations of Social Theory.* Cambridge, Mass.: Harvard University Press.

Coleman, James, and Lee Rainwater. 1978. *Social Standing in America.* New York: Basic Books.

Cooper, Suzanne. 1998. "A Positive Theory of Income Redistribution." *Journal of Economic Growth* 3(2): 171–95.

Corcoran, Mary. 1995. "Rags to Rags: Poverty and Mobility in the United States." *Annual Review of Sociology* 21(4): 237–67.

Corcoran, Mary, and Terry Adams. 1997a. "Race, Sex, and Intergenerational Inequality." In *The Consequences of Growing up Poor,* edited by Jeanne Brooks-Gunn and Greg Duncan. New York: Russell Sage Foundation.

———. 1997b. "Race, Poverty, Welfare, and Neighborhood Influences on Men's Economic Outcomes." Institute for Social Research, University of Michigan, Ann Arbor. Unpublished paper.

Corcoran, Mary, R. Gordon, D. Laren, and Gary Solon. 1992. "The Association Between Men's Economic Status and Their Family and Community Origins." *Journal of Human Resources* 27: 575–601.

Corcoran, Mary, and J. Kunz. 1997. "Do Unmarried Births Among African American Teens Lead to Adult Poverty?" *Social Service Review* 71: 274–87.

———. 1999. "Background Determinants of Male Joblessness." School of Public Policy Studies, University of Michigan, Ann Arbor. Unpublished paper.

Coronado, Julia Lynn, Don Fullerton, and Thomas Glass. 2000. "The Progressivity of Social Security." Working Paper 7520. Cambridge, Mass.: National Bureau of Economic Research.

Coulson, N. Edward. 1991. "Really Useful Tests of the Monocentric Model." *Land Economics* 67(August): 299–307.

Coulton, Claudia, Jill Korbin, Marilyn Su, and Julian Chow. 1995. "Community-Level Factors and Child Maltreatment Rates." *Child Development* 66: 1262–76.

Crane, Jonathan. 1991. "The Epidemic Theory of Ghettos and Neighborhood Effects on Dropping out and Teenage Childbearing." *American Journal of Sociology* 96(5): 1226–59.

Cummings, Jean L., and Denise DiPasquale. 1999. "The Low-Income Housing Tax Credit: An Analysis of the First Ten Years." *Housing Policy Debate* 10(2): 251–307.

Cuomo, Andrew, and Harold Lucas. 2000. *Promise Being Fulfilled: The Transformation of America's Public Housing.* Washington: U.S. Department of Housing and Urban Development (July).

Currie, Janet. 2000. "Food and Nutrition Programs." Paper presented at National Bureau of Economic Research Conference on Means-Tested Transfers, Cambridge, Mass.(May 11–12).

———. In press. "Early Childhood Intervention Programs: What Do We Know?" *Journal of Economic Perspectives.*

Currie, Janet, and Jonathan Gruber. 1995. "Health Insurance Eligibility, Utilization of Medical Care, and Child Health." Working Paper 5052. Cambridge, Mass.: National Bureau of Economic Research (March).

———. 1996. "Health Insurance Eligibility, Utilization of Medical Care, and Child Health." *Quarterly Journal of Economics* 111(2): 431–66.

Currie, Janet, and Duncan Thomas. 1995. "Does Head Start Make a Difference?" *American Economic Review* 83(3): 341–64.

————. 1998. "School Quality and the Longer-term Effects of Head Start." Working Paper 6362. Cambridge, Mass.: National Bureau of Economic Research.

————. 2000. "Does Head Start Help Hispanic Children?" *Journal of Public Economics* 74(2): 235–62.

Cutler, David M., and Edward L. Glaeser. 1997. "Are Ghettos Good or Bad?" *Quarterly Journal of Economics* 112(August): 827–72.

Cutler, David M., Edward L. Glaeser, and Jacob L. Vigdor. 1999. "The Rise and Decline of the American Ghetto." *Journal of Political Economy* 107(June): 455–506.

————. 1991. "Macroeconomic Performance and the Disadvantaged." *Brookings Papers on Economic Activity* 2: 1–61.

Cutler, David M., and Lawrence F. Katz. 1993. "Macroeconomic Performance and the Disadvantaged." *Brookings Papers on Economic Activity* 2: 285–339.

Daly, Mary, and Robert Valletta. 2000. "Inequality and Poverty in the United States: The Effects of Changing Family Behavior and Rising Wage Dispersion." Federal Reserve Board of San Francisco. Unpublished paper.

Danziger, Sandra, Mary Corcoran, Sheldon Danziger, Colleen Heflin, Ariel Kalil, Judith Levine, Daniel Rosen, Kristin Seefeldt, Kristine Siefert, and Richard Tolman. 2000. "Barriers to Employment for Welfare Recipients." In *Prosperity for All? The Economic Boom and African Americans*, edited by Robert Cherry and William M. Rodgers III. New York: Russell Sage.

Danziger, Sheldon. 2000. "Approaching the Limit: Early Lessons from Welfare Reform." Paper presented at the conference Rural Dimensions of Welfare Reform, Joint Center for Poverty Research, Northwestern University and University of Chicago (May).

————. ed. 1999. *Economic Conditions and Welfare Reform.* Kalamazoo, Mich.: W. E. Upjohn Institute for Employment Research.

Danziger, Sheldon, and Peter Gottschalk. 1995. *America Unequal.* New York and Cambridge, Mass.: Russell Sage Foundation and Harvard University Press.

Danziger, Sheldon, Robert Haveman, and Robert Plotnick. 1981. "How Income Transfer Programs Affect Work, Savings, and Income Distribution: A Critical Assessment." *Journal of Economic Literature* 19(3): 975–1028.

Danziger, Sheldon, Colleen M. Heflin, Mary E. Corcoran, and Elizabeth Oltmans. 2001. "Does It Pay to Move from Welfare to Work?" Ann Arbor: Poverty Research and Training Center, University of Michigan (August). Available at: *www.ssw.umich.edu/poverty/pubs.html.*

Danziger, Sheldon H., Gary Sandefur, and Daniel H. Weinberg, eds. 1994. *Confronting Poverty: Prescriptions for Change.* Cambridge, Mass.: Harvard University Press.

Danziger, Sheldon, and Jane Waldfogel, eds. 2000. *Securing the Future: Investing in Children from Birth to College.* New York: Russell Sage Foundation.

Danziger, Sheldon H., and Daniel H. Weinberg, eds. 1986. *Fighting Poverty: What Works and What Doesn't.* Cambridge, Mass.: Harvard University Press.

Danziger, Sheldon, et al. 1999. "Barriers to Work Among Welfare Recipients." *Focus* 20(2): 31–34.

Danzon, Patricia. 1992. "Hidden Overhead Costs: Is Canada's System Really Less Expensive?" *Health Affairs* 11(Spring): 21–43.

Datcher, Linda. 1982. "Effects of Community and Family Background on Achievement." *Review of Economics and Statistics* 64(1): 32–41.

Dechter, Aimée. 1992. "The Effect of Women's Economic Independence on Union Dissolution." Working Paper 92–28. Madison: Center for Demography and Ecology, University of Wisconsin.

Denton, Nancy A. 1994. "Are African Americans Still Hypersegregated?" In *Residential Apartheid: The American Legacy,* edited by Robert D. Bullard, J. Eugene Grigsby III, and Charles Lee. Los Angeles: CAAS Publications.

Dickens, William T. 1999. "Rebuilding Urban Labor Markets: What Community Development Can Accomplish." In *Urban Problems and Community Development,* edited by Ronald F. Ferguson and William T. Dickens. Washington, D.C.: Brookings Institution.

Dickert, Stacy, Scott Houser, and John Karl Scholz. 1995. "The Earned Income Tax Credit and Transfer Programs: A Study of Labor Market and Program Participation." In *Tax Policy and the Economy,* edited by James M. Poterba. Cambridge, Mass.: National Bureau of Economic Research and MIT Press.

Dion, Robin, and LaDonna Pavetti. 2000. *Access to and Participation in Medicaid and the Food Stamp Program: A Review of the Recent Literature.* Washington, D.C.: Mathematica Policy Research.

Donahoe, Debra, and Marta Tienda. 2000. "The Transition from School to Work: Is There a Crisis? What Can Be Done?" in *Securing the Future: Investing in Children from Birth to College,* edited by Sheldon Danziger and Jane Waldfogel. New York: Russell Sage Foundation.

Donelan, Karen, Robert J. Blendon, Craig A. Hill, Catherine Hoffman, Diane Rowland, Martin Frankel, and Drew Altman. 1996. "Whatever Happened to the Health Insurance Crisis in the United States?: Voices from a National Survey." *Journal of the American Medical Association* 276(16): 1346–50.

Downey, Greg, and Alice Shabecoff. 1996. "Can This Business Succeed?: Nonprofits and Community Economic Development." *Strategy Alert: Quarterly Report of the Community Information Exchange* 48(Fall-Winter): 1–16.

Downs, Anthony. 1968. "Alternative Futures for the American Ghetto." *Daedalus* 97(Fall): 1331–78.

Du Bois, W. E. B. 1899. *The Negro in Business.* Atlanta: Atlanta University Press.

Duca, John, and Stuart Rosenthal. 1994. "Borrowing Constraints and Access to Owner-Occupied Housing." *Regional Science and Urban Economics* 24(June): 301–22.

Duncan, Greg. 1991. "The Economic Environment of Childhood." In *Children in Poverty: Child Development and Public Policy,* edited by Aletha Huston. New York: Cambridge University Press.

———. 1994. "Families and Neighbors as Sources of Disadvantage in the Schooling Decisions of White and Black Adolescents." *American Journal of Education* 103(1): 20–53.

Duncan, Greg J., and Jeanne Brooks-Gunn, eds. 1997. *Consequences of Growing up Poor.* New York: Russell Sage Foundation.

Duncan, Greg, Jeanne Brooks-Gunn, and Paula Klebanov. 1994. "Economic Deprivation and Early Childhood Development." *Child Development* 65: 296–318.

Duncan, Greg J., and Willard Rodgers. 1988. "Longitudinal Aspects of Childhood Poverty." *Journal of Marriage and the Family* 50(November): 1007–21.

———. 1991. "Has Children's Poverty Become More Persistent?" *American Sociological Review* 56(August): 538–50.

Duncan, Greg J., and Wei-Jun J. Yeung. 1994. "Extent and Consequences of Welfare Dependence Among America's Children." Ann Arbor: Survey Research Center, University of Michigan. Unpublished paper.

Duncan, Greg J., Wei-Jun J. Yeung, Jeanne Brooks-Gunn, and Judith R. Smith. 1998. "How Much Does Childhood Poverty Affect the Life Chances of Children?" *American Sociological Review* 63(3): 406–23.

Duncombe, William, and John Yinger. 1998. "School Finance Reform: Aid Formulas and Equity Objectives." *National Tax Journal* 51(June): 239–62.

Duneier, Mitchell. 1992. *Slim's Table.* Chicago: University of Chicago Press.

Durlauf, Steven. 1996a. "A Theory of Persistent Income Inequality." *Journal of Economic Growth* 1: 75–93.

———. 1996b. "Neighborhood Feedbacks, Endogenous Stratification, and Income Inequality." In *Dynamic Disequilibrium Modelling,* edited by William Barnett, Giancarlo Gandolfo, and Claud Hillinger. Cambridge: Cambridge University Press.

———. 1996c. "Associational Redistribution: A Defense." *Politics and Society* 24: 391–410.

———. 1997. "Statistical Mechanics Approaches to Socioeconomic Behavior." In *The Economy as a Complex Evolving System II,* edited by W. Brian Arthur, Steven Durlauf, and David Lane. Redwood City, Calif.: Addison-Wesley.

———. 1999a. "The Memberships Theory of Inequality: Ideas and Implications." In *Elites, Minorities, and Economic Growth,* edited by Elise Brezis and Peter Temin. Amsterdam: North-Holland.

———. 1999b. "The Case 'Against' Social Capital." *Focus* 20(2): 1–5.

———. 2000. "A Framework for Modeling Individual Behavior and Social Interactions." University of Wisconsin, Madison. Unpublished paper.

———. 2001. "On the Empirics of Social Capital." University of Wisconsin, Madison. Unpublished paper.

———. In press. "Bowling Alone: A Review Essay." *Journal of Economic Behavior and Organization.*

Edin, Kathryn, and Laura Lein. 1997. *Making Ends Meet: How Single Mothers Survive Welfare and Low-Wage Work.* New York: Russell Sage Foundation.

Eisinger, Peter. 1995. "State Economic Development in the 1990s." *Economic Development Quarterly* 9(May): 146–58.

Ellen, Ingrid Gould, and Margery Austin Turner. 1997. "Does Neighborhood Matter?: Assessing Recent Evidence." *Housing Policy Debate* 8(4): 833–66.

Elliot, Mark, and Elisabeth King. 1999. *Labor Market Leverage: Sectoral Employment Field Report*. Field Report Series. Philadelphia: Public/Private Ventures.

Elliot, Mark, Beth Palubinsky, and Joseph Tierney. 1999. *Overcoming Roadblocks on the Way to Work: Bridges to Work Field Report*. Philadelphia: Public/Private Venture.

Ellwood, David T. 1986. "The Spatial Mismatch Hypothesis: Are There Teenage Jobs Missing in the Ghetto?" In *The Black Youth Employment Crisis*, edited by Richard B. Freeman and Harry J. Holzer. Chicago: University of Chicago Press.

———. 1999. "The Impact of the EITC on Work and Social Policy Reforms on Work, Marriage, and Living Arrangements." John F. Kennedy School of Government, Cambridge, Mass. Unpublished paper (November).

———. 2000. "Antipoverty Policy for Families in the Next Century: From Welfare to Work—and Worries." *Journal of Economic Perspectives* 14(1): 187–98.

Ellwood, Deborah A., and Daniel J. Boyd. 2000. *Changes in State Spending on Social Services Since the Implementation of Welfare Reform*. Albany, N.Y.: Nelson A. Rockefeller Institute of Government.

Ellwood, Marilyn, and Carol Irvin. 2000. *Welfare Leavers and Medicaid Dynamics: Five States in 1995*. Cambridge, Mass.: Mathematica Policy Research.

Ellwood, Marilyn, and Leighton Ku. 1998. *Welfare and Immigration Reforms: Unintended Side Effects for Medicaid*. Washington, D.C.: Urban Institute.

Employee Benefit Research Institute. 1999. "EBRI Issue Brief: Public Attitudes on the U.S. Health Care System: Findings from the 1999 Health Confidence Survey." EBRI, Washington, D.C. (October).

Engberg, John, and Robert Greenbaum. 1999. "State Enterprise Zones and Local Housing Markets." *Journal of Housing Research* [Fannie Mae Foundation, Washington] 10: 163–87.

Ettner, Susan L., Richard G. Frank, and Ronald C. Kessler. 1997. "The Impact of Psychiatric Disorders on Labor Market Outcomes." *Industrial and Labor Relations Review* 51(1): 64–81.

European Community. 2000. *The Social Situation in the European Union, 2000*. Brussels: Unit E.1, Directorate General for Employment and Social Affairs (April).

Eurostat. 1998. "Recommendations of the Task Force on Statistics on Social Exclusion and Poverty." Luxembourg: European Statistical Office. Available at: *europa.eu.int/eurostat.html*.

———. 2000. "Report of the Working Group: Statistics on Income, Social Exclusion, and Poverty." Luxembourg: European Statistical Office. Available at: *europa.eu.int/eurostat.html*.

Evans, Geoffrey. 1993. "Class Conflict and Inequality." In *International Social Attitudes: The Tenth British Social Attitudes Report*, edited by Roger Jowell, Lindsay Brook, and Lizanne Dowds, with Daphne Arendt. Aldershot, Eng.: Dartmouth Publishing.

Evans, William N., Wallace Oates, and Robert M. Schwab. 1992. "Measuring Peer Group Effects: A Study of Teenage Behavior." *Journal of Political Economy* 100(5): 966–91.

Fair Housing Center of Metropolitan Detroit. 1999. *$115,000,000 and Counting*. Detroit: Fair Housing Center of Metropolitan Detroit.

Farkas, George. 1996. *Human Capital or Cultural Capital?: Ethnicity and Poverty Groups in an Urban School District*. New York: Aldine de Gruyter.

Farley, Reynolds, Howard Schuman, Suzanne Bianchi, Diane Colasanto, and Shirley Hatchett. 1978. "'Chocolate City, Vanilla Suburbs': Will the Trend Toward Racially Separate Communities Continue?" *Social Science Research* 7: 319–44.

Feagin, Joe R. 1994. "A House Is Not a Home: White Racism and U.S. Housing Practices." In *Residential Apartheid: The American Legacy*, edited by Robert D. Bullard, J. Eugene Grigsby III, and Charles Lee. Los Angeles: CAAS Publications.

Federal Financial Institutions Examination Council. 2000. "HMDA National Aggregate Reports." Available at: *ffiec.gov/hmda_rpt/agggnat_99.htm.*

Federman, Mary, T. I. Garner, K. Short, W. B. Cutter IV, J. Kiely, D. Levine, D. McGought, and M. McMillen. 1996. "What Does It Mean to Be Poor in America?" *Monthly Labor Review* 119(5): 3–17.

Feldstein, Martin. 1996. "Social Security and Saving: New Time Series Evidence." *National Tax Journal* 49(2): 151–64.

Feldstein, Martin, and Andrew Samwick. 1998. "Two Percent Personal Retirement Accounts: Their Potential Effects on Social Security Tax Rates and National Saving." Working Paper 6540. Cambridge, Mass.: National Bureau of Economic Research.

Ferguson, Ronald F., and William T. Dickens, eds. 1999. *Urban Problems and Community Development*. Washington, D.C.: Brookings Institution.

Ferguson, Ronald, and Helen F. Ladd. 1996. "Additional Evidence on How and Why Money Matters: A Production Function Analysis of Alabama Schools." In *Holding Schools Accountable: Performance-Based Reform in Education*, edited by Helen F. Ladd. Washington, D.C.: Brookings Institution.

Ferguson, Ronald F., and Sara E. Stoutland. 1999. "Reconceiving the Community Development Field." In *Urban Problems and Community Development*, edited by Ronald F. Ferguson and William T. Dickens. Washington, D.C.: Brookings Institution.

Fernandez, Raquel, and Richard Rogerson. 1999. "Sorting and Long-Run Inequality." New York University, New York. Unpublished paper.

Finn, Jeremy, and Charles M. Achilles. 1999. "Tennessee's Class Size Study: Findings, Implications, Misconceptions." *Educational Evaluation and Policy Analysis* 21(2): 97–110.

Fisher, G. M. 1992. "The Development and History of the Poverty Thresholds." *Social Security Bulletin* 55(4, Winter): 3–14.

———. 1996. "Relative or Absolute: New Light on the Behavior of Poverty Lines over Time." *Newsletter of the Government Statistics Section of the American Statistical Association* (Summer): 10–12.

———. 1997. "The Development of the Orshansky Poverty Thresholds and Their Subsequent History as the Official U.S. Poverty Measure." Working Paper. Washington: U.S. Department of Health and Human Services.

Fisher, Peter S., and Alan H. Peters. 1997. "Tax and Spending Incentives and Enterprise Zones." *New England Economic Review* [Federal Reserve Bank of Boston] (March-April): 109–30.

———. 1998. *Industrial Incentives: Competition Among American States and Cities.* Kalamazoo, Mich.: W. E. Upjohn Institute for Employment Research.

Fishkin, James S. 1983. *Justice, Equal Opportunity, and the Family.* New Haven, Conn.: Yale University Press.

Fiss, Owen. 2000. "What Should Be Done for Those Who Have Been Left Behind?" *Boston Review* (September).

Fix, Michael, and Jeffrey S. Passel 1994. *Immigration and Immigrants: Setting the Record Straight.* Washington, D.C.: Urban Institute.

———. 1999. *Trends in Noncitizens' and Citizens' Use of Public Benefits Following Welfare Reform: 1994–1997.* Washington, D.C.: Urban Institute.

Fix, Michael, Jeffrey S. Passel, and Wendy Zimmerman. 1996a. "The Use of SSI and Other Welfare Programs by Immigrants." Testimony before the U.S. House of Representatives, Committee on Ways and Means, May 23, 1966. Washington, D.C.: Urban Institute.

———. 1996b. "Summary of Facts About Immigrants' Use of Welfare." Washington, D.C.: Urban Institute.

Fix, Michael, and Raymond J. Struyk, eds. 1993. *Clear and Convincing Evidence: Measurement of Discrimination in America.* Washington, D.C.: Urban Institute.

Fix, Michael, and Karen Tumlin. 1997. "Welfare Reform and the Devolution of Immigrant Policy." *New Federalism: Issues and Options for States,* Series A, No. A-15 (October). Washington, D.C.: Urban Institute.

Fleming, Michael F., Marlon P. Mundt, Michael T. French, Kristen L. Barry, Linda B. Manwell, and Ellyn A. Stauffacher. 2000. "Benefit-Cost Analysis of Brief Physician Advice with Problem Drinkers in Primary Care Settings." *Medical Care* 38(1): 7–18.

Follain, James R., David Ling, and Gary McGill. 1993. "The Preferential Tax Treatment of Owner-Occupied Housing: Who Really Benefits?" *Housing Policy Debate* 4(1): 1–24.

Fordham, Signithia, and John U. Ogbu. 1986. "Black Students' School Success: Coping with the 'Burden of *Acting White.*'" *Urban Review* 18: 176–206.

Förster, Michael. 1993. "Comparing Poverty in 13 OECD Countries: Traditional and Synthetic Approaches." Studies in Social Policy 10. Paris: Organization for Economic Cooperation and Development (October). Available at: *www.oecd.org.*

———. 2000. "Trends and Driving Factors in Income Distribution and Poverty in the OECD Area." Social Policies Studies Division Paper 42. Paris: Organization for Economic Cooperation and Development (September).

Frank, Richard, and Paul Gertler. 1991. "An Assessment of Measurement Error Bias for Estimating the Impact of Mental Distress on Earnings." *Journal of Human Resources* 26(1): 154–64.

Franks, Peter, Carolyn M. Clancy, and Marthe R. Gold. 1993. "Health Insurance and Mortality: Evidence from a National Cohort." *Journal of the American Medical Association* 270(6): 737–41.

Freedman, Stephen, Jean Tansey Knab, Lisa A. Gennetian, and David Navarro.

2000. *The Los Angeles Jobs-First GAIN Evaluation.* New York: Manpower Demonstration Research Corporation.

Freeman, Howard E., Linda H. Aiken, Robert J. Blendon, and Christopher R. Covey. 1990. "Uninsured Working-Age Adults: Characteristics and Consequences." *Health Services Research* 24(February): 811–24.

Freeman, Richard. 1999. "The New Inequality in the U.S." In *Growing Apart,* edited by Albert Fishlow and Karen Parker. New York: Council on Foreign Relations.

———. 2001. "Does the Booming Economy Help Explain the Fall in Crime?" *Perspectives on Crime and Justice: 1999–2000 Lecture Series,* vol. 4, NCJ 184245 (March). Washington, D.C.: National Institute of Justice.

Freeman, Richard, and William Rodgers. 2000. "Area Economic Conditions and the Labor Market Outcomes of Young Men in the 1990s Expansion." In *Prosperity for All? The Economic Boom and African Americans,* edited by Robert Cherry and William M. Rodgers. New York: Russell Sage Foundation.

Freeman, Richard, and Jane Waldfogel. 1997. "Dunning Delinquent Dads: The Effects of Child Support Enforcement Policy on Child Support Receipt by Never-Married Women." Working Paper 6664. Cambridge, Mass.: National Bureau of Economic Research.

Friedlander, Daniel, and Gary Burtless. 1995. *Five Years After: The Long-term Effects of Welfare-to-Work Programs.* New York: Russell Sage Foundation.

Frongillo, Edward A., Barbara S. Rauschenbach, Christine M. Olson, Anne Kendall, and Ana G. Colmenares. 1997. "Questionnaire-Based Measures Are Valid for the Identification of Rural Households with Hunger and Food Insecurity." *Journal of Nutrition* 127: 699–705.

Fullerton, Howard N. 1999. "Labor Force Participation: Seventy-five Years of Change, 1950–1998 and 1998–2025." *Monthly Labor Review* (December): 3–12.

Galster, George C. 1990a. "Federal Fair Housing Policy: The Great Misapprehension." In *Building Foundations,* edited by Denise DiPasquale and Langley C. Keyes. Philadelphia: University of Pennsylvania Press.

———. 1990b. "Racial Steering by Real Estate Agents: Mechanisms and Motives." *Review of Black Political Economy* 19(Summer): 39–63.

———. 1991. "Housing Discrimination and Urban Poverty of African Americans." *Journal of Housing Research* 2(2): 87–122.

———. 1998. *An Econometric Model of the Urban Opportunity Structure: Cumulative Causation Among City Markets, Social Problems, and Underserved Areas.* Research Report. Washington: Fannie Mae Foundation.

Garbarino, James, and Kathleen Kostelny. 1992. "Child Maltreatment as a Community Problem." *Child Abuse and Neglect* 16: 455–64.

Garbarino, James, and Deborah Sherman. 1980. "High-Risk Neighborhoods and High-Risk Families: The Human Ecology of Child Maltreatment." *Child Development* 51: 188–98.

Garfinkel, Irwin, and Robert Haveman. 1977. *Earnings Capacity, Poverty, and Inequality.* New York: Academic Press.

Garfinkel, Irwin, and Sara McLanahan. 2000. "Fragile Families and Child Well-being: A Survey of New Parents." *Focus* 21(1): 9–11.

Garfinkel, Irwin, Daniel R. Meyer, and Judith Seltzer, eds. 1998. *Fathers Under Fire: The Revolution in Child Support Enforcement.* New York: Russell Sage Foundation.

Geldhof, Corine. 2000. "The Workforce Investment Act." *Alaska Economic Trends* (March). Available at: *www.ajcn.state.ak.us/wia0300.html.*

Geronimus, Arlene. 1997. "Teenage Childbearing and Personal Responsibility: An Alternative View." *Political Science Quarterly* 112(3): 405–30.

Geronimus, Arline, and Sanders Korenman. 1992. "The Socioeconomic Consequences of Teen Childbearing Reconsidered." *Quarterly Journal of Economics* 107(4): 1187–1214.

Geronimus, Arline T., Sanders Korenman, and M. H. M. M. Hillemeier. 1994. "Young Maternal Age Adversely Affect Child Development." *Population and Development Review* 20(3): 585–602.

Giloth, Robert P., ed. 1998. *Jobs and Economic Development: Strategies and Practices.* Thousand Oaks, Calif.: Sage Publications.

Ginther, Donna, Robert Haveman, and Barbara Wolfe. 2000. "Neighborhood Attributes as Determinants of Children's Outcomes: How Robust Are the Relationships?" University of Wisconsin, Madison. Unpublished paper.

Gittell, Ross, and J. Phillip Thompson. 1999. "Inner-City Business Development and Entrepreneurship: New Frontiers for Policy and Research." In *Urban Problems and Community Development,* edited by Ronald F. Ferguson and William T. Dickens. Washington, D.C.: Brookings Institution.

Glaeser, Edward L. 2000a. "Places, People, Policies: An Agenda for America's Urban Poor." *Harvard Magazine* (November-December): 34–35.

———. 2000b. "Demand for Density?: Functions of the City in the Twenty-first Century." *Brookings Review* 18(Summer): 12–15.

Glaeser, Edward L., Matthew E. Kahn, and Jordan Rappaport. 2000. "Why Do the Poor Live in Cities?" Working Paper 7636. Cambridge, Mass.: National Bureau of Economic Research.

Glaeser, Edward, Bruce Sacerdote, and José Scheinkman. 1996. "Crime and Social Interactions." *Quarterly Journal of Economics* 111: 507–48.

Goering, J. 1996. "Expanding Housing Choices for HUD-Assisted Families: First Biennial Report on the Moving To Opportunity for Fair Housing Demonstration." Washington: Office of Policy Development and Research, U.S. Department of Housing and Urban Development.

Goldberger, Arthur S. 1979. "Heritability." *Econometrica* 46(184): 327–47.

Gomby, Deanna S. 1999. "Home Visiting: Recent Program Evaluations—Analysis and Recommendations." *The Future of Children* 9(1): 4–26.

Goodman, Allen C. 1988. "An Econometric Model of Housing Price, Permanent Income, Tenure Choice, and Housing Demand." *Journal of Urban Economics* 23(May): 327–53.

Gottschalk, Peter. 1992. "The Intergenerational Transmission of Welfare Participation: Facts and Possible Causes." *Journal of Policy Analysis and Management* 11: 254–72.

———. 1997. "Inequality, Income Growth, and Mobility: The Basic Facts." *Journal of Economic Perspectives* 11(2): 21–50.

Gottschalk, Peter, and Sheldon Danziger. 1993. "Family Structure, Family Size, and Family Income: Accounting for Changes in the Economic Well-being of Children, 1968–1986." In *Uneven Tides: Rising Inequality in America*, edited by Sheldon Danziger and Peter Gottschalk. New York: Russell Sage Foundation.

———. 1998. "Family Income Mobility—How Much Is There, and Has It Changed?" In *The Inequality Paradox: Growth of Income Disparity*, edited by James A. Auerbach and Richard S. Belous. Washington, D.C.: National Policy Association.

Gottschalk, Peter, Sara McLanahan, and Gary D. Sandefur. 1994. "The Dynamics and Intergenerational Transmission of Poverty and Welfare Participation." In *Confronting Poverty: Prescriptions for Change*, edited by Sheldon H. Danziger, Gary D. Sandefur, and Daniel H. Weinberg. Cambridge, Mass.: Harvard University Press.

Gottschalk, Peter, and Timothy M. Smeeding. 1997. "Cross-National Comparisons of Earnings and Income Inequality." *Journal of Economic Literature* 35(2): 633–87.

———. 2000. "Empirical Evidence on Income Inequality in Industrialized Countries." In *Handbook of Income Distribution*, edited by Anthony B. Atkinson and François Bourguignon. New York: Elsevier-North-Holland.

Gould, Eric, David B. Mustard, and Bruce A. Weinberg. 2000. "Crime Rates and Local Labor Market Opportunities in the United States: 1979–1997. Working paper.

Granovetter, Mark. 1974. *Getting a Job: A Study of Contacts and Careers*. Cambridge, Mass.: Harvard University Press.

Granovetter, Mark, and R. Soong. 1988. "Threshold Models of Diversity: Chinese Restaurants, Residential Segregation, and the Spiral of Silence." In *Sociological Methodology*, vol. 18, edited by C. Clogg. Cambridge: Basil Blackwell.

Green, Richard K., and Michele J. White. 1997. "Measuring the Benefits of Homeowning: Effects on Children." *Journal of Urban Economics* 41(May): 441–61.

Green, Roy E. 1991. *Enterprise Zones: New Directions in Economic Development*. Newbury Park, Calif.: Sage Publications.

Greenbaum, Robert T., and John B. Engberg. 1999. "The Impact of State Enterprise Zones on Urban Manufacturing Establishments." H. John Heinz III School of Public Policy and Management, Carnegie Mellon University, Pittsburgh. Unpublished paper.

Greenberg, Mark, and Steve Savner. 1999. *The Final TANF Regulations: A Preliminary Analysis*. Washington, D.C.: Center for Law and Social Policy.

Greenstein, Theodore N. 1995. "Gender Ideology, Marital Disruption, and the Employment of Married Women." *Journal of Marriage and the Family* 52: 657–76.

Grissmer, David, Ann Flanagan, Jennifer Kawata, and Stephanie Williamson. 2000. *Improving Student Achievement: What State NAEP Test Scores Tell Us*. MR-924. Santa Monica, Calif.: RAND Corporation.

Grogan, Paul S., and Tony Proscio. 2000. *Comeback Cities: A Blueprint for Urban Neighborhood Revival*. Boulder, Colo.: Westview Press.

Grubb, W. Norton. 1996. *Learning to Work: The Case for Reintegrating Job Training and Education*. New York: Russell Sage Foundation.

Gruber, Jonathan. 1997. "The Consumption Smoothing Benefits of Unemployment Insurance." *American Economic Review* 87(1): 192–205.

———. 2000. "Medicaid." Paper presented at National Bureau of Economic Research Conference on Means-Tested Transfers, Cambridge, Mass. (May 11–12).

Gruber, Jonathan, John Kim, and Dina Mayzlin. 1999. "Physician Fees and Procedure Intensity: The Case of Cesarean Delivery." *Journal of Health Economics* 18(4): 473–90.

Gruber, Jonathan, and Aaron Yelowitz. 1999. "Public Health Insurance and Private Saving." *Journal of Political Economy* 107(6): 1249–74.

Gueron, Judith, and Edward Pauly. 1991. *From Welfare to Work*. New York: Russell Sage Foundation.

Gundersen, Craig, and Jonathan Gruber. In press. "The Dynamics of Food Insufficiency." *Papers and Proceedings of the Second Food Security Measurement and Research Conferences.*

Gustafson, Cynthia K., and Phillip B. Levine. 1998. "Less-Skilled Workers, Welfare Reform, and the Unemployment Insurance System." Working Paper 6489. Cambridge, Mass.: National Bureau of Economic Research.

Gustman, Alan L., and Thomas L. Steinmeier. 2000. "How Effective Is Redistribution Under the Social Security Benefit Formula?" Working Paper 7597. Cambridge, Mass.: National Bureau of Economic Research.

Gyourko, Joseph, and Peter Linneman. 1997. "The Changing Influences of Education, Income, Family Structure, and Race on Homeownership by Age over Time." *Journal of Housing Research* 8(1): 1–26.

Gyourko, Joseph, Peter Linneman, and Susan Wachter. 1999. "Analyzing the Relationships Among Race, Wealth, and Home Ownership in America." *Journal of Housing Economics* 8(2): 63–89.

Hadley, Jack, Earl P. Steinberg, and Judith Feder. 1991. "Comparison of Uninsured and Privately Insured Hospital Patients: Condition on Admission, Resource Use, and Outcome." *Journal of the American Medical Association* 265(3): 374–79.

Hagenaars, Aldi, Klaas de Vos, and Asghar Zaidi. 1994. "Patterns of Poverty in Europe." Final report to the European Statistical Office. Luxembourg: Eurostat (September).

Hahn, Andrew, Tom Leavitt, and Paul Aaron. 1994. *Evaluation of the Quantum Opportunities Program (QOP): Did the Program Work?: A Report on the Postsecondary Outcomes and Cost-effectiveness of the QOP Program (1989–1993)*. Waltham, Mass.: Brandeis University.

Halpern, Robert. 1995. *Rebuilding the Inner City: A History of Neighborhood Initiatives to Address Poverty in the United States*. New York: Columbia University Press.

Hamilton, Gayle, Stephen Freedman, and Sharon M. McGroder. 2000. *Do Mandatory Welfare-to-Work Programs Affect the Well-being of Children?* New York: Manpower Demonstration Research Corporation.

Hampton, Robert, and Eli Newberger. 1985. "Child Abuse Incidence and Reporting by Hospitals: Significance of Severity, Class, and Race." *American Journal of Public Health* 75: 56–60.

Hanson, Thomas L., Sara McLanahan, and Elizabeth Thomson. 1997. "Economic Resources, Parental Practices, and Children's Well-being." In *Consequences of Growing up Poor,* edited by Greg J. Duncan and Jeanne Brooks-Gunn. New York: Russell Sage Foundation.

Hanushek, Eric A. 1986. "The Economics of Schooling: Production and Efficiency in Public Schools." *Journal of Economic Literature* 24(3): 1141–77.

———. 1989. "The Impact of Differential Expenditures on School Performance." *Educational Researcher* 18(4): 45–51.

———. 1994. *Making Schools Work: Improving Performance and Controlling Costs.* Washington, D.C.: Brookings Institution.

———. 1996a. "Measuring Investment in Education." *Journal of Economic Perspectives* 10(4): 9–30.

———. 1996b. "A More Complete Picture of School Resource Policies." *Review of Educational Research* 66: 397–409.

———. 1996c. "School Resources and Student Performance." In *Does Money Matter?: The Effect of School Resources on Student Achievement and Adult Success,* edited by Gary Burtless. Washington: Brookings Institution.

———. 1997. "Assessing the Effects of School Resources on Student Performance: An Update." *Educational Evaluation and Policy Analysis* 19(2): 141–64.

Harris, David R. 1999. "'Property Values Drop When Blacks Move in, Because . . . ': Racial and Socioeconomic Determinants of Neighborhood Desirability." *American Sociological Review* 64(June): 461–79.

Harris Poll. 1999. Harris poll 65 (November 5).

Harrison, Bennett 1968. "Economic Development Planning for American Urban Slums." *International Development Review* (March): 23–29.

———. 1974. "Ghetto Economic Development: A Survey." *Journal of Economic Literature* 12(1): 1–37.

Harrison, Bennett, and Marcus Weiss. 1998. *Workforce Development Networks: Community-Based Organizations and Regional Alliances.* Newbury Park, Calif.: Sage Publications.

Harrison, Bennett, Marcus Weiss, and Jon Gant. 1995. *Building Bridges: CDC's and the World of Employment Training.* New York: Ford Foundation.

Hatry, Harry P., Mark Fall, Thomas O. Singer, and Blaine Liner. 1990. *Monitoring the Outcomes of Economic Development Programs.* Washington: Urban Institute Press.

Hauser, Richard. 1970. "Context and Consex: A Cautionary Tale." *American Journal of Sociology* 75(4): 645–64.

———. 1998. "Intergenerational Mobility in the United States: Measures, Differentials, and Trends." Center for Demography and Ecology, University of Wisconsin, Madison. Unpublished paper.

Haveman, Robert H., ed. 1977. *A Decade of Federal Antipoverty Programs: Achievements, Failures, and Lessons.* New York: Academic Press.

———. 2000, "Poverty and the Distribution of Economic Well-being Since the 1960s." In *Economic Events, Ideas, and Policies: The 1960s and After,* edited by George L. Perry and James Tobin. Washington, D.C.: Brookings Institution.

Haveman, Robert, and A. Bershadker. 2001. "The 'Inability to Be Self-reliant' as an Indicator of Poverty: Trends for the U.S., 1975–1997." Department of Economics, University of Wisconsin, Madison. Unpublished paper.

Haveman, Robert, and M. Mullikin. 1999. "Alternatives to the Official Poverty Measure." University of Wisconsin, Madison. Unpublished paper (November).

Haveman, Robert, and Johnathan Schwabish. 1999. "Economic Growth and Poverty: A Return to Normalcy?" *Focus* 20(2): 1–7.

———. 2000. "Has Macroeconomic Performance Regained Its Antipoverty Bite?" *Contemporary Economic Policy* 18(4): 415–27.

Haveman, Robert, and Barbara Wolfe. 1994. *Succeeding Generations: On the Effect of Investments in Children.* New York: Russell Sage Foundation.

———. 1995. "The Determinants of Children's Attainments: A Review of Methods and Findings." *Journal of Economic Literature* 33(4): 1829–78.

———. 1999. "Review of the Research on Genetic Causes of Inequality." Institute for Research on Poverty, University of Wisconsin, Madison. Unpublished paper.

———. 2000. "The Economics of Disability and Disability Policy." In *Handbook of Health Economics,* vol. 1A, edited by Anthony J. Culyer and Joseph P. Newhouse. Amsterdam: North-Holland.

Haveman, Robert, and Edward N. Wolff. 2001. "Who Are the Asset Poor?: Levels, Trends, and Composition, 1983–1998." Unpublished working paper. Madison, Wisc.: Department of Economics, University of Wisconsin.

Haveman, Robert, Edward N. Wolff, and E. Peterson. 1996. "Children of Early Childbearers as Young Adults." In *Kids Having Kids: Economic Costs and Social Consequences of Teen Pregnancy,* edited by Rebecca Maynard. Washington, D.C.: Urban Institute.

Health Care Financing Administration, Office of the Actuary. 2000a. "Brief Summaries of Medicare and Medicaid" (July). Washington: Health Care Financing Administration.

———. 2000b. "National Health Expenditures" (January). Washington: Health Care Financing Administration.

Health Policy Tracking Service. 1999. "Q&A on Immigrant Benefits." Available at: *stateserv.hpts.org/hpts2000.*

Hebel, J. Richard, Patricia Nowicki, and Mary Sexton. 1985. "The Effect of an Antismoking Intervention During Pregnancy: An Assessment of Interaction with Maternal Characteristics." *American Journal of Epidemiology* 122: 135–48.

Heckman, James, Anne Layne-Farrar, and Petra Todd. 1996. "Does Measured School Quality Really Matter?: An Examination of the Earnings-Quality Relationship." In *Does Money Matter?: The Effect of School Resources on Student Achievement and Adult Success,* edited by Gary Burtless. Washington, D.C.: Brookings Institution.

Heckman, James J., and Lance Lochner. 2000. "Rethinking Education and Training Policy: Understanding the Sources of Skill Formation in a Modern Economy." In *Securing the Future: Investing in Children from Birth to College,* edited by Sheldon Danziger and Jane Waldfogel. New York: Russell Sage Foundation.

Hedges, Larry V., Richard D. Laine, and Rob Greenwald. 1994. "Does Money Matter?: A Meta-analysis of Studies of the Effects of Differential School Inputs on Student Outcomes." *Education Researcher* 23(3): 5–14.

Henderson, J. V., P. Mieszkowski, and Y. Sauvageau. 1978. "Peer Group Effects and Education Production Functions." *Journal of Public Economics* 10: 97–106.

Hernandez, Donald J. 1993. *America's Children*. New York: Russell Sage Foundation.

Herrnstein, Richard, and Charles Murray. 1994. *The Bell Curve: Intelligence and Class Structure in American Life*. New York: Free Press.

Hershey, Alan M., and LaDonna Pavetti. 1997. "Turning Job Finders into Job Keepers." *The Future of Children: Welfare to Work* 1: 74–86.

Hershey, Alan, and L. Rosemberg. 1994. "The Study of the Replication of the CET Job Training Model." Report for the U.S. Department of Labor. Cambridge, Mass.: Mathematica Policy Research (June 27).

Hills, John. 1999. "Social Exclusion in the UK: The State of Current Research." Paper presented at the Statistics Users Conference on Social Exclusion Statistics, London (November).

———. In press. "Taxation for the Enabling State." In *Making Public Policy for the Twenty-first Century*, edited by N. Fraser and John Hills. Bristol, Eng.: Policy Press.

Hills, John, and Orsolya Lelkes. 1999. "Social Security, Selective Universalism, and Patchwork Redistribution." In *British Social Attitudes: Fifteenth Report*, edited by Richard Jowell et al. Aldershot, Eng.: Ashgate.

HM Treasury. 2000. *Budget 2000: Prudent for a Purpose*. London: Stationery Office.

Hoffman, Saul D., E. Michael Foster, and Frank Furstenberg Jr. 1993. "Reevaluating the Costs of Teenage Childbearing." *Demography* 30(2): 1–13.

Hollister, Robinson G. 1990. *The Minority Female Single Parent Demonstration: New Evidence About Effective Training Strategies*. New York: Rockefeller Foundation.

Holzer, Harry J. 1996. *What Employers Want: Job Prospects for Less-Educated Workers*. New York: Russell Sage Foundation.

Holzer, Harry J., and Keith R. Ihlanfeldt. 1996. "Spatial Factors and the Employment of Blacks at the Firm Level." *New England Economic Review* [Federal Reserve Bank of Boston] (May-June, special issue).

———. 1998. "Customer Discrimination and Employment Outcomes for Minority Workers." *Quarterly Journal of Economics* 106(August): 835–67.

Hotz, J., S. McElroy, and S. Sanders. 1996. "The Costs and Consequences of Teenage Childbearing for Mothers." *Chicago Policy Review* (Fall): 54–94.

Hotz, Joseph, and John Karl Scholz. 2000. "The Earned Income Tax Credit." Paper presented at National Bureau of Economic Research Conference on Means-Tested Transfers, Cambridge, Mass.(May 11–12).

———. 2001. "Measuring Employment and Income Outcomes for Low-Income Populations with Administrative and Survey Data." In *Evaluating Welfare Reform in an Era of Transition*, edited by Robert Moffitt and Michele Ver Ploeg. Washington, D.C.: National Academy Press.

Hubbard, R. Glenn, Jonathan Skinner, and Steven P. Zeldes. 1995. "Precautionary Saving and Social Insurance." *Journal of Political Economy* 103(2): 360–99.

Hurst, Erik, Ming Ching Luoh, and Frank P. Stafford. 1998. "The Wealth Dynamics of American Families, 1984–1994." *Brookings Papers on Economic Activity* 1: 267–338.

Iceland, John, and Joshua Masnick Kim. 2000. "Poverty Among Working Families: New Insights from an Improved Poverty Measure." Paper presented at the annual meeting of the Population Association of America, Los Angeles(March 23–25).

Ihlanfeldt, Keith R. 1993. "Intra-Urban Job Accessibility and Hispanic Youth Unemployment Rates." *Journal of Urban Economics* 33(March): 254–71.

———. 1999. "The Geography of Economic and Social Opportunity in Metropolitan Areas." In *Governance and Opportunity in Metropolitan America,* edited by Alan Altshuler, William Morrill, Harold Wolman, and Faith Mitchell. Washington, D.C.: National Academy Press.

Ihlanfeldt, Keith R., and David L. Sjoquist. 1990. "Job Accessibility and Racial Differences in Youth Unemployment Rates." *American Economic Review* 80(March): 267–76.

———. 1998. "The Spatial Mismatch Hypothesis: A Review of Recent Studies and Their Implications for Welfare Reform." *Housing Policy Debate* 9(4): 849–92.

Indiana Department of Commerce. 1992. "Indiana Enterprise Zone: A Program Evaluation for 1989 and 1990." Indianapolis: Indiana Department of Commerce (October).

INTERFACE. 1985. "Crossing the Hudson: A Survey of New York Manufacturers Who Have Moved to New Jersey." New York: INTERFACE.

Jackson, Kenneth T. 1985. *Crabgrass Frontier: The Suburbanization of America.* New York: Oxford University Press.

Jäntti, Marcus, and Sheldon Danziger. 2000. "Income Poverty in Advanced Countries." In *Handbook of Income Distribution,* edited by Anthony B. Atkinson and François Bourguignon. New York: Elsevier-North-Holland.

Jargowsky, Paul A. 1997. *Poverty and Place: Ghettos, Barrios, and the American City.* New York: Russell Sage Foundation.

Jencks, Christopher, and S. Mayer. 1990. "The Social Consequences of Growing up in a Poor Neighborhood." In *Inner-City Poverty in the United States,* edited by Laurence Lynn and Michael McGreary. Washington, D.C.: National Academy Press.

———. 1996. "Do Official Poverty Rates Provide Useful Information About Trends in Children's Economic Welfare?" Harris Graduate School of Public Policy, University of Chicago. Unpublished paper.

Johnson, D., and Timothy Smeeding. 1997. "Measuring the Trends in Inequality of Individuals and Families: Income and Consumption." Washington: U.S. Bureau of Labor Statistics (June).

Jorenby, Douglas E., Scott J. Leischow, Mitchell A. Nides, Stephen I. Rennard, Andrew Johnston, Arlene R. Hughes, Stevens S. Smith, Myra L. Muramoto, David M. Daughton, Kimberli Dean, Michael C. Fiore, and Timothy B. Baker. 1999. "A Controlled Trial of Sustained-Release Bupropion, a Nicotine Patch, or Both for Smoking Cessation." *New England Journal of Medicine* 340(9): 685–91.

Kahn, James A. 1988. "Social Security, Liquidity, and Early Retirement." *Journal of Public Economics* 35(1): 97–117.

Kain, John F. 1968. "Housing Segregation, Negro Employment, and Metropolitan Decentralization." *Quarterly Journal of Economics* 82(2): 175–97.

———. 1992. "The Spatial Mismatch Hypothesis: Three Decades Later." *Housing Policy Debate* 3(2): 371–460.

Kain, John F., and Joseph J. Persky. 1969. "Alternatives to the Gilded Ghetto." *Public Interest* 14(Winter): 74–87.

Kaiser Family Foundation. 1999. *1999 Annual Employer Health Benefits Survey.* Available at *www.kff.org/content/1999/1538.*

———. 2001. *CHIP Program Enrollment: June 2000.* Available at: *www.kff.org/content/2001/2224/2224.pdf.*

Kamerman, Sheila B., and Alfred Kahn. 1995. *Starting Right: How America Neglects Its Youngest Children and What We Can Do About It.* New York: Oxford University Press.

Kaplan, April. 1998. "Transportation: The Essential Need to Address the 'To' in Welfare-to-Work." *Welfare Information Network Issue Notes* 2(10).

Kaplan, Thomas, and Ingrid Rothe. 1999. "New Hope and W-2: Common Challenges, Different Responses." *Focus* 20(2): 44–50.

Karoly, Lynn, Peter W. Greenwood, Susan S. Everingham, Jill Hoube, Rebecca Kilburn, C. Peter Rydell, Matthew Sanders, and Jim Chiesa. 1998. *Investing in Our Children: What We Know and Don't Know About the Costs and Benefits of Early Childhood Interventions.* MR-898. Santa Monica, Calif.: RAND Corporation.

Kasarda, John D. 1993. "Inner-City Poverty and Neighborhood Distress: 1970 to 1990." *Housing Policy Debate* 4(3): 253–302.

———. 1995. "Industrial Restructuring and the Changing Location of Jobs." In *State of the Union: America in the 1990s,* vol. 1, *Economic Trends,* edited by Reynolds Farley. New York: Russell Sage Foundation.

Kasarda, John D., and Kwok-fai Ting. 1996. "Joblessness and Poverty in America's Central Cities: Causes and Policy Prescriptions." *Housing Policy Debate* 7(2): 387–419.

Kasinitz, Philip, and Jan Rosenberg. 1996. "Missing the Connection: Social Isolation and Employment on the Brooklyn Waterfront." *Social Problems* 43: 180–96.

Kasprow, Wesley J., and Robert A. Rosenheck. 2000. "Mortality Among Homeless and Domiciled Veterans with Mental Disorders." *Journal of Nervous and Mental Disease* 188(3): 141–47.

Katz, Lawrence F., Jeffrey R. Kling, and Jeffrey B. Liebman. 2000. "Moving To Opportunity in Boston: Early Impacts of a Randomized Mobility Experiment." *Quarterly Journal of Economics* 116: 607–54.

Katz, Michael. 1996. *In the Shadow of the Poorhouse: A Social History of Welfare in America.* New York: Basic Books.

Keil, Julien E., Susan E. Sutherland, Rebecca Knapp, and Herman A. Tyroler. 1992. "Does Equal Socioeconomic Status in Black and White Men Mean Equal Risk of Mortality?" *American Journal of Public Health* 82(8): 1133–36.

Kemple, James J., and Jason C. Snipes. 2000. *Career Academies: Impacts on Students' Engagement and Performance in High School.* New York: Manpower Demonstration Research Corporation.

Kenkel, Donald S. 1991. "Health Behavior, Health Knowledge, and Schooling." *Journal of Political Economy* 99(2): 287–305.

———. 2000. "The Cost of Healthy People." Department of Policy Analysis and Management, Cornell University, Ithaca, N.Y. Unpublished paper.

Kenworthy, Lane. 1998. "Do Social-Welfare Policies Reduce Poverty?: A Cross-National Assessment." Luxembourg Income Study Working Paper 188. Syracuse, N.Y.: Center for Policy Research, Maxwell School, Syracuse University (September). Available at: *www.lis.ceps.lu.*

Kerachsky, S. 1994. *The Minority Female Single Parent Demonstration: Making a Difference—Does an Integrated Program Model Promote More Jobs and Higher Pay?* Washington, D.C.: Mathematica Policy Research.

Kiel, Katherine A., and Jeffrey E. Zabel. 1996. "House Price Differentials in U.S. Cities: Household and Neighborhood Racial Effects." *Journal of Housing Economics* 5(June): 143–65.

Kim, Hwanjoon. 2000. "Anti-Poverty Effectiveness of Taxes and Income Transfers in Welfare States." Luxembourg Income Study Working Paper 228. Syracuse, N.Y.: Center for Policy Research, Maxwell School, Syracuse University (March). Available at: *www.lis.ceps.lu.*

Kindig, David, Harmoz Movassaghi, Nancy Cross Dunham, Daniel I. Zwick, and Charles M. Taylor. 1987. "Trends in Physician Availability in Ten Urban Areas from 1963 to 1980." *Inquiry* 24(2): 136–46.

Kinzer, Robert, and Edward Sagarin. 1971. "Roots of the Integrationist-Separatist Dilemma." In *Black Business Enterprise,* edited by Ronald W. Bailey. New York: Basic Books.

Kirschenman, Joleen, and Kathyrn M. Neckerman. 1991. "'We'd Love to Hire Them, but . . . ': The Meaning of Race for Employers." In *The Urban Underclass,* edited by Christopher Jencks and Paul E. Peterson. Washington, D.C.: Brookings Institution.

Klerman, Jacob A., and Lynn A. Karoly. 1995. *The Transition to Stable Employment: The Experience of U.S. Youth in Their Early Labor Market Career.* MR-564. Santa Monica, Calif.: RAND Corporation.

Knox, Virginia, Cynthia Miller, and Lisa A. Gennetian. 2000. *Reforming Welfare and Rewarding Work: A Summary of the Final Report on the Minnesota Family Investment Program.* New York: Manpower Demonstration Research Corporation. Available at: *www.mdrc.org/Reports2000/MFIP/MFIPSummary.htm.*

Kozol, Jonathan. 1991. *Savage Inequalities.* New York: Crown.

Kremer, Michael, and Eric Maskin. 1996. "Segregation by Skill and the Rise in Inequality." Massachusetts Institute of Technology, Cambridge, Mass. Unpublished paper.

Krueger, Alan B. 1999a. "An Economist's View of Class Size Research." Unpublished paper. Princeton University.

———. 1999b. "Experimental Estimates of Education Production Functions." *Quarterly Journal of Economics* 114(2): 497–532.

Ku, Leighton, and B. Bruen. 1999. *The Continuing Decline in Medicaid Coverage: Assessing the New Federalism.* Brief A-37. Washington, D.C.: Urban Institute.

Ladd, Helen F. 1994. "Spatially Targeted Economic Development Strategies." *Cityscape: A Journal of Policy Development and Research* 1: 194–218. August.

———. 1998. "Evidence on Discrimination in Credit Markets." *Journal of Economic Perspectives* 12(Spring): 41–62.

LaLonde, Robert J. 1995. "The Promise of Public Sector–Sponsored Training Programs." *Journal of Economic Perspectives* 9(2): 149–68.

Lampmann, Robert J. 1959. *The Low-Income Population and Economic Growth.* Washington: U.S. Government Printing Office.

Lave, Judith R., Christopher R. Keane, Chyongchiou J. Lin, Edmund M. Ricci, Gabriele Amersbach, and Charles P. LaVallee. 1999. "Impact of a Children's Health Insurance Program on Newly Enrolled Children." *Journal of the American Medical Association* 279(22): 1820–25.

Lazar, Irving, and Richard Darlington. 1982. "Lasting Effects of Early Education: A Report from the Consortium for Longitudinal Studies." *Monographs of the Society for Research in Child Development* 47(2–4), serial no. 195.

Leary, Warren E. 1997. "Cockroaches Cited as Big Cause of Asthma." *New York Times,* May 8.

Leigh, Duane E. 2000. "Training Programs for Dislocated Workers." In *Improving the Odds: Increasing the Effectiveness of Publicly Funded Training,* edited by Burt S. Barnow and Christopher T. King. Washington, D.C.: Urban Institute.

Lemann, Nicholas. 1994. "The Myth of Community Development." *New York Times Magazine* (January 9): 26–31.

Lenhart, Amanda. 2000. "Who's Not Online: 57 Percent of Those Without Internet Access Say They Do Not Plan to Log On." Pew Internet and American Life Project Working Paper. Washington, D.C.: Pew Internet and American Life Project Working Paper.

Leonard, Jonathan S. 1987. "The Interaction of Residential Segregation and Employment Discrimination." *Journal of Urban Economics* 21(May): 323–46.

Lerman, Robert. 1996. The Impact of the Changing U.S. Family Structure on Child Poverty and Income Inequality. *Economica* 63(supp.): S119–40.

Lerman, Robert, and Elaine Sorensen. 2000. "Child Support: Interactions Between Private and Public Transfers." Paper presented at National Bureau of Economic Research Conference on Means-Tested Transfers, Cambridge, Mass.(May 11–12).

Levit, Katherine, Cathy Cowan, Helen Lazenby, Arthur Sensenig, Patricia McDonnell, Jean Stiller, and Anne Martin. 2000. "Health Spending in 1998: Signals of Change." *Health Affairs* 19(1): 124–32.

Levy, Frank, and Richard M. Murnane. 1992. "U.S. Earnings Levels and Earnings Inequality: A Review of the Trends and Proposed Explanations." *Journal of Economic Literature* 30(September): 1333–81.

Lewis, Oscar. 1966. *La Vida: A Puerto Rican Family in the Culture of Poverty.* New York: Random House.

Liebow, Elliott. 1967. *Tally's Corner.* Boston: Little, Brown.

Lindsey, Duncan. 1994. *The Welfare of Children.* New York: Oxford University Press.

Link, Bruce G., Ezra Susser, Ann Stueve, Jo Phalen, Robert E. Moore, and Elmer Struening. 1994. "Lifetime and Five-Year Prevalence of Homelessness in the United States." *American Journal of Public Health* 84(12): 1907–12.

Linneman, Peter, Isaac F. Megbolugbe, Susan M. Wachter, and Man Cho. 1997. "Do Borrowing Constraints Change U.S. Homeownership Rates?" *Journal of Housing Economics* 6(December): 318–33.

London, Rebecca. 1998. "Trends in Single Mothers' Living Arrangements from 1970 to 1995: Correcting the Current Population Survey." *Demography* 35(1): 125–31.

Loury, Glenn. 1977. "A Dynamic Theory of Racial Income Differences." In *Women, Minorities, and Employment Discrimination,* edited by Phyllis Wallace and Annette LaMond. Lexington, Mass.: Lexington Books.

———. 1987. "Why Should We Care About Group Inequality?" *Social Philosophy and Policy:* 249–71.

———. 2000. "Who Cares About Racial Inequality?" *Journal of Sociology and Social Welfare* 27: 133–51.

Ludwig, Jens, et al. 1998. "Socioeconomic Inequality and Race Differences in Homicides, Other Injuries, and Other Mortality Causes." Unpublished paper.

Lupton, J., and F. Stafford. 2000. "Five Years Older: Much Richer or Deeper in Debt?" Paper presented to the Allied Social Science Association meetings, Boston (January).

Luxembourg Income Study. 2000a. *LIS Quick Reference Guide.* Syracuse, N.Y.: Center for Policy Research, Maxwell School, Syracuse University. Available at: www.lis.ceps.lu/lisquick.htm.

———. 2000b. "Tabulations on Health Care Expenses." Center for Policy Research, Maxwell School, Syracuse University, Syracuse, N.Y. (August). Unpublished.

Lyall, Victoria, and William Schweke. 1996. *Using Alliance-Based Development Strategies for Economic Empowerment.* Washington: Corporation for Enterprise Development.

Lynch, Lisa M. 2000. "Trends in and Consequences of Investments in Children." In *Securing the Future: Investing in Children from Birth to College,* edited by Sheldon Danziger and Jane Waldfogel. New York: Russell Sage Foundation.

Ma, Patricia, and Tony Proscio. 1998. "Working Close to Home: Wire-Net's Hire Locally Program." Workforce Development Report to the Field Series. Philadelphia: Public/Private Ventures.

Manski, Charles F. 1993. "Identification of Endogenous Social Effects: The Reflection Problem." *Review of Economic Studies* 60(3): 531–42.

———. In press. "Economic Analysis of Social Interactions." *Journal of Economic Perspectives.*

Mare, R. D. 1992. "Trends in the Process of Social Stratification." *Contemporary Sociology* 21: 654–58.

Martinez, John M., and Cynthia Miller. 2000. "The Effects of Parents' Fair Share on the Employment and Earnings of Low-Income, Noncustodial Fathers." *Focus* 21(Spring): 23—26.

Massey, Douglas S. 1990. "American Apartheid: Segregation and the Making of the Underclass." *American Journal of Sociology* 96(2): 329–58.

———. 1996. "The Age of Extremes: Concentrated Affluence and Poverty in the Twenty-first Century." *Demography* 33(4): 396–412.

Massey, Douglas S., and Nancy A. Denton. 1993. *American Apartheid: Segregation and the Making of the Underclass.* Cambridge, Mass.: Harvard University Press.

Massey, Douglas, and Shawn Kanaiaupuni. 1993. "Public Housing and the Concentration of Poverty." *Social Science Quarterly* 74: 109–22.

Mayer, Susan E. 1997. *What Money Can't Buy: The Effect of Parental Income on Children's Outcomes.* Cambridge, Mass.: Harvard University Press.

Mayer, Susan E., and Christopher Jencks. 1993. "Recent Trends in Economic Inequality in the United States: Income Versus Expenditures Versus Material Well-being." In *Poverty and Prosperity in the USA in the Late Twentieth Century,* edited by Dimitri B. Papadimitriou and Edward Wolff. New York: St. Martin's Press.

Mayer, Susan E., and L. Lopoo. 2000. "Has the Intergenerational Transmission of Economic Status Changed?" University of Chicago. Unpublished paper.

McCarton, Cecelia M., Jeanne Brooks-Gunn, Ina F. Wallace, et al. 1997. "Results at Age Eight Years of Early Intervention for Low-Birthweight Premature Infants: The Infant Health and Development Program." *Journal of the American Medical Association* 265: 2212–17.

McClure, Kirk. 1998. "Housing Vouchers Versus Housing Production: Assessing Long-term Costs." *Housing Policy Debate* 9(2): 355–71.

———. 2000. "The Low-Income Housing Tax Credit as an Aid to Housing Finance: How Well Has It Worked?" *Housing Policy Debate* 11(1): 91–114.

McKey, Ruth Hubbell, Larry Condelli, Harriet Ganson, et al. 1985. *The Impact of Head Start on Children, Families, and Communities: Final Report of the Head Start Evaluation, Synthesis, and Utilization Project.* 85–31193. Washington: U.S. Department of Health and Human Services.

McLanahan, Sara. 1995. "The Consequences of Nonmarital Childbearing for Women, Children, and Society." In *Report to Congress on Out-of-Wedlock Childbearing.* Washington: U.S. Department of Health and Human Services.

———. 1997. "Parent Absence or Poverty: Which Matters More?" In *Consequences of Growing up Poor,* edited by Greg Duncan and Jeanne Brooks-Gunn. New York: Russell Sage Foundation.

———. 1998. "Building Human Capital: A Two-Generation Approach." Paper presented at the Ford Foundation conference Investing in Children, Columbia University (October).

McLanahan, Sara, and Gary Sandefur. 1994. *Growing up with a Single Parent: What Hurts, What Helps.* Cambridge, Mass.: Harvard University Press.

McLoyd, Vonnie. 1990. "The Impact of Economic Hardship on Black Families and Children: Psychological Distress, Parenting, and Socio-emotional Development." *Child Development* 61: 311–46.

———. 1998. "Socioeconomic Disadvantage and Child Development." *American Psychologist* 53: 185–204.

McMurrer, Daniel P., and Isabel V. Sawhill. 1998. *Getting Ahead: Economic and Social Mobility in America.* Washington, D.C.: Urban Institute.

Mead, Lawrence M. 1986. *Beyond Entitlement: The Social Obligations of Citizenship.* New York: Free Press.

———. 1992. *The New Politics of Poverty: The Non-Working Poor in America.* New York: Basic Books.

Melendez, Edwin. 1996. *Working on Jobs: The Center for Employment Training.* Boston: Gaston Institute, University of Massachusetts, Boston.

Melendez, Edwin, and Bennett Harrison. 1998. "Matching the Disadvantaged to Job Opportunities: Structural Explanations for the Past Successes of the Center for Employment Training." *Economic Development Quarterly* 12: 3–11.

Meyer, Bruce D., and Dan T. Rosenbaum. 2001. "Welfare, the Earned Income Tax Credit, and the Labor Supply of Single Mothers." *Quarterly Journal of Economics* 96(3): 1063–1114.

Meyer, Daniel R., Maria Cancian, et al. 2001. *The Child Support Demonstration Evaluation: Summary of Experimental Impacts.* Madison: Institute for Research on Poverty, University of Wisconsin.

Meyer, Daniel R., and Mei-Chen Hu. 1999. "A Note on the Antipoverty Effectiveness of Child Support Among Mother-Only Families." *Journal of Human Resources* 34(1): 225–34.

Michael, Robert, and Connie Citro. 1995. *Measuring Poverty: A New Approach.* Washington, D.C.: National Academy Press.

Michalopoulos, Charles, David Card, Lisa Gennetian, Kristen Harknett, and Philip K. Robins. 2000. *The Self-Sufficiency Project at Thirty-six Months: Effects of a Financial Work Incentive on Employment and Income.* New York: Manpower Demonstration Research Corporation.

Michalopoulos, Charles, Christine Schwartz, and Diana Adams-Ciardullo. 2000. *What Works Best for Whom: Impacts of Twenty Welfare-to-Work Programs by Subgroup (Executive Summary).* New York: Manpower Demonstration Research Corporation. Available at: *www.mdrc.org/Reports2000/NEWWS-Subgroup-ExecSumm.htm.*

Milgram, Stanley. 1974. *Obedience to Authority.* New York: Harper and Row.

Miller, Daniel S., and Elizabeth H. Lin. 1988. "Children in Sheltered Homeless Families: Reported Health Status and Use of Health Services." *Pediatrics* 81(5): 668–73.

Moffitt, Robert A. 1992. "The Incentive Effects of the U.S. Welfare System." *Journal of Economic Literature* 30(1): 1–61.

———. 1998. "The Effect of Welfare on Marriage and Fertility." In *Welfare, the Family, and Reproductive Behavior,* edited by Robert Moffitt. Washington, D.C.: National Academy Press.

———. 2000a. "TANF." Paper presented at National Bureau of Economic Research Conference on Means-Tested Transfers, Cambridge, Mass.(May 11–12).

———. 2000b. "Welfare benefits and Female Headship in the U.S. Time Series." *American Economic Review* 90(2): 373–77.

———. 2001. "Policy Interventions, Low-Level Equilibria, and Social Interactions," in *Social Dynamics,* Steven N. Durlauf and H. Peyton Young, eds., Cambridge: MIT Press.

Moffitt, Robert, and Barbara Wolfe. 1992. "The Effect of the Medicaid Program on Welfare Participation and Labor Supply." *Review of Economics and Statistics* 74(4): 615–26.

Molnar, Alex, Philip Smith, and Karen Ehrle. 1999. "Evaluating the SAGE Program: A Pilot Program in Targeted Pupil-Teacher Reduction in Wisconsin." *Educational Evaluation and Policy Analysis* 21(2): 165–78.

Montgomery, James. 1992. "Social Networks and Persistent Inequality in Labor Markets." Northwestern University, Chicago. Unpublished paper.

———. 1994a. "Weak Ties, Employment, and Inequality: An Equilibrium Analysis." *American Journal of Sociology* 99(5): 1212–36.

———. 1994b. "Revisiting Tally's Corner: Mainstream Norms, Dissonance, and Underclass Behavior." *Rationality and Society* 6: 462–88.

Moore, K. A., D. R. Morrison, and A. D. Green. 1996. "Effects on the Children Born to Adolescent Mothers." In *Kids Having Kids: Economic Costs and Social Consequences of Teen Pregnancy,* edited by Rebecca Maynard. Washington, D.C.: Urban Institute.

Moore, Mark. 1999. "Security and Community Development." In *Urban Problems and Community Development,* edited by Ronald F. Ferguson and William T. Dickens. Washington, D.C.: Brookings Institution.

Mort, Elizabeth A., Jennifer N. Edwards, David W. Emmons, Karen Convery, and David Blumenthal. 1996. "Physician Response to Patient Insurance Status in Ambulatory Care Clinical Decisionmaking: Implications for Quality of Care." *Medical Care* 34(8): 783–97.

Moskos, George, and John Sibley Butler. 1996. *All That We Can Be.* New York: Basic Books.

Moss, Philip, and Chris Tilly. 2001. *Stories Employers Tell: Race, Skill, and Hiring in America.* New York: Russell Sage Foundation.

Moynihan, Daniel Patrick. 1965. *The Negro Family: The Case for National Action.* U.S. Department of Labor. Washington: U.S. Government Printing Office

Mullahy, John, and Jody L. Sindelar. 1990. "Gender Differences in the Effects of Mental Health on Labor Force Participation." In *Research in Human Capital and Development: Female Labor Force Participation,* edited by Ismail Sirageldin. Greenwich, Conn.: JAI Press.

Mumford Center for Comparative Urban and Regional Research, State University of New York, Albany. 2001. "Metro Racial and Ethnic Change—Census 2000." Available at: *mumford1.dydns.org/cen2000.*

Munnell, Alicia H., Lynn E. Browne, James McEneaney, and Geoffrey M. B. Tootell. 1996. "Mortgage Lending in Boston: Interpreting the HMDA Data." *American Economic Review* 86(March): 25–53.

Murray, Charles. 1984. *Losing Ground: American Social Policy 1950–1980.* New York: Basic Books.

———. 1993. "The Coming White Underclass." *Wall Street Journal,* October 23.

———. 1995. "The Key to Welfare Reform: Reducing Illegitimacy." Washington, D.C.: American Enterprise Institute.

National Center for Health Statistics. 1998. *Health, United States, 1998.* Hyattsville, Md.: Public Health Service, U.S. Department of Health and Human Services.

———. 1999. *Health, United States, 1999.* Hyattsville, Md.: Public Health Service, U.S. Department of Health and Human Services.

———. 2000a. *National Vital Statistics Reports* 48(3). Available at: *www.cdc.gov/nchs.*

———. 2000b. *National Vital Statistics Reports* 47(18). Available at: *www.cdc.gov/nchs.*

———. 2000c. *Health, United States, 2000.* Hyattsville, Md.: Public Health Service, U.S. Department of Health and Human Services.

National Commission on Children. 1991. *Beyond Rhetoric: A New American Agenda for Children and Families: Final Report of the National Commission on Children.* Washington: National Commission on Children.

National Telecommunications and Information Administration. 2000. "Falling Through the Net: Toward Digital Inclusion." Available at: *digitaldivide.gov/reports.htm.*

Neumark, David, and Elizabeth Powers. 1998. "The Effect of Means-Tested Income Support for the Elderly on Pre-Retirement Saving: Evidence from the SSI Program in the U.S." *Journal of Public Economics* 68(2): 181–206.

Newburger, Harriet. 1995. "Sources of Difference in Information Used by Black and White Housing Seekers: An Exploratory Analysis." *Urban Studies* 32(April): 445–50.

Newman, Katherine. 1999. *No Shame in My Game.* New York: Alfred A. Knopf and Russell Sage Foundation.

Newman, Katherine, and Chancy Lennon. 1995. "Finding Work in the Inner City: How Hard Is It Now? How Hard Will It Be for AFDC Recipients?" Working Paper 76. New York: Russell Sage Foundation.

Newman, Sandra J., and Ann B. Schnare. 1997. "And a Suitable Living Environment: The Failure of Housing Programs to Deliver on Neighborhood Quality." *Housing Policy Debate* 8(4): 703–42.

Nicholson, Sean. 1997. "The Effect of Federal Policy on Hospital Care for the Poor." Department of Economics, University of Wisconsin, Madison. Unpublished paper.

Noble, Holcomb B. 1999. "Study Shows Asthma Risk for Children in Poor Areas." *New York Times,* July 27.

Nyden, Philip, John Lukehart, Michael T. Maly, and William Peterman. 1998. "Neighborhood Racial and Ethnic Diversity in U.S. Cities." *Cityscape* 4(2): 1–18.

Nye, Barbara A., Larry V. Hedges, and Spyros Konstantopoulos. 1999. "The Long-term Effects of Small Classes: A Five-Year Follow-up of the Tennessee Class Size Experiment." *Educational Evaluation and Policy Analysis* 21(2): 127–42.

O'Brien, Ellen, and Judith Feder. 1999. "Employment-Based Health Insurance Coverage and Its Decline: The Growing Plight of Low-Wage Workers." Paper prepared for the Kaiser Commission on Medicaid and the Uninsured.

O'Connor, Alice. 1999. "Swimming Against the Tide: A Brief History of Federal Policy in Poor Communities." In *Urban Problems and Community Development,* edited by Ronald F. Ferguson and William T. Dickens. Washington, D.C.: Brookings Institution.

Okun, Arthur M. 1975. *Equality and Efficiency: The Big Tradeoff.* Washington, D.C.: Brookings Institution.

Oliker, Stacey J. 1995. "The Proximate Contexts of Workfare and Work: A Framework for Studying Poor Women's Economic Choices." *Sociological Quarterly* 36(2): 251–72.

Oliver, Melvin L., and Thomas M. Shapiro. 1995. *Black Wealth: White Wealth: A New Perspective on Racial Inequality.* New York: Routledge.

Olsen, Edgar. 2000. "Housing Assistance." Paper presented at National Bureau of Economic Research Conference on Means-Tested Transfers, Cambridge, Mass. (May 11–12).

Ondrich, Jan, Stephen Ross, and John Yinger. 2000. "How Common Is Housing Discrimination?: Improving on Traditional Measures." *Journal of Urban Economics* 47(May): 470–500.

Ondrich, Jan, Alex Stricker, and John Yinger. 1998. "Do Real Estate Brokers Choose to Discriminate?: Evidence from the 1989 Housing Discrimination Study." *Southern Economic Journal* 64(April): 880–901.

Oppenheimer, Valerie K. 1988. "A Theory of Marriage Timing." *American Journal of Sociology* 94: 563–91.

Orfield, Gary, and Susan E. Eaton. 1996. *Dismantling Desegregation.* New York: New Press.

Orfield, Gary, with the assistance of Sara Schley, Diane Glass, and Sean Reardon. 1993. "The Growth of Segregation in American Schools: Changing Patterns of Separation and Poverty Since 1968." Report to the National School Boards Association. Harvard Project on School Desegregation, Cambridge, Mass.

Organization for Economic Cooperation and Development. 1996. "Employment Outlook 1996." *OECD Employment Outlook* 59, 60 (June, December).

———. 1999. *Social Expenditure Database 1980–1996.* Paris: Organization for Economic Cooperation and Development.

———. 2001. "Purchasing Power Parities for OECD Countries, 1970–1999." Available at: *www.oecd.org/std/pppoecd.xls.*

Orshansky, M. 1965. "Counting the Poor." *Social Security Bulletin* 28(January): 3.

Osterman, Paul, and Brenda A. Lautsch. 1996. "Project Quest: A Report to the Ford Foundation." Massachusetts Institute of Technology, Cambridge, Mass.

O'Sullivan, Arthur. 2000. *Urban Economics.* 4th ed. Boston: Irwin McGraw-Hill.

Pafenberg, Forrest, and Kevin A. Roth. 1999. "Realtors and the Internet: The Impact of Online Technologies on the Real Estate Industry." Available from the National Association of Realtors at: *www.onerealtorplace.com/online.nsf.*

Page, Marianne. 1995. "Racial and Ethnic Discrimination in Urban Housing Markets: Evidence from a Recent Audit Study." *Journal of Urban Economics* 38(September): 183–206.

Page, Marianne, and G. Solon. 2000. "Correlations Between Sisters and Neighboring Girls in Their Subsequent Income as Adults." University of Michigan, Ann Arbor. Unpublished paper.

Painter, Gary, Stuart Gabriel, and Dowell Myers. 2001. "Race, Immigrant Status, and Housing Tenure Choice." *Journal of Urban Economics* 49(September): 121–49.

Pamuk, E., D. Makuc, K. Heck, C. Reuben, and K. Lochner. 1998. *Socioeconomic Status and Health Chartbook: Health, United States, 1998.* Hyattsville, Md.: National Center for Health Statistics.

Papke, James A. 1990. "The Role of Market-Based Public Policy in Economic Development and Urban Revitalization: A Retrospective Analysis and Appraisal of the Indiana Enterprise Zone Program—Year Three Report." West Lafayette, Ind.: Center for Tax Policy Studies, Purdue University.

Papke, Leslie. 1993. "What Do We Know About Enterprise Zones?" In *Tax Policy and the Economy,* edited by James Poterba. Cambridge, Mass.: MIT Press.

———. 1994. "Tax Policy and Urban Development: Evidence from the Indiana Enterprise Zone Program." *Journal of Public Economics* 54: 37–49.

Parrott, Sharon. 1998. *Welfare Recipients Who Find Jobs.* Washington: Center on Budget and Policy Priorities.

Pastor, Manuel Jr., et al. 2000. *Regions at Work: How Cities and Suburbs Can Grow Together.* Minneapolis: University of Minnesota Press.

Pate, David, and Earl S. Johnson. 2000. "The Ethnographic Study for the W-2 Child Support Demonstration Evaluation: Some Preliminary Findings." *Focus* 21(1): 18–22.

Pauly, Mark, Patricia Danzon, Paul Feldstein, and John Hoff. 1991. "A Plan for Responsible National Health Insurance." *Health Affairs* 10(1): 5–25.

Pavetti, LaDonna. 1999. "How Much More Can Welfare Mothers Work?" *Focus* 20(2): 16–19.

Pavetti, LaDonna, and Dan Bloom. 2001. "Sanctions and Time Limits: State Policies and Early Outcomes." In *New World of Welfare,* edited by Rebecca Blank and Ron Haskins. Washington, D.C.: Brookings Institution.

Pavetti, LaDonna, Michelle Derr, Jacquie Anderson, Carole Trippe, and Sidnee Paschal. 2000. *The Role of Intermediaries in Helping TANF Recipients Find Jobs.* Washington, D.C.: Mathematica Policy Research.

Pavetti, LaDonna, and Debra Strong. 2001. *Work-Based Strategies for Hard-to-Employ TANF Recipients: A Preliminary Assessment of Program Models and Dimensions.* Washington, D.C.: Mathematica Policy Research.

Paxson, Christina, and Jane Waldfogel. 1999a. "Parental Resources and Child Abuse and Neglect." *American Economic Review: Papers and Proceedings* (May): 239–44.

———. 1999b. "Work, Welfare, and Child Maltreatment." Working Paper. Cambridge, Mass.: National Bureau of Economic Research.

Pelton, Leroy. 1978. "Child Abuse and Neglect: The Myth of Classlessness." *American Journal of Orthopsychiatry* 48: 608–17.

Pepper Commission. 1990. *A Call for Action.* Final Report of the U.S. Bipartisan Commission on Comprehensive Health Care. Washington: U.S. Government Printing Office.

Perry, Stewart. 1987. *Communities on the Way: Rebuilding Local Economies in the United States and Canada.* Albany: State University of New York.

Peters, H. Elizabeth, and Natalie C. Mullis. 1997 "The Role of Family Income and Sources of Income in Adolescent Achievement." In *Consequences of Growing up Poor,* edited by Greg Duncan and Jeanne Brooks-Gunn. New York: Russell Sage Foundation.

Peterson, Paul E. 1995. "State Response to Welfare Reform: A Race to the Bottom?"

In *Welfare Reform: An Analysis of the Issues,* edited by Isabel V. Sawhill. Washington, D.C.: Urban Institute.

Piachaud, David, and Holly Sutherland. 2000. "How Effective Is the British Government's Attempt to Reduce Child Poverty?" Working Paper 38. London: Centre for Analysis of Social Exclusion (CASE), London School of Economics.

Plotnick, Robert D., and Irwin Garfinkel, Daniel S. Gaylin, Sara S. McLanahan, and Inhoe Ku. 1999. "Better Child Support Enforcement: Can It Reduce Teenage Premarital Childbearing?" University of Washington, Seattle. Unpublished paper.

Plotnick, Robert, and Felicity Skidmore. 1975. *Progress Against Poverty: A Review of the 1964–1974 Decade.* New York: Academic Press.

Popkin, Susan, James E. Rosenbaum, and Patricia Meaden. 1993. "Labor Market Experiences of Low-Income Black Women in Middle-Class Suburbs: Evidence from a Survey of Gautreaux Program Participants." *Journal of Policy Analysis and Management* 12(Summer): 556–74.

Porter, Kathryn, and Wendell Primus. 1999. *Changes Since 1995 in the Safety Net's Impact on Child Poverty.* Washington: Center on Budget and Policy Priorities.

Porter, Michael E. 1995. "The Competitive Advantage of the Inner City." *Harvard Business Review* (May-June): 55.

Portes, Alejandro. 1998. "Social Capital: Its Origins and Applications in Modern Sociology." *Annual Review of Sociology* 24: 1–14.

Powell, Walter W. 1990. "Neither Market Nor Hierarchy: Network Forms of Organization." *Research in Organizational Behavior* 12: 295–336.

Powers, Elizabeth T. 1998. "Does Means-Testing Welfare Discourage Saving?: Evidence from a Change in AFDC Policy in the United States." *Journal of Public Economics* 68(1): 33–53.

Primus, Wendell, Lynette Rawlings, Kathy Larin, and Kathryn Porter. 1999. *The Initial Impacts of Welfare Reform on the Incomes of Single-Mother Families.* Washington: Center on Budget and Policy Priorities.

Quigley, John M. 2000. "A Decent Home: Housing Policy in Perspective." *Brookings Papers in Urban Affairs* 1(1): 1–47.

Rabinowitz J., et al. 1998. "Relationship Between Types of Insurance and Care During the Early Course of Psychosis." *American Journal of Psychology* 155: 1392–97.

Rainwater, Lee. 1990. "Poverty and Equivalence as Social Constructions." Luxembourg Income Study Working Paper 91. Syracuse, N.Y.: Center for Policy Research, Maxwell School, Syracuse University.

Rainwater, Lee, and Timothy M. Smeeding. 1999. "From 'Relative' to 'Real' Income: Purchase Power Parities and Household Microdata: Problems and Prospects." In *Papers and Final Report of the Third Meeting on Household Income Statistics.* Ottawa: Statistics Canada. Available at: *www.lis.ceps.lu/canberra/ottawareport/ ottasession5.PDF.*

———. 2000. "Doing Poorly: The Real Income of American Children in Comparative Perspective." In *Crisis in American Institutions,* edited by Jerome H. Skolnick and Elliott Currie. Boston: Allyn and Bacon.

Rangarajan, Anu, and Tim Novak. 1999. *The Struggle to Sustain Employment: The Effec-*

tiveness of the Postemployment Services Demonstration. Princeton, N.J.: Mathematica Policy Research.

Rangarajan, Anu, Peter Schochet, and Dexter Chu. 1998. *Employment Experiences of Welfare Recipients Who Find Jobs: Is Targeting Possible?* Princeton, N.J.: Mathematica Policy Research.

Raphael, Steven. 1998. "Inter- and Intra-Ethnic Comparisons of the Central City–Suburban Youth Employment Differential: Evidence from the Oakland Metropolitan Area." *Industrial and Labor Relations Review* 51(3): 505–24.

Raphael, Steven, and Rudolf Winter-Ebmer. 2000. "Identifying the Effect of Unemployment on Crime." University of California, Los Angeles (January). Unpublished paper.

Raudenbush, Stephen, and Robert Sampson. 1999. "Ecometrics: Toward a Science of Assessing Ecological Settings, with Application to the Systematic Social Observation of Neighborhoods." *Sociological Methodology* 29, edited by Mark Becker and Michael Sobel. Cambridge: Basil Blackwell.

Ravallion, Martin. 1994. "Poverty Comparisons." *Fundamentals of Pure and Applied Economics* 56. Chur, Switzerland: Harwood Academic Press.

———. 1996. "Issues in Measuring and Modeling Poverty," *Economic Journal* 106(September): 1328–44.

Rector, Robert. 1995. *Combating Family Disintegration, Crime, and Dependence: Welfare Reform and Beyond.* Washington, D.C.: Heritage Foundation.

———. 1998. "The Myth of Widespread American Poverty." Washington, D.C.: Heritage Foundation.

Rector, Robert, Kirk A. Johnson, and Sarah Youssef. 1999. "The Extent of Material Hardship and Poverty in the United States." *Review of Social Economy* 57(3): 351–87.

Rector, Robert, K. W. O'Beirne, and M. McLaughlin. 1990. *How "Poor" Are America's Poor?* Washington, D.C.: Heritage Foundation.

Rees, Albert. 1966. "Information Networks in Labor Markets." *American Economic Review: Papers and Proceedings* (May): 559–56.

Rees, Albert, and George Schultz. 1970. *Workers in an Urban Labor Market.* Chicago: University of Chicago Press.

Reville, Robert T. 1995. "Intertemporal and Life-Cycle Variation in Measured Intergenerational Earnings Mobility." Working paper. Santa Monica, Calif.: RAND Corporation.

Reville, Robert T., and Jacob A. Klerman. 1996. "Job Training: The Impact on California of Further Consolidation and Devolution." In *The New Fiscal Federalism and the Social Safety Net,* edited by J. Hosek and R. Levine. Santa Monica, Calif.: RAND Corporation.

Reynolds, Arthur. 1998. "The Chicago Child-Parent Center and Expansion Program: A Study of Extended Early Childhood Intervention." In *Social Programs That Work,* edited by Jonathan Crane. New York: Russell Sage Foundation.

Reynolds, Arthur J., Emily Mann, Wendy Miedel, and Paul Smokowski. 1997. "The State of Early Childhood Intervention: Effectiveness, Myths and Realities, New Directions." *Focus* 19(1): 5–11.

———. 2000. "Long-term Benefits of Participation in the Title I Chicago Child-Parent Centers." Paper presented at the biennial meeting of the Society for Research on Adolescence, Chicago (March 30).

———. 2001. "Long-term Effects of an Early Childhood Intervention on Educational Achievement and Juvenile Arrest: A Fifteen-Year Follow-up of Low-Income Children in Public Schools." *Journal of the American Medical Association* 285(18): 2339–46.

Rivo, Marc L., and David A. Kindig. 1996. "A Report Card on the Physician Work Force in the United States." *New England Journal of Medicine* 334: 892–96.

Robert, Stephanie A. 1998. "Community-Level Socioeconomic Status Effects on Adult Health." *Journal of Health and Social Behavior* 39(1): 18–37.

———. 1999. "Socioeconomic Position and Health: The Independent Contribution of Community Context." *Annual Review of Sociology* 25: 489–516.

Robert Wood Johnson Foundation. 1987. *Access to Health Care in the United States: Results of a 1986 Survey.* Special Report 2. Princeton, N.J.: Robert Wood Johnson Foundation.

Roemer, John. 1993. "A Pragmatic Theory of Responsibility for the Egalitarian Planner." *Philosophy and Public Affairs* 22: 146–66.

———. 1998. *Equality of Opportunity: A Theory and Applications.* Cambridge, Mass.: Harvard University Press.

Roemer, John, and Roger Wets. 1995. "Neighborhood Effects on the Distribution of Income." University of California, Davis. Unpublished paper.

Rogers, Cynthia L. 1997. "Job Search and Unemployment Duration: Implications for the Spatial Mismatch Hypothesis." *Journal of Urban Economics* 42: 108–32.

Rose, S. 1993. "Declining Family Incomes in the 1980s: New Evidence from Longitudinal Data." *Challenge* (November–December): 29–36.

Rosenbaum, James. 1995. "Changing the Geography of Opportunity by Expanding Residential Choice: Lessons from the Gautreaux Program." *Housing Policy Debate* 6: 231–69.

Rosenbaum, James, S. DeLuca, and Shazia R. Miller. 1999. "The Long-term Effects of Residential Mobility on AFDC Receipt: Studying the Gautreaux Program with Administrative Data." Northwestern University, Chicago. Unpublished paper.

Rosenbaum, James E., Nancy Fishman, Alison Brett, and Patricia Meaden. 1993. "Can the Kerner Commission's Housing Strategy Improve Employment, Education, and Social Integration for Low-Income Blacks?" *North Carolina Law Review* 71(June): 1519–56.

Rosenbaum, James, and S. Popkin. 1991. "Employment and Earnings of Low-Income Blacks Who Move to Middle-Class Suburbs." In *The Urban Underclass,* edited by Christopher Jencks and Paul Peterson. Washington, D.C.: Brookings Institution.

Rosenbloom, Sandra. 1992. *Reverse Commute Transportation: Emerging Provider Roles.* Washington: U.S. Department of Transportation.

Rosenzweig, Mark R. 1999. "Welfare, Marital Prospects, and Nonmarital Childbearing." *Journal of Political Economy* 107(6): S3–32.

Ross, Stephen, and John Yinger. 1999. "Sorting and Voting: A Review of the Literature on Urban Public Finance." In *Handbook of Urban and Regional Economics,* vol. 3, *Applied Urban Economics,* edited by P. Cheshire and Edwin S. Mills. Amsterdam: North-Holland.

Ross, Stephen, and John Yinger. Forthcoming. *The Color of Credit: What is Known About Mortgage Lending Discrimination.* Cambridge, Mass.: MIT Press.

Rossi, Peter H. 1998. *Feeding the Poor: Assessing Federal Food Aid.* Washington, D.C.: American Enterprise Institute.

Roth, Kevin A. 2000. "The 2000 National Association of Realtors Profile of Home Buyers and Sellers." Available at: *www.nar.realtor.com/research/images/668prof.pdf.*

Rouse, Cecelia Elena. 1997. "Private School Vouchers and Student Achievement: An Evaluation of the Milwaukee Parental Choice Program." Working Paper 5964. Cambridge, Mass.: National Bureau of Economic Research.

Roychoudhry, Canopy, and Allen C. Goodman. 1996. "Evidence of Racial Discrimination in Different Dimensions of Housing Search." *Real Estate Economics* 24(Summer): 161–78.

Rubin, Barry M., and Craig M. Richards. 1992. "A Transatlantic Comparison of Enterprise Zone Impacts: The British and American Experience." *Economic Development Quarterly* 6(4, November).

Ruggles, Patricia. 1990. *Drawing the Line: Alternative Poverty Measures and Their Implications for Public Policy.* Washington, D.C.: Urban Institute.

Rust, John, and Christopher Phelan. 1997. "How Social Security and Medicare Affect Retirement Behavior in a World of Incomplete Markets." *Econometrica* 65(4, July): 781–831.

Sabel, Charles F. 1993. "Studied Trust: Building New Forms of Cooperation in a Volatile Economy." *Human Relations* 46(9): 1133–70.

Sampson, Robert J. 1999. "What 'Community' Supplies." In *Urban Problems and Community Development,* edited by Ronald F. Ferguson and William T. Dickens. Washington, D.C.: Brookings Institution.

Sampson, Robert, Jeffrey Morenoff, and Felton Earls. 1999. "Beyond Social Capital: Collective Efficacy for Children." *American Sociological Review* 64(5): 633–60.

Sampson, Robert, Stephen Raudenbush, and Felton Earls. 1997. "Neighborhoods and Violent Crime: A Study of Collective Efficacy." *Science* 277: 918–24.

Sard, Barbara, and Jeff Kubell. 2000. *The Increasing Use of TANF and State Matching Funds to Provide Housing Assistance to Families Moving from Welfare to Work.* Washington: Center on Budget and Policy Priorities.

Sawhill, Isabel. 1999. "Investing in Children." Children's Roundtable Report 1. Washington, D.C.: Brookings Institution (April).

Schelling, Thomas. 1971. "Dynamic Models of Segregation." *Journal of Mathematical Sociology* 1: 143–86.

Schill, Michael H., and Samantha Friedman. 1999. "The Fair Housing Amendments Act of 1988: The First Decade." *Cityscape* 4(3): 57–78.

Schochet, Peter Z., John Burghardt, and Steven Glazerman. 2000. *National Job Corps Study: The Short-term Impacts of Job Corps on Participants' Employment and Related Outcomes.* Princeton, N.J.: Mathematica Policy Research.

Schuchter, Arnold. 1971. "Conjoining Black Revolution and Private Enterprise." In *Black Business Enterprise,* edited by Ronald W. Bailey. New York: Basic Books.

Schweinhart, Lawrence J., and David P. Weikart. 1998. "High/Scope Perry Preschool Program Effects at Age Twenty-seven." In *Social Programs That Work,* edited by Jonathan Crane. New York: Russell Sage Foundation.

Schweke, William, Brian Dabson, and Carl Rist. 1996. *Improving Your Business Climate.* Washington, D.C.: Corporation for Enterprise Development.

Schweke, William, Carl Rist, and Brian Dabson. 1994. *Bidding for Business: Are Cities and States Selling Themselves Short?* Washington, D.C.: Corporation for Enterprise Development.

Seltzer, Judith A. 2000. "Families Formed Outside of Marriage." *Journal of Marriage and the Family* 62(4): 1247–68.

Selwyn, Neil, Stephen Gorard, and Sara Williams. 2001. "Digital Divide or Digital Opportunity?: The Role of Technology in Overcoming Social Exclusion in U.S. Education." *Educational Policy* 15: 258–77.

Sen, Amartya. 1983. "Poor, Relatively Speaking." *Oxford Economic Papers* 35: 153–69

———. 1992. *Inequality Reexamined.* Cambridge, Mass.: Harvard University Press.

Servon, Lisa J., and Timothy Bates. 1998. "Microenterprise as an Exit Route from Poverty: Recommendations for Programs and Policy Makers." *Journal of Urban Affairs* 20: 419–41.

Sheils, John, Paul Hogan, and Randall Haught. 1999. "Health Insurance and Taxes: The Impact of Proposed Changes in Current Federal Policy." Paper prepared for the National Coalition on Health Care.

Short, Kathleen, T. Garner, D. Johnson, and P. Doyle. 1999. *Experimental Poverty Measures, 1990–1997.* P60–205. Washington: U.S. Bureau of the Census.

Short, Kathleen, and Martina Shea. 1995. "Beyond Poverty, Extended Measures of Well-being: 1992." Current Population Reports Series P70, no. 50RV. Washington: U.S. Bureau of the Census.

Sipe, Cynthia L. 1996. *Mentoring: A Synthesis of Public/Private Venture's Research, 1988–1995.* Philadelphia: Public/Private Ventures.

Slesnick, D. T. 1993. "Gaining Ground: Poverty in the Postwar United States." *Journal of Political Economy* 101(1): 1–38.

Smeeding, Timothy M. 1977. "The Antipoverty Effectiveness of In-kind Transfers." *Journal of Human Resources* 12(Summer): 360–78.

———. 1982. "Alternative Methods for Valuing Selected In-kind Transfers and Measuring Their Impact on Poverty." Technical Report 50. Washington: U.S. Bureau of the Census (March).

———. 1997. "Poverty in Developed Countries: The Evidence from the Luxembourg Income Study." In *Poverty and Human Development.* New York: United Nations Development Programme.

———. 2000. "Changing Income Inequality in OECD Countries: Updated Results from the Luxembourg Income Study (LIS)." In *The Personal Distribution of Income in an International Perspective,* edited by Richard Hauser and Irene Becker. Berlin: Springer-Verlag.

Smeeding, Timothy M., Michael O'Higgins, and Lee Rainwater. 1990. *Poverty, Inequality, and the Distribution of Income in a Comparative Context: The Luxembourg Income Study (LIS)*. London/Washington: Harvester Wheatsheaf/Urban Institute.

Smeeding, Timothy M., and Katherin Ross Phillips. 2001. "Social Protection for the Poor in the Developed World." In *Shielding the Poor: Social Protection in the Developing World*, edited by Nora Lustig. Washington, D.C.: Brookings Institution.

Smeeding, Timothy M., and Lee Rainwater. 2001. "Comparing Living Standards Across Nations: Real Incomes at the Top, the Bottom, and the Middle." Paper prepared for the Levy Institute conference The Quality of Life in America and Other Advanced Industrialized Nations, Bard College, Annandale-on-Hudson, N.Y. (June 6–7).

Smeeding, Timothy M., Peter Saunders, John Coder, Stephen Jenkins, Johan Fontall, Aldi J. M. Hagenaars, Richard Hauser, and Michael Wolfson. 1993. "Poverty, Inequality, and Family Living Standards Impacts across Seven Nations: The Effect of Noncash Subsidies for Health, Education, and Housing." *Review of Income and Wealth* 39(3, September): 229–56.

Smeeding, Timothy M., and Dennis Sullivan. 1998. "Generations and the Distribution of Economic Well-Being: A Cross-National View." *American Economic Review: Papers and Proceedings* 88(2): 254–58.

Smeeding, Timothy M., Michael Ward, Ian Castles, and Haeduck Lee. 2000. "Making Cross-Country Comparisons of Income Distributions." Paper presented at the twenty-sixth general conference of the International Association for Research in Income and Wealth, Cracow, Poland (August 3). Available at: *www.stat.gov.pl* and *www.econ.nyu.edu/dept/iariw.*

Smith, Judith R., Jeanne Brooks-Gunn, and Pamela Klebanov. 1997. "The Consequences of Living in Poverty for Young Children's Cognitive and Verbal Ability and Early School Achievement." In *Consequences of Growing up Poor*, edited by Greg Duncan and Jeanne Brooks-Gunn. New York: Russell Sage Foundation.

Smith, Robin, and Michelle DeLair. 1999. "New Evidence from Lender Testing: Discrimination at the Preapplication Stage." In *Mortgage Lending Discrimination: A Review of Existing Evidence*, edited by M. A. Turner and Felicity Skidmore. Washington, D.C.: Urban Institute.

Social Exclusion Unit. 1997. (Brochure on the Social Exclusion Unit). London: Cabinet Office.

Solon, Gary. 1999a. "Intergenerational Mobility in the Labor Market." In *Handbook of Labor Economics*, vol. 3A, edited by Orley Ashenfelter and Davis Card. Amsterdam: North-Holland.

———. 1999b. "Mobility Within and Across Generations." Economics Department, University of Michigan, Ann Arbor. Unpublished paper.

Solon, Gary, Marianne Page, and Greg Duncan. 1999. "Correlations Between Neighboring Children in Their Subsequent Educational Attainment." University of Michigan, Ann Arbor. Unpublished paper.

Sorensen, Elaine, and Chava Zibman. 2000. "To What Extent Do Children Benefit from Child Support?: New Information from the National Survey of America's Families, 1997." *Focus* 21(1): 34–37.

South, Scott, and Kyle Crowder. 1999. "Neighborhood Effects on Family Formation: Concentrated Poverty and Beyond." *American Sociological Review* 64(1): 113–32.

Spain, Daphne, and Suzanne M. Bianchi. 1996. *Balancing Act: Motherhood, Marriage, and Employment Among American Women.* New York: Russell Sage Foundation.

Squires, Gregory D., and William Velez. 1988. "Insurance Redlining and the Process of Discrimination." *Review of Black Political Economy* 16(Winter): 63–75.

Stack, Carol. 1974. *All Our Kin.* New York: Basic Books.

State Capitals Newsletters [Alexandria, Va.]. 2000. "Arizona Conservatives Want Surplus Money Spent on Marriage Training; Substance Abuse Programs May Suffer." *Public Assistance and Welfare Trends* 54(15, April 10).

State Policy Documentation Project. 1999. "State Time Limits on TANF Cash Assistance." Washington, D.C.: State Policy Documentation Project.

———. 2000a. "Financial Eligibility for TANF Cash Assistance." Available at *www.spdp.org/tanf/financial/.* Washington, D.C.: State Policy Documentation Project.

———. 2000b. "States Exercising the Option to Terminate the Medicaid Coverage of a Nonpregnant Head of Household Who Loses TANF for Refusal to Work." Available at *www.spdp.org/medicaid/table_8.html/.* Washington, D.C.: State Policy Documentation Project.

Stegman, Michael A., and Michael I. Luger. 1993. "Issues in the Design of Locally Sponsored Homeownership Programs." *Journal of the American Planning Association* 59(Autumn): 417–32.

Steuerle, C. Eugene. 1991. "Finance-Based Reform: The Search for Adaptable Health Policy." Paper presented at the American Enterprise Institute conference American Health Policy: Critical Issues for Reform, Washington (October).

Stevens, A. H. 1995. "Measuring the Persistence of Poverty over Multiple Spells." Ph.D. diss., Department of Economics, University of Michigan.

Stewart, K. J., and S. B. Reed. 1999. "Consumer Price Index Research Series Using Current Methods, 1978–1998." *Monthly Labor Review* (June): 29–38.

Stillman, Joseph. 1999. *Working to Learn: Skills Development Under Work First.* Philadelphia: Public/Private Ventures.

Stolberg, Sheryl Gay. 1999. "Gasping for Breath: Poor Fight Baffling Surge in Asthma." *New York Times,* October 18.

Stoutland, Sara E. 1999. "Community Development Corporations: Mission, Strategy, and Accomplishments." In *Urban Problems and Community Development,* edited by Ronald F. Ferguson and William T. Dickens. Washington, D.C.: Brookings Institution.

Strawn, Julie, and Karin Martinson. 2000. *Steady Work and Better Jobs: How to Help Low-Income Parents Sustain Employment and Advance in the Workplace.* New York: Manpower Demonstration Research Corporation.

Streufert, Peter. 1991. "The Effect of Underclass Isolation on Schooling Choice." University of Wisconsin, Madison. Unpublished paper.

Sucoff, Clea, and Dawn Upchurch. 1998. "Neighborhood Context and the Risk of Childbearing Among Metropolitan-Area Black Adolescents." *American Sociological Review* 63(4): 571–85.

Summers, Robert, and Alan Heston. 1991. "The Penn World Table (Mark 5): An Expanded Set of International Comparisons, 1950–1988." *Quarterly Journal of Economics* 106(2): 327–68.

Sweeney, Eileen, Liz Schott, Ed Lazere, Shawn Fremsted, Heidi Goldberg, Jocelyn Guyer, David Super, and Clifford Johnson. 2000. *Windows of Opportunity.* Washington: Center on Budget and Policy Priorities.

Taggart, Robert. 1995. *Quantum Opportunity Program.* Philadelphia: Opportunities Industrialization Centers of America.

Tate, Charles. 1970. "Brimmer and Black Capitalism: An Analysis." *Review of Black Political Economy* (Spring-Summer): 84–90.

Teachman, Jay D., Kathleen M. Paasch, Randal D. Day, and Karen P. Carver. 1997. "Poverty During Adolescence and Subsequent Educational Attainment." In *Consequences of Growing up Poor,* edited by Greg Duncan and Jeanne Brooks-Gunn. New York: Russell Sage Foundation.

Temkin, Kenneth, George Galster, Roberto Quercia, and Sheila O'Leary. 1999. *A Study of the GSEs' Single-Family Underwriting Guidelines.* Washington, D.C.: Urban Institute.

Tierney, Joseph P., Jean Baldwin Grossman, and Nancy L. Resch. 1995. *Making a Difference: An Impact Study of Big Brothers/Big Sisters.* Philadelphia: Public/Private Ventures.

Tilly, Chris, and Charles Tilly. 1994. "Capitalist Work and Labor Markets." In *The Handbook of Economic Sociology,* edited by Neil J. Smelser and Richard Swedberg. Princeton, N.J.: Princeton University Press.

Topa, Giorgio. 1997. "Social Interactions, Local Spillovers, and Unemployment." New York University. Unpublished paper.

Townsend, Peter. 1979. *Poverty in the United Kingdom.* Harmondsworth, Eng.: Penguin Books.

Trickett, Penelope, Lawrence Aber, Vicki Carlson, and Dante Cicchetti. 1991. "Relationship of Socioeconomic Status to the Etiology and Developmental Sequelae of Physical Child Abuse." *Developmental Psychology* 27: 148–58.

Triest, Robert K. 1998. "Has Poverty Gotten Worse?" *Journal of Economic Perspectives* 12(1): 97–114.

Tucker, Robert C. 1978. *The Marx-Engels Reader.* New York: W. W. Norton.

Tumlin, Karen C., Wendy Zimmerman, and Jason Ost. 1999. *State Snapshots of Public Benefits for Immigrants: A Supplemental Report to "Patchwork Policies."* Washington, D.C.: Urban Institute.

Turner, Margery Austin. 1992. "Discrimination in Urban Housing Markets: Lessons from Fair Housing Audits." *Housing Policy Debate* 3(2): 185–215.

———. 1998. "Moving Out of Poverty: Expanding Mobility and Choice Through Tenant-Based Housing Assistance." *Housing Policy Debate* 9(2): 373–94.

Turner, Margery Austin, and Maris Mickelsons. 1992. "Patterns of Racial Steering in Four Metropolitan Areas." *Journal of Housing Economics* 2(September): 199–234.

Turner, R. H. 1960. "Contest Mobility Versus Sponsored Mobility." In *Class, Status, and Power,* edited by Reinhard Bendix and S. H. Lipset. Glencoe, Ill.: Free Press.

Tweedie, Jack. 1999. *Tracking Recipients After They Leave Welfare.* Denver: National Conference of State Legislatures.

Tym, Roger, et al. 1984. *Monitoring Enterprise Zones: Year Three Report.* London: Department of the Environment, HMSO.

UNICEF Innocenti Research Centre. 2000. "A League Table of Child Poverty in Rich Nations." Innocenti Report Card 1. Florence: UNICEF (June). Available at: *www.unicef-icdc.org.*

United Kingdom Department of Social Security. 1993. *Households Below Average Income.* London: Government Statistical Service.

United Nations Development Programme. 1998. *Human Development Report: Consumption for Human Development.* New York: United Nations. Available at: *www.undp.org/hdro/98.htm.*

————. 1999. *Human Development Report 1999: Globalization with a Human Face.* New York: United Nations. Available at: *www.undp.org/hdro/99.htm.*

Urban Institute. 1997. "The Medicaid Disproportionate Share Hospital Payment Program: Background and Issues." Washington, D.C.: Urban Institute.

U.S. Bureau of the Census. *Historical Poverty Tables.* Available at *www.census.gov/hhes/income/histinc/histpovtb.html.*

————. 1996. "Income, Poverty, and the Valuation of Noncash Benefits." Current Population Reports Series P60–189. Washington: U.S. Government Printing Office.

————. 1998a. *Statistical Abstract 1997.* Washington: U.S. Government Printing Office.

————. 1998b. *Educational Attainment in the United States: March 1998.* P20–513. Available at: *www.census.gov/prod/3/98pubs/p20-513u.pdf.*

————. 1998c. *School Enrollment: Social and Economic Characteristics of Students.* P20–521. Available at: *www.census.gov/prod/3/98pubs/p20-521u.pdf.*

————. 1999a. "Poverty in the United States: 1998." Current Population Reports Series P60–207. Washington: U.S. Government Printing Office (September).

————. 1999b. *Experimental Poverty Measures: 1990–1997.* Current Population Reports (Consumer Income) Series P60–205. Washington: U.S. Government Printing Office (June).

————. 2000. *Poverty in the United States.* Current Population Reports Series P60–210. Washington: U.S. Government Printing Office (September).

————. 2001. "Population and Household Economic Topics." Available at: *www.census.gov/population/www/index.html.*

U.S. Conference of Mayors. 2000. "Hunger and Homelessness in America'a Cities: 16th Annual Survey. Available at *www.usmayors.org/uscm/news/press_releases/documents/hunger_release.htm*

U.S. Council of Economic Advisers. 1999a. "Technical Report: The Effects of Welfare Policy and the Economic Expansion on Welfare Caseloads: An Update." August 3.

————. 1999b. *Economic Report of the President.* Washington: U.S. Government Printing Office.

————. 2000. *Economic Report of the President.* Washington: U.S. Government Printing Office.

U.S. Department of Health and Human Services. 1995. *Report to Congress on Out-of-Wedlock Childbearing.* Available at: *www.cdc.gov/nchs/data/wedlock.pdf.*

———. 1997. *Setting the Baseline: A Report on State Welfare Waivers.* Washington: Office of Human Services Policy, Office of the Assistant Secretary for Planning and Evaluation, U.S. Department of Health and Human Services.

———. 1998a. *Aid to Families with Dependent Children: The Baseline.* Washington: Office of Human Services Policy, Office of the Assistant Secretary for Planning and Evaluation, U.S. Department of Health and Human Services.

———. 1998b. "State Spending Under the Child Care Block Grant." Available at: *www.acf.dhhs.gov/news/press/1998/cc97fund.htm.*

———. 1998c. *Trends in the Well-being of America's Children and Youth 1998.* Washington: U.S. Department of Health and Human Services.

———. 1999a. *Health, United States, 1999, with Health and Aging Chartbook.* Available at: *www.cdc.gov/nchs/data/hus99.pdf.*

———. 1999b. "Change in TANF Caseloads." Washington: Administration for Children and Families, U.S. Department of Health and Human Services. Available at: *www.acf.dhhs.gov/news/stats/caseload.htm.*

———. 1999c. "TANF Percent of Total U.S. Population, 1960–1999." Washington: Administration for Children and Families, U.S. Department of Health and Human Services. Available at: *www.acf.dhhs.gov/news/stats/6097rf.htm.*

———. 1999d. *Helping Families Achieve Self-sufficiency: A Guide for Funding Services for Children and Families Through the TANF Program.* Washington: Administration for Children and Families, Office of Family Assistance, U.S. Department of Health and Human Services.

———. 2000a. *Temporary Assistance for Needy Families (TANF) Program.* Third Annual Report to Congress. Washington: U.S. Department of Health and Human Services.

———. 2000b. *Healthy People 2010: Understanding and Improving Health.* Washington: U.S. Department of Health and Human Services.

———. 2000c. *1999 Head Start Fact Sheet.* Available at: *www2.acf.dhhs.gov/programs/hsb/about/99_hsfs.htm.*

U.S. Department of Housing and Urban Development. 1994. *Priority: Home! The Federal Plan to Break the Cycle of Homelessness.* Washington: U.S. Department of Housing and Urban Development.

———. 1995. *The State of Fair Housing, 1993.* Washington: U.S. Department of Housing and Urban Development.

———. 1996. *Evaluation of HOPE 3 Program: Final Report.* Washington: U.S. Department of Housing and Urban Development.

———. 2000. *Rental Housing Assistance—The Worsening Crisis: A Report to Congress on Worst-Case Housing Needs.* Washington: U.S. Department of Housing and Urban Development. Available at: *www.hud.gov.*

U.S. Department of Justice, Immigration and Naturalization Service. 1999. *The Triennial Comprehensive Report on Immigration.* Washington: Immigration and Naturalization Service.

U.S. Department of Labor. 2001. "Employment Characteristics of Families in 2000."

USDL News Release 01–103, April 19, 2001. Washington: Bureau of Labor Statistics.

———. 2000. *Employer Costs for Employee Compensation.* Washington: Bureau of Labor Statistics (June).

U.S. General Accounting Office. 1995. *Multiple Employment Training Programs: Major Overhaul Needed to Create a More Efficient, Customer-Driven System.* Washington: U.S. General Accounting Office.

———. 1998. *Welfare Reform: Early Fiscal Effects of the TANF Block Grant.* Report GAO/HEHS-98–137. Washington: U.S. General Accounting Office.

———. 1999a. *Food Stamp Program: Various Factors Have Led to Declining Participation.* GAO/RCED-99–195. Washington: U.S. General Accounting Office.

———. 1999b. *Welfare Reform: Information on Former Recipients' Status.* Report GAO/HEHS-99–48. Washington: U.S. General Accounting Office.

———. 1999c. *Food Stamp Program: Various Factors Have Led to Declining Participation.* Report GAO/HEHS-99–48. Washington: U.S. General Accounting Office.

———. 1999d. *Lead Poisoning: Federal Health Care Programs Are Not Effectively Reaching At-Risk Children.* GAO/HEHS-99–18. Washington: U.S. General Accounting Office (January).

———. 2000. *Welfare Reform: State Sanction Policies and Number of Families Affected.* Report GAO/HEHS-00–44. Washington: U.S. General Accounting Office.

U.S. House of Representatives, Committee on Ways and Means. 1992. *Background Material and Data on Programs Within the Jurisdiction of the Committee on Ways and Means.* Washington: U.S. Government Printing Office.

———. 1998. *Background Material and Data on Programs Within the Jurisdiction of the Committee on Ways and Means.* Washington: U.S. Government Printing Office.

———. 2000. *Background Material and Data on Programs Within the Jurisdiction of the Committee on Ways and Means.* Washington: U.S. Government Printing Office.

U.S. Surgeon General. 1999. *Mental Health: A Report of the Surgeon General.* Washington: U.S. Department of Health and Human Services.

Vandell, Deborah L., and Kim M. Pierce. In press. "Child Care Quality and Children's Success at School." In *Early Childhood Learning: Programs for a New Age,* edited by M. Wang. Mahwah, N.J.: Erlbaum.

Vandell, Deborah L., and Lee Shumow. 1999. "After-School Child Care Programs." *The Future of Children* 9(2): 64–80.

Vandell, Deborah L., and Barbara Wolfe. 2000. *Child Care Quality: Does It Matter and Does It Need to Be Improved?* Washington: Office of the Assistant Secretary for Planning and Evaluation, U.S. Department of Health and Human Services.

Vandell, Kerry D. 1995. "Market Factors Affecting Spatial Heterogeneity Among Urban Neighborhoods." *Housing Policy Debate* 6(1): 103–40.

Vanness, David, and Barbara Wolfe. 1999. "Government Mandates and Employer-Based Health Insurance: Who Is Still Not Covered?" Discussion Paper 1198–99. Madison: Institute for Research on Poverty, University of Wisconsin.

Varacy, David P., and Carole C. Walker. 2000. "Vouchering out Distressed Subsidized Developments: Does Moving Lead to Improvements in Housing and Neighborhood Conditions?" *Housing Policy Debate* 11(1): 115–62.

Ventura, Stephanie J., K. D. Peters, J. A. Martin, and J. D. Maurer. 1997. *Births and Deaths: United States, 1996.* Monthly Vital Statistics Report 46(1, supp. 2). Hyattsville, Md.: National Center for Health Statistics.

Vidal, Avis. 1992. *Rebuilding Communities: A National Study of Urban Community Development Corporations.* New York: Community Development Research Center, New School for Social Research.

Vietorisz, Thomas, and Bennett Harrison. 1970. *The Economic Development of Harlem.* New York: Praeger.

Waitzman, Norman, and Ken Smith. 1998. "Separate but Lethal: The Effects of Economic Segregation on Mortality in Metropolitan Areas." *Milbank Quarterly* 76(3): 341–58.

Waldfogel, Jane. 1998. *The Future of Child Protection: How to Break the Cycle of Abuse and Neglect.* Cambridge, Mass.: Harvard University Press.

Walker, Robert. 1999. "Introduction." In *Ending Child Poverty: Popular Welfare for the Twenty-first Century,* edited by Robert Walker. Bristol, Eng.: Policy Press.

Waller, Maureen, and Robert Plotnick. 1999. *Child Support and Low-Income Families: Perceptions, Practices, and Policy.* San Francisco: Public Policy Institute of California.

Waring, Marily. 1999. *Counting for Nothing: What Men Value and What Women Are Worth.* Toronto: University of Toronto Press.

Weinberg, Bruce A., Patricia B. Reagan, and Jeffrey J. Yankow. 1999. "Do Neighborhoods Affect Work Behavior?: Evidence from the NLSY79." Department of Economics, Ohio State University, Columbus. Unpublished paper.

Weinberg, Daniel H. 1985. "Filling the 'Poverty Gap': Multiple Transfer Program Participation." *Journal of Human Resources* 20(1): 64–89.

———. 1987. "Filling the 'Poverty Gap': 1979–1984." *Journal of Human Resources* 22(4): 563–73.

———. 1991. "Poverty Dynamics and the Poverty Gap, 1984–1986." *Journal of Human Resources* 26(3): 535–44.

Weiner, Rebecca. 2001. "Finding Free Internet Access for Those Without." *New York Times,* May 23.

Weissman, Joel S., Constantine Gastonis, and Arnold M. Epstein. 1992. "Rates of Avoidable Hospitalization by Insurance Status in Massachusetts and Maryland." *Journal of the American Medical Association* 268(17): 2388–94.

Welch, Finis. 1999. "In Defense of Inequality." *American Economic Review: Papers and Proceedings* 89(2): 1–17.

White, Karl R. 1985. "Efficacy of Early Intervention." *Journal of Special Education* 19(4): 401–16.

Wienk, Ronald E., Clifford E. Reid, John C. Simonson, and Frederick J. Eggers. 1979. *Measuring Discrimination in American Housing Markets: The Housing Market Practices Survey.* Washington: U.S. Department of Housing and Urban Development.

Wilder, Margaret G., and Barry M. Rubin. 1996. "Rhetoric Versus Reality: A Review of Studies on State Enterprise Zone Programs." *Journal of the American Planning Association* 62(4): 473–91.

Wilson, Franklin. 1985. "The Impact of School Desegregation Programs on White Public School Enrollment, 1968–1976." *Sociology of Education* 58(3): 137–53.

Wilson, Franklin D., and Pamela Smock. 1991. "Desegregation and the Stability of White Enrollments: A School-Level Analysis, 1968–1984." *Sociology of Education* 64(4): 278–92.

Wilson, William Julius. 1987. *The Truly Disadvantaged: The Inner City, the Underclass, and Public Policy.* Chicago: University of Chicago Press.

———. 1996. *When Work Disappears.* New York: Alfred A. Knopf.

———. 1999. *The Bridge over the Racial Divide: Rising Inequality and Coalition Politics.* New York: Russell Sage Foundation.

Wissoker, Douglas, Wendy Zimmerman, and George Galster. 1998. *Testing for Discrimination in Home Insurance.* Research Report. Washington, D.C.: Urban Institute.

Wolfe, Barbara, and Timothy M. Smeeding. 1999. "Poverty, Health, and Health Care Utilization: The Health Needs of the Poor." Paper presented to the annual meeting of the American Economic Association, New York (January 4).

Wolfe, Barbara, and David Vanness. 1999. "Inequality in Health Care Access and Utilization and the Potential Role for the Public Sector." In *Fighting Poverty: Caring for Children, Parents, the Elderly, and Health,* edited by Stein Ringen and Philip de Jong. Aldershot, Eng.: Ashgate.

Wolfe, Barbara, Amy Wolaver, and Timothy McBride. 1998. "Government Mandates, Health Insurance, and the Deterioration of the Low-Wage Labor Market: Are They Connected?" In *The State of Social Welfare, 1997,* edited by Peter Flore, Philip de Jong, Julian LeGrand, and Jun-Young Kim. Aldershot, Eng.: Ashgate.

Yinger, John. 1995. *Closed Doors, Opportunities Lost: The Continuing Costs of Housing Discrimination.* New York: Russell Sage Foundation.

———. 1997. "Cash in Your Face: The Cost of Racial and Ethnic Discrimination in Housing." *Journal of Urban Economics* 42(November): 339–65.

———. 1998. "Evidence on Discrimination in Consumer Markets." *Journal of Economic Perspectives* 12(Spring): 23–40.

Zabrowski, A., and A. Gordon. 1993. *Evaluation of Minority Female Single Parent Demonstration: Fifth Year Impacts at CET.* Report for the Rockefeller Foundation. New York: Mathematica Policy Research.

Zellman, Gail. 1992. "The Impact of Case Characteristics on Child Abuse Reporting Decisions." *Child Abuse and Neglect* 16: 57–74.

Zigler, Edward F., and Susan Muenchow. 1992. *Head Start: The Inside Story of America's Most Successful Educational Experiment.* New York: Basic Books.

Ziliak, J. 1999. "Income Transfers and Assets of the Poor." Working Paper DP1202–99. Madison: Institute for Research on Poverty, University of Wisconsin.

Zimmerman, Wendy, and Michael Fix. 1998. *Declining Applications for Medi-Cal and Welfare Benefits in Los Angeles County.* Washington, D.C.: Urban Institute.

Zimmerman, Wendy, and Karen C. Tumlin. 1999. Patchwork Policies: State Assistance for Immigrants Under Welfare Reform. Washington, D.C.: Urban Institute.